LECTIONARY FOR MASS

THE ROMAN MISSAL
RESTORED BY DECREE OF THE SECOND ECUMENICAL
COUNCIL OF THE VATICAN AND PROMULGATED BY
AUTHORITY OF POPE PAUL VI

LECTIONARY FOR MASS

FOR USE IN THE DIOCESES
OF THE UNITED STATES OF AMERICA

SECOND TYPICAL EDITION

Volume IV:
Common of Saints
Ritual Masses, Masses for Various Needs and Occasions,
Votive Masses, and Masses for the Dead

UNITED STATES CONFERENCE OF CATHOLIC BISHOPS

A Liturgical Press Book

THE LITURGICAL PRESS COLLEGEVILLE, MINNESOTA

Concordat cum originali:

Reverend James P. Moroney
Executive Director, Secretariat for the Liturgy
United States Conference of Catholic Bishops

Published by the authority of the Bishops' Committee on the Liturgy,
United States Conference of Catholic Bishops.

ACKNOWLEDGMENTS

Design by Frank Kacmarcik, Obl.S.B.

ISBN 0-8146-2880-X

CONTENTS

SACRED CONGREGATION FOR DIVINE WORSHIP

Prot. n. 106/69

DECREE

The Order of Readings from the Sacred Scriptures to be used at Mass was prepared by the Consilium for the Implementation of the Constitution on the Sacred Liturgy in accordance with the requirement of the Constitution that a more lavish table of the word of God be spread before the faithful, that the treasures of the Bible be opened up more widely, and that the more important part of the Holy Scriptures be read to the people over a prescribed number of years (art. 51). The Supreme Pontiff Paul VI approved it by the Apostolic Constitution *Missale Romanum*, on 3 April 1969.

Accordingly, this Sacred Congregation for Divine Worship, by special mandate of the Supreme Pontiff, promulgates this same Order of Readings for Mass, establishing that it enter into force on 30 November, the First Sunday of Advent, in the year 1969. However, in the coming liturgical year series B will be used for the Sunday readings and series II for the first reading on weekdays of Ordinary Time.

Since in the present Order of Readings only the references are given for the individual readings, the Episcopal Conferences will have complete texts prepared in the vernacular languages, observing the norms laid down in the Instruction on vernacular translations issued by the Consilium for the Implementation of the Constitution on the Sacred Liturgy on 25 January 1969. The vernacular texts may either be taken from translations of the Sacred Scriptures already lawfully approved for particular regions, and confirmed by the Apostolic See, or, newly translated, in which case they should be submitted for confirmation to this Sacred Congregation.

All things to the contrary notwithstanding.

From the offices of the Sacred Congregation for Divine Worship, 25 May 1969, Pentecost Sunday.

✠ Benno Cardinal Gut
Prefect

✠ A. Bugnini
Secretary

SACRED CONGREGATION
FOR THE SACRAMENTS AND DIVINE WORSHIP

Prot. CD 240/81

DECREE

REGARDING THE SECOND TYPICAL EDITION

The Order of Readings for Mass, first published in *editio typica* in 1969, was promulgated on 25 May of that year by special mandate of the Supreme Pontiff Paul VI, in accordance with the requirement of the Constitution on the Sacred Liturgy, in order to provide Bishops' Conferences with the references for the individual biblical readings at Mass with a view to the preparation of lectionaries in the vernacular languages in the different regions.

In that edition were lacking the biblical references of readings for celebration of the sacraments and other rites that have been published since May 1969. Moreover, following the issuing of the Neo-Vulgate edition of the Sacred Scriptures, it was laid down by the Apostolic Constitution *Scripturarum thesaurus* of 25 April 1979 that thereafter the text of the Neo-Vulgate must be adopted as the typical edition for liturgical use. Since the first *editio typica* is no longer available, it seemed opportune to prepare a second edition, having the following features with regard to the previous one:

1. The text of the Introduction has been expanded.

2. In compliance with the Apostolic Constitution *Scripturarum thesaurus*, the Neo-Vulgate edition of the Sacred Scriptures has been used in indicating the biblical references.

3. There have been incorporated all the biblical references to be found in the lectionaries for the celebration of sacraments and sacramentals that have been published since the first edition of the Order of Readings for Mass.

4. The biblical references have also been added for readings for certain Masses "for various needs" and for readings in other Masses which were inserted into the Roman Missal for the first time in its second edition of 1975.

5. As regards the celebrations of the Holy Family, the Baptism of the Lord, the Ascension, and Pentecost, references have been added for optional read-

ings in such a way that biblical texts arranged for cycles A, B, and C in the Lectionary for Sundays and feasts are completed.

The Supreme Pontiff John Paul II has by his authority approved this second edition of the Order of Readings for Mass and the Sacred Congregation for the Sacraments and Divine Worship now promulgates it and declares it to be the *editio typica.*

The Episcopal Conferences will introduce the changes found in this second edition into the editions to be prepared in the vernacular.

All things to the contrary notwithstanding.

From the offices of the Sacred Congregation for the Sacraments and Divine Worship, 21 January 1981.

✝ James R. Cardinal Knox
Prefect

✝ Virgilio Noè
Associate Secretary

CONGREGATION FOR DIVINE WORSHIP
AND THE DISCIPLINE OF THE SACRAMENTS

Prot. 492/00/L

THE UNITED STATES OF AMERICA

At the request of His Excellency, Joseph A. Fiorenza, Bishop of Galveston–Houston, President of the Conference of Bishops of the United States of America, made in a letter dated February 25, 2001, and in virtue of the faculties granted to this Congregation by the Supreme Pontiff JOHN PAUL II, we gladly confirm and approve also according to the norms of the Instruction, *Liturgiam authenticam*, dated March 28, 2001, Volume II of the *Lectionarium Missae*, drawn up in English, as in the attached copy, with the title of *Lectionary for Mass for use in the Dioceses of the United States of America.*

In printed editions of the text there should be inserted in its entirety this Decree by which the Apostolic See accords the requested confirmation of the sole translation to be used in the celebration of holy Mass in all the dioceses of the United States of America. Moreover, two copies of the printed text should be forwarded to this Congregation.

All things to the contrary notwithstanding.

From the offices of the Congregation for Divine Worship and the Discipline of the Sacraments, June 6, 2001.

✢ Jorge A. Cardinal Medina Estévez
Prefect

✢ Franciscus Pius Tamburrino
Archbishop-Secretary

NATIONAL CONFERENCE OF CATHOLIC BISHOPS
UNITED STATES OF AMERICA

DECREE

In accord with the norms established by decree of the Sacred Congregation of Rites in *Cum, nostra ætate* (January 27, 1966), this edition of the *Lectionary for Mass, Volume II: Proper of Seasons for Weekdays, Proper of Saints, Ritual Masses, Masses for Various Needs, Votive Masses and Masses for the Dead,* is declared to be the vernacular typical edition of the *Ordo Lectionum Missæ, editio typica altera* in the dioceses of the United States of America, and is published by authority of the National Conference of Catholic Bishops.

The second volume of the *Lectionary for Mass* was canonically approved for use by the National Conference of Catholic Bishops on June 20, 1992, and was subsequently confirmed by the Apostolic See by decree of the Congregation for Divine Worship and the Discipline of the Sacraments on June 6, 2001 (Prot. 492/00/L).

On Ash Wednesday, February 13, 2002, the second volume of the *Lectionary for Mass* may be used in the liturgy. On Pentecost Sunday, May 19, 2002, the use of the entire *Lectionary for Mass* is mandatory. After that date no other edition of the *Lectionary for Mass* may be used in the dioceses of the United States of America.

Given at the General Secretariat of the National Conference of Catholic Bishops, Washington, D.C. on June 29, 2001, the Solemnity of Saints Peter and Paul.

☩ Most Reverend Joseph A. Fiorenza
Bishop of Galveston-Houston

President
National Conference of Catholic Bishops

Reverend Monsignor William P. Fay
General Secretary

INTRODUCTION

PREAMBLE

CHAPTER ONE

GENERAL PRINCIPLES
FOR THE LITURGICAL CELEBRATION OF THE WORD OF GOD

1. CERTAIN PRELIMINARIES

a) The Importance of the Word of God in Liturgical Celebration

1. The Second Vatican Council,[1] the magisterium of the Popes,[2] and various documents promulgated after the Council by the organisms of the Holy See[3] have already had many excellent things to say about the importance of the word of God and about reestablishing the use of Sacred Scripture in every celebration of the Liturgy. The Introduction to the 1969 edition of the Order of Readings for Mass has clearly stated and briefly explained some of the more important principles.[4]

On the occasion of this new edition of the Order of Readings for Mass, requests have come from many quarters for a more detailed exposition of the same principles. Hence, this expanded and more suitable arrangement of the Introduction first gives a general statement on the essential bond between the word of God and the liturgical celebration,[5] then deals in greater detail with the word of God in the celebration of Mass, and, finally, explains the precise structure of the Order of Readings for Mass.

b) Terms Used to Refer to the Word of God

2. For the sake of clear and precise language on this topic, a definition of terms might well be expected as a prerequisite. Nevertheless this Introduction will simply use the same terms employed in conciliar and postconciliar documents. Furthermore it will use "Sacred Scripture" and "word of God" interchangeably throughout when referring to the books written under the inspiration of the Holy Spirit, thus avoiding any confusion of language or meaning.[6]

c) The Significance of the Word of God in the Liturgy

3. The many riches contained in the one word of God are admirably brought out in the different kinds of liturgical celebration and in the different gatherings of the faithful who take part in those celebrations. This takes place as the unfolding mystery of Christ is recalled during the course of the liturgical year, as the Church's sacraments and sacramentals are celebrated, or as the faithful respond individually to the Holy Spirit working within them.[7] For then the liturgical celebration, founded primarily on the word of God and sustained by it, becomes a new event and enriches the word itself with new meaning and power. Thus in the Liturgy the Church faithfully adheres to the way Christ himself read and explained the Sacred Scriptures, beginning with the "today" of his coming forward in the synagogue and urging all to search the Scriptures.[8]

2. LITURGICAL CELEBRATION OF THE WORD OF GOD
a) The Proper Character of the Word of God in the Liturgical Celebration

4. In the celebration of the Liturgy the word of God is not announced in only one way[9] nor does it always stir the hearts of the hearers with the same efficacy. Always, however, Christ is present in his word,[10] as he carries out the mystery of salvation, he sanctifies humanity and offers the Father perfect worship.[11]

Moreover, the word of God unceasingly calls to mind and extends the economy of salvation, which achieves its fullest expression in the Liturgy. The liturgical celebration becomes therefore the continuing, complete, and effective presentation of God's word.

The word of God constantly proclaimed in the Liturgy is always, then, a living and effective word[12] through the power of the Holy Spirit. It expresses the Father's love that never fails in its effectiveness toward us.

b) The Word of God in the Economy of Salvation

5. When in celebrating the Liturgy the Church proclaims both the Old and New Testament, it is proclaiming one and the same mystery of Christ.

The New Testament lies hidden in the Old; the Old Testament comes fully to light in the New.[13] Christ himself is the center and fullness of the whole of Scripture, just as he is of all liturgical celebration.[14] Thus the Scriptures are the living waters from which all who seek life and salvation must drink.

The more profound our understanding of the celebration of the Liturgy, the higher our appreciation of the importance of God's word. Whatever we say of the one, we can in turn say of the other, because each recalls the mystery of Christ and each in its own way causes the mystery to be carried forward.

c) The Word of God in the Liturgical Participation of the Faithful

6. In celebrating the Liturgy the Church faithfully echoes the "Amen" that Christ, the mediator between God and men and women, uttered once for all as he shed his blood to seal God's new covenant in the Holy Spirit.[15]

When God communicates his word, he expects a response, one, that is, of listening and adoring "in Spirit and in truth" (Jn 4:23). The Holy Spirit makes that response effective, so that what is heard in the celebration of the Liturgy may be carried out in a way of life: "Be doers of the word and not hearers only" (Jas 1:22).

The liturgical celebration and the participation of the faithful receive outward expression in actions, gestures, and words. These derive their full meaning not simply from their origin in human experience but from the word of God and the economy of salvation, to which they refer. Accordingly, the participation of the faithful in the Liturgy increases to the degree that, as they listen to the word of God proclaimed in the Liturgy, they strive harder to commit themselves to the Word of God incarnate in Christ. Thus, they endeavor to conform their way of life to what they celebrate in the Liturgy, and then in turn to bring to the celebration of the Liturgy all that they do in life.[16]

3. THE WORD OF GOD IN THE LIFE OF THE PEOPLE OF THE COVENANT
a) The Word of God in the Life of the Church

7. In the hearing of God's word the Church is built up and grows, and in the signs of the liturgical celebration God's wonderful, past works in the history of salvation are presented anew

as mysterious realities. God in turn makes use of the congregation of the faithful that celebrates the Liturgy in order that his word may speed on and be glorified and that his name be exalted among the nations.[17]

Whenever, therefore, the Church, gathered by the Holy Spirit for liturgical celebration,[18] announces and proclaims the word of God, she is aware of being a new people in whom the covenant made in the past is perfected and fulfilled. Baptism and confirmation in the Spirit have made all Christ's faithful into messengers of God's word because of the grace of hearing they have received. They must therefore be the bearers of the same word in the Church and in the world, at least by the witness of their lives.

The word of God proclaimed in the celebration of God's mysteries does not only address present conditions but looks back to past events and forward to what is yet to come. Thus God's word shows us what we should hope for with such a longing that in this changing world our hearts will be set on the place where our true joys lie.[19]

b) The Church's Explanation of the Word of God

8. By Christ's own will there is a marvelous diversity of members in the new people of God and each has different duties and responsibilities with respect to the word of God. Accordingly, the faithful listen to God's word and meditate on it, but only those who have the office of teaching by virtue of sacred ordination or who have been entrusted with exercising that ministry expound the word of God.

This is how in doctrine, life, and worship the Church keeps alive and passes on to every generation all that she is, all that she believes. Thus with the passage of the centuries, the Church is ever to advance toward the fullness of divine truth until God's word is wholly accomplished in her.[20]

c) The Connection between the Word of God Proclaimed and the Working of the Holy Spirit

9. The working of the Holy Spirit is needed if the word of God is to make what we hear outwardly have its effect inwardly. Because of the Holy Spirit's inspiration and support, the word of God becomes the foundation of the liturgical celebration and the rule and support of all our life.

The working of the Holy Spirit precedes, accompanies, and brings to completion the whole celebration of the Liturgy. But the Spirit also brings home[21] to each person individually everything that in the proclamation of the word of God is spoken for the good of the whole gathering of the faithful. In strengthening the unity of all, the Holy Spirit at the same time fosters a diversity of gifts and furthers their multiform operation.

d) The Essential Bond between the Word of God and the Mystery of the Eucharist

10. The Church has honored the word of God and the Eucharistic mystery with the same reverence, although not with the same worship, and has always and everywhere insisted upon and sanctioned such honor. Moved by the example of its Founder, the Church has never ceased to celebrate his paschal mystery by coming together to read "what referred to him in all the Scriptures" (Lk 24:27) and to carry out the work of salvation through the celebration of the memorial of the Lord and through the sacraments. "The preaching of the word is necessary for the ministry of the sacraments, for these are sacraments of faith, which is born and nourished from the word."[22]

The Church is nourished spiritually at the twofold table of God's word and of the Eucharist:[23] from the one it grows in wisdom and from the other in holiness. In the word of God the divine covenant is announced; in the Eucharist the new and everlasting covenant is renewed. On the one hand the history of salvation is brought to mind by means of human sounds; on the other it is made manifest in the sacramental signs of the Liturgy.

It can never be forgotten, therefore, that the divine word read and proclaimed by the Church in the Liturgy has as its one purpose the sacrifice of the New Covenant and the banquet of grace, that is, the Eucharist. The celebration of Mass in which the word is heard and the Eucharist is offered and received forms but one single act of divine worship.[24] That act offers the sacrifice of praise to God and makes available to God's creatures the fullness of redemption.

FIRST PART

THE WORD OF GOD IN THE CELEBRATION OF MASS

CHAPTER TWO

THE CELEBRATION OF THE LITURGY OF THE WORD AT MASS

1. THE ELEMENTS OF THE LITURGY OF THE WORD AND THEIR RITES

11. "Readings from Sacred Scripture and the chants between the readings form the main part of the Liturgy of the Word. The homily, the profession of faith, and the universal prayer or prayer of the faithful carry it forward and conclude it."[25]

a) The Biblical Readings

12. In the celebration of Mass the biblical readings with their accompanying chants from the Sacred Scriptures may not be omitted, shortened, or, worse still, replaced by nonbiblical readings.[26] For it is out of the word of God handed down in writing that even now "God speaks to his people"[27] and it is from the continued use of Sacred Scripture that the people of God, docile to the Holy Spirit under the light of faith, is enabled to bear witness to Christ before the world by its manner of life.

13. The reading of the Gospel is the high point of the Liturgy of the Word. For this the other readings, in their established sequence from the Old to the New Testament, prepare the assembly.

14. A speaking style on the part of the readers that is audible, clear, and intelligent is the first means of transmitting the word of God properly to the congregation. The readings, taken from the approved editions,[28] may be sung in a way suited to different languages. This singing, however, must serve to bring out the sense of the words, not obscure them. On occasions when the readings are in Latin, the manner given in the *Ordo cantus Missae* is to be maintained.[29]

15. There may be concise introductions before the readings, especially the first. The style proper to such comments must be respected, that is, they must be simple, faithful to the text, brief, well prepared, and properly varied to suit the text they introduce.[30]

16. In a Mass with the people the readings are always to be proclaimed at the ambo.[31]

17. Of all the rites connected with the Liturgy of the Word, the reverence due to the Gospel reading must receive special attention.[32] Where there is an Evangeliary or Book of Gospels that has been carried in by the deacon or reader during the entry procession,[33] it is most fitting that the deacon or a priest, when there is no deacon, take the book from the altar[34] and carry it to the ambo. He is preceded by servers with candles and incense or other symbols of reverence that may be customary. As the faithful stand and acclaim the Lord, they show honor to the Book of Gospels. The deacon who is to read the Gospel, bowing in front of the one presiding, asks and receives the blessing. When no deacon is present, the priest, bowing before the altar, prays inaudibly, *Almighty God, cleanse my heart . . . .*[35]

At the ambo the one who proclaims the Gospel greets the people, who are standing, and announces the reading as he makes the sign of the cross on forehead, mouth, and breast. If incense is used, he next incenses the book, then reads the Gospel. When finished, he kisses the book, saying the appointed words inaudibly.

Even if the Gospel itself is not sung, it is appropriate for the greeting *The Lord be with you,* and *A reading from the holy Gospel according to . . .,* and at the end *The Gospel of the Lord* to be sung, in order that the congregation may also sing its acclamations. This is a way both of bringing out the importance of the Gospel reading and of stirring up the faith of those who hear it.

18. At the conclusion of the other readings, *The word of the Lord* may be sung, even by someone other than the reader; all respond with the acclamation. In this way the assembled congregation pays reverence to the word of God it has listened to in faith and gratitude.

b) The Responsorial Psalm

19. The responsorial psalm, also called the gradual, has great liturgical and pastoral significance because it is an "integral part of the liturgy of the word."[36] Accordingly, the faithful must be continually instructed on the way to perceive the word of God speaking in the psalms and to turn these psalms into the prayer of the Church. This, of course, "will be achieved more readily if a deeper understanding of the psalms, according to the meaning with which they are sung in the sacred Liturgy, is more diligently promoted among the clergy and communicated to all the faithful by means of appropriate catechesis."[37]

Brief remarks about the choice of the psalm and response as well as their correspondence to the readings may be helpful.

20. As a rule the responsorial psalm should be sung. There are two established ways of singing the psalm after the first reading: responsorially and directly. In responsorial singing, which, as far as possible, is to be given preference, the psalmist, or cantor of the psalm, sings the psalm verse and the whole congregation joins in by singing the response. In direct singing of the psalm there is no intervening response by the community; either the psalmist, or cantor of the psalm, sings the psalm alone as the community listens or else all sing it together.

21. The singing of the psalm, or even of the response alone, is a great help toward understanding and meditating on the psalm's spiritual meaning.

To foster the congregation's singing, every means available in each individual culture is to be employed. In particular, use is to be made of all the relevant options provided in the Order of Readings for Mass[38] regarding responses corresponding to the different liturgical seasons.

22. When not sung, the psalm after the reading is to be recited in a manner conducive to meditation on the word of God.[39]

The responsorial psalm is sung or recited by the psalmist or cantor at the ambo.[40]

c) The Acclamation before the Reading of the Gospel

23. The *Alleluia* or, as the liturgical season requires, the verse before the Gospel, is also a "rite or act standing by itself."[41] It serves as the greeting of welcome of the assembled faithful to the Lord who is about to speak to them and as an expression of their faith through song.

The *Alleluia* or the verse before the Gospel must be sung and during it all stand. It is not to be sung only by the cantor who intones it or by the choir, but by the whole of the people together.[42]

d) The Homily

24. Through the course of the liturgical year the homily sets forth the mysteries of faith and the standards of the Christian life on the basis of the sacred text. Beginning with the Constitution on the Liturgy, the homily as part of the Liturgy of the Word[43] has been repeatedly and strongly recommended and in some cases it is obligatory. As a rule it is to be given by the one presiding.[44] The purpose of the homily at Mass is that the spoken word of God and the Liturgy of the Eucharist may together become "a proclamation of God's wonderful works in the history of salvation, the mystery of Christ."[45] Through the readings and homily Christ's paschal mystery is proclaimed; through the sacrifice of the Mass it becomes present.[46] Moreover Christ himself is always present and active in the preaching of his Church.[47]

Whether the homily explains the text of the Sacred Scriptures proclaimed in the readings or some other text of the Liturgy,[48] it must always lead the community of the faithful to celebrate the Eucharist actively, "so that they may hold fast in their lives to what they have grasped by faith."[49] From this living explanation, the word of God proclaimed in the readings and the Church's celebration of the day's Liturgy will have greater impact. But this demands that the homily be truly the fruit of meditation, carefully prepared, neither too long nor too short, and suited to all those present, even children and the uneducated.[50]

At a concelebration, the celebrant or one of the concelebrants as a rule gives the homily.[51]

25. On the prescribed days, that is, Sundays and holydays of obligation, there must be a homily in all Masses celebrated with a congregation, even Masses on the preceding evening; the homily may not be omitted without a serious reason.[52] There is also to be a homily in Masses with children and with special groups.[53]

A homily is strongly recommended on the weekdays of Advent, Lent, and the Easter season for the sake of the faithful who regularly take part in the celebration of Mass; also on other feasts and occasions when a large congregation is present.[54]

26. The priest celebrant gives the homily, standing either at the chair or at the ambo.[55]

27. Any necessary announcements are to be kept completely separate from the homily; they must take place following the prayer after Communion.[56]

e) Silence

28. The Liturgy of the Word must be celebrated in a way that fosters meditation; clearly, any sort of haste that hinders recollection must be avoided. The dialogue between God and his people taking place through the Holy Spirit demands short intervals of silence, suited to the assembled congregation, as an opportunity to take the word of God to heart and to prepare a response to it in prayer.

Proper times for silence during the Liturgy of the Word are, for example, before this Liturgy begins, after the first and the second reading, after the homily.[57]

f) The Profession of Faith

29. The symbol, creed, or profession of faith, said when the rubrics require, has as its purpose in the celebration of Mass that the assembled congregation may respond and give assent to the word of God heard in the readings and through the homily, and that before beginning to celebrate in the Eucharist the mystery of faith it may call to mind the rule of faith in a formulary approved by the Church.[58]

g) The Universal Prayer or Prayer of the Faithful

30. In the light of God's word and in a sense in response to it, the congregation of the faithful prays in the universal prayer as a rule for the needs of the universal Church and the local community, for the salvation of the world and those oppressed by any burden, and for special categories of people.

The celebrant introduces the prayer; a deacon, another minister, or some of the faithful may propose intentions that are short and phrased with a measure of freedom. In these petitions "the people, exercising its priestly function, makes intercession for all men and women,"[59] with the result that, as the Liturgy of the Word has its full effects in the faithful, they are better prepared to proceed to the Liturgy of the Eucharist.

31. For the prayer of the faithful the celebrant presides at the chair and the intentions are announced at the ambo.[60]

The assembled congregation takes part in the prayer of the faithful while standing and by saying or singing a common response after each intention or by silent prayer.[61]

2. AIDS TO THE PROPER CELEBRATION OF THE LITURGY OF THE WORD

a) The Place for the Proclamation of the Word of God

32. There must be a place in the church that is somewhat elevated, fixed, and of a suitable design and nobility. It should reflect the dignity of God's word and be a clear reminder to the people that in the Mass the table of God's word and of Christ's body is placed before them.[62] The place for the readings must also truly help the people's listening and attention during the Liturgy of the Word. Great pains must therefore be taken, in keeping with the design of each church, over the harmonious and close relationship of the ambo with the altar.

33. Either permanently or at least on occasions of greater solemnity, the ambo should be decorated simply and in keeping with its design.

Since the ambo is the place from which the word of God is proclaimed by the ministers, it must of its nature be reserved for the readings, the responsorial psalm, and the Easter Proclamation (the *Exsultet*). The ambo may rightly be used for the homily and the prayer of the faithful, however, because of their close connection with the entire Liturgy of the Word. It is better for the commentator, cantor, or director of singing, for example, not to use the ambo.[63]

34. In order that the ambo may properly serve its liturgical purpose, it is to be rather large, since on occasion several ministers must use it at the same time. Provision must also be made for the readers to have enough light to read the text and, as required, to have modern sound equipment enabling the faithful to hear them without difficulty.

b) The Books for Proclamation of the Word of God in the Liturgy

35. Along with the ministers, the actions, the allocated places, and other elements, the books containing the readings of the word of God remind the hearers of the presence of God speaking to his people. Since in liturgical celebrations the books too serve as signs and symbols of the higher realities, care must be taken to ensure that they truly are worthy, dignified, and beautiful.[64]

36. The proclamation of the Gospel always stands as the high point of the Liturgy of the Word. Thus the liturgical tradition of both West and East has consistently made a certain distinction between the books for the readings. The Book of Gospels was always fabricated and decorated with the utmost care and shown greater respect than any of the other books of readings. In our times also, then, it is very desirable that cathedrals and at least the larger, more populous parishes and the churches with a larger attendance possess a beautifully designed Book of Gospels, separate from any other book of readings. For good reason it is the Book of Gospels that is presented to a deacon at his ordination and that at an ordination to the episcopate is laid upon the head of the bishop-elect and held there.[65]

37. Because of the dignity of the word of God, the books of readings used in the celebration are not to be replaced by other pastoral aids, for example, by leaflets printed for the preparation of the readings by the faithful or for their personal meditation.

CHAPTER THREE

OFFICES AND MINISTRIES
IN THE CELEBRATION OF THE LITURGY OF THE WORD WITHIN MASS

1. THE FUNCTION OF THE PRESIDENT AT THE LITURGY OF THE WORD

38. The one presiding at the Liturgy of the Word communicates the spiritual nourishment it contains to those present, especially in the homily. Even if he too is a listener to the word of God proclaimed by others, the duty of proclaiming it has been entrusted above all to him. Personally or through others he sees to it that the word of God is properly proclaimed. He then as a rule reserves to himself the tasks of composing comments to help the people listen more attentively and of preaching a homily that fosters in them a richer understanding of the word of God.

39. The first requirement for one who is to preside over the celebration is a thorough knowledge of the structure of the Order of Readings, so that he will know how to work a fruitful effect in the hearts of the faithful. Through study and prayer he must also develop a full understanding of the coordination and connection of the various texts in the Liturgy of the Word, so that the Order of Readings will become the source of a sound understanding of the mystery of Christ and his saving work.

40. The one presiding is to make ready use of the various options provided in the Lectionary regarding readings, responses, responsorial psalms, and Gospel acclamations;[66] but he is to do so in harmony[67] with all concerned and after listening to the opinions of the faithful in what concerns them.[68]

41. The one presiding exercises his proper office and the ministry of word of God also as he preaches the homily.[69] In this way he leads his brothers and sisters to an affective knowledge of Scripture. He opens their minds to thanksgiving for the wonderful works of God. He strengthens the faith of those present in the word that in the celebration becomes sacrament through the Holy Spirit. Finally, he prepares them for a fruitful reception of Communion and invites them to take upon themselves the demands of the Christian life.

42. The president is responsible for preparing the faithful for the Liturgy of the Word on occasion by means of introductions before the readings.[70] These comments can help the assembled congregation toward a better hearing of the word of God, because they stir up an attitude of faith and good will. He may also carry out this responsibility through others, a deacon, for example, or a commentator.[71]

43. As he directs the prayer of the faithful and through their introduction and conclusion connects them, if possible, with the day's readings and the homily, the president leads the faithful toward the Liturgy of the Eucharist.[72]

2. THE ROLE OF THE FAITHFUL IN THE LITURGY OF THE WORD

44. Christ's word gathers the people of God as one and increases and sustains them. "This applies above all to the Liturgy of the Word in the celebration of Mass, where there are inseparably united the proclamation of the death of the Lord, the response of the people listening, and the very offering through which Christ has confirmed the New Covenant in his Blood, and in which the people share by their intentions and by reception of the sacrament."[73] For "not only when things are read 'that were written for our instruction' (Rom 15:4), but also when the Church prays or sings or acts, the faith of those taking part is nourished and their minds are raised to God, so that they may offer him rightful worship and receive his grace more abundantly."[74]

45. In the Liturgy of the Word, the congregation of Christ's faithful even today receives from God the word of his covenant through the faith that comes by hearing, and must respond to that word in faith, so that they may become more and more truly the people of the New Covenant.

The people of God have a spiritual right to receive abundantly from the treasury of God's word. Its riches are presented to them through use of the Order of Readings, the homily, and pastoral efforts.

For their part, the faithful at the celebration of Mass are to listen to the word of God with an inward and outward reverence that will bring them continuous growth in the spiritual life and draw them more deeply into the mystery which is celebrated.[75]

46. As a help toward celebrating the memorial of the Lord with eager devotion, the faithful should be keenly aware of the one presence of Christ in both the word of God—it is he himself "who speaks when the Sacred Scriptures are read in the Church"—and "above all under the Eucharistic species."[76]

47. To be received and integrated into the life of Christ's faithful, the word of God demands a living faith.[77] Hearing the word of God unceasingly proclaimed arouses that faith.

The Sacred Scriptures, above all in their liturgical proclamation, are the source of life and strength. As the Apostle Paul attests, the Gospel is the saving power of God for everyone who believes.[78] Love of the Scriptures is therefore a force reinvigorating and renewing the entire people of God.[79] All the faithful without exception must therefore always be ready to listen gladly to God's word.[80] When this word is proclaimed in the Church and put into living practice, it enlightens the faithful through the working of the Holy Spirit and draws them into the entire mystery of the Lord as a reality to be lived.[81] The word of God reverently received moves the heart and its desires toward conversion and toward a life resplendent with both individual and community faith,[82] since God's word is the food of Christian life and the source of the prayer of the whole Church.[83]

48. The intimate connection between the Liturgy of the Word and the Liturgy of the Eucharist in the Mass should prompt the faithful to be present right from the beginning of the celebration,[84] to take part attentively, and to prepare themselves in so far as possible to hear the word, especially by learning beforehand more about Sacred Scripture. That same connection should also awaken in them a desire for a liturgical understanding of the texts read and a readiness to respond through singing.[85]

When they hear the word of God and reflect deeply on it, Christ's faithful are enabled to respond to it actively with full faith, hope, and charity through prayer and self-giving, and not only during Mass but in their entire Christian life.

3. MINISTRIES IN THE LITURGY OF THE WORD

49. Liturgical tradition assigns responsibility for the biblical readings in the celebration of Mass to ministers: to readers and the deacon. But when there is no deacon or no other priest present, the priest celebrant is to read the Gospel[86] and when there is no reader present, all the readings.[87]

50. It pertains to the deacon in the Liturgy of the Word at Mass to proclaim the Gospel, sometimes to give the homily, as occasion suggests, and to propose to the people the intentions of the prayer of the faithful.[88]

51. "The reader has his own proper function in the Eucharistic celebration and should exercise this even though ministers of a higher rank may be present."[89] The ministry of reader, conferred through a liturgical rite, must be held in respect. When there are instituted readers available, they are to carry out their office at least on Sundays and festive days, especially at the principal Mass of the day. These readers may also be given responsibility for assisting in the arrangement of the Liturgy of the Word, and, to the extent necessary, of seeing to the preparation of others of the faithful who may be appointed on a given occasion to read at Mass.[90]

52. The liturgical assembly truly requires readers, even those not instituted. Proper measures must therefore be taken to ensure that there are certain suitable laypeople who have been trained to carry out this ministry.[91] Whenever there is more than one reading, it is better to assign the readings to different readers, if available.

53. In Masses without a deacon, the function of announcing the intentions for the prayer of the faithful is to be assigned to the cantor, particularly when they are to be sung, to a reader, or to someone else.[92]

54. During the celebration of Mass with a congregation a second priest, a deacon, and an instituted reader must wear the distinctive vestment of their office when they go up to the ambo

to read the word of God. Those who carry out the ministry of reader just for the occasion or even regularly but without institution may go to the ambo in ordinary attire, but this should be in keeping with the customs of the different regions.

55. "It is necessary that those who exercise the ministry of reader, even if they have not received institution, be truly suited and carefully prepared, so that the faithful may develop a warm and living love for Sacred Scripture from listening to the sacred readings."[93]

Their preparation must above all be spiritual, but what may be called a technical preparation is also needed. The spiritual preparation presupposes at least a biblical and liturgical formation. The purpose of their biblical formation is to give readers the ability to understand the readings in context and to perceive by the light of faith the central point of the revealed message. The liturgical formation ought to equip the readers to have some grasp of the meaning and structure of the Liturgy of the Word and of the significance of its connection with the Liturgy of the Eucharist. The technical preparation should make the readers more skilled in the art of reading publicly, either with the power of their own voice or with the help of sound equipment.

56. The psalmist, or cantor of the psalm, is responsible for singing, responsorially or directly, the chants between the readings—the psalm or other biblical canticle, the gradual and *Alleluia*, or other chant. The psalmist may, as occasion requires, intone the *Alleluia* and verse.[94]

For carrying out the function of psalmist it is advantageous to have in each ecclesial community laypeople with the ability to sing and read with correct diction. The points made about the formation of readers apply to cantors as well.

57. The commentator also fulfills a genuine liturgical ministry, which consists in presenting to the congregation of the faithful, from a suitable place, relevant explanations and comments that are clear, of marked sobriety, meticulously prepared, and as a rule written out and approved beforehand by the celebrant.[95]

SECOND PART

THE STRUCTURE OF THE ORDER OF READINGS FOR MASS

CHAPTER FOUR

THE GENERAL ARRANGEMENT OF READINGS FOR MASS

1. THE PASTORAL PURPOSE OF THE ORDER OF READINGS FOR MASS

58. On the basis of the intention of the Second Vatican Council, the Order of Readings provided by the Lectionary of the Roman Missal has been composed above all for a pastoral purpose.

To achieve this aim, not only the principles underlying this new Order of Readings but also the lists of texts that it provides have been discussed and revised over and over again, with the cooperation of a great many experts in exegetical, liturgical, catechetical, and pastoral studies from all parts of the world. The Order of Readings is the fruit of this combined effort.

The prolonged use of this Order of Readings to proclaim and explain Sacred Scripture in the Eucharistic celebration will, it is hoped, prove to be an effective step toward achieving the objective stated repeatedly by the Second Vatican Council.[96]

59. The decision on revising the Lectionary for Mass was to draw up and edit a single, rich, and full Order of Readings that would be in complete accord with the intent and prescriptions of the Second Vatican Council.[97] At the same time, however, the Order was meant to be of a kind that would meet the requirements and usages of particular Churches and celebrating congregations. For this reason, those responsible for the revision took pains to safeguard the liturgical tradition of the Roman Rite, but valued highly the merits of all the systems of selecting, arranging, and using the biblical readings in other liturgical families and in certain particular Churches. The revisers made use of those elements that experience has confirmed, but with an effort to avoid certain shortcomings found in the preceding form of the tradition.

60. The present Order of Readings for Mass, then, is an arrangement of biblical readings that provides the faithful with a knowledge of the whole of God's word, in a pattern suited to the purpose. Throughout the liturgical year, but above all during the seasons of Easter, Lent, and Advent, the choice and sequence of readings are aimed at giving Christ's faithful an ever-deepening perception of the faith they profess and of the history of salvation.[98] Accordingly, the Order of Readings corresponds to the requirements and interests of the Christian people.

61. The celebration of the Liturgy is not in itself simply a form of catechesis, but it does contain an element of teaching. The Lectionary of the Roman Missal brings this out[99] and therefore deserves to be regarded as a pedagogical resource aiding catechesis.

This is so because the Order of Readings for Mass aptly presents from Sacred Scripture the principal deeds and words belonging to the history of salvation. As its many phases and events are recalled in the Liturgy of the Word, it will become clear to the faithful that the history of salvation is continued here and now in the representation of Christ's paschal mystery celebrated through the Eucharist.

62. The pastoral advantage of having in the Roman Rite a single Order of Readings for the Lectionary is obvious on other grounds. All the faithful, particularly those who for various reasons do not always take part in Mass with the same assembly, will everywhere be able to hear the same readings on any given day or in any liturgical season and to meditate on the application of these readings to their own concrete circumstances. This is the case even in places that have no priest and where a deacon or someone else deputed by the bishop conducts a celebration of the word of God.[100]

63. Pastors may wish to respond specifically from the word of God to the concerns of their own congregations. Although they must be mindful that they are above all to be heralds of the entire mystery of Christ and of the Gospel, they may rightfully use the options provided in the Order of Readings for Mass. This applies particularly to the celebration of a ritual or votive Mass, a Mass in honor of the Saints, or one of the Masses for various needs and occasions. With due regard for the general norms, special faculties are granted concerning the readings in Masses celebrated for particular groups.[101]

2. THE PRINCIPLES OF COMPOSITION OF THE ORDER OF READINGS FOR MASS

64. To achieve the purpose of the Order of Readings for Mass, the parts have been selected and arranged in such a way as to take into account the sequence of the liturgical seasons and the hermeneutical principles whose understanding and definition has been facilitated by modern biblical research.

It was judged helpful to state here the principles guiding the composition of the Order of Readings for Mass.

a) The Choice of Texts

65. The course of readings in the Proper of Seasons is arranged as follows. Sundays and festive days present the more important biblical passages. In this way the more significant parts of God's revealed word can be read to the assembled faithful within an appropriate period of time. Weekdays present a second series of texts from Sacred Scripture and in a sense these complement the message of salvation explained on festive days. But neither series in these main parts of the Order of Readings—the series for Sundays and festive days and that for weekdays—is dependent on the other. The Order of Readings for Sundays and festive days extends over three years; for weekdays, over two. Thus each runs its course independently of the other.

The sequence of readings in other parts of the Order of Readings is governed by its own rules. This applies to the series of readings for celebrations of the Saints, ritual Masses, Masses for various needs and occasions, votive Masses, or Masses for the dead.

b) The Arrangement of the Readings for Sundays and Festive Days

66. The following are features proper to the readings for Sundays and festive days:

1. Each Mass has three readings: the first from the Old Testament, the second from an Apostle (that is, either from a Letter or from the Book of Revelation, depending on the season), and the third from the Gospels. This arrangement brings out the unity of the Old and New Testaments and of the history of salvation, in which Christ is the central figure, commemorated in his paschal mystery.

2. A more varied and richer reading of Sacred Scripture on Sundays and festive days results from the three-year cycle provided for these days, in that the same texts are read only every fourth year.[102]

3. The principles governing the Order of Reading for Sundays and festive days are called the principles of "harmony" and of "semicontinuous reading." One or the other applies according to the different seasons of the year and the distinctive character of the particular liturgical season.

67. The best instance of harmony between the Old and New Testament readings occurs when it is one that Scripture itself suggests. This is the case when the doctrine and events recounted in texts of the New Testament bear a more or less explicit relationship to the doctrine and events of the Old Testament. The present Order of Readings selects Old Testament texts mainly because of their correlation with New Testament texts read in the same Mass, and particularly with the Gospel text.

Harmony of another kind exists between texts of the readings for each Mass during Advent, Lent, and Easter, the seasons that have a distinctive importance or character.

In contrast, the Sundays in Ordinary Time do not have a distinctive character. Thus the text of both the apostolic and Gospel readings are arranged in order of semicontinuous reading, whereas the Old Testament reading is harmonized with the Gospel.

68. The decision was made not to extend to Sundays the arrangement suited to the liturgical seasons mentioned, that is, not to have an organic harmony of themes devised with a view to facilitating homiletic instruction. Such an arrangement would be in conflict with the genuine conception of liturgical celebration, which is always the celebration of the mystery of Christ and which by its own tradition makes use of the word of God not only at the prompting of logical or extrinsic concerns but spurred by the desire to proclaim the Gospel and to lead those who believe to the fullness of truth.

c) The Arrangement of the Readings for Weekdays

69. The weekday readings have been arranged in the following way:

1. Each Mass has two readings: the first is from the Old Testament or from an Apostle (that is, either from a Letter or from the Book of Revelation), and during the Easter season from the Acts of the Apostles; the second, from the Gospels.

2. The yearly cycle for Lent has its own principles of arrangement, which take into account the baptismal and penitential character of this season.

3. The cycle for the weekdays of Advent, the Christmas season, and the Easter season is also yearly and the readings thus remain the same each year.

4. For the thirty-four weeks of Ordinary Time, the weekday Gospel readings are arranged in a single cycle, repeated each year. But the first reading is arranged in a two-year cycle and is thus read every other year. Year I is used during odd-numbered years; Year II, during even-numbered years.

Like the Order for Sundays and festive days, then, the weekday Order of Readings is governed by similar application of the principles of harmony and of semicontinuous reading, especially in the case of seasons with their own distinctive character.

d) The Readings for Celebrations of the Saints

70. Two series of readings are provided for celebrations of the Saints.

1. The Proper of Saints provides the first series, for solemnities, feasts, or memorials and particularly when there are proper texts for one or other such celebration. Sometimes in the Proper, however, there is a reference to the most appropriate among the texts in the Commons as the one to be given preference.

2. The Commons of Saints provide the second, more extensive group of readings. There are, first, appropriate texts for the different classes of Saints (martyrs, pastors, virgins, etc.), then numerous texts that deal with holiness in general. These may be freely chosen whenever the Commons are indicated as the source for the choice of readings.

71. As to their sequence, all the texts in this part of the Order of Readings appear in the order in which they are to be read at Mass. Thus the Old Testament texts are first, then the texts from the Apostles, followed by the psalms and verses between the readings, and finally the texts from the Gospels. The rationale of this arrangement is that, unless otherwise noted, the celebrant may choose at will from such texts, in view of the pastoral needs of the congregation taking part in the celebration.

e) Readings for Ritual Masses, Masses for Various Needs and Occasions, Votive Masses, and Masses for the Dead

72. For ritual Masses, Masses for various needs and occasions, votive Masses, and Masses for the dead, the texts for the readings are arranged as just described, that is, numerous texts are grouped together in the order of their use, as in the Commons of Saints.

f) The Main Criteria Applied in Choosing and Arranging the Readings

73. In addition to the guiding principles already given for the arrangement of readings in the individual parts of the Order of Readings, others of a more general nature follow.

1) THE RESERVATION OF SOME BOOKS TO PARTICULAR LITURGICAL SEASONS

74. In this Order of Readings, some biblical books are set aside for particular liturgical seasons on the basis both of the intrinsic importance of subject matter and of liturgical tradition. For example, the Western (Ambrosian and Hispanic) and Eastern tradition of reading the Acts of the Apostles during the Easter season is maintained. This usage results in a clear presentation of how the Church's entire life derives its beginning from the paschal mystery. The tradition of both West and East is also retained, namely the reading of the Gospel of John in the latter weeks of Lent and in the Easter season.

Tradition assigns the reading of Isaiah, especially the first part, to Advent. Some texts of this book, however, are read during the Christmas season, to which the First Letter of John is also assigned.

2) THE LENGTH OF THE TEXTS

75. A *middle way* is followed in regard to the length of texts. A distinction has been made between narratives, which require reading a fairly long passage but which usually hold the attention of the faithful, and texts that should not be lengthy because of the profundity of their doctrine.

In the case of certain rather lengthy texts, longer and shorter versions are provided to suit different situations. The editing of the shorter version has been carried out with great caution.

3) DIFFICULT TEXTS

76. In readings for Sundays and solemnities, texts that present real difficulties are avoided for pastoral reasons. The difficulties may be objective, in that the texts themselves raise profound literary, critical, or exegetical problems; or the difficulties may lie, at least to a certain extent, in the ability of the faithful to understand the texts. But there could be no justification for concealing from the faithful the spiritual riches of certain texts on the grounds of difficulty if the problem arises from the inadequacy either of the religious education that every Christian should have or of the biblical formation that every pastor of souls should have. Often a difficult reading is clarified by its correlation with another in the same Mass.

4) THE OMISSION OF CERTAIN VERSES

77. The omission of verses in readings from Scripture has at times been the tradition of many liturgies, including the Roman liturgy. Admittedly such omissions may not be made lightly, for fear of distorting the meaning of the text or the intent and style of Scripture. Yet on pastoral grounds it was decided to continue the traditional practice in the present Order of Readings, but at the same time to ensure that the essential meaning of the text remained intact. One

reason for the decision is that otherwise some texts would have been unduly long. It would also have been necessary to omit completely certain readings of high spiritual value for the faithful because those readings include some verse that is pastorally less useful or that involves truly difficult questions.

3. PRINCIPLES TO BE FOLLOWED IN THE USE OF THE ORDER OF READINGS
a) The Freedom of Choice Regarding Some Texts

78. The Order of Readings sometimes leaves it to the celebrant to choose between alternative texts or to choose one from the several listed together for the same reading. The option seldom exists on Sundays, solemnities, or feasts, in order not to obscure the character proper to the particular liturgical season or needlessly interrupt the semicontinuous reading of some biblical book. On the other hand, the option is given readily in celebrations of the Saints, in ritual Masses, Masses for various needs and occasions, votive Masses, and Masses for the dead.

These options, together with those indicated in the General Instruction of the Roman Missal and the *Ordo cantus Missae,*[103] have a pastoral purpose. In arranging the Liturgy of the Word, then, the priest should "consider the general spiritual good of the congregation rather than his personal outlook. He should be mindful that the choice of texts is to be made in harmony with the ministers and others who have a role in the celebration and should listen to the opinions of the faithful in what concerns them more directly."[104]

1) THE TWO READINGS BEFORE THE GOSPEL

79. In Masses to which three readings are assigned, all three are to be used. If, however, for pastoral reasons the Conference of Bishops has given permission for two readings only to be used,[105] the choice between the two first readings is to be made in such a way as to safeguard the Church's intent to instruct the faithful more completely in the mystery of salvation. Thus, unless the contrary is indicated in the text of the Lectionary, the reading to be chosen as the first reading is the one that is more closely in harmony with the Gospel, or, in accord with the intent just mentioned, the one that is more helpful toward a coherent catechesis over an extended period, or that preserves the semicontinuous reading of some biblical book.[106]

2) THE LONGER AND SHORTER FORMS OF TEXTS

80. A pastoral criterion must also guide the choice between the longer and shorter forms of the same text. The main consideration must be the capacity of the hearers to listen profitably either to the longer or to the shorter reading; or to listen to a more complete text that will be explained through the homily.

3) WHEN TWO TEXTS ARE PROVIDED

81. When a choice is allowed between alternative texts, whether they are fixed or optional, the first consideration must be the best interest of those taking part. It may be a matter of using the easier texts or the one more relevant to the assembled congregation or, as pastoral advantage may suggest, of repeating or replacing a text that is assigned as proper to one celebration and optional to another.

The issue may arise when it is feared that some text will create difficulties for a particular congregation or when the same text would have to be repeated within a few days, as on a Sunday and on a day during the week following.

4) THE WEEKDAY READINGS

82. The arrangement of weekday readings provides texts for every day of the week through-out the year. In most cases, therefore, these readings are to be used on their assigned days, unless a solemnity, a feast, or else a memorial with proper readings occurs.[107]

In using the Order of Readings for weekdays attention must be paid to whether one read-ing or another from the same biblical book will have to be omitted because of some celebra-tion occurring during the week. With the arrangement of readings for the entire week in mind, the priest in that case arranges to omit the less significant passages or combines them in the most appropriate manner with other readings, if they contribute to an integral view of a par-ticular theme.

5) THE CELEBRATIONS OF THE SAINTS

83. When they exist, proper readings are given for celebrations of the Saints, that is, biblical passages about the Saint or the mystery that the Mass is celebrating. Even in the case of a memorial these readings must take the place of the weekday readings for the same day. This Order of Readings makes explicit note of every case of proper readings on a memorial.

In some cases there are accommodated readings, those, namely, that bring out some par-ticular aspect of a Saint's spiritual life or work. Use of such readings does not seem binding, except for compelling pastoral reasons. For the most part references are given to readings in the Commons in order to facilitate choice. But these are merely suggestions: in place of an ac-commodated reading or the particular reading proposed from a Common, any other reading from the Commons referred to may be selected.

The first concern of a priest celebrating with a congregation is the spiritual benefit of the faithful and he will be careful not to impose his personal preference on them. Above all he will make sure not to omit too often or without sufficient cause the readings assigned for each day in the weekday Lectionary: the Church's desire is that a more lavish table of the word of God be spread before the faithful.[108]

There are also common readings, that is, those placed in the Commons either for some de-termined class of Saints (martyrs, virgins, pastors) or for the Saints in general. Because in these cases several texts are listed for the same reading, it will be up to the priest to choose the one best suited to those listening.

In all celebrations of Saints the readings may be taken not only from the Commons to which the references are given in each case, but also from the Common of Holy Men and Women, whenever there is special reason for doing so.

84. For celebrations of the Saints the following should be observed:

1. On solemnities and feasts the readings must be those that are given in the Proper or in the Commons. For solemnities and feasts of the General Roman Calendar proper readings are always assigned.

2. On solemnities inscribed in particular calendars, three readings are to be assigned, un-less the Conference of Bishops has decreed that there are to be only two readings.[109] The first reading is from the Old Testament (but during the Easter season, from the Acts of the Apostles or the Book of Revelation); the second, from an Apostle; the third, from the Gospels.

3. On feasts and memorials, which have only two readings, the first reading can be chosen from either the Old Testament or from an Apostle; the second is from the Gospels. Following the Church's traditional practice, however, the first reading during the Easter season is to be taken from an Apostle; the second, as far as possible, from the Gospel of John.

6) OTHER PARTS OF THE ORDER OF READINGS

85. In the Order of Readings for ritual Masses the references given are to the texts already published for the individual rites. This obviously does not include the texts belonging to celebrations that must not be integrated with Mass.[110]

86. The Order of Readings for Masses for various needs and occasions, votive Masses, and Masses for the dead provides many texts that can be of assistance in adapting such celebrations to the situation, circumstances, and concerns of the particular groups taking part.[111]

87. In ritual Masses, Masses for various needs and occasions, votive Masses, and Masses for the dead, since many texts are given for the same reading, the choice of readings follows the criteria already indicated for the choice of readings from the Common of Saints.

88. On a day when some ritual Mass is not permitted and when the norms in the individual rite allow the choice of one reading from those provided for ritual Masses, the general spiritual welfare of the participants must be considered.[112]

b) The Responsorial Psalm and the Acclamation before the Gospel Reading

89. Among the chants between the readings, the psalm which follows the first reading is of great importance. As a rule the psalm to be used is the one assigned to the reading. But in the case of readings for the Common of Saints, ritual Masses, Masses for various needs and occasions, votive Masses, and Masses for the dead the choice is left up to the priest celebrating. He will base his choice on the principle of the pastoral benefit of those present.

But to make it easier for the people to join in the response to the psalm, the Order of Readings lists certain other texts of psalms and responses that have been chosen according to the various seasons or classes of Saints. Whenever the psalm is sung, these texts may replace the text corresponding to the reading.[113]

90. The chant between the second reading and the Gospel is either specified in each Mass and correlated with the Gospel or else it is left as a choice to be made from those in the series given for a liturgical season or one of the Commons.

91. During Lent one of the acclamations from those given in the Order of Readings may be used, depending on the occasion.[114] This acclamation precedes and follows the verse before the Gospel.

CHAPTER FIVE

DESCRIPTION OF THE ORDER OF READINGS

92. It seems useful to provide here a brief description of the Order of Readings, at least for the principal celebrations and the different seasons of the liturgical year. With these in mind, readings were selected on the basis of the rules already stated. This description is meant to assist

pastors of souls to understand the structure of the Order of Readings, so that their use of it will become more perceptive and the Order of Readings a source of good for Christ's faithful.

1. ADVENT

a) The Sundays

93. Each Gospel reading has a distinctive theme: the Lord's coming at the end of time (First Sunday of Advent), John the Baptist (Second and Third Sunday), and the events that prepared immediately for the Lord's birth (Fourth Sunday).

The Old Testament readings are prophecies about the Messiah and the Messianic age, especially from the Book of Isaiah.

The readings from an Apostle contain exhortations and proclamations, in keeping with the different themes of Advent.

b) The Weekdays

94. There are two series of readings: one to be used from the beginning of Advent until 16 December; the other from 17 to 24 December.

In the first part of Advent there are readings from the Book of Isaiah, distributed in accord with the sequence of the book itself and including the more important texts that are also read on the Sundays. For the choice of the weekday Gospel the first reading has been taken into consideration.

On Thursday of the second week the readings from the Gospel concerning John the Baptist begin. The first reading is either a continuation of Isaiah or a text chosen in view of the Gospel.

In the last week before Christmas the events that immediately prepared for the Lord's birth are presented from the Gospels of Matthew (chapter 1) and Luke (chapter 1). The texts in the first reading, chosen in view of the Gospel reading, are from different Old Testament books and include important Messianic prophecies.

2. THE CHRISTMAS SEASON

a) The Solemnities, Feasts, and Sundays

95. For the vigil and the three Masses of Christmas both the prophetic readings and the others have been chosen from the Roman tradition.

The Gospel on the Sunday within the Octave of Christmas, Feast of the Holy Family, is about Jesus' childhood and the other readings are about the virtues of family life.

On the Octave Day of Christmas, Solemnity of the Blessed Virgin Mary, the Mother of God, the readings are about the Virgin Mother of God and the giving of the holy Name of Jesus.

On the second Sunday after Christmas, the readings are about the mystery of the Incarnation.

On the Epiphany of the Lord, the Old Testament reading and the Gospel continue the Roman tradition; the text for the reading from the Letters of the Apostles is about the calling of the nations to salvation.

On the Feast of the Baptism of the Lord, the texts chosen are about this mystery.

b) The Weekdays

96. From 29 December on, there is a continuous reading of the whole of the First Letter of John, which actually begins earlier, on 27 December, the Feast of St. John the Evangelist, and on 28 December, the Feast of the Holy Innocents. The Gospels relate manifestations of the

Lord: events of Jesus' childhood from the Gospel of Luke (29–30 December); passages from the first chapter of the Gospel of John (31 December–5 January); other manifestations of the Lord from the four Gospels (7–12 January).

3. LENT

a) The Sundays

97. The Gospel readings are arranged as follows:

The first and second Sundays maintain the accounts of the Temptation and Transfiguration of the Lord, with readings, however, from all three Synoptics.

On the next three Sundays, the Gospels about the Samaritan woman, the man born blind, and the raising of Lazarus have been restored in Year A. Because these Gospels are of major importance in regard to Christian initiation, they may also be read in Year B and Year C, especially in places where there are catechumens.

Other texts, however, are provided for Year B and Year C: for Year B, a text from John about Christ's coming glorification through his Cross and Resurrection and for Year C, a text from Luke about conversion.

On Palm Sunday of the Lord's Passion the texts for the procession are selections from the Synoptic Gospels concerning the Lord's solemn entry into Jerusalem. For the Mass the reading is the account of the Lord's Passion.

The Old Testament readings are about the history of salvation, which is one of the themes proper to the catechesis of Lent. The series of texts for each Year presents the main elements of salvation history from its beginning until the promise of the New Covenant.

The readings from the Letters of the Apostles have been selected to fit the Gospel and the Old Testament readings and, to the extent possible, to provide a connection between them.

b) The Weekdays

98. The readings from the Gospels and the Old Testament were selected because they are related to each other. They treat various themes of the Lenten catechesis that are suited to the spiritual significance of this season. Beginning with Monday of the Fourth Week of Lent, there is a semicontinuous reading of the Gospel of John, made up of texts that correspond more closely to the themes proper to Lent.

Because the readings about the Samaritan woman, the man born blind, and the raising of Lazarus are now assigned to Sundays, but only for Year A (in Year B and Year C they are optional), provision has been made for their use on weekdays. Thus at the beginning of the Third, Fourth, and Fifth Weeks of Lent optional Masses with these texts for the Gospel have been inserted and may be used in place of the readings of the day on any weekday of the respective week.

In the first days of Holy Week the readings are about the mystery of Christ's passion. For the Chrism Mass the readings bring out both Christ's Messianic mission and its continuation in the Church by means of the sacraments.

4. THE SACRED TRIDUUM AND THE EASTER SEASON

a) The Sacred Easter Triduum

99. On Holy Thursday at the evening Mass the remembrance of the meal preceding the Exodus casts its own special light because of Christ's example in washing the feet of his disciples and Paul's account of the institution of the Christian Passover in the Eucharist.

On Good Friday the liturgical service has as its center John's narrative of the Passion of him who was proclaimed in Isaiah as the Servant of the LORD and who became the one High Priest by offering himself to the Father.

At the Vigil on the holy night of Easter there are seven Old Testament readings which recall the wonderful works of God in the history of salvation. There are two New Testament readings, the announcement of the Resurrection according to one of the Synoptic Gospels and a reading from St. Paul on Christian baptism as the sacrament of Christ's Resurrection.

The Gospel reading for the Mass on Easter day is from John on the finding of the empty tomb. There is also, however, the option to use the Gospel texts from the Easter Vigil or, when there is an evening Mass on Easter Sunday, to use the account in Luke of the Lord's appearance to the disciples on the road to Emmaus. The first reading is from the Acts of the Apostles, which throughout the Easter season replaces the Old Testament reading. The reading from the Apostle Paul concerns the living out of the paschal mystery in the Church.

b) The Sundays

100. The Gospel readings for the first three Sundays recount the appearances of the risen Christ. The readings about the Good Shepherd are assigned to the Fourth Sunday. On the Fifth, Sixth, and Seventh Sundays, there are excerpts from the Lord's discourse and prayer at the end of the Last Supper.

The first reading is from the Acts of the Apostles, in a three-year cycle of parallel and progressive selections: material is presented on the life of the early Church, its witness, and its growth.

For the reading from the Apostles, the First Letter of Peter is in Year A, the First Letter of John in Year B, the Book of Revelation in Year C. These are the texts that seem to fit in especially well with the spirit of joyous faith and sure hope proper to this season.

c) The Weekdays

101. As on the Sundays, the first reading is a semicontinuous reading from the Acts of the Apostles. The Gospel readings during the Easter octave are accounts of the Lord's appearances. After that there is a semicontinuous reading of the Gospel of John, but with texts that have a paschal character, in order to complete the reading from John during Lent. This paschal reading is made up in large part of the Lord's discourse and prayer at the end of the Last Supper.

d) The Solemnities of the Ascension and of Pentecost

102. For the first reading the Solemnity of the Ascension retains the account of the Ascension according to the Acts of the Apostles. This text is complemented by the second reading from the Apostle on Christ in exaltation at the right hand of the Father. For the Gospel reading, each of the three Years has its own text in accord with the differences in the Synoptic Gospels.

In the evening Mass celebrated on the Vigil of Pentecost four Old Testament texts are provided; any one of them may be used, in order to bring out the many aspects of Pentecost. The reading from the Apostles shows the actual working of the Holy Spirit in the Church. The Gospel reading recalls the promise of the Spirit made by Christ before his own glorification.

For the Mass on Pentecost day itself, in accord with received usage, the account in the Acts of the Apostles of the great occurrence on Pentecost day is taken as the first reading. The texts from the Apostle Paul bring out the effect of the action of the Spirit in the life of the Church. The Gospel reading is a remembrance of Jesus bestowing his Spirit on the disciples on the evening of Easter day; other optional texts describe the action of the Spirit on the disciples and on the Church.

5. ORDINARY TIME

a) *The Arrangement and Choice of Texts*

103. Ordinary Time begins on the Monday after the Sunday following 6 January; it lasts until the Tuesday before Lent inclusive. It begins again on the Monday after Pentecost Sunday and finishes before evening prayer I of the First Sunday of Advent.

The Order of Readings provides readings for thirty-four Sundays and the weeks following them. In some years, however, there are only thirty-three weeks of Ordinary Time. Further, some Sundays either belong to another season (the Sunday on which the Feast of the Baptism of the Lord falls and Pentecost Sunday) or else are impeded by a solemnity that coincides with Sunday (e.g., The Most Holy Trinity or Christ the King).

104. For the correct arrangement in the use of the readings for Ordinary Time, the following are to be respected:

1. The Sunday on which the Feast of the Baptism of the Lord falls replaces the First Sunday in Ordinary Time. Therefore the readings of the First Week of Ordinary Time begin on the Monday after the Sunday following 6 January. When the Feast of the Baptism of the Lord is celebrated on Monday because the Epiphany has been celebrated on the Sunday, the readings of the First Week begin on Tuesday.

2. The Sunday following the Feast of the Baptism of the Lord is the Second Sunday of Ordinary Time. The remaining Sundays are numbered consecutively up to the Sunday preceding the beginning of Lent. The readings for the week in which Ash Wednesday falls are interrupted after the Tuesday readings.

3. For the resumption of the readings of Ordinary Time after Pentecost Sunday:

—when there are thirty-four Sundays in Ordinary Time, the week to be used is the one that immediately follows the last week used before Lent;[115]

—when there are thirty-three Sundays in Ordinary Time, the first week that would have been used after Pentecost is omitted, in order to reserve for the end of the year the eschatological texts that are assigned to the last two weeks.[116]

b) *The Sunday Readings*

1) THE GOSPEL READINGS

105. On the Second Sunday of Ordinary Time the Gospel continues to center on the manifestation of the Lord, which is celebrated on the Solemnity of the Epiphany, through the traditional passage about the wedding feast at Cana and two other passages from the Gospel of John.

Beginning with the Third Sunday, there is a semicontinuous reading of the Synoptic Gospels. This reading is arranged in such a way that as the Lord's life and preaching unfold the doctrine proper to each of these Gospels is presented.

This distribution also provides a certain coordination between the meaning of each Gospel and the progress of the liturgical year. Thus after Epiphany the readings are on the beginning of the Lord's preaching and they fit in well with Christ's baptism and the first events in which he manifests himself. The liturgical year leads quite naturally to a conclusion in the eschatological theme proper to the last Sundays, since the chapters of the Synoptics that precede the account of the Passion treat this eschatological theme rather extensively.

After the Sixteenth Sunday in Year B, five readings are incorporated from John chapter 6 (the discourse on the bread of life). This is the natural place for these readings because the multiplication of the loaves from the Gospel of John takes the place of the same account in Mark. In the semicontinuous reading of Luke for Year C, the introduction of this Gospel has been prefixed to the first text (that is, on the Third Sunday). This passage expresses the author's intention very beautifully and there seemed to be no better place for it.

2) THE OLD TESTAMENT READINGS

106. These readings have been chosen to correspond to the Gospel passages in order to avoid an excessive diversity between the readings of different Masses and above all to bring out the unity between the Old and the New Testament. The connection between the readings of the same Mass is shown by a precise choice of the readings prefixed to the individual readings.

To the degree possible, the readings were chosen in such a way that they would be short and easy to grasp. But care has been taken to ensure that many Old Testament texts of major significance would be read on Sundays. Such readings are distributed not according to a logical order but on the basis of what the Gospel reading requires. Still, the treasury of the word of God will be opened up in such a way that nearly all the principal pages of the Old Testament will become familiar to those taking part in the Mass on Sundays.

3) THE READINGS FROM THE APOSTLES

107. There is a semicontinuous reading of the Letters of Paul and James (the Letters of Peter and John being read during the Easter and Christmas seasons).

Because it is quite long and deals with such diverse issues, the First Letter to the Corinthians has been spread over the three years of the cycle at the beginning of Ordinary Time. It also was thought best to divide the Letter to the Hebrews into two parts; the first part is read in Year B and the second in Year C.

Only readings that are short and readily grasped by the people have been chosen.

Table II at the end of this Introduction[117] indicates the distribution of Letters of the Apostles over the three-year cycle of the Sundays of Ordinary Time.

c) The Readings for Solemnities of the Lord during Ordinary Time

108. On the solemnities of Holy Trinity, Corpus Christi, and the Sacred Heart, the texts chosen correspond to the principal themes of these celebrations.

The readings of the Thirty-Fourth and last Sunday of Ordinary Time celebrate Christ the universal King. He was prefigured by David and proclaimed as King amid the humiliations of his Passion and Cross; he reigns in the Church and will come again at the end of time.

d) The Weekday Readings

109. The *Gospels* are so arranged that Mark is read first (First to Ninth Week), then Matthew (Tenth to Twenty-First Week), then Luke (Twenty-Second to Thirty-Fourth Week). Mark chapters 1–12 are read in their entirety, with the exception only of the two passages of Mark chapter 6 that are read on weekdays in other seasons. From Matthew and Luke the readings comprise all the material not contained in Mark. All the passages that either are distinctively presented in each Gospel or are needed for a proper understanding of its progression are read

two or three times. Jesus' eschatological discourse as contained in its entirety in Luke is read at the end of the liturgical year.

110. The *First Reading* is taken in periods of several weeks at a time first from one then from the other Testament; the number of weeks depends on the length of the biblical books read.

Rather large sections are read from the New Testament books in order to give the substance, as it were, of each of the Letters.

From the Old Testament there is room only for select passages that, as far as possible, bring out the character of the individual books. The historical texts have been chosen in such a way as to provide an overall view of the history of salvation before the Incarnation of the Lord. But lengthy narratives could hardly be presented; sometimes verses have been selected that make for a reading of moderate length. In addition, the religious significance of the historical events is sometimes brought out by means of certain texts from the wisdom books that are placed as prologues or conclusions to a series of historical readings.

Nearly all the Old Testament books have found a place in the Order of Readings for weekdays in the Proper of Seasons. The only omissions are the shortest of the prophetic books (Obadiah and Zephaniah) and a poetic book (the Song of Songs). Of those narratives of edification requiring a lengthy reading if they are to be understood, Tobit and Ruth are included, but the others (Esther and Judith) are omitted. Texts from these latter two books are assigned, however, to Sundays and weekdays at other times of the year.

Table III at the end of this Introduction[118] lists the way the books of the Old and the New Testaments are distributed over the weekdays in Ordinary Time in the course of two years.

At the end of the liturgical year the readings are from the books that correspond to the eschatological character of this period, Daniel and the Book of Revelation.

CHAPTER SIX

ADAPTATIONS, TRANSLATIONS, AND FORMAT OF THE ORDER OF READINGS

1. ADAPTATIONS AND TRANSLATIONS

111. In the liturgical assembly the word of God must always be read either from the Latin texts prepared by the Holy See or from vernacular translations approved for liturgical use by the Conferences of Bishops, according to existing norms.[119]

112. The Lectionary for Mass must be translated integrally in all its parts, including the Introduction. If the Conference of Bishops has judged it necessary and useful to add certain adaptations, these are to be incorporated after their confirmation by the Holy See.[120]

113. The size of the Lectionary will necessitate editions in more than one volume; no particular division of the volumes is prescribed. But each volume is to contain the explanatory texts on the structure and purpose of the section it contains.

The ancient custom is recommended of having separate books, one for the Gospels and the other for the other readings for the Old and New Testaments.

It may also be useful to publish separately a Sunday lectionary (which could also contain selected excerpts from the sanctoral cycle), and a weekday lectionary. A practical basis for dividing the Sunday lectionary is the three-year cycle, so that all the readings for each year are presented in sequence.

But there is freedom to adopt other arrangements that may be devised and seem to have pastoral advantages.

114. The texts for the chants are always to be adjoined to the readings, but separate books containing the chants alone are permitted. It is recommended that the texts be printed with divisions into stanzas.

115. Whenever a text consists of different parts, the typography must make this structure of the text clear. It is likewise recommended that even non-poetic texts be printed with division into sense lines to assist the proclamation of the readings.

116. Where there are longer and shorter forms of a text, they are to be printed separately, so that each can be read with ease. But if such a separation does not seem feasible, a way is to be found to ensure that each text can be proclaimed without mistakes.

117. In vernacular editions the texts are not to be printed without headings prefixed. If it seems advisable, an introductory note on the general meaning of the passage may be added to the heading. This note is to carry some distinctive symbol or is to be set in different type to show clearly that it is an optional text.[121]

118. It would be useful for every volume to have an index of the passages of the Bible, modeled on the biblical index of the present volume.[122] This will provide ready access to texts of the lectionaries for Mass that may be needed or helpful for specific occasions.

2. THE FORMAT OF INDIVIDUAL READINGS

For each reading the present volume carries the textual reference, the headings, and the *incipit*.

a) The Biblical References

119. The text reference (that is, to chapter and verses) is always given according to the Neo-Vulgate edition for the psalms.[123] But a second reference according to the original text (Hebrew, Aramaic, or Greek) has been added wherever there is a discrepancy. Depending on the decrees of the competent Authorities for the individual languages, vernacular versions may retain the enumeration corresponding to the version of the Bible approved for liturgical use by the same Authorities. Exact references to chapter and verses, however, must always appear and may be given in the text or in the margin.

120. These references provide liturgical books with the basis of the "announcement" of the text that must be read in the celebration, but which is not printed in this volume. This "announcement" of the text will observe the following norms, but they may be altered by decree of the competent Authorities on the basis of what is customary and useful for different places and languages.

121. The formula to be used is always: "A *reading* from the Book of . . .," "A *reading* from the Letter of . . .," or "A *reading* from the holy Gospel according to . . .," and not: "The *beginning* of . . .," (unless this seems advisable in particular instances), nor: "The *continuation* of . . . ."

122. The traditionally accepted titles for books are to be retained with the following exceptions:

1. Where there are two books with the same name, the title is to be: The first Book, The second Book (for example, of Kings, of Maccabees) or The first Letter, The second Letter.

2. The title more common in current usage is to be accepted for the following books:

—I and II Samuel instead of I and II Kings;

—I and II Kings instead of III and IV Kings;

—I and II Chronicles instead of I and II Paralipomenon;

—The Books of Ezra and Nehemiah instead of I and II Ezra.

3. The distinguishing titles for the wisdom books are: The Book of Job, the Book of Proverbs, the Book of Ecclesiastes, the Song of Songs, the Book of Wisdom, and the Book of Sirach.

4. For all the books that are included among the prophets in the Neo-Vulgate, the formula is to be: "A reading from the Book of the Prophet Isaiah, or of the Prophet Jeremiah or of the Prophet Baruch" and: "A reading from the Book of the Prophet Ezekiel, of the Prophet Daniel, of the Prophet Hosea, of the Prophet Malachi," even in the case of books not regarded by some as being in actual fact prophetic.

5. The title is to be Book of Lamentations and Letter to the Hebrews, with no mention of Jeremiah or Paul.

b) The Heading

123. There is a *heading* prefixed to each text, chosen carefully (usually from the words of the text itself) in order to point out the main theme of the reading and, when necessary, to make the connection between the readings of the same Mass clear.

c) The "Incipit"

124. In this Order of Readings the first element of the *incipit* is the customary introductory phrase: "At that time," "In those days," "Brothers and sisters," "Beloved," "Dearly beloved," "Dearest brothers and sisters," or "Thus says the Lord," "Thus says the Lord God." These words are not given when the text itself provides sufficient indication of the time or the persons involved or where such phrases would not fit in with the very nature of the text. For the individual languages, such phrases may be changed or omitted by decree of the competent Authorities.

After the first words of the *incipit* the Order of Readings gives the proper beginning of the reading, with some words deleted or supplied for intelligibility, inasmuch as the text is separated from its context. When the text for a reading is made up of non-consecutive verses and this has required changes in wording, these are appropriately indicated.

d) The Final Acclamation

125. In order to facilitate the congregation's acclamation, the words for the reader *The word of the Lord,* or similar words suited to local custom, are to be printed at the end of the reading for use by the reader.

NOTES

[1] Cf. especially Second Vatican Council, Constitution on the Sacred Liturgy, *Sacrosanctum Concilium*, nn. 7, 24, 33, 35, 48, 51, 52, 56; Dogmatic Constitution on Divine Revelation, *Dei Verbum*, nn. 1, 21, 25, 26; Decree on the Missionary Activity of the Church, *Ad gentes*, n. 6; Decree on the Ministry and Life of Priests, *Presbyterorum Ordinis*, n. 18.

[2] Among the spoken or written statements of the Supreme Pontiffs, see especially: Paul VI, Motu Proprio, *Ministeria quaedam*, 15 August 1972, n. V: *Acta Apostolicae Sedis* [*AAS*] 64 (1972) 532; Apostolic Exhortation, *Marialis cultus*, 2 February 1974, n. 12: *AAS* 66 (1974) 125–126; Apostolic Exhortation, *Evangelii nuntiandi*, 8 December 1975, n. 28: *AAS* 68 (1976) 24–25, n. 43: *ibid.*, pp. 33–34, n. 47: *ibid.*, pp. 36–37; John Paul II, Apostolic Constitution, *Scripturarum thesaurus*, 25 April 1979 in *Nova Vulgata Bibliorum Sacrorum editione*, Typis Polyglottis Vaticanis 1979, pp. V–VIII; Apostolic Exhortation, *Catechesi tradendae*, 16 October 1979, nn. 23, 27, 48: *AAS* 71 (1979) 1296–1297, 1298–1299, 1316; Letter, *Dominicae Cenae*, 24 February 1980, n. 10: *AAS* 72 (1980) 134–137.

[3] Cf. V. gr. Sacred Congregation of Rites, Instruction, *Eucharisticum Mysterium*, 25 May 1967, n. 10: *AAS* 59 (1967) 547–548; Sacred Congregation for Divine Worship, Instruction, *Liturgicae instaurationes*, 5 September 1970, n. 2: *AAS* 62 (1970) 695–696; Sacred Congregation for the Clergy, *Directorum catechesticum generale,* 11 April 1971: *AAS* 64 (1972) 106–107; n. 25: *ibid.*, p. 114; Sacred Congregation for Divine Worship, *Institutio Generalis Missalis Romani*, nn. 9, 11, 24, 33, 60, 62, 316, 320; Sacred Congregation for Catholic Education, Instruction on liturgical formation in seminaries, *In ecclesiasticam futurorum sacerdotum*, 3 June 1979, nn. 11, 52; *ibid.*, Appendix, n. 15; Sacred Congregation for the Sacraments and Divine Worship, Instruction, *Inaestimabile Donum*, 3 April 1980, nn. 1, 2, 3; *AAS* 72 (1980) 333–334.

[4] Cf. Missale Romanum ex Decreto Sacrosancti Oecumenici Concilii Vaticani II instauratum auctoritate Pauli VI promulgatum, *Ordo lectionum Missae* (Typis Polyglottis Vaticanis, 1969) pp. IX–XII (Praenotanda); Decree of promulgation: *AAS* 61 (1969) 548–549.

[5] Cf. Second Vatican Council, Constitution on the Sacred Liturgy, *Sacrosanctum Concilium*, nn. 35, 56; Paul VI, Apostolic Exhortation, *Evangelii nuntiandi*, 8 December 1975, nn. 28, 47: *AAS* 68 (1976) 24–25, 36–37; John Paul II, Letter, *Dominicae Cenae*, 24 February 1980, nn. 10, 11, 12: *AAS* 72 (1980) 134–146.

[6] For example, the terms "word of God," "Sacred Scripture," "Old" and "New Testament," "Reading (readings) of the word of God," "Reading (readings) from Sacred Scripture," "Celebration (celebrations) of the word of God," etc.

[7] Thus one and the same text may be read or used for various reasons on various occasions and celebrations of the Church's liturgical year. This is to be recalled in the homily, in pastoral exegesis, and in catechesis. The indexes of this volume will show, for example, that Romans chapter 6 or Romans chapter 8 is used in various seasons of the liturgical year and in various celebrations of the sacraments and sacramentals.

[8] Cf. Lk 4:16-21; 24:25-35, 44-49.

[9] Thus, for example, in the celebration of Mass, there is proclamation, reading, etc. (cf. *Institutio Generalis Missalis Romani*, nn. 21, 23, 95, 131, 146, 234, 235). There are also other celebrations of the word of God in the *Pontificale Romanum*, the *Rituale Romanum*, and the *Liturgia Horarum*, as restored by decree of Second Vatican Council.

[10] Cf. Second Vatican Council, Constitution on the Sacred Liturgy, *Sacrosanctum Concilium*, nn. 7, 33; Mk 16:19-20; Mt 28:20; St. Augustine, *Sermo* 85, 1: "The Gospel is the mouth of Christ. He is seated in heaven yet does not cease to speak on earth": *PL* 38, 520; cf. also *In Io. Ev. tract.* XXX, 1: *PL* 35, 1632; *CCL* 36, 289; *Pontificale Romano–Germanicum*: "The Gospel is read, in which Christ speaks by his own mouth to the people . . . the Gospel resounds in the church as though Christ himself were speaking to the

people" (see C. Vogel & R. Elze, edd., *Le Pontifical romano–germanique du dixième siècle. Le Texte I*, Città del Vaticano, 1963, XCIV, 18, p. 334); or "At the approach of Christ, that is the Gospel, we put aside our staffs, because we have no need of human assistance" (*ibid.* XCIV, 23, p. 335).

[11] Cf. Second Vatican Council, Constitution on the Sacred Liturgy, *Sacrosanctum Concilium*, n. 7.

[12] Cf. Heb 4:12.

[13] Cf. St. Augustine, *Quaestionum in Heptateuchum liber* 2, 73: *PL* 34, 623; *CCL* 33, 106; Second Vatican Council, Dogmatic Constitution on Divine Revelation, *Dei Verbum*, n. 16.

[14] Cf. St. Jerome: "If, as St. Paul says (1 Cor 1:24), Christ is the power of God and the wisdom of God, anyone who is ignorant of the Scriptures is ignorant of the power of God and his wisdom. For ignorance of the Scriptures is ignorance of Christ" (*Commentarii in Isaiam prophetam, Prologus: PL* 24, 17A; *CCL* 73, 1); Second Vatican Council, Dogmatic Constitution on Divine Revelation, *Dei Verbum*, n. 25.

[15] Cf. 2 Cor 1:20-22.

[16] Cf. Second Vatican Council, Constitution on the Sacred Liturgy, *Sacrosanctum Concilium*, n. 10.

[17] Cf. 2 Thes 3:1.

[18] Cf. *Collectae, Pro Sancta Ecclesia,* in *Missale Romanum ex Decreto Sacrosancti Oecumenici Concilii Vaticani II instauratum auctoritate Pauli VI promulgatum* (Typis Polyglottis Vaticanis, 1975) pp. 786, 787, 790: St. Cyprian, *De oratione dominica* 23: *PL* 4, 553; *CSEL* 3/2, 285; *CCL* 3A, 105; St. Augustine, *Sermo* 71, 20, 33: *PL* 38, 463f.

[19] Cf. *Collecta, Dominica XXI "per annum,"* in *Missale Romanum*, p. 360.

[20] Cf. Second Vatican Council, Dogmatic Constitution on Divine Revelation, *Dei Verbum*, n. 8.

[21] Cf. Jn 14:15-17, 25-26–16:15.

[22] Second Vatican Council, Decree on the Ministry and Life of Priests, *Presbyterorum Ordinis*, n. 4.

[23] Cf. Second Vatican Council, Constitution on the Sacred Liturgy, *Sacrosanctum Concilium*, n. 51; Decree on the Ministry and Life of Priests, *Presbyterorum Ordinis*, n. 18; also Dogmatic Constitution on Divine Revelation, *Dei Verbum*, n. 21; Decree on the Missionary Activity of the Church, *Ad gentes*, n. 6. Cf. *Institutio Generalis Missalis Romani*, n. 8.

[24] Second Vatican Council, Constitution on the Sacred Liturgy, *Sacrosanctum Concilium*, n. 56.

[25] *Institutio Generalis Missalis Romani*, n. 33.

[26] Cf. Sacred Congregation for Divine Worship, Instruction, *Liturgicae instaurationes*, 5 September 1970, n. 2: *AAS* 62 (1970) 695–696; John Paul II, Letter, *Dominicae Cenae*, 24 February 1980, n. 10: *AAS* 72 (1980) 134–137; Sacred Congregation for the Sacraments and Divine Worship, Instruction, *Inaestimabile Donum*, 3 April 1980, n. 1: *AAS* 72 (1980) 333.

[27] Second Vatican Council, Constitution on the Sacred Liturgy, *Sacrosanctum Concilium*, n. 33.

[28] Cf. below, n. 111 of this Introduction.

[29] Cf. *Missale Romanum ex Decreto Sacrosancti Oecumenici Concilii Vaticani II instauratum auctoritate Pauli VI promulgatum, Ordo cantus Missae, editio typica* 1972, *Praenotanda*, nn. 4, 6, 10.

[30] Cf. *Institutio Generalis Missalis Romani*, n. 11.

[31] Cf. *ibid.*, n. 272; and nn. 32–34 of this Introduction.

[32] Cf. *ibid.*, nn. 35, 95.

[33] Cf. *ibid.*, nn. 82–84.

[34] Cf. *ibid.*, nn. 94, 131.

[35] Cf. *Ordo Missae cum populo*, 11, in: *Missale Romanum ex Decreto Sacrosancti Oecumenici Concilii Vaticani II instauratum auctoritate Pauli VI promulgatum* (Typis Polyglottis Vaticanis, 1975) p. 388.

[36] *Institutio Generalis Missalis Romani*, n. 36.

[37] Paul VI, Apostolic Constitution, *Laudis canticum,* in *Liturgia Horarum ex Decreto Sacrosancti Oecumenici Concilii Vaticani II instaurata, auctoritate Pauli VI promulgata* (Typis Polyglottis Vaticanis, 1971); cf. also Second Vatican Council, Constitution on the Sacred Liturgy, *Sacrosanctum Concilium*, nn. 24, 90; Sacred Congregation of Rites, Instruction, *Musicam sacram*, 5 March 1967, n. 39: *AAS* 59 (1967) 311; *Liturgia Horarum, Institutio Generalis*, nn. 23, 109; Sacred Congregation for Catholic Education, *Ratio fundamentalis,* n. 53.

[38] Cf. below, nn. 89–90 of this Introduction.

[39] Cf. *Institutio Generalis Missalis Romani*, nn. 18, 39.

[40] Cf. *ibid.*, n. 272; and below, nn. 32ff. of this Introduction.

[41] Cf. *ibid.*, n. 39.

[42] Cf. *ibid.*, nn. 37–39; *Missale Romanum ex Decreto Sacrosancti Oecumenici Concilii Vaticani II instauratum auctoritate Pauli VI promulgatum, Ordo cantus Missae, Praenotanda*, nn. 7–9; *Graduale Romanum*, 1974, *Praenotanda*, n. 7; *Graduale simplex, editio typica altera* 1975, *Praenotanda*, n. 16.

[43] Second Vatican Council, Constitution on the Sacred Liturgy, *Sacrosanctum Concilium*, n. 52; Sacred Congregation of Rites, Instruction, *Inter Oecumenici*, 26 September 1964, n. 54: *AAS* 56 (1964) 890.

[44] Cf. *Institutio Generalis Missalis Romani*, n. 42.

[45] Second Vatican Council, Constitution on the Sacred Liturgy, *Sacrosanctum Concilium*, n. 35, 2.

[46] Cf. Second Vatican Council, Constitution on the Sacred Liturgy, *Sacrosanctum Concilium*, nn. 6 and 47.

[47] Cf. Paul VI, Encyclical, *Mysterium Fidei*, 3 September 1965, n. 36: *AAS* 57 (1965) 753; Second Vatican Council, Decree on the Missionary Activity of the Church, *Ad gentes*, n. 9; Paul VI, Apostolic Exhortation, *Evangelii nuntiandi*, 8 December 1975, n. 43: *AAS* 69 (1976) 33–34.

[48] Cf. Second Vatican Council, Constitution on the Sacred Liturgy, *Sacrosanctum Concilium*, n. 35, 2; *Institutio Generalis Missalis Romani*, n. 41.

[49] Second Vatican Council, Constitution on the Sacred Liturgy, *Sacrosanctum Concilium*, n. 10.

[50] Cf. John Paul II, Apostolic Exhortation, *Catechesi tradendae*, 16 October 1979, n. 48: *AAS* 71 (1979) 1316.

[51] Cf. *Institutio Generalis Missalis Romani*, n. 165.

[52] Cf. *ibid.*, n. 42; and also Sacred Congregation of Rites, Instruction, *Eucharisticum Mysterium*, 25 May 1967, n. 28: *AAS* 59 (1967) 556–557.

[53] Cf. Sacred Congregation for Divine Worship, Instruction, *Actio pastoralis*, 15 May 1969, n. 6g: *AAS* 61 (1969) 809; *Directorium de Missis cum pueris*, 1 November 1973, n. 48: *AAS* 66 (1974) 44.

[54] Cf. *Institutio Generalis Missalis Romani*, nn. 42, 338; *Rituale Romanum ex Decreto Sacrosancti Oecumenici Concilii Vaticani II instauratum, auctoritate Pauli VI promulgatum, Ordo celebrandi Matrimonium*

(Typis Polyglottis Vaticanis, 1969) nn. 22, 42, 57; *Ordo Exsequiarum* (Typis Polyglottis Vaticanis, 1969) nn. 41, 64.

[55] Cf. *Institutio Generalis Missalis Romani*, n. 97.

[56] Cf. *ibid.*, n. 139.

[57] Cf. *ibid.*, n. 23.

[58] Cf. *ibid.*, n. 43.

[59] Cf. *ibid.*, n. 45.

[60] Cf. *ibid.*, n. 99.

[61] Cf. *ibid.*, n 47.

[62] Cf. above, note 23 of this Introduction.

[63] Cf. *Institutio Generalis Missalis Romani*, n. 272.

[64] Cf. Second Vatican Council, Constitution on the Sacred Liturgy, *Sacrosanctum Concilium*, n. 122.

[65] Cf. *Pontificale Romanum ex Decreto Sacrosancti Oecumenici Concilii Vaticani II instauratum auctoritate Pauli VI promulgatum, De Ordinatione Diaconi, Presbyteri et Episcopi* (Typis Polyglottis Vaticanis, 1968) p. 28, n. 24; p. 58, n. 21; p. 85, n. 24; p. 70, n. 25; p. 110, n. 25.

[66] Cf. below, nn. 78–91 of this Introduction.

[67] Cf. *Institutio Generalis Missalis Romani*, nn. 318–320, 324–325.

[68] Cf. *ibid.*, n. 313.

[69] Cf. *ibid.*, n. 42; Sacred Congregation for the Sacraments and Divine Worship, Instruction, *Inaestimabile Donum*, 3 April 1980, n. 3: *AAS* 72 (1980) 334.

[70] Cf. *Institutio Generalis Missalis Romani*, n. 11.

[71] Cf. *ibid.*, n. 68.

[72] Cf. *ibid.*, nn. 33, 47.

[73] Second Vatican Council, Decree on the Ministry and Life of Priests, *Presbyterorum Ordinis*, n. 4.

[74] Second Vatican Council, Constitution on the Sacred Liturgy, *Sacrosanctum Concilium*, n. 33.

[75] Cf. *Institutio Generalis Missalis Romani*, n. 9.

[76] Second Vatican Council, Constitution on the Sacred Liturgy, *Sacrosanctum Concilium*, n. 7.

[77] Cf. *ibid.*, n. 9.

[78] Cf. Rom 1:16.

[79] Cf. Second Vatican Council, Dogmatic Constitution on Divine Revelation, *Dei Verbum*, n. 21.

[80] Quoted *ibid.*

[81] Cf. Jn 14:15-26; 15:26–16:4, 5-15.

[82] Cf. Second Vatican Council, Decree on the Missionary Activity of the Church, *Ad gentes*, nn. 6 and 15; and also Dogmatic Constitution on Divine Revelation, *Dei Verbum*, n. 26.

[83] Cf. Second Vatican Council, Constitution on the Sacred Liturgy, *Sacrosanctum Concilium*, n. 24; and also Sacred Congregation for the Clergy, *Directorium Catechisticum Generale*, 11 April 1971, n. 25: *AAS* 64 (1972) 114.

[84] Cf. Second Vatican Council, Constitution on the Sacred Liturgy, *Sacrosanctum Concilium*, n. 56; see also Sacred Congregation for the Sacraments and Divine Worship, Instruction, *Inaestimabile Donum*, 3 April 1980, n. 1: *AAS* 72 (1980) 333–334.

[85] Cf. Second Vatican Council, Constitution on the Sacred Liturgy, *Sacrosanctum Concilium*, nn. 24 and 35.

[86] Cf. *Institutio Generalis Missalis Romani*, n. 34.

[87] Cf. *ibid.*, n. 96.

[88] Cf. *ibid.*, nn. 47, 61, 132; Sacred Congregation for the Sacraments and Divine Worship, Instruction, *Inaestimabile Donum*, 3 April 1980, n. 3: *AAS* 72 (1980) 334.

[89] Cf. *Institutio Generalis Missalis Romani*, n. 66.

[90] Cf. Paul VI, Motu Proprio, *Ministeria quaedam*, 15 August 1972, n. V: *AAS* 64 (1972) 532.

[91] Cf. Sacred Congregation for the Sacraments and Divine Worship, Instruction, *Inaestimabile Donum*, 3 April 1980, nn. 2 and 18: *AAS* 72 (1980) 334; cf. also Sacred Congregation for Divine Worship, *Directorium de Missis cum pueris*, 1 November 1973, nn. 22, 24, 27: *AAS* 66 (1974) 43.

[92] Cf. *Institutio Generalis Missalis Romani*, nn. 47, 66, 151; cf. also Consilium ad exsequendam Constitutionem de Sacra Liturgia, *De oratione communi fidelium* (Città del Vaticano, 1966) n. 8.

[93] Cf. *Institutio Generalis Missalis Romani*, n. 66.

[94] Cf. *ibid.*, nn. 37a and 67.

[95] Cf. *ibid.*, n. 68.

[96] Cf., for example, Pope Paul VI, Apostolic Constitution, *Missale Romanum*, 3 April 1969, in *Missale Romanum ex Decreto Sacrosancti Oecumenici Concilii Vaticani II instauratum auctoritate Pauli VI promulgatum* (Typis Polyglottis Vaticanis, 1975) p. 15, quoted in *Missale Romanum ex Decreto Sacrosancti Oecumenici Concilii Vaticani II instauratum auctoritate Pauli VI promulgatum, Ordo lectionum Missae, editio typica altera* (Typis Polyglottis Vaticanis, 1981) p. XXX.

[97] Cf. Second Vatican Council, Constitution on the Sacred Liturgy, *Sacrosanctum Concilium*, nn. 35 and 51.

[98] Cf. Pope Paul VI, Apostolic Constitution, *Missale Romanum*: in *Missale Romanum ex Decreto Sacrosancti Oecumenici Concilii Vaticani II instauratum auctoritate Pauli VI promulgatum* (Typis Polyglottis Vaticanis, 1975) p. 15, quoted in *Missale Romanum ex Decreto Sacrosancti Oecumenici Concilii Vaticani II instauratum auctoritate Pauli VI promulgatum, Ordo lectionum Missae, editio typica altera* (Typis Polyglottis Vaticanis, 1981) p. XXXI.

[99] Cf. Second Vatican Council, Constitution on the Sacred Liturgy, *Sacrosanctum Concilium*, nn. 9 and 33; Sacred Congregation of Rites, Instruction, *Inter Oecumenici*, 26 September 1964, n. 7: *AAS* 56 (1964) 878; John Paul II, Apostolic Exhortation, *Catechesi tradendae*, 16 October 1979, n. 23: *AAS* 71 (1979) 1296–1297.

[100] Cf. Second Vatican Council, Constitution on the Sacred Liturgy, *Sacrosanctum Concilium*, n. 35, 4; Sacred Congregation of Rites, Instruction, *Inter Oecumenici*, 26 September 1964, nn. 37–38: *AAS* 56 (1964) 884.

[101] Cf. Sacred Congregation for Divine Worship, Instruction, *Actio pastoralis*, 15 May 1969, n. 6: *AAS* 61 (1969) 809; Sacred Congregation for Divine Worship, *Directorium de Missis cum pueris*, 1 November 1973,

nn. 41–47: *AAS* 66 (1974) 43; Paul VI, Apostolic Exhortation *Marialis cultus*, 2 February 1974, n. 12: *AAS* 66 (1974) 125–126.

[102] Each of the years is designated by the letter A, B, or C. The following is the procedure to determine which year is A, B, or C. The letter C designates a year whose number is divisible into three equal parts, as though the cycle had taken its beginning from the first year of the Christian era. Thus the year 1 would have been Year A; year 2, Year B; year 3, Year C (as would years 6, 9, and 12). Thus, for example, year 1980 is Year C; 1981, Year A; 1982, Year B; and 1983, Year C again. And so forth. Obviously each cycle runs in accord with the plan of the liturgical year, that is, it begins with the First Week of Advent, which falls in the preceding year of the civil calendar.

The years in each cycle are marked in a sense by the principal characteristic of the Synoptic Gospel used for the semicontinuous reading of Ordinary Time. Thus the first Year of the cycle is the Year for the reading of the Gospel of Matthew and is so named; the second and third Years are the Year of Mark and the Year of Luke.

[103] Cf. *Institutio Generalis Missalis Romani*, nn. 36–40; *Missale Romanum ex Decreto Sacrosancti Oecumenici Concilii Vaticani II instauratum auctoritate Pauli VI promulgatum*, *Ordo cantus Missae* (Typis Polyglottis Vaticanis) nn. 5–9.

[104] Cf. *Institutio Generalis Missalis Romani*, n. 313.

[105] Cf. *ibid.*, n. 318; Sacred Congregation for the Sacraments and Divine Worship, Instruction, *Inaestimabile donum*, n. 1: *AAS* 72 (1980) 333–334.

[106] For example: in Lent the continuity of the Old Testament readings corresponds to the unfolding of the history of salvation; the Sundays in Ordinary Time provide the semicontinuous reading of one of the Letters of the Apostles. In these cases it is right that the pastor of souls choose one or other of the readings in a systematic way over a series of Sundays, so that he may establish a coherent plan for catechesis. It is not right to read indiscriminately on one day from the Old Testament, on another from the Letter of an Apostle, without any orderly plan for the texts that follow.

[107] Cf. *Institutio Generalis Missalis Romani*, n. 319.

[108] Cf. *ibid.*, n. 316c; see Second Vatican Council, Constitution on the Sacred Liturgy, *Sacrosanctum Concilium*, n. 51.

[109] Cf. *Institutio Generalis Missalis Romani*, n. 318.

[110] Cf. *Rituale Romanum ex Decreto Sacrosancti Oecumenici Concilii Vaticani II instauratum, auctoritate Pauli VI promulgatum, Ordo Paenitentiae* (Typis Polyglottis Vaticanis, 1974) *Praenotanda*, n. 13.

[111] Cf. *Institutio Generalis Missalis Romani*, n. 320.

[112] Cf. *ibid.*, n. 313.

[113] Cf. nn. 173–174, of this Order of Readings.

[114] Cf. n. 233, of this Order of Readings.

[115] So, for example, when there are six weeks before Lent, the seventh week begins on the Monday after Pentecost. The Solemnity of the Most Holy Trinity replaces the Sunday of Ordinary Time.

[116] When there are, for example, five weeks before Lent, the Monday after Pentecost begins with the Seventh Week of Ordinary Time and the Sixth Week is omitted.

[117] Cf. Table II at the end of this Introduction [found in volume I].

[118] Cf. Table III at the end of this Introduction [Table II in this volume] .

[119] Cf. Consilium ad exsequendam Constitutionem de Sacra Liturgia, Instruction, *De popularibus interpretationibus conficiendis*, 25 January 1969: Notitiae 5 (1969), pp. 3–12; *Declaratio circa interpretationes textuum liturgicorum "ad interim" paratas*: Notitiae 5 (1969), p. 69; Sacred Congregation for Divine Worship, *Declaratio de interpretatione textuum liturgicorum*: Notitiae 5 (1969), pp. 333–334 (cf. also *Responsiones ad dubia*, in Notitiae 9 (1973) pp. 153–154); *De unica interpretatione textuum liturgicorum*: Notitiae 6 (1970), pp. 84–85; Sacred Congregation for the Sacraments and Divine Worship, *Epistula ad Praesides Conferentiarum Episcopalium de linguis vulgaribus in S. Liturgiam inducendis*: Notitiae 12 (1976), pp. 300–302.

[120] Cf. Sacred Congregation for Divine Worship, Instruction, *Liturgicae instaurationes*, 5 September 1970, n. 11: *AAS* 62 (1970) 702–703; *Institutio Generalis Missalis Romani*, n. 325.

[121] Cf. *ibid., Institutio Generalis Missalis Romani*, nn. 11, 29, 68a, 139.

[122] Cf. Index of Readings, p. 1229, of this Order of Readings.

[123] The references for the psalms follow the order of the *Liber Psalmorum*, published by the Pontifical Commission for the Neo-Vulgate (Typis Polyglottis Vaticanis, 1969).

TABLE IA
PRINCIPAL CELEBRATIONS OF
THE LITURGICAL YEAR

Year	Lectionary Cycle Sunday	Lectionary Cycle Weekday	Ash Wednesday	Easter	Ascension Thursday	Pentecost
1998	C	II	25 Feb	12 Apr	21 May	31 May
1999	A	I	17 Feb	4 Apr	13 May	23 May
2000	B	II	8 Mar	23 Apr	1 June	11 June
2001	C	I	28 Feb	15 Apr	24 May	3 June
2002	A	II	13 Feb	31 Mar	9 May	19 May
2003	B	I	5 Mar	20 Apr	29 May	8 June
2004	C	II	25 Feb	11 Apr	20 May	30 May
2005	A	I	9 Feb	27 Mar	5 May	15 May
2006	B	II	1 Mar	16 Apr	25 May	4 June
2007	C	I	21 Feb	8 Apr	17 May	27 May
2008	A	II	6 Feb	23 Mar	1 May	11 May
2009	B	I	25 Feb	12 Apr	21 May	31 May
2010	C	II	17 Feb	4 Apr	13 May	23 May
2011	A	I	9 Mar	24 Apr	2 June	12 June
2012	B	II	22 Feb	8 Apr	17 May	27 May
2013	C	I	13 Feb	31 Mar	9 May	19 May
2014	A	II	5 Mar	20 Apr	29 May	8 June
2015	B	I	18 Feb	5 Apr	14 May	24 May
2016	C	II	10 Feb	27 Mar	5 May	15 May
2017	A	I	1 Mar	16 Apr	25 May	4 June
2018	B	II	14 Feb	1 Apr	10 May	20 May
2019	C	I	6 Mar	21 Apr	30 May	9 June
2020	A	II	26 Feb	12 Apr	21 May	31 May
2021	B	I	17 Feb	4 Apr	13 May	23 May
2022	C	II	2 Mar	17 Apr	26 May	5 June
2023	A	I	22 Feb	9 Apr	18 May	28 May
2024	B	II	14 Feb	31 Mar	9 May	19 May
2025	C	I	5 Mar	20 Apr	29 May	8 June

TABLE IB

PRINCIPAL CELEBRATIONS OF
THE LITURGICAL YEAR

| | | | Weeks in Ordinary Time | | | | |
| | | | before Lent | | after Easter Season | | |
Year	Lectionary Cycle Sunday	Lectionary Cycle Weekday	Number of Weeks	Ending	Beginning	Week Number	First Sunday of Advent
1998	C	II	7	24 Feb	1 June	9	29 Nov
1999	A	I	6	16 Feb	24 May	8	28 Nov
2000	B	II	9	7 Mar	12 June	10	3 Dec
2001	C	I	7	27 Feb	4 June	9	2 Dec
2002	A	II	5	12 Feb	20 May	7	1 Dec
2003	B	I	8	4 Mar	9 June	10	30 Nov
2004	C	II	7	24 Feb	31 May	9	28 Nov
2005	A	I	5	8 Feb	16 May	7	27 Nov
2006	B	II	8	28 Feb	5 June	9	3 Dec
2007	C	I	7	20 Feb	28 May	8	2 Dec
2008	A	II	4	5 Feb	12 May	6	30 Nov
2009	B	I	7	24 Feb	1 June	9	29 Nov
2010	C	II	6	16 Feb	24 May	8	28 Nov
2011	A	I	9	8 Mar	13 June	11	27 Nov
2012	B	II	7	21 Feb	28 May	8	2 Dec
2013	C	I	5	12 Feb	20 May	7	1 Dec
2014	A	II	8	4 Mar	9 June	10	30 Nov
2015	B	I	6	17 Feb	25 May	8	29 Nov
2016	C	II	5	9 Feb	16 May	7	27 Nov
2017	A	I	8	28 Feb	5 June	9	3 Dec
2018	B	II	6	13 Feb	21 May	7	2 Dec
2019	C	I	8	5 Mar	10 June	10	1 Dec
2020	A	II	7	25 Feb	1 June	9	29 Nov
2021	B	I	6	16 Feb	24 May	8	28 Nov
2022	C	II	8	1 Mar	6 June	10	27 Nov
2023	A	I	7	21 Feb	29 May	8	3 Dec
2024	B	II	6	13 Feb	20 May	7	1 Dec
2025	C	I	8	4 Mar	9 June	10	30 Nov

TABLE II

ORDER OF THE FIRST READING FOR
WEEKDAYS IN ORDINARY TIME

Week	Year I	Year II
1	Hebrews	1 Samuel
2	Hebrews	1 Samuel
3	Hebrews	2 Samuel
4	Hebrews	2 Samuel; 1 Kings, 1–16
5	Genesis, 1–11	1 Kings, 1–16
6	Genesis, 1–11	James
7	Sirach	James
8	Sirach	1 Peter; Jude
9	Tobit	2 Peter; 2 Timothy
10	2 Corinthians	1 Kings, 17–22
11	2 Corinthians	1 Kings, 17–22; 2 Kings
12	Genesis, 12–50	2 Kings; Lamentations
13	Genesis, 12–50	Amos
14	Genesis, 12–50	Hosea; Isaiah
15	Exodus	Isaiah; Micah
16	Exodus	Micah; Jeremiah
17	Exodus; Leviticus	Jeremiah
18	Numbers; Deuteronomy	Jeremiah; Nahum; Habakkuk
19	Deuteronomy; Joshua	Ezekiel
20	Judges; Ruth	Ezekiel
21	1 Thessalonians	2 Thessalonians; 1 Corinthians
22	1 Thessalonians; Colossians	1 Corinthians
23	Colossians; 1 Timothy	1 Corinthians
24	1 Timothy	1 Corinthians
25	Ezra; Haggai; Zechariah	Proverbs; Ecclesiastes
26	Zechariah; Nehemiah; Baruch	Job
27	Jonah; Malachi; Joel	Galatians
28	Romans	Galatians; Ephesians
29	Romans	Ephesians
30	Romans	Ephesians
31	Romans	Ephesians; Philippians
32	Wisdom	Titus; Philemon; 2 and 3 John
33	1 and 2 Maccabees	Revelation
34	Daniel	Revelation

TABLE III

ABBREVIATIONS OF THE BOOKS OF THE BIBLE

Acts	Acts of the Apostles	2 Kgs	2 Kings
Am	Amos	Lam	Lamentations
Bar	Baruch	Lk	Luke
1 Chr	1 Chronicles	Lv	Leviticus
2 Chr	2 Chronicles	Mal	Malachi
1 Cor	1 Corinthians	1 Mc	1 Maccabees
2 Cor	2 Corinthians	2 Mc	2 Maccabees
Col	Colossians	Mi	Micah
Dn	Daniel	Mk	Mark
Dt	Deuteronomy	Mt	Matthew
Eccl	Ecclesiastes	Na	Nahum
Eph	Ephesians	Neh	Nehemiah
Est	Esther	Nm	Numbers
Ex	Exodus	Ob	Obadiah
Ez	Ezekiel	Phil	Philippians
Ezr	Ezra	Phlm	Philemon
Gal	Galatians	Prv	Proverbs
Gen	Genesis	Ps(s)	Psalm(s)
Hab	Habakkuk	1 Pt	1 Peter
Heb	Hebrews	2 Pt	2 Peter
Hg	Haggai	Rom	Romans
Hos	Hosea	Ru	Ruth
Is	Isaiah	Rv	Revelation
Jas	James	Sg	Song of Songs
Jb	Job	Sir	Sirach
Jdt	Judith	1 Sm	1 Samuel
Jer	Jeremiah	2 Sm	2 Samuel
Jgs	Judges	1 Thes	1 Thessalonians
Jl	Joel	2 Thes	2 Thessalonians
Jn	John	Ti	Titus
1 Jn	1 John	1 Tm	1 Timothy
2 Jn	2 John	2 Tm	2 Timothy
3 Jn	3 John	Tb	Tobit
Jon	Jonah	Wis	Wisdom
Jos	Joshua	Zec	Zechariah
Jud	Jude	Zep	Zephaniah
1 Kgs	1 Kings		

COMMONS

THE COMMON OF THE ANNIVERSARY OF THE DEDICATION OF A CHURCH

701 READING I FROM THE OLD TESTAMENT

1.

1 Kings 8:22-23, 27-30   May your eyes watch night and day over this temple.

A reading from the first Book of Kings

In those days:
Solomon stood before the altar of the LORD
   in the presence of the whole community of Israel,
   and stretching forth his hands toward heaven, he said,
   "LORD, God of Israel, there is no God like you
   in heaven above or on earth below;
   you keep your covenant of mercy with your servants
   who are faithful to you with their whole heart.

"Can it indeed be that God dwells on earth?
If the heavens and the highest heavens cannot contain you,
   how much less this temple which I have built!
Look kindly on the prayer and petition of your servant,
   O LORD, my God,
   and listen to the cry of supplication I, your servant,
   utter before you this day.
May your eyes watch night and day over this temple,
   the place where you have decreed you shall be honored;
   may you heed the prayer which I, your servant, offer in this place.
Listen to the petitions of your servant
   and of your people Israel
   which they offer in this place.
Listen from your heavenly dwelling and grant pardon."

The word of the Lord.

2.

2 Chronicles 5:6-10, 13–6:2   I have truly built a princely house and
dwelling, where you may abide forever.

A reading from the second Book of Chronicles

King Solomon and the entire community of Israel
   gathered about him before the ark
   were sacrificing sheep and oxen so numerous
   that they could not be counted or numbered.
The priests brought the ark of the covenant of the LORD
   to its place beneath the wings of the cherubim in the sanctuary,
   the holy of holies of the temple.
The cherubim had their wings spread out over the place of the ark,
   sheltering the ark and its poles from above.
The poles were long enough so that their ends could be seen
   from that part of the holy place nearest the sanctuary;
   however, they could not be seen beyond.
The ark has remained there to this day.
There was nothing in it but the two tablets
   which Moses put there on Horeb,
   the tablets of the covenant which the LORD made
   with the children of Israel at their departure from Egypt.

When the trumpeters and singers were heard as a single voice
   praising and giving thanks to the LORD,
   and when they raised the sound
   of the trumpets, cymbals and other musical instruments
   to "give thanks to the LORD, for he is good,
   for his mercy endures forever,"
   the building of the LORD's temple was filled with a cloud.
The priests could not continue to minister because of the cloud,
   since the LORD's glory filled the house of God.

Then Solomon said:
   "The LORD intends to dwell in the dark cloud.
I have truly built you a princely house and dwelling,
   where you may abide forever."

The word of the Lord.

3.

Isaiah 56:1, 6-7   My house shall be called a house of prayer for
all peoples.

A reading from the Book of the Prophet Isaiah

> **Thus says the LORD:**
> **Observe what is right, do what is just;**
> > **for my salvation is about to come,**
> > **my justice, about to be revealed.**
>
> **The foreigners who join themselves to the LORD,**
> > **ministering to him,**
> **Loving the name of the LORD,**
> > **and becoming his servants—**
> **All who keep the sabbath free from profanation**
> > **and hold to my covenant,**
> **Them I will bring to my holy mountain**
> > **and make joyful in my house of prayer;**
> **Their burnt offerings and sacrifices**
> > **will be acceptable on my altar,**
> **For my house shall be called**
> > **a house of prayer for all peoples.**

The word of the Lord.

4.

Ezekiel 43:1-2, 3c-7a   The temple was filled with the glory of the Lord.

A reading from the Book of the Prophet Ezekiel

The angel led me to the gate which faces the east,
  and there I saw the glory of the God of Israel
  coming from the east.
I heard a sound like the roaring of many waters,
  and the earth shone with his glory.
I fell prone as the glory of the Lord entered the temple
  by way of the gate which faces the east,
  but spirit lifted me up and brought me to the inner court.
And I saw that the temple was filled with the glory of the Lord.
Then I heard someone speaking to me from the temple,
  while the man stood beside me.
The voice said to me:
  Son of man, this is where my throne shall be,
  this is where I will set the soles of my feet;
  here I will dwell among the children of Israel forever.

The word of the Lord.

5.

Ezekiel 47:1-2, 8-9, 12   I saw water flowing from the temple, and all who were touched by it were saved (see Roman Missal, antiphon for the blessing and sprinkling of water during the season of Easter).

A reading from the Book of the Prophet Ezekiel

The angel brought me back to the entrance of the temple,
  and I saw water flowing out
  from beneath the threshold of the temple toward the east,
  for the façade of the temple was toward the east;
  the water flowed down from the right side of the temple,
  south of the altar.
He led me outside by the north gate,
  and around to the outer gate facing the east,
  where I saw water trickling from the right side.
He said to me,
  "This water flows into the eastern district down upon the Arabah,
  and empties into the sea, the salt waters, which it makes fresh.
Wherever the river flows,
  every sort of living creature that can multiply shall live,
  and there shall be abundant fish,
  for wherever this water comes the sea shall be made fresh.
Along both banks of the river, fruit trees of every kind shall grow;
  their leaves shall not fade, nor their fruit fail.
Every month they shall bear fresh fruit,
  for they shall be watered by the flow from the sanctuary.
Their fruit shall serve for food, and their leaves for medicine."

The word of the Lord.

702 READING I FROM THE NEW TESTAMENT DURING THE SEASON OF EASTER

First Option

Acts 7:44-50   The Most High does not dwell in houses made by human hands.

A reading from the Acts of the Apostles

Stephen said to the people, the elders and the scribes:
"Our ancestors had the tent of testimony in the desert
  just as the One who spoke to Moses directed him
  to make it according to the pattern he had seen.
Our ancestors who inherited it
  brought it with Joshua when they dispossessed the nations
  that God drove out from before our ancestors,
  up to the time of David,
  who found favor in the sight of God
  and asked that he might find a dwelling place
  for the house of Jacob.
But Solomon built a house for him.
Yet the Most High does not dwell in houses made by human hands.
As the prophet says:

> *The heavens are my throne,*
>   *the earth is my footstool.*
> *What kind of house can you build for me?*
>   *says the Lord,*
>   *or what is to be my resting place?*
> *Did not my hand make all these things?"*

The word of the Lord.

Second Option

Revelation 21:1-5a   Behold, God's dwelling is with the human race.

A reading from the Book of Revelation

I, John, saw a new heaven and a new earth.
The former heaven and the former earth had passed away,
  and the sea was no more.
I also saw the holy city, a new Jerusalem,
  coming down out of heaven from God,
  prepared as a bride adorned for her husband.

I heard a loud voice from the throne saying,
    "Behold, God's dwelling is with the human race.
He will dwell with them and they will be his people
    and God himself will always be with them as their God.
He will wipe every tear from their eyes,
    and there shall be no more death or mourning, wailing or pain,
    for the old order has passed away."

The One who sat on the throne said,
    "Behold, I make all things new."

The word of the Lord.

Third Option

Revelation 21:9-14   I will show you the bride, the wife of the Lamb.

A reading from the Book of Revelation

The angel spoke to me, saying:
"Come here. I will show you the bride, the wife of the Lamb."
He took me in spirit to a great, high mountain
    and showed me the holy city Jerusalem
    coming down out of heaven from God.
It gleamed with the splendor of God.
Its radiance was like that of a precious stone,
    like jasper, clear as crystal.
It had a massive, high wall,
    with twelve gates where twelve angels were stationed
    and on which names were inscribed,
    the names of the twelve tribes of the children of Israel.
There were three gates facing east,
    three north, three south, and three west.
The wall of the city had twelve courses of stones as its foundation,
    on which were inscribed the twelve names
    of the twelve Apostles of the Lamb.

The word of the Lord.

703 RESPONSORIAL PSALM

1.

1 Chronicles 29:10, 11, 12

R̪. (13b) **We praise your glorious name, O mighty God.**

"Blessed may you be, O Lord,
   God of Israel our father,
   from eternity to eternity."

R̪. **We praise your glorious name, O mighty God.**

"Yours, O Lord, are grandeur and power,
   majesty, splendor, and glory.
For all in heaven and on earth is yours."

R̪. **We praise your glorious name, O mighty God.**

"Yours, O Lord, is the sovereignty;
   you are exalted as head over all.
Riches and honor are from you."

R̪. **We praise your glorious name, O mighty God.**

"You have dominion over all.
In your hands are power and might;
   it is yours to give grandeur and strength to all."

R̪. **We praise your glorious name, O mighty God.**

2.

Psalm 46:2-3, 5-6, 8-9

R̪. (5) **There is a stream whose runlets gladden the city of God, the holy dwelling of the Most High!**

God is our refuge and our strength,
   an ever-present help in distress.
Therefore we fear not, though the earth be shaken
   and mountains plunge into the depths of the sea.

℟. There is a stream whose runlets gladden the city of God, the holy dwelling of the Most High!

There is a stream whose runlets gladden the city of God,
   the holy dwelling of the Most High.
God is in its midst; it shall not be disturbed;
   God will help it at the break of dawn.

℟. There is a stream whose runlets gladden the city of God, the holy dwelling of the Most High!

The LORD of hosts is with us;
   our stronghold is the God of Jacob.
Come! behold the deeds of the LORD,
   the astounding things he has wrought on earth.

℟. There is a stream whose runlets gladden the city of God, the holy dwelling of the Most High!

3.

Psalm 84:3, 4, 5 and 10, 11

℟. How lovely is your dwelling-place, Lord, mighty God!
   or:
℟. Here God lives among his people.

My soul yearns and pines
   for the courts of the LORD.
My heart and my flesh
   cry out for the living God.

℟. How lovely is your dwelling-place, Lord, mighty God!
   or:
℟. Here God lives among his people.

Even the sparrow finds a home,
   and the swallow a nest
   in which she puts her young—
Your altars, O LORD of hosts,
   my king and my God!

(cont.)

℟. How lovely is your dwelling-place, Lord, mighty God!
   or:
℟. Here God lives among his people.

Blessed they who dwell in your house!
   continually they praise you.
O God, behold our shield,
   and look upon the face of your anointed.

℟. How lovely is your dwelling-place, Lord, mighty God!
   or:
℟. Here God lives among his people.

I had rather one day in your courts
   than a thousand elsewhere;
I had rather lie at the threshold of the house of my God
   than dwell in the tents of the wicked.

℟. How lovely is your dwelling-place, Lord, mighty God!
   or:
℟. Here God lives among his people.

4.

Psalm 95:1-2, 3-5, 6-7

℟. (2) **Let us come before the Lord and praise him.**

Come, let us sing joyfully to the LORD;
   let us acclaim the Rock of our salvation.
Let us come into his presence with thanksgiving;
   let us joyfully sing psalms to him.

℟. **Let us come before the Lord and praise him.**

For the LORD is a great God,
   and a great king above all gods;
In his hands are the depths of the earth,
   and the tops of the mountains are his.
His is the sea, for he has made it,
   and the dry land, which his hands have formed.

℟. Let us come before the Lord and praise him.

Come, let us bow down in worship;
  let us kneel before the LORD who made us.
For he is our God,
  and we are the people he shepherds, the flock he guides.

℟. Let us come before the Lord and praise him.

  5.

Psalm 122:1-2, 3-4ab, 8-9

℟. (1) Let us go rejoicing to the house of the Lord!

I rejoiced because they said to me,
  "We will go up to the house of the LORD."
And now we have set foot
  within your gates, O Jerusalem.

℟. Let us go rejoicing to the house of the Lord!

Jerusalem, built as a city
  with compact unity.
To it the tribes go up,
  the tribes of the LORD.

℟. Let us go rejoicing to the house of the Lord!

Because of my relatives and friends
  I will say, "Peace be within you!"
Because of the house of the LORD, our God,
  I will pray for your good.

℟. Let us go rejoicing to the house of the Lord!

704 READING II FROM THE NEW TESTAMENT

First Option

1 Corinthians 3:9c-11, 16-17   You are God's temple.

A reading from the first Letter of Saint Paul to the Corinthians

Brothers and sisters:
You are God's building.

According to the grace of God given to me,
like a wise master builder I laid a foundation,
and another is building upon it.
But each one must be careful how he builds upon it,
for no one can lay a foundation other than the one that is there,
namely, Jesus Christ.
Do you not know that you are the temple of God,
and that the Spirit of God dwells in you?
If anyone destroys God's temple,
God will destroy that person;
for the temple of God, which you are, is holy.

The word of the Lord.

Second Option

Ephesians 2:19-22   Through him the whole structure is held together and grows into a temple sacred in the Lord.

A reading from the Letter of Saint Paul to the Ephesians

Brothers and sisters:
You are no longer strangers and sojourners,
but you are fellow citizens with the holy ones
and members of the household of God,
built upon the foundation of the Apostles and prophets,
with Christ Jesus himself as the capstone.
Through him the whole structure is held together
and grows into a temple sacred in the Lord;
in him you also are being built together
into a dwelling place of God in the Spirit.

The word of the Lord.

Third Option

Hebrews 12:18-19, 22-24   You have approached Mount Zion and the city of the living God.

A reading from the Letter to the Hebrews

Brothers and sisters:
You have not approached that which could be touched
   and a blazing fire and gloomy darkness
   and storm and a trumpet blast
   and a voice speaking words such that those who heard
   begged that no message be further addressed to them.
No, you have approached Mount Zion
   and the city of the living God, the heavenly Jerusalem,
   and countless angels in festal gathering,
   and the assembly of the firstborn enrolled in heaven,
   and God the judge of all,
   and the spirits of the just made perfect,
   and Jesus, the mediator of a new covenant,
   and the sprinkled Blood that speaks more eloquently
   than that of Abel.

The word of the Lord.

Fourth Option

1 Peter 2:4-9   Like living stones, let yourselves be built into a spiritual house.

A reading from the first Letter of Saint Peter

Beloved:
Come to the Lord, a living stone, rejected by human beings
but chosen and precious in the sight of God,
and, like living stones,
let yourselves be built into a spiritual house
to be a holy priesthood to offer spiritual sacrifices
acceptable to God through Jesus Christ.
For it says in Scripture:

Behold, I am laying a stone in Zion,
a cornerstone, chosen and precious,
and whoever believes in it shall not be put to shame.

Therefore, its value is for you who have faith,
but for those without faith:

The stone which the builders rejected
has become the cornerstone,

and

A stone which will make people stumble,
and a rock that will make them fall.

They stumble by disobeying the word, as is their destiny.

You are "a chosen race, a royal priesthood,
a holy nation, a people of his own,
so that you may announce the praises" of him
who called you out of darkness into his wonderful light.

The word of the Lord.

705 ALLELUIA VERSE AND VERSE BEFORE THE GOSPEL

1.

2 Chronicles 7:16

**I have chosen and consecrated this house, says the Lord,
that my name may be there forever.**

2.

Isaiah 66:1

**"The heavens are my throne, the earth is my footstool," says the LORD;
What kind of house can you build for me?**

3.

Ezekiel 37:27

**My dwelling shall be with them, says the Lord;
I will be their God and they shall be my people.**

4.

See Matthew 7:8

**In my house, says the Lord, everyone who asks will receive;
The one who seeks, finds; and to the one who knocks, the door will be
   opened.**

5.

Matthew 16:18

**You are Peter, and upon this rock I will build my Church,
and the gates of the netherworld shall not prevail against it.**

706 GOSPEL

First Option

Matthew 16:13-19   You are Peter: I will give you the keys to the Kingdom of heaven.

✠ **A reading from the holy Gospel according to Matthew**

When Jesus went into the region of Caesarea Philippi
he asked his disciples,
"Who do people say that the Son of Man is?"
They replied, "Some say John the Baptist, others Elijah,
still others Jeremiah or one of the prophets."
He said to them, "But who do you say that I am?"
Simon Peter said in reply,
"You are the Christ, the Son of the living God."
Jesus said to him in reply, "Blessed are you, Simon son of Jonah.
For flesh and blood has not revealed this to you, but my heavenly Father.
And so I say to you, you are Peter,
and upon this rock I will build my Church,
and the gates of the netherworld shall not prevail against it.
I will give you the keys to the Kingdom of heaven.
Whatever you bind on earth shall be bound in heaven;
and whatever you loose on earth shall be loosed in heaven."

The Gospel of the Lord.

Second Option

Luke 19:1-10   Today salvation has come to this house.

☩ **A reading from the holy Gospel according to Luke**

At that time, Jesus came to Jericho and intended to pass through the town.
Now a man there named Zacchaeus,
   who was a chief tax collector and also a wealthy man,
   was seeking to see who Jesus was;
   but he could not see him because of the crowd,
   for he was short in stature.
So he ran ahead and climbed a sycamore tree in order to see Jesus,
   who was about to pass that way.
When he reached the place, Jesus looked up and said,
   "Zacchaeus, come down quickly,
   for today I must stay at your house."
And he came down quickly and received him with joy.
When they saw this, they began to grumble, saying,
   "He has gone to stay at the house of a sinner."
But Zacchaeus stood there and said to the Lord,
   "Behold, half of my possessions, Lord, I shall give to the poor,
   and if I have extorted anything from anyone
   I shall repay it four times over."
And Jesus said to him,
   "Today salvation has come to this house
   because this man too is a descendant of Abraham.
For the Son of Man has come to seek
   and to save what was lost."

The Gospel of the Lord.

Third Option

John 2:13-22   Jesus was speaking about the temple of his Body.

✠ **A reading from the holy Gospel according to John**

Since the Passover of the Jews was near,
   Jesus went up to Jerusalem.
He found in the temple area those who sold oxen, sheep, and doves,
   as well as the money-changers seated there.
He made a whip out of cords
   and drove them all out of the temple area, with the sheep and oxen,
   and spilled the coins of the money-changers
   and overturned their tables,
   and to those who sold doves he said,
   "Take these out of here,
   and stop making my Father's house a marketplace."
His disciples recalled the words of Scripture,
   Zeal for your house will consume me.
At this the Jews answered and said to him,
   "What sign can you show us for doing this?"
Jesus answered and said to them,
   "Destroy this temple and in three days I will raise it up."
The Jews said,
   "This temple has been under construction for forty-six years,
   and you will raise it up in three days?"
But he was speaking about the temple of his Body.
Therefore, when he was raised from the dead,
   his disciples remembered that he had said this,
   and they came to believe the Scripture
   and the word Jesus had spoken.

The Gospel of the Lord.

Fourth Option

John 4:19-24   True worshipers will worship the Father in Spirit and truth.

☩ **A reading from the holy Gospel according to John**

The Samaritan woman said to Jesus,
   "Sir, I can see that you are a prophet.
Our ancestors worshiped on this mountain;
   but you people say that the place to worship is in Jerusalem."
Jesus said to her,
   "Believe me, woman, the hour is coming
   when you will worship the Father
   neither on this mountain nor in Jerusalem.
You people worship what you do not understand;
   we worship what we understand,
   because salvation is from the Jews.
But the hour is coming, and is now here,
   when true worshipers will worship the Father in Spirit and truth;
   and indeed the Father seeks such people to worship him.
God is Spirit, and those who worship him
   must worship in Spirit and truth."

The Gospel of the Lord.

THE COMMON OF THE BLESSED VIRGIN MARY

707 READING I FROM THE OLD TESTAMENT

1.

Genesis 3:9-15, 20   I will put enmity between your offspring and the offspring of the woman.

A reading from the Book of Genesis

After the man, Adam, had eaten of the tree,
  the Lord God called to the man and asked him, "Where are you?"
He answered, "I heard you in the garden;
  but I was afraid, because I was naked,
  so I hid myself."
Then he asked, "Who told you that you were naked?
You have eaten, then,
  from the tree of which I had forbidden you to eat!"
The man replied, "The woman whom you put here with me—
  she gave me fruit from the tree, and so I ate it."
The Lord God then asked the woman,
  "Why did you do such a thing?"
The woman answered, "The serpent tricked me into it, so I ate it."

Then the Lord God said to the serpent:

  "Because you have done this, you shall be banned
    from all the animals
    and from all the wild creatures;
  On your belly shall you crawl,
    and dirt shall you eat
    all the days of your life.
  I will put enmity between you and the woman,
    and between your offspring and hers;
  He will strike at your head,
    while you strike at his heel."

The man called his wife Eve,
  because she became the mother of all the living.

The word of the Lord.

2.

Genesis 12:1-7   The Lord spoke to our ancestors, to Abraham and to his descendants for ever (Luke 1:55).

A reading from the Book of Genesis

The LORD said to Abram:
"Go forth from the land of your kinsfolk
   and from your father's house to a land that I will show you.

   "I will make of you a great nation,
     and I will bless you;
I will make your name great,
   so that you will be a blessing.
I will bless those who bless you
   and curse those who curse you.
All the communities of the earth
   shall find blessing in you."

Abram went as the LORD directed him, and Lot went with him.
Abram was seventy-five years old when he left Haran.
Abram took his wife Sarai, his brother's son Lot,
   all the possessions that they had accumulated,
   and the persons they had acquired in Haran,
   and they set out for the land of Canaan.
When they came to the land of Canaan, Abram passed through the land
   as far as the sacred place at Shechem,
   by the terebinth of Moreh.
(The Canaanites were then in the land.)

The LORD appeared to Abram and said,
   "To your descendants I will give this land."
So Abram built an altar there to the LORD who had appeared to him.

The word of the Lord.

3.

2 Samuel 7:1-5, 8b-11, 16   The Lord God will give him the throne of David
his father (Luke 1:32).

A reading from the second Book of Samuel

When King David was settled in his palace,
   and the LORD **had given him rest from his enemies on every side,**
   he said to Nathan the prophet,
   "Here I am living in a house of cedar,
   while the ark of God dwells in a tent!"
Nathan answered the king,
   "Go, do whatever you have in mind,
   for the LORD **is with you."**
But that night the LORD **spoke to Nathan and said:**
   "Go tell my servant David, 'Thus says the LORD**:**
   Should you build me a house to dwell in?'

"'It was I who took you from the pasture
   and from the care of the flock
   to be commander of my people Israel.
I have been with you wherever you went,
   and I have destroyed all your enemies before you.
And I will make you famous like the great ones of the earth.
I will fix a place for my people Israel;
   I will plant them so that they may dwell in their place
   without further disturbance.
Neither shall the wicked continue to afflict them as they did of old,
   since the time I first appointed judges over my people Israel.
I will give you rest from all your enemies.
The LORD **also reveals to you**
   that he will establish a house for you.
Your house and your kingdom shall endure forever before me;
   your throne shall stand firm forever.'"

The word of the Lord.

4.

1 Chronicles 15:3-4, 15-16; 16:1-2   They brought in the ark of God and set it within the tent which David had pitched for it.

A reading from the first Book of Chronicles

David assembled all Israel in Jerusalem to bring the ark of the Lord
   to the place which he had prepared for it.
David also called together the sons of Aaron and the Levites.

The Levites bore the ark of God on their shoulders with poles,
   as Moses had ordained according to the word of the Lord.

David commanded the chiefs of the Levites
   to appoint their brethren as chanters,
   to play on musical instruments, harps, lyres, and cymbals
   to make a loud sound of rejoicing.

They brought in the ark of God and set it within the tent
   which David had pitched for it.
Then they offered up burnt offerings and peace offerings to God.
When David had finished offering up the burnt offerings and peace
   offerings,
   he blessed the people in the name of the Lord.

The word of the Lord.

5.

Proverbs 8:22-31   Mary, seat of Wisdom.

A reading from the Book of Proverbs

The Wisdom of God says:
"The LORD begot me, the first-born of his ways,
  the forerunner of his prodigies of long ago;
From of old I was poured forth,
  at the first, before the earth.
When there were no depths I was brought forth,
  when there were no fountains or springs of water;
Before the mountains were settled into place,
  before the hills, I was brought forth;
While as yet the earth and fields were not made,
  nor the first clods of the world.

"When he established the heavens I was there,
  when he marked out the vault over the face of the deep;
When he made firm the skies above,
  when he fixed fast the foundations of the earth;
When he set for the sea its limit,
  so that the waters should not transgress his command;
Then was I beside him as his craftsman,
  and I was his delight day by day,
Playing before him all the while,
  playing on the surface of his earth;
  and I found delight in the sons of men."

The word of the Lord.

6.

Sirach 24:1-2, 3-4, 8-12, 18-21   Mary, seat of Wisdom.

A reading from the Book of Sirach

Wisdom sings her own praises and is honored in God,
before her own people she proclaims her glory;
In the assembly of the Most High she opens her mouth,
in the presence of his power she declares her worth.

"From the mouth of the Most High I came forth
the first-born before all creatures.
I made that in the heavens there should arise
light that never fades
and mistlike covered the earth.
In the highest heavens did I dwell,
my throne on a pillar of cloud.

"Then the Creator of all gave me his command,
and he who formed me chose the spot for my tent,
Saying, 'In Jacob make your dwelling,
in Israel your inheritance
and among my chosen put down your roots.'
Before all ages, in the beginning, he created me,
and through all ages I shall not cease to be.
In the holy tent I ministered before him,
and in Zion I fixed my abode.
Thus in the chosen city he has given me rest,
in Jerusalem is my domain.
I have struck root among the glorious people,
in the portion of the LORD, his heritage
and in the company of the holy ones do I linger.

"Come to me, all you that yearn for me,
and be filled with my fruits;
You will remember me as sweeter than honey,
better to have than the honeycomb
my memory is unto everlasting generations.
Whoever eats of me will hunger still,
whoever drinks of me will thirst for more;
Whoever obeys me will not be put to shame,
whoever serves me will never fail."

The word of the Lord.

7.

Isaiah 7:10-14; 8:10   The virgin shall conceive and bear a son.

A reading from the Book of the Prophet Isaiah

The LORD spoke to Ahaz:
Ask for a sign from the LORD, your God;
  let it be deep as the nether world, or high as the sky!
But Ahaz answered,
  "I will not ask! I will not tempt the LORD!"
Then Isaiah said:
  Listen, O house of David!
Is it not enough for you to weary people,
  must you also weary my God?
Therefore the Lord himself will give you this sign:
  the virgin shall conceive, and bear a son,
  and shall name him Emmanuel
  which means "God is with us."

The word of the Lord.

8.

Isaiah 9:1-6   A son is given us.

A reading from the Book of the Prophet Isaiah

The people who walked in darkness
  have seen a great light;
Upon those who dwelt in the land of gloom
  a light has shone.
You have brought them abundant joy
  and great rejoicing,
As they rejoice before you as at the harvest,
  as people make merry when dividing spoils.
For the yoke that burdened them,
  the pole on their shoulder,
And the rod of their taskmaster
  you have smashed, as on the day of Midian.
For every boot that tramped in battle,
  every cloak rolled in blood,
  will be burned as fuel for flames.

For a child is born to us, a son is given us;
   upon his shoulder dominion rests.
They name him Wonder-Counselor, God-Hero,
   Father-Forever, Prince of Peace.
His dominion is vast
   and forever peaceful,
From David's throne, and over his kingdom,
   which he confirms and sustains
By judgment and justice,
   both now and forever.
The zeal of the LORD of hosts will do this!

The word of the Lord.

9.

Isaiah 61:9-11   I rejoice heartily in the LORD.

A reading from the Book of the Prophet Isaiah

Thus says the LORD:
Their descendants shall be renowned among the nations,
   and their offspring among the peoples;
All who see them shall acknowledge them
   as a race the LORD has blessed.

I rejoice heartily in the LORD,
   in my God is the joy of my soul;
For he has clothed me with a robe of salvation,
   and wrapped me in a mantle of justice,
Like a bridegroom adorned with a diadem,
   like a bride bedecked with her jewels.
As the earth brings forth its plants,
   and a garden makes its growth spring up,
So will the Lord GOD make justice and praise
   spring up before all the nations.

The word of the Lord.

10.

Micah 5:1-4a   Until the time when she who is to give birth has borne.

A reading from the Book of the Prophet Micah

The LORD says:
You, Bethlehem-Ephrathah,
  too small to be among the clans of Judah,
From you shall come forth for me
  one who is to be ruler in Israel;
Whose origin is from of old,
  from ancient times.
(Therefore the Lord will give them up, until the time
  when she who is to give birth has borne,
And the rest of his brethren shall return
  to the children of Israel.)
He shall stand firm and shepherd his flock
  by the strength of the LORD,
  in the majestic name of the LORD, his God;
And they shall remain, for now his greatness
  shall reach to the ends of the earth;
  he shall be peace.

The word of the Lord.

11.

Zechariah 2:14-17   Rejoice, O daughter Zion! See, I am coming.

A reading from the Book of the Prophet Zechariah

Sing and rejoice, O daughter Zion!
See, I am coming to dwell among you, says the LORD.
Many nations shall join themselves to the LORD on that day,
  and they shall be his people,
  and he will dwell among you,
  and you shall know that the LORD of hosts has sent me to you.
The LORD will possess Judah as his portion in the holy land,
  and he will again choose Jerusalem.
Silence, all mankind, in the presence of the LORD!
  for he stirs forth from his holy dwelling.

The word of the Lord.

708 READING I FROM THE NEW TESTAMENT DURING THE SEASON OF EASTER

1.

Acts 1:12-14   All these devoted themselves with one accord to prayer with Mary, the mother of Jesus.

A reading from the Acts of the Apostles

After Jesus had been taken up to heaven,
the Apostles returned to Jerusalem
from the mount called Olivet, which is near Jerusalem,
a sabbath day's journey away.

When they entered the city
they went to the upper room where they were staying,
Peter and John and James and Andrew,
Philip and Thomas, Bartholomew and Matthew,
James son of Alphaeus, Simon the Zealot,
and Judas son of James.
All these devoted themselves with one accord to prayer,
together with some women,
and Mary the mother of Jesus, and his brothers.

The word of the Lord.

2.

Revelation 11:19a; 12:1-6a, 10ab   A great sign appeared in the sky.

A reading from the Book of Revelation

**God's temple in heaven was opened,
    and the ark of his covenant could be seen in the temple.**

**A great sign appeared in the sky, a woman clothed with the sun,
    with the moon under her feet,
    and on her head a crown of twelve stars.
She was with child and wailed aloud in pain
    as she labored to give birth.
Then another sign appeared in the sky;
    it was a huge red dragon, with seven heads and ten horns,
    and on its heads were seven diadems.
Its tail swept away a third of the stars in the sky
    and hurled them down to the earth.
Then the dragon stood before the woman about to give birth,
    to devour her child when she gave birth.
She gave birth to a son, a male child,
    destined to rule all the nations with an iron rod.
Her child was caught up to God and his throne.
The woman herself fled into the desert
    where she had a place prepared by God.**

**Then I heard a loud voice in heaven say:
    "Now have salvation and power come,
        and the Kingdom of our God
        and the authority of his Anointed."**

The word of the Lord.

3.

Revelation 21:1-5a   I also saw a new Jerusalem, prepared as a bride adorned for her husband.

A reading from the Book of Revelation

I, John, saw a new heaven and a new earth.
The former heaven and the former earth had passed away,
  and the sea was no more.
I also saw the holy city, a new Jerusalem,
  coming down out of heaven from God,
  prepared as a bride adorned for her husband.
I heard a loud voice from the throne saying,
  "Behold, God's dwelling is with the human race.
He will dwell with them and they will be his people
  and God himself will always be with them as their God.
He will wipe every tear from their eyes,
  and there shall be no more death or mourning, wailing or pain,
  for the old order has passed away."

The One who sat on the throne said,
  "Behold, I make all things new."

The word of the Lord.

709 RESPONSORIAL PSALM

1.

1 Samuel 2:1, 4-5, 6-7, 8abcd

R̸. (see 1b) **My heart exults in the Lord, my Savior.**

"My heart exults in the LORD,
  my horn is exalted in my God.
I have swallowed up my enemies;
  I rejoice in my victory."

R̸. My heart exults in the Lord, my Savior.

"The bows of the mighty are broken,
  while the tottering gird on strength.
The well-fed hire themselves out for bread,
  while the hungry batten on spoil.
The barren wife bears seven sons,
  while the mother of many languishes."

R̸. My heart exults in the Lord, my Savior.

"The LORD puts to death and gives life;
  he casts down to the nether world;
  he raises up again.
The LORD makes poor and makes rich,
  he humbles, he also exalts."

R̸. My heart exults in the Lord, my Savior.

"He raises the needy from the dust;
  from the dung heap he lifts up the poor,
To seat them with nobles
  and make a glorious throne their heritage."

R̸. My heart exults in the Lord, my Savior.

2.

Judith 13:18bcde, 19

℟. (15:9d) **You are the highest honor of our race.**

"Blessed are you, daughter, by the Most High God,
    above all the women on earth;
    and blessed be the LORD **God,**
    the creator of heaven and earth."

℟. **You are the highest honor of our race.**

"Your deed of hope will never be forgotten
    by those who tell of the might of God."

℟. **You are the highest honor of our race.**

3.

Psalm 45:11-12, 14-15, 16-17

℟. (11) **Listen to me, daughter; see and bend your ear.**

Hear, O daughter, and see; turn your ear,
   forget your people and your father's house.
So shall the king desire your beauty;
   for he is your lord, and you must worship him.

℟. **Listen to me, daughter; see and bend your ear.**

All glorious is the king's daughter as she enters;
   her raiment is threaded with spun gold.
In embroidered apparel she is borne in to the king;
   behind her the virgins of her train are brought to you.

℟. **Listen to me, daughter; see and bend your ear.**

They are borne in with gladness and joy;
   they enter the palace of the king.
The place of your fathers your sons shall have;
   you shall make them princes through all the land.

℟. **Listen to me, daughter; see and bend your ear.**

4.

Psalm 113:1b-2, 3-4, 5-6, 7

℟. **Blessed be the name of the Lord for ever.**
   or:
℟. **Alleluia.**

Praise, you servants of the LORD,
   praise the name of the LORD.
Blessed be the name of the LORD
   both now and forever.

℟. **Blessed be the name of the Lord for ever.**
   or:
℟. **Alleluia.**

From the rising to the setting of the sun
   is the name of the LORD to be praised.
High above all nations is the LORD;
   above the heavens is his glory.

℟. **Blessed be the name of the Lord for ever.**
   or:
℟. **Alleluia.**

Who is like the LORD, our God, who is enthroned on high
   and looks upon the heavens and the earth below?

℟. **Blessed be the name of the Lord for ever.**
   or:
℟. **Alleluia.**

He raises up the lowly from the dust;
   from the dunghill he lifts up the poor
To seat them with princes,
   with the princes of his own people.

℟. **Blessed be the name of the Lord for ever.**
   or:
℟. **Alleluia.**

5.

Luke 1:46-47, 48-49, 50-51, 52-53, 54-55

℟. (49) **The Almighty has done great things for me, and holy is his Name.**
   or:

℟. **O Blessed Virgin Mary, you carried the Son of the eternal Father.**

"My soul proclaims the greatness of the Lord,
   my spirit rejoices in God my Savior."

℟. **The Almighty has done great things for me, and holy is his Name.**
   or:

℟. **O Blessed Virgin Mary, you carried the Son of the eternal Father.**

"For he has looked with favor on his lowly servant.
From this day all generations will call me blessed:
   the Almighty has done great things for me
   and holy is his Name."

℟. **The Almighty has done great things for me, and holy is his Name.**
   or:

℟. **O Blessed Virgin Mary, you carried the Son of the eternal Father.**

"He has mercy on those who fear him
   in every generation.
He has shown the strength of his arm,
   he has scattered the proud in their conceit."

℟. **The Almighty has done great things for me, and holy is his Name.**
   or:

℟. **O Blessed Virgin Mary, you carried the Son of the eternal Father.**

"He has cast down the mighty from their thrones,
   and has lifted up the lowly.
He has filled the hungry with good things,
   and the rich he has sent away empty."

℟. **The Almighty has done great things for me, and holy is his Name.**
   or:

℟. **O Blessed Virgin Mary, you carried the Son of the eternal Father.**

"He has come to the help of his servant Israel
   for he has remembered his promise of mercy,
the promise he made to our fathers,
   to Abraham and his children for ever."

℟. **The Almighty has done great things for me, and holy is his name.**
   or:

℟. **O Blessed Virgin Mary, you carried the Son of the eternal Father.**

710 READING II FROM THE NEW TESTAMENT

First Option

Romans 5:12, 17-19   Where sin increased, grace overflowed all the more.

A reading from the Letter of Saint Paul to the Romans

Brothers and sisters:
Through one man sin entered the world,
    and through sin, death,
    and thus death came to all men, inasmuch as all sinned.

For if, by the transgression of the one,
    death came to reign through that one,
    how much more will those who receive the abundance of grace
    and of the gift of justification
    come to reign in life through the one Jesus Christ.
In conclusion, just as through one transgression
    condemnation came upon all,
    so, through one righteous act,
    acquittal and life came to all.
For just as through the disobedience of the one man
    the many were made sinners,
    so, through the obedience of the one,
    the many will be made righteous.

The word of the Lord.

Second Option

Romans 8:28-30   Those he foreknew he also predestined.

A reading from the Letter of Saint Paul to the Romans

Brothers and sisters:
We know that all things work for good for those who love God,
    who are called according to his purpose.
For those he foreknew he also predestined
    to be conformed to the image of his Son,
    so that he might be the firstborn
    among many brothers.
And those he predestined he also called;
    and those he called he also justified;
    and those he justified he also glorified.

The word of the Lord.

Third Option

Galatians 4:4-7   God sent his Son, born of a woman.

A reading from the Letter of Saint Paul to the Galatians

Brothers and sisters:
When the fullness of time had come, God sent his Son,
    born of a woman, born under the law,
    to ransom those under the law,
    so that we might receive adoption as sons.
As proof that you are sons,
    God sent the spirit of his Son into our hearts,
    crying out, "Abba, Father!"
So you are no longer a slave but a son,
    and if a son then also an heir, through God.

The word of the Lord.

Fourth Option

Ephesians 1:3-6, 11-12   God chose us in Christ, before the world began.

A reading from the Letter of Saint Paul to the Ephesians

Blessed be the God and Father of our Lord Jesus Christ,
    who has blessed us in Christ
    with every spiritual blessing in the heavens,
      as he chose us in him, before the foundation of the world,
      to be holy and without blemish before him.
In love he destined us for adoption to himself through Jesus Christ,
    in accord with the favor of his will,
    for the praise of the glory of his grace
    that he granted us in the beloved.

In him we were also chosen,
    destined in accord with the purpose of the One
    who accomplishes all things according to the intention of his will,
    so that we might exist for the praise of his glory,
    we who first hoped in Christ.

The word of the Lord.

711 ALLELUIA VERSE AND VERSE BEFORE THE GOSPEL

1.

See Luke 1:28

**Hail, Mary, full of grace, the Lord is with you;
blessed are you among women.**

2.

See Luke 1:45

**Blessed are you, O Virgin Mary, who believed
that what was spoken to you by the Lord would be fulfilled.**

3.

See Luke 2:19

**Blessed is the Virgin Mary who kept the word of God
and pondered it in her heart.**

4.

Luke 11:28

**Blessed are those who hear the word of God
and observe it.**

5.

**Blessed are you, holy Virgin Mary, deserving of all praise;
from you rose the sun of justice, Christ our God.**

6.

**Blessed are you, O Virgin Mary;
without dying you won the martyr's crown
beneath the Cross of the Lord.**

712 GOSPEL

1. Long Form

Matthew 1:1-16, 18-23   For it is through the Holy Spirit that this child has been conceived in her.

✠ **A reading from the holy Gospel according to Matthew**

The book of the genealogy of Jesus Christ,
  the son of David, the son of Abraham.

Abraham became the father of Isaac,
  Isaac the father of Jacob,
  Jacob the father of Judah and his brothers.
Judah became the father of Perez and Zerah,
  whose mother was Tamar.
Perez became the father of Hezron,
  Hezron the father of Ram,
  Ram the father of Amminadab.
Amminadab became the father of Nahshon,
  Nahshon the father of Salmon,
  Salmon the father of Boaz,
  whose mother was Rahab.
Boaz became the father of Obed,
  whose mother was Ruth.
Obed became the father of Jesse,
  Jesse the father of David the king.

David became the father of Solomon,
  whose mother had been the wife of Uriah.
Solomon became the father of Rehoboam,
  Rehoboam the father of Abijah,
  Abijah the father of Asaph.
Asaph became the father of Jehoshaphat,
  Jehoshaphat the father of Joram,
  Joram the father of Uzziah.
Uzziah became the father of Jotham,
  Jotham the father of Ahaz,
  Ahaz the father of Hezekiah.
Hezekiah became the father of Manasseh,
  Manasseh the father of Amos,
  Amos the father of Josiah.

Josiah became the father of Jechoniah and his brothers
    at the time of the Babylonian exile.

After the Babylonian exile,
    Jechoniah became the father of Shealtiel,
    Shealtiel the father of Zerubbabel,
    Zerubbabel the father of Abiud.
Abiud became the father of Eliakim,
    Eliakim the father of Azor,
    Azor the father of Zadok.
Zadok became the father of Achim,
    Achim the father of Eliud,
    Eliud the father of Eleazar.
Eleazar became the father of Matthan,
    Matthan the father of Jacob,
    Jacob the father of Joseph, the husband of Mary.
Of her was born Jesus who is called the Christ.

Now this is how the birth of Jesus Christ came about.
When his mother Mary was betrothed to Joseph,
    but before they lived together,
    she was found with child through the Holy Spirit.
Joseph her husband, since he was a righteous man,
    yet unwilling to expose her to shame,
    decided to divorce her quietly.
Such was his intention when, behold,
    the angel of the Lord appeared to him in a dream and said,
    "Joseph, son of David,
    do not be afraid to take Mary your wife into your home.
For it is through the Holy Spirit
    that this child has been conceived in her.
She will bear a son and you are to name him Jesus,
    because he will save his people from their sins."
All this took place to fulfill
    what the Lord had said through the prophet:

> *Behold, the virgin shall be with child and bear a son,*
> *and they shall name him Emmanuel,*

which means "God is with us."

The Gospel of the Lord.

OR Short Form

Matthew 1:18-23   For it is through the Holy Spirit that this child has been conceived in her.

✠   **A reading from the holy Gospel according to Matthew**

This is how the birth of Jesus Christ came about.
When his mother Mary was betrothed to Joseph,
 but before they lived together,
 she was found with child through the Holy Spirit.
Joseph her husband, since he was a righteous man,
 yet unwilling to expose her to shame,
 decided to divorce her quietly.
Such was his intention when, behold,
 the angel of the Lord appeared to him in a dream and said,
 "Joseph, son of David,
 do not be afraid to take Mary your wife into your home.
For it is through the Holy Spirit
 that this child has been conceived in her.
She will bear a son and you are to name him Jesus,
 because he will save his people from their sins."
All this took place to fulfill
 what the Lord had said through the prophet:

> ***Behold, the virgin shall be with child and bear a son,***
> ***and they shall name him Emmanuel,***

which means "God is with us."

The Gospel of the Lord.

2.

Matthew 2:13-15, 19-23   Take the child and his mother and flee to Egypt.

✠   **A reading from the holy Gospel according to Matthew**

When the magi had departed, behold,
 the angel of the Lord appeared to Joseph in a dream and said,
 "Rise, take the child and his mother, flee to Egypt,
 and stay there until I tell you.
Herod is going to search for the child to destroy him."
Joseph rose and took the child and his mother by night
 and departed for Egypt.

He stayed there until the death of Herod,
   that what the Lord had said through the prophet might be fulfilled,
   Out of Egypt I called my son.

When Herod had died, behold,
   the angel of the Lord appeared in a dream
   to Joseph in Egypt and said,
   "Rise, take the child and his mother and go to the land of Israel,
   for those who sought the child's life are dead."
He rose, took the child and his mother,
   and went to the land of Israel.
But when he heard that Archelaus was ruling over Judea
   in place of his father Herod,
   he was afraid to go back there.
And because he had been warned in a dream,
   he departed for the region of Galilee.
He went and dwelt in a town called Nazareth,
   so that what had been spoken through the prophets might be fulfilled,
   He shall be called a Nazorean.

The Gospel of the Lord.

3.

Matthew 12:46-50   Stretching out his hand toward his disciples, he said, here are my mother and my brothers.

☩   **A reading from the holy Gospel according to Matthew**

While Jesus was speaking to the crowds,
   his mother and his brothers appeared outside,
   wishing to speak with him.
Someone told him, "Your mother and your brothers are standing outside,
   asking to speak with you."
But he said in reply to the one who told him,
   "Who is my mother? Who are my brothers?"
And stretching out his hand toward his disciples, he said,
   "Here are my mother and my brothers.
For whoever does the will of my heavenly Father
   is my brother, and sister, and mother."

The Gospel of the Lord.

4.

Luke 1:26-38   Behold, you will conceive in your womb and bear a son.

✠ **A reading from the holy Gospel according to Luke**

The angel Gabriel was sent from God
   to a town of Galilee called Nazareth,
   to a virgin betrothed to a man named Joseph,
   of the house of David,
   and the virgin's name was Mary.
And coming to her, he said,
   "Hail, full of grace! The Lord is with you."
But she was greatly troubled at what was said
   and pondered what sort of greeting this might be.
Then the angel said to her,
   "Do not be afraid, Mary,
   for you have found favor with God.
Behold, you will conceive in your womb and bear a son,
   and you shall name him Jesus.
He will be great and will be called Son of the Most High,
   and the Lord God will give him the throne of David his father,
   and he will rule over the house of Jacob forever,
   and of his Kingdom there will be no end."
But Mary said to the angel,
   "How can this be,
   since I have no relations with a man?"
And the angel said to her in reply,
   "The Holy Spirit will come upon you,
   and the power of the Most High will overshadow you.
Therefore the child to be born
   will be called holy, the Son of God.
And behold, Elizabeth, your relative,
   has also conceived a son in her old age,
   and this is the sixth month for her who was called barren;
   for nothing will be impossible for God."
Mary said, "Behold, I am the handmaid of the Lord.
May it be done to me according to your word."
Then the angel departed from her.

The Gospel of the Lord.

5.

Luke 1:39-47   Blessed is she who believed.

✛   **A reading from the holy Gospel according to Luke**

Mary set out
and traveled to the hill country in haste
to a town of Judah,
where she entered the house of Zechariah
and greeted Elizabeth.
When Elizabeth heard Mary's greeting,
the infant leaped in her womb,
and Elizabeth, filled with the Holy Spirit,
cried out in a loud voice and said,
"Most blessed are you among women,
and blessed is the fruit of your womb.
And how does this happen to me,
that the mother of my Lord should come to me?
For at the moment the sound of your greeting reached my ears,
the infant in my womb leaped for joy.
Blessed are you who believed
that what was spoken to you by the Lord
would be fulfilled."

And Mary said:

"My soul proclaims the greatness of the Lord;
my spirit rejoices in God my savior."

The Gospel of the Lord.

6.

Luke 2:1-14   She gave birth to her firstborn son.

☩   **A reading from the holy Gospel according to Luke**

In those days a decree went out from Caesar Augustus
   that the whole world should be enrolled.
This was the first enrollment,
   when Quirinius was governor of Syria.
So all went to be enrolled, each to his own town.
And Joseph too went up from Galilee from the town of Nazareth
   to Judea, to the city of David that is called Bethlehem,
   because he was of the house and family of David,
   to be enrolled with Mary, his betrothed, who was with child.
While they were there,
   the time came for her to have her child,
   and she gave birth to her firstborn son.
She wrapped him in swaddling clothes and laid him in a manger,
   because there was no room for them in the inn.

Now there were shepherds in that region living in the fields
   and keeping the night watch over their flock.
The angel of the Lord appeared to them
   and the glory of the Lord shone around them,
   and they were struck with great fear.
The angel said to them,
   "Do not be afraid;
   for behold, I proclaim to you good news of great joy
   that will be for all the people.
For today in the city of David
   a savior has been born for you who is Christ and Lord.
And this will be a sign for you:
   you will find an infant wrapped in swaddling clothes
   and lying in a manger."
And suddenly there was a multitude of the heavenly host with the angel,
   praising God and saying:

   "Glory to God in the highest
   and on earth peace to those on whom his favor rests."

The Gospel of the Lord.

7.

Luke 2:15b-19   Mary kept all these things, reflecting on them in her heart.

✝   **A reading from the holy Gospel according to Luke**

**The shepherds said to one another,
    "Let us go, then, to Bethlehem
    to see this thing that has taken place,
    which the Lord has made known to us."
So they went in haste and found Mary and Joseph
    and the infant lying in the manger.
When they saw this,
    they made known the message
    that had been told them about this child.
All who heard it were amazed
    by what had been told them by the shepherds.
And Mary kept all these things,
    reflecting on them in her heart.**

The Gospel of the Lord.

8.

Luke 2:27-35   You yourself a sword will pierce.

☩ **A reading from the holy Gospel according to Luke**

Simeon came in the Spirit into the temple;
  and when the parents brought in the child Jesus
  to perform the custom of the law in regard to him,
  he took him into his arms and blessed God, saying:

"Lord, now let your servant go in peace;
  your word has been fulfilled;
my own eyes have seen the salvation
  which you prepared in the sight of every people:
a light to reveal you to the nations
  and the glory of your people Israel."

The child's father and mother were amazed at what was said about him;
  and Simeon blessed them and said to Mary his mother,
  "Behold, this child is destined
  for the fall and rise of many in Israel,
  and to be a sign that will be contradicted
  and you yourself a sword will pierce
  so that the thoughts of many hearts may be revealed."

The Gospel of the Lord.

9.

Luke 2:41-52   Your father and I have been looking for you.

☩ **A reading from the holy Gospel according to Luke**

Each year Jesus' parents went to Jerusalem for the feast of Passover,
  and when he was twelve years old,
  they went up according to festival custom.
After they had completed its days, as they were returning,
  the boy Jesus remained behind in Jerusalem,
  but his parents did not know it.
Thinking that he was in the caravan,
  they journeyed for a day
  and looked for him among their relatives and acquaintances,
  but not finding him,
  they returned to Jerusalem to look for him.

After three days they found him in the temple,
   sitting in the midst of the teachers,
   listening to them and asking them questions,
   and all who heard him were astounded
   at his understanding and his answers.
When his parents saw him,
   they were astonished,
   and his mother said to him,
   "Son, why have you done this to us?
Your father and I have been looking for you with great anxiety."
And he said to them,
   "Why were you looking for me?
Did you not know that I must be in my Father's house?"
But they did not understand what he said to them.
He went down with them and came to Nazareth,
   and was obedient to them;
   and his mother kept all these things in her heart.
And Jesus advanced in wisdom and age and favor
   before God and man.

The Gospel of the Lord.

10.

Luke 11:27-28   Blessed is the womb that carried you.

✠   **A reading from the holy Gospel according to Luke**

While Jesus was speaking,
   a woman from the crowd called out and said to him,
   "Blessed is the womb that carried you
   and the breasts at which you nursed."
He replied, "Rather, blessed are those
   who hear the word of God and observe it."

The Gospel of the Lord.

11.

John 2:1-11   The mother of Jesus was there.

✠ **A reading from the holy Gospel according to John**

There was a wedding in Cana at Galilee,
  and the mother of Jesus was there.
Jesus and his disciples were also invited to the wedding.
When the wine ran short,
  the mother of Jesus said to him,
  "They have no wine."
And Jesus said to her,
  "Woman, how does your concern affect me?
My hour has not yet come."
His mother said to the servers,
  "Do whatever he tells you."
Now there were six stone water jars there for Jewish ceremonial washings,
  each holding twenty to thirty gallons.
Jesus told them,
  "Fill the jars with water."
So they filled them to the brim.
Then he told them,
  "Draw some out now and take it to the headwaiter."
So they took it.
And when the headwaiter tasted the water that had become wine,
  without knowing where it came from
  although the servers who had drawn the water knew,
  the headwaiter called the bridegroom and said to him,
  "Everyone serves good wine first,
  and then when people have drunk freely, an inferior one;
  but you have kept the good wine until now."
Jesus did this as the beginning of his signs in Cana in Galilee
  and so revealed his glory,
  and his disciples began to believe in him.

The Gospel of the Lord.

12.

John 19:25-27   Behold, your son. Behold, your mother.

✝ **A reading from the holy Gospel according to John**

Standing by the cross of Jesus were his mother
  and his mother's sister, Mary the wife of Clopas,
  and Mary Magdalene.
When Jesus saw his mother and the disciple there whom he loved,
  he said to his mother, "Woman, behold, your son."
Then he said to the disciple,
  "Behold, your mother."
And from that hour the disciple took her into his home.

The Gospel of the Lord.

THE COMMON OF MARTYRS

713 READING I FROM THE OLD TESTAMENT

1.

2 Chronicles 24:18-22   Zechariah was stoned to death in the court of the LORD's temple.

A reading from the second Book of Chronicles

The princes of Judah forsook the temple of the LORD,
    the God of their fathers,
    and began to serve the sacred poles and the idols;
    and because of this crime of theirs,
    wrath came upon Judah and Jerusalem.
Although prophets were sent to them to convert them to the LORD,
    the people would not listen to their warnings.
Then the spirit of God possessed Zechariah,
    son of Jehoiada the priest.
He took his stand above the people and said to them:
    "God says, 'Why are you transgressing the LORD's commands,
    so that you cannot prosper?
Because you have abandoned the LORD, he has abandoned you.'"
But the people conspired against him,
    and at the king's order they stoned him to death
    in the court of the LORD's temple.
Thus King Joash was unmindful of the devotion shown him
    by Jehoiada, Zechariah's father, and slew his son.
And as he was dying, he said, "May the LORD see and avenge."

The word of the Lord.

2.

2 Maccabees 6:18, 21, 24-31   I am suffering it with joy in my soul because of my devotion to him.

A reading from the second Book of Maccabees

Eleazar, one of the foremost scribes,
    a man of advanced age and noble appearance,
    was being forced to open his mouth to eat pork.

Those in charge of that unlawful ritual meal took the man aside privately,
   because of their long acquaintance with him,
   and urged him to bring meat of his own providing,
   such as he could legitimately eat,
   and to pretend to be eating some of the meat of the sacrifice
   prescribed by the king.

He told them:
   "At our age it would be unbecoming to make such a pretense;
   many young men would think the ninety-year-old Eleazar
   had gone over to an alien religion.
Should I thus pretend for the sake of a brief moment of life,
   they would be led astray by me,
   while I would bring shame and dishonor on my old age.
Even if, for the time being, I avoid the punishment of men,
   I shall never, whether alive or dead,
   escape the hands of the Almighty.
Therefore, by manfully giving up my life now,
   I will prove myself worthy of my old age,
   and I will leave to the young a noble example
   of how to die willingly and generously for the revered and holy laws."

He spoke thus,
   and went immediately to the instrument of torture.
Those who shortly before had been kindly disposed
   now became hostile toward him because what he had said
   seemed to them utter madness.
When he was about to die under the blows,
   he groaned and said:
   "The LORD in his holy knowledge knows full well that,
   although I could have escaped death,
   I am not only enduring terrible pain in my body from this scourging,
   but also suffering it with joy in my soul
   because of my devotion to him."
This is how he died,
   leaving in his death a model of courage
   and an unforgettable example of virtue
   not only for the young but for the whole nation.

The word of the Lord.

3.

2 Maccabees 7:1-2, 9-14   We are ready to die rather than transgress the laws of our ancestors.

A reading from the second Book of Maccabees

It happened that seven brothers with their mother were arrested
   and tortured with whips and scourges by the king,
   to force them to eat pork in violation of God's law.
One of the brothers, speaking for the others, said:
   "What do you expect to achieve by questioning us?
We are ready to die rather than transgress the laws of our ancestors."

At the point of death, the second brother said:
   "You accursed fiend, you are depriving us of this present life,
   but the King of the world will raise us up to live again forever.
It is for his laws that we are dying."

After him the third suffered their cruel sport.
He put out his tongue at once when told to do so,
   and bravely held out his hands, as he spoke these noble words:
   "It was from Heaven that I received these;
   for the sake of his laws I disdain them;
   from him I hope to receive them again."
Even the king and his attendants marveled at the young man's courage,
   because he regarded his sufferings as nothing.

After he had died,
   they tortured and maltreated the fourth brother in the same way.
When he was near death, he said,
   "It is my choice to die at the hands of men
   with the hope God gives of being raised up by him;
   but for you, there will be no resurrection to life."

The word of the Lord.

4.

2 Maccabees 7:1, 20-23, 27b-29   This most admirable mother bore it
courageously because of her hope in the Lord.

A reading from the second Book of Maccabees

It happened that seven brothers with their mother were arrested
    and tortured with whips and scourges by the king,
    to force them to eat pork in violation of God's law.

Most admirable and worthy of everlasting remembrance was the mother,
    who saw her seven sons perish in a single day,
    yet bore it courageously because of her hope in the Lord.
Filled with a noble spirit that stirred her womanly heart with manly
        courage
    she exhorted each of them
    in the language of their forefathers with these words:
    "I do not know how you came into existence in my womb;
    it was not I who gave you the breath of life,
    nor was it I who set in order
    the elements of which each of you is composed.
Therefore, since it is the Creator of the universe
    who shapes each man's beginning,
    as he brings about the origin of everything,
    he, in his mercy,
    will give you back both breath and life,
    because you now disregard yourselves for the sake of his law."

"Son, have pity on me, who carried you in my womb for nine months,
    nursed you for three years, brought you up,
    educated and supported you to your present age.
I beg you, child, to look at the heavens and the earth
    and see all that is in them;
    then you will know that God did not make them out of existing things;
    and in the same way the human race came into existence.
Do not be afraid of this executioner,
    but be worthy of your brothers and accept death,
    so that in the time of mercy I may receive you again with them."

The word of the Lord.

5.

Wisdom 3:1-9   As sacrificial offerings he took them to himself.

A reading from the Book of Wisdom

The souls of the just are in the hand of God,
 and no torment shall touch them.
They seemed, in the view of the foolish, to be dead;
 and their passing away was thought an affliction
 and their going forth from us, utter destruction.
But they are in peace.
For if before men, indeed, they be punished,
 yet is their hope full of immortality;
Chastised a little, they shall be greatly blessed,
 because God tried them
 and found them worthy of himself.
As gold in the furnace, he proved them,
 and as sacrificial offerings he took them to himself.
In the time of their visitation they shall shine,
 and shall dart about as sparks through stubble;
They shall judge nations and rule over peoples,
 and the LORD shall be their King forever.
Those who trust in him shall understand truth,
 and the faithful shall abide with him in love:
Because grace and mercy are with his holy ones,
 and his care is with his elect.

The word of the Lord.

6.

Sirach 51:1-8   You redeemed me, true to the greatness of your mercy and of your name.

A reading from the Book of Sirach

I give you thanks, O Lord and King;
   I praise you, O God my savior!
I will make known your name,
   for you have been a helper and a protector to me.
You have kept back my body from the pit,
   and from the scourge of a slanderous tongue,
   from lips that went over to falsehood.
And in the sight of those who stood by,
   you have delivered me,
According to the multitude of the mercy of your name,
   and from them that did roar, prepared to devour me,
And from the power of those who sought my life;
   from many a danger you have saved me,
   from flames that hemmed me in on every side;
From the midst of unremitting fire when I was not burnt
   from the deep belly of the nether world;
From deceiving lips and painters of lies,
   from the arrows of dishonest tongues.
My soul was at the point of death,
   my life was nearing the depths of the nether world;
They encompassed me on every side, but there was no one to help me,
   I looked for one to sustain me, but could find no one.
But then I remembered the mercies of the LORD,
   his kindness through ages past;
For he saves those who take refuge in him,
   and rescues them from every evil.

The word of the Lord.

714 READING I FROM THE NEW TESTAMENT DURING THE SEASON OF EASTER

First Option

Acts 7:55-60   Lord Jesus, receive my spirit.

A reading from the Acts of the Apostles

Stephen, filled with the Holy Spirit,
looked up intently to heaven and saw the glory of God
and Jesus standing at the right hand of God,
and he said, "Behold, I see the heavens opened
and the Son of Man standing at the right hand of God."
But they cried out in a loud voice,
covered their ears, and rushed upon him together.
They threw him out of the city, and began to stone him.
The witnesses laid down their cloaks
at the feet of a young man named Saul.
As they were stoning Stephen, he called out,
"Lord Jesus, receive my spirit."
Then he fell to his knees and cried out in a loud voice,
"Lord, do not hold this sin against them";
and when he said this, he fell asleep.

The word of the Lord.

Second Option

Revelation 7:9-17   These are the ones who have survived the time of great distress.

A reading from the Book of Revelation

I, John, had a vision of a great multitude,
which no one could count,
from every nation, race, people, and tongue.
They stood before the throne and before the Lamb,
wearing white robes and holding palm branches in their hands.
They cried out in a loud voice:

"Salvation comes from our God, who is seated on the throne,
and from the Lamb."

All the angels stood around the throne
and around the elders and the four living creatures.

They prostrated themselves before the throne,
  worshiped God, and exclaimed:

  "Amen. Blessing and glory, wisdom and thanksgiving,
    honor, power, and might
    be to our God forever and ever. Amen."

Then one of the elders spoke up and said to me,
  "Who are these wearing white robes, and where did they come from?"
I said to him, "My lord, you are the one who knows."
He said to me,
  "These are the ones who have survived the time of great distress;
  they have washed their robes
  and made them white in the Blood of the Lamb.

  "For this reason they stand before God's throne
    and worship him day and night in his temple.
    The One who sits on the throne will shelter them.
  They will not hunger or thirst anymore,
    nor will the sun or any heat strike them.
  For the Lamb who is in the center of the throne will shepherd them
    and lead them to springs of life-giving water,
    and God will wipe away every tear from their eyes."

The word of the Lord.

Third Option

Revelation 12:10-12b   Love for life did not deter them from death.

A reading from the Book of Revelation

I, John, heard a loud voice in heaven say:
"Now have salvation and power come,
   and the Kingdom of our God
   and the authority of his Anointed.
For the accuser of our brothers is cast out,
   who accuses them before our God day and night.
They conquered him by the Blood of the Lamb
   and by the word of their testimony;
   love for life did not deter them from death.
Therefore, rejoice, you heavens,
   and you who dwell in them."

The word of the Lord.

Fourth Option

Revelation 21:5-7   The victor will inherit these gifts.

A reading from the Book of Revelation

The One who was seated on the throne said:
"Behold, I make all things new."
Then he said, "Write these words down,
   for they are trustworthy and true."
He said to me, "They are accomplished.
I am the Alpha and the Omega, the beginning and the end.
To the thirsty I will give a gift
   from the spring of life-giving water.
The victor will inherit these gifts,
   and I shall be his God,
   and he will be my son."

The word of the Lord.

715 RESPONSORIAL PSALM

First Option

Psalm 31:3cd-4, 6 and 8ab, 16bc and 17

℞. (6) **Into your hands, O Lord, I commend my spirit.**

Be my rock of refuge,
   a stronghold to give me safety.
You are my rock and my fortress;
   for your name's sake you will lead and guide me.

℞. **Into your hands, O Lord, I commend my spirit.**

Into your hands I commend my spirit;
   you will redeem me, O Lord, O faithful God.
I will rejoice and be glad because of your mercy.

℞. **Into your hands, O Lord, I commend my spirit.**

Rescue me from the clutches of my enemies and my persecutors,
Let your face shine upon your servant;
   save me in your kindness.

℞. **Into your hands, O Lord, I commend my spirit.**

Second Option

Psalm 34:2-3, 4-5, 6-7, 8-9

℞. (5) **The Lord delivered me from all my fears.**

I will bless the Lord at all times;
   his praise shall be ever in my mouth.
Let my soul glory in the Lord;
   the lowly will hear me and be glad.

℞. **The Lord delivered me from all my fears.**

Glorify the Lord with me,
   let us together extol his name.
I sought the Lord, and he answered me
   and delivered me from all my fears.

(cont.)

℞. **The Lord delivered me from all my fears.**

Look to him that you may be radiant with joy,
   and your faces may not blush with shame.
When the afflicted man called out, the LORD heard,
   and from all his distress he saved him.

℞. **The Lord delivered me from all my fears.**

The angel of the LORD encamps
   around those who fear him, and delivers them.
Taste and see how good the LORD is;
   blessed the man who takes refuge in him.

℞. **The Lord delivered me from all my fears.**

Third Option

Psalm 124:2-3, 4-5, 7cd-8

℞. (7) **Our soul has been rescued like a bird from the fowler's snare.**

Had not the LORD been with us—
When men rose up against us,
   then would they have swallowed us alive
When their fury was inflamed against us.

℞. **Our soul has been rescued like a bird from the fowler's snare.**

Then would the waters have overwhelmed us;
The torrent would have swept over us;
   over us then would have swept
   the raging waters.

℞. **Our soul has been rescued like a bird from the fowler's snare.**

Broken was the snare,
   and we were freed.
Our help is in the name of the LORD,
   who made heaven and earth.

℞. **Our soul has been rescued like a bird from the fowler's snare.**

Fourth Option

Psalm 126:1bc-2ab, 2cd-3, 4-5, 6

℞. (5) **Those who sow in tears shall reap rejoicing.**

When the Lord brought back the captives of Zion,
  we were like men dreaming.
Then our mouth was filled with laughter,
  and our tongue with rejoicing.

℞. **Those who sow in tears shall reap rejoicing.**

Then they said among the nations,
  "The Lord has done great things for them."
The Lord has done great things for us;
  we are glad indeed.

℞. **Those who sow in tears shall reap rejoicing.**

Restore our fortunes, O Lord,
  like the torrents in the southern desert.
Those who sow in tears
  shall reap rejoicing.

℞. **Those who sow in tears shall reap rejoicing.**

Although they go forth weeping,
  carrying the seed to be sown,
They shall come back rejoicing,
  carrying their sheaves.

℞. **Those who sow in tears shall reap rejoicing.**

716 READING II FROM THE NEW TESTAMENT

1.

Romans 5:1-5   We even boast of our afflictions.

A reading from the Letter of Saint Paul to the Romans

Brothers and sisters:
Since we have been justified by faith,
  we have peace with God through our Lord Jesus Christ,
  through whom we have gained access by faith
  to this grace in which we stand,
  and we boast in hope of the glory of God.
Not only that, but we even boast of our afflictions,
  knowing that affliction produces endurance,
  and endurance, proven character,
  and proven character, hope,
  and hope does not disappoint,
  because the love of God has been poured out into our hearts
  through the Holy Spirit that has been given to us.

The word of the Lord.

2.

Romans 8:31b-39   Neither death nor life will be able to separate us from the love of God.

A reading from the Letter of Saint Paul to the Romans

Brothers and sisters:
If God is for us, who can be against us?
He who did not spare his own Son
  but handed him over for us all,
  how will he not also give us everything else along with him?
Who will bring a charge against God's chosen ones?
It is God who acquits us.
Who will condemn?
Christ Jesus it is who died—or, rather, was raised—
  who also is at the right hand of God,
  who indeed intercedes for us.
What will separate us from the love of Christ?
Will anguish, or distress, or persecution, or famine,
  or nakedness, or peril, or the sword?

As it is written:

> *For your sake we are being slain all the day;*
>   *we are looked upon as sheep to be slaughtered.*

No, in all these things we conquer overwhelmingly
  through him who loved us.
For I am convinced that neither death, nor life,
  nor angels, nor principalities,
  nor present things, nor future things,
  nor powers, nor height, nor depth,
  nor any other creature will be able to separate us
  from the love of God in Christ Jesus our Lord.

The word of the Lord.

3.

2 Corinthians 4:7-15   Always carrying about in the body the dying of Jesus.

A reading from the second Letter of Saint Paul to the Corinthians

Brothers and sisters:
We hold this treasure in earthen vessels,
  that the surpassing power may be of God and not from us.
We are afflicted in every way, but not constrained;
  perplexed, but not driven to despair;
  persecuted, but not abandoned;
  struck down, but not destroyed;
  always carrying about in the body the dying of Jesus,
  so that the life of Jesus may also be manifested in our body.
For we who live are constantly being given up to death
  for the sake of Jesus,
  so that the life of Jesus may be manifested in our mortal flesh.

So death is at work in us, but life in you.
Since, then, we have the same spirit of faith,
  according to what is written, *I believed, therefore I spoke,*
  we too believe and therefore speak,
  knowing that the one who raised the Lord Jesus
  will raise us also with Jesus
  and place us with you in his presence.
Everything indeed is for you,
  so that the grace bestowed in abundance on more and more people
  may cause the thanksgiving to overflow for the glory of God.

The word of the Lord.

4.

2 Corinthians 6:4-10   We are treated as dying and behold we live.

A reading from the second Letter of Saint Paul to the Corinthians

Brothers and sisters:
In everything we commend ourselves as ministers of God,
   through much endurance, in afflictions, hardships, constraints,
   beatings, imprisonments, riots, labors, vigils, fasts;
   by purity, knowledge, patience, kindness,
   in the Holy Spirit, in unfeigned love, in truthful speech,
   in the power of God;
   with weapons of righteousness at the right and at the left;
   through glory and dishonor, insult and praise.
We are treated as deceivers and yet are truthful;
   as unrecognized and yet acknowledged;
   as dying and behold we live;
   as chastised and yet not put to death;
   as sorrowful yet always rejoicing;
   as poor yet enriching many;
   as having nothing and yet possessing all things.

The word of the Lord.

5.

2 Timothy 2:8-13; 3:10-12   All who want to live religiously in Christ Jesus
will be persecuted.

A reading from the second Letter of Saint Paul to Timothy

Beloved:
Remember Jesus Christ, raised from the dead, a descendant of David:
   such is my Gospel, for which I am suffering,
   even to the point of chains, like a criminal.
But the word of God is not chained.
Therefore, I bear with everything for the sake of those who are chosen,
   so that they too may obtain the salvation that is in Christ Jesus,
   together with eternal glory.

This saying is trustworthy:

> If we have died with him
>> we shall also live with him;
> if we persevere
>> we shall also reign with him.
> But if we deny him
>> he will deny us.
> If we are unfaithful
>> he remains faithful,
>>> for he cannot deny himself.

You have followed my teaching, way of life,
>> purpose, faith, patience, love,
>> endurance, persecutions, and sufferings,
>> such as happened to me in Antioch, Iconium, and Lystra,
>> persecutions that I endured.
Yet from all these things the Lord delivered me.
In fact, all who want to live religiously in Christ Jesus
>> will be persecuted.

The word of the Lord.

6.

Hebrews 10:32-36   You endured a great contest of suffering.

A reading from the Letter to the Hebrews

Brothers and sisters:
Remember the days past when, after you had been enlightened,
>> you endured a great contest of suffering.
At times you were publicly exposed to abuse and affliction;
>> at other times you associated yourselves with those so treated.
You even joined in the sufferings of those in prison
>> and joyfully accepted the confiscation of your property,
>> knowing that you had a better and lasting possession.
Therefore, do not throw away your confidence;
>> it will have great recompense.
You need endurance to do the will of God and receive what he has
>> promised.

The word of the Lord.

7.

James 1:2-4, 12   Blessed is the man who perseveres in the face
of temptation.

A reading from the Letter of Saint James

Consider it all joy, my brothers and sisters,
  when you encounter various trials,
  for you know that the testing of your faith produces perseverance.
And let perseverance be perfect,
  so that you may be perfect and complete, lacking in nothing.

Blessed is the man who perseveres in temptation,
  for when he has been proved he will receive the crown of life
  that he promised to those who love him.

The word of the Lord.

8.

1 Peter 3:14-17   Do not be afraid or terrified with fear of them.

A reading from the first Letter of Saint Peter

Beloved:
Even if you should suffer because of righteousness, blessed are you.
Do not be afraid or terrified with fear of them,
  but sanctify Christ as Lord in your hearts.
Always be ready to give an explanation
  to anyone who asks you for a reason for your hope,
  but do it with gentleness and reverence,
  keeping your conscience clear,
  so that, when you are maligned,
  those who defame your good conduct in Christ
  may themselves be put to shame.
For it is better to suffer for doing good,
  if that be the will of God, than for doing evil.

The word of the Lord.

9.

1 Peter 4:12-19   Rejoice to the extent that you share in the sufferings
of Christ.

A reading from the first Letter of Saint Peter

Beloved, do not be surprised that a trial by fire is occurring among you,
   as if something strange were happening to you.
But rejoice to the extent that you share in the sufferings of Christ,
   so that when his glory is revealed
   you may also rejoice exultantly.
If you are insulted for the name of Christ, blessed are you,
   for the Spirit of glory and of God rests upon you.
But let no one among you be made to suffer
   as a murderer, a thief, an evildoer, or as an intriguer.
But whoever is made to suffer as a Christian should not be ashamed
   but glorify God because of the name.
For it is time for the judgment to begin with the household of God;
   if it begins with us, how will it end
   for those who fail to obey the Gospel of God?

   And if the righteous one is barely saved,
      where will the godless and the sinner appear?

As a result, those who suffer in accord with God's will
   hand their souls over to a faithful creator as they do good.

The word of the Lord.

10.

1 John 5:1-5   The victory that conquers the world is our faith.

A reading from the first Letter of Saint John

Beloved:
Everyone who believes that Jesus is the Christ is begotten by God,
     and everyone who loves the Father
     loves also the one begotten by him.
In this way we know that we love the children of God
     when we love God and obey his commandments.
For the love of God is this,
     that we keep his commandments.
And his commandments are not burdensome,
     for whoever is begotten by God conquers the world.
And the victory that conquers the world is our faith.
Who indeed is the victor over the world
     but the one who believes that Jesus is the Son of God?

The word of the Lord.

717 ALLELUIA VERSE AND VERSE BEFORE THE GOSPEL

1.

Matthew 5:10

**Blessed are they who are persecuted for the sake of righteousness,
for theirs is the Kingdom of heaven.**

2.

John 17:19

**I consecrate myself for them,
so that they also may be consecrated in the truth.**

3.

2 Corinthians 1:3b-4a

**Blessed be the Father of compassion and God of all encouragement,
who encourages us in our every affliction.**

4.

James 1:12

**Blessed is the man who perseveres in temptation,
for when he has been proved he will receive the crown of life.**

5.

1 Peter 4:14

**If you are insulted for the name of Christ, blessed are you,
for the Spirit of God rests upon you.**

6.

See *Te Deum*

**We praise you, O God,
we acclaim you as Lord;
the white-robed army of martyrs praise you.**

718   GOSPEL

1.

Matthew 10:17-22   You will be led before governors and kings for my sake, as a witness before them and the pagans.

☩   **A reading from the holy Gospel according to Matthew**

Jesus said to his Apostles:
"Beware of men, for they will hand you over to courts
   and scourge you in their synagogues,
   and you will be led before governors and kings for my sake
   as a witness before them and the pagans.
When they hand you over,
   do not worry about how you are to speak
   or what you are to say.
You will be given at that moment what you are to say.
For it will not be you who speak
   but the Spirit of your Father speaking through you.
Brother will hand over brother to death,
   and the father his child;
   children will rise up against parents and have them put to death.
You will be hated by all because of my name,
   but whoever endures to the end will be saved."

The Gospel of the Lord.

2.

Matthew 10:28-33   Do not be afraid of those who kill the body.

☩   **A reading from the holy Gospel according to Matthew**

Jesus said to his Apostles:
"Do not be afraid of those who kill the body
   but cannot kill the soul;
   rather, be afraid of the one who can destroy
   both soul and body in Gehenna.
Are not two sparrows sold for a small coin?
Yet not one of them falls to the ground without your Father's knowledge.
Even all the hairs of your head are counted.
So do not be afraid; you are worth more than many sparrows.
Everyone who acknowledges me before others
   I will acknowledge before my heavenly Father.

But whoever denies me before others,
   I will deny before my heavenly Father."

The Gospel of the Lord.

   3.

Matthew 10:34-39   I have come to bring not peace but the sword.

✝ **A reading from the holy Gospel according to Matthew**

Jesus said to his Apostles:
"Do not think that I have come to bring peace upon the earth.
I have come to bring not peace but the sword.
For I have come to set
   a man 'against his father,
      a daughter against her mother,
   and a daughter-in-law against her mother-in-law;
      and one's enemies will be those of one's household.'

"Whoever loves father or mother more than me is not worthy of me,
   and whoever loves son or daughter more than me is not worthy of me;
   and whoever does not take up his cross
   and follow after me is not worthy of me.
Whoever finds his life will lose it,
   and whoever loses his life for my sake will find it."

The Gospel of the Lord.

   4.

Luke 9:23-26   Whoever loses his life for my sake will save it.

✝ **A reading from the holy Gospel according to Luke**

Jesus said to all,
   "If anyone wishes to come after me, he must deny himself
   and take up his cross daily and follow me.
For whoever wishes to save his life will lose it,
   but whoever loses his life for my sake will save it.
What profit is there for one to gain the whole world
   yet lose or forfeit himself?
Whoever is ashamed of me and of my words,
   the Son of Man will be ashamed of when he comes in his glory
   and in the glory of the Father and of the holy angels."

The Gospel of the Lord.

5.

John 12:24-26   If a grain of wheat falls to the ground and dies, it produces much fruit.

✠   **A reading from the holy Gospel according to John**

Jesus said to his disciples:
"Amen, amen, I say to you,
     unless a grain of wheat falls to the ground and dies,
     it remains just a grain of wheat;
     but if it dies, it produces much fruit.
Whoever loves his life loses it,
     and whoever hates his life in this world
     will preserve it for eternal life.
Whoever serves me must follow me,
     and where I am, there also will my servant be.
The Father will honor whoever serves me."

The Gospel of the Lord.

6.

John 15:18-21   If they persecuted me, they will also persecute you.

✠   **A reading from the holy Gospel according to John**

Jesus said to his disciples:
"If the world hates you, realize that it hated me first.
If you belonged to the world, the world would love its own;
     but because you do not belong to the world,
     and I have chosen you out of the world,
     the world hates you.
Remember the word I spoke to you,
     'No slave is greater than his master.'
If they persecuted me, they will also persecute you.
If they kept my word, they will also keep yours.
And they will do all these things to you on account of my name,
     because they do not know the one who sent me."

The Gospel of the Lord.

7.

John 17:11b-19   The world hated them.

✠ **A reading from the holy Gospel according to John**

Lifting his eyes to heaven, Jesus prayed, saying:
"Holy Father, keep them in your name that you have given me,
so that they may be one just as we are one.
When I was with them I protected them in your name that you gave me,
and I guarded them, and none of them was lost
except the son of destruction,
in order that the Scripture might be fulfilled.
But now I am coming to you.
I speak this in the world
so that they may share my joy completely.
I gave them your word, and the world hated them,
because they do not belong to the world
any more than I belong to the world.
I do not ask that you take them out of the world
but that you keep them from the Evil One.
They do not belong to the world
any more than I belong to the world.
Consecrate them in the truth.
Your word is truth.
As you sent me into the world,
so I sent them into the world.
And I consecrate myself for them,
so that they also may be consecrated in truth."

The Gospel of the Lord.

THE COMMON OF PASTORS

719   READING I FROM THE OLD TESTAMENT OUTSIDE THE EASTER SEASON

1.

Exodus 32:7-14   Then he spoke of exterminating them, but Moses, his chosen one, withstood him in the breach to turn back his destructive wrath (Psalm 106:23).

A reading from the Book of Exodus

The LORD said to Moses,
   "Go down at once to your people,
      whom you brought out of the land of Egypt,
      for they have become depraved.
They have soon turned aside from the way I pointed out to them,
      making for themselves a molten calf and worshiping it,
      sacrificing to it and crying out,
      'This is your God, O Israel,
      who brought you out of the land of Egypt!'
I see how stiff necked this people is," continued the LORD to Moses.
"Let me alone, then,
      that my wrath may blaze up against them to consume them.
Then I will make of you a great nation."

But Moses implored the LORD, his God, saying,
   "Why, O LORD, should your wrath blaze up against your own people,
      whom you brought out of the land of Egypt
      with such great power and with so strong a hand?
Why should the Egyptians say,
      'With evil intent he brought them out,
      that he might kill them in the mountains
      and exterminate them from the face of the earth'?
Let your blazing wrath die down;
      relent in punishing your people.
Remember your servants Abraham, Isaac, and Israel,
      and how you swore to them by your own self, saying,
      'I will make your descendants as numerous as the stars in the sky;
      and all this land that I promised,
      I will give your descendants as their perpetual heritage.'"

So the Lord relented in the punishment
  he had threatened to inflict on his people.

The word of the Lord.

2.

Deuteronomy 10:8-9   The Lord himself is his heritage.

A reading from the Book of Deuteronomy

**Moses summoned all of Israel and said to them:
"At that time the Lord set apart the tribe of Levi
  to carry the ark of the covenant of the Lord,
  to be in attendance before the Lord and minister to him,
  and to give blessings in his name,
  as they have done to this day.
For this reason,
  Levi has no share in the heritage with his brothers;
  the Lord himself is his heritage,
  as the Lord, your God, has told him."**

The word of the Lord.

3.

1 Samuel 16:1b, 6-13a   There—anoint him, for this is he!

A reading from the first Book of Samuel

The Lord said to Samuel:
"Fill your horn with oil, and be on your way.
I am sending you to Jesse of Bethlehem,
  for I have chosen my king from among his sons."

As Jesse and his sons came to the sacrifice,
  Samuel looked at Eliab and thought,
  "Surely the Lord's anointed is here before him."
But the Lord said to Samuel:
  "Do not judge from his appearance or from his lofty stature,
  because I have rejected him.
Not as man sees does God see,
  because he sees the appearance
  but the Lord looks into the heart."
Then Jesse called Abinadab and presented him before Samuel,
  who said, "The Lord has not chosen him."
Next Jesse presented Shammah, but Samuel said,
  "The Lord has not chosen this one either."
In the same way Jesse presented seven sons before Samuel,
  but Samuel said to Jesse,
  "The Lord has not chosen any one of these."
Then Samuel asked Jesse,
  "Are these all the sons you have?"
Jesse replied,
  "There is still the youngest, who is tending the sheep."
Samuel said to Jesse,
  "Send for him;
  we will not begin the sacrificial banquet until he arrives here."
Jesse sent and had the young man brought to them.
He was ruddy, a youth handsome to behold
  and making a splendid appearance.
The Lord said,
  "There—anoint him, for this is he!"
Then Samuel, with the horn of oil in hand,
  anointed him in the midst of his brothers;
  and from that day on, the spirit of the Lord rushed upon David.

The word of the Lord.

4.

Isaiah 6:1-8   Whom shall I send? Who will go for us?

A reading from the Book of the Prophet Isaiah

In the year King Uzziah died,
    I saw the Lord seated on a high and lofty throne,
    with the train of his garment filling the temple.
Seraphim were stationed above; each of them had six wings:
    with two they veiled their faces,
    with two they veiled their feet,
    and with two they hovered aloft.

"Holy, holy, holy is the LORD of hosts!"
    they cried, one to the other.
"All the earth is filled with his glory!"
At the sound of that cry, the frame of the door shook
    and the house was filled with smoke.

Then I said, "Woe is me, I am doomed!
For I am a man of unclean lips,
    living among a people of unclean lips;
    yet my eyes have seen the King, the LORD of hosts!"
Then one of the seraphim flew to me,
    holding an ember which he had taken with tongs from the altar.

He touched my mouth with it and said,
    "See, now that this has touched your lips,
    your wickedness is removed, your sin purged."

Then I heard the voice of the Lord saying,
    "Whom shall I send? Who will go for us?"
"Here I am," I said; "send me!"

The word of the Lord.

5. For Missionaries

Isaiah 52:7-10   All the ends of the earth will behold the salvation of our God.

A reading from the Book of the Prophet Isaiah

> **How beautiful upon the mountains**
> **   are the feet of him who brings glad tidings,**
> **Announcing peace, bearing good news,**
> **   announcing salvation, and saying to Zion,**
> **   "Your God is King!"**
> **Hark! Your sentinels raise a cry,**
> **   together they shout for joy,**
> **For they see directly, before their eyes,**
> **   the LORD restoring Zion.**
> **Break out together in song,**
> **   O ruins of Jerusalem!**
> **For the LORD comforts his people,**
> **   he redeems Jerusalem.**
> **The LORD has bared his holy arm**
> **   in the sight of all the nations;**
> **All the ends of the earth will behold**
> **   the salvation of our God.**

The word of the Lord.

6.

Isaiah 61:1-3a   The LORD has anointed me; he has sent me to bring glad tidings to the lowly.

A reading from the Book of the Prophet Isaiah

> **The spirit of the Lord GOD is upon me,**
> **   because the LORD has anointed me;**
> **He has sent me to bring glad tidings to the lowly,**
> **   to heal the brokenhearted,**
> **To proclaim liberty to the captives**
> **   and release to the prisoners,**
> **To announce a year of favor from the LORD**
> **   and a day of vindication by our God,**
> **   to comfort all who mourn;**
> **To place on those who mourn in Zion**
> **   a diadem instead of ashes,**

To give them oil of gladness in place of mourning,
   a glorious mantle instead of a listless spirit.

The word of the Lord.

7.

Jeremiah 1:4-9   To whomever I send you, you shall go.

A reading from the Book of the Prophet Jeremiah

The word of the Lord came to me thus:

Before I formed you in the womb I knew you,
   before you were born I dedicated you,
   a prophet to the nations I appointed you.

"Ah, Lord, God!" I said,
   "I know not how to speak; I am too young."

But the Lord answered me,

Say not, "I am too young."
To whomever I send you, you shall go;
   whatever I command you, you shall speak.
Have no fear before them,
   because I am with you to deliver you, says the Lord.

Then the Lord extended his hand and touched my mouth, saying,

See, I place my words in your mouth!

The word of the Lord.

8.

Ezekiel 3:17-21   I have appointed you a watchman for the house of Israel.

A reading from the Book of the Prophet Ezekiel

The word of the LORD came to me:
  Son of man, I have appointed you a watchman
  for the house of Israel.
When you hear a word from my mouth,
  you shall warn them for me.

If I say to the wicked man,
  You shall surely die;
  and you do not warn him or speak out
  to dissuade him from his wicked conduct so that he may live:
  the wicked man shall die for his sin,
  but I will hold you responsible for his death.
If, on the other hand, you have warned the wicked man,
  yet he has not turned away from his evil
  nor from his wicked conduct,
  then he shall die for his sin,
  but you shall save your life.

If a virtuous man turns away from virtue and does wrong
  when I place a stumbling block before him, he shall die.
He shall die for his sin,
  and his virtuous deeds shall not be remembered;
  but I will hold you responsible for his death
  if you did not warn him.
When, on the other hand, you have warned a virtuous man not to sin,
  and he has in fact not sinned,
  he shall surely live because of the warning,
  and you shall save your own life.

The word of the Lord.

9.

Ezekiel 34:11-16   As a shepherd tends his flock, so will I tend my sheep.

A reading from the Book of the Prophet Ezekiel

Thus says the Lord GOD:
   I myself will look after and tend my sheep.
As a shepherd tends his flock
      when he finds himself among his scattered sheep,
      so will I tend my sheep.
I will rescue them from every place where they were scattered
      when it was cloudy and dark.
I will lead them out from among the peoples
      and gather them from the foreign lands;
      I will bring them back to their own country
      and pasture them upon the mountains of Israel
      in the land's ravines and all its inhabited places.
In good pastures will I pasture them,
      and on the mountain heights of Israel
      shall be their grazing ground.
There they shall lie down on good grazing ground,
      and in rich pastures shall they be pastured
      on the mountains of Israel.
I myself will pasture my sheep;
      I myself will give them rest, says the Lord GOD.
The lost I will seek out,
      the strayed I will bring back,
      the injured I will bind up,
      the sick I will heal,
      but the sleek and the strong I will destroy,
      shepherding them rightly.

The word of the Lord.

720 READING I FROM THE NEW TESTAMENT DURING THE SEASON OF EASTER

1. For Missionaries

Acts 13:46-49   We now turn to the Gentiles.

A reading from the Acts of the Apostles

Paul and Barnabas spoke out boldly and said,
   "It was necessary that the word of God be spoken to you first,
   but since you reject it
   and condemn yourselves as unworthy of eternal life,
   we now turn to the Gentiles.
For so the Lord has commanded us,
   I have made you a light to the Gentiles,
   that you may be an instrument of salvation
   to the ends of the earth."

The Gentiles were delighted when they heard this
   and glorified the word of the Lord.
All who were destined for eternal life came to believe,
   and the word of the Lord continued to spread
   through the whole region.

The word of the Lord.

2.

Acts 20:17-18a, 28-32, 36   Keep watch over yourselves and over the whole flock of which the Holy Spirit has appointed you overseers, in which you tend the Church of God.

A reading from the Acts of the Apostles

From Miletus Paul had the presbyters
   of the Church at Ephesus summoned.
When they came to him, he addressed them,
   "Keep watch over yourselves and over the whole flock
   of which the Holy Spirit has appointed you overseers,
   in which you tend the Church of God
   that he acquired with his own Blood.
I know that after my departure savage wolves will come among you,
   and they will not spare the flock.

And from your own group,
>   men will come forward perverting the truth
>   to draw the disciples away after them.
So be vigilant and remember that for three years, night and day,
>   I unceasingly admonished each of you with tears.
And now I commend you to God
>   and to that gracious word of his that can build you up
>   and give you the inheritance among all who are consecrated."

When he had finished speaking
>   he knelt down and prayed with them all.

The word of the Lord.

3. For Missionaries

Acts 26:19-23   He would proclaim light both to our people and to the Gentiles.

A reading from the Acts of the Apostles

Paul said:
"King Agrippa, I was not disobedient to the heavenly vision.
On the contrary, first to those in Damascus and in Jerusalem
>   and throughout the whole country of Judea,
>   and then to the Gentiles,
>   I preached the need to repent and turn to God,
>   and to do works giving evidence of repentance.
That is why the Jews seized me when I was in the temple
>   and tried to kill me.
But I have enjoyed God's help to this very day,
>   and so I stand here testifying to small and great alike,
>   saying nothing different from what the prophets and Moses foretold,
>   that the Christ must suffer and that,
>   as the first to rise from the dead,
>   he would proclaim light both to our people and to the Gentiles."

The word of the Lord.

721 RESPONSORIAL PSALM

1.

Psalm 16:1-2a and 5, 7-8, 11

℟. (see 5a) **You are my inheritance, O Lord.**

Keep me, O God, for in you I take refuge;
   I say to the Lord, **"My Lord are you."**
O Lord, **my allotted portion and my cup,**
   you it is who hold fast my lot.

℟. **You are my inheritance, O Lord.**

I bless the Lord **who counsels me;**
   even in the night my heart exhorts me.
I set the Lord **ever before me;**
   with him at my right hand I shall not be disturbed.

℟. **You are my inheritance, O Lord.**

You will show me the path to life,
   fullness of joys in your presence,
   the delights at your right hand forever.

℟. **You are my inheritance, O Lord.**

2.

Psalm 23:1-3a, 4, 5, 6

℟. (1) **The Lord is my shepherd; there is nothing I shall want.**

The Lord **is my shepherd; I shall not want.**
   In verdant pastures he gives me repose;
Beside restful waters he leads me;
   he refreshes my soul.

℟. **The Lord is my shepherd; there is nothing I shall want.**

Even though I walk in the dark valley
   I fear no evil; for you are at my side
With your rod and your staff
   that give me courage.

℟. **The Lord is my shepherd; there is nothing I shall want.**

You spread the table before me
   in the sight of my foes;
You anoint my head with oil;
   my cup overflows.

℟. **The Lord is my shepherd; there is nothing I shall want.**

Only goodness and kindness follow me
   all the days of my life;
And I shall dwell in the house of the LORD
   for years to come.

℟. **The Lord is my shepherd; there is nothing I shall want.**

3.

Psalm 40:2 and 4, 7-8a, 8b-9, 10

℟. (8a and 9a) **Here I am, Lord; I come to do your will.**

I have waited, waited for the LORD,
   and he stooped toward me and heard my cry.
And he put a new song into my mouth,
   a hymn to our God.

℟. **Here I am, Lord; I come to do your will.**

Sacrifice or offering you wished not,
   but ears open to obedience you gave me.
Burnt offerings or sin-offerings you sought not;
   then said I, "Behold I come."

℟. **Here I am, Lord; I come to do your will.**

"In the written scroll it is prescribed for me,
To do your will, O my God, is my delight,
   and your law is within my heart!"

℟. **Here I am, Lord; I come to do your will.**

I announced your justice in the vast assembly;
   I did not restrain my lips, as you, O LORD, know.

℟. **Here I am, Lord; I come to do your will.**

4.

Psalm 89:2-3, 4-5, 21-22, 25 and 27

R̸. (2) **For ever I will sing the goodness of the Lord.**

The favors of the LORD I will sing forever;
   through all generations my mouth shall proclaim your faithfulness.
For you have said, "My kindness is established forever";
   in heaven you have confirmed your faithfulness.

R̸. **For ever I will sing the goodness of the Lord.**

"I have made a covenant with my chosen one,
   I have sworn to David my servant:
Forever will I confirm your posterity
   and establish your throne for all generations."

R̸. **For ever I will sing the goodness of the Lord.**

"I have found David, my servant;
   with my holy oil I have anointed him,
That my hand may be always with him,
   and that my arm may make him strong."

R̸. **For ever I will sing the goodness of the Lord.**

"My faithfulness and my mercy shall be with him,
   and through my name shall his horn be exalted.
He shall say of me, 'You are my father,
   my God, the Rock, my savior.'"

R̸. **For ever I will sing the goodness of the Lord.**

5.

Psalm 96:1-2a, 2b-3, 7-8a, 10

R̸. (3) **Proclaim God's marvelous deeds to all the nations.**

Sing to the LORD a new song;
   sing to the LORD, all you lands.
Sing to the LORD; bless his name.

R̸. **Proclaim God's marvelous deeds to all the nations.**

Announce his salvation, day after day.
Tell his glory among the nations;
   among all peoples, his wondrous deeds.

R℣. **Proclaim God's marvelous deeds to all the nations.**

Give to the LORD, you families of nations,
   give to the LORD glory and praise;
   give to the LORD the glory due his name!

R℣. **Proclaim God's marvelous deeds to all the nations.**

Say among the nations: The LORD is king.
He has made the world firm, not to be moved;
   he governs the peoples with equity.

R℣. **Proclaim God's marvelous deeds to all the nations.**

6.

Psalm 106:19-20, 21-22, 23

R℣. (4a) **Remember us, O Lord, as you favor your people.**

Our fathers made a calf in Horeb
   and adored a molten image;
They exchanged their glory
   for the image of a grass-eating bullock.

R℣. **Remember us, O Lord, as you favor your people.**

They forgot the God who had saved them,
   who had done great deeds in Egypt,
Wondrous deeds in the land of Ham,
   terrible things at the Red Sea.

R℣. **Remember us, O Lord, as you favor your people.**

Then he spoke of exterminating them,
   but Moses, his chosen one,
Withstood him in the breach
   to turn back his destructive wrath.

R℣. **Remember us, O Lord, as you favor your people.**

7.

Psalm 110:1, 2, 3, 4

℟. (4b) **You are a priest for ever, in the line of Melchizedek.**

The Lord said to my Lord: "Sit at my right hand
  till I make your enemies your footstool."

℟. **You are a priest for ever, in the line of Melchizedek.**

The scepter of your power the Lord will stretch forth from Zion:
  "Rule in the midst of your enemies."

℟. **You are a priest for ever, in the line of Melchizedek.**

"Yours is princely power in the day of your birth, in holy splendor;
  before the daystar, like the dew, I have begotten you."

℟. **You are a priest for ever, in the line of Melchizedek.**

The Lord has sworn, and he will not repent:
  "You are a priest forever, according to the order of Melchizedek."

℟. **You are a priest for ever, in the line of Melchizedek.**

8.

Psalm 117:1bc, 2

℟. (Mark 16:15) **Go out to all the world and tell the Good News.**
  or:
℟. **Alleluia.**

Praise the Lord, all you nations;
  glorify him, all you peoples!

℟. **Go out to all the world, and tell the Good News.**
  or:
℟. **Alleluia.**

For steadfast is his kindness toward us,
  and the fidelity of the Lord endures forever.

℟. **Go out to all the world, and tell the Good News.**
  or:
℟. **Alleluia.**

722 READING II FROM THE NEW TESTAMENT

1.

Romans 12:3-13   Since we have gifts that differ according to the grace
given to us.

A reading from the Letter of Saint Paul to the Romans

Brothers and sisters:
By the grace given to me I tell everyone among you
  not to think of himself more highly than one ought to think,
  but to think soberly,
  each according to the measure of faith that God has apportioned.
For as in one body we have many parts,
  and all the parts do not have the same function,
  so we, though many, are one Body in Christ
  and individually parts of one another.
Since we have gifts that differ according to the grace given to us,
  let us exercise them:
  if prophecy, in proportion to the faith;
  if ministry, in ministering;
  if one is a teacher, in teaching;
  if one exhorts, in exhortation;
  if one contributes, in generosity;
  if one is over others, with diligence;
  if one does acts of mercy, with cheerfulness.

Let love be sincere;
  hate what is evil,
  hold on to what is good;
  love one another with mutual affection;
  anticipate one another in showing honor.
Do not grow slack in zeal,
  be fervent in spirit,
  serve the Lord.
Rejoice in hope,
  endure in affliction,
  persevere in prayer.
Contribute to the needs of the holy ones,
  exercise hospitality.

The word of the Lord.

2. For Missionaries

1 Corinthians 1:18-25   It was the will of God through the foolishness of
the proclamation to save those who have faith.

A reading from the first Letter of Saint Paul to the Corinthians

Brothers and sisters:
The message of the cross is foolishness to those who are perishing,
   but to us who are being saved it is the power of God.
For it is written:
   I will destroy the wisdom of the wise,
      and the learning of the learned I will set aside.

Where is the wise one?
Where is the scribe?
Where is the debater of this age?
Has not God made the wisdom of the world foolish?
For since in the wisdom of God
   the world did not come to know God through wisdom,
   it was the will of God through the foolishness of the proclamation
   to save those who have faith.
For Jews demand signs and Greeks look for wisdom,
   but we proclaim Christ crucified,
   a stumbling block to Jews and foolishness to Gentiles,
   but to those who are called, Jews and Greeks alike,
   Christ the power of God and the wisdom of God.
For the foolishness of God is wiser than human wisdom,
   and the weakness of God is stronger than human strength.

The word of the Lord.

3.

1 Corinthians 4:1-5   Thus should one regard us: as servants of Christ and
stewards of the mysteries of God.

A reading from the first Letter of Saint Paul to the Corinthians

Brothers and sisters:
Thus should one regard us: as servants of Christ
   and stewards of the mysteries of God.
Now it is of course required of stewards that they be found trustworthy.

It does not concern me in the least
   that I be judged by you or any human tribunal;
   I do not even pass judgment on myself;
   I am not conscious of anything against me,
   but I do not thereby stand acquitted;
   the one who judges me is the Lord.
Therefore do not make any judgment
   before the appointed time,
   until the Lord comes,
   for he will bring to light what is hidden in darkness
   and will manifest the motives of our hearts,
   and then everyone will receive praise from God.

The word of the Lord.

   4.

1 Corinthians 9:16-19, 22-23   Woe to me if I do not preach it!

A reading from the first Letter of Saint Paul to the Corinthians

Brothers and sisters:
If I preach the Gospel, this is no reason for me to boast,
   for an obligation has been imposed on me,
   and woe to me if I do not preach it!
If I do so willingly, I have a recompense,
   but if unwillingly, then I have been entrusted with a stewardship.
What then is my recompense?
That, when I preach,
   I offer the Gospel free of charge
   so as not to make full use of my right in the Gospel.

Although I am free in regard to all,
   I have made myself a slave to all
   so as to win over as many as possible.
To the weak I became weak, to win over the weak.
I have become all things to all, to save at least some.
All this I do for the sake of the Gospel,
   so that I too may have a share in it.

The word of the Lord.

5.

2 Corinthians 3:1-6a   He has indeed qualified us as ministers of a
new covenant.

A reading from the second Letter of Saint Paul to the Corinthians

Brothers and sisters:
Are we beginning to commend ourselves again?
Do we need, as some do,
   letters of recommendation to you or from you?
You are our letter, written on our hearts,
   known and read by all,
   shown to be a letter of Christ administered by us,
   written not in ink but by the Spirit of the living God,
   not on tablets of stone but on tablets that are hearts of flesh.

Such confidence we have through Christ toward God.
Not that of ourselves we are qualified
   to take credit for anything as coming from us;
   rather, our qualification comes from God,
   who has indeed qualified us as ministers of a new covenant,
   not of letter but of spirit.

The word of the Lord.

6.

2 Corinthians 4:1-2, 5-7   We preach Jesus Christ as Lord, and ourselves
as your slaves for the sake of Jesus.

A reading from the second Letter of Saint Paul to the Corinthians

Brothers and sisters:
Since we have this ministry through the mercy shown us,
   we are not discouraged.
Rather, we have renounced shameful, hidden things;
   not acting deceitfully or falsifying the word of God,
   but by the open declaration of the truth
   we commend ourselves to everyone's conscience in the sight of God.
For we do not preach ourselves but Jesus Christ as Lord,
   and ourselves as your slaves for the sake of Jesus.
For God who said, *Let light shine out of darkness*,
   has shone in our hearts to bring to light
   the knowledge of the glory of God on the face of Jesus Christ.

But we hold this treasure in earthen vessels,
   that the surpassing power may be of God and not from us.

The word of the Lord.

   7.

2 Corinthians 5:14-20   He gave us the ministry of reconciliation.

A reading from the second Letter of Saint Paul to the Corinthians

Brothers and sisters:
The love of Christ impels us,
   once we have come to the conviction that one died for all;
   therefore, all have died.
He indeed died for all,
   so that those who live might no longer live for themselves
   but for him who for their sake died and was raised.

Consequently, from now on we regard no one according to the flesh;
   even if we once knew Christ according to the flesh,
   yet now we know him so no longer.
So whoever is in Christ is a new creation:
   the old things have passed away;
   behold, new things have come.
And all this is from God,
   who has reconciled us to himself through Christ
   and given us the ministry of reconciliation,
   namely, God was reconciling the world to himself in Christ,
   not counting their trespasses against them
   and entrusting to us the message of reconciliation.
So we are ambassadors for Christ,
   as if God were appealing through us.
We implore you on behalf of Christ,
   be reconciled to God.

The word of the Lord.

8.

Ephesians 4:1-7, 11-13   In the work of ministry, in building up the Body of Christ.

A reading from the Letter of Saint Paul to the Ephesians

Brothers and sisters,
I, a prisoner for the Lord,
  urge you to live in a manner worthy of the call you have received,
  with all humility and gentleness, with patience,
  bearing with one another through love,
  striving to preserve the unity of the spirit
  through the bond of peace:
  one Body and one Spirit,
  as you were also called to the one hope of your call;
  one Lord, one faith, one baptism;
  one God and Father of all,
  who is over all and through all and in all.

But grace was given to each of us
  according to the measure of Christ's gift.

And he gave some as Apostles, others as prophets,
  others as evangelists, others as pastors and teachers,
  to equip the holy ones for the work of ministry,
  for building up the Body of Christ,
  until we all attain to the unity of faith
  and knowledge of the Son of God, to mature to manhood,
  to the extent of the full stature of Christ.

The word of the Lord.

9.

Colossians 1:24-29   On behalf of his Body, which is the Church, of which I am a minister in accordance with God's stewardship given to me to bring to completion for you the word of God.

A reading from the Letter of Saint Paul to the Colossians

Brothers and sisters:
I rejoice in my sufferings for your sake,
  and in my flesh I am filling up
  what is lacking in the afflictions of Christ
  on behalf of his Body, which is the Church,

of which I am a minister
    in accordance with God's stewardship given to me
    to bring to completion for you the word of God,
    the mystery hidden from ages and from generations past.
But now it has been manifested to his holy ones,
    to whom God chose to make known the riches of the glory
    of this mystery among the Gentiles;
    it is Christ in you, the hope for glory.
It is he whom we proclaim,
    admonishing everyone and teaching everyone with all wisdom,
    that we may present everyone perfect in Christ.
For this I labor and struggle,
    in accord with the exercise of his power working within me.

The word of the Lord.

10.

1 Thessalonians 2:2b-8   We were determined to share with you not only the Gospel of God but our very selves as well.

A reading from the first Letter of Saint Paul to the Thessalonians

Brothers and sisters:
We drew courage through our God
    to speak to you the Gospel of God with much struggle.
Our exhortation was not from delusion or impure motives,
    nor did it work through deception.
But as we were judged worthy by God to be entrusted with the Gospel,
    that is how we speak,
    not as trying to please men,
    but rather God, who judges our hearts.
Nor, indeed, did we ever appear with flattering speech, as you know,
    or with a pretext for greed—God is witness—nor did we seek praise
    from men, either from you or from others,
    although we were able to impose our weight as Apostles of Christ.
Rather, we were gentle among you,
    as a nursing mother cares for her children.
With such affection for you,
    we were determined to share with you not only the Gospel of God,
    but our very selves as well, so dearly beloved had you become to us.

The word of the Lord.

11.

2 Timothy 1:13-14; 2:1-3   Guard this rich trust with the help of the Holy Spirit who dwells within us.

A reading from the second Letter of Saint Paul to Timothy

Beloved:
Take as your norm the sound words that you heard from me,
  in the faith and love that are in Christ Jesus.
Guard this rich trust with the help of the Holy Spirit
  who dwells within us.
So you, my child, be strong in the grace that is in Christ Jesus.
And what you heard from me through many witnesses
  entrust to faithful people
  who will have the ability to teach others as well.
Bear your share of hardship along with me
  like a good soldier of Christ Jesus.

The word of the Lord.

12.

2 Timothy 4:1-5   Perform the work of an evangelist, fulfill your ministry.

A reading from the second Letter of Saint Paul to Timothy

Beloved:
I charge you in the presence of God and of Christ Jesus,
  who will judge the living and the dead,
  and by his appearing and his kingly power:
  proclaim the word;
  be persistent whether it is convenient or inconvenient;
  convince, reprimand, encourage through all patience and teaching.
For the time will come when people will not tolerate sound doctrine but,
  following their own desires and insatiable curiosity,
  will accumulate teachers and will stop listening to the truth
  and will be diverted to myths.
But you, be self-possessed in all circumstances;
  put up with hardship;
  perform the work of an evangelist;
  fulfill your ministry.

The word of the Lord.

13.

1 Peter 5:1-4   Tend the flock of God in your midst.

A reading from the first Letter of Saint Peter

Beloved:
I exhort the presbyters among you,
   as a fellow presbyter and witness to the sufferings of Christ
   and one who has a share in the glory to be revealed.
Tend the flock of God in your midst,
   overseeing it not by constraint but willingly,
   as God would have it, not for shameful profit but eagerly.
Do not lord it over those assigned to you,
   but be examples to the flock.
And when the chief Shepherd is revealed,
   you will receive the unfading crown of glory.

The word of the Lord.

723 ALLELUIA VERSE AND VERSE BEFORE THE GOSPEL

1.

Matthew 23:9b, 10b

**You have but one Father in heaven;
you have but one master, the Christ!**

2.

Matthew 28:19a, 20bc

**Go, and teach all nations, says the Lord;
I am with you always, until the end of the world.**

3.

Mark 1:17

**Come after me, says the Lord,
and I will make you fishers of men.**

4.

Luke 4:18

**The Lord sent me to bring glad tidings to the poor
and to proclaim liberty to captives.**

5.

John 10:14

**I am the good shepherd, says the Lord;
I know my sheep, and mine know me.**

6.

John 15:5

**I am the vine, you are the branches, says the Lord:
whoever remains in me and I in him will bear much fruit.**

7.

John 15:15b

**I call you my friends, says the Lord,
for I have made known to you all that the Father has told me.**

8.

2 Corinthians 5:19

**God was reconciling the world to himself in Christ,
and entrusting to us the message of reconciliation.**

724 GOSPEL

1.

Matthew 9:35-38   The harvest is abundant but the laborers are few.

✠ **A reading from the holy Gospel according to Matthew**

Jesus went around to all the towns and villages,
teaching in their synagogues,
proclaiming the Gospel of the Kingdom,
and curing every disease and illness.
At the sight of the crowds, his heart was moved with pity for them
because they were troubled and abandoned,
like sheep without a shepherd.
Then he said to his disciples,
"The harvest is abundant but the laborers are few;
so ask the master of the harvest
to send out laborers for his harvest."

The Gospel of the Lord.

2. For a Pope

Matthew 16:13-19   You are Peter, and upon this rock I will build my Church.

✠ **A reading from the holy Gospel according to Matthew**

Jesus went into the region of Caesarea Philippi
and he asked his disciples,
"Who do people say that the Son of Man is?"
They replied, "Some say John the Baptist, others Elijah,
still others Jeremiah or one of the prophets."
He said to them, "But who do you say that I am?"
Simon Peter said in reply,
"You are the Christ, the Son of the living God."
Jesus said to him in reply, "Blessed are you, Simon son of Jonah.
For flesh and blood has not revealed this to you, but my heavenly Father.
And so I say to you, you are Peter,
and upon this rock I will build my Church,
and the gates of the netherworld shall not prevail against it.
I will give you the keys to the Kingdom of heaven.
Whatever you bind on earth shall be bound in heaven;
and whatever you loose on earth shall be loosed in heaven."

The Gospel of the Lord.

3.

Matthew 23:8-12   The greatest among you must be your servant.

✝ **A reading from the holy Gospel according to Matthew**

Jesus spoke to his disciples:
"Do not be called 'Rabbi.'
You have but one teacher, and you are all brothers.
Call no one on earth your father;
    you have but one Father in heaven.
Do not be called 'Master';
    you have but one master, the Christ.
The greatest among you must be your servant.
Whoever exalts himself will be humbled;
    but whoever humbles himself will be exalted."

The Gospel of the Lord.

4. For Missionaries

Matthew 28:16-20   Go, therefore, and make disciples of all nations.

✝ **A reading from the holy Gospel according to Matthew**

The Eleven disciples went to Galilee,
    to the mountain to which Jesus had ordered them.
When they saw him, they worshiped, but they doubted.
Then Jesus approached and said to them,
    "All power in heaven and on earth has been given to me.
Go, therefore, and make disciples of all nations,
    baptizing them in the name of the Father,
    and of the Son, and of the Holy Spirit,
    teaching them to observe all that I have commanded you.
And behold, I am with you always, until the end of the age."

The Gospel of the Lord.

5.

Mark 1:14-20　I will make you fishers of men.

✠ **A reading from the holy Gospel according to Mark**

After John had been arrested,
　　Jesus came to Galilee proclaiming the Gospel of God:
　　"This is the time of fulfillment.
The Kingdom of God is at hand.
Repent, and believe in the Gospel."

As he passed by the Sea of Galilee,
　　he saw Simon and his brother Andrew casting their nets into the sea;
　　they were fishermen.
Jesus said to them,
　　"Come after me, and I will make you fishers of men."
Then they abandoned their nets and followed him.
He walked along a little farther
　　and saw James, the son of Zebedee, and his brother John.
They too were in a boat mending their nets.
Then he called them.
So they left their father Zebedee in the boat
　　along with the hired men and followed him.

The Gospel of the Lord.

6. For Missionaries

Mark 16:15-20　Go into the whole world and proclaim the Gospel to
every creature.

✠ **A reading from the holy Gospel according to Mark**

Jesus appeared to the Eleven and said to them:
"Go into the whole world
　　and proclaim the Gospel to every creature.
Whoever believes and is baptized will be saved;
　　whoever does not believe will be condemned.
These signs will accompany those who believe:
　　in my name they will drive out demons,
　　they will speak new languages.
They will pick up serpents with their hands,
　　and if they drink any deadly thing, it will not harm them.
They will lay hands on the sick, and they will recover."

So then the Lord Jesus, after he spoke to them,
  was taken up into heaven
  and took his seat at the right hand of God.
But they went forth and preached everywhere,
  while the Lord worked with them
  and confirmed the word through accompanying signs.

The Gospel of the Lord.

7. For Missionaries

Luke 5:1-11   At your command I will lower the nets.

✢   **A reading from the holy Gospel according to Luke**

While the crowd was pressing in on Jesus and listening to the word of God,
  he was standing by the Lake of Gennesaret.
He saw two boats there alongside the lake;
  the fishermen had disembarked and were washing their nets.
Getting into one of them, the one belonging to Simon,
  he asked him to put out a short distance from the shore.
Then he sat down and taught the crowds from the boat.
After he had finished speaking, he said to Simon,
  "Put out into deep water and lower your nets for a catch."
Simon said in reply,
  "Master, we have worked hard all night and have caught nothing,
  but at your command I will lower the nets."
When they had done this, they caught a great number of fish
  and their nets were tearing.
They signaled to their partners in the other boat
  to come to help them.
They came and filled both boats
  so that the boats were in danger of sinking.
When Simon Peter saw this, he fell at the knees of Jesus and said,
  "Depart from me, Lord, for I am a sinful man."
For astonishment at the catch of fish they had made seized him
  and all those with him,
  and likewise James and John, the sons of Zebedee,
  who were partners of Simon.
Jesus said to Simon, "Do not be afraid;
  from now on you will be catching men."
When they brought their boats to the shore,
  they left everything and followed him.

The Gospel of the Lord.

8.

Luke 10:1-9   The harvest is abundant but the laborers are few.

✠ **A reading from the holy Gospel according to Luke**

The Lord Jesus appointed seventy-two disciples
  whom he sent ahead of him in pairs
  to every town and place he intended to visit.
He said to them,
  "The harvest is abundant but the laborers are few;
  so ask the master of the harvest
  to send out laborers for his harvest.
Go on your way;
  behold, I am sending you like lambs among wolves.
Carry no money bag, no sack, no sandals;
  and greet no one along the way.
Into whatever house you enter,
  first say, 'Peace to this household.'
If a peaceful person lives there,
  your peace will rest on him;
  but if not, it will return to you.
Stay in the same house and eat and drink what is offered to you,
  for the laborer deserves his payment.
Do not move about from one house to another.
Whatever town you enter and they welcome you,
  eat what is set before you,
  cure the sick in it and say to them,
  'The Kingdom of God is at hand for you.'"

The Gospel of the Lord.

9.

Luke 22:24-30   I confer a kingdom on you, just as my Father has conferred one on me.

✠ **A reading from the holy Gospel according to Luke**

An argument broke out among the Apostles
  about which of them should be regarded as the greatest.
Jesus said to them,
  "The kings of the Gentiles lord it over them
  and those in authority over them are addressed as 'Benefactors;'
  but among you it shall not be so.

Rather, let the greatest among you be as the youngest,
   and the leader as the servant.
For who is greater:
   the one seated at table or the one who serves?
Is it not the one seated at table?
I am among you as the one who serves.
It is you who have stood by me in my trials;
   and I confer a kingdom on you,
   just as my Father has conferred one on me,
   that you may eat and drink at my table in my Kingdom;
   and you will sit on thrones
   judging the twelve tribes of Israel."

The Gospel of the Lord.

10.

John 10:11-16   A good shepherd lays down his life for the sheep.

✝   **A reading from the holy Gospel according to John**

Jesus said:
"I am the good shepherd.
A good shepherd lays down his life for the sheep.
A hired man, who is not a shepherd
   and whose sheep are not his own,
   sees a wolf coming and leaves the sheep and runs away,
   and the wolf catches and scatters them.
This is because he works for pay and has no concern for the sheep.
I am the good shepherd,
   and I know mine and mine know me,
   just as the Father knows me and I know the Father;
   and I will lay down my life for the sheep.
I have other sheep that do not belong to this fold.
These also I must lead, and they will hear my voice,
   and there will be one flock, one shepherd."

The Gospel of the Lord.

11.

John 15:9-17   I no longer call you slaves; I have called you friends.

✠ **A reading from the holy Gospel according to John**

Jesus said to his disciples:
"As the Father loves me, so I also love you.
Remain in my love.
If you keep my commandments, you will remain in my love,
 just as I have kept my Father's commandments
 and remain in his love.

"I have told you this so that my joy might be in you
 and your joy might be complete.
This is my commandment: love one another as I love you.
No one has greater love than this,
 to lay down one's life for one's friends.
You are my friends if you do what I command you.
I no longer call you slaves,
 because a slave does not know what his master is doing.
I have called you friends,
 because I have told you everything I have heard from my Father.
It was not you who chose me, but I who chose you
 and appointed you to go and bear fruit that will remain,
 so that whatever you ask the Father in my name he may give you.
This I command you: love one another."

The Gospel of the Lord.

12. For a Pope

John 21:15-17   Feed my lambs, feed my sheep.

✠ **A reading from the holy Gospel according to John**

**After Jesus had revealed himself to his disciples and
    eaten breakfast with them, he said to Simon Peter,
    "Simon, son of John, do you love me more than these?"
Simon Peter answered him, "Yes, Lord, you know that I love you."
Jesus said to him, "Feed my lambs."
He then said to Simon Peter a second time,
    "Simon, son of John, do you love me?"
Simon Peter answered him, "Yes, Lord, you know that I love you."
He said to him, "Tend my sheep."
He said to him the third time,
    "Simon, son of John, do you love me?"
Peter was distressed that he had said to him a third time,
    "Do you love me?" and he said to him,
    "Lord, you know everything; you know that I love you."
Jesus said to him, "Feed my sheep."**

The Gospel of the Lord.

THE COMMON OF DOCTORS OF THE CHURCH

725 READING I FROM THE OLD TESTAMENT

First Option

1 Kings 3:11-14   I give you a wise and understanding heart.

A reading from the first Book of Kings

The LORD said to Solomon:
"Because you have asked for this—not for a long life for yourself,
nor for riches, nor for the life of your enemies,
but for understanding so that you may know what is right—
I do as you requested.
I give you a heart so wise and understanding
that there has never been anyone like you up to now,
and after you there will come no one to equal you.
In addition, I give you what you have not asked for,
such riches and glory that among kings there is not your like.
And if you follow me by keeping my statutes and commandments,
as your father David did,
I will give you a long life."

The word of the Lord.

Second Option

Wisdom 7:7-10, 15-16   Beyond health and comeliness I loved her.

A reading from the Book of Wisdom

I prayed, and prudence was given me;
I pleaded, and the spirit of wisdom came to me.
I preferred her to scepter and throne,
And deemed riches nothing in comparison with her,
nor did I liken any priceless gem to her;
Because all gold, in view of her, is a little sand,
and before her, silver is to be accounted mire.
Beyond health and comeliness I loved her,
And I chose to have her rather than the light,
because the splendor of her never yields to sleep.

Now God grant I speak suitably
   and value these endowments at their worth:
For he is the guide of Wisdom
   and the director of the wise.
For both we and our words are in his hand,
   as well as all prudence and knowledge of crafts.

The word of the Lord.

Third Option

Sirach 15:1-6   She will fill him with the spirit of wisdom
and understanding.

A reading from the Book of Sirach

He who fears the LORD will do this;
   he who is practiced in the law will come to wisdom.
Motherlike she will meet him,
   like a young bride she will embrace him,
Nourish him with the bread of understanding,
   and give him the water of learning to drink.
He will lean upon her and not fall,
   he will trust in her and not be put to shame.
She will exalt him above his fellows;
   and in the midst of the assembly she will open his mouth
   and fill him with the spirit of wisdom and understanding,
   and clothe him with the robe of glory.
Joy and gladness he will find,
   an everlasting name he will inherit.

The word of the Lord.

Fourth Option

Sirach 39:6e-10   He who studies the law of the Most High will be filled with the spirit of understanding.

A reading from the Book of Sirach

If it pleases the Lord Almighty,
    he who studies the law of the Most High
    will be filled with the spirit of understanding;
He will pour forth his words of wisdom
    and in prayer give thanks to the Lord,
Who will direct his knowledge and his counsel,
    as he meditates upon his mysteries.
He will show the wisdom of what he has learned
    and glory in the law of the Lord's covenant.
Many will praise his understanding;
    his fame can never be effaced;
Unfading will be his memory,
    through all generations his name will live;
Peoples will speak of his wisdom,
    and in assembly sing his praises.

The word of the Lord.

726 READING I FROM THE NEW TESTAMENT DURING THE SEASON OF EASTER

First Option

Acts 2:14a, 22-24, 32-36   God has made him both Lord and Christ.

A reading from the Acts of the Apostles

On the day of the Pentecost, Peter stood up with the Eleven,
   raised his voice, and proclaimed to them:

"You who are children of Israel, hear these words.
Jesus the Nazorean was a man commended to you by God
   with mighty deeds, wonders, and signs,
   which God worked through him in your midst, as you yourselves know.
This man, delivered up by the set plan and foreknowledge of God,
   you killed, using lawless men to crucify him.
But God raised him up, releasing him from the throes of death,
   because it was impossible for him to be held by it.

"God raised this Jesus; of this we are all witnesses.
Exalted at the right hand of God,
   he received the promise of the Holy Spirit from the Father
   and poured it forth, as you both see and hear.
For David did not go up into heaven, but he himself said:

   The Lord said to my Lord,
   'Sit at my right hand
      until I make your enemies your footstool.'

Therefore let the whole house of Israel know for certain
   that God has made him both Lord and Christ,
   this Jesus whom you crucified."

The word of the Lord.

Second Option

Acts 13:26-33   What God promised to our fathers he has brought to fulfillment by raising up Jesus.

A reading from the Acts of the Apostles

When Paul came to Antioch in Pisidia, he said in the synagogue:
   "My brothers, sons of the family of Abraham,
   and those others among you who are God-fearing,
   to us this word of salvation has been sent.
The inhabitants of Jerusalem and their leaders failed to recognize him,
   and by condemning him they fulfilled the oracles of the prophets
   that are read sabbath after sabbath.
For even though they found no grounds for a death sentence,
   they asked Pilate to have him put to death,
   and when they had accomplished all that was written about him,
   they took him down from the tree and placed him in a tomb.
But God raised him from the dead,
   and for many days he appeared to those
   who had come up with him from Galilee to Jerusalem.
These are now his witnesses before the people.
We ourselves are proclaiming this good news to you
   that what God promised our fathers
   he has brought to fulfillment for us, their children, by raising up Jesus,
   as it is written in the second psalm,
   You are my Son; this day I have begotten you."

The word of the Lord.

727 RESPONSORIAL PSALM

First Option

Psalm 19:8, 9, 10, 11

R℣. (10) **The judgments of the Lord are true, and all of them are just.**
or:
R℣. (John 6:63) **Your words, Lord, are Spirit and life.**

The law of the LORD **is perfect,**
   refreshing the soul;
The decree of the LORD **is trustworthy,**
   giving wisdom to the simple.

R℣. **The judgments of the Lord are true, and all of them are just.**
or:
R℣. **Your words, Lord, are Spirit and life.**

The precepts of the LORD **are right,**
   rejoicing the heart;
The command of the LORD **is clear,**
   enlightening the eye.

R℣. **The judgments of the Lord are true, and all of them are just.**
or:
R℣. **Your words, Lord, are Spirit and life.**

The fear of the LORD **is pure,**
   enduring forever;
The ordinances of the LORD **are true,**
   all of them just.

R℣. **The judgments of the Lord are true, and all of them are just.**
or:
R℣. **Your words, Lord, are Spirit and life.**

They are more precious than gold,
   than a heap of purest gold;
Sweeter also than syrup
   or honey from the comb.

R℣. **The judgments of the Lord are true, and all of them are just.**
or:
R℣. **Your words, Lord, are Spirit and life.**

Second Option

Psalm 37:3-4, 5-6, 30-31

℟. (30a) **The mouth of the just murmurs wisdom.**

Trust in the L**ORD** **and do good,**
   that you may dwell in the land and be fed in security.
Take delight in the L**ORD**,
   and he will grant you your heart's requests.

℟. **The mouth of the just murmurs wisdom.**

Commit to the L**ORD** **your way;**
   trust in him, and he will act.
He will make justice dawn for you like the light;
   bright as the noonday shall be your vindication.

℟. **The mouth of the just murmurs wisdom.**

The mouth of the just tells of wisdom
   and his tongue utters what is right.
The law of his God is in his heart,
   and his steps do not falter.

℟. **The mouth of the just murmurs wisdom.**

Third Option

Psalm 119:9, 10, 11, 12, 13, 14

℟. (12b) **Lord, teach me your statutes.**

How can a young man be faultless in his way?
  By keeping to your words.

℟. **Lord, teach me your statutes.**

With all my heart I seek you;
  let me not stray from your commands.

℟. **Lord, teach me your statutes.**

Within my heart I treasure your promise,
  that I may not sin against you.

℟. **Lord, teach me your statutes.**

Blessed are you, O LORD;
  teach me your statutes.

℟. **Lord, teach me your statutes.**

With my lips I declare
  all the ordinances of your mouth.

℟. **Lord, teach me your statutes.**

In the way of your decrees
  I rejoice as much as in all riches.

℟. **Lord, teach me your statutes.**

728   READING II FROM THE NEW TESTAMENT

1.

1 Corinthians 1:18-25   It was the will of God through the foolishness of the proclamation to save those who have faith.

A reading from the first Letter of Saint Paul to the Corinthians

Brothers and sisters:
The message of the cross is foolishness to those who are perishing,
   but to us who are being saved it is the power of God.
For it is written:

   I will destroy the wisdom of the wise,
      and the learning of the learned I will set aside.

Where is the wise one?
Where is the scribe?
Where is the debater of this age?
Has not God made the wisdom of the world foolish?
For since in the wisdom of God
   the world did not come to know God through wisdom,
   it was the will of God through the foolishness of the proclamation
   to save those who have faith.
For Jews demand signs and Greeks look for wisdom,
   but we proclaim Christ crucified,
   a stumbling block to Jews and foolishness to Gentiles,
   but to those who are called, Jews and Greeks alike,
   Christ the power of God and the wisdom of God.
For the foolishness of God is wiser than human wisdom,
   and the weakness of God is stronger than human strength.

The word of the Lord.

2.

1 Corinthians 2:1-10a   We speak God's wisdom, mysterious, hidden.

A reading from the first Letter of Saint Paul to the Corinthians

When I came to you, brothers and sisters,
    proclaiming the mystery of God,
    I did not come with sublimity of words or of wisdom.
For I resolved to know nothing while I was with you
    except Jesus Christ, and him crucified.
I came to you in weakness and fear and much trembling,
    and my message and my proclamation
    were not with persuasive words of wisdom,
    but with a demonstration of Spirit and power,
    so that your faith might rest not on human wisdom
    but on the power of God.

Yet we speak a wisdom to those who are mature,
    but not a wisdom of this age,
    nor of the rulers of this age who are passing away.
Rather we speak God's wisdom, mysterious, hidden,
    which God predetermined before the ages for our glory,
    and which none of the rulers of this age knew;
    for, if they had known it,
    they would not have crucified the Lord of glory.
But as it is written:

> ***What eye has not seen, and ear has not heard,***
>   ***and what has not entered the human heart,***
>   ***what God has prepared for those who love him,***

this God has revealed to us through the Spirit.

The word of the Lord.

3.

1 Corinthians 2:10b-16   But we have the mind of Christ.

A reading from the first Letter of Saint Paul to the Corinthians

Brothers and sisters:
The Spirit scrutinizes everything, even the depths of God.
Among men, who knows what pertains to the man
  except his spirit that is within?
Similarly, no one knows what pertains to God except the Spirit of God.
We have not received the spirit of the world
  but the Spirit who is from God,
  so that we may understand the things freely given us by God.
And we speak about them not with words taught by human wisdom,
  but with words taught by the Spirit,
  describing spiritual realities in spiritual terms.

Now the natural man does not accept what pertains to the Spirit of God,
  for to him it is foolishness, and he cannot understand it,
  because it is judged spiritually.
The one who is spiritual, however, can judge everything
  but is not subject to judgment by anyone.

For *who has known the mind of the Lord, so as to counsel him?*
But we have the mind of Christ.

The word of the Lord.

4.

Ephesians 3:8-12   This grace was given, to preach to the Gentiles the inscrutable riches of Christ.

A reading from the Letter of Saint Paul to the Ephesians

Brothers and sisters:
To me, the very least of all the holy ones, this grace was given,
  to preach to the Gentiles the inscrutable riches of Christ,
  and to bring to light for all what is the plan of the mystery
  hidden from ages past in God who created all things,
  so that the manifold wisdom of God
  might now be made known through the Church
  to the principalities and authorities in the heavens.

This was according to the eternal purpose
   that he accomplished in Christ Jesus our Lord,
    in whom we have boldness of speech
    and confidence of access through faith in him.

The word of the Lord.

5.

Ephesians 4:1-7, 11-13   In the work of ministry, in building up the Body
of Christ.

A reading from the Letter of Saint Paul to the Ephesians

Brothers and sisters:
I, a prisoner for the Lord,
   urge you to live in a manner worthy of the call you have received,
   with all humility and gentleness, with patience,
   bearing with one another through love,
   striving to preserve the unity of the Spirit
   through the bond of peace:
   one Body and one Spirit,
   as you were also called to the one hope of your call;
   one Lord, one faith, one baptism;
   one God and Father of all,
   who is over all and through all and in all.

But grace was given to each of us
   according to the measure of Christ's gift.

And he gave some as Apostles, others as prophets,
   others as evangelists, others as pastors and teachers,
   to equip the holy ones for the work of ministry,
   for building up the Body of Christ,
   until we all attain to the unity of faith
   and knowledge of the Son of God, to mature manhood,
   to the extent of the full stature of Christ.

The word of the Lord.

6.

2 Timothy 1:13-14; 2:1-3   Guard this rich trust with the help of the Holy Spirit who dwells within us.

A reading from the second Letter of Saint Paul to Timothy

Beloved:
Take as your norm the sound words that you heard from me,
  in the faith and love that are in Christ Jesus.
Guard this rich trust with the help of the Holy Spirit
  that dwells within us.

My child, be strong in the grace that is in Christ Jesus.
And what you heard from me through many witnesses
  entrust to faithful people
  who will have the ability to teach others as well.
Bear your share of hardship along with me
  like a good soldier of Christ Jesus.

The word of the Lord.

7.

2 Timothy 4:1-5   Perform the work of an evangelist; fulfill your ministry.

A reading from the second Letter of Saint Paul to Timothy

Beloved:
I charge you in the presence of God and of Christ Jesus,
  who will judge the living and the dead,
  and by his appearing and his kingly power:
  proclaim the word;
  be persistent whether it is convenient or inconvenient;
  convince, reprimand, encourage through all patience and teaching.
For the time will come
  when people will not tolerate sound doctrine but,
  following their own desires and insatiable curiosity,
  will accumulate teachers and will stop listening to the truth
  and will be diverted to myths.
But you, be self-possessed in all circumstances;
  put up with hardship;
  perform the work of an evangelist;
  fulfill your ministry.

The word of the Lord.

729 ALLELUIA VERSE AND VERSE BEFORE THE GOSPEL

1.

Matthew 5:16

**Let your light shine before others,
that they may see your good deeds and glorify your heavenly Father.**

2.

Matthew 23:9b, 10b

**You have but one Father in heaven.
You have but one master, the Christ.**

3.

See John 6:63c, 68c

**Your words, Lord, are Spirit and life;
you have the words of everlasting life.**

4.

John 15:5

**I am the vine, you are the branches, says the Lord:
whoever remains in me and I in him will bear much fruit.**

5.

See Acts 16:14b

**Open our hearts, O Lord,
to listen to the words of your Son.**

6.

1 Corinthians 1:18

**The message about the cross is foolishness to those who are perishing,
but to us who are being saved it is the power of God.**

7.

1 Corinthians 2:7

**We speak God's wisdom, mysterious, hidden,
which God predetermined before the ages for our glory.**

8.

**The seed is the word of God, Christ is the sower;
all who come to him will live for ever.**

730 GOSPEL

1.

Matthew 5:13-19   You are the light of the world.

✠ **A reading from the holy Gospel according to Matthew**

Jesus said to his disciples:
"You are the salt of the earth.
But if salt loses its taste, with what can it be seasoned?
It is no longer good for anything
  but to be thrown out and trampled underfoot.
You are the light of the world.
A city set on a mountain cannot be hidden.
Nor do they light a lamp and then put it under a bushel basket;
  it is set on a lampstand,
  where it gives light to all in the house.
Just so, your light must shine before others,
  that they may see your good deeds
  and glorify your heavenly Father.

"Do not think that I have come to abolish the law or the prophets.
I have come not to abolish but to fulfill.
Amen, I say to you, until heaven and earth pass away,
  not the smallest letter or the smallest part of a letter
  will pass from the law,
  until all things have taken place.
Therefore, whoever breaks one of the least of these commandments
  and teaches others to do so
  will be called least in the Kingdom of heaven.
But whoever obeys and teaches these commandments
  will be called greatest in the Kingdom of heaven."

The Gospel of the Lord.

2.

Matthew 7:21-29   He taught them as one having authority.

☩   **A reading from the holy Gospel according to Matthew**

Jesus said to his disciples:
"Not everyone who says to me, 'Lord, Lord,'
   will enter the Kingdom of heaven,
   but only the one who does the will of my Father in heaven.
Many will say to me on that day,
   'Lord, Lord, did we not prophesy in your name?
Did we not drive out demons in your name?
Did we not do mighty deeds in your name?'
Then I will declare to them solemnly,
   'I never knew you. Depart from me, you evildoers.'

"Everyone who listens to these words of mine and acts on them
   will be like a wise man who built his house on rock.
The rain fell, the floods came,
   and the winds blew and buffeted the house.
But it did not collapse; it had been set solidly on rock.
And everyone who listens to these words of mine
   but does not act on them
   will be like a fool who built his house on sand.
The rain fell, the floods came,
   and the winds blew and buffeted the house.
And it collapsed and was completely ruined."

When Jesus finished these words,
   the crowds were astonished at his teaching,
   for he taught them as one having authority,
   and not as their scribes.

The Gospel of the Lord.

3.

Matthew 13:47-52   The new and the old.

☩ **A reading from the holy Gospel according to Matthew**

Jesus said to the crowds:
"The Kingdom of heaven is like a net thrown into the sea,
which collects fish of every kind.
When it is full they haul it ashore
and sit down to put what is good into buckets.
What is bad they throw away.
Thus it will be at the end of the age.
The angels will go out and separate the wicked from the righteous
and throw them into the fiery furnace,
where there will be wailing and grinding of teeth.

"Do you understand all these things?"
They answered, "Yes."
And he replied,
"Then every scribe who has been instructed in the Kingdom of heaven
is like the head of a household who brings from his storeroom
both the new and the old."

The Gospel of the Lord.

4.

Matthew 23:8-12   Do not be called "Rabbi." You have but one teacher,
who is Christ.

☩ **A reading from the holy Gospel according to Matthew**

Jesus said to his disciples:
"Do not be called 'Rabbi.'
You have but one teacher, and you are all brothers.
Call no one on earth your father;
you have but one Father in heaven.
Do not be called 'Master';
you have but one master, the Christ.
The greatest among you must be your servant.
Whoever exalts himself will be humbled;
whoever humbles himself will be exalted."

The Gospel of the Lord.

5. Long Form

Mark 4:1-10, 13-20   The sower went out to sow.

✠   **A reading from the holy Gospel according to Mark**

On another occasion, Jesus began to teach by the sea.
A very large crowd gathered around him
   so that he got into a boat on the sea and sat down.
And the whole crowd was beside the sea on land.
And he taught them at length in parables,
   and in the course of his instruction he said to them,
   "Hear this! A sower went out to sow.
And as he sowed, some seed fell on the path,
   and the birds came and ate it up.
Other seed fell on rocky ground where it had little soil.
It sprang up at once because the soil was not deep.
And when the sun rose, it was scorched and it withered for lack of roots.
Some seed fell among thorns,
   and the thorns grew up and choked it
   and it produced no grain.
And some seed fell on rich soil and produced fruit.
It came up and grew and yielded thirty, sixty, and a hundredfold."
He added, "Whoever has ears to hear ought to hear."

And when he was alone,
   those present along with the Twelve
   questioned him about the parables.
He said to them,
   "Do you not understand this parable?
Then how will you understand any of the parables?
The sower sows the word.
These are the ones on the path where the word is sown.
As soon as they hear, Satan comes at once
   and takes away the word sown in them.
And these are the ones sown on rocky ground who,
   when they hear the word, receive it at once with joy.
But they have no roots; they last only for a time.
Then when tribulation or persecution comes because of the word,
   they quickly fall away.
Those sown among thorns are another sort.

They are the people who hear the word,
   but worldly anxiety, the lure of riches,
   and the craving for other things intrude and choke the word,
   and it bears no fruit.
But those sown on rich soil are the ones who hear the word and accept it
   and bear fruit thirty and sixty and a hundredfold."

The Gospel of the Lord.

OR Short Form

Mark 4:1-9   A sower went out to sow.

☩ **A reading from the holy Gospel according to Mark**

On another occasion, Jesus began to teach by the sea.
A very large crowd gathered around him
   so that he got into a boat on the sea and sat down.
And the whole crowd was beside the sea on land.
And he taught them at length in parables,
   and in the course of his instruction he said to them,
   "Hear this! A sower went out to sow.
And as he sowed, some seed fell on the path,
   and the birds came and ate it up.
Other seed fell on rocky ground where it had little soil.
It sprang up at once because the soil was not deep.
And when the sun rose, it was scorched and it withered for lack of roots.
Some seed fell among thorns,
   and the thorns grew up and choked it
   and it produced no grain.
And some seed fell on rich soil and produced fruit.
It came up and grew and yielded thirty, sixty, and a hundredfold."
He added, "Whoever has ears to hear ought to hear."

The Gospel of the Lord.

6.

Luke 6:43-45   From the fullness of the heart the mouth speaks.

✠ **A reading from the holy Gospel according to Luke**

Jesus said to his disciples:
"A good tree does not bear rotten fruit,
   nor does a rotten tree bear good fruit.
For every tree is known by its own fruit.
For people do not pick figs from thorn bushes,
   nor do they gather grapes from brambles.
A good person out of the store of goodness in his heart produces good,
   but an evil person out of a store of evil produces evil;
   for from the fullness of the heart the mouth speaks."

The Gospel of the Lord.

THE COMMON OF VIRGINS

731 READING I FROM THE OLD TESTAMENT

First Option

Song of Songs 8:6-7   Stern as death is love.

A reading from the Song of Songs

Set me as a seal on your heart,
   as a seal on your arm;
For stern as death is love,
   relentless as the nether world is devotion;
   its flames are a blazing fire.
Deep waters cannot quench love,
   nor floods sweep it away.
Were one to offer all he owns to purchase love,
   he would be roundly mocked.

The word of the Lord.

Second Option

Hosea 2:16bc, 17cd, 21-22   I will espouse you to me forever.

A reading from the Book of the Prophet Hosea

Thus says the Lord:
I will lead her into the desert
   and speak to her heart.
She shall respond there as in the days of her youth,
   when she came up from the land of Egypt.
I will espouse you to me forever:
   I will espouse you in right and in justice,
   in love and in mercy;
I will espouse you in fidelity,
   and you shall know the Lord.

The word of the Lord.

732 READING I FROM THE NEW TESTAMENT DURING THE SEASON OF EASTER

First Option

Revelation 19:1, 5-9a　Blessed are those who have been called to the wedding feast of the Lamb.

A reading from the Book of Revelation

**I, John, heard what sounded like the loud voice
of a great multitude in heaven, saying:**

> **"Alleluia!
> Salvation, glory, and might belong to our God."**

A voice coming from the throne said:

> **"Praise our God, all you his servants,
> and you who revere him, small and great."**

**Then I heard something like the sound of a great multitude
or the sound of rushing water or mighty peals of thunder,
as they said:**

> **"Alleluia!
> The Lord has established his reign,
> our God, the almighty.
> Let us rejoice and be glad
> and give him glory.
> For the wedding day of the Lamb has come,
> his bride has made herself ready.
> She was allowed to wear
> a bright, clean linen garment."**

The linen represents the righteous deeds of the holy ones.

**Then the angel said to me,
"Write this:
Blessed are those who have been called
to the wedding feast of the Lamb."**

The word of the Lord.

Second Option

Revelation 21:1-5a   I saw the new Jerusalem, prepared as a bride
adorned for her husband.

A reading from the Book of Revelation

I, John, saw a new heaven and a new earth.
The former heaven and the former earth had passed away,
 and the sea was no more.
I also saw the holy city, a new Jerusalem,
 coming down out of heaven from God,
 prepared as a bride adorned for her husband.
I heard a loud voice from the throne saying,
 "Behold, God's dwelling is with the human race.
He will dwell with them and they will be his people
 and God himself will always be with them as their God.
He will wipe every tear from their eyes,
 and there shall be no more death or mourning, wailing or pain,
 for the old order has passed away."

The One who sat on the throne said,
 "Behold, I make all things new."

The word of the Lord.

733 RESPONSORIAL PSALM

First Option

Psalm 45:11-12, 14-15, 16-17

R℣. (11) **Listen to me, daughter; see and bend your ear.**
   or:
R℣. **The bridegroom is here; let us go out to meet Christ the Lord.**

Hear, O daughter, and see; turn your ear,
   forget your people and your father's house.
So shall the king desire your beauty;
   for he is your lord, and you must worship him.

R℣. **Listen to me, daughter; see and bend your ear.**
   or:
R℣. **The bridegroom is here; let us go out to meet Christ the Lord.**

All glorious is the king's daughter as she enters;
   her raiment is threaded with spun gold.
In embroidered apparel she is borne in to the king;
   behind her the virgins of her train are brought to you.

R℣. **Listen to me, daughter; see and bend your ear.**
   or:
R℣. **The bridegroom is here; let us go out to meet Christ the Lord.**

They are borne in with gladness and joy;
   they enter the palace of the king.
The place of your fathers your sons shall have;
   you shall make them princes through all the land.

R℣. **Listen to me, daughter; see and bend your ear.**
   or:
R℣. **The bridegroom is here; let us go out to meet Christ the Lord.**

Second Option

Psalm 148:1bc-2, 11-12, 13, 14

R℣. (see 12a and 13a) **Young men and women, praise the name of the Lord.**
   or:
R℣. **Alleluia.**

Praise the LORD from the heavens;
   praise him in the heights;
Praise him, all you his angels,
   praise him, all you his hosts.

R℣. **Young men and women, praise the name of the Lord.**
   or:
R℣. **Alleluia.**

Let the kings of the earth and all peoples,
   the princes and all the judges of the earth,
Young men, too, and maidens,
   old men and boys,
Praise the name of the LORD,
   for his name alone is exalted.

R℣. **Young men and women, praise the name of the Lord.**
   or:
R℣. **Alleluia.**

His majesty is above earth and heaven.
He has lifted up the horn of his people.
Be this his praise from all his faithful ones;
   from the children of Israel, the people close to him. Alleluia.

R℣. **Young men and women, praise the name of the Lord.**
   or:
R℣. **Alleluia.**

734 READING II FROM THE NEW TESTAMENT

First Option

1 Corinthians 7:25-35   A virgin is anxious about the things of the Lord.

A reading from the first Letter of Saint Paul to the Corinthians

Brothers and sisters:
In regard to virgins, I have no commandment from the Lord,
   but I give my opinion as one who by the Lord's mercy is trustworthy.
So this is what I think best because of the present distress:
   that it is a good thing for a person to remain as he is.
Are you bound to a wife? Do not seek a separation.
Are you free of a wife? Then do not look for a wife.
If you marry, however, you do not sin,
   nor does an unmarried woman sin if she marries;
   but such people will experience affliction in their earthly life,
   and I would like to spare you that.

I tell you, brothers, the time is running out.
From now on, let those having wives act as not having them,
   those weeping as not weeping,
   those rejoicing as not rejoicing,
   those buying as not owning,
   those using the world as not using it fully.
For the world in its present form is passing away.

I should like you to be free of anxieties.
An unmarried man is anxious about the things of the Lord,
   how he may please the Lord.
But a married man is anxious about the things of the world,
   how he may please his wife, and he is divided.
An unmarried woman or a virgin is anxious about the things of the Lord,
   so that she may be holy in both body and spirit.
A married woman, on the other hand,
   is anxious about the things of the world,
   how she may please her husband.
I am telling you this for your own benefit,
   not to impose a restraint upon you,
   but for the sake of propriety
   and adherence to the Lord without distraction.

The word of the Lord.

Second Option

2 Corinthians 10:17–11:2   I betrothed you to one husband, to present you
as a chaste virgin to Christ.

A reading from the second Letter of Saint Paul to the Corinthians

Brothers and sisters:
"Whoever boasts, should boast in the Lord."
For it is not the one who recommends himself who is approved,
but the one whom the Lord recommends.

If only you would put up with a little foolishness from me!
Please put up with me.
For I am jealous of you with the jealousy of God,
since I betrothed you to one husband
to present you as a chaste virgin to Christ.

The word of the Lord.

735 ALLELUIA VERSE AND VERSE BEFORE THE GOSPEL

1.

John 14:23

**Whoever loves me will keep my word
and my Father will love him,
and we will come to him.**

2.

**This is the wise virgin, whom the Lord found waiting;
at his coming, she went in with him to the wedding feast.**

3.

**Come, bride of Christ, and receive the crown,
which the Lord has prepared for you for ever.**

736 GOSPEL

First Option

Matthew 19:3-12   For the sake of the Kingdom of heaven.

✠ **A reading from the holy Gospel according to Matthew**

**Some Pharisees approached Jesus, and tested him, saying,
    "Is it lawful for a man to divorce his wife for any cause whatever?"
He said in reply,
    "Have you not read that from the beginning
    the Creator *made them male and female* and said,
    *For this reason a man shall leave his father and mother
    and be joined to his wife, and the two shall become one flesh?*
So they are no longer two, but one flesh.
Therefore, what God has joined together, man must not separate."
They said to him,
    "Then why did Moses command that the man give the woman
    a bill of divorce and dismiss her?"
He said to them,
    "Because of the hardness of your hearts
    Moses allowed you to divorce your wives,
    but from the beginning it was not so.
I say to you, whoever divorces his wife
    (unless the marriage is unlawful)
    and marries another commits adultery."
His disciples said to him,
    "If that is the case of a man with his wife,
    it is better not to marry."
He answered, "Not all can accept this word,
    but only those to whom that is granted.
Some are incapable of marriage because they were born so;
    some, because they were made so by others;
    some, because they have renounced marriage
    for the sake of the Kingdom of heaven.
Whoever can accept this ought to accept it."**

The Gospel of the Lord.

Second Option

Matthew 25:1-13   Behold, the bridegroom! Come out to meet him!

☩ **A reading from the holy Gospel according to Matthew**

Jesus told his disciples this parable:
"The Kingdom of heaven will be like ten virgins
  who took their lamps and went out to meet the bridegroom.
Five of them were foolish and five were wise.
The foolish ones, when taking their lamps,
  brought no oil with them,
  but the wise brought flasks of oil with their lamps.
Since the bridegroom was long delayed,
  they all became drowsy and fell asleep.
At midnight, there was a cry,
  'Behold, the bridegroom! Come out to meet him!'
Then all those virgins got up and trimmed their lamps.
The foolish ones said to the wise,
  'Give us some of your oil,
  for our lamps are going out.'
But the wise ones replied,
  'No, for there may not be enough for us and you.
Go instead to the merchants and buy some for yourselves.'
While they went off to buy it,
  the bridegroom came
  and those who were ready went into the wedding feast with him.
Then the door was locked.
Afterwards the other virgins came and said,
  'Lord, Lord, open the door for us!'
But he said in reply,
  'Amen, I say to you, I do not know you.'
Therefore, stay awake,
  for you know neither the day nor the hour."

The Gospel of the Lord.

Third Option

Luke 10:38-42   Martha welcomed him. Mary has chosen the better part.

✠ **A reading from the holy Gospel according to Luke**

Jesus entered a village
 where a woman whose name was Martha welcomed him.
She had a sister named Mary
 who sat beside the Lord at his feet listening to him speak.
Martha, burdened with much serving, came to him and said,
  "Lord, do you not care
  that my sister has left me by myself to do the serving?
Tell her to help me."
The Lord said to her in reply,
  "Martha, Martha, you are anxious and worried about many things.
There is need of only one thing.
Mary has chosen the better part
 and it will not be taken from her."

The Gospel of the Lord.

THE COMMON OF HOLY MEN AND WOMEN

737 READING I FROM THE OLD TESTAMENT

1.

Genesis 12:1-4a   Go forth from the land of your kinsfolk and from your father's house.

A reading from the Book of Genesis

The LORD said to Abram:
"Go forth from the land of your kinsfolk
    and from your father's house to a land that I will show you.

    "I will make of you a great nation,
        and I will bless you;
    I will make your name great,
        so that you will be a blessing.
    I will bless those who bless you
        and curse those who curse you.
    All the communities of the earth
        shall find blessing in you."

Abram went as the LORD directed him.

The word of the Lord.

2.

Leviticus 19:1-2, 17-18   You shall love your neighbor as yourself.

A reading from the Book of Leviticus

The LORD said to Moses,
    "Speak to the whole assembly of the children of Israel and tell them:
    Be holy, for I, the LORD, your God, am holy.

"You shall not bear hatred for your brother in your heart.
Though you may have to reprove your fellow citizen
    do not incur sin because of him.
Take no revenge and cherish no grudge against any of your people.
You shall love your neighbor as yourself.
I am the LORD."

The word of the Lord.

3.

Deuteronomy 6:3-9   Love the LORD your God with all your heart.

A reading from the Book of Deuteronomy

Moses said to the people:
"Hear, Israel, and be careful to observe these commandments,
  that you may grow and prosper the more,
  in keeping with the promise of the LORD, the God of your fathers,
  to give you a land flowing with milk and honey.

"Hear, O Israel! The LORD is our God, the LORD alone!
Therefore, you shall love the LORD, your God,
  with all your heart,
  and with all your soul,
  and with all your strength.
Take to heart these words which I enjoin on you today.
Drill them into your children.
Speak of them at home and abroad, whether you are busy or at rest.
Bind them at your wrist as a sign
  and let them be as a pendant on your forehead.
Write them on the doorposts of your houses and on your gates."

The word of the Lord.

4. For Religious

Deuteronomy 10:8-9   The Lord himself is our heritage.

A reading from the Book of Deuteronomy

Moses summoned all of Israel and said to them:
"At that time the LORD set apart the tribe of Levi
  to carry the ark of the covenant of the LORD,
  to be in attendance before the LORD and minister to him,
  and to give blessings in his name,
  as they have done to this day.
For this reason,
  Levi has no share in the heritage with his brothers;
  the LORD himself is his heritage,
  as the LORD, your God, has told him."

The word of the Lord.

5. For Religious

1 Kings 19:4-9a, 11-15a   Go outside and stand on the mountain before the LORD.

A reading from the first Book of Kings

Elijah went a day's journey into the desert,
   until he came to a broom tree and sat beneath it.
He prayed for death saying:
   "This is enough, O LORD!
Take my life, for I am no better than my fathers."
He lay down and fell asleep under the broom tree,
   but then an angel touched him and ordered him to get up and eat.
He looked and there at his head was a hearth cake
   and a jug of water.
After he ate and drank, he lay down again,
   but the angel of the LORD came back a second time,
   touched him, and ordered,
   "Get up and eat, else the journey will be too long for you!"
He got up, ate, and drank;
   then strengthened by that food,
   he walked forty days and forty nights to the mountain of God, Horeb.

There he came to a cave, where he took shelter.
Then the LORD said to him,
   "Go outside and stand on the mountain before the LORD;
   the LORD will be passing by."
A strong and heavy wind was rending the mountains
   and crushing rocks before the LORD—
   but the LORD was not in the wind.
After the wind there was an earthquake—
   but the LORD was not in the earthquake.
After the earthquake there was fire—
   but the LORD was not in the fire.
After the fire there was a tiny whispering sound.
When he heard this,
   Elijah hid his face in his cloak
   and went and stood at the entrance of the cave.
A voice said to him, "Elijah, why are you here?"
He replied, "I have been most zealous for the LORD, the God of hosts.
But the children of Israel have forsaken your covenant,
   torn down your altars, and put your prophets to the sword.

I alone am left, and they seek to take my life."
The LORD said to him,
   "Go, take the road back to the desert near Damascus."

The word of the Lord.

6. For Religious

1 Kings 19:16b, 19-21   Elisha left and followed Elijah.

A reading from the first Book of Kings

The LORD said to Elijah:
"You shall anoint Elisha, son of Shaphat of Abel-meholah,
   as prophet to succeed you."

Elijah set out and came upon Elisha, son of Shaphat,
   as he was plowing with twelve yoke of oxen;
   he was following the twelfth.
Elijah went over to him and threw his cloak over him.
Elisha left the oxen, ran after Elijah, and said,
   "Please, let me kiss my father and mother goodbye,
   and I will follow you."
Elijah answered, "Go back!
Have I done anything to you?"
Elisha left him, and taking the yoke of oxen, slaughtered them;
   he used the plowing equipment for fuel to boil their flesh,
   and gave it to his people to eat.
Then he left and followed Elijah as his attendant.

The word of the Lord.

7.

Tobit 8:4b-8   Allow us to live together to a happy old age.

A reading from the Book of Tobit

On their wedding night Tobiah arose from bed and said to his wife,
  "My love, get up. Let us pray and beg our Lord
  to have mercy on us and to grant us deliverance."
She got up, and they started to pray
  and beg that deliverance might be theirs.
He began with these words:

  "Blessed are you, O God of our fathers;
    praised be your name forever and ever.
  Let the heavens and all your creation
    praise you forever.
  You made Adam and you gave him his wife Eve
    to be his help and support;
    and from these two the human race descended.
  You said, 'It is not good for the man to be alone;
    let us make him a partner like himself.'
  Now, Lord, you know that I take this wife of mine
    not because of lust,
    but for a noble purpose.
  Call down your mercy on me and on her,
    and allow us to live together to a happy old age."

They said together, "Amen, amen."

The word of the Lord.

8. For Those Who Work for the Underprivileged

Tobit 12:6-14a   Prayer and fasting are good, but better than either is almsgiving accompanied by righteousness.

A reading from the Book of Tobit

The angel Raphael said to Tobit and his son:
"Thank God!
Give him the praise and the glory.
Before all the living,
    acknowledge the many good things he has done for you,
    by blessing and extolling his name in song.
Before all people, honor and proclaim God's deeds,
    and do not be slack in praising him.
A king's secret it is prudent to keep,
    but the works of God are to be declared and made known.
Praise them with due honor.
Do good, and evil will not find its way to you.
Prayer and fasting are good,
    but better than either is almsgiving accompanied by righteousness.
A little with righteousness is better than abundance with wickedness.
It is better to give alms than to store up gold;
    for almsgiving saves one from death and expiates every sin.
Those who regularly give alms shall enjoy a full life;
    but those habitually guilty of sin are their own worst enemies.

"I will now tell you the whole truth;
    I will conceal nothing at all from you.
I have already said to you,
    'A king's secret it is prudent to keep,
    but the works of God are to be made known with due honor.'
I can now tell you that when you, Tobit, and Sarah prayed,
    it was I who presented and read the record of your prayer
    before the Glory of the Lord;
    and I did the same thing when you used to bury the dead.
When you did not hesitate to get up
    and leave your dinner in order to go and bury the dead,
    I was sent to put you to the test."

The word of the Lord.

9. For Widows

Judith 8:2-8   She was a very God-fearing woman.

A reading from the Book of Judith

Judith's husband, Manasseh, of her own tribe and clan,
had died at the time of the barley harvest.
While he was in the field supervising those who bound the sheaves,
he suffered sunstroke;
and he died of this illness in Bethulia, his native city.
Manasseh was buried with his fathers
in the field between Dothan and Balamon.
The widowed Judith remained three years and four months at home,
where she set up a tent for herself on the roof of her house.
She put sackcloth about her loins and wore widow's weeds.
She fasted all the days of her widowhood,
except sabbath eves and sabbaths, new moon eves and new moons,
feastdays and holidays of the house of Israel.
She was beautifully formed and lovely to behold.

Her husband, Manasseh, the son of Joseph,
the son of Ahitub, the son of Melchis,
the son of Eliab, the son of Nathanael,
the son of Sarasadai, the son of Simeon,
had left her gold and silver,
servants and maids, livestock and fields,
which she was maintaining.
No one had a bad word to say about her,
for she was a very God-fearing woman.

The word of the Lord.

10.

Esther C:1-7, 10   I acted as I did so as not to place the honor of man above that of God.

A reading from the Book of Esther

Mordecai prayed:
"O God of Abraham, God of Isaac, God of Jacob, blessed are you;
O Lord God, almighty King, all things are in your power,
and there is no one to oppose you in your will to save Israel.

You made heaven and earth
  and every wonderful thing under the heavens.
You are LORD of all,
  and there is no one who can resist you, LORD.
You know all things.
You know, O LORD, that
  gladly would I have kissed the soles of Haman's feet
  for the salvation of Israel.
But I acted as I did so as not to place the honor of man
  above that of God.
I will not bow down to anyone but you, my LORD and God.
Hear my prayer; have pity on your inheritance
  and turn our sorrow into joy:
    thus we shall live to sing praise to your name, O LORD.
Do not silence those who praise you."

The word of the Lord.

11.

Proverbs 31:10-13, 19-20, 30-31   The woman who fears the LORD is to
be praised.

A reading from the Book of Proverbs

When one finds a worthy wife,
  her value is far beyond pearls.
Her husband, entrusting his heart to her,
  has an unfailing prize.
She brings him good, and not evil,
  all the days of her life.
She obtains wool and flax
  and cloth with skillful hands.
She puts her hands to the distaff,
  and her fingers ply the spindle.
She reaches out her hands to the poor,
  and extends her arms to the needy.
Charm is deceptive and beauty fleeting;
  the woman who fears the LORD is to be praised.
Give her a reward of her labors,
  and let her works praise her at the city gates.

The word of the Lord.

12.

Sirach 2:7-13   You who fear the LORD, believe him, hope in him, love him.

A reading from the Book of Sirach

You who fear the LORD, wait for his mercy,
   turn not away lest you fall.
You who fear the LORD, trust him,
   and your reward will not be lost.
You who fear the LORD, hope for good things,
   for lasting joy and mercy.
You who fear the Lord, love him
   and your hearts will be enlightened.
Study the generations long past and understand;
   has anyone hoped in the LORD and been disappointed?
Has anyone persevered in his commandments and been forsaken?
   Has anyone called upon him and been rebuffed?
Compassionate and merciful is the LORD;
   he forgives sins, he saves in time of trouble
   and he is a protector to all who seek him in truth.

The word of the Lord.

13.

Sirach 3:17-24   Humble yourself and you will find favor with God.

A reading from the Book of Sirach

My child, conduct your affairs with humility,
   and you will be loved more than a giver of gifts.
Humble yourself the more, the greater you are,
   and you will find favor with God.
The greater you are,
   the more you must humble yourself in all things,
   and you will find grace before God.
For great is the power of God;
   by the humble he is glorified.
What is too sublime for you, seek not,
   into things beyond your strength search not.
What is committed to you, attend to;
   for it is not necessary for you to see with your eyes
   those things which are hidden.

With what is too much for you meddle not,
   when shown things beyond human understanding.
Their own opinion has misled many,
   and false reasoning unbalanced their judgment.
Where the pupil of the eye is missing, there is no light,
   and where there is no knowledge, there is no wisdom.

The word of the Lord.

   14.

Sirach 26:1-4, 13-16   Like the sun rising in the LORD's heavens, the beauty
of a virtuous wife is the radiance of her home.

A reading from the Book of Sirach

Blessed the husband of a good wife,
   twice-lengthened are his days;
A worthy wife brings joy to her husband,
   peaceful and full is his life.
A good wife is a generous gift
   bestowed upon him who fears the LORD;
Be he rich or poor, his heart is content,
   and a smile is ever on his face.

A gracious wife delights her husband,
   her thoughtfulness puts flesh on his bones;
A gift from the LORD is her governed speech,
   and her firm virtue is of surpassing worth.
Choicest of blessings is a modest wife,
   priceless her chaste soul.
A holy and decent woman adds grace upon grace;
   indeed, no price is worthy of her temperate soul.
Like the sun rising in the LORD's heavens,
   the beauty of a virtuous wife is the radiance of her home.

The word of the Lord.

15. For Those Who Work for the Underprivileged

Isaiah 58:6-11   Share your bread with the hungry.

A reading from the Book of the Prophet Isaiah

Thus says the LORD:
This is the fasting that I wish:
   releasing those bound unjustly,
   untying the thongs of the yoke;
Setting free the oppressed,
   breaking every yoke;
Sharing your bread with the hungry,
   sheltering the oppressed and the homeless;
Clothing the naked when you see them,
   and not turning your back on your own.
Then your light shall break forth like the dawn,
   and your wound shall quickly be healed;
Your vindication shall go before you,
   and the glory of the LORD shall be your rear guard.
Then you shall call, and the LORD will answer,
   you shall cry for help, and he will say: Here I am!
If you remove from your midst oppression,
   false accusation and malicious speech;
If you bestow your bread on the hungry
   and satisfy the afflicted;
Then light shall rise for you in darkness,
   and the gloom shall become for you like midday;
Then the LORD will guide you always
   and give you plenty even on the parched land.
He will renew your strength,
   and you shall be like a watered garden,
   like a spring whose water never fails.

The word of the Lord.

16.

Jeremiah 20:7-9   It becomes like fire burning in my heart.

A reading from the Book of the Prophet Jeremiah

You duped me, O Lord, and I let myself be duped;
  you were too strong for me, and you triumphed.
All the day I am an object for laughter;
  everyone mocks me.
Whenever I speak, I must cry out,
  violence and outrage is my message;
The word of the Lord has brought me
  derision and reproach all the day.
I say to myself, I will not mention him,
  I will speak in his name no more.
But then it becomes like fire burning in my heart,
  imprisoned in my bones;
I grow weary holding it in,
  I cannot endure it.

The word of the Lord.

17.

Micah 6:6-8   You have been told, O man, what the Lord requires of you.

A reading from the Book of the Prophet Micah

With what shall I come before the Lord,
  and bow before God most high?
Shall I come before him with burnt offerings,
  with calves a year old?
Will the Lord be pleased with thousands of rams,
  with myriad streams of oil?
Shall I give my first-born for my crime,
  the fruit of my body for the sin of my soul?
You have been told, O man, what is good,
  and what the Lord requires of you:
Only to do the right and to love goodness,
  and to walk humbly with your God.

The word of the Lord.

18.

Zephaniah 2:3; 3:12-13   But I will leave as a remnant in your midst a people humble and lowly.

A reading from the Book of the Prophet Zephaniah

Seek the Lord**, all you humble of the earth,**
who have observed his law;
Seek justice, seek humility;
perhaps you may be sheltered
on the day of the Lord**'s anger.**

But I will leave as a remnant in your midst
a people humble and lowly,
Who shall take refuge in the name of the Lord:
the remnant of Israel.
They shall do no wrong
and speak no lies;
Nor shall there be found in their mouths
a deceitful tongue;
They shall pasture and couch their flocks
with none to disturb them.

The word of the Lord.

738 READING I FROM THE NEW TESTAMENT DURING THE SEASON OF EASTER

First Option   For Religious

Acts 4:32-35   The community of believers was of one heart and mind.

A reading from the Acts of the Apostles

The community of believers was of one heart and mind,
   and no one claimed that any of his possessions was his own,
   but they had everything in common.
With great power the Apostles bore witness
   to the resurrection of the Lord Jesus,
   and great favor was accorded them all.
There was no needy person among them,
   for those who owned property or houses would sell them,
   bring the proceeds of the sale,
   and put them at the feet of the Apostles,
   and they were distributed to each according to need.

The word of the Lord.

Second Option

Revelation 3:14b, 20-22   I will dine with him and he with me.

A reading from the Book of Revelation

"'The Amen, the faithful and true witness,
   the source of God's creation, says this:

"'"Behold, I stand at the door and knock.
If anyone hears my voice and opens the door,
   then I will enter his house and dine with him,
   and he with me.
I will give the victor the right to sit with me on my throne,
   as I myself first won the victory
   and sit with my Father on his throne.

"'"Whoever has ears ought to hear
   what the Spirit says to the churches."'"

The word of the Lord.

Third Option

Revelation 19:1, 5-9a   Blessed are those who have been called to the wedding feast of the Lamb.

A reading from the Book of Revelation

I, John, heard what sounded like the loud voice
of a great multitude in heaven, saying:
"Alleluia!
Salvation, glory, and might belong to our God."

A voice coming from the throne said:

"Praise our God, all you his servants,
and you who revere him, small and great."

Then I heard something like the sound of a great multitude
or the sound of rushing water or mighty peals of thunder,
as they said:

"Alleluia!
The Lord has established his reign,
our God, the almighty.
Let us rejoice and be glad
and give him glory.
For the wedding day of the Lamb has come,
his bride has made herself ready.
She was allowed to wear
a bright, clean linen garment."
(The linen represents the righteous deeds of the holy ones.)

Then the angel said to me,
"Write this:
Blessed are those who have been called
to the wedding feast of the Lamb."

The word of the Lord.

Fourth Option

Revelation 21:5-7   To the thirsty I will give a gift from the spring of life-giving water.

A reading from the Book of Revelation

The One who was seated on the throne said:
"Behold, I make all things new."
Then he said, "Write these words down,
for they are trustworthy and true."
He said to me, "They are accomplished.
I am the Alpha and the Omega,
the beginning and the end.
To the thirsty I will give a gift
from the spring of life-giving water.
The victor will inherit these gifts,
and I shall be his God,
and he will be my son."

The word of the Lord.

739 RESPONSORIAL PSALM

1.

Psalm 1:1-2, 3, 4 and 6

℟. (40:5a) **Blessed are they who hope in the Lord.**
   or:
℟. (2a) **Blessed are they who delight in the law of the Lord.**
   or:
℟. (92:13-14) **The just will flourish like the palm tree in the garden of the Lord.**

Blessed the man who follows not
   the counsel of the wicked
Nor walks in the way of sinners,
   nor sits in the company of the insolent,
But delights in the law of the LORD
   and meditates on his law day and night.

℟. **Blessed are they who hope in the Lord.**
   or:
℟. **Blessed are they who delight in the law of the Lord.**
   or:
℟. **The just will flourish like the palm tree in the garden of the Lord.**

He is like a tree
   planted near running water,
That yields its fruit in due season,
   and whose leaves never fade.
   Whatever he does, prospers.

℟. **Blessed are they who hope in the Lord.**
   or:
℟. **Blessed are they who delight in the law of the Lord.**
   or:
℟. **The just will flourish like the palm tree in the garden of the Lord.**

Not so, the wicked, not so;
    they are like chaff which the wind drives away.
For the LORD watches over the way of the just,
    but the way of the wicked vanishes.

℟. Blessed are they who hope in the Lord.
    or:
℟. Blessed are they who delight in the law of the Lord.
    or:
℟. The just will flourish like the palm tree in the garden of the Lord.

    2.

Psalm 15:2-3a, 3bc-4ab, 5

℟. (1) The just one shall live on your holy mountain, O Lord.

He who walks blamelessly and does justice;
    who thinks the truth in his heart
    and slanders not with his tongue.

℟. The just one shall live on your holy mountain, O Lord.

Who harms not his fellow man,
    nor takes up a reproach against his neighbor;
By whom the reprobate is despised,
    while he honors those who fear the LORD.

℟. The just one shall live on your holy mountain, O Lord.

Who lends not his money at usury
    and accepts no bribe against the innocent.
He who does these things
    shall never be disturbed.

℟. The just one shall live on your holy mountain, O Lord.

3.

Psalm 16:1-2ab and 5, 7-8, 11

℟. (see 5a) **You are my inheritance, O Lord.**

Keep me, O God, for in you I take refuge;
   I say to the L{ORD}**, "My Lord are you."**
O L{ORD}**, my allotted portion and my cup,**
   you it is who hold fast my lot.

℟. **You are my inheritance, O Lord.**

I bless the L{ORD} **who counsels me;**
   even in the night my heart exhorts me.
I set the L{ORD} **ever before me;**
   with him at my right hand I shall not be disturbed.

℟. **You are my inheritance, O Lord.**

You will show me the path to life,
   fullness of joys in your presence,
   the delights at your right hand forever.

℟. **You are my inheritance, O Lord.**

4.

Psalm 23:1-3, 4, 5, 6

℟. (1) **The Lord is my shepherd; there is nothing I shall want.**

The LORD is my shepherd; I shall not want.
    In verdant pastures he gives me repose;
Beside restful waters he leads me;
    he refreshes my soul.
He guides me on right paths
    for his name's sake.

℟. **The Lord is my shepherd; there is nothing I shall want.**

Even though I walk in the dark valley
    I fear no evil; for you are at my side
With your rod and your staff
    that give me courage.

℟. **The Lord is my shepherd; there is nothing I shall want.**

You spread the table before me
    in the sight of my foes;
You anoint my head with oil;
    my cup overflows.

℟. **The Lord is my shepherd; there is nothing I shall want.**

Only goodness and kindness follow me
    all the days of my life;
And I shall dwell in the house of the LORD
    for years to come.

℟. **The Lord is my shepherd; there is nothing I shall want.**

5.

Psalm 34:2-3, 4-5, 6-7, 8-9, 10-11

℟. (2) **I will bless the Lord at all times.**
　　or:
℟. (9) **Taste and see the goodness of the Lord.**

I will bless the Lord at all times;
　　his praise shall be ever in my mouth.
Let my soul glory in the Lord;
　　the lowly will hear and be glad.

℟. **I will bless the Lord at all times.**
　　or:
℟. **Taste and see the goodness of the Lord.**

Glorify the Lord with me,
　　let us together extol his name.
I sought the Lord, and he answered me
　　and delivered me from all my fears.

℟. **I will bless the Lord at all times.**
　　or:
℟. **Taste and see the goodness of the Lord.**

Look to him that you may be radiant with joy,
　　and your faces may not blush with shame.
When the poor one called out, the Lord heard,
　　and from all his distress he saved him.

℟. **I will bless the Lord at all times.**
　　or:
℟. **Taste and see the goodness of the Lord.**

The angel of the Lord encamps
　　around those who fear him, and delivers them.
Taste and see how good the Lord is;
　　blessed the man who takes refuge in him.

℟. **I will bless the Lord at all times.**
　　or:
℟. **Taste and see the goodness of the Lord.**

Fear the LORD, you his holy ones,
   for nought is lacking to those who fear him.
The great grow poor and hungry;
   but those who seek the LORD want for no good thing.

℟. I will bless the Lord at all times.
   or:
℟. Taste and see the goodness of the Lord.

   6.

Psalm 103:1bc-2, 3-4, 8-9, 13-14, 17-18a

℟. (1) O bless the Lord, my soul!

Bless the LORD, O my soul;
   and all my being, bless his holy name.
Bless the LORD, O my soul,
   and forget not all his benefits.

℟. O bless the Lord, my soul!

He pardons all your iniquities,
   he heals all your ills,
He redeems your life from destruction,
   crowns you with kindness and compassion.

℟. O bless the Lord, my soul!

Merciful and gracious is the LORD,
   slow to anger and abounding in kindness.
He will not always chide,
   nor does he keep his wrath forever.

℟. O bless the Lord, my soul!

As a father has compassion on his children,
   so the LORD has compassion on those who fear him,
For he knows how we are formed;
   he remembers that we are dust.

℟. O bless the Lord, my soul!

But the kindness of the LORD is from eternity
   to eternity toward those who fear him,
And his justice toward his children's children
   among those who keep his covenant.

℟. O bless the Lord, my soul!

7.

Psalm 112:1-2, 3-4, 5-7a, 7b-8, 9

R̸. (1) **Blessed the man who fears the Lord.**
   or:
R̸. **Alleluia.**

Blessed the man who fears the LORD,
   who greatly delights in his commands.
His posterity shall be mighty upon the earth;
   the upright generation shall be blessed.

R̸. **Blessed the man who fears the Lord.**
   or:
R̸. **Alleluia.**

Wealth and riches shall be in his house;
   his generosity shall endure forever.
Light shines through the darkness for the upright;
   he is gracious and merciful and just.

R̸. **Blessed the man who fears the Lord.**
   or:
R̸. **Alleluia.**

Well for the man who is gracious and lends,
   who conducts his affairs with justice;
He shall never be moved;
   the just one shall be in everlasting remembrance.

R̸. **Blessed the man who fears the Lord.**
   or:
R̸. **Alleluia.**

An evil report he shall not fear;
   his heart is firm, trusting in the LORD.
His heart is steadfast; he shall not fear
   till he looks down upon his foes.

℟. **Blessed the man who fears the Lord.**
   or:
℟. **Alleluia.**

Lavishly he gives to the poor,
   his generosity shall endure forever;
his horn shall be exalted in glory.

℟. **Blessed the man who fears the Lord.**
   or:
℟. **Alleluia.**

8.

Psalm 128:1-2, 3, 4-5

℟. **Blessed are those who fear the Lord.**

Blessed are you who fear the LORD,
   who walk in his ways!
For you shall eat the fruit of your handiwork;
   blessed shall you be, and favored.

℟. **Blessed are those who fear the Lord.**

Your wife shall be like a fruitful vine
   in the recesses of your home;
Your children like olive plants
   around your table.

℟. **Blessed are those who fear the Lord.**

Behold, thus is the man blessed
   who fears the LORD.
The LORD bless you from Zion:
   may you see the prosperity of Jerusalem
   all the days of your life.

℟. **Blessed are those who fear the Lord.**

9.

Psalm 131:1bcde, 2, 3

℟. In you, Lord, I have found my peace.

O LORD, my heart is not proud,
  nor are my eyes haughty;
I busy not myself with great things,
  nor with things too sublime for me.

℟. In you, Lord, I have found my peace.

Nay rather, I have stilled and quieted
  my soul like a weaned child.
Like a weaned child on its mother's lap,
  so is my soul within me.

℟. In you, Lord, I have found my peace.

O Israel, hope in the LORD,
  both now and forever.

℟. In you, Lord, I have found my peace.

740 READING II FROM THE NEW TESTAMENT

1.

Romans 8:26-30   Those he justified he also glorified.

A reading from the Letter of Saint Paul to the Romans

Brothers and sisters:
The Spirit comes to the aid of our weakness;
    for we do not know how to pray as we ought,
    but the Spirit himself intercedes with inexpressible groanings.
And the one who searches hearts
    knows what is the intention of the Spirit,
    because he intercedes for the holy ones
    according to God's will.

We know that all things work for good for those who love God,
    who are called according to his purpose.
For those he foreknew he also predestined
    to be conformed to the image of his Son,
    so that he might be the firstborn
    among many brothers.
And those he predestined he also called;
    and those he called he also justified;
    and those he justified he also glorified.

The word of the Lord.

2.

1 Corinthians 1:26-31   God chose the weak of the world.

A reading from the first Letter of Saint Paul to the Corinthians

Consider your own calling, brothers and sisters.
Not many of you were wise by human standards,
   not many were powerful,
   not many were of noble birth.
Rather, God chose the foolish of the world to shame the wise,
   and God chose the weak of the world to shame the strong,
   and God chose the lowly and despised of the world,
   those who count for nothing,
   to reduce to nothing those who are something,
   so that no human being might boast before God.
It is due to him that you are in Christ Jesus,
   who became for us wisdom from God,
   as well as righteousness, sanctification, and redemption,
   so that, as it is written,
   Whoever boasts, should boast in the Lord.

The word of the Lord.

3. Long Form

1 Corinthians 12:31–13:13   Love never fails.

A reading from the first Letter of Saint Paul to the Corinthians

Brothers and sisters:
Strive eagerly for the greatest spiritual gifts.
But I shall show you a still more excellent way.

If I speak in human and angelic tongues
   but do not have love,
   I am a resounding gong or a clashing cymbal.
And if I have the gift of prophecy
   and comprehend all mysteries and all knowledge;
   if I have all faith so as to move mountains,
   but do not have love, I am nothing.
If I give away everything I own,
   and if I hand my body over so that I may boast
   but do not have love, I gain nothing.

Love is patient, love is kind.

It is not jealous, love is not pompous,
   it is not inflated, it is not rude,
   it does not seek its own interests,
   it is not quick-tempered, it does not brood over injury,
      it does not rejoice over wrongdoing
   but rejoices with the truth.

It bears all things, believes all things,
   hopes all things, endures all things.

Love never fails.

If there are prophecies, they will be brought to nothing;
   if tongues, they will cease;
   if knowledge, it will be brought to nothing.

For we know partially and we prophesy partially,
   but when the perfect comes, the partial will pass away.

When I was a child, I used to talk as a child,
   think as a child, reason as a child;
   when I became a man, I put aside childish things.

At present we see indistinctly, as in a mirror,
   but then face to face.

At present I know partially;
   then I shall know fully, as I am fully known.

So faith, hope, love remain, these three;
   but the greatest of these is love.

The word of the Lord.

OR Short Form

1 Corinthians 13:4-13   Love never fails.

A reading from the first Letter of Saint Paul to the Corinthians

Brothers and sisters:
Love is patient, love is kind.
It is not jealous, love is not pompous,
   it is not inflated, it is not rude,
   it does not seek its own interests,
   it is not quick-tempered, it does not brood over injury,
   it does not rejoice over wrongdoing but rejoices with the truth.
It bears all things, believes all things,
   hopes all things, endures all things.

Love never fails.
If there are prophecies, they will be brought to nothing;
   if tongues, they will cease;
   if knowledge, it will be brought to nothing.
For we know partially and we prophesy partially,
   but when the perfect comes, the partial will pass away.
When I was a child, I used to talk as a child,
   think as a child, reason as a child;
   when I became a man, I put aside childish things.
At present we see indistinctly, as in a mirror,
   but then face to face.
At present I know partially;
   then I shall know fully, as I am fully known.
So faith, hope, love remain, these three;
   but the greatest of these is love.

The word of the Lord.

4.

2 Corinthians 10:17–11:2   I betrothed you to one husband, to present you as a chaste virgin to Christ.

A reading from the second Letter of Saint Paul to the Corinthians

Brothers and sisters:
Whoever boasts, should boast in the Lord.
For it is not the one who recommends himself who is approved,
but the one whom the Lord recommends.

If only you would put up with a little foolishness from me!
Please put up with me.
For I am jealous of you with the jealousy of God,
since I betrothed you to one husband
to present you as a chaste virgin to Christ.

The word of the Lord.

5.

Galatians 2:19-20   I live, no longer I, but Christ lives in me.

A reading from the Letter of Saint Paul to the Galatians

Brothers and sisters:
Through the law I died to the law,
that I might live for God.
I have been crucified with Christ;
yet I live, no longer I, but Christ lives in me;
insofar as I now live in the flesh,
I live by faith in the Son of God
who has loved me and given himself up for me.

The word of the Lord.

6.

Galatians 6:14-16   Through which the world has been crucified to me and I to the world.

A reading from the Letter of Saint Paul to the Galatians

Brothers and sisters:
May I never boast except in the cross of our Lord Jesus Christ,
   through which the world has been crucified to me,
   and I to the world.
For neither does circumcision mean anything, nor does uncircumcision,
   but only a new creation.
Peace and mercy be to all who follow this rule
   and to the Israel of God.

The word of the Lord.

7.

Ephesians 3:14-19   To know the love of Christ which surpasses knowledge.

A reading from the Letter of Saint Paul to the Ephesians

Brothers and sisters:
I kneel before the Father,
   from whom every family in heaven and on earth is named,
   that he may grant you in accord with the riches of his glory
   to be strengthened with power through his Spirit in the inner self,
   and that Christ may dwell in your hearts through faith;
   that you, rooted and grounded in love,
   may have strength to comprehend with all the holy ones
   what is the breadth and length and height and depth,
   and to know the love of Christ that surpasses knowledge,
   so that you may be filled with all the fullness of God.

The word of the Lord.

8.

Ephesians 6:10-13, 18   Put on the armor of God.

A reading from the Letter of Saint Paul to the Ephesians

Brothers and sisters:
Draw your strength from the Lord and from his mighty power.
Put on the armor of God so that you may be able to stand firm
    against the tactics of the Devil.
For our struggle is not with flesh and blood
    but with the principalities, with the powers,
    with the world rulers of this present darkness,
    with the evil spirits in the heavens.
Therefore, put on the armor of God,
    that you may be able to resist on the evil day
    and, having done everything, to hold your ground.

With all prayer and supplication,
    pray at every opportunity in the Spirit.
To that end, be watchful with all perseverance and supplication
    for all the holy ones.

The word of the Lord.

9.

Philippians 3:8-14   I continue my pursuit toward the goal, the prize of God's upward calling, in Christ Jesus.

A reading from the Letter of Saint Paul to the Philippians

Brothers and sisters:
I consider everything as a loss
    because of the supreme good of knowing Christ Jesus my Lord.
For his sake I have accepted the loss of all things
    and I consider them so much rubbish,
    that I may gain Christ and be found in him,
    not having any righteousness of my own based on the law
    but that which comes through faith in Christ,
    the righteousness from God,
    depending on faith to know him and the power of his resurrection
    and the sharing of his sufferings by being conformed to his death,
    if somehow I may attain the resurrection from the dead.

It is not that I have already taken hold of it
    or have already attained perfect maturity,
    but I continue my pursuit in hope that I may possess it,
    since I have indeed been taken possession of by Christ Jesus.
Brothers and sisters, I for my part
    do not consider myself to have taken possession.
Just one thing: forgetting what lies behind
    but straining forward to what lies ahead,
    I continue my pursuit toward the goal,
    the prize of God's upward calling, in Christ Jesus.

The word of the Lord.

10.

Philippians 4:4-9   Think about whatever is worthy of praise.

A reading from the Letter of Saint Paul to the Philippians

Brothers and sisters:
Rejoice in the Lord always.
I shall say it again: rejoice!
Your kindness should be known to all.
The Lord is near.

Have no anxiety at all, but in everything,
  by prayer and petition, with thanksgiving,
  make your requests known to God.
Then the peace of God that surpasses all understanding
  will guard your hearts and minds in Christ Jesus.

Finally, brothers and sisters,
  whatever is true, whatever is honorable,
  whatever is just, whatever is pure,
  whatever is lovely, whatever is gracious,
  if there is any excellence
  and if there is anything worthy of praise,
  think about these things.
Keep on doing what you have learned and received
  and heard and seen in me.
Then the God of peace will be with you.

The word of the Lord.

11.

Colossians 3:12-17   Over all these put on love, that is, the bond
of perfection.

A reading from the Letter of Saint Paul to the Colossians

Brothers and sisters:
Put on, as God's chosen ones, holy and beloved,
  heartfelt compassion, kindness, humility, gentleness, and patience,
  bearing with one another and forgiving one another,
  if one has a grievance against another;
  as the Lord has forgiven you, so must you also do.
And over all these put on love,
  that is, the bond of perfection.
And let the peace of Christ control your hearts,
  the peace into which you were also called in one Body.
And be thankful.
Let the word of Christ dwell in you richly,
  as in all wisdom you teach and admonish one another,
  singing psalms, hymns, and spiritual songs
  with gratitude in your hearts to God.
And whatever you do, in word or in deed,
  do everything in the name of the Lord Jesus,
  giving thanks to God the Father through him.

The word of the Lord.

12. For Widows

1 Timothy 5:3-10   The real widow, who is all alone, has set her hope on God.

A reading from the first Letter of Saint Paul to Timothy

Beloved:
Honor widows who are truly widows.
But if a widow has children or grandchildren,
**   let these first learn to perform their religious duty**
**   to their own family and to make recompense to their parents,**
**   for this is pleasing to God.**
The real widow, who is all alone,
**   has set her hope on God**
**   and continues in supplications and prayers night and day.**
But the one who is self-indulgent is dead while she lives.
Command this, so that they may be irreproachable.
And whoever does not provide for relatives and especially family members
**   has denied the faith and is worse than an unbeliever.**

Let a widow be enrolled if she is not less than sixty years old,
**   married only once, with a reputation for good works,**
**   namely, that she has raised children, practiced hospitality,**
**   washed the feet of the holy ones, helped those in distress,**
**   involved herself in every good work.**

The word of the Lord.

13.

James 2:14-17   Faith of itself, if it does not have works, is dead.

A reading from the Letter of Saint James

What good is it, my brothers and sisters,
**   if someone says he has faith but does not have works?**
Can that faith save him?
If a brother or sister has nothing to wear
**   and has no food for the day,**
**   and one of you says to them,**
**   "Go in peace, keep warm, and eat well,"**
**   but you do not give them the necessities of the body,**
**   what good is it?**
So also faith of itself,
**   if it does not have works, is dead.**

The word of the Lord.

14.

1 Peter 3:1-9   Holy women hoped in God.

A reading from the first Letter of Saint Peter

You wives should be subordinate to your husbands so that,
 even if some disobey the word,
 they may be won over without a word by their wives' conduct
 when they observe your reverent and chaste behavior.
Your adornment should not be an external one:
 braiding the hair, wearing gold jewelry, or dressing in fine clothes,
 but rather the hidden character of the heart,
 expressed in the imperishable beauty
 of a gentle and calm disposition,
 which is precious in the sight of God.
For this is also how the holy women who hoped in God
 once used to adorn themselves
 and were subordinate to their husbands;
 thus Sarah obeyed Abraham, calling him "lord."
You are her children when you do what is good and fear no intimidation.

Likewise, you husbands should live with your wives in understanding,
 showing honor to the weaker female sex,
 since we are joint heirs of the gift of life,
 so that your prayers may not be hindered.

Finally, all of you, be of one mind, sympathetic,
 loving toward one another, compassionate, humble.
Do not return evil for evil, or insult for insult;
 but, on the contrary, a blessing, because to this you were called,
 that you might inherit a blessing.

The word of the Lord.

15.

1 Peter 4:7b-11   As each one has received a gift, use it to serve one another.

A reading from the first Letter of Saint Peter

Beloved:
Be serious and sober-minded
    so that you will be able to pray.
Above all, let your love for one another be intense,
    because love covers a multitude of sins.
Be hospitable to one another without complaining.
As each one has received a gift, use it to serve one another
    as good stewards of God's varied grace.
Whoever preaches, let it be with the words of God;
    whoever serves, let it be with the strength that God supplies,
    so that in all things God may be glorified through Jesus Christ,
    to whom belong glory and dominion forever and ever. Amen.

The word of the Lord.

16. For Those Who Work for the Underprivileged

1 John 3:14-18   We ought to lay down our lives for our brothers.

A reading from the first Letter of Saint John

Beloved:
We know that we have passed from death to life
    because we love our brothers.
Whoever does not love remains in death.
Everyone who hates his brother is a murderer,
    and you know that anyone who is a murderer
    does not have eternal life remaining in him.
The way we came to know love
    was that he laid down his life for us;
    so we ought to lay down our lives for our brothers.
If someone who has worldly means
    sees a brother in need and refuses him compassion,
    how can the love of God remain in him?
Children, let us love not in word or speech
    but in deed and truth.

The word of the Lord.

17.

1 John 4:7-16   If we love one another, God remains in us.

A reading from the first Letter of Saint John

Beloved, let us love one another,
  because love is of God;
  everyone who loves is begotten by God and knows God.
Whoever is without love does not know God, for God is love.
In this way the love of God was revealed to us:
  God sent his only-begotten Son into the world
  so that we might have life through him.
In this is love:
  not that we have loved God, but that he loved us
  and sent his Son as expiation for our sins.
Beloved, if God so loved us,
  we also must love one another.
No one has ever seen God.
Yet, if we love one another, God remains in us,
  and his love is brought to perfection in us.

This is how we know that we remain in him and he in us,
  that he has given us of his Spirit.
Moreover, we have seen and testify
  that the Father sent his Son as savior of the world.
Whoever acknowledges that Jesus is the Son of God,
  God remains in him and he in God.
We have come to know and to believe in the love God has for us.

God is love, and whoever remains in love
  remains in God and God in him.

The word of the Lord.

18.

1 John 5:1-5   The victory that conquers the world is our faith.

A reading from the first Letter of Saint John

Beloved:
Everyone who believes that Jesus is the Christ is begotten by God,
> **and everyone who loves the Father**
> **loves also the one begotten by him.**

In this way we know that we love the children of God
> **when we love God and obey his commandments.**

For the love of God is this,
> **that we keep his commandments.**

And his commandments are not burdensome,
> **for whoever is begotten by God conquers the world.**

And the victory that conquers the world is our faith.
Who indeed is the victor over the world
> **but the one who believes that Jesus is the Son of God?**

The word of the Lord.

741 ALLELUIA VERSE AND VERSE
BEFORE THE GOSPEL

1.

Matthew 5:3

Blessed are the poor in spirit;
for theirs is the Kingdom of heaven.

2.

Matthew 5:6

Blessed are those who hunger and thirst for righteousness,
for they will be satisfied.

3.

Matthew 5:8

Blessed are the clean of heart,
for they will see God.

4.

See Matthew 11:25

Blessed are you, Father, Lord of heaven and earth;
you have revealed to little ones the mysteries of the Kingdom.

5.

Matthew 11:28

Come to me, all you who labor and are burdened,
and I will give you rest, says the Lord.

6.

Matthew 23:11, 12b

The greatest among you must be your servant.
Whoever humbles himself will be exalted.

7.

Luke 21:36

Be vigilant at all times
and pray that you may have the strength to stand before the Son of Man.

8.

John 8:12

**I am the light of the world, says the Lord;
whoever follows me will have the light of life.**

9.

John 8:31b-32

**If you remain in my word, you will truly be my disciples,
and you will know the truth, says the Lord.**

10.

John 13:34

**I give you a new commandment:
love one another as I have loved you.**

11.

John 14:23

**Whoever loves me will keep my word
and my Father will love him
and we will come to him.**

12.

John 15:4a, 5b

**Remain in me, as I remain in you, says the Lord;
whoever remains in me will bear much fruit.**

13.

John 15:9b, 5b

**Remain in my love, says the Lord;
whoever remains in me and I in him will bear much fruit.**

742 GOSPEL

1.

Matthew 5:1-12a   Rejoice and be glad, for your reward will be great in heaven.

✠ **A reading from the holy Gospel according to Matthew**

When Jesus saw the crowds, he went up the mountain,
   and after he had sat down, his disciples came to him.
He began to teach them, saying:

   "Blessed are the poor in spirit,
      for theirs is the Kingdom of heaven.
   Blessed are they who mourn,
      for they will be comforted.
   Blessed are the meek,
      for they will inherit the land.
   Blessed are they who hunger and thirst for righteousness,
      for they will be satisfied.
   Blessed are the merciful,
      for they will be shown mercy.
   Blessed are the clean of heart,
      for they will see God.
   Blessed are the peacemakers,
      for they will be called children of God.
   Blessed are they who are persecuted for the sake of righteousness,
      for theirs is the Kingdom of heaven.
   Blessed are you when they insult you and persecute you
      and utter every kind of evil against you falsely because of me.
   Rejoice and be glad,
      for your reward will be great in heaven."

The Gospel of the Lord.

2.

Matthew 5:13-16   You are the light of the world.

☩ **A reading from the holy Gospel according to Matthew**

Jesus said to his disciples:
"You are the salt of the earth.
But if salt loses its taste, with what can it be seasoned?
It is no longer good for anything
but to be thrown out and trampled underfoot.
You are the light of the world.
A city set on a mountain cannot be hidden.
Nor do they light a lamp and then put it under a bushel basket;
it is set on a lamp stand,
where it gives light to all in the house.
Just so, your light must shine before others,
that they may see your good deeds
and glorify your heavenly Father."

The Gospel of the Lord.

3.

Matthew 7:21-27   The house built on rock and the house built on sand.

☩ **A reading from the holy Gospel according to Matthew**

Jesus said to his disciples:
"Not everyone who says to me, 'Lord, Lord,'
will enter the Kingdom of heaven,
but only the one who does the will of my Father in heaven.
Many will say to me on that day,
'Lord, Lord, did we not prophesy in your name?
Did we not drive out demons in your name?
Did we not do mighty deeds in your name?'
Then I will declare to them solemnly,
'I never knew you. Depart from me, you evildoers.'

"Everyone who listens to these words of mine and acts on them
will be like a wise man who built his house on rock.
The rain fell, the floods came,
and the winds blew and buffeted the house.
But it did not collapse; it had been set solidly on rock.

And everyone who listens to these words of mine
   but does not act on them
   will be like a fool who built his house on sand.
The rain fell, the floods came,
   and the winds blew and buffeted the house.
And it collapsed and was completely ruined."

The Gospel of the Lord.

4.

Matthew 11:25-30   Although you have hidden these things from the wise
and the learned, you have revealed them to the childlike.

✠ **A reading from the holy Gospel according to Matthew**

At that time Jesus exclaimed:
"I give praise to you, Father, Lord of heaven and earth,
   for although you have hidden these things
   from the wise and the learned
   you have revealed them to the childlike.
Yes, Father, such has been your gracious will.
All things have been handed over to me by my Father.
No one knows the Son except the Father,
   and no one knows the Father except the Son
   and anyone to whom the Son wishes to reveal him."

"Come to me, all you who labor and are burdened,
   and I will give you rest.
Take my yoke upon you and learn from me,
   for I am meek and humble of heart;
   and you will find rest for yourselves.
For my yoke is easy, and my burden light."

The Gospel of the Lord.

5.

Matthew 13:44-46   He sells all that he has and buys that field.

✠ **A reading from the holy Gospel according to Matthew**

Jesus said to the crowds:
"The Kingdom of heaven is like a treasure buried in a field,
  which a person finds and hides again,
  and out of joy goes and sells all that he has and buys that field.
Again, the Kingdom of heaven is like a merchant
  searching for fine pearls.
When he finds a pearl of great price,
  he goes and sells all that he has and buys it."

The Gospel of the Lord.

6.

Matthew 16:24-27   Whoever loses his life for my sake will find it.

✠ **A reading from the holy Gospel according to Matthew**

Jesus said to his disciples,
  "Whoever wishes to come after me must deny himself,
  take up his cross, and follow me.
For whoever wishes to save his life will lose it,
  but whoever loses his life for my sake will find it.
What profit would there be for one to gain the whole world
  and forfeit his life?
Or what can one give in exchange for his life?
For the Son of Man will come with his angels in his Father's glory,
  and then he will repay each one according to his conduct."

The Gospel of the Lord.

7.

Matthew 18:1-5   Unless you turn and become like children, you will not
enter the Kingdom of heaven.

✠ **A reading from the holy Gospel according to Matthew**

The disciples approached Jesus and said,
  "Who is the greatest in the Kingdom of heaven?"
He called a child over, placed it in their midst, and said,
  "Amen, I say to you, unless you turn and become like children,
  you will not enter the Kingdom of heaven.

Whoever humbles himself like this child
   is the greatest in the Kingdom of heaven.
And whoever receives one child such as this in my name receives me."

The Gospel of the Lord.

8. For Religious

Matthew 19:3-12   For the sake of the Kingdom of heaven.

✠ **A reading from the holy Gospel according to Matthew**

Some Pharisees approached Jesus and tested him, saying,
   "Is it lawful for a man to divorce his wife for any cause whatever?"
He said in reply,
   "Have you not read that from the beginning
   the Creator *made them male and female* and said,
   For this reason a man shall leave his father and mother
   and be joined to his wife, and the two shall become one flesh?
So they are no longer two, but one flesh.
Therefore, what God has joined together, man must not separate."
They said to him,
   "Then why did Moses command that the man give the woman
   a bill of divorce and dismiss her?"
He said to them, "Because of the hardness of your hearts
   Moses allowed you to divorce your wives,
   but from the beginning it was not so.
I say to you, whoever divorces his wife
   (unless the marriage is unlawful)
   and marries another commits adultery."
His disciples said to him,
   "If that is the case of a man with his wife,
   it is better not to marry."
He answered, "Not all can accept this word,
   but only those to whom that is granted.
Some are incapable of marriage because they were born so;
   some, because they were made so by others;
   some, because they have renounced marriage
   for the sake of the Kingdom of heaven.
Whoever can accept this ought to accept it."

The Gospel of the Lord.

9.

Matthew 19:27-29   You who have followed me will receive a hundred times more.

✝   **A reading from the holy Gospel according to Matthew**

Peter said to Jesus,
   "We have given up everything and followed you.
What will there be for us?"
Jesus said to them, "Amen, I say to you
   that you who have followed me, in the new age,
   when the Son of Man is seated on his throne of glory,
   will yourselves sit on twelve thrones,
   judging the twelve tribes of Israel.
And everyone who has given up houses or brothers or sisters
   or father or mother or children or lands
   for the sake of my name will receive a hundred times more,
   and will inherit eternal life."

The Gospel of the Lord.

10.

Matthew 22:34-40   Love the Lord your God and your neighbor as yourself.

✝   **A reading from the holy Gospel according to Matthew**

When the Pharisees heard that Jesus had silenced the Sadducees,
   they gathered together, and one of them
   a scholar of the law, tested him by asking,
   "Teacher, which commandment in the law is the greatest?"
He said to him,
   "You shall love the Lord, your God, with all your heart,
   with all your soul, and with all your mind.
This is the greatest and the first commandment.
The second is like it:
   You shall love your neighbor as yourself.
The whole law and the prophets depend on these two commandments."

The Gospel of the Lord.

11.

Matthew 25:1-13   Behold, the bridegroom! Come out to meet him!

☩ **A reading from the holy Gospel according to Matthew**

Jesus told his disciples this parable:
"The Kingdom of heaven will be like ten virgins
  who took their lamps and went out to meet the bridegroom.
Five of them were foolish and five were wise.
The foolish ones, when taking their lamps,
  brought no oil with them,
  but the wise brought flasks of oil with their lamps.
Since the bridegroom was long delayed,
  they all became drowsy and fell asleep.
At midnight, there was a cry,
  'Behold, the bridegroom!
  Come out to meet him!'
Then all those virgins got up and trimmed their lamps.
The foolish ones said to the wise,
  'Give us some of your oil,
  for our lamps are going out.'
But the wise ones replied,
  'No, for there may not be enough for us and you.
Go instead to the merchants and buy some for yourselves.'
While they went off to buy it,
  the bridegroom came
  and those who were ready went into the wedding feast with him.
Then the door was locked.
Afterwards the other virgins came and said,
  'Lord, Lord, open the door for us!'
But he said in reply,
  'Amen, I say to you, I do not know you.'
Therefore, stay awake,
  for you know neither the day nor the hour."

The Gospel of the Lord.

12. Long Form

Matthew 25:14-30   Since you were faithful in small matters, come, share your master's joy.

✠   **A reading from the holy Gospel according to Matthew**

Jesus told his disciples this parable:
"A man who was going on a journey called in his servants
   and entrusted his possessions to them.
To one he gave five talents;
   to another, two; to a third, one—
   to each according to his ability.
Then he went away.
Immediately the one who received five talents went and traded with them,
   and made another five.
Likewise, the one who received two made another two.
But the man who received one went off and dug a hole in the ground
   and buried his master's money.
After a long time
   the master of those servants came back
   and settled accounts with them.
The one who had received five talents
   came forward bringing the additional five.
He said, 'Master, you gave me five talents.
See, I have made five more.'
His master said to him, 'Well done, my good and faithful servant.
Since you were faithful in small matters,
   I will give you great responsibilities.
Come, share your master's joy.'
Then the one who had received two talents also came forward and said,
   'Master, you gave me two talents.
See, I have made two more.'
His master said to him, 'Well done, my good and faithful servant.
Since you were faithful in small matters,
   I will give you great responsibilities.
Come, share your master's joy.'
Then the one who had received the one talent came forward and said,
   'Master, I knew you were a demanding person,
   harvesting where you did not plant
   and gathering where you did not scatter;
   so out of fear I went off and buried your talent in the ground.

Here it is back.'

His master said to him in reply, 'You wicked, lazy servant!

So you knew that I harvest where I did not plant
   and gather where I did not scatter?

Should you not then have put my money in the bank
   so that I could have got it back with interest on my return?

Now then! Take the talent from him and give it to the one with ten.

For to everyone who has
   more will be given and he will grow rich;
   but from the one who has not
   even what he has will be taken away.

And throw this useless servant into the darkness outside,
   where there will be wailing and grinding of teeth.'"

The Gospel of the Lord.

OR Short Form

Matthew 25:14-23   Since you were faithful in small matters, come, share your master's joy.

✠   **A reading from the holy Gospel according to Matthew**

Jesus told his disciples this parable:
"A man who was going on a journey
**   called in his servants and entrusted his possessions to them.**
To one he gave five talents;
**   to another, two; to a third, one—**
**   to each according to his ability.**
Then he went away.
Immediately the one who received five talents went and traded with them,
**   and made another five.**
Likewise, the one who received two made another two.
But the man who received one went off and dug a hole in the ground
**   and buried his master's money.**
After a long time
**   the master of those servants came back and settled accounts with them.**
The one who had received five talents came forward
**   bringing the additional five.**
He said, 'Master, you gave me five talents.
See, I have made five more.'
His master said to him, 'Well done, my good and faithful servant.
Since you were faithful in small matters,
**   I will give you great responsibilities.**
Come, share your master's joy.'
Then the one who had received two talents also came forward and said,
**   'Master, you gave me two talents.**
See, I have made two more.'
His master said to him, 'Well done, my good and faithful servant.

Since you were faithful in small matters,
  I will give you great responsibilities.
Come, share your master's joy.'"

The Gospel of the Lord.

13. For Those Who Work for the Underprivileged

Long Form

Matthew 25:31-46   Whatever you did for the least of my brothers, you did for me.

✠   **A reading from the holy Gospel according to Matthew**

Jesus said to his disciples:
"When the Son of Man comes in his glory,
  and all the angels with him,
  he will sit upon his glorious throne,
  and all the nations will be assembled before him.
And he will separate them one from another,
  as a shepherd separates the sheep from the goats.
He will place the sheep on his right and the goats on his left.
Then the king will say to those on his right,
  'Come, you who are blessed by my Father.
Inherit the kingdom prepared for you from the foundation of the world.
For I was hungry and you gave me food,
  I was thirsty and you gave me drink,
  a stranger and you welcomed me,
  naked and you clothed me,
  ill and you cared for me,
  in prison and you visited me.'
Then the righteous will answer him and say,
  'Lord, when did we see you hungry and feed you,
  or thirsty and give you drink?
When did we see you a stranger and welcome you,
  or naked and clothe you?
When did we see you ill or in prison, and visit you?'
And the king will say to them in reply,
  'Amen, I say to you, whatever you did
  for one of the least brothers of mine, you did for me.'
Then he will say to those on his left,
  'Depart from me, you accursed,
  into the eternal fire prepared for the Devil and his angels.
For I was hungry and you gave me no food,
  I was thirsty and you gave me no drink,
  a stranger and you gave me no welcome,
  naked and you gave me no clothing,
  ill and in prison, and you did not care for me.'

Then they will answer and say,
  'Lord, when did we see you hungry or thirsty
  or a stranger or naked or ill or in prison,
  and not minister to your needs?'
He will answer them, 'Amen, I say to you,
  what you did not do for one of these least ones,
  you did not do for me.'
And these will go off to eternal punishment,
  but the righteous to eternal life."

The Gospel of the Lord.

OR Short Form

Matthew 25:31-40   Whatever you did for the least of my brothers, you did for me.

✝ **A reading from the holy Gospel according to Matthew**

Jesus said to his disciples:
"When the Son of Man comes in his glory,
and all the angels with him,
he will sit upon his glorious throne,
and all the nations will be assembled before him.
And he will separate them one from another,
as a shepherd separates the sheep from the goats.
He will place the sheep on his right and the goats on his left.
Then the king will say to those on his right,
'Come, you who are blessed by my Father.
Inherit the kingdom prepared for you from the foundation of the world.
For I was hungry and you gave me food,
I was thirsty and you gave me drink,
a stranger and you welcomed me,
naked and you clothed me,
ill and you cared for me,
in prison and you visited me.'
Then the righteous will answer him and say,
'Lord, when did we see you hungry and feed you,
or thirsty and give you drink?
When did we see you a stranger and welcome you,
or naked and clothe you?
When did we see you ill or in prison, and visit you?'
And the king will say to them in reply,
'Amen, I say to you, whatever you did
for the least brothers of mine you did for me.'"

The Gospel of the Lord.

14.

Mark 3:31-35   Whoever does the will of God is my brother and sister and mother.

✠ **A reading from the holy Gospel according to Mark**

The mother of Jesus and his brothers arrived.
Standing outside they sent word to him and called him.
A crowd seated around him told him,
 "Your mother and your brothers and your sisters
 are outside asking for you."
But he said to them in reply,
 "Who are my mother and my brothers?"
And looking around at those seated in the circle he said,
 "Here are my mother and my brothers.
For whoever does the will of God
 is my brother and sister and mother."

The Gospel of the Lord.

15. For Teachers

Mark 9:34-37   Whoever receives such a child as this, receives me.

✠ **A reading from the holy Gospel according to Mark**

Jesus' disciples had been discussing among themselves
 who was the greatest.
Then he sat down, called the Twelve, and said to them,
 "If anyone wishes to be first,
 he shall be the last of all and the servant of all."
Taking a child he placed it in their midst,
 and putting his arms around it he said to them,
 "Whoever receives one child such as this in my name, receives me;
 and whoever receives me,
 receives not me but the One who sent me."

The Gospel of the Lord.

16. For Teachers

Mark 10:13-16   Let the children come to me; do not prevent them.

✠ **A reading from the holy Gospel according to Mark**

People were bringing children to Jesus that he might touch them,
  but the disciples rebuked them.
When Jesus saw this he became indignant and said to them,
  "Let the children come to me; do not prevent them,
  for the Kingdom of God belongs to such as these.
Amen, I say to you,
  whoever does not accept the Kingdom of God like a child
  will not enter it."
Then he embraced them and blessed them,
  placing his hands on them.

The Gospel of the Lord.

17. For Religious

Long Form

Mark 10:17-30   Go, sell what you have, and give to the poor; then come,
follow me.

✠ **A reading from the holy Gospel according to Mark**

As Jesus was setting out on a journey,
  a man ran up, knelt down before him, and asked him,
  "Good teacher, what must I do to inherit eternal life?"
Jesus answered him, "Why do you call me good?
No one is good but God alone.
You know the commandments:
  You shall not kill;
  you shall not commit adultery;
  you shall not steal;
  you shall not bear false witness;
  you shall not defraud;
  honor your father and your mother."
He replied and said to him,
  "Teacher, all of these I have observed from my youth."
Jesus, looking at him, loved him and said to him,
  "You are lacking in one thing.

Go, sell what you have, and give to the poor
    and you will have treasure in heaven; then come, follow me."
At that statement his face fell,
    and he went away sad, for he had many possessions.

Jesus looked around and said to his disciples,
    "How hard it is for those who have wealth
    to enter the Kingdom of God!"
The disciples were amazed at his words.
So Jesus again said to them in reply,
    "Children, how hard it is to enter the Kingdom of God!
It is easier for a camel to pass through the eye of a needle
    than for one who is rich to enter the Kingdom of God."
They were exceedingly astonished
    and said among themselves, "Then who can be saved?"
Jesus looked at them and said,
    "For men it is impossible, but not for God.
All things are possible for God."
Peter began to say to him,
    "We have given up everything and followed you."
Jesus said, "Amen, I say to you,
    there is no one who has given up house or brothers or sisters
    or mother or father or children or lands for my sake
    and for the sake of the Gospel
    who will not receive a hundred times more now in this present age:
    houses and brothers and sisters and mothers and children and lands,
    with persecutions, and eternal life in the age to come."

The Gospel of the Lord.

OR Short Form

Mark 10:17-27   Go, sell what you have, and give to the poor; then come, follow me.

✠   **A reading from the holy Gospel according to Mark**

As Jesus was setting out on a journey,
  a man ran up, knelt down before him, and asked him,
  "Good teacher, what must I do to inherit eternal life?"
Jesus answered him, "Why do you call me good?
No one is good but God alone.
You know the commandments:
  You shall not kill;
  you shall not commit adultery;
  you shall not steal;
  you shall not bear false witness;
  you shall not defraud;
  honor your father and your mother."
He replied and said to him,
  "Teacher, all of these I have observed from my youth."
Jesus, looking at him, loved him and said to him,
  "You are lacking in one thing.
Go, sell what you have, and give to the poor
  and you will have treasure in heaven; then come, follow me."
At that statement his face fell,
  and he went away sad, for he had many possessions.

Jesus looked around and said to his disciples,
  "How hard it is for those who have wealth
  to enter the Kingdom of God!"
The disciples were amazed at his words.
So Jesus again said to them in reply,
  "Children, how hard it is to enter the Kingdom of God!
It is easier for a camel to pass through the eye of a needle
  than for one who is rich to enter the Kingdom of God."
They were exceedingly astonished
  and said among themselves, "Then who can be saved?"
Jesus looked at them and said,
  "For men it is impossible, but not for God.
All things are possible for God."

The Gospel of the Lord.

18.

Luke 6:27-38   Be merciful, just as your Father is merciful.

✛ **A reading from the holy Gospel according to Luke**

Jesus said to his disciples:
"To you who hear I say,
   love your enemies, do good to those who hate you,
   bless those who curse you, pray for those who mistreat you.
To the person who strikes you on one cheek,
   offer the other one as well,
   and from the person who takes your cloak,
   do not withhold even your tunic.
Give to everyone who asks of you,
   and from the one who takes what is yours do not demand it back.
Do to others as you would have them do to you.
For if you love those who love you,
   what credit is that to you?
Even sinners love those who love them.
And if you do good to those who do good to you,
   what credit is that to you?
Even sinners do the same.
If you lend money to those from whom you expect repayment,
   what credit is that to you?
Even sinners lend to sinners,
   and get back the same amount.
But rather, love your enemies and do good to them,
   and lend expecting nothing back;
   then your reward will be great
   and you will be children of the Most High,
   for he himself is kind to the ungrateful and the wicked.
Be merciful, just as also your Father is merciful.

"Stop judging and you will not be judged.
Stop condemning and you will not be condemned.
Forgive and you will be forgiven.
Give and gifts will be given to you;
   a good measure, packed together, shaken down, and overflowing,
   will be poured into your lap.
For the measure with which you measure
   will in return be measured out to you."

The Gospel of the Lord.

19. For Religious

Luke 9:57-62   I will follow you wherever you go.

✠   **A reading from the holy Gospel according to Luke**

As Jesus and his disciples were proceeding on their journey,
  someone said to him, "I will follow you wherever you go."
Jesus answered him,
  "Foxes have dens and birds of the sky have nests,
  but the Son of Man has nowhere to rest his head."
And to another he said, "Follow me."
But he replied, "Lord, let me go first and bury my father."
But he answered him, "Let the dead bury their dead.
But you, go and proclaim the Kingdom of God."
And another said, "I will follow you, Lord,
  but first let me say farewell to my family at home."
Jesus said to him, "No one who sets a hand to the plow
  and looks to what was left behind is fit for the Kingdom of God."

The Gospel of the Lord.

20.

Luke 10:38-42   Martha welcomed him. Mary has chosen the better part.

✠   **A reading from the holy Gospel according to Luke**

Jesus entered a village
  where a woman whose name was Martha welcomed him.
She had a sister named Mary
  who sat beside the Lord at his feet listening to him speak.
Martha, burdened with much serving, came to him and said,
  "Lord, do you not care
  that my sister has left me by myself to do the serving?
Tell her to help me."
The Lord said to her in reply,
  "Martha, Martha, you are anxious and worried about many things.
There is need of only one thing.
Mary has chosen the better part and it will not be taken from her."

The Gospel of the Lord.

21. For Religious

Luke 12:32-34   Your Father is pleased to give you the Kingdom.

✠ **A reading from the holy Gospel according to Luke**

Jesus said to his disciples:
"Do not be afraid any longer, little flock,
  for your Father is pleased to give you the Kingdom.
Sell your belongings and give alms.
Provide money bags for yourselves that do not wear out,
  an inexhaustible treasure in heaven
  that no thief can reach nor moth destroy.
For where your treasure is, there also will your heart be."

The Gospel of the Lord.

22.

Luke 12:35-40   You also must be prepared.

✠ **A reading from the holy Gospel according to Luke**

Jesus said to his disciples:
"Gird your loins and light your lamps
  and be like servants who await their master's return from a wedding,
  ready to open immediately when he comes and knocks.
Blessed are those servants whom the master finds vigilant on his arrival.
Amen, I say to you, he will gird himself,
  have them recline at table, and proceed to wait on them.
And should he come in the second or third watch
  and find them prepared in this way,
  blessed are those servants.
Be sure of this:
  if the master of the house had known the hour
  when the thief was coming,
  he would not have let his house be broken into.
You also must be prepared, for at an hour you do not expect,
  the Son of Man will come."

The Gospel of the Lord.

23. For Religious

Luke 14:25-33   Everyone of you who does not renounce all his possessions cannot be my disciple.

☩   **A reading from the holy Gospel according to Luke**

Great crowds were traveling with Jesus,
   and he turned and addressed them,
   "If anyone comes to me without hating his father and mother,
   wife and children, brothers and sisters,
   and even his own life,
   he cannot be my disciple.
Whoever does not carry his own cross and come after me
   cannot be my disciple.
Which of you wishing to construct a tower
   does not first sit down and calculate the cost
   to see if there is enough for its completion?
Otherwise, after laying the foundation
   and finding himself unable to finish the work
   the onlookers should laugh at him and say,
   'This one began to build but did not have the resources to finish.'
Or what king marching into battle would not first sit down
   and decide whether with ten thousand troops
   he can successfully oppose another king
   advancing upon him with twenty thousand troops?
But if not, while he is still far away,
   he will send a delegation to ask for peace terms.
In the same way,
   everyone of you who does not renounce all his possessions
   cannot be my disciple."

The Gospel of the Lord.

24.

John 15:1-8   Whoever remains in me, and I in him, will bear much fruit.

☩   **A reading from the holy Gospel according to John**

Jesus said to his disciples:
"I am the true vine, and my Father is the vine grower.
He takes away every branch in me that does not bear fruit,
   and everyone that does he prunes so that it bears more fruit.
You are already pruned because of the word that I spoke to you.
Remain in me, as I remain in you.

Just as a branch cannot bear fruit on its own
    unless it remains on the vine,
    so neither can you unless you remain in me.
I am the vine, you are the branches.
Whoever remains in me and I in him will bear much fruit,
    because without me you can do nothing.
Anyone who does not remain in me
    will be thrown out like a branch and wither;
    people will gather them and throw them into a fire
    and they will be burned.
If you remain in me and my words remain in you,
    ask for whatever you want and it will be done for you.
By this is my Father glorified,
    that you bear much fruit and become my disciples."

The Gospel of the Lord.

25.

John 15:9-17   You are my friends if you do what I command you.

✛ **A reading from the holy Gospel according to John**

Jesus said to his disciples:
"As the Father loves me, so I also love you.
Remain in my love.
If you keep my commandments, you will remain in my love,
    just as I have kept my Father's commandments
    and remain in his love.

"I have told you this so that my joy might be in you
    and your joy might be complete.
This is my commandment: love one another as I love you.
No one has greater love than this,
    to lay down one's life for one's friends.
You are my friends if you do what I command you.
I no longer call you slaves,
    because a slave does not know what his master is doing.
I have called you friends,
    because I have told you everything I have heard from my Father.
It was not you who chose me, but I who chose you
    and appointed you to go and bear fruit that will remain,
    so that whatever you ask the Father in my name he may give you.
This I command you: love one another."

The Gospel of the Lord.

26.

John 17:20-26   I wish that where I am they also may be with me.

✠   **A reading from the holy Gospel according to John**

Jesus raised his eyes to heaven and said:
"Holy Father, I pray not only for these,
   but also for those who will believe in me through their word,
   so that they may all be one,
   as you, Father, are in me and I in you,
   that they also may be in us,
   that the world may believe that you sent me.
And I have given them the glory you gave me,
   so that they may be one, as we are one,
   I in them and you in me,
   that they may be brought to perfection as one,
   that the world may know that you sent me,
   and that you loved them even as you loved me.
Father, they are your gift to me.
I wish that where I am they also may be with me,
   that they may see my glory that you gave me,
   because you loved me before the foundation of the world.
Righteous Father, the world also does not know you,
   but I know you, and they know that you sent me.
I made known to them your name and I will make it known,
   that the love with which you loved me
   may be in them and I in them."

The Gospel of the Lord.

RITUAL MASSES

I. FOR THE CONFERRAL OF CHRISTIAN INITIATION

1. CATECHUMENATE AND CHRISTIAN INITIATION OF ADULTS

743 ENTRANCE INTO THE ORDER OF CATECHUMENS

The following texts may be used or other appropriate texts may be chosen.

FIRST READING

Genesis 12:1-4a   Go forth from the land of your kinsfolk to a land that I will show you.

A reading from the Book of Genesis

The LORD said to Abram:
"Go forth from the land of your kinsfolk
  and from your father's house to a land that I will show you.

    "I will make of you a great nation,
      and I will bless you;
    I will make your name great,
      so that you will be a blessing.
    I will bless those who bless you
      and curse those who curse you.
    All the communities of the earth
      shall find blessing in you."

Abram went as the LORD directed him.

The word of the Lord.

RESPONSORIAL PSALM

Psalm 33:4-5, 12-13, 18-19, 20 and 22

℟. (12) **Blessed the people the Lord has chosen to be his own.**
　 or:
℟. (22) **Lord, let your mercy be on us, as we place our trust in you.**

For upright is the word of the LORD,
　 and all his works are trustworthy.
He loves justice and right;
　 of the kindness of the LORD the earth is full.

℟. **Blessed the people the Lord has chosen to be his own.**
　 or:
℟. **Lord, let your mercy be on us, as we place our trust in you.**

Blessed the nation whose God is the LORD,
　 the people he has chosen for his own inheritance.
From heaven the LORD looks down; he sees all mankind.

℟. **Blessed the people the Lord has chosen to be his own.**
　 or:
℟. **Lord, let your mercy be on us, as we place our trust in you.**

But see, the eyes of the LORD are upon those who fear him,
　 upon those who hope for his kindness,
To deliver them from death
　 and preserve them in spite of famine.

℟. **Blessed the people the Lord has chosen to be his own.**
　 or:
℟. **Lord, let your mercy be on us, as we place our trust in you.**

Our soul waits for the LORD,
　 who is our help and our shield.
May your kindness, O LORD, be upon us
　 who have put our hope in you.

℟. **Blessed the people the Lord has chosen to be his own.**
　 or:
℟. **Lord, let your mercy be on us, as we place our trust in you.**

VERSE BEFORE THE GOSPEL

John 1:41, 17b

We have found the Messiah:
Jesus Christ, through whom came truth and grace.

GOSPEL

John 1:35-42   Behold, the Lamb of God. We have found the Messiah.

✠ **A reading from the holy Gospel according to John**

John was standing with two of his disciples,
and as he watched Jesus walk by, he said,
"Behold, the Lamb of God."
The two disciples of John heard what he said and followed Jesus.
Jesus turned and saw them following him and said to them,
"What are you looking for?"
They said to him, "Rabbi," which translated means Teacher,
"where are you staying?"
Jesus said to them, "Come, and you will see."
So they went and saw where he was staying,
and they stayed with him that day.
It was about four in the afternoon.
Andrew, the brother of Simon Peter,
was one of the two who heard John and followed Jesus.
He first found his own brother Simon and told him,
"We have found the Messiah," which is translated Christ.
Then he brought him to Jesus.
Jesus looked at him and said,
"You are Simon the son of John;
you will be called Cephas," which is translated Peter.

The Gospel of the Lord.

744 ELECTION OR ENROLLMENT OF NAMES

If this is done on the first Sunday of Lent, the readings of any series in the three-year cycle of readings for this Sunday may be used.

If this is done outside of this Sunday and the readings of the day are not appropriate, readings from those assigned to the First Sunday of Lent (nos. 22–24), or other suitable readings, should be selected.

745 FIRST SCRUTINY

The readings and chants are always taken from the Third Sunday of Lent, Year A (no. 28).

746 SECOND SCRUTINY

The readings and chants are always taken from the Fourth Sunday of Lent, Year A (no. 31). The following reading may also be chosen: Exodus 13:21-22.

747 THIRD SCRUTINY

The readings and chants are always taken from the Fifth Sunday of Lent, Year A (no. 34).

748 PRESENTATION OF THE CREED

The following texts may be used or other appropriate texts may be chosen.

FIRST READING

Deuteronomy 6:1-7   Hear, O Israel! You shall love the Lord, your God, with all your heart.

A reading from the Book of Deuteronomy

Moses said to the people:
"These then are the commandments, the statutes, and decrees
  which the LORD, your God, has ordered
  that you be taught to observe in the land
  into which you are crossing for conquest,
  so that you and your son and your grandson
  may fear the LORD, your God,
  and keep, throughout the days of your lives,
  all his statutes and commandments which I enjoin on you,
  and thus have long life.
Hear then, Israel, and be careful to observe them,
  that you may grow and prosper the more,
  in keeping with the promise of the LORD, the God of your fathers,
  to give you a land flowing with milk and honey.

"Hear, O Israel! The LORD is our God, the LORD alone!
Therefore, you shall love the LORD, your God,
  with all your heart,
  and with all your soul,
  and with all your strength.
Take to heart these words which I enjoin on you today.
Drill them into your children.
Speak of them at home and abroad, whether you are busy or at rest."

The word of the Lord

RESPONSORIAL PSALM

Psalm 19:8, 9, 10, 11

R℣. (John 6:68c) **Lord, you have the words of everlasting life.**

**The law of the Lord is perfect,
    refreshing the soul;
The decree of the Lord is trustworthy,
    giving wisdom to the simple.**

R℣. **Lord, you have the words of everlasting life.**

**The precepts of the Lord are right,
    rejoicing the heart;
The command of the Lord is clear,
    enlightening the eye.**

R℣. **Lord, you have the words of everlasting life.**

**The fear of the Lord is pure,
    enduring forever;
The ordinances of the Lord are true,
    all of them just.**

R℣. **Lord, you have the words of everlasting life.**

**They are more precious than gold,
    than a heap of purest gold;
Sweeter also than syrup
    or honey from the comb.**

R℣. **Lord, you have the words of everlasting life.**

SECOND READING

First Option

Romans 10:8-13   The confession of faith of those believing in Christ.

A reading from the Letter of Saint Paul to the Romans

**Brothers and sisters:
What does the Scripture say?**

> ***The word is near you,
>   in your mouth and in your heart,***

that is, the word of faith that we preach,

for, if you confess with your mouth that Jesus is Lord

and believe in your heart that God raised him from the dead,

you will be saved.

For one believes with the heart and so is justified,

and one confesses with the mouth and so is saved.

For the Scripture says,

No one who believes in him will be put to shame.

For there is no distinction between Jew and Greek;

the same Lord is Lord of all,

enriching all who call upon him.

For *everyone who calls on the name of the Lord will be saved.*

The word of the Lord.

Second Option

Long Form

1 Corinthians 15:1-8   Through the Gospel you are also being saved if you hold fast to the word I preached to you.

A reading from the first Letter of Saint Paul to the Corinthians

I am reminding you, brothers and sisters,

of the Gospel I preached to you,

which you indeed received and in which you also stand.

Through it you are also being saved,

if you hold fast to the word I preached to you,

unless you believed in vain.

For I handed on to you as of first importance what I also received:

that Christ died for our sins in accordance with the Scriptures;

that he was buried;

that he was raised on the third day in accordance with the Scriptures;

that he appeared to Cephas, then to the Twelve.

After that, he appeared to more

than five hundred brothers at once,

most of whom are still living,

though some have fallen asleep.

After that he appeared to James,

then to all the Apostles.

Last of all, as to one born abnormally,

he appeared to me.

The word of the Lord.

OR Short Form

1 Corinthians 15:1-4   Through the Gospel you are also being saved if you
hold fast to the word I preached to you.

A reading from the first Letter of Saint Paul to the Corinthians

I am reminding you, brothers and sisters,
   of the Gospel I preached to you,
   which you indeed received and in which you also stand.
Through it you are also being saved,
   if you hold fast to the word I preached to you,
   unless you believed in vain.
For I handed on to you as of first importance what I also received:
   that Christ died for our sins in accordance with the Scriptures;
   that he was buried;
   that he was raised on the third day in accordance with the Scriptures.

The word of the Lord.

VERSE BEFORE THE GOSPEL

John 3:16

God so loved the world that he gave his only-begotten Son,
so that everyone who believes in him might have eternal life.

GOSPEL

   First Option

Matthew 16:13-18   You are Peter, and upon this rock I will build
my Church.

✠ **A reading from the holy Gospel according to Matthew**

When Jesus went into the region of Caesarea Philippi
   he asked his disciples,
   "Who do people say that the Son of Man is?"
They replied, "Some say John the Baptist,
   others Elijah,
   still others Jeremiah or one of the prophets."
He said to them, "But who do you say that I am?"
Simon Peter said in reply,
   "You are the Christ, the Son of the living God."

Jesus said to him in reply, "Blessed are you, Simon son of Jonah.
For flesh and blood has not revealed this to you, but my heavenly Father.
And so I say to you, you are Peter,
    and upon this rock I will build my Church,
    and the gates of the netherworld shall not prevail against it."

The Gospel of the Lord.

OR Second Option

John 12:44-50   I came into the world as light, so that anyone who believes in me might not remain in darkness.

✠   **A reading from the holy Gospel according to John**

Jesus cried out and said,
    "Whoever believes in me believes not only in me
    but also in the one who sent me,
    and whoever sees me sees the one who sent me.
I came into the world as light,
    so that everyone who believes in me might not remain in darkness.
And if anyone hears my words and does not observe them,
    I do not condemn him,
    for I did not come to condemn the world but to save the world.
Whoever rejects me and does not accept my words
    has something to judge him: the word that I spoke,
    it will condemn him on the last day,
    because I did not speak on my own,
    but the Father who sent me commanded me what to say and speak.
And I know that his commandment is eternal life.
So what I say, I say as the Father told me."

The Gospel of the Lord.

749 PRESENTATION OF THE LORD'S PRAYER

The following texts may be used or other appropriate texts may be chosen.

FIRST READING

Hosea 11:1, 3-4, 8e-9   I drew them with human cords, with bands of love.

A reading from the Book of the Prophet Hosea

The LORD says:
When Israel was a child I loved him,
   out of Egypt I called my son.
Yet it was I who taught Ephraim to walk,
   who took them in my arms;
I drew them with human cords,
   with bands of love;
I fostered them like one
   who raises an infant to his cheeks;
Yet, though I stooped to feed my child,
   they did not know that I was their healer.

My heart is overwhelmed,
   my pity is stirred.
I will not give vent to my blazing anger,
   I will not destroy Ephraim again;
For I am God and not man,
   the Holy One present among you;
   I will not let the flames consume you.

The word of the Lord.

RESPONSORIAL PSALM

First Option

Psalm 23:1b-3a, 3b-4, 5, 6

R̰. (1) **The Lord is my shepherd; there is nothing I shall want.**

The LORD is my shepherd; I shall not want.
   In verdant pastures he gives me repose;
Beside restful waters he leads me;
   he refreshes my soul.

R̰. **The Lord is my shepherd; there is nothing I shall want.**

He guides me in right paths
    for his name's sake.
Even though I walk in the dark valley
    I fear no evil; for you are at my side
With your rod and your staff
    that give me courage.

℞. The Lord is my shepherd; there is nothing I shall want.

You spread the table before me
    in the sight of my foes;
You anoint my head with oil;
    my cup overflows.

℞. The Lord is my shepherd; there is nothing I shall want.

Only goodness and kindness follow me
    all the days of my life;
And I shall dwell in the house of the LORD
    for years to come.

℞. The Lord is my shepherd; there is nothing I shall want.

OR Second Option

Psalm 103:1-2, 8 and 10, 11-12, 13 and 14

℞. (13) **As a father is kind to his children, so kind is the Lord to those who fear him.**

Bless the LORD, O my soul;
    and all my being, bless his holy name.
Bless the LORD, O my soul,
    and forget not all his benefits.

℞. **As a father is kind to his children, so kind is the Lord to those who fear him.**

Merciful and gracious is the LORD,
    slow to anger and abounding in kindness.
Not according to our sins does he deal with us,
    nor does he requite us according to our crimes.

(cont.)

℟. **As a father is kind to his children, so kind is the Lord to those who fear him.**

For as the heavens are high above the earth
   so surpassing is his kindness toward those who fear him.
As far as the east is from the west,
   so far has he put our transgressions from us.

℟. **As a father is kind to his children, so kind is the Lord to those who fear him.**

As a father has compassion on his children,
   so the LORD has compassion on those who fear him,
For he knows how we are formed;
   he remembers that we are dust.

℟. **As a father is kind to his children, so kind is the Lord to those who fear him.**

SECOND READING

First Option

Romans 8:14-17, 26-27   You received a spirit of adoption, through which we cry, *"Abba!"*

A reading from the Letter of Saint Paul to the Romans

Brothers and sisters:
Those who are led by the Spirit of God are sons of God.
For you did not receive a spirit of slavery to fall back into fear,
   but you received a spirit of adoption,
   through which we cry, "*Abba,* Father!"
The Spirit himself bears witness with our spirit
   that we are children of God,
   and if children, then heirs,
   heirs of God and joint heirs with Christ,
   if only we suffer with him
   so that we may also be glorified with him.

In the same way, the Spirit too comes to the aid of our weakness;
   for we do not know how to pray as we ought,
   but the Spirit himself intercedes with inexpressible groanings.

And the one who searches hearts
    knows what is the intention of the Spirit,
    because he intercedes for the holy ones
    according to God's will.

The word of the Lord.

OR Second Option

Galatians 4:4-7   God sent the Spirit of his Son into our hearts, crying out, *"Abba!* Father!"

A reading from the Letter of Saint Paul to the Galatians

Brothers and sisters:
When the fullness of time had come, God sent his Son,
    born of a woman, born under the law,
    to ransom those under the law,
    so that we might receive adoption as sons.
As proof that you are sons,
    God sent the Spirit of his Son into our hearts,
    crying out, "*Abba,* Father!"
So you are no longer a slave but a son,
    and if a son then also an heir, through God.

The word of the Lord.

VERSE BEFORE THE GOSPEL

Romans 8:15

**For you did not receive a spirit of slavery to fall back into fear,
but you received a spirit of adoption, through which we cry, "*Abba!* Father!"**

GOSPEL

Matthew 6:9-13   Lord, teach us to pray.

✠ **A reading from the holy Gospel according to Matthew**

Jesus said to his disciples,

"This is how you are to pray:

**Our Father who art in heaven,
    hallowed be thy name,
    thy Kingdom come,
thy will be done,
    on earth as it is in heaven.
Give us this day our daily bread;
and forgive us our trespasses,
    as we forgive those who trespass against us;
and lead us not into temptation,
    but deliver us from evil."**

The Gospel of the Lord.

750 BAPTISM DURING THE EASTER VIGIL

The readings are taken from those assigned to the Easter Vigil (above, no. 42); Isaiah 55 (reading 5) and Ezekiel 36 (reading 7) may be chosen in addition to Exodus (reading 3).

CHRISTIAN INITIATION APART FROM THE EASTER VIGIL

751 READING FROM THE OLD TESTAMENT

The following readings from the Old Testament may be used or the readings from the Old Testament for the Easter Vigil may be chosen.

1.

Genesis 15:1-6, 18a   Just so shall your descendants be. To your descendants I give the land.

A reading from the Book of Genesis

The word of the LORD came to Abram in a vision:

> **Fear not, Abram!**
>   **I am your shield;**
>   **I will make your reward very great.**

But Abram said,
>   **"O Lord GOD, what good will your gifts be,**
>   **if I keep on being childless**
>   **and have as my heir the steward of my house, Eliezer?"**

Abram continued,
>   **"See, you have given me no offspring,**
>   **and so one of my servants will be my heir."**

Then the word of the LORD came to him:
>   **"No, that one shall not be your heir;**
>   **your own issue shall be your heir."**

He took him outside and said:
>   **"Look up at the sky and count the stars, if you can.**

Just so," he added, "shall your descendants be."

Abram put his faith in the LORD,
>   **who credited it to him as an act of righteousness.**

It was on that occasion that the LORD made a covenant with Abram,
>   **saying: "To your descendants I give this land."**

The word of the Lord.

2.

Genesis 17:1-8   Between you and me I will establish my covenant and with your descendants after you as an everlasting pact.

A reading from the Book of Genesis

When Abram was ninety-nine years old,
   the Lord appeared to him and said:
   "I am God the Almighty.
Walk in my presence and be blameless.
Between you and me I will establish my covenant,
   and I will multiply you exceedingly."
When Abram prostrated himself, God continued to speak to him:
   "My covenant with you is this:
   you are to become the father of a host of nations.
No longer shall you be called Abram;
   your name shall be Abraham,
   for I am making you the father of a host of nations.
I will render you exceedingly fertile,
   I will make nations of you;
   kings shall stem from you.
I will maintain my covenant with you
   and your descendants after you
   throughout the ages as an everlasting pact,
   to be your God and the God of your descendants after you.
I will give to you and to your descendants after you
   the land in which you are now staying,
   the whole land of Canaan,
   as a permanent possession; and I will be their God."

The word of the Lord.

3.

Genesis 35:1-4, 6-7a   Get rid of the foreign gods you have among you.

A reading from the Book of Genesis

God said to Jacob: "Go up now to Bethel.
Settle there and build an altar there to the God
   who appeared to you while you were fleeing from your brother Esau."
So Jacob told his family and all the others who were with him:
   "Get rid of the foreign gods that you have among you;
   then purify yourselves and put on fresh clothes.
We are now to go up to Bethel,
   and I will build an altar there to the God who answered me
   in my hour of distress
   and who has been with me wherever I have gone."
They therefore handed over to Jacob
   all the foreign gods in their possession
   and also the rings they had in their ears.

Thus Jacob and all the people who were with him arrived in Luz,
   that is, Bethel, in the land of Canaan.
There he built an altar and named the place Bethel.

The word of the Lord.

4.

Deuteronomy 30:15-20   Choose life, then, so that you and your
descendants may live.

A reading from the Book of Deuteronomy

Moses said to the people:
"Today I have set before you
    life and prosperity, death and doom.
If you obey the commandments of the Lord, your God,
    that I enjoin on you today,
    loving him, and walking in his ways,
    and keeping his commandments, statutes and decrees,
    you will live and grow numerous,
    and the Lord, your God,
    will bless you in the land you are entering to occupy.
If, however, you turn away your hearts and will not listen,
    but are led astray and adore and serve other gods,
    I tell you now that you will certainly perish;
    you will not have a long life
    on the land that you are crossing the Jordan to enter and occupy.
I call heaven and earth today to witness against you:
    I have set before you life and death,
    the blessing and the curse.
Choose life, then,
    that you and your descendants may live, by loving the Lord, your God,
    heeding his voice, and holding fast to him.
For that will mean life for you,
    a long life for you to live on the land that the Lord swore
    he would give to your fathers Abraham, Isaac and Jacob."

The word of the Lord.

5.

Joshua 24:1-2a, 15-17, 18b-25a   We also will serve the Lord, for he is our God.

A reading from the Book of Joshua

Joshua gathered together all the tribes of Israel at Shechem,
  summoning their elders, their leaders,
  their judges and their officers.
When they stood in ranks before God,
  Joshua addressed all the people:

"If it does not please you to serve the LORD,
  decide today whom you will serve,
  the gods your ancestors served beyond the River
  or the gods of the Amorites in whose country you are dwelling.
As for me and my household, we will serve the LORD."

But the people answered,
  "Far be it from us to forsake the LORD
  for the service of other gods.
For it was the LORD, our God,
  who brought us and our ancestors up out of the land of Egypt,
  out of a state of slavery.
He performed those great miracles before our very eyes
  and protected us along our entire journey
  and among all the peoples through whom we passed.
Therefore we also will serve the LORD, for he is our God."

Joshua in turn said to the people,
  "You may not be able to serve the LORD, for he is a holy God;
  he is a jealous God
  who will not forgive your transgressions or your sins.
If, after the good he has done for you,
  you forsake the LORD and serve strange gods,
  he will do evil to you and destroy you."

But the people answered Joshua,
  "We will still serve the LORD."
Joshua therefore said to the people,
  "You are your own witnesses that you have chosen to serve the LORD."
They replied, "We are, indeed!"
Joshua said:
  "Now, therefore, put away the strange gods that are among you
  and turn your hearts to the LORD, the God of Israel."

Then the people promised Joshua,
 "We will serve the LORD, our God, and obey his voice."

So Joshua made a covenant with the people that day.

The word of the Lord.

6.

2 Kings 5:9-15a   So Naaman went down and plunged into the Jordan seven times and he was clean.

A reading from the second Book of Kings

Naaman, the army commander of the king of Aram,
 came with his horses and chariots
 and stopped at the door of Elisha's house.
The prophet sent him the message:
 "Go and wash seven times in the Jordan,
 and your flesh will heal, and you will be clean."
But Naaman went away angry, saying,
 "I thought that he would surely come out
 and stand there to invoke the LORD his God,
 and would move his hand over the spot,
 and thus cure the leprosy.
Are not the rivers of Damascus, the Abana and Pharpar,
 better than all the waters of Israel?
Could I not wash in them and be cleansed?"
With this, he turned about in anger and left.

But his servants came up and reasoned with him.
"My father," they said,
 "if the prophet had told you to do something extraordinary,
 would you not have done it?
All the more now, since he said to you,
 'Wash and be clean,' should you do as he said."
So Naaman went down and plunged into the Jordan seven times
 at the word of the man of God.
His flesh became again like the flesh of a little child, and he was clean.

He returned with his whole retinue to the man of God.
On his arrival he stood before him and said,
 "Now I know that there is no God in all the earth,
 except in Israel."

The word of the Lord.

7.

Isaiah 44:1-3   I will pour out my Spirit upon your descendants.

A reading from the Book of the Prophet Isaiah

Hear, O Jacob, my servant,
   Israel, whom I have chosen.
Thus says the LORD who made you,
   your help, who formed you from the womb:
Fear not, O Jacob, my servant,
   the darling whom I have chosen.
I will pour out water upon the thirsty ground,
   and streams upon the dry land;
I will pour out my Spirit upon your offspring,
   and my blessing upon your descendants.

The word of the Lord.

8.

Jeremiah 31:31-34   I will place my law within them and write it upon their hearts.

A reading from the Book of the Prophet Jeremiah

The days are coming, says the LORD,
   when I will make a new covenant with the house of Israel
   and the house of Judah.
It will not be like the covenant I made with their fathers
   the day I took them by the hand
   to lead them forth from the land of Egypt;
   for they broke my covenant,
   and I had to show myself their master, says the LORD.
But this is the covenant which I will make
   with the house of Israel after those days, says the LORD.
I will place my law within them, and write it upon their hearts;
   I will be their God, and they shall be my people.
No longer will they have need to teach their friends and relatives
   how to know the LORD.
All, from least to greatest, shall know me, says the LORD,
   for I will forgive their evildoing and remember their sin no more.

The word of the Lord.

9.

Ezekiel 36:24-28   I shall pour clean water over you and you shall be cleansed of all your sins.

A reading from the Book of the Prophet Ezekiel

Thus says the Lord:
I will take you away from among the nations,
   gather you from all the foreign lands,
   and bring you back to your own land.
I will sprinkle clean water upon you
   to cleanse you from all your impurities,
   and from all your idols I will cleanse you.
I will give you a new heart and place a new spirit within you,
   taking from your bodies your stony hearts
   and giving you natural hearts.
I will put my spirit within you and make you live by my statutes,
   careful to observe my decrees.
You shall live in the land I gave your fathers;
   you shall be my people, and I will be your God.

The word of the Lord.

752 READING FROM THE NEW TESTAMENT

1.

Acts 2:14a, 36-40a, 41-42   Repent and be baptized, every one of you, in the name of Jesus Christ.

A reading from the Acts of the Apostles

On the day of Pentecost, Peter stood up with the Eleven,
  raised his voice, and proclaimed:

  "Let the whole house of Israel know for certain
  that God has made him both Lord and Christ,
  this Jesus whom you crucified."

Now when they heard this, they were cut to the heart,
  and they asked Peter and the other Apostles,
  "What are we to do, my brothers?"
Peter said to them,
  "Repent and be baptized, every one of you,
  in the name of Jesus Christ for the forgiveness of your sins;
  and you will receive the gift of the Holy Spirit.
For the promise is made to you and to your children
  and to all those far off,
  whomever the Lord our God will call."
He testified with many other arguments, and was exhorting them.
Those who accepted his message were baptized,
  and about three thousand persons were added that day.

They devoted themselves to the teaching of the Apostles
  and to the communal life,
  to the breaking of the bread and to the prayers.

The word of the Lord.

2.

Acts 8:26-38   Look, there is water. What is to prevent my being baptized?

A reading from the Acts of the Apostles

The angel of the Lord spoke to Philip,
  "Get up and head south on the road
  that goes down from Jerusalem to Gaza, the desert route."

So he got up and set out.
Now there was an Ethiopian eunuch,
  a court official of the Candace,
  that is, the queen of the Ethiopians,
  in charge of her entire treasury,
  who had come to Jerusalem to worship, and was returning home.
Seated in his chariot, he was reading the prophet Isaiah.
The Spirit said to Philip,
  "Go and join up with that chariot."
Philip ran up and heard him reading Isaiah the prophet and said,
  "Do you understand what you are reading?"
He replied,
  "How can I, unless someone instructs me?"
So he invited Philip to get in and sit with him.
This was the Scripture passage he was reading:

  Like a sheep he was led to the slaughter,
    and as a lamb before its shearer is silent,
      so he opened not his mouth.
  In his humiliation justice was denied him.
    Who will tell of his posterity?
      For his life is taken from the earth.

Then the eunuch said to Philip in reply,
  "I beg you, about whom is the prophet saying this?
About himself, or about someone else?"
Then Philip opened his mouth and, beginning with this Scripture passage,
  he proclaimed Jesus to him.
As they traveled along the road
  they came to some water,
  and the eunuch said, "Look, there is water.
What is to prevent my being baptized?"
Then he ordered the chariot to stop,
  and Philip and the eunuch both went down into the water,
  and he baptized him.

The word of the Lord.

3.

Long Form

Romans 6:3-11   When we were indeed buried with him through baptism into death, so that we too might live in newness of life.

A reading from the Letter of Saint Paul to the Romans

Brothers and sisters:
Are you unaware that we who were baptized into Christ Jesus
were baptized into his death?
We were indeed buried with him through baptism into death,
so that, just as Christ was raised from the dead
by the glory of the Father,
we too might live in newness of life.

For if we have grown into union with him through a death like his,
we shall also be united with him in the resurrection.
We know that our old self was crucified with him,
so that our sinful body might be done away with,
that we might no longer be in slavery to sin.
For a dead person has been absolved from sin.
If, then, we have died with Christ,
we believe that we shall also live with him.
We know that Christ, raised from the dead, dies no more;
death no longer has power over him.
As to his death, he died to sin once and for all;
as to his life, he lives for God.
Consequently, you too must think of yourselves as being dead to sin
and living for God in Christ Jesus.

The word of the Lord.

OR Short Form

Romans 6:3-4, 8-11   When we were indeed buried with him through baptism into death, so that we too might live in newness of life.

A reading from the Letter of Saint Paul to the Romans

Brothers and sisters:
Are you unaware that we who were baptized into Christ Jesus
   were baptized into his death?
We were indeed buried with him through baptism into death,
   so that, just as Christ was raised from the dead
   by the glory of the Father,
   we too might live in newness of life.

If, then, we have died with Christ,
   we believe that we shall also live with him.
We know that Christ, raised from the dead, dies no more;
   death no longer has power over him.
As to his death, he died to sin once and for all;
   as to his life, he lives for God.
Consequently, you too must think of yourselves as being dead to sin
   and living for God in Christ Jesus.

The word of the Lord.

4.

Romans 8:28-32, 35, 37-39   What will separate us from the love of Christ?

A reading from the Letter of Saint Paul to the Romans

Brothers and sisters:
We know that all things work for good for those who love God,
 who are called according to his purpose.
For those he foreknew he also predestined
 to be conformed to the image of his Son,
 so that he might be the firstborn
 among many brothers.
And those he predestined he also called;
 and those he called he also justified;
 and those he justified he also glorified.

What then shall we say to this?
If God is for us, who can be against us?
He who did not spare his own Son
 but handed him over for us all,
 how will he not also give us everything else along with him?
What will separate us from the love of Christ?
Will anguish, or distress, or persecution, or famine,
 or nakedness, or peril, or the sword?

No, in all these things we conquer overwhelmingly
 through him who loved us.
For I am convinced that neither death, nor life,
 nor angels, nor principalities,
 nor present things, nor future things,
 nor powers, nor height, nor depth,
 nor any other creature will be able to separate us
 from the love of God in Christ Jesus our Lord.

The word of the Lord.

5.

1 Corinthians 12:12-13   In one Spirit we were all baptized into one Body.

A reading from the first Letter of Saint Paul to the Corinthians

Brothers and sisters:
As a body is one though it has many parts,
   and all the parts of the body, though many, are one body,
      so also Christ.
For in one Spirit we were all baptized into one Body,
   whether Jews or Greeks, slaves or free persons,
   and we were all given to drink of one Spirit.

The word of the Lord.

6.

Galatians 3:26-28   For all of you who were baptized into Christ have clothed yourselves with Christ.

A reading from the Letter of Saint Paul to the Galatians

Brothers and sisters:
Through faith you are all children of God in Christ Jesus.
For all of you who were baptized into Christ
   have clothed yourselves with Christ.
There is neither Jew nor Greek,
   there is neither slave nor free person,
   there is not male and female;
   for you are all one in Christ Jesus.

The word of the Lord.

7.

Ephesians 1:3-10, 13-14   He destined us for adoption to himself through Jesus Christ.

A reading from the Letter of Saint Paul to the Ephesians

Blessed be the God and Father of our Lord Jesus Christ,
   who has blessed us in Christ
   with every spiritual blessing in the heavens,
   as he chose us in him before the foundation of the world,
   to be holy and without blemish before him.
In love he destined us for adoption to himself through Jesus Christ,
   in accord with the favor of his will,
   for the praise of the glory of his grace
   that he granted us in the beloved.

In him we have redemption by his Blood,
   the forgiveness of transgressions,
   in accord with the riches of his grace that he lavished upon us.
In all wisdom and insight, he has made known to us
   the mystery of his will in accord with his favor
   that he set forth in him as a plan for the fullness of times,
   to sum up all things in Christ, in heaven and on earth.

In him you also, who have heard the word of truth,
   the Gospel of your salvation, and have believed in him,
   were sealed with the promised Holy Spirit,
   which is the first installment of our inheritance
   toward redemption as God's possession, to the praise of his glory.

The word of the Lord.

8.

Ephesians 4:1-6   There is one Lord, one faith, one baptism.

A reading from the Letter of Saint Paul to the Ephesians

Brothers and sisters:
I, a prisoner for the Lord,
   urge you to live in a manner worthy of the call you have received,
   with all humility and gentleness, with patience,
   bearing with one another through love,
   striving to preserve the unity of the spirit
   through the bond of peace:

one Body and one Spirit,
  as you were also called to the one hope of your call;
  one Lord, one faith, one baptism;
  one God and Father of all,
  who is over all and through all and in all.

The word of the Lord.

  9.

Colossians 3:9b-17   Put on, then, as God's chosen ones, the new man.

A reading from the Letter of Saint Paul to the Colossians

Brothers and sisters:
You have taken off the old self with its practices
  and have put on the new self,
  which is being renewed, for knowledge,
  in the image of its creator.
Here there is not Greek and Jew,
  circumcision and uncircumcision,
  barbarian, Scythian, slave, free;
  but Christ is all and in all.

Put on then, as God's chosen ones, holy and beloved,
  heartfelt compassion, kindness, humility, gentleness, and patience,
  bearing with one another and forgiving one another,
  if one has a grievance against another;
  as the Lord has forgiven you, so must you also do.
And over all these put on love,
  that is, the bond of perfection.
And let the peace of Christ control your hearts,
  the peace into which you were also called in one Body.
And be thankful.
Let the word of Christ dwell in you richly,
  as in all wisdom you teach and admonish one another,
  singing psalms, hymns, and spiritual songs
  with gratitude in your hearts to God.
And whatever you do, in word or in deed,
  do everything in the name of the Lord Jesus,
  giving thanks to God the Father through him.

The word of the Lord.

10.

Titus 3:4-7   He saved us through the bath of rebirth and renewal by the
Holy Spirit.

A reading from the Letter of Saint Paul to Titus

Beloved:
When the kindness and generous love
  of God our savior appeared,
not because of any righteous deeds we had done
  but because of his mercy,
he saved us through the bath of rebirth
  and renewal by the Holy Spirit,
whom he richly poured out on us
  through Jesus Christ our savior,
so that we might be justified by his grace
  and become heirs in hope of eternal life.

The word of the Lord.

11.

Hebrews 10:22-25   With our hearts sprinkled clean from an evil
conscience and our bodies washed in pure water.

A reading from the Letter to the Hebrews

Brothers and sisters:
Let us approach with a sincere heart and in absolute trust,
  with our hearts sprinkled clean from an evil conscience
  and our bodies washed in pure water.
Let us hold unwaveringly to our confession that gives us hope,
  for he who made the promise is trustworthy.
We must consider how to rouse one another to love and good works.
We should not stay away from our assembly,
  as is the custom of some, but encourage one another,
  and this all the more as you see the day drawing near.

The word of the Lord.

12.

1 Peter 2:4-5, 9-10   You are a chosen race, a royal priesthood.

A reading from the first Letter of Saint Peter

Beloved:
Come to the Lord, a living stone, rejected by human beings
  but chosen and precious in the sight of God,
  and, like living stones,
  let yourselves be built into a spiritual house
  to be a holy priesthood to offer spiritual sacrifices
  acceptable to God through Jesus Christ.

You are "a chosen race, a royal priesthood,
  a holy nation, a people of his own,
  so that you may announce the praises" of him
  who called you out of darkness into his wonderful light.

  Once you were "no people"
    but now you are God's people;
  you "had not received mercy"
    but now you have received mercy.

The word of the Lord.

13.

Revelation 19:1, 5-9a   Blessed are those who have been called to the
wedding feast of the Lamb.

A reading from the Book of Revelation

I, John, heard what sounded like the loud voice
    of a great multitude in heaven, saying:

"Alleluia!
Salvation, glory, and might belong to our God."

A voice coming from the throne said:

"Praise our God, all you his servants,
    and you who revere him, small and great."

Then I heard something like the sound of a great multitude
    or the sound of rushing water or mighty peals of thunder, as they said:

"Alleluia!
The Lord has established his reign,
    our God, the almighty.
Let us rejoice and be glad
    and give him glory.
For the wedding day of the Lamb has come,
    his bride has made herself ready.
She was allowed to wear
    a bright, clean linen garment."

The linen represents the righteous deeds of the holy ones.

Then the angel said to me,
    "Write this:
Blessed are those who have been called
    to the wedding feast of the Lamb."

The word of the Lord.

753 RESPONSORIAL PSALM

1.

Psalm 8:4-5, 6-7, 8-9

℞. (2a) **O Lord, our God, how wonderful is your name in all the earth!**
   or:
℞. (Ephesians 5:14) **Wake up and rise from death: Christ will shine upon you!**

When I behold your heavens, the work of your fingers,
   the moon and the stars which you set in place—
What is man that you should be mindful of him,
   or the son of man that you should care for him?

℞. **O Lord, our God, how wonderful is your name in all the earth!**
   or:
℞. **Wake up and rise from death: Christ will shine upon you!**

You have made him little less than the angels,
   and crowned him with glory and honor.
You have given him rule over the works of your hands,
   putting all things under his feet.

℞. **O Lord, our God, how wonderful is your name in all the earth!**
   or:
℞. **Wake up and rise from death: Christ will shine upon you!**

All sheep and oxen,
   yes, and the beasts of the field,
The birds of the air, the fishes of the sea,
   and whatever swims the paths of the seas.

℞. **O Lord, our God, how wonderful is your name in all the earth!**
   or:
℞. **Wake up and rise from death: Christ will shine upon you!**

2.

Psalm 23:1b-3a, 4, 5, 6

℟. (1) **The Lord is my shepherd; there is nothing I shall want.**
   or:
℟. (1 Peter 2:25) **You were all like lost sheep; but now you have returned to the shepherd of your souls.**

The Lord is my shepherd; I shall not want.
   In verdant pastures he gives me repose;
Beside restful waters he leads me;
   he refreshes my soul.

℟. **The Lord is my shepherd; there is nothing I shall want.**
   or:
℟. **You were all like lost sheep; but now you have returned to the shepherd of your souls.**

Even though I walk in the dark valley
   I fear no evil; for you are at my side
With your rod and your staff
   that give me courage.

℟. **The Lord is my shepherd; there is nothing I shall want.**
   or:
℟. **You were all like lost sheep; but now you have returned to the shepherd of your souls.**

You spread the table before me
   in the sight of my foes;
You anoint my head with oil;
   my cup overflows.

℟. **The Lord is my shepherd; there is nothing I shall want.**
   or:
℟. **You were all like lost sheep; but now you have returned to the shepherd of your souls.**

Only goodness and kindness follow me
   all the days of my life;
And I shall dwell in the house of the LORD
   for years to come.

℟. **The Lord is my shepherd; there is nothing I shall want.**
   or:
℟. **You were all like lost sheep; but now you have returned to the shepherd of your souls.**

3.

Psalm 27:1bcde, 4, 8b-9, 13-14

℟. (1a) **The Lord is my light and my salvation.**
    or:
℟. (Ephesians 5:14) **Wake up and rise from death: Christ will shine upon you!**

The Lᴏʀᴅ is my light and my salvation;
    whom should I fear?
The Lᴏʀᴅ is my life's refuge;
    of whom should I be afraid?

℟. **The Lord is my light and my salvation.**
    or:
℟. **Wake up and rise from death: Christ will shine upon you!**

One thing I ask of the Lᴏʀᴅ;
    this I seek:
To dwell in the house of the Lᴏʀᴅ
    all the days of my life,
That I may gaze on the loveliness of the Lᴏʀᴅ
    and contemplate his temple.

℟. **The Lord is my light and my salvation.**
    or:
℟. **Wake up and rise from death: Christ will shine upon you!**

Your presence, O Lᴏʀᴅ, I seek.
Hide not your face from me;
    do not in anger repel your servant.
You are my helper: cast me not off;
    forsake me not, O God my savior.

℟. **The Lord is my light and my salvation.**
    or:
℟. **Wake up and rise from death: Christ will shine upon you!**

I believe that I shall see the bounty of the Lᴏʀᴅ
    in the land of the living.
Wait for the Lᴏʀᴅ with courage;
    be stouthearted, and wait for the Lᴏʀᴅ.

(cont.)

℟. The Lord is my light and my salvation.
   or:
℟. Wake up and rise from death: Christ will shine upon you!

   4.

Psalm 32:1bc-2, 5, 11

℟. (1a) Blessed are those whose sins are forgiven.
   or:
℟. (11a) Let the just exult and rejoice in the Lord.

Blessed is he whose fault is taken away,
   whose sin is covered.
Blessed the man to whom the LORD imputes not guilt,
   in whose spirit there is no guile.

℟. Blessed are those whose sins are forgiven.
   or:
℟. Let the just exult and rejoice in the Lord.

Then I acknowledged my sin to you,
   my guilt I covered not.
I said, "I confess my faults to the LORD,"
   and you took away the guilt of my sin.

℟. Blessed are those whose sins are forgiven.
   or:
℟. Let the just exult and rejoice in the Lord.

Be glad in the LORD and rejoice, you just;
   exult, all you upright of heart.

℟. Blessed are those whose sins are forgiven.
   or:
℟. Let the just exult and rejoice in the Lord.

5.

Psalm 34:2-3, 6-7, 8-9, 14-15, 16-17, 18-19

℟. (6a) **Look to him, that you may be radiant with joy!**

I will bless the LORD at all times;
 his praise shall be ever in my mouth.
Let my soul glory in the LORD;
 the lowly will hear me and be glad.

℟. **Look to him, that you may be radiant with joy!**

Look to him that you may be radiant with joy
 and your faces may not blush with shame.
When the poor one called out, the Lord heard
 and from all of his distress he saved him.

℟. **Look to him, that you may be radiant with joy!**

The angel of the LORD encamps
 around those who fear him, and delivers them.
Taste and see how good the LORD is;
 blessed the man who takes refuge in him.

℟. **Look to him, that you may be radiant with joy!**

Keep your tongue from evil,
 and your lips from speaking guile.
Turn from evil, and do good;
 seek peace, and follow after it.

℟. **Look to him, that you may be radiant with joy!**

The LORD has eyes for the just
 and ears for their cry.
The LORD confronts the evildoers,
 to destroy the remembrance of them from the earth.

℟. **Look to him, that you may be radiant with joy!**

When the just cry out, the LORD hears them,
 and from all their distress he rescues them.
The LORD is close to the brokenhearted;
 and those who are crushed in spirit he saves.

℟. **Look to him, that you may be radiant with joy!**

6.

Psalm 42:2-3; 43:3, 4

℟. (42:3a) **My soul is thirsting for the living God.**

As the hind longs for the running waters,
  so my soul longs for you, O God.
Athirst is my soul for God, the living God.
  When shall I go and behold the face of God?

℟. **My soul is thirsting for the living God.**

Send forth your light and your fidelity;
  they shall lead me on
And bring me to your holy mountain,
  to your dwelling-place.

℟. **My soul is thirsting for the living God.**

Then will I go in to the altar of God,
  the God of my gladness and joy;
Then will I give you thanks upon the harp,
  O God, my God!

℟. **My soul is thirsting for the living God.**

7.

Psalm 51:3-4, 8-9, 12-13, 14 and 17

℟. (12a) **Create a clean heart in me, O God.**
  or:
℟. (Ezekiel 36:26) **I will give you a new heart, a new spirit within you.**

Have mercy on me, O God, in your goodness;
  in the greatness of your compassion wipe out my offense.
Thoroughly wash me from my guilt
  and of my sin cleanse me.

℟. **Create a clean heart in me, O God.**
  or:
℟. **I will give you a new heart, a new spirit within you.**

Behold, you are pleased with sincerity of heart,
   and in my inmost being you teach me wisdom.
Cleanse me of sin with hyssop, that I may be purified;
   wash me, and I shall be whiter than snow.

R̝. Create a clean heart in me, O God.
   or:
R̝. I will give you a new heart, a new spirit within you.

A clean heart create for me, O God,
   and a steadfast spirit renew within me.
Cast me not out from your presence,
   and your Holy Spirit take not from me.

R̝. Create a clean heart in me, O God.
   or:
R̝. I will give you a new heart, a new spirit within you.

Give me back the joy of your salvation,
   and a willing spirit sustain in me.
O Lord, open my lips,
   and my mouth shall proclaim your praise.

R̝. Create a clean heart in me, O God.
   or:
R̝. I will give you a new heart, a new spirit within you.

8.

Psalm 63:2, 3-4, 5-6, 8-9a

R̝. (2b) **My soul is thirsting for you, O Lord my God.**

O God, you are my God whom I seek;
   for you my flesh pines and my soul thirsts
   like the earth, parched, lifeless and without water.

R̝. My soul is thirsting for you, O Lord my God.

Thus have I gazed toward you in the sanctuary
   to see your power and your glory,
For your kindness is a greater good than life;
   my lips shall glorify you.

(cont.)

R℣. **My soul is thirsting for you, O Lord my God.**

Thus will I bless you while I live;
  lifting up my hands, I will call upon your name.
As with the riches of a banquet shall my soul be satisfied,
  and with exultant lips my mouth shall praise you.

R℣. **My soul is thirsting for you, O Lord my God.**

You are my help,
  and in the shadow of your wings I shout for joy.
My soul clings fast to you.

R℣. **My soul is thirsting for you, O Lord my God.**

9.

Psalm 66:1b-3a, 5-6, 8-9, 16-17

R℣. (1) **Let all the earth cry out to God with joy.**

Shout joyfully to God, all the earth,
  sing praise to the glory of his name;
  proclaim his glorious praise.
Say to God, "How tremendous are your deeds!"

R℣. **Let all the earth cry out to God with joy.**

Come and see the works of God,
  his tremendous deeds among the children of Adam.
He has changed the sea into dry land;
  through the river they passed on foot;
  therefore let us rejoice in him.

R℣. **Let all the earth cry out to God with joy.**

Bless our God, you peoples;
  loudly sound his praise,
He has given life to our souls,
  and has not let our feet slip.

R℣. **Let all the earth cry out to God with joy.**

Hear now, all you who fear God, while I declare
  what he has done for me.
When I appealed to him in words,
  praise was on the tip of my tongue.

℞. Let all the earth cry out to God with joy.

10.

Psalm 89:3-4, 16-17, 21-22, 25 and 27

℞. (2a) For ever I will sing the goodness of the Lord.

You have said, "My kindness is established forever";
  in heaven you have confirmed your faithfulness:
I have made a covenant with my chosen one,
  I have sworn to David my servant.

℞. For ever I will sing the goodness of the Lord.

Blessed the people who know the joyful shout;
  in the light of your countenance, O LORD, they walk.
At your name they rejoice all the day,
  and through your justice they are exalted.

℞. For ever I will sing the goodness of the Lord.

"I have found David, my servant;
  with my holy oil I have anointed him,
That my hand may be always with him,
  and that my arm may make him strong."

℞. For ever I will sing the goodness of the Lord.

"My faithfulness and my mercy shall be with him,
  and through my name shall his horn be exalted.
He shall say of me, 'You are my father,
  my God, the Rock, my savior.'"

℞. For ever I will sing the goodness of the Lord.

11.

Psalm 126:1bc-2ab, 2cd-3, 4-5, 6

℞. (3) **The Lord has done great things for us; we are filled with joy.**

When the Lord brought back the captives of Zion,
   we were like men dreaming.
Then our mouth was filled with laughter,
   and our tongue with rejoicing.

℞. **The Lord has done great things for us; we are filled with joy.**

Then they said among the nations,
   "The Lord has done great things for them."
The Lord has done great things for us;
   we are glad indeed.

℞. **The Lord has done great things for us; we are filled with joy.**

Restore our fortunes, O Lord,
   like the torrents in the southern desert.
Those that sow in tears
   shall reap rejoicing.

℞. **The Lord has done great things for us; we are filled with joy.**

Although they go forth weeping,
   carrying the seed to be sown,
They shall come back rejoicing,
   carrying their sheaves.

℞. **The Lord has done great things for us; we are filled with joy.**

754 ALLELUIA VERSE AND VERSE BEFORE THE GOSPEL

1.

Mark 16:15

**Go into the whole world
and proclaim the Gospel.**

2.

John 3:16

**God so loved the world that he gave his only-begotten Son
so that everyone who believes in him might have eternal life.**

3.

John 8:12

**I am the light of the world, says the Lord;
whoever follows me will have the light of life.**

4.

John 14:6

**I am the way and the truth and the life, says the Lord;
no one comes to the Father except through me.**

5.

Ephesians 4:5-6a

**There is one Lord, and one faith, one baptism,
one God and Father of all.**

6.

See Colossians 2:12

**We were buried with Christ in baptism;
in baptism we have been raised with him.**

7.

Colossians 3:1

If then you were raised with Christ,
seek what is above,
where Christ is seated at the right hand of God.

8.

See 2 Timothy 1:10

Our Savior Jesus Christ has destroyed death
and brought life to light through the Gospel.

9.

1 Peter 2:9

You are a chosen race, a royal priesthood, a holy nation;
announce the praises of him who called you
out of darkness into his wonderful light.

755 GOSPEL

1.

Matthew 16:24-27   Whoever wishes to come after me must deny himself.

✠ **A reading from the holy Gospel according to Matthew**

Jesus said to his disciples,
> **"Whoever wishes to come after me must deny himself,**
> **take up his cross, and follow me.**

For whoever wishes to save his life will lose it,
> **but whoever loses his life for my sake will find it.**

What profit would there be for one to gain the whole world
> **and forfeit his life?**

Or what can one give in exchange for his life?

For the Son of Man will come with his angels in his Father's glory,
> **and then he will repay each one according to his conduct."**

The Gospel of the Lord.

2.

Matthew 28:18-20   Go, therefore, and make disciples of all nations, baptizing them in the name of the Father, and of the Son, and of the Holy Spirit.

✠ **A reading from the holy Gospel according to Matthew**

Jesus said to the Eleven disciples:
"All power in heaven and on earth has been given to me.
Go, therefore, and make disciples of all nations,
> **baptizing them in the name of the Father,**
> **and of the Son, and of the Holy Spirit,**
> **teaching them to observe all that I have commanded you.**

And behold, I am with you always, until the end of the age."

The Gospel of the Lord.

3.

Mark 1:9-11 Jesus was baptized in the Jordan by John.

✠ **A reading from the holy Gospel according to Mark**

Jesus came from Nazareth of Galilee
   and was baptized in the Jordan by John.
On coming up out of the water he saw the heavens being torn open
   and the Spirit, like a dove, descending upon him.
And a voice came from the heavens,
   "You are my beloved Son; with you I am well pleased."

The Gospel of the Lord.

4.

Mark 10:13-16 Whoever does not accept the Kingdom of God like a child will not enter it.

✠ **A reading from the holy Gospel according to Mark**

People were bringing children to Jesus that he might touch them,
   but the disciples rebuked them.
When Jesus saw this he became indignant and said to them,
   "Let the children come to me; do not prevent them,
   for the Kingdom of God belongs to such as these.
Amen, I say to you,
   whoever does not accept the Kingdom of God like a child
   will not enter it."
Then he embraced them and blessed them,
   placing his hands on them.

The Gospel of the Lord.

5.

Mark 16:15-16, 19-20 Whoever believes and is baptized will be saved.

✠ **A reading from the holy Gospel according to Mark**

Jesus appeared to the Eleven and said to them:
"Go into the whole world
   and proclaim the Gospel to every creature.
Whoever believes and is baptized will be saved;
   whoever does not believe will be condemned."

The Lord Jesus, after he spoke to them,
   was taken up into heaven
   and took his seat at the right hand of God.
But they went forth and preached everywhere,
   while the Lord worked with them
   and confirmed the word through accompanying signs.

The Gospel of the Lord.

6.

Luke 24:44-53   Repentance, for the forgiveness of sins, will be preached in his name to all the nations.

✠ **A reading from the holy Gospel according to Luke**

Jesus said to his disciples:
"These are my words that I spoke to you while I was still with you,
   that everything written about me in the law of Moses
   and in the prophets and psalms must be fulfilled."
Then he opened their minds to understand the Scriptures.
And he said to them,
   "Thus it is written that the Christ would suffer
   and rise from the dead on the third day
   and that repentance, for the forgiveness of sins,
   would be preached in his name
   to all the nations, beginning from Jerusalem.
You are witnesses of these things.
And behold I am sending the promise of my Father upon you;
   but stay in the city
   until you are clothed with power from on high."

Then he led them out as far as Bethany,
   raised his hands, and blessed them.
As he blessed them he parted from them
   and was taken up to heaven.
They did him homage
   and then returned to Jerusalem with great joy,
   and they were continually in the temple praising God.

The Gospel of the Lord.

7.

John 1:1-5, 9-14, 16-18   He gave power to become children of God to
those who believe in his name.

✠   **A reading from the holy Gospel according to John**

In the beginning was the Word,
and the Word was with God,
and the Word was God.
He was in the beginning with God.
All things came to be through him,
and without him nothing came to be.
What came to be through him was life,
and this life was the light of the human race;
the light shines in the darkness,
and the darkness has not overcome it.
The true light, which enlightens everyone, was coming into the world.

He was in the world,
and the world came to be through him,
but the world did not know him.
He came to what was his own,
but his own people did not accept him.

But to those who did accept him
he gave power to become children of God,
to those who believe in his name,
who were born not by natural generation
nor by human choice nor by a man's decision but of God.

And the Word became flesh
and made his dwelling among us,
and we saw his glory,
the glory as of the Father's only-begotten Son,
full of grace and truth.

From his fullness we have all received,
grace in place of grace,
because while the law was given through Moses,
grace and truth came through Jesus Christ.
No one has ever seen God.
The only-begotten Son, God, who is at the Father's side,
has revealed him.

The Gospel of the Lord.

8.

John 1:29-34   Behold, the Lamb of God, who takes away the sin of
the world.

✠   **A reading from the holy Gospel according to John**

John saw Jesus coming toward him and said,
   "Behold, the Lamb of God, who takes away the sin of the world.
He is the one of whom I said,
   'A man is coming after me who ranks ahead of me
   because he existed before me.'
I did not know him,
   but the reason why I came baptizing with water
   was that he might be made known to Israel."
John testified further, saying,
   "I saw the Spirit come down like a dove from the sky
   and remain upon him.
I did not know him,
   but the one who sent me to baptize with water told me,
   'On whomever you see the Spirit come down and remain,
   he is the one who will baptize with the Holy Spirit.'
Now I have seen and testified that he is the Son of God."

The Gospel of the Lord.

9.

John 3:1-6   No one can see the Kingdom of God without being born from above.

✛ **A reading from the holy Gospel according to John**

There was a Pharisee named Nicodemus, a ruler of the Jews.
He came to Jesus at night and said to him,
   "Rabbi, we know that you are a teacher who has come from God,
   for no one can do these signs that you are doing
   unless God is with him."
Jesus answered and said to him,
   "Amen, amen, I say to you,
   unless one is born from above,
   he cannot see the Kingdom of God."
Nicodemus said to him,
   "How can a man once grown old be born again?
Surely he cannot reenter his mother's womb and be born again, can he?"
Jesus answered,
   "Amen, amen, I say to you,
   unless one is born of water and Spirit
   he cannot enter the Kingdom of God.
What is born of flesh is flesh
   and what is born of spirit is spirit.

The Gospel of the Lord.

10.

John 3:16-21   So that anyone who believes in him might have eternal life.

✛ **A reading from the holy Gospel according to John**

God so loved the world that he gave his only Son,
   so that everyone who believes in him might not perish
   but might have eternal life.
For God did not send his Son into the world to condemn the world,
   but that the world might be saved through him.
Whoever believes in him will not be condemned,
   but whoever does not believe has already been condemned,
   because he has not believed in the name of the only Son of God.

And this is the verdict,

> that the light came into the world,

> but people preferred darkness to light,

> because their works were evil.

For everyone who does wicked things hates the light

> and does not come toward the light,

> so that his works might not be exposed.

But whoever lives the truth comes to the light,

> so that his works may be clearly seen as done in God.

The Gospel of the Lord.

11.

John 12:44-50   I came into the world as light.

✠ **A reading from the holy Gospel according to John**

Jesus cried out and said,

> "Whoever believes in me believes not only in me

> but also in the one who sent me,

> and whoever sees me sees the one who sent me.

I came into the world as light,

> so that everyone who believes in me might not remain in darkness.

And if anyone hears my words and does not observe them,

> I do not condemn him,

> for I did not come to condemn the world but to save the world.

Whoever rejects me and does not accept my words

> has something to judge him: the word that I spoke,

> it will condemn him on the last day,

> because I did not speak on my own,

> but the Father who sent me commanded me what to say and speak.

And I know that his commandment is eternal life.

So what I say, I say as the Father told me."

The Gospel of the Lord.

12.

John 15:1-11   Anyone who remains in me and I in him will bear much fruit.

✠   **A reading from the holy Gospel according to John**

Jesus said to his disciples:
"I am the true vine, and my Father is the vine grower.
He takes away every branch in me that does not bear fruit,
  and every one that does he prunes so that it bears more fruit.
You are already pruned because of the word that I spoke to you.
Remain in me, as I remain in you.
Just as a branch cannot bear fruit on its own
    unless it remains on the vine,
      so neither can you unless you remain in me.
I am the vine, you are the branches.
Anyone who remains in me and I in him will bear much fruit,
    because without me you can do nothing.
Anyone who does not remain in me
    will be thrown out like a branch and wither;
    people will gather them and throw them into a fire
    and they will be burned.
If you remain in me and my words remain in you,
    ask for whatever you want and it will be done for you.
By this is my Father glorified,
    that you bear much fruit and become my disciples.
As the Father loves me, so I also love you.
Remain in my love.
If you keep my commandments, you will remain in my love,
    just as I have kept my Father's commandments
    and remain in his love.

"I have told you this so that my joy may be in you
    and your joy may be complete."

The Gospel of the Lord.

2. CONFERRAL OF INFANT BAPTISM

756 READING FROM THE OLD TESTAMENT

First Option

Exodus 17:3-7   Give us water to drink (Exodus 17:2).

A reading from the Book of Exodus

In their thirst for water,
 the people grumbled against Moses,
  saying, "Why did you ever make us leave Egypt?
Was it just to have us die here of thirst
 with our children and our livestock?"
So Moses cried out to the LORD,
 "What shall I do with this people?
A little more and they will stone me!"
The LORD answered Moses,
 "Go over there in front of the people,
  along with some of the elders of Israel,
  holding in your hand, as you go,
  the staff with which you struck the river.
I will be standing there in front of you on the rock in Horeb.
Strike the rock, and the water will flow from it
 for the people to drink."
This Moses did, in the presence of the elders of Israel.
The place was called Massah and Meribah,
 because the children of Israel quarreled there
 and tested the LORD, saying,
 "Is the LORD in our midst or not?"

The word of the Lord.

Second Option

Ezekiel 36:24-28   I shall pour clean water upon you to cleanse you from all your impurities.

A reading from the Book of the Prophet Ezekiel

Thus says the Lord GOD:
I will take you away from among the nations,
   gather you from all the foreign lands,
   and bring you back to your own land.
I will sprinkle clean water upon you
   to cleanse you from all your impurities,
   and from all your idols I will cleanse you.
I will give you a new heart and place a new spirit within you,
   taking from your bodies your stony hearts
   and giving you natural hearts.
I will put my spirit within you and make you live by my statutes,
   careful to observe my decrees.
You shall live in the land I gave your fathers;
   you shall be my people, and I will be your God.

The word of the Lord.

Third Option

Ezekiel 47:1-9, 12   I saw water flowing from the temple, and all who were touched by it were saved (see *Roman Missal,* antiphon for blessing and sprinkling holy water during the season of Easter).

A reading from the Book of the Prophet Ezekiel

The angel brought me, Ezekiel,
   back to the entrance of the temple of the Lord,
   and I saw water flowing out
   from beneath the threshold of the temple toward the east,
   for the façade of the temple was toward the east;
   the water flowed down from the right side of the temple,
   south of the altar.
He led me outside by the north gate,
   and around to the outer gate facing the east,
   where I saw water trickling from the right side.

Then when he had walked off to the east
>with a measuring cord in his hand,
>he measured off a thousand cubits
>and had me wade through the water,
>which was ankle-deep.

He measured off another thousand
>and once more had me wade through the water,
>which was now knee-deep.

Again he measured off a thousand and had me wade;
>the water was up to my waist.

Once more he measured off a thousand,
>but there was now a river through which I could not wade;
>for the water had risen so high it had become a river
>that could not be crossed except by swimming.

He asked me, "Have you seen this, son of man?"

Then he brought me to the bank of the river, where he had me sit.

Along the bank of the river I saw very many trees on both sides.

He said to me,
>"This water flows into the eastern district down upon the Arabah,
>and empties into the sea, the salt waters, which it makes fresh.

Wherever the river flows,
>every sort of living creature that can multiply shall live,
>and there shall be abundant fish,
>for wherever this water comes the sea shall be made fresh.

Along both banks of the river, fruit trees of every kind shall grow;
>their leaves shall not fade, nor their fruit fail.

Every month they shall bear fresh fruit,
>for they shall be watered by the flow from the sanctuary.

Their fruit shall serve for food, and their leaves for medicine."

The word of the Lord.

757 READING FROM THE NEW TESTAMENT

1.

Romans 6:3-5   Buried with him through baptism into death, we too might live in newness of life.

A reading from the Letter of Saint Paul to the Romans

Brothers and sisters:
Are you unaware that we who were baptized into Christ Jesus
    were baptized into his death?
We were indeed buried with him through baptism into death,
    so that, just as Christ was raised from the dead
    by the glory of the Father,
    we too might live in newness of life.

For if we have grown into union with him through a death like his,
    we shall also be united with him in the resurrection.

The word of the Lord.

2.

Romans 8:28-32   To be conformed to the image of his Son.

A reading from the Letter of Saint Paul to the Romans

Brothers and sisters:
We know that all things work for good for those who love God,
    who are called according to his purpose.
For those he foreknew he also predestined
    to be conformed to the image of his Son,
    so that he might be the firstborn
    among many brothers.
And those he predestined he also called;
    and those he called he also justified;
    and those he justified he also glorified.

What then shall we say to this?
If God is for us, who can be against us?
He who did not spare his own Son
    but handed him over for us all,
    how will he not also give us everything else along with him?

The word of the Lord.

3.

1 Corinthians 12:12-13   For in one Spirit we were all baptized into one Body.

A reading from the first Letter of Saint Paul to the Corinthians

Brothers and sisters:
As a body is one though it has many parts,
  and all the parts of the body, though many, are one body,
  so also Christ.
For in one Spirit we were all baptized into one Body,
  whether Jews or Greeks, slaves or free persons,
  and we were all given to drink of one Spirit.

The word of the Lord.

4.

Galatians 3:26-28   All of you who were baptized into Christ have clothed yourselves with Christ.

A reading from the Letter of Saint Paul to the Galatians

Brothers and sisters:
Through faith you are all children of God in Christ Jesus.
For all of you who were baptized into Christ
  have clothed yourselves with Christ.
There is neither Jew nor Greek,
  there is neither slave nor free person,
  there is not male and female;
  for you are all one in Christ Jesus.

The word of the Lord.

5.

Ephesians 4:1-6   There is one Lord, one faith, one baptism.

A reading from the Letter of Saint Paul to the Ephesians

Brothers and sisters:
I, a prisoner for the Lord,
 urge you to live in a manner worthy of the call you have received,
 with all humility and gentleness, with patience,
 bearing with one another through love,
 striving to preserve the unity of the spirit
 through the bond of peace:
 one Body and one Spirit,
 as you were also called to the one hope of your call;
 one Lord, one faith, one baptism;
 one God and Father of all,
 who is over all and through all and in all.

The word of the Lord.

6.

1 Peter 2:4-5, 9-10   You are a chosen race, a royal priesthood.

A reading from the first Letter of Saint Peter

Beloved:
Come to the Lord, a living stone, rejected by human beings
 but chosen and precious in the sight of God,
 and, like living stones,
 let yourselves be built into a spiritual house
 to be a holy priesthood to offer spiritual sacrifices
  acceptable to God through Jesus Christ.

You are "a chosen race, a royal priesthood,
 a holy nation, a people of his own,
 so that you may announce the praises" of him
 who called you out of darkness into his wonderful light.

 Once you were "no people"
  but now you are God's people;
 you "had not received mercy"
  but now you have received mercy.

The word of the Lord.

758 RESPONSORIAL PSALM

First Option

Psalm 23:1b-3a, 3b-4, 5, 6

R℣. (1) **The Lord is my shepherd; there is nothing I shall want.**

The LORD is my shepherd; I shall not want.
   In verdant pastures he gives me repose;
Beside restful waters he leads me;
   he refreshes my soul.

R℣. **The Lord is my shepherd; there is nothing I shall want.**

He guides me in right paths
   for his name's sake.
Even though I walk in the dark valley
   I fear no evil; for you are at my side
With your rod and your staff
   that give me courage.

R℣. **The Lord is my shepherd; there is nothing I shall want.**

You spread the table before me
   in the sight of my foes;
You anoint my head with oil;
   my cup overflows.

R℣. **The Lord is my shepherd; there is nothing I shall want.**

Only goodness and kindness follow me
   all the days of my life;
And I shall dwell in the house of the LORD
   for years to come.

R℣. **The Lord is my shepherd; there is nothing I shall want.**

Second Option

Psalm 27:1bcde, 4, 8b-9abc, 13-14

℟. (1b) **The Lord is my light and my salvation.**
or:
℟. (Ephesians 5:14) **Wake up and rise from death: Christ will shine upon you!**

The LORD is my light and my salvation;
  whom should I fear?
The LORD is my life's refuge;
  of whom should I be afraid?

℟. **The Lord is my light and my salvation.**
or:
℟. **Wake up and rise from death: Christ will shine upon you!**

One thing I ask of the Lord;
  this I seek:
To dwell in the house of the LORD
  all the days of my life,
That I may gaze on the loveliness of the LORD
  and contemplate his temple.

℟. **The Lord is my light and my salvation.**
or:
℟. **Wake up and rise from death: Christ will shine upon you!**

Your presence, O LORD, I seek.
Hide not your face from me;
  do not in anger repel your servant.
You are my helper: cast me not off.

℟. **The Lord is my light and my salvation.**
or:
℟. **Wake up and rise from death: Christ will shine upon you!**

I believe that I shall see the bounty of the LORD
  in the land of the living.
Wait for the LORD with courage;
  be stouthearted, and wait for the LORD.

℟. **The Lord is my light and my salvation.**
or:
℟. **Wake up and rise from death: Christ will shine upon you!**

Third Option

Psalm 34:2-3, 6-7, 8-9, 14-15, 16-17, 18-19

℟. (6a) **Look to him, that you may be radiant with joy!**
   or:
℟. (9a) **Taste and see the goodness of the Lord.**

I will bless the LORD **at all times;**
   his praise shall ever be in my mouth.
Let my soul glory in the LORD**;**
   the lowly will hear me and be glad.

℟. **Look to him, that you may be radiant with joy!**
   or:
℟. **Taste and see the goodness of the Lord.**

Look to him that you may be radiant with joy,
   and your faces may not blush with shame.
When the poor one called out, the LORD **heard,**
   and from all his distress he saved him.

℟. **Look to him, that you may be radiant with joy!**
   or:
℟. **Taste and see the goodness of the Lord.**

The angel of the LORD **encamps**
   around those who fear him, and delivers them.
Taste and see how good the LORD **is;**
   blessed the man who takes refuge in him.

℟. **Look to him, that you may be radiant with joy!**
   or:
℟. **Taste and see the goodness of the Lord.**

Keep your tongue from evil,
   your lips from speaking guile;
Turn from evil, and do good;
   seek peace and follow after it.

(cont.)

R̸. **Look to him, that you may be radiant with joy!**
   or:
R̸. **Taste and see the goodness of the Lord.**

The LORD has eyes for the just
   and ears for their cry.
The LORD confronts the evildoers,
   to destroy remembrance of them from the earth.

R̸. **Look to him, that you may be radiant with joy!**
   or:
R̸. **Taste and see the goodness of the Lord.**

When the just cry out, the LORD hears them,
   and from all their distress he rescues them.
The LORD is close to the brokenhearted,
   and those who are crushed in spirit he saves.

R̸. **Look to him, that you may be radiant with joy!**
   or:
R̸. **Taste and see the goodness of the Lord.**

759 ALLELUIA VERSE AND VERSE BEFORE THE GOSPEL

1.

John 3:16

**God so loved the world that he gave his only-begotten Son,
so that everyone who believes in him might have eternal life.**

2.

John 8:12

**I am the light of the world, says the Lord;
whoever follows me will have the light of life.**

3.

John 14:6

**I am the way and the truth and the life, says the Lord;
no one comes to the Father, except through me.**

4.

Ephesians 4:5-6a

**There is one Lord, one faith, one baptism,
one God and the Father of all.**

5.

See 2 Timothy 1:10

**Our Savior Jesus Christ has destroyed death
and brought life to light through the Gospel.**

6.

1 Peter 2:9

**You are a chosen race, a royal priesthood, a holy nation:
announce the praises of him who called you
out of darkness into his wonderful light.**

760 GOSPEL

1.

Matthew 22:35-40   This is the greatest and the first commandment.

✠ **A reading from the holy Gospel according to Matthew**

One of the Pharisees, a scholar of the law, tested Jesus by asking,
"Teacher, which commandment in the law is the greatest?"
He said to him,
"You shall love the Lord, your God, with all your heart,
with all your soul, and with all your mind.
This is the greatest and the first commandment.
The second is like it:
You shall love your neighbor as yourself.
The whole law and the prophets depend on these two commandments."

The Gospel of the Lord.

2.

Matthew 28:18-20   Go, therefore, and make disciples of all nations,
baptizing them in the name of the Father, and of the Son, and of the
Holy Spirit.

✠ **A reading from the holy Gospel according to Matthew**

Jesus said to the Eleven disciples:
"All power in heaven and on earth has been given to me.
Go, therefore, and make disciples of all nations,
baptizing them in the name of the Father,
and of the Son, and of the Holy Spirit,
teaching them to observe all that I have commanded you.
And behold, I am with you always, until the end of the age."

The Gospel of the Lord.

3.

Mark 1:9-11   Jesus was baptized in the Jordan by John.

☩   **A reading from the holy Gospel according to Mark**

Jesus came from Nazareth of Galilee
  and was baptized in the Jordan by John.
On coming up out of the water he saw the heavens being torn open
  and the Spirit, like a dove, descending upon him.
And a voice came from the heavens,
  "You are my beloved Son; with you I am well pleased."

The Gospel of the Lord.

4.

Mark 10:13-16   Let the children come to me; do not prevent them.

☩   **A reading from the holy Gospel according to Mark**

People were bringing children to Jesus that he might touch them,
  but the disciples rebuked them.
When Jesus saw this he became indignant and said to them,
  "Let the children come to me; do not prevent them,
  for the Kingdom of God belongs to such as these.
Amen, I say to you,
  whoever does not accept the Kingdom of God like a child
  will not enter it."
Then he embraced them and blessed them,
  placing his hands on them.

The Gospel of the Lord.

5.

Long Form

Mark 12:28-34   Hear O Israel! You shall love the Lord, your God, with all your heart.

✠ **A reading from the holy Gospel according to Mark**

One of the scribes came to Jesus and asked him,
   "Which is the first of all the commandments?"
Jesus replied, "The first is this:
   Hear, O Israel!
   The Lord our God is Lord alone!
You shall love the Lord your God with all your heart,
   with all your soul, with all your mind,
   and with all your strength.
The second is this:
   You shall love your neighbor as yourself.
There is no other commandment greater than these."
The scribe said to him,
   "Well said, teacher. You are right in saying,
   'He is One and there is no other than he.'
And 'to love him with all your heart,
   with all your understanding,
   with all your strength,
   and to love your neighbor as yourself'
   is worth more than all burnt offerings and sacrifices."
And when Jesus saw that he answered with understanding,
   he said to him,
   "You are not far from the Kingdom of God."
And no one dared to ask him any more questions.

The Gospel of the Lord.

OR Short Form

Mark 12:28-31   Hear O Israel! You shall love the Lord, your God, with all your heart.

✠ **A reading from the holy Gospel according to Mark**

One of the scribes came to Jesus and asked him,
   "Which is the first of all the commandments?"

Jesus replied, "The first is this:
 'Hear, O Israel! The Lord our God is Lord alone!
You shall love the Lord your God with all your heart,
 with all your soul, with all your mind,
 and with all your strength.'
The second is this:
 'You shall love your neighbor as yourself.'
There is no other commandment greater than these."

The Gospel of the Lord.

 6.

John 3:1-6 No one can see the Kingdom of God without being born from above.

✝ **A reading from the holy Gospel according to John**

There was a Pharisee named Nicodemus, a ruler of the Jews.
He came to Jesus at night and said to him,
 "Rabbi, we know that you are a teacher who has come from God,
 for no one can do these signs that you are doing
 unless God is with him."
Jesus answered and said to him,
 "Amen, amen, I say to you,
 unless one is born from above,
 he cannot see the Kingdom of God."
Nicodemus said to him,
 "How can a man once grown old be born again?
Surely he cannot reenter his mother's womb and be born again, can he?"
Jesus answered,
 "Amen, amen, I say to you,
 unless one is born of water and Spirit
 he cannot enter the Kingdom of God.
What is born of flesh is flesh
 and what is born of spirit is spirit."

The Gospel of the Lord.

7.

John 4:5-14   A spring of water welling up to eternal life.

✠ **A reading from the holy Gospel according to John**

Jesus came to a town of Samaria called Sychar,
   near the plot of land that Jacob had given to his son Joseph.
Jacob's well was there.
Jesus, tired from his journey, sat down there at the well.
It was about noon.

A woman of Samaria came to draw water.
Jesus said to her,
   "Give me a drink."
His disciples had gone into the town to buy food.
The Samaritan woman said to him,
   "How can you, a Jew, ask me, a Samaritan woman, for a drink?"
—For Jews use nothing in common with Samaritans.—
Jesus answered and said to her,
   "If you knew the gift of God
   and who is saying to you, 'Give me a drink,'
   you would have asked him
   and he would have given you living water."
The woman said to him,
   "Sir, you do not even have a bucket and the cistern is deep;
   where then can you get this living water?
Are you greater than our father Jacob,
   who gave us this cistern and drank from it himself
   with his children and his flocks?"
Jesus answered and said to her,
   "Everyone who drinks this water will be thirsty again;
   but whoever drinks the water I shall give will never thirst;
   the water I shall give will become in him
   a spring of water welling up to eternal life."

The Gospel of the Lord.

8.

John 6:44-47   Whoever believes has eternal life.

✠   **A reading from the holy Gospel according to John**

Jesus said to the crowds:
"No one can come to me unless the Father who sent me draw him,
   and I shall raise him on the last day.
It is written in the prophets:

   They shall all be taught by God.

Everyone who listens to my Father and learns from him comes to me.
Not that anyone has seen the Father
   except the one who is from God;
   he has seen the Father.
Amen, amen, I say to you,
   whoever believes has eternal life."

The Gospel of the Lord.

9.

John 7:37b-39a   Rivers of living water will flow.

✠   **A reading from the holy Gospel according to John**

Jesus stood up and exclaimed,
   "Let anyone who thirsts come to me and drink.
Whoever believes in me, as Scripture says:

   Rivers of living water will flow from within him."

He said this in reference to the Spirit
   that those who came to believe in him were to receive.

The Gospel of the Lord.

10.

John 9:1-7   So he went and washed and came back able to see.

✝ **A reading from the holy Gospel according to John**

As Jesus passed by he saw a man blind from birth.
His disciples asked him,
  "Rabbi, who sinned, this man or his parents,
  that he was born blind?"
Jesus answered,
  "Neither he nor his parents sinned;
  it is so that the works of God might be made visible through him.
We have to do the works of the one who sent me while it is day.
Night is coming when no one can work.
While I am in the world, I am the light of the world."
When he had said this, he spat on the ground
  and made clay with the saliva,
  and smeared the clay on his eyes, and said to him,
  "Go wash in the Pool of Siloam" (which means Sent).
So he went and washed, and came back able to see.

The Gospel of the Lord.

11.

John 15:1-11   Whoever remains in me and I in him will bear much fruit.

✝ **A reading from the holy Gospel according to John**

Jesus said to his disciples:
"I am the true vine, and my Father is the vine grower.
He takes away every branch in me that does not bear fruit,
  and everyone that does he prunes so that it bears more fruit.
You are already pruned because of the word that I spoke to you.
Remain in me, as I remain in you.
Just as a branch cannot bear fruit on its own
  unless it remains on the vine,
  so neither can you unless you remain in me.
I am the vine, you are the branches.
Whoever remains in me and I in him will bear much fruit,
  because without me you can do nothing.

Anyone who does not remain in me
  will be thrown out like a branch and wither;
  people will gather them and throw them into a fire
  and they will be burned.
If you remain in me and my words remain in you,
  ask for whatever you want and it will be done for you.
By this is my Father glorified,
  that you bear much fruit and become my disciples.
As the Father loves me, so I also love you.
Remain in my love.
If you keep my commandments, you will remain in my love,
  just as I have kept my Father's commandments
  and remain in his love.

"I have told you this so that my joy may be in you
  and your joy may be complete."

The Gospel of the Lord.

12.

John 19:31-35 One soldier thrust his lance into his side, and
immediately Blood and water flowed out.

✝ **A reading from the holy Gospel according to John**

Since it was preparation day,
  in order that the bodies might not remain on the cross on the sabbath,
  for the sabbath day of that week was a solemn one,
  the Jews asked Pilate that their legs be broken
  and they be taken down.
So the soldiers came and broke the legs of the first
  and then of the other one who was crucified with Jesus.
But when they came to Jesus and saw that he was already dead,
  they did not break his legs,
  but one soldier thrust his lance into his side,
  and immediately Blood and water flowed out.
An eyewitness has testified, and his testimony is true;
  he knows that he is speaking the truth,
  so that you also may come to believe.

The Gospel of the Lord.

3. RECEPTION OF BAPTIZED CHRISTIANS INTO THE FULL COMMUNION OF THE CATHOLIC CHURCH

Readings, responsorial psalms, and verses before the Gospel may be taken in whole or in part from the Mass of the day, or from the Mass for the Unity of Christians (nos. 867–871), or from the Mass for Christian Initiation (nos. 751–755), or from the following:

761 READING FROM THE NEW TESTAMENT

1.

Romans 8:28-39   He predestined us to be conformed to the image of his Son.

A reading from the Letter of Saint Paul to the Romans

Brothers and sisters:
We know that all things work for good for those who love God
    who are called according to his purpose.
For those he foreknew he also predestined
    to be conformed to the image of his Son,
    so that he might be the firstborn
    among many brothers.
And those he predestined he also called;
    and those he called he also justified;
    and those he justified he also glorified.

What then shall we say to this?
If God is for us, who can be against us?
He who did not spare his own Son
    but handed him over for us all,
    how will he not also give us everything else along with him?
Who will bring a charge against God's chosen ones?
It is God who acquits us.
Who will condemn?
It is Christ Jesus who died, rather, was raised,
    who also is at the right hand of God,
    who indeed intercedes for us.
What will separate us from the love of Christ?
Will anguish, or distress, or persecution, or famine,
    or nakedness, or peril, or the sword?

As it is written:

> *For your sake we are being slain all the day;*
>   *we are looked upon as sheep to be slaughtered.*

No, in all these things we conquer overwhelmingly
   through him who loved us.
For I am convinced that neither death, nor life,
   nor angels, nor principalities,
   nor present things, nor future things,
   nor powers, nor height, nor depth,
   nor any other creature will be able to separate us
   from the love of God in Christ Jesus our Lord.

The word of the Lord.

2.

1 Corinthians 12:31–13:13   Love never fails.

A reading from the first Letter of Saint Paul to the Corinthians

Brothers and sisters:
Strive eagerly for the greatest spiritual gifts.

But I shall show you a still more excellent way.

If I speak in human and angelic tongues
    but do not have love,
    I am a resounding gong or a clashing cymbal.
And if I have the gift of prophecy
    and comprehend all mysteries and all knowledge;
    if I have all faith so as to move mountains,
    but do not have love, I am nothing.
If I give away everything I own,
    and if I hand my body over so that I may boast
    but do not have love, I gain nothing.

Love is patient, love is kind.
It is not jealous, love is not pompous,
    it is not inflated, it is not rude,
    it does not seek its own interests,
    it is not quick-tempered, it does not brood over injury, it does not rejoice
        over wrongdoing
    but rejoices with the truth.
It bears all things, believes all things,
    hopes all things, endures all things.

Love never fails.
If there are prophecies, they will be brought to nothing;
    if tongues, they will cease;
    if knowledge, it will be brought to nothing.
For we know partially and we prophesy partially,
    but when the perfect comes, the partial will pass away.
When I was a child, I used to talk as a child,
    think as a child, reason as a child;
    when I became a man, I put aside childish things.
At present we see indistinctly, as in a mirror,
    but then face to face.

At present I know partially;
  then I shall know fully, as I am fully known.
So faith, hope, love remain, these three;
  but the greatest of these is love.

The word of the Lord.

3.

Ephesians 1:3-14   He chose us to be holy and without blemish before him.

A reading from the Letter of Saint Paul to the Ephesians

Blessed be the God and Father of our Lord Jesus Christ,
  who has blessed us in Christ
  with every spiritual blessing in the heavens,
  as he chose us in him, before the foundation of the world,
  to be holy and without blemish before him.
In love he destined us for adoption to himself through Jesus Christ,
  in accord with the favor of his will,
  for the praise of the glory of his grace
  that he granted us in the beloved.

In him we have redemption by his Blood,
  the forgiveness of transgressions,
  in accord with the riches of his grace that he lavished upon us.
In all wisdom and insight, he has made known to us
  the mystery of his will in accord with his favor
  that he set forth in him as a plan for the fullness of times,
  to sum up all things in Christ, in heaven and on earth.

In him we were also chosen,
  destined in accord with the purpose of the One
  who accomplishes all things according to the intention of his will,
  so that we might exist for the praise of his glory,
  we who first hoped in Christ.
In him you also, who have heard the word of truth,
  the Gospel of your salvation, and have believed in him,
  were sealed with the promised Holy Spirit,
  which is the first installment of our inheritance
  toward redemption as his possession, to the praise of his glory.

The word of the Lord.

4.

Ephesians 4:1-7, 11-13   One Lord, one faith, one baptism, one God, the Father of all.

A reading from the Letter of Saint Paul to the Ephesians

Brothers and sisters:
I, a prisoner for the Lord,
  urge you to live in a manner worthy of the call you have received,
  with all humility and gentleness, with patience,
  bearing with one another through love,
  striving to preserve the unity of the Spirit
  through the bond of peace:
  one Body and one Spirit,
  as you were also called to the one hope of your call;
  one Lord, one faith, one baptism;
  one God and Father of all,
  who is over all and through all and in all.

But grace was given to each of us
  according to the measure of Christ's gift.

And he gave some as Apostles, others as prophets,
  others as evangelists, others as pastors and teachers,
  to equip the holy ones for the work of ministry,
  for building up the Body of Christ,
  until we all attain to the unity of faith
  and knowledge of the Son of God, to mature manhood,
  to the extent of the full stature of Christ.

The word of the Lord.

5.

Philippians 4:4-8   Whatever is pure, think about these things.

A reading from the Letter of Saint Paul to the Philippians

Brothers and sisters:
Rejoice in the Lord always.
I shall say it again: rejoice!
Your kindness should be known to all.
The Lord is near.

Have no anxiety at all, but in everything,
　　by prayer and petition, with thanksgiving,
　　make your requests known to God.
Then the peace of God that surpasses all understanding
　　will guard your hearts and minds in Christ Jesus.

Finally, brothers and sisters,
　　whatever is true, whatever is honorable,
　　whatever is just, whatever is pure,
　　whatever is lovely, whatever is gracious,
　　if there is any excellence
　　and if there is anything worthy of praise,
　　think about these things.

The word of the Lord.

6.

1 Thessalonians 5:16-24　May you entirely, spirit, soul and body, be
preserved blameless, for the coming of our Lord Jesus Christ.

A reading from the first Letter of Saint Paul to the Thessalonians

Brothers and sisters:
Rejoice always. Pray without ceasing.
In all circumstances give thanks,
　　for this is the will of God for you in Christ Jesus.
Do not quench the Spirit.
Do not despise prophetic utterances.
Test everything; retain what is good.
Refrain from every kind of evil.

May the God of peace himself make you perfectly holy
　　and may you entirely, spirit, soul, and body,
　　be preserved blameless for the coming of our Lord Jesus Christ.
The one who calls you is faithful,
　　and he will also accomplish it.

The word of the Lord.

762 RESPONSORIAL PSALM

1.

Psalm 27:1, 4, 8b-9abc, 13-14

℟. (1b) **The Lord is my light and my salvation.**

The LORD is my light and my salvation;
   whom should I fear?
The LORD is my life's refuge;
   of whom should I be afraid?

℟. The Lord is my light and my salvation.

One thing I ask of the LORD;
   this I seek:
To dwell in the house of the LORD
   all the days of my life,
That I may gaze on the loveliness of the LORD
   and contemplate his temple.

℟. The Lord is my light and my salvation.

Your presence, O LORD, I seek.
Hide not your face from me;
   do not in anger repel your servant.
You are my helper: cast me not off.

℟. The Lord is my light and my salvation.

I believe that I shall see the bounty of the LORD
   in the land of the living.
Wait for the LORD with courage;
   be stouthearted, and wait for the LORD.

℟. The Lord is my light and my salvation.

2.

Psalm 42:2-3; 43:3, 4

R̷. (42:3a) **My soul is thirsting for the living God.**

As the hind longs for the running waters,
   so my soul longs for you, O God.
Athirst is my soul for God, the living God.
   When shall I go and behold the face of God?

R̷. **My soul is thirsting for the living God.**

Send forth your light and your fidelity;
   they shall lead me on
And bring me to your holy mountain,
   to your dwelling-place.

R̷. **My soul is thirsting for the living God.**

Then will I go in to the altar of God,
   the God of my gladness and joy;
Then will I give you thanks upon the harp,
   O God, my God!

R̷. **My soul is thirsting for the living God.**

3.

Psalm 61:2-3b, 3c-4, 5-6, 9

℞. (4a) **Lord, you are my refuge.**

Hear my cry, O God,
 listen to my prayer!
From the earth's end I call to you
 as my heart grows faint.

℞. **Lord, you are my refuge.**

You will set me high above a rock;
 you will give me rest,
For you are my refuge,
 a tower of strength against the enemy.

℞. **Lord, you are my refuge.**

Oh, that I might lodge in your tent forever,
 take refuge in the shelter of your wings!
You indeed, O God, have accepted my vows;
 you granted me the heritage of those who fear your name.

℞. **Lord, you are my refuge.**

So will I sing the praises of your name forever,
 fulfilling my vows day by day.

℞. **Lord, you are my refuge.**

4.

Psalm 63:2, 3-4, 5-6, 8-9

℞. (2b) **My soul is thirsting for you, O Lord my God.**

O God, you are my God whom I seek;
 for you my flesh pines and my soul thirsts
 like the earth, parched, lifeless and without water.

℞. **My soul is thirsting for you, O Lord my God.**

Thus I have gazed toward you in the sanctuary
 to see your power and your glory,
For your kindness is a greater good than life;
 my lips shall glorify you.

℞. **My soul is thirsting for you, O Lord my God.**

Thus will I bless you while I live;
  lifting up my hands, I will call upon your name.
As with the riches of a banquet shall my soul be satisfied,
  and with exultant lips my mouth shall praise you.

℟. **My soul is thirsting for you, O Lord my God.**

You are my help,
  and in the shadow of your wings I shout for joy.
My soul clings fast to you;
  your right hand upholds me.

℟. **My soul is thirsting for you, O Lord my God.**

  5.

Psalm 65:2, 3-4, 5, 6

℟. (2a) **It is right to praise you in Zion, O God.**

To you we owe our hymn of praise,
  O God in Zion;
To you must vows be fulfilled
  in Jerusalem.

℟. **It is right to praise you in Zion, O God.**

To you all flesh must come
  because of wicked deeds.
We are overcome by our sins;
  it is you who pardon them.

℟. **It is right to praise you in Zion, O God.**

Blessed is the man you choose,
  and bring to dwell in your courts.
May we be filled with good things of your house,
  the holy things of your temple!

℟. **It is right to praise you in Zion, O God.**

With awe-inspiring deeds of justice you answer us,
  O God our savior,
The hope of all the ends of the earth
  and of the distant seas.

℟. **It is right to praise you in Zion, O God.**

6.

Psalm 121:1bc-2, 3-4, 5-6, 7-8

℟. (2a) **Our help is from the Lord.**

I lift up my eyes toward the mountains;
   whence shall help come to me?
My help is from the Lord,
   who made heaven and earth.

℟. **Our help is from the Lord.**

May he not suffer your foot to slip;
   may he slumber not who guards you:
Indeed he neither slumbers nor sleeps,
   the guardian of Israel.

℟. **Our help is from the Lord.**

The Lord is your guardian; the Lord is your shade;
   he is beside you at your right hand.
The sun shall not harm you by day,
   nor the moon by night.

℟. **Our help is from the Lord.**

The Lord will guard you from all evil;
   he will guard your life.
The Lord will guard your coming and your going,
   both now and forever.

℟. **Our help is from the Lord.**

763 GOSPEL

1.

Matthew 5:2-12a   Rejoice and be glad, for your reward will be great in heaven.

✝ **A reading from the holy Gospel according to Matthew**

Jesus began to teach his disciples, saying:

"Blessed are the poor in spirit,
    for theirs is the Kingdom of heaven.
Blessed are they who mourn,
    for they will be comforted.
Blessed are the meek,
    for they will inherit the land.
Blessed are they who hunger and thirst for righteousness,
    for they will be satisfied.
Blessed are the merciful,
    for they will be shown mercy.
Blessed are the clean of heart,
    for they will see God.
Blessed are the peacemakers,
    for they will be called children of God.
Blessed are they who are persecuted for the sake of righteousness,
    for theirs is the Kingdom of heaven.
Blessed are you when they insult you and persecute you
    and utter every kind of evil against you falsely because of me.
Rejoice and be glad,
    for your reward will be great in heaven."

The Gospel of the Lord.

2.

Matthew 5:13-16   Let your light shine before others.

✠ **A reading from the holy Gospel according to Matthew**

Jesus said to his disciples:
"You are the salt of the earth.
But if salt loses its taste, with what can it be seasoned?
It is no longer good for anything
  but to be thrown out and trampled underfoot.
You are the light of the world.
A city set on a mountain cannot be hidden.
Nor do they light a lamp and then put it under a bushel basket;
  it is set on a lampstand,
    where it gives light to all in the house.
Just so, your light must shine before others,
  that they may see your good deeds
  and glorify your heavenly Father."

The Gospel of the Lord.

3.

Matthew 11:25-30   You have hidden these things from the wise and the
learned; you have revealed them to the childlike.

✠ **A reading from the holy Gospel according to Matthew**

At that time Jesus answered:
"I give praise to you, Father, Lord of heaven and earth,
  for although you have hidden these things
  from the wise and the learned
  you have revealed them to the childlike.
Yes, Father, such has been your gracious will.
All things have been handed over to me by my Father.
No one knows the Son except the Father,
  and no one knows the Father except the Son
  and anyone to whom the Son wishes to reveal him.
"Come to me, all you who labor and are burdened,
  and I will give you rest.

Take my yoke upon you and learn from me,
for I am meek and humble of heart;
and you will find rest for yourselves.
For my yoke is easy, and my burden light."

The Gospel of the Lord.

4.

John 3:16-21   So that everyone who believes in him might not perish.

✠ **A reading from the holy Gospel according to John**

God so loved the world that he gave his only-begotten Son,
so that everyone who believes in him might not perish
but might have eternal life.
For God did not send his Son into the world to condemn the world,
but that the world might be saved through him.
Whoever believes in him will not be condemned,
but whoever does not believe has already been condemned,
because he has not believed in the name of the only-begotten Son of God.
And this is the verdict,
that the light came into the world,
but people preferred darkness to light,
because their works were evil.
For everyone who does wicked things hates the light
and does not come toward the light,
so that his works might not be exposed.
But whoever lives the truth comes to the light,
so that his works may be clearly seen as done in God.

The Gospel of the Lord.

5.

John 14:15-23, 26-27   We will come to him and make our dwelling with him.

✝ **A reading from the holy Gospel according to John**

Jesus said to his disciples:
"If you love me, you will keep my commandments.
And I will ask the Father,
    and he will give you another Advocate to be with you always,
    the Spirit of truth, which the world cannot accept,
    because it neither sees nor knows it.
But you know it, because it remains with you,
    and will be in you.
I will not leave you orphans; I will come to you.
In a little while the world will no longer see me,
    but you will see me, because I live and you will live.
On that day you will realize that I am in my Father
    and you are in me and I in you.
Whoever has my commandments and observes them
    is the one who loves me.
And whoever loves me will be loved by my Father,
    and I will love him and reveal myself to him."
Judas, not the Iscariot, said to him,
    "Master, then what happened that you will reveal yourself to us
    and not to the world?"
Jesus answered and said to him,
    "Whoever loves me will keep my word,
    and my Father will love him,
    and we will come to him and make our dwelling with him.

"The Advocate, the Holy Spirit
    that the Father will send in my name—
    he will teach you everything
    and remind you of all that I told you.
Peace I leave with you; my peace I give to you.
Not as the world gives do I give it to you.
Do not let your hearts be troubled or afraid."

The Gospel of the Lord.

6.

John 15:1-6   I am the vine, you are the branches.

✠ **A reading from the holy Gospel according to John**

Jesus said to his disciples:
"I am the true vine, and my Father is the vine grower.
He takes away every branch in me that does not bear fruit,
   and every one that does he prunes so that it bears more fruit.
You are already pruned because of the word that I spoke to you.
Remain in me, as I remain in you.
Just as a branch cannot bear fruit on its own
   unless it remains on the vine,
   so neither can you unless you remain in me.
I am the vine, you are the branches.
Whoever remains in me and I in him will bear much fruit,
   because without me you can do nothing.
Anyone who does not remain in me
   will be thrown out like a branch and wither;
   people will gather them and throw them into a fire
   and they will be burned."

The Gospel of the Lord.

4. CONFIRMATION

764 READING FROM THE OLD TESTAMENT

1.

Isaiah 11:1-4ab   The Spirit of the Lord shall rest upon him.

A reading from the Book of the Prophet Isaiah

On that day, a shoot shall sprout from the stump of Jesse,
and from his roots a bud shall blossom.
The Spirit of the LORD shall rest upon him:
a Spirit of wisdom and of understanding,
A Spirit of counsel and of strength,
a Spirit of knowledge and of fear of the LORD,
and his delight shall be the fear of the LORD.
Not by appearance shall he judge,
nor by hearsay shall he decide,
But he shall judge the poor with justice,
and decide aright for the land's afflicted.

The word of the Lord.

2.

Isaiah 42:1-3   Here is my servant upon whom I have put my Spirit.

A reading from the Book of the Prophet Isaiah

Thus says the Lord:
Here is my servant whom I uphold,
my chosen one with whom I am pleased,
Upon whom I have put my Spirit;
he shall bring forth justice to the nations,
Not crying out, not shouting,
not making his voice heard in the street.
A bruised reed he shall not break,
and a smoldering wick he shall not quench.

The word of the Lord.

3.

Isaiah 61:1-3abcd, 6ab, 8c-9   The Lord has anointed me; he has sent me
to bring glad tidings to the lowly and to give them the oil of gladness.

A reading from the Book of the Prophet Isaiah

The Spirit of the Lord G<small>OD</small> is upon me,
because the L<small>ORD</small> has anointed me;
He has sent me to bring glad tidings to the lowly,
to heal the brokenhearted,
To proclaim liberty to the captives
and release to the prisoners,
To announce a year of favor from the L<small>ORD</small>
and a day of vindication by our God,
to comfort all who mourn;
To place on those who mourn in Zion
a diadem instead of ashes,
To give them oil of gladness in place of mourning,
a glorious mantle instead of a listless spirit.
You yourselves shall be named priests of the L<small>ORD</small>,
ministers of our God you shall be called.
I will give them their recompense faithfully,
a lasting covenant I will make with them.
Their descendants shall be renowned among the nations,
and their offspring among the peoples;
All who see them shall acknowledge them
as a race the L<small>ORD</small> has blessed.

The word of the Lord.

4.

Ezekiel 36:24-28　I will put a new spirit within you.

A reading from the Book of the Prophet Ezekiel

Thus says the Lord GOD:
I will take you away from among the nations,
　　gather you from all the foreign lands,
　　and bring you back to your own land.
I will sprinkle clean water upon you
　　to cleanse you from all your impurities,
　　and from all your idols I will cleanse you.
I will give you a new heart and place a new Spirit within you,
　　taking from your bodies your stony hearts
　　and giving you natural hearts.
I will put my Spirit within you and make you live by my statutes,
　　careful to observe my decrees.
You shall live in the land I gave your fathers;
　　you shall be my people, and I will be your God.

The word of the Lord.

5.

Joel 2:23a, 26–3:1-3a   I will pour out my Spirit upon the servants
and handmaids.

A reading from the Book of the Prophet Joel

Children of Zion, exult
    and rejoice in the LORD, your God!

You shall eat and be filled,
    and shall praise the name of the LORD, your God,
Because he has dealt wondrously with you;
    my people shall nevermore be put to shame.
And you shall know that I am in the midst of Israel;
    I am the LORD, your God, and there is no other;
    my people shall nevermore be put to shame.

Then afterward I will pour out
    my Spirit upon all mankind.
Your sons and daughters shall prophesy,
    your old men shall dream dreams,
    your young men shall see visions;
Even upon the servants in those days,
    I will pour out my Spirit.
And I will work wonders in the heavens and on the earth.

The word of the Lord.

765 READING FROM THE NEW TESTAMENT

1.

Acts 1:3-8   You will receive the power when the Holy Spirit comes upon you, and you will be my witnesses.

A reading from the Acts of the Apostles

Jesus showed the Apostles that he was alive
by many proofs after he had suffered,
appearing to them during forty days
and speaking about the Kingdom of God.
While meeting with them,
he enjoined them not to depart from Jerusalem,
but to wait for "the promise of the Father
about which you have heard me speak;
for John baptized with water,
but in a few days you will be baptized with the Holy Spirit."

When they had gathered together they asked him,
"Lord, are you at this time going to restore
the kingdom to Israel?"
He answered them, "It is not for you to know the times or seasons
that the Father has established by his own authority.
But you will receive power when the Holy Spirit comes upon you,
and you will be my witnesses in Jerusalem,
throughout Judea and Samaria,
and to the ends of the earth."

The word of the Lord.

2.

Acts 2:1-6, 14, 22b-23, 32-33 All were filled with the Holy Spirit, and began to speak in different tongues.

A reading from the Acts of the Apostles

When the time for Pentecost was fulfilled,
   they were all in one place together.
And suddenly there came from the sky
   a noise like a strong driving wind,
   and it filled the entire house in which they were.
Then there appeared to them tongues as of fire,
   which parted and came to rest on each one of them.
And they were all filled with the Holy Spirit
   and began to speak in different tongues,
   as the Spirit enabled them to proclaim.

Now there were devout Jews from every nation under heaven staying in
   Jerusalem.
At this sound, they gathered in a large crowd,
   but they were confused
   because each one heard them speaking in his own language.

Then Peter stood up with the Eleven, raised his voice, and proclaimed to
   them:
   "You who are Jews, indeed all of you staying in Jerusalem.
Let this be known to you, and listen to my words.

"Jesus the Nazorean was a man commended to you by God
   with mighty deeds, wonders, and signs,
   which God worked through him in your midst,
   as you yourselves know.
This man, delivered up by the set plan and foreknowledge of God,
   you killed, using lawless men to crucify him.

"God raised this Jesus;
   of this we are all witnesses.
Exalted at the right hand of God,
   he received the promise of the Holy Spirit from the Father
   and poured it forth, as you both see and hear."

The word of the Lord.

3.

Acts 8:1bc, 4, 14-17   They laid hands on them and they received the Holy Spirit.

A reading from the Acts of the Apostles

On that day, there broke out a severe persecution
of the Church in Jerusalem,
and all were scattered throughout the countryside
of Judea and Samaria, except the Apostles.

Those who had been scattered went about preaching the word.

When the Apostles in Jerusalem
heard that Samaria had accepted the word of God,
they sent them Peter and John,
who went down and prayed for them,
that they might receive the Holy Spirit,
for he had not yet fallen upon any of them;
they had only been baptized in the name of the Lord Jesus.
Then they laid hands on them
and they received the Holy Spirit.

The word of the Lord.

4.

Acts 10:1, 33-34a, 37-44   The Holy Spirit fell upon all those who were listening to the word.

A reading from the Acts of the Apostles

In Caesarea there was a man named Cornelius,
a centurion of the Cohort called the Italica.

Cornelius said to Peter:
"I sent for you immediately,
and you were kind enough to come.
Now therefore we are all here in the presence of God
to listen to all that you have been commanded by the Lord."

Then Peter proceeded to speak and said,
"You know what has happened all over Judea,
beginning in Galilee after the baptism that John preached,
how God anointed Jesus of Nazareth
with the Holy Spirit and power.

He went about doing good
    and healing all those oppressed by the Devil,
    for God was with him.
We are witnesses of all that he did
    both in the country of the Jews and in Jerusalem.
They put him to death by hanging him on a tree.
This man God raised on the third day and granted that he be visible,
    not to all the people, but to us,
    the witnesses chosen by God in advance,
    who ate and drank with him after he rose from the dead.
He commissioned us to preach to the people
    and testify that he is the one appointed by God
    as judge of the living and the dead.
To him all the prophets bear witness,
    that everyone who believes in him
    will receive forgiveness of sins through his name."

While Peter was still speaking these things,
    the Holy Spirit fell upon all who were listening to the word.

The word of the Lord.

5.

Acts 19:1b-6a   Did you receive the Holy Spirit when you became believers?

A reading from the Acts of the Apostles

Paul came to Ephesus where he found some disciples.
He said to them,
    "Did you receive the Holy Spirit when you became believers?"
They answered him,
    "We have never even heard that there is a Holy Spirit."
He said, "How were you baptized?"
They replied, "With the baptism of John."
Paul then said,
    "John baptized with a baptism of repentance,
    telling the people to believe in the one who was to come after him,
    that is, in Jesus."
When they heard this,
    they were baptized in the name of the Lord Jesus.
And when Paul laid his hands on them,
    the Holy Spirit came upon them.

The word of the Lord.

6.

Romans 5:1-2, 5-8   The love of God has been poured into our hearts
through the Holy Spirit who has been given to us.

A reading from the Letter of Saint Paul to the Romans

Brothers and sisters:
Since we have been justified by faith,
   we have peace with God through our Lord Jesus Christ,
   through whom we have gained access by faith
   to this grace in which we stand,
   and we boast in hope of the glory of God.
And hope does not disappoint,
   because the love of God has been poured out into our hearts
   through the Holy Spirit who has been given to us.
For Christ, while we were still helpless,
   died at the appointed time for the ungodly.
Indeed, only with difficulty does one die for a just person,
   though perhaps for a good person one might even find courage to die.
But God proves his love for us
   in that while we were still sinners Christ died for us.

The word of the Lord.

7.

Romans 8:14-17   The Spirit himself bears witness with our spirit that we
are children of God.

A reading from the Letter of Saint Paul to the Romans

Brothers and sisters:
For those who are led by the Spirit of God are sons of God.
For you did not receive a spirit of slavery to fall back into fear,
   but you received a spirit of adoption,
   through which we cry, "*Abba*, Father!"
The Spirit himself bears witness with our spirit
   that we are children of God,
   and if children, then heirs,
   heirs of God and joint heirs with Christ,
   if only we suffer with him
   so that we may also be glorified with him.

The word of the Lord.

8.

Romans 8:26-27   The Spirit himself intercedes with inexpressible groanings.

A reading from the Letter of Saint Paul to the Romans

Brothers and sisters:
The Spirit comes to the aid of our weakness;
 for we do not know how to pray as we ought,
 but the Spirit himself intercedes with inexpressible groanings.
And the one who searches hearts
 knows what is the intention of the Spirit,
 because it intercedes for the holy ones
 according to God's will.

The word of the Lord.

9.

1 Corinthians 12:4-13   But one and the same Spirit produces all these gifts, distributing them individually to each person as he wishes.

A reading from the first Letter of Saint Paul to the Corinthians

Brothers and sisters:
There are different kinds of spiritual gifts but the same Spirit;
there are different forms of service but the same Lord;
there are different workings but the same God
who produces all of them in everyone.
To each individual the manifestation of the Spirit
is given for some benefit.
To one is given through the Spirit the expression of wisdom;
another the expression of knowledge according to the same Spirit;
another faith by the same Spirit;
another gifts of healing by the one Spirit;
another mighty deeds;
another prophecy;
another discernment of spirits;
another varieties of tongues;
another interpretation of tongues.
But one and the same Spirit produces all of these,
distributing them individually to each person as he wishes.

As a body is one though it has many parts,
and all the parts of the body, though many, are one body,
so also Christ.
For in one Spirit we were all baptized into one Body,
whether Jews or Greeks, slaves or free persons,
and we were all given to drink of one Spirit.

The word of the Lord.

10.

Galatians 5:16-17, 22-23a, 24-25   If we live in the Spirit, let us also follow the Spirit.

A reading from the Letter of Saint Paul to the Galatians

Brothers and sisters:
Live by the Spirit
and you will certainly not gratify the desire of the flesh.

For the flesh has desires against the Spirit,
  and the Spirit against the flesh;
  these are opposed to each other,
  so that you may not do what you want.
In contrast, the fruit of the Spirit is love, joy, peace,
  patience, kindness, generosity,
  faithfulness, gentleness, self-control.
Now those who belong to Christ Jesus have crucified their flesh
  with its passions and desires.
If we live in the Spirit, let us also follow the Spirit.

The word of the Lord.

11.

Ephesians 1:3a, 4a, 13-19a   You were sealed with the promised Holy Spirit.

A reading from the Letter of Saint Paul to the Ephesians

Blessed be the God and Father of our Lord Jesus Christ.
He chose us in Christ, before the foundation of the world.
In him you also, who have heard the word of truth,
  the Gospel of your salvation, and have believed in him,
  were sealed with the promised Holy Spirit,
  which is the first installment of our inheritance
  toward redemption as God's possession, to the praise of his glory.

Therefore, I, too, hearing of your faith in the Lord Jesus
  and of your love for all the holy ones,
  do not cease giving thanks for you,
  remembering you in my prayers,
  that the God of our Lord Jesus Christ, the Father of glory,
  may give you a spirit of wisdom and revelation
  resulting in knowledge of him.
May the eyes of your hearts be enlightened,
  that you may know what is the hope that belongs to his call,
  what are the riches of glory
  in his inheritance among the holy ones,
  and what is the surpassing greatness of his power
  for us who believe.

The word of the Lord.

12.

Ephesians 4:1-6   One Body and one Spirit, one baptism.

A reading from the Letter of Saint Paul to the Ephesians

Brothers and sisters:
I, a prisoner for the Lord,
   urge you to live in a manner worthy of the call you have received,
   with all humility and gentleness, with patience,
   bearing with one another through love,
   striving to preserve the unity of the Spirit
   through the bond of peace:
   one Body and one Spirit,
   as you were also called to the one hope of your call;
   one Lord, one faith, one baptism;
   one God and Father of all,
   who is over all and through all and in all.

   The word of the Lord.

766 RESPONSORIAL PSALM

1.

Psalm 22:23-24ab, 26-27, 28 and 31-32

R̸. (23a) **I will proclaim your name to my brothers and sisters.**
   or:
R̸. (John 15:26-27) **When the Holy Spirit comes to you, you will be my witnesses.**

I will proclaim your name to my brothers and sisters;
   in the midst of the assembly I will praise you:
"You who fear the LORD, praise him;
   all you descendants of Jacob, give glory to him."

R̸. **I will proclaim your name to my brothers and sisters.**
   or:
R̸. **When the Holy Spirit comes to you, you will be my witnesses.**

By your gift will I utter praise in the vast assembly;
   I will fulfill my vows before those who fear him.
The lowly shall eat their fill;
   they who seek the LORD shall praise him:
   "May your hearts be ever merry!"

R̸. **I will proclaim your name to my brothers and sisters.**
   or:
R̸. **When the Holy Spirit comes to you, you will be my witnesses.**

All the ends of the earth
   shall remember and turn to the LORD;
All the families of the nations
   shall bow down before him;
   my descendants shall serve him.
Let the coming generation be told of the LORD
   that they may proclaim to a people yet to be born
   the justice he has shown.

R̸. **I will proclaim your name to my brothers and sisters.**
   or:
R̸. **When the Holy Spirit comes to you, you will be my witnesses.**

2.

Psalm 23:1b-3a, 3bc-4, 5-6

℟. (1) **The Lord is my shepherd; there is nothing I shall want.**

The LORD **is my shepherd; I shall not want.**
   In verdant pastures he gives me repose;
Beside restful waters he leads me;
   he refreshes my soul.

℟. **The Lord is my shepherd; there is nothing I shall want.**

He guides me in right paths
   for his name's sake.
Even though I walk in the dark valley
   I fear no evil; for you are at my side
With your rod and your staff
   that give me courage.

℟. **The Lord is my shepherd; there is nothing I shall want.**

You spread the table before me
   in the sight of my foes;
You anoint my head with oil;
   my cup overflows.

℟. **The Lord is my shepherd; there is nothing I shall want.**

Only goodness and kindness follow me
   all the days of my life;
And I shall dwell in the house of the LORD
   for years to come.

℟. **The Lord is my shepherd; there is nothing I shall want.**

3.

Psalm 96:1-2a, 2b-3, 9-10a, 11-12

℟. (3) **Proclaim God's marvelous deeds to all the nations.**

Sing to the LORD a new song;
 sing to the LORD, all you lands;
Sing to the LORD; bless his name.

℟. **Proclaim God's marvelous deeds to all the nations.**

Announce his salvation, day after day.
Tell his glory among the nations;
 among all peoples, his wondrous deeds.

℟. **Proclaim God's marvelous deeds to all the nations.**

Worship the LORD in his holy attire.
Tremble before him, all the earth;
 say among the nations: The LORD is king.

℟. **Proclaim God's marvelous deeds to all the nations.**

Let the heavens be glad and the earth rejoice;
 let the sea and what fills it resound;
 let the plains be joyful and all that is in them!
Then shall all the trees of the forest exult.

℟. **Proclaim God's marvelous deeds to all the nations.**

4.

Psalm 104:1ab and 24, 27-28, 30-31, 33-34

℟. (see 30) **Lord, send out your Spirit, and renew the face of the earth.**

Bless the LORD, O my soul!
    O LORD, my God, you are great indeed!
How manifold are your works, O LORD!
    In wisdom you have wrought them all—
    the earth is full of your creatures.

℟. Lord, send out your Spirit, and renew the face of the earth.

They all look to you
    to give them food in due time.
When you give it to them, they gather it;
    when you open your hand, they are filled with good things.

℟. Lord, send out your Spirit, and renew the face of the earth.

When you send forth your spirit, they are created,
    and you renew the face of the earth.
May the glory of the LORD endure forever;
    may the LORD be glad in his works!

℟. Lord, send out your Spirit, and renew the face of the earth.

I will sing to the LORD all my life;
    I will sing praise to my God while I live.
Pleasing to him be my theme;
    I will be glad in the LORD.

℟. Lord, send out your Spirit, and renew the face of the earth.

5.

Psalm 117:1bc, 2

℟. (Acts 1:8) **You will be my witnesses to all the world.**
  or:
℟. **Alleluia.**

Praise the LORD, all you nations,
  glorify him, all you peoples!

℟. **You will be my witnesses to all the world.**
  or:
℟. **Alleluia.**

For steadfast is his kindness toward us,
  and the fidelity of the LORD endures forever.

℟. **You will be my witnesses to all the world.**
  or:
℟. **Alleluia.**

6.

Psalm 145:2-3, 4-5, 8-9, 10-11, 15-16, 21

℟. (see 1) **I will praise your name for ever, Lord.**

Every day will I bless you,
and I will praise your name forever and ever.
Great is the LORD and highly to be praised;
his greatness is unsearchable.

℟. **I will praise your name for ever, Lord.**

Generation after generation praises your works
and proclaims your might.
They speak of the splendor of your glorious majesty
and tell of your wondrous works.

℟. **I will praise your name for ever, Lord.**

The LORD is gracious and merciful,
slow to anger and of great kindness.
The LORD is good to all
and compassionate toward all his works.

℟. **I will praise your name for ever, Lord.**

Let all your works give you thanks, O LORD,
and let your faithful ones bless you.
Let them discourse of the glory of your Kingdom
and speak of your might.

℟. **I will praise your name for ever, Lord.**

The eyes of all look hopefully to you
and you give them their food in due season;
You open your hand
and satisfy the desire of every living thing.

℟. **I will praise your name for ever, Lord.**

May my mouth speak the praise of the LORD,
and may all flesh bless his holy name forever and ever.

℟. **I will praise your name for ever, Lord.**

767 ALLELUIA VERSE AND VERSE BEFORE THE GOSPEL

1.

John 14:16

**I will ask the Father
and he will give you another Advocate
to be with you always.**

2.

John 15:26b, 27a

**The Spirit of truth will testify to me, says the Lord;
and you also will testify.**

3.

John 16:13a; 14:26d

**When the Spirit of truth comes,
he will guide you to all truth
and remind you of all I told you.**

4.

Revelation 1:5a, 6a

**Jesus Christ, you are the faithful witness, firstborn from the dead;
you have made us a kingdom of priests to serve our God and Father.**

5.

**Come, Holy Spirit;
shine on us the radiance of your light.**

6.

**Come, Holy Spirit, fill the hearts of your faithful,
and kindle in them the fire of your love.**

768 GOSPEL

1.

Matthew 5:1-12a   Theirs is the Kingdom of heaven.

✝ **A reading from the holy Gospel according to Matthew**

When Jesus saw the crowds, he went up the mountain,
  and after he had sat down, his disciples came to him.
He began to teach them, saying:

  "Blessed are the poor in spirit,
    for theirs is the Kingdom of heaven.
  Blessed are they who mourn,
    for they will be comforted.
  Blessed are the meek,
    for they will inherit the land.
  Blessed are they who hunger and thirst for righteousness,
    for they will be satisfied.
  Blessed are the merciful,
    for they will be shown mercy.
  Blessed are the clean of heart,
    for they will see God.
  Blessed are the peacemakers,
    for they will be called children of God.
  Blessed are they who are persecuted for the sake of righteousness,
    for theirs is the Kingdom of heaven.
  Blessed are you when they insult you and persecute you
    and utter every kind of evil against you falsely because of me.
  Rejoice and be glad,
    for your reward will be great in heaven."

The Gospel of the Lord.

2.

Matthew 16:24-27   Whoever wishes to come after me must deny himself.

✠ **A reading from the holy Gospel according to Matthew**

Jesus said to his disciples,
  "Whoever wishes to come after me must deny himself,
  take up his cross, and follow me.
For whoever wishes to save his life will lose it,
  but whoever loses his life for my sake will find it.
What profit would there be for one to gain the whole world
  and forfeit his life?
Or what can one give in exchange for his life?
For the Son of Man will come with his angels in his Father's glory,
  and then he will repay each one according to his conduct."

The Gospel of the Lord.

3.

Matthew 25:14-30   Since you were faithful in small matters, come, share
your master's joy.

☩ **A reading from the holy Gospel according to Matthew**

Jesus told his disciples this parable:
"A man going on a journey
    called in his servants and entrusted his possessions to them.
To one he gave five talents; to another, two; to a third, one—
    to each according to his ability.
Then he went away.
Immediately the one who received five talents went and traded with them,
    and made another five.
Likewise, the one who received two made another two.
But the one who received one went off and dug a hole in the ground
    and buried his master's money.
After a long time
    the master of those servants came back and settled accounts with them.
The one who had received five talents
    came forward bringing the additional five.
He said, 'Master, you gave me five talents.
See, I have made five more.'
His master said to him, 'Well done, my good and faithful servant.
Since you were faithful in small matters,
    I will give you great responsibilities.
Come, share your master's joy.'
Then the one who had received two talents also came forward and said,
    'Master, you gave me two talents.
See, I have made two more.'
His master said to him, 'Well done, my good and faithful servant.
Since you were faithful in small matters,
    I will give you great responsibilities.
Come, share your master's joy.'
Then the one who had received the one talent came forward and said,
    'Master, I knew you were a demanding person,
      harvesting where you did not plant
      and gathering where you did not scatter;
      so out of fear I went off and buried your talent in the ground.
Here it is back.'
His master said to him in reply, 'You wicked, lazy servant!

So you knew that I harvest where I did not plant
    and gather where I did not scatter?
Should you not then have put my money in the bank
    so that I could have got it back with interest on my return?
Now then! Take the talent from him and give it to the one with ten.
For to everyone who has,
    more will be given and he will grow rich;
    but from the one who has not,
    even what he has will be taken away.
And throw this useless servant into the darkness outside,
    where there will be wailing and grinding of teeth.'"

The Gospel of the Lord.

4.

Mark 1:9-11   Jesus saw the Spirit descending upon him.

✠ **A reading from the holy Gospel according to Mark**

**Jesus came from Nazareth of Galilee
    and was baptized in the Jordan by John.
On coming up out of the water he saw the heavens being torn open
    and the Spirit, like a dove, descending upon him.
And a voice came from the heavens,
    "You are my beloved Son; with you I am well pleased."**

The Gospel of the Lord.

5.

Luke 4:16-22a   The Spirit of the Lord is upon me.

✠   **A reading from the holy Gospel according to Luke**

Jesus came to Nazareth, where he had grown up,
   and went according to his custom
   into the synagogue on the sabbath day.
He stood up to read and was handed a scroll of the prophet Isaiah.
Jesus unrolled the scroll and found the passage where it was written:

   The Spirit of the Lord is upon me,
      because he has anointed me
         to bring glad tidings to the poor.
   He has sent me to proclaim liberty to captives
      and recovery of sight to the blind,
         to let the oppressed go free,
   and to proclaim a year acceptable to the Lord.

Rolling up the scroll, he handed it back to the attendant and sat down,
   and the eyes of all in the synagogue looked intently at him.
He said to them,
   "Today this Scripture passage is fulfilled in your hearing."
And all spoke highly of him
   and were amazed at the gracious words that came from his mouth.

The Gospel of the Lord.

6.

Luke 8:4-10a, 11b-15   The seed that fell on rich soil: they are the ones
who, when they have heard the word, bear fruit through perseverance.

✠   **A reading from the holy Gospel according to Luke**

When a large crowd gathered, with people from one town after another
   journeying to Jesus, he spoke in a parable.
"A sower went out to sow his seed.
And as he sowed, some seed fell on the path and was trampled,
   and the birds of the sky ate it up.
Some seed fell on rocky ground,
   and when it grew, it withered for lack of moisture.
Some seed fell among thorns,
   and the thorns grew with it and choked it.

And some seed fell on good soil, and when it grew,
 it produced fruit a hundredfold."
After saying this, he called out,
 "Whoever has ears to hear ought to hear."

Then his disciples asked him
 what the meaning of this parable might be.
He answered,
 "The seed is the word of God.
Those on the path are the ones who have heard,
 but the Devil comes and takes away the word from their hearts
 that they may not believe and be saved.
Those on rocky ground are the ones who, when they hear,
 receive the word with joy, but they have no root;
 they believe only for a time and fall away in time of temptation.
As for the seed that fell among thorns,
 they are the ones who have heard,
 but as they go along,
 they are choked by the anxieties and riches and pleasures of life,
 and they fail to produce mature fruit.
But as for the seed that fell on rich soil,
 they are the ones who, when they have heard the word,
 embrace it with a generous and good heart,
 and bear fruit through perseverance."

The Gospel of the Lord.

7.

Luke 10:21-24   I give you praise, Father, for you have revealed hidden things to the childlike.

✠ **A reading from the holy Gospel according to Luke**

Jesus rejoiced in the Holy Spirit and said,
    "I give you praise, Father, Lord of heaven and earth,
        for although you have hidden these things
        from the wise and the learned
        you have revealed them to the childlike.
Yes, Father, such has been your gracious will.
All things have been handed over to me by my Father.
No one knows who the Son is except the Father,
        and who the Father is except the Son
        and anyone to whom the Son wishes to reveal him."

Turning to the disciples in private he said,
    "Blessed are the eyes that see what you see.
For I say to you, many prophets and kings desired to see what you see,
        but did not see it,
        and to hear what you hear,
        but did not hear it."

The Gospel of the Lord.

8.

John 7:37b-39   Rivers of living water will flow.

✠ **A reading from the holy Gospel according to John**

Jesus stood up and exclaimed,
    "Let anyone who thirsts come to me and drink.
Whoever believes in me, as Scripture says:

    Rivers of living water will flow from within him.

He said this in reference to the Spirit
    that those who came to believe in him were to receive.
There was, of course, no Spirit yet,
    because Jesus had not yet been glorified.

The Gospel of the Lord.

9.

John 14:15-17   The Spirit of truth will remain with you.

✠ **A reading from the holy Gospel according to John**

Jesus said to his disciples:
"If you love me, you will keep my commandments.
And I will ask the Father,
   and he will give you another Advocate to be with you always,
   the Spirit of truth, which the world cannot accept,
   because it neither sees nor knows it.
But you know it, because it remains with you,
   and will be in you."

The Gospel of the Lord.

10.

John 14:23-26   The Holy Spirit will teach you everything.

✠ **A reading from the holy Gospel according to John**

Jesus said to his disciples:
"Whoever loves me will keep my word,
   and my Father will love him,
   and we will come to him and make our dwelling with him.
Whoever does not love me does not keep my words;
   yet the word you hear is not mine
   but that of the Father who sent me.

"I have told you this while I am with you.
The Advocate, the Holy Spirit
   that the Father will send in my name—
   he will teach you everything
   and remind you of all that I told you."

The Gospel of the Lord.

11.

John 15:18-21, 26-27   When the Spirit of truth that proceeds from the Father comes, he will testify to me.

✠   **A reading from the holy Gospel according to John**

Jesus said to his disciples:
"If the world hates you, realize that it hated me first.
If you belonged to the world, the world would love its own;
  but because you do not belong to the world,
  and I have chosen you out of the world,
  the world hates you.
Remember the word I spoke to you,
  'No slave is greater than his master.'
If they persecuted me, they will also persecute you.
If they kept my word, they will also keep yours.
And they will do all these things to you on account of my name,
  because they do not know the one who sent me.

"When the Advocate comes whom I will send you from the Father,
  the Spirit of truth that proceeds from the Father,
  he will testify to me.
And you also testify,
  because you have been with me from the beginning."

The Gospel of the Lord.

12.

John 16:5-7, 12-13a   The Spirit of truth will guide you to all truth.

✠   **A reading from the holy Gospel according to John**

Jesus said to his disciples:
"Now I am going to the one who sent me,
  and not one of you asks me, 'Where are you going?'
But because I told you this, grief has filled your hearts.
But I tell you the truth, it is better for you that I go.
For if I do not go, the Advocate will not come to you.
But if I go, I will send him to you.

"I have much more to tell you, but you cannot bear it now.
But when he comes, the Spirit of truth,
  he will guide you to all truth."

The Gospel of the Lord.

5. FIRST COMMUNION FOR CHILDREN

769

Readings may be taken either in whole or in part from the Mass of the day, or from the Mass of Christian Initiation (nos. 751–755), or from the votive Mass of the Holy Eucharist (nos. 976–981).

II. FOR THE CONFERRAL OF HOLY ORDERS

770 READING FROM THE OLD TESTAMENT

First Option (For Deacons)

Numbers 3:5-9   Summon the tribe of Levi and present them to Aaron the priest, as his assistants.

A reading from the Book of Numbers

The LORD said to Moses:
"Summon the tribe of Levi
  and present them to Aaron the priest, as his assistants.
They shall discharge his obligations
  and those of the whole community
    before the meeting tent by serving at the Dwelling.
They shall have custody of all the furnishings of the meeting tent
  and discharge the duties of the children of Israel
    in the service of the Dwelling.
You shall give the Levites to Aaron and his sons;
  they have been set aside from among the children of Israel
    as dedicated to me."

The word of the Lord.

Second Option (For Priests)

Numbers 11:11b-12, 14-17, 24-25   I will take some of the Spirit that is on you and I will bestow it on them.

A reading from the Book of Numbers

Moses asked the LORD:
"Why are you so displeased with me
  that you burden me with all this people?
Was it I who conceived all this people?
Or was it I who gave them birth,
  that you tell me to carry them at my bosom,
  like a foster father carrying an infant,
  to the land you have promised under oath to their fathers?
I cannot carry all this people by myself,
  for they are too heavy for me.
If this is the way you will deal with me,
  then please do me the favor of killing me at once,
  so that I need no longer face this distress."

Then the L<small>ORD</small> said to Moses,
   "Assemble for me seventy of the elders of Israel,
     men you know for true elders and authorities among the people,
     and bring them to the meeting tent.
When they are in place beside you,
     I will come down and speak with you there.
I will also take some of the Spirit that is on you
     and will bestow it on them,
     that they may share the burden of the people with you.
You will then not have to bear it by yourself."

So Moses went out and told the people what the L<small>ORD</small> had said.
Gathering seventy elders of the people,
     he had them stand around the tent.
The L<small>ORD</small> then came down in the cloud and spoke to him.
Taking some of the Spirit that was on Moses,
     he bestowed it on the seventy elders,
     and as the Spirit came to rest on them, they prophesied.

The word of the Lord.

Third Option (For Bishops and Priests)

Isaiah 61:1-3abcd   The L<small>ORD</small> has anointed me; he has sent me to bring glad tidings to the lowly and to give them the oil of gladness.

A reading from the Book of the Prophet Isaiah

The Spirit of the Lord G<small>OD</small> is upon me,
     because the L<small>ORD</small> has anointed me;
He has sent me to bring glad tidings to the lowly,
     to heal the brokenhearted,
To proclaim liberty to the captives
     and release to the prisoners,
To announce a year of favor from the L<small>ORD</small>
     and a day of vindication by our God,
     to comfort all who mourn;
To place on those who mourn in Zion
     a diadem instead of ashes,
To give them oil of gladness in place of mourning,
     a glorious mantle instead of a listless spirit.

The word of the Lord.

Fourth Option

Jeremiah 1:4-9   To whomever I send you, you shall go.

A reading from the Book of the Prophet Jeremiah

The word of the LORD **came to me thus:**

Before I formed you in the womb I knew you,
before you were born I dedicated you,
a prophet to the nations I appointed you.

"Ah, Lord GOD**!" I said,**
"I know not how to speak; I am too young."

But the LORD **answered me,**

Say not, "I am too young."
To whomever I send you, you shall go;
whatever I command you, you shall speak.
Have no fear before them,
because I am with you to deliver you, says the LORD**.**

Then the LORD **extended his hand and touched my mouth, saying,**
See, I place my words in your mouth!

The word of the Lord.

771 READING FROM THE NEW TESTAMENT

1. (For Deacons)

Acts 6:1-7b   Select from among you seven reputable men.

A reading from the Acts of the Apostles

As the number of disciples continued to grow,
 the Hellenists complained against the Hebrews
 because their widows were being neglected in the daily distribution.
So the Twelve called together the community of the disciples and said,
 "It is not right for us to neglect the word of God to serve at table.
Brothers, select from among you seven reputable men,
 filled with the Spirit and wisdom,
 whom we shall appoint to this task,
 whereas we shall devote ourselves to prayer
 and to the ministry of the word."
The proposal was acceptable to the whole community,
 so they chose Stephen, a man filled with faith and the Holy Spirit,
 also Philip, Prochorus, Nicanor, Timon, Parmenas,
 and Nicholas of Antioch, a convert to Judaism.
They presented these men to the Apostles
 who prayed and laid hands on them.
The word of God continued to spread,
 and the number of the disciples in Jerusalem increased greatly.

The word of the Lord.

2. (For Deacons)

Acts 8:26-40   Beginning with this Scripture passage, Philip proclaimed Jesus to him.

A reading from the Acts of the Apostles

The angel of the Lord spoke to Philip,
   "Get up and head south on the road
   that goes down from Jerusalem to Gaza, the desert route."
So he got up and set out.
Now there was an Ethiopian eunuch,
   a court official of the Candace,
   that is, the queen of the Ethiopians,
   in charge of her entire treasury,
   who had come to Jerusalem to worship, and was returning home.
Seated in his chariot, he was reading the prophet Isaiah.
The Spirit said to Philip,
   "Go and join up with that chariot."
Philip ran up and heard him reading Isaiah the prophet and said,
   "Do you understand what you are reading?"
He replied,
   "How can I, unless someone instructs me?"
So he invited Philip to get in and sit with him.
This was the Scripture passage he was reading:

   Like a sheep he was led to the slaughter,
      and as a lamb before its shearer is silent,
         so he opened not his mouth.
   In his humiliation justice was denied him.
      Who will tell of his posterity?
         For his life is taken from the earth.

Then the eunuch said to Philip in reply,
   "I beg you, about whom is the prophet saying this?
About himself, or about someone else?"
Then Philip opened his mouth and, beginning with this Scripture passage,
   he proclaimed Jesus to him.
As they traveled along the road
   they came to some water,
   and the eunuch said, "Look, there is water.
What is to prevent my being baptized?"

Then he ordered the chariot to stop,
    and Philip and the eunuch both went down into the water,
    and he baptized him.
When they came out of the water,
    the Spirit of the Lord snatched Philip away,
    and the eunuch saw him no more,
    but continued on his way rejoicing.
Philip came to Azotus,
    and went about proclaiming the good news
    to all the towns until he reached Caesarea.

The word of the Lord.

3.

Acts 10:37-43   We are witnesses of all that he did both in the country of
the Jews and in Jerusalem.

A reading from the Acts of the Apostles

Peter proceeded to speak and said:
"You know what has happened all over Judea,
    beginning in Galilee after the baptism
    that John preached,
    how God anointed Jesus of Nazareth
    with the Holy Spirit and power.
He went about doing good
    and healing all those oppressed by the Devil,
    for God was with him.
We are witnesses of all that he did
    both in the country of the Jews and in Jerusalem.
They put him to death by hanging him on a tree.
This man God raised on the third day and granted that he be visible,
    not to all the people, but to us,
    the witnesses chosen by God in advance,
    who ate and drank with him after he rose from the dead.
He commissioned us to preach to the people
    and testify that he is the one appointed by God
    as judge of the living and the dead.
To him all the prophets bear witness,
    that everyone who believes in him
    will receive forgiveness of sins through his name."

The word of the Lord.

4. (For Bishops and Priests)

Acts 20:17-18a, 28-32, 36   Keep watch over yourselves and over the whole flock of which the Holy Spirit has appointed you overseers, in which you tend the Church of God.

A reading from the Acts of the Apostles

From Miletus Paul had the presbyters
  of the Church at Ephesus summoned.
When they came to him, he addressed them,

> **"Keep watch over yourselves and over the whole flock**
> **of which the Holy Spirit has appointed you overseers,**
> **in which you tend the Church of God**
> **that he acquired with his own Blood.**
I know that after my departure savage wolves will come among you,
  and they will not spare the flock.
And from your own group,
  men will come forward perverting the truth
  to draw the disciples away after them.
So be vigilant and remember that for three years, night and day,
  I unceasingly admonished each of you with tears.
And now I commend you to God
  and to that gracious word of his that can build you up
  and give you the inheritance among all who are consecrated."

When Paul had finished speaking
  he knelt down and prayed with them all.

The word of the Lord.

5.

Romans 12:4-8   We have gifts that differ according to the grace given to us.

A reading from the Letter of Saint Paul to the Romans

Brothers and sisters:
As in one body we have many parts,
  and all the parts do not have the same function,
  so we, though many, are one Body in Christ
  and individually parts of one another.

Since we have gifts that differ according to the grace given to us,
> let us exercise them:
> if prophecy, in proportion to the faith;
> if ministry, in ministering;
> if one is a teacher, in teaching;
> if one exhorts, in exhortation;
> if one contributes, in generosity;
> if one is over others, with diligence;
> if one does acts of mercy, with cheerfulness.

The word of the Lord.

6.

2 Corinthians 4:1-2, 5-7   For we do not preach ourselves but Jesus Christ as Lord, and ourselves as your slaves for the sake of Jesus.

A reading from the second Letter of Saint Paul to the Corinthians

Brothers and sisters:
Since we have this ministry through the mercy shown us,
> we are not discouraged.

Rather, we have renounced shameful, hidden things;
> not acting deceitfully or falsifying the word of God,
> but by the open declaration of the truth
> we commend ourselves to everyone's conscience in the sight of God.

For we do not preach ourselves but Jesus Christ as Lord,
> and ourselves as your slaves for the sake of Jesus.

For God who said, *Let light shine out of darkness,*
> has shone in our hearts to bring to light
> the knowledge of the glory of God on the face of Jesus Christ.

But we hold this treasure in earthen vessels,
> that the surpassing power may be of God and not from us.

The word of the Lord.

7.

2 Corinthians 5:14-20   He has given us the ministry of reconciliation.

A reading from the second Letter of Saint Paul to the Corinthians

Brothers and sisters:
The love of Christ impels us,
once we have come to the conviction that one died for all;
therefore, all have died.
He indeed died for all,
so that those who live might no longer live for themselves
but for him who for their sake died and was raised.

Consequently, from now on we regard no one according to the flesh;
even if we once knew Christ according to the flesh,
yet now we know him so no longer.
So whoever is in Christ is a new creation:
the old things have passed away;
behold, new things have come.
And all this is from God,
who has reconciled us to himself through Christ
and given us the ministry of reconciliation,
namely, God was reconciling the world to himself in Christ,
not counting their trespasses against them
and entrusting to us the message of reconciliation.
So we are ambassadors for Christ,
as if God were appealing through us.
We implore you on behalf of Christ,
be reconciled to God.

The word of the Lord.

8.

Ephesians 4:1-7, 11-13   In the work of ministry, in building up the Body of Christ.

A reading from the Letter of Saint Paul to the Ephesians

Brothers and sisters:
I, a prisoner for the Lord,
urge you to live in a manner worthy of the call you have received,
with all humility and gentleness, with patience,
bearing with one another through love,

striving to preserve the unity of the Spirit
through the bond of peace:
one Body and one Spirit,
as you were also called to the one hope of your call;
one Lord, one faith, one baptism;
one God and Father of all,
who is over all and through all and in all.

But grace was given to each of us
according to the measure of Christ's gift.

And he gave some as Apostles, others as prophets,
others as evangelists, others as pastors and teachers,
to equip the holy ones for the work of ministry,
for building up the Body of Christ,
until we all attain to the unity of faith
and knowledge of the Son of God, to mature manhood,
to the extent of the full stature of Christ.

The word of the Lord.

9. (For Deacons)

1 Timothy 3:8-10, 12-13   Holding fast to the mystery of the faith with a clear conscience.

A reading from the first Letter of Saint Paul to Timothy

Deacons must be dignified, not deceitful,
not addicted to drink, not greedy for sordid gain,
holding fast to the mystery of the faith with a clear conscience.
Moreover, they should be tested first;
then, if there is nothing against them,
let them serve as deacons.
Deacons may be married only once
and must manage their children and their households well.
Thus those who serve well as deacons gain good standing
and much confidence in their faith in Christ Jesus.

The word of the Lord.

10. (For Priests)

1 Timothy 4:12-16   Do not neglect the gift you have, which was conferred on you with the imposition of hands by the presbyterate.

A reading from the first Letter of Saint Paul to Timothy

Beloved:
Let no one have contempt for your youth,
   but set an example for those who believe,
   in speech, conduct, love, faith, and purity.
Until I arrive, attend to the reading, exhortation, and teaching.
Do not neglect the gift you have,
   which was conferred on you through the prophetic word
   with the imposition of hands by the presbyterate.
Be diligent in these matters, be absorbed in them,
   so that your progress may be evident to everyone.
Attend to yourself and to your teaching;
   persevere in both tasks,
   for by doing so you will save
   both yourself and those who listen to you.

The word of the Lord.

   OR (For Bishops)

1 Timothy 4:12b-16   Do not neglect the gift you have, which was conferred on you with the imposition of hands by the presbyterate.

A reading from the first Letter of Saint Paul to Timothy

Beloved:
Set an example for those who believe,
   in speech, conduct, love, faith, and purity.
Until I arrive, attend to the reading, exhortation, and teaching.
Do not neglect the gift you have,
   which was conferred on you through the prophetic word
   with the imposition of hands by the presbyterate.
Be diligent in these matters, be absorbed in them,
   so that your progress may be evident to everyone.
Attend to yourself and to your teaching;
   persevere in both tasks,
   for by doing so you will save
   both yourself and those who listen to you.

The word of the Lord.

11. (For Bishops)

2 Timothy 1:6-14   To stir into flame the gift of God that you have through the laying on of hands.

A reading from the second Letter of Saint Paul to Timothy

Beloved:
I remind you to stir into flame
    the gift of God that you have through the imposition of my hands.
For God did not give us a spirit of cowardice
    but rather of power and love and self-control.
So do not be ashamed of your testimony to our Lord,
    nor of me, a prisoner for his sake;
    but bear your share of hardship for the Gospel
    with the strength that comes from God.

He saved us and called us to a holy life,
    not according to our works
    but according to his own design
    and the grace bestowed on us in Christ Jesus before time began,
    but now made manifest
    through the appearance of our savior Christ Jesus,
    who destroyed death and brought life and immortality
    to light through the Gospel,
    for which I was appointed preacher and Apostle and teacher.
On this account I am suffering these things;
    but I am not ashamed,
    for I know him in whom I have believed
    and am confident that he is able to guard
    what has been entrusted to me until that day.
Take as your norm the sound words that you heard from me,
    in the faith and love that are in Christ Jesus.
Guard this rich trust with the help of the Holy Spirit
    that dwells within us.

The word of the Lord.

344 Forthe Conferral of Holy Orders

12.

Hebrews 5:1-10 Christ was acclaimed by God as high priest, in the line of Melchizedek.

A reading from the Letter to the Hebrews

Every high priest is taken from among men
   and made their representative before God,
     to offer gifts and sacrifices for sins.
He is able to deal patiently with the ignorant and erring,
   for he himself is beset by weakness
   and so, for this reason, must make sin offerings for himself
   as well as for the people.
No one takes this honor upon himself
   but only when called by God,
     just as Aaron was.
In the same way,
   it was not Christ who glorified himself in becoming high priest,
   but rather the one who said to him:

   You are my son:
     this day I have begotten you;

   just as he says in another place:

   You are a priest forever
     according to the order of Melchizedek.

In the days when he was in the flesh,
   he offered prayers and supplications with loud cries and tears
   to the one who was able to save him from death,
   and he was heard because of his reverence.
Son though he was, he learned obedience from what he suffered;
   and when he was made perfect,
   he became the source of eternal salvation for all who obey him,
   declared by God high priest according to the order of Melchizedek.

The word of the Lord.

13.

1 Peter 4:7b-11   As good stewards of God's varied grace.

A reading from the first Letter of Saint Peter

Beloved:
Be serious and sober-minded
    so that you will be able to pray.
Above all, let your love for one another be intense,
    because love covers a multitude of sins.
Be hospitable to one another without complaining.
As each one has received a gift, use it to serve one another
    as good stewards of God's varied grace.
Whoever preaches, let it be with the words of God;
    whoever serves, let it be with the strength that God supplies,
    so that in all things God may be glorified through Jesus Christ,
    to whom belong glory and dominion forever and ever. Amen.

The word of the Lord.

14.

1 Peter 5:1-4   Tend the flock of God in your midst.

A reading from the first Letter of Saint Peter

Beloved:
I exhort the presbyters among you,
    as a fellow presbyter and witness to the sufferings of Christ
    and one who has a share in the glory to be revealed.
Tend the flock of God in your midst,
    overseeing it not by constraint but willingly,
    as God would have it,
    not for shameful profit but eagerly.
Do not lord it over those assigned to you,
    but be examples to the flock.
And when the chief Shepherd is revealed,
    you will receive the unfading crown of glory.

The word of the Lord.

772 RESPONSORIAL PSALM

1.

Psalm 23:1-3, 4, 5, 6

℟. (1) **The Lord is my shepherd; there is nothing I shall want.**

The LORD is my shepherd; I shall not want.
   In verdant pastures he gives me repose;
Beside restful waters he leads me;
   he refreshes my soul.

℟. **The Lord is my shepherd; there is nothing I shall want.**

He guides me in right paths
   for his name's sake.
Even though I walk in the dark valley
   I fear no evil; for you are at my side
With your rod and your staff
   that give me courage.

℟. **The Lord is my shepherd; there is nothing I shall want.**

You spread the table before me
   in the sight of my foes;
You anoint my head with oil;
   my cup overflows.

℟. **The Lord is my shepherd; there is nothing I shall want.**

Only goodness and kindness follow me
   all the days of my life;
And I shall dwell in the house of the LORD
   for years to come.

℟. **The Lord is my shepherd; there is nothing I shall want.**

2.

Psalm 84:3-4, 5, 11

R̸. (5a) **Blessed are they who dwell in your house, O Lord.**

My soul yearns and pines
for the courts of the Lᴏʀᴅ.
My heart and my flesh
cry out for the living God.
Even the sparrow finds a home,
and the swallow a nest
in which she puts her young—
Your altars, O Lᴏʀᴅ of hosts,
my king and my God!

R̸. **Blessed are they who dwell in your house, O Lord.**

Blessed they who dwell in your house!
continually they praise you.

R̸. **Blessed are they who dwell in your house, O Lord.**

I had rather one day in your courts
than a thousand elsewhere;
I had rather lie at the threshold of the house of my God
than dwell in the tents of the wicked.

R̸. **Blessed are they who dwell in your house, O Lord.**

3.

Psalm 89:21-22, 25 and 27

R̸. (2a) **For ever I will sing the goodness of the Lord.**

"I have found David, my servant;
with my holy oil I have anointed him,
That my hand may be always with him,
and that my arm may make him strong."

R̸. **For ever I will sing the goodness of the Lord.**

"My faithfulness and my mercy shall be with him,
and through my name shall his horn be exalted.
He shall say of me, 'You are my father,
my God, the Rock, my savior.'"

R̸. **For ever I will sing the goodness of the Lord.**

4.

Psalm 96:1-2a, 2b-3, 10

R⁊. (see Matthew 28:19) **Go out to the world and teach all nations, alleluia.**

Sing to the LORD a new song;
  sing to the LORD, all you lands.
Sing to the LORD; bless his name.

R⁊. **Go out to the world and teach all nations, alleluia.**

Announce his salvation, day after day.
Tell his glory among the nations;
  among all peoples, his wondrous deeds.

R⁊. **Go out to the world and teach all nations, alleluia.**

Say among the nations: The LORD is king.
He has made the world firm, not to be moved;
  he governs the peoples with equity.

R⁊. **Go out to the world and teach all nations, alleluia.**

5.

Psalm 100:1b-2, 3, 4, 5

R⁊. (John 15:14) **You are my friends, says the Lord, if you do what I command you.**

Sing joyfully to the LORD, all you lands;
  serve the LORD with gladness;
  come before him with joyful song.

R⁊. **You are my friends, says the Lord, if you do what I command you.**

Know that the LORD is God;
  he made us, his we are;
  his people, the flock he tends.

R⁊. **You are my friends, says the Lord, if you do what I command you.**

Enter his gates with thanksgiving,
  his courts with praise;
Give thanks to him; bless his name.

R⁊. **You are my friends, says the Lord, if you do what I command you.**

For he is good:
  the LORD**, whose kindness endures forever,**
  and his faithfulness, to all generations.

R̶. **You are my friends, says the Lord, if you do what I command you.**

  6.

Psalm 110:1, 2, 3, 4

R̶. **Christ the Lord, a priest for ever in the line of Melchizedek, offered bread and wine.**
  or:
R̶. **(4b) You are a priest for ever, in the line of Melchizedek.**

The LORD **said to my Lord: "Sit at my right hand**
  till I make your enemies your footstool."

R̶. **Christ the Lord, a priest for ever in the line of Melchizedek, offered bread and wine.**
  or:
R̶. **You are a priest for ever, in the line of Melchizedek.**

The scepter of your power the LORD **will stretch forth from Zion:**
  "Rule in the midst of your enemies."

R̶. **Christ the Lord, a priest for ever in the line of Melchizedek, offered bread and wine.**
  or:
R̶. **You are a priest for ever, in the line of Melchizedek.**

"Yours is princely power in the day of your birth, in holy splendor;
  before the daystar, like the dew, I have begotten you."

R̶. **Christ the Lord, a priest for ever in the line of Melchizedek, offered bread and wine.**
  or:
R̶. **You are a priest for ever, in the line of Melchizedek.**

The LORD **has sworn, and he will not repent:**
  "You are a priest forever, according to the order of Melchizedek."

R̶. **Christ the Lord, a priest for ever in the line of Melchizedek, offered bread and wine.**
  or:
R̶. **You are a priest for ever, in the line of Melchizedek.**

7.

Psalm 116:12-13, 17-18

℟. (see 1 Corinthians 10:16) **Our blessing-cup is a communion with the Blood of Christ.**
   or:
℟. **Alleluia.**

How shall I make a return to the Lord
   for all the good he has done for me?
The cup of salvation I will take up,
   and I will call upon the name of the Lord.

℟. **Our blessing-cup is a communion with the Blood of Christ.**
   or:
℟. **Alleluia.**

To you will I offer sacrifice of thanksgiving,
   and I will call upon the name of the Lord.
My vows to the Lord I will pay
   in the presence of all his people.

℟. **Our blessing-cup is a communion with the Blood of Christ.**
   or:
℟. **Alleluia.**

8.

Psalm 117:1, 2

℟. (Mark 16:15) **Go out to all the world and tell the Good News.**
   or:
℟. **Alleluia.**

Praise the Lord, all you nations,
   glorify him, all you peoples!

℟. **Go out to all the world and tell the Good News.**
   or:
℟. **Alleluia.**

For steadfast is his kindness toward us,
   and the fidelity of the Lord endures forever.

℟. **Go out to all the world and tell the Good News.**
   or:
℟. **Alleluia.**

773 ALLELUIA VERSE AND VERSE BEFORE THE GOSPEL

1.

Matthew 28:19a, 20b

Go and teach all nations, says the Lord;
I am with you always, until the end of the world.

2.

Luke 4:18

The Lord sent me to bring glad tidings to the poor
and to proclaim liberty to captives.

3.

John 10:14

I am the good shepherd, says the Lord;
I know my sheep, and mine know me.

4.

John 15:15b

I call you my friends, says the Lord,
for I have made known to you all that the Father has told me.

774 GOSPEL

1.

Matthew 5:13-16   You are the light of the world.

✠ **A reading from the holy Gospel according to Matthew**

Jesus said to his disciples:
"You are the salt of the earth.
But if salt loses its taste, with what can it be seasoned?
It is no longer good for anything
   but to be thrown out and trampled underfoot.
You are the light of the world.
A city set on a mountain cannot be hidden.
Nor do they light a lamp and then put it under a bushel basket;
   it is set on a lampstand,
   where it gives light to all in the house.
Just so, your light must shine before others,
   that they may see your good deeds
   and glorify your heavenly Father."

The Gospel of the Lord.

2.

Matthew 9:35-38   Ask the master of the harvest to send out laborers for his harvest.

✠ **A reading from the holy Gospel according to Matthew**

Jesus went around to all the towns and villages,
   teaching in their synagogues,
   proclaiming the Gospel of the Kingdom,
   and curing every disease and illness.
At the sight of the crowds, his heart was moved with pity for them
   because they were troubled and abandoned,
   like sheep without a shepherd.
Then he said to his disciples,
   "The harvest is abundant but the laborers are few;
   so ask the master of the harvest
   to send out laborers for his harvest."

The Gospel of the Lord.

3.

Matthew 10:1-5a   Jesus chose twelve Apostles and sent them out.

✠ **A reading from the holy Gospel according to Matthew**

Jesus summoned his Twelve disciples
   and gave them authority over unclean spirits to drive them out
   and to cure every disease and every illness.
The names of the Twelve Apostles are these:
   first, Simon called Peter, and his brother Andrew;
   James, the son of Zebedee, and his brother John;
   Philip and Bartholomew,
   Thomas and Matthew the tax collector;
   James, the son of Alphaeus, and Thaddeus;
   Simon the Cananean, and Judas Iscariot
   who betrayed him.

Jesus sent out these Twelve after instructing them.

The Gospel of the Lord.

4.

Matthew 20:25b-28   Whoever wishes to be first among you shall be
your slave.

✠ **A reading from the holy Gospel according to Matthew**

Jesus summoned his disciples and said to them:
"You know that the rulers of the Gentiles lord it over them,
   and the great ones make their authority over them felt.
But it shall not be so among you.
Rather, whoever wishes to be great among you shall be your servant;
   whoever wishes to be first among you shall be your slave.
Just so, the Son of Man did not come to be served
   but to serve and to give his life as a ransom for many."

The Gospel of the Lord.

5.

Luke 10:1-9   The harvest is abundant but the laborers are few.

✝ **A reading from the holy Gospel according to Luke**

The Lord Jesus appointed seventy-two other disciples
   whom he sent ahead of him in pairs
   to every town and place he intended to visit.
He said to them,
   "The harvest is abundant but the laborers are few;
   so ask the master of the harvest
   to send out laborers for his harvest.
Go on your way;
   behold, I am sending you like lambs among wolves.
Carry no money bag, no sack, no sandals;
   and greet no one along the way.
Into whatever house you enter,
   first say, 'Peace to this household.'
If a peaceful person lives there,
   your peace will rest on him;
   but if not, it will return to you.
Stay in the same house and eat and drink what is offered to you,
   for the laborer deserves payment.
Do not move about from one house to another.
Whatever town you enter and they welcome you,
   eat what is set before you,
   cure the sick in it and say to them,
   'The Kingdom of God is at hand for you.'"

The Gospel of the Lord.

6.

Luke 12:35-44   Blessed are those servants whom the master finds awake on his arrival.

✝ **A reading from the holy Gospel according to Luke**

Jesus said to his disciples:
"Gird your loins and light your lamps
   and be like servants who await their master's return from a wedding,
   ready to open immediately when he comes and knocks.
Blessed are those servants
   whom the master finds vigilant on his arrival.
Amen, I say to you, he will gird himself,
   have them recline at table, and proceed to wait on them.
And should he come in the second or third watch
   and find them prepared in this way,
   blessed are those servants.
Be sure of this:
   if the master of the house had known the hour
   when the thief was coming,
   he would not have let his house be broken into.
You also must be prepared, for at an hour you do not expect,
   the Son of Man will come."

Then Peter said,
   "Lord, is this parable meant for us or for everyone?"
And the Lord replied,
   "Who, then, is the faithful and prudent steward
   whom the master will put in charge of his servants
   to distribute the food allowance at the proper time?
Blessed is that servant whom his master on arrival finds doing so.
Truly, I say to you, he will put the servant
   in charge of all his property."

The Gospel of the Lord.

7.

Luke 22:14-20, 24-30   Do this in memory of me. I am among you as the one who serves.

☩ **A reading from the holy Gospel according to Luke**

When the hour came,
   Jesus took his place at table with the Apostles.
He said to them,
   "I have eagerly desired to eat this Passover with you before I suffer,
   for, I tell you, I shall not eat it again
   until there is fulfillment in the Kingdom of God."
Then he took a cup, gave thanks, and said,
   "Take this and share it among yourselves;
   for I tell you that from this time on
   I shall not drink of the fruit of the vine
   until the Kingdom of God comes."
Then he took the bread, said the blessing,
   broke it, and gave it to them, saying,
   "This is my Body, which will be given for you;
   do this in memory of me."
And likewise the cup after they had eaten, saying,
   "This cup is the new covenant in my Blood,
   which will be shed for you."

Then an argument broke out among them
   about which of them should be regarded as the greatest.
He said to them,
   "The kings of the Gentiles lord it over them
   and those in authority over them are addressed as 'Benefactors';
   but among you it shall not be so.
Rather, let the greatest among you be as the youngest,
   and the leader as the servant.
For who is greater:
   the one seated at table or the one who serves?
Is it not the one seated at table?
I am among you as the one who serves.
It is you who have stood by me in my trials;
   and I confer a kingdom on you,
   just as my Father has conferred one on me,
   that you may eat and drink at my table in my Kingdom;

**and you will sit on thrones
judging the twelve tribes of Israel.”**

The Gospel of the Lord.

8.

John 10:11-16   A good shepherd lays down his life for the sheep.

✢ **A reading from the holy Gospel according to John**

**Jesus said:
“I am the good shepherd.
A good shepherd lays down his life for the sheep.
A hired man, who is not a shepherd
   and whose sheep are not his own,
   sees a wolf coming and leaves the sheep and runs away,
   and the wolf catches and scatters them.
This is because he works for pay and has no concern for the sheep.
I am the good shepherd,
   and I know mine and mine know me,
   just as the Father knows me and I know the Father;
   and I will lay down my life for the sheep.
I have other sheep that do not belong to this fold.
These also I must lead, and they will hear my voice,
   and there will be one flock, one shepherd.”**

The Gospel of the Lord.

9.

John 12:24-26   Whoever serves me must follow me.

✠   **A reading from the holy Gospel according to John**

Jesus answered Andrew and Philip, saying:
"Amen, amen, I say to you,
    unless a grain of wheat falls to the ground and dies,
    it remains just a grain of wheat;
    but if it dies, it produces much fruit.
Whoever loves his life loses it,
    and whoever hates his life in this world
    will preserve it for eternal life.
Whoever serves me must follow me,
    and where I am, there also will my servant be.
The Father will honor whoever serves me."

The Gospel of the Lord.

10.

John 15:9-17   It was not you who chose me, but I who chose you.

✠   **A reading from the holy Gospel according to John**

Jesus said to his disciples:
"As the Father loves me, so I also love you.
Remain in my love.
If you keep my commandments, you will remain in my love,
    just as I have kept my Father's commandments
    and remain in his love.

"I have told you this so that my joy may be in you
    and your joy may be complete.
This is my commandment: love one another as I love you.
No one has greater love than this,
    to lay down one's life for one's friends.
You are my friends if you do what I command you.
I no longer call you slaves,
    because a slave does not know what his master is doing.
I have called you friends,
    because I have told you everything I have heard from my Father.

It was not you who chose me, but I who chose you
  and appointed you to go and bear fruit that will remain,
  so that whatever you ask the Father in my name he may give you.
This I command you: love one another."

The Gospel of the Lord.

11.

John 17:6, 14-19   I consecrate myself for them, so that they also may be
consecrated in truth.

✠ **A reading from the holy Gospel according to John**

Jesus raised his eyes to heaven and prayed, saying:
"Holy Father, I revealed your name
  to those whom you gave me out of the world.
They belonged to you and you gave them to me,
  and they have kept your word.
I gave them your word, and the world hated them,
  because they do not belong to the world
  any more than I belong to the world.
I do not ask that you take them out of the world
  but that you keep them from the Evil One.
They do not belong to the world
  any more than I belong to the world.
Consecrate them in the truth.
Your word is truth.
As you sent me into the world,
  so I sent them into the world.
And I consecrate myself for them,
  so that they also may be consecrated in truth."

The Gospel of the Lord.

12.

John 20:19-23   As the Father has sent me, so I send you. Receive the Holy Spirit.

✠ **A reading from the holy Gospel according to John**

On the evening of that first day of the week,
  when the doors were locked, where the disciples were,
  for fear of the Jews,
  Jesus came and stood in their midst
  and said to them, "Peace be with you."
When he had said this, he showed them his hands and his side.
The disciples rejoiced when they saw the Lord.
Jesus said to them again, "Peace be with you.
As the Father has sent me, so I send you."
And when he had said this, he breathed on them and said to them,
  "Receive the Holy Spirit.
Whose sins you forgive are forgiven them,
  and whose sins you retain are retained."

The Gospel of the Lord.

13.

John 21:15-17   Feed my lambs, feed my sheep.

✠ **A reading from the holy Gospel according to John**

After Jesus had revealed himself to his disciples
  and eaten breakfast with them, he said to Simon Peter,
  "Simon, son of John, do you love me more than these?"
Simon Peter answered him, "Yes, Lord, you know that I love you."
Jesus said to him, "Feed my lambs."
He then said to Simon Peter a second time,
  "Simon, son of John, do you love me?"
Simon Peter answered him, "Yes, Lord, you know that I love you."
He said to him, "Tend my sheep."
He said to him the third time,
  "Simon, son of John, do you love me?"
Peter was distressed that he had said to him a third time,
  "Do you love me?" and he said to him,
  "Lord, you know everything; you know that I love you."
Jesus said to him, "Feed my sheep."

The Gospel of the Lord.

III. FOR THE ADMISSION TO CANDIDACY FOR THE DIACONATE AND THE PRIESTHOOD

775 READING FROM THE OLD TESTAMENT

First Option

Deuteronomy 1:9-14   Choose wise, intelligent, and experienced men from each of your tribes, that I may appoint them as your leaders.

A reading from the Book of Deuteronomy

Moses summoned all of Israel and said to them:
"Alone, I am unable to carry you.
The Lord, your God, has so multiplied you
  that you are now as numerous as the stars in the sky.
May the Lord, the God of your fathers,
  increase you a thousand times over,
  and bless you as he promised!
But how can I alone bear the crushing burden that you are,
  along with your bickering?
Choose wise, intelligent, and experienced men from each of your tribes,
  that I may appoint them as your leaders."
They answered, "We agree to do as you have proposed."

The word of the Lord.

Second Option

Sirach 39:1b, 5-8   He will give his heart early to the Lord, his maker.

A reading from the Book of Sirach

The one who studies the law of God
  explores the wisdom of the men of old
  and occupies himself with the prophecies.
He travels among the peoples of foreign lands
  to learn what is good and evil among men.

He will give his heart early to the Lord, his Maker,
  to petition the Most High,
  to open his lips in prayer,
  to ask pardon for his sins.
Then, if it pleases the Lord Almighty,
  he will be filled with the spirit of understanding.

The word of the Lord.

Third Option

Isaiah 6:1-2a, 3-8   Whom shall I send? Who will go for us?

A reading from the Book of the Prophet Isaiah

In the year King Uzziah died,
   I saw the Lord seated on a high and lofty throne,
   with the train of his garment filling the temple.
Seraphim were stationed above.

They cried one to the other,
   "Holy, holy, holy is the Lord of hosts!
All the earth is filled with his glory!"
At the sound of that cry, the frame of the door shook
   and the house was filled with smoke.

Then I said, "Woe is me, I am doomed!
For I am a man of unclean lips,
   living among a people of unclean lips;
   yet my eyes have seen the King, the Lord of hosts!"
Then one of the seraphim flew to me,
   holding an ember which he had taken with tongs from the altar.

He touched my mouth with it,
   "See," he said, "now that this has touched your lips,
   your wickedness is removed, your sin purged."

Then I heard the voice of the Lord saying,
   "Whom shall I send? Who will go for us?"
"Here I am," I said; "send me!"

The word of the Lord.

Fourth Option

Jeremiah 1:4-9   To whomever I send you, you shall go.

A reading from the Book of the Prophet Jeremiah

The word of the LORD came to me thus:

> **Before I formed you in the womb I knew you,**
> **before you were born I dedicated you,**
> **a prophet to the nations I appointed you.**

> **"Ah, Lord GOD!" I said,**
> **"I know not how to speak; I am too young."**

But the LORD answered me,

> **Say not, "I am too young."**
> **To whomever I send you, you shall go;**
> **whatever I command you, you shall speak.**
> **Have no fear before them,**
> **because I am with you to deliver you, says the LORD.**

Then the LORD extended his hand and touched my mouth, saying,
> **See, I place my words in your mouth!**

The word of the Lord.

776 READING FROM THE NEW TESTAMENT

First Option

Acts 14:21-23   They appointed presbyters for them in each Church.

A reading from the Acts of the Apostles

Paul and Barnabas returned to Lystra and to Iconium
   and to Antioch.
They strengthened the spirits of the disciples
   and exhorted them to persevere in the faith, saying,
   "It is necessary for us to undergo many hardships
   to enter the Kingdom of God."
They appointed presbyters for them in each Church and,
   with prayer and fasting, commended them to the Lord
   in whom they had put their faith.

The word of the Lord.

Second Option

1 Corinthians 9:16-19, 22-23   Woe to me if I do not preach the Gospel!

A reading from the first Letter of Saint Paul to the Corinthians

Brothers and sisters:
If I preach the Gospel, this is no reason for me to boast,
   for an obligation has been imposed on me,
   and woe to me if I do not preach it!
If I do so willingly, I have a recompense,
   but if unwillingly, then I have been entrusted with a stewardship.
What then is my recompense?
That, when I preach,
   I offer the Gospel free of charge
   so as not to make full use of my right in the Gospel.
Although I am free in regard to all,
   I have made myself a slave to all
   so as to win over as many as possible.
To the weak I became weak, to win over the weak.
I have become all things to all, to save at least some.
All this I do for the sake of the Gospel,
   so that I too may have a share in it.

The word of the Lord.

Third Option

1 Corinthians 12:4-11   To each individual the manifestation of the Spirit is given for some benefit.

A reading from the first Letter of Saint Paul to the Corinthians

Brothers and sisters:
There are different kinds of spiritual gifts but the same Spirit;
  there are different forms of service but the same Lord;
  there are different workings but the same God
  who produces all of them in everyone.
To each individual the manifestation of the Spirit
  is given for some benefit.
To one is given through the Spirit the expression of wisdom;
  to another the expression of knowledge according to the same Spirit;
  to another faith by the same Spirit;
  to another gifts of healing by the one Spirit;
  to another mighty deeds;
  to another prophecy;
  to another discernment of spirits;
  to another varieties of tongues;
  to another interpretation of tongues.
But one and the same Spirit produces all of these,
  distributing them individually to each person as he wishes.

The word of the Lord.

Fourth Option

2 Timothy 3:10-12, 14-15   Remain faithful to what you have learned.

A reading from the second Letter of Saint Paul to Timothy

Beloved:
You have followed my teaching, way of life,
  purpose, faith, patience, love, endurance, persecutions,
  and sufferings, such as happened to me
  in Antioch, Iconium, and Lystra,
  persecutions that I endured.
Yet from all these things the Lord delivered me.
In fact, all who want to live religiously in Christ Jesus
  will be persecuted.
But you, remain faithful to what you have learned and believed,
  because you know from whom you learned it,
  and that from infancy you have known the sacred Scriptures,
  which are capable of giving you wisdom for salvation
  through faith in Christ Jesus.

The word of the Lord.

777 RESPONSORIAL PSALM

First Option

Psalm 16:1b-2a and 5, 7-8, 11

℟. (see 5a) **You are my inheritance, O Lord.**

Keep me, O God, for in you I take refuge;
  I say to the LORD, "My Lord are you."
O LORD, my allotted portion and my cup,
  you it is who hold fast my lot.

℟. **You are my inheritance, O Lord.**

I bless the LORD who counsels me;
  even in the night my heart exhorts me.
I set the LORD ever before me;
  with him at my right hand I shall not be disturbed.

℟. **You are my inheritance, O Lord.**

You will show me the path to life,
  fullness of joys in your presence,
  the delights at your right hand forever.

℟. **You are my inheritance, O Lord.**

Second Option

Psalm 24:1bc-2, 3-4ab, 5-6

℟. (see 6) **Lord, this is the people that longs to see your face.**

The LORD's are the earth and its fullness;
  the world and those who dwell in it.
For he founded it upon the seas
  and established it upon the rivers.

℟. **Lord, this is the people that longs to see your face.**

Who can ascend the mountain of the LORD?
  or who may stand in his holy place?
He whose hands are sinless, whose heart is clean,
  who desires not what is vain.

(cont.)

R̂. **Lord, this is the people that longs to see your face.**

He shall receive a blessing from the LORD,
  a reward from God his savior.
Such is the race that seeks for him,
  that seeks the face of the God of Jacob.

R̂. **Lord, this is the people that longs to see your face.**

Third Option

Psalm 98:1, 2-3ab, 3cd-4, 5-6

R̂. (see 2b) **The Lord has revealed to the nations his saving power.**

Sing to the LORD a new song,
  for he has done wondrous deeds;
His right hand has won victory for him,
  his holy arm.

R̂. **The Lord has revealed to the nations his saving power.**

The LORD has made his salvation known:
  in the sight of the nations he has revealed his justice.
He has remembered his kindness and his faithfulness
  toward the house of Israel.

R̂. **The Lord has revealed to the nations his saving power.**

All the ends of the earth have seen
  the salvation by our God.
Sing joyfully to the LORD, all you lands;
  break into song; sing praise.

R̂. **The Lord has revealed to the nations his saving power.**

Sing praise to the LORD with the harp,
  with the harp and melodious song.
With trumpets and the sound of the horn
  sing joyfully before the King, the LORD.

R̂. **The Lord has revealed to the nations his saving power.**

778 ALLELUIA VERSE AND VERSE BEFORE THE GOSPEL

1.

Mark 1:17

**Come after me, says the Lord,
and I will make you fishers of men.**

2.

Luke 4:18

**The Lord sent me to bring glad tidings to the poor,
and to proclaim liberty to captives.**

3.

John 12:26

**Whoever serves me must follow me, says the Lord;
and where I am, there also will my servant be.**

779 GOSPEL

1.

Matthew 9:35-38   Ask the master of the harvest to send out laborers for his harvest.

✝ **A reading from the holy Gospel according to Matthew**

**Jesus went around to all the towns and villages,
    teaching in their synagogues,
    proclaiming the Gospel of the Kingdom,
    and curing every disease and illness.
At the sight of the crowds, his heart was moved with pity for them
    because they were troubled and abandoned,
    like sheep without a shepherd.
Then he said to his disciples,
    "The harvest is abundant but the laborers are few;
    so ask the master of the harvest
    to send out laborers for his harvest."**

The Gospel of the Lord.

2.

Mark 1:14-20   I will make you fishers of men.

✝ **A reading from the holy Gospel according to Mark**

**After John the Baptist had been arrested,
    Jesus came to Galilee proclaiming the Gospel of God:
    "This is the time of fulfillment.
The Kingdom of God is at hand.
Repent, and believe in the Gospel."**

**As he passed by the Sea of Galilee,
    he saw Simon and his brother Andrew casting their nets into the sea;
    they were fishermen.
Jesus said to them,
    "Come after me, and I will make you fishers of men."
Then they left their nets and followed him.
He walked along a little farther
    and saw James, the son of Zebedee, and his brother John.
They too were in a boat mending their nets.
Then he called them.**

So they left their father Zebedee in the boat
along with the hired men and followed him.

The Gospel of the Lord.

3.

Luke 5:1-11   At your command I will lower the nets.

✠ **A reading from the holy Gospel according to Luke**

While the crowd was pressing in on Jesus and listening to the word of God,
he was standing by the Lake of Gennesaret.
He saw two boats there alongside the lake;
the fishermen had disembarked and were washing their nets.
Getting into one of the boats, the one belonging to Simon,
he asked him to put out a short distance from the shore.
Then he sat down and taught the crowds from the boat.
After he had finished speaking, he said to Simon,
"Put out into deep water and lower your nets for a catch."
Simon said in reply,
"Master, we have worked hard all night and have caught nothing,
but at your command I will lower the nets."
When they had done this, they caught a great number of fish
and their nets were tearing.
They signaled to their partners in the other boat
to come to help them.
They came and filled both boats
so that they were in danger of sinking.
When Simon Peter saw this, he fell at the knees of Jesus and said,
"Depart from me, Lord, for I am a sinful man."
For astonishment at the catch of fish they had made seized him
and all those with him,
and likewise James and John, the sons of Zebedee,
who were partners of Simon.
Jesus said to Simon, "Do not be afraid;
from now on you will be catching men."
When they brought their boats to the shore,
they left everything and followed him.

The word of the Lord.

4.

John 1:35-42   Behold the Lamb of God. We have found the Messiah.

✠   **A reading from the holy Gospel according to John**

John was standing with two of his disciples,
   and as he watched Jesus walk by, he said,
   "Behold, the Lamb of God."
The two disciples of John heard what he said and followed Jesus.
Jesus turned and saw them following him and said to them,
   "What are you looking for?"
They said to him, "Rabbi" (which translated means Teacher),
   "where are you staying?"
He said to them, "Come, and you will see."
So they went and saw where he was staying,
   and they stayed with him that day.
It was about four in the afternoon.
Andrew, the brother of Simon Peter,
   was one of the two who heard John and followed Jesus.
He first found his own brother Simon and told him,
   "We have found the Messiah" (which is translated Christ).
Then he brought him to Jesus.
Jesus looked at him and said,
   "You are Simon the son of John;
   you will be called Cephas" (which is translated Peter).

The Gospel of the Lord.

5.

John 1:45-51   Here is a true child of Israel. There is no duplicity in him.

✠ **A reading from the holy Gospel according to John**

Philip found Nathanael and told him,
> **"We have found the one about whom Moses wrote in the law,**
> **and also the prophets, Jesus, son of Joseph, from Nazareth."**

But Nathanael said to him,
> **"Can anything good come from Nazareth?"**

Philip said to him, "Come and see."

Jesus saw Nathanael coming toward him and said of him,
> **"Here is a true child of Israel.**

There is no duplicity in him."

Nathanael said to him, "How do you know me?"

Jesus answered and said to him,
> **"Before Philip called you, I saw you under the fig tree."**

Nathanael answered him,
> **"Rabbi, you are the Son of God; you are the King of Israel."**

Jesus answered and said to him,
> **"Do you believe**
> **because I told you that I saw you under the fig tree?**

You will see greater things than this."

And he said to him,
> **"Amen, amen, I say to you, you will see heaven opened**
> **and the angels of God ascending and descending on the Son of Man."**

The Gospel of the Lord.

IV. FOR THE CONFERRAL OF MINISTRIES

1. INSTITUTION OF READERS

780 READING FROM THE OLD TESTAMENT

First Option

Deuteronomy 6:3-9   Take to heart these words.

A reading from the Book of Deuteronomy

Moses said to the people of Israel:
"Hear, Israel, and be careful to observe these commandments,
that you may grow and prosper the more,
in keeping with the promise of the LORD, the God of your fathers,
to give you a land flowing with milk and honey.

"Hear, O Israel! The LORD is our God, the LORD alone!
Therefore, you shall love the LORD, your God,
with all your heart,
and with all your soul,
and with all your strength.
Take to heart these words which I enjoin on you today.
Drill them into your children.
Speak of them at home and abroad, whether you are busy or at rest.
Bind them at your wrist as a sign
and let them be as a pendant on your forehead.
Write them on the doorposts of your houses and on your gates."

The word of the Lord.

Second Option

Deuteronomy 30:10-14   It is something very near to you. You have only
to carry it out.

A reading from the Book of Deuteronomy

Moses said to the people:
"Heed the voice of the LORD, your God,
   and keep his commandments and statutes
   that are written in this book of the law,
   when you return to the LORD, your God,
   with all your heart and all your soul.

"For this command which I enjoin on you today
   is not too mysterious and remote for you.
It is not up in the sky, that you should say,
   'Who will go up in the sky to get it for us
   and tell us of it, that we may carry it out?'
Nor is it across the sea, that you should say,
   'Who will cross the sea to get it for us
   and tell us of it, that we may carry it out?'
No, it is something very near to you,
   already in your mouths and in your hearts;
   you have only to carry it out."

The word of the Lord.

Third Option

Nehemiah 8:2-4a, 5-6, 8-10   Ezra read plainly from the book of the law, interpreting it.

A reading from the Book of Nehemiah

Ezra the priest brought the law before the assembly,
   which consisted of men, women,
    and those children old enough to understand.
Standing at one end of the open place that was before the Water Gate,
   he read out of the book from daybreak till midday,
    in the presence of the men, the women,
    and those children old enough to understand;
    and all the people listened attentively to the book of the law.
Ezra the scribe stood on a wooden platform
   that had been made for the occasion.
He opened the scroll
   so that all the people might see it
   (for he was standing higher up than any of the people);
    and, as he opened it, all the people rose.
Ezra blessed the LORD, the great God,
   and all the people, their hands raised high, answered,
    "Amen, amen!"
Then they bowed down and prostrated themselves before the LORD,
   their faces to the ground.
Ezra read plainly from the book of the law of God,
   interpreting it so that all could understand what was read.
Then Nehemiah, that is, His Excellency, and Ezra the priest-scribe
   and the Levites who were instructing the people
   said to all the people:
   "Today is holy to the LORD your God.
Do not be sad, and do not weep"—
   for all the people were weeping as they heard the words of the law.
He said further: "Go, eat rich foods and drink sweet drinks,
   and allot portions to those who had nothing prepared;
   for today is holy to our LORD.
Do not be saddened this day,
   for rejoicing in the LORD must be your strength!"

The word of the Lord.

Fourth Option

Isaiah 55:10-11   The rain watered the earth, making it fertile.

A reading from the Book of the Prophet Isaiah

The Lord says:
> **Just as from the heavens**
>> **the rain and snow come down**
> **And do not return there**
>> **till they have watered the earth,**
>> **making it fertile and fruitful,**
> **Giving seed to the one who sows**
>> **and bread to the one who eats,**
> **So shall my word be**
>> **that goes forth from my mouth;**
> **My word shall not return to me void,**
>> **but shall do my will,**
>> **achieving the end for which I sent it.**

The word of the Lord.

781   READING FROM THE NEW TESTAMENT

1.

1 Corinthians 2:1-5   Proclaiming the mystery of God.

A reading from the first Letter of Saint Paul to the Corinthians

When I came to you, brothers and sisters,
   proclaiming the mystery of God,
   I did not come with sublimity of words or of wisdom.
For I resolved to know nothing while I was with you
   except Jesus Christ, and him crucified.
I came to you in weakness and fear and much trembling,
   and my message and my proclamation
   were not with persuasive words of wisdom,
   but with a demonstration of spirit and power,
   so that your faith might rest not on human wisdom
   but on the power of God.

The word of the Lord.

2.

2 Timothy 3:14-17   All Scripture is inspired by God and is useful
for teaching.

A reading from the second Letter of Saint Paul to Timothy

Beloved:
Remain faithful to what you have learned and believed,
   because you know from whom you learned it,
   and that from infancy you have known the sacred Scriptures,
   which are capable of giving you wisdom for salvation
   through faith in Christ Jesus.
All Scripture is inspired by God
   and is useful for teaching, for refutation, for correction,
   and for training in righteousness,
   so that one who belongs to God may be competent,
   equipped for every good work.

The word of the Lord.

3.

2 Timothy 4:1-5   Perform the work of an evangelist; fulfill your ministry.

A reading from the second Letter of Saint Paul to Timothy

Beloved:
I charge you in the presence of God and Christ Jesus,
    who will judge the living and the dead,
    and by his appearing and his kingly power:
    proclaim the word;
    be persistent whether it is convenient or inconvenient;
    convince, reprimand, encourage through all patience and teaching.
For the time will come when people will not tolerate sound doctrine
    but, following their own desires and insatiable curiosity,
    will accumulate teachers and will stop listening to the truth
    and will be diverted to myths.
But you, be self-possessed in all circumstances;
    put up with hardship;
    perform the work of an evangelist;
    fulfill your ministry.

The word of the Lord.

4.

Hebrews 4:12-13   The word of God is able to discern reflections and thoughts of the heart.

A reading from the Letter to the Hebrews

The word of God is living and effective,
    sharper than any two-edged sword,
    penetrating even between soul and spirit, joints and marrow,
    and able to discern reflections and thoughts of the heart.
No creature is concealed from him,
    but everything is naked and exposed to the eyes of him
    to whom we must render an account.

The word of the Lord.

5.

1 John 1:1-4   What we have seen and heard we now proclaim to you.

A reading from the first Letter of Saint John

Beloved:
   What was from the beginning,
   what we have heard,
   what we have seen with our eyes,
   what we looked upon
   and touched with our hands
   concerns the Word of life—
   for the life was made visible;
   we have seen it and testify to it
   and proclaim to you the eternal life
   that was with the Father and was made visible to us—
   what we have seen and heard
   we proclaim now to you,
   so that you too may have fellowship with us;
   for our fellowship is with the Father
   and with his Son, Jesus Christ.
   We are writing this so that our joy may be complete.

The word of the Lord.

782 RESPONSORIAL PSALM

First Option

Psalm 19:8, 9, 10, 11

℟. (see John 6:63c) **Your words, Lord, are Spirit and life.**

The law of the LORD is perfect,
 refreshing the soul;
The decree of the LORD is trustworthy,
 giving wisdom to the simple.

℟. **Your words, Lord, are Spirit and life.**

The precepts of the LORD are right,
 rejoicing the heart;
The command of the LORD is clear,
 enlightening the eye.

℟. **Your words, Lord, are Spirit and life.**

The fear of the LORD is pure,
 enduring forever;
The ordinances of the LORD are true,
 all of them just.

℟. **Your words, Lord, are Spirit and life.**

They are more precious than gold,
 than a heap of purest gold;
Sweeter also than syrup
 or honey from the comb.

℟. **Your words, Lord, are Spirit and life.**

Second Option

Psalm 119:9, 10, 11, 12

℟. (12b) **Lord, teach me your statutes.**

How shall a young man be faultless in his way?
 By keeping to your words.

(cont.)

℞. **Lord, teach me your statutes.**

With all my heart I seek you;
**   let me not stray from your commands.**

℞. **Lord, teach me your statutes.**

Within my heart I treasure your promise,
**   that I may not sin against you.**

℞. **Lord, teach me your statutes.**

Blessed are you, O LORD;
**   teach me your statutes.**

℞. **Lord, teach me your statutes.**

Third Option

Psalm 147:15-16, 17-18, 19-20

℞. (12a) **Praise the Lord, Jerusalem.**

He sends forth his command to the earth;
**   swiftly runs his word!**
He spreads snow like wool;
**   frost he strews like ashes.**

℞. **Praise the Lord, Jerusalem.**

He scatters his hail like crumbs;
**   before his cold the waters freeze.**
He sends his word and melts them;
**   he lets his breeze blow and the waters run.**

℞. **Praise the Lord, Jerusalem.**

He has proclaimed his word to Jacob,
**   his statutes and his ordinances to Israel.**
He has not done thus for any other nation;
**   his ordinances he has not made known to them. Alleluia.**

℞. **Praise the Lord, Jerusalem.**

783 ALLELUIA VERSE AND VERSE BEFORE THE GOSPEL

1.

Luke 4:18

The Spirit of the Lord is upon me
he has sent me to bring glad tidings to the poor.

2.

See John 6:63c, 68c

Your words, Lord, are Spirit and life;
you have the words of everlasting life.

3.

See Acts 16:14b

Open our hearts, O Lord,
to listen to the words of your Son.

4.

The seed is the word of God, Christ is the sower;
all who come to him will live for ever.

784 GOSPEL

1.

Matthew 5:14-19   You are the light of the world.

☩ **A reading from the holy Gospel according to Matthew**

Jesus said to his disciples:
"You are the light of the world.
A city set on a mountain cannot be hidden.
Nor do they light a lamp and then put it under a bushel basket;
  it is set on a lampstand,
  where it gives light to all in the house.
Just so, your light must shine before others,
  that they may see your good deeds
  and glorify your heavenly Father.

"Do not think that I have come to abolish the law or the prophets.
I have come not to abolish but to fulfill.
Amen, I say to you, until heaven and earth pass away,
  not the smallest letter or the smallest part of a letter
  will pass from the law,
  until all things have taken place.
Therefore, whoever breaks one of the least of these commandments
  and teaches others to do so
  will be called least in the Kingdom of heaven.
But whoever obeys and teaches these commandments
  will be called greatest in the Kingdom of heaven."

The Gospel of the Lord.

2.

Mark 1:35-39   He went into their synagogues, preaching.

☩ **A reading from the holy Gospel according to Mark**

Rising very early before dawn,
  Jesus left and went off to a deserted place, where he prayed.
Simon and those who were with him pursued him
  and on finding him said,
  "Everyone is looking for you."
He told them, "Let us go on to the nearby villages
  that I may preach there also.
For this purpose have I come."

So he went into their synagogues, preaching and driving out demons
   throughout the whole of Galilee.

The Gospel of the Lord.

   3.

Luke 4:16-21   The Spirit of the Lord is upon me.

✠ **A reading from the holy Gospel according to Luke**

Jesus came to Nazareth, where he had grown up,
   and went according to his custom
   into the synagogue on the sabbath day.
He stood up to read and was handed a scroll of the prophet Isaiah.
He unrolled the scroll and found the passage where it was written:

> *The Spirit of the Lord is upon me,*
>   *because he has anointed me*
>   *to bring glad tidings to the poor.*
> *He has sent me to proclaim liberty to captives*
>   *and recovery of sight to the blind,*
>   *to let the oppressed go free,*
> *and to proclaim a year acceptable to the Lord.*

Rolling up the scroll, he handed it back to the attendant and sat down,
   and the eyes of all in the synagogue looked intently at him.
He said to them,
   "Today this Scripture passage is fulfilled in your hearing."

The Gospel of the Lord.

4.

Luke 24:44-48   Jesus sent the Apostles to preach repentance, for the forgiveness of sins.

✠   **A reading from the holy Gospel according to Luke**

Jesus said to his disciples:
"These are my words that I spoke to you while I was still with you,
 that everything written about me in the law of Moses
 and in the prophets and psalms must be fulfilled."
Then he opened their minds to understand the Scriptures.
And Jesus said to them,
 "Thus it is written that the Christ would suffer
 and rise from the dead on the third day
 and that repentance, for the forgiveness of sins,
 would be preached in his name
 to all the nations, beginning from Jerusalem.
You are witnesses of these things."

The Gospel of the Lord.

5.

John 7:14-18   My teaching is not my own, but is from the One who sent me.

✠   **A reading from the holy Gospel according to John**

When the feast was already half over,
 Jesus went up into the temple area and began to teach.
The Jews were amazed and said,
 "How does he know Scripture without having studied?"
Jesus answered them and said,
 "My teaching is not my own
 but is from the One who sent me.
Whoever chooses to do his will
 shall know whether my teaching is from God
 or whether I speak on my own.
Whoever speaks on his own seeks his own glory,
 but whoever seeks the glory of the one who sent him is truthful,
 and there is no wrong in him."

The Gospel of the Lord.

2. INSTITUTION OF ACOLYTES

785 READING FROM THE OLD TESTAMENT

1.

Genesis 14:18-20   Melchizedek brought out bread and wine.

A reading from the Book of Genesis

**Melchizedek, king of Salem, brought out bread and wine,
    and being a priest of God Most High,
    he blessed Abram with these words:**

**"Blessed be Abram by God Most High,
    the creator of heaven and earth;
And blessed be God Most High,
    who delivered your foes into your hand."**

Then Abram gave him a tenth of everything.

The word of the Lord.

2.

Exodus 16:2-4, 12-15   I will rain down bread from heaven for you.

A reading from the Book of Exodus

The whole assembly of the children of Israel grumbled against Moses and
    Aaron.
The children of Israel said to them,
    "Would that we had died at the LORD's hand in the land of Egypt,
    as we sat by our fleshpots and ate our fill of bread!
But you had to lead us into this desert
    to make the whole community die of famine!"

Then the LORD said to Moses,
    "I will now rain down bread from heaven for you.
Each day the people are to go out and gather their daily portion;
    thus will I test them,
    to see whether they follow my instructions or not."

"I have heard the grumbling of the children of Israel.
Tell them: In the evening twilight you shall eat flesh,
    and in the morning you shall have your fill of bread,
    so that you may know that I, the LORD, am your God."

In the evening quail came up and covered the camp.
In the morning a dew lay all about the camp,
    and when the dew evaporated, there on the surface of the desert
    were fine flakes like hoarfrost on the ground.
On seeing it, the children of Israel asked one another, "What is this?"
    for they did not know what it was.
But Moses told them,
    "This is the bread which the LORD has given you to eat."

The word of the Lord.

3.

Exodus 24:3-8   This is the blood of the covenant that the Lord has made with you.

A reading from the Book of Exodus

When Moses came to the people
   and related all the words and ordinances of the LORD,
   they all answered with one voice,
   "We will do everything that the LORD has told us."
Moses then wrote down all the words of the LORD and,
   rising early the next day,
   he erected at the foot of the mountain an altar
   and twelve pillars for the twelve tribes of Israel.
Then, having sent certain young men of the children of Israel
   to offer burnt offerings and sacrifice young bulls
   as peace offerings to the LORD,
   Moses took half of the blood and put it in large bowls;
   the other half he splashed on the altar.
Taking the book of the covenant, he read it aloud to the people,
   who answered, "All that the LORD has said, we will heed and do."
Then he took the blood and sprinkled it on the people, saying,
   "This is the blood of the covenant
   that the LORD has made with you
   in accordance with all these words of his."

The word of the Lord.

4.

Deuteronomy 8:2-3, 14b-16a   He fed you with manna, a food unknown to you and your fathers.

A reading from the Book of Deuteronomy

Moses said to the people:
"Remember how for forty years now the LORD**, your God,**
   has directed all your journeying in the desert,
   so as to test you by affliction
   and find out whether or not it was your intention
   to keep his commandments.
He therefore let you be afflicted with hunger,
   and then fed you with manna,
   a food unknown to you and your fathers,
   in order to show you that not by bread alone does man live,
   but by every word that comes forth from the mouth of the LORD.

"Do not forget the LORD**, your God,**
   who brought you out of the land of Egypt,
   that place of slavery;
   who guided you through the vast and terrible desert
   with its saraph serpents and scorpions,
   its parched and waterless ground;
   who brought forth water for you from the flinty rock
   and fed you in the desert with manna,
   a food unknown to your fathers."

The word of the Lord.

5.

1 Kings 19:4-8   He walked forty days and forty nights to the mountain of God.

A reading from the first Book of Kings

Elijah went a day's journey into the desert,
   until he came to a broom tree and sat beneath it.
He prayed for death:
   "This is enough, O LORD**!**
Take my life, for I am no better than my fathers."
He lay down and fell asleep under the broom tree,
   but then an angel touched him and ordered him to get up and eat.

He looked and there at his head was a hearth cake and a jug of water.
After he ate and drank, he lay down again,
  but the angel of the LORD came back a second time,
  touched him, and ordered,
  "Get up and eat, else the journey will be too long for you!"
He got up, ate, and drank;
  then strengthened by that food,
  he walked forty days and forty nights to the mountain of God, Horeb.

The word of the Lord.

6.

Proverbs 9:1-6   Come, eat my food, and drink the wine I have mixed.

A reading from the Book of Proverbs

Wisdom has built her house,
  she has set up her seven columns;
She has dressed her meat, mixed her wine,
  yes, she has spread her table.
She has sent out her maidens; she calls
  from the heights out over the city:
"Let whoever is simple turn in here;
  to him who lacks understanding, I say,
Come, eat of my food,
  and drink of the wine I have mixed!
Forsake foolishness that you may live;
  advance in the way of understanding."

The word of the Lord.

786   READING FROM THE NEW TESTAMENT

1.

Acts 2:42-47   They devoted themselves to meeting together and breaking bread.

A reading from the Acts of the Apostles

The disciples devoted themselves
   to the teaching of the Apostles and to the communal life,
   to the breaking of the bread and to the prayers.
Awe came upon everyone,
   and many wonders and signs were done through the Apostles.
All who believed were together and had all things in common;
   they would sell their property and possessions
   and divide them among all according to each one's need.
Every day they devoted themselves
   to meeting together in the temple area
   and to breaking bread in their homes.
They ate their meals with exultation and sincerity of heart,
   praising God and enjoying favor with all the people.
And every day the Lord added to their number those who were being
      saved.

The word of the Lord.

2.

Acts 10:34a, 37-43   To us, who ate and drank with him after he rose from the dead.

A reading from the Acts of the Apostles

Peter proceeded to speak, saying:
"You know what has happened all over Judea,
   beginning in Galilee after the baptism
   that John preached,
   how God anointed Jesus of Nazareth
   with the Holy Spirit and power.
He went about doing good
   and healing all those oppressed by the Devil,
   for God was with him.
We are witnesses of all that he did
   both in the country of the Jews and in Jerusalem.

They put him to death by hanging him on a tree.
This man God raised on the third day and granted that he be visible,
   not to all the people, but to us,
   the witnesses chosen by God in advance,
   who ate and drank with him after he rose from the dead.
He commissioned us to preach to the people
   and testify that he is the one appointed by God
   as judge of the living and the dead.
To him all the prophets bear witness,
   that everyone who believes in him
   will receive forgiveness of sins through his name."

The word of the Lord.

3.

1 Corinthians 10:16-17   Because the loaf of bread is one, we, though many, are one Body.

A reading from the first Letter of Saint Paul to the Corinthians

Brothers and sisters:
The cup of blessing that we bless,
   is it not a participation in the Blood of Christ?
The bread that we break,
   is it not a participation in the Body of Christ?
Because the loaf of bread is one,
   we, though many, are one Body,
   for we all partake of the one loaf.

The word of the Lord.

4.

1 Corinthians 11:23-26   As often as you eat this bread and drink the cup,
you proclaim the death of the Lord.

A reading from the first Letter of Saint Paul to the Corinthians

Brothers and sisters:
I received from the Lord what I also handed on to you,
  that the Lord Jesus, on the night he was handed over,
  took bread, and, after he had given thanks,
  broke it and said, "This is my Body that is for you.
Do this in remembrance of me."
In the same way also the cup, after supper, saying,
  "This cup is the new covenant in my Blood.
Do this, as often as you drink it, in remembrance of me."
For as often as you eat this bread and drink the cup,
  you proclaim the death of the Lord until he comes.

The word of the Lord.

5.

Hebrews 9:11-15   The Blood of Christ will cleanse our conscience.

A reading from the Letter to the Hebrews

When Christ came as high priest
  of the good things that have come to be,
  passing through the greater and more perfect tabernacle
  not made by hands, that is, not belonging to this creation,
  he entered once for all into the sanctuary,
  not with the blood of goats and calves
  but with his own Blood, thus obtaining eternal redemption.
For if the blood of goats and bulls
  and the sprinkling of a heifer's ashes
  can sanctify those who are defiled
  so that their flesh is cleansed,
  how much more will the Blood of Christ,
  who through the eternal spirit offered himself unblemished to God,
  cleanse our consciences from dead works to worship the living God.

For this reason he is mediator of a new covenant:
  since a death has taken place for deliverance from transgressions
  under the first covenant,
  those who are called may receive the promised eternal inheritance.

The word of the Lord.

787 RESPONSORIAL PSALM

1.

Psalm 23:1-3a, 3b-4, 5, 6

℟. (1) **The Lord is my shepherd; there is nothing I shall want.**

The LORD is my shepherd; I shall not want.
  In verdant pastures he gives me repose;
Beside restful waters he leads me;
  he refreshes my soul.

℟. **The Lord is my shepherd; there is nothing I shall want.**

He guides me in right paths
  for his name's sake.
Even though I walk in the dark valley
  I fear no evil; for you are at my side
With your rod and your staff
  that give me courage.

℟. **The Lord is my shepherd; there is nothing I shall want.**

You spread the table before me
  in the sight of my foes;
You anoint my head with oil;
  my cup overflows.

℟. **The Lord is my shepherd; there is nothing I shall want.**

Only goodness and kindness follow me
  all the days of my life;
And I shall dwell in the house of the LORD
  for years to come.

℟. **The Lord is my shepherd; there is nothing I shall want.**

2.

Psalm 34:2-3, 4-5, 6-7, 8-9, 10-11

℟. (9a) **Taste and see the goodness of the Lord.**

I will bless the Lord at all times;
  his praise shall be ever in my mouth.
Let my soul glory in the Lord;
  the lowly will hear me and be glad.

℟. **Taste and see the goodness of the Lord.**

Glorify the Lord with me,
  let us together extol his name.
I sought the Lord, and he answered me
  and delivered me from all my fears.

℟. **Taste and see the goodness of the Lord.**

Look to him that you may be radiant with joy,
  and your faces may not blush with shame.
When the poor one called out, the Lord heard,
  and from all his distress he saved him.

℟. **Taste and see the goodness of the Lord.**

The angel of the Lord encamps
  around those who fear him, and delivers them.
Taste and see how good the Lord is;
  blessed the man who takes refuge in him.

℟. **Taste and see the goodness of the Lord.**

Fear the Lord, you his holy ones,
  for nought is lacking to those who fear him.
The great grow poor and hungry;
  but those who seek the Lord want for no good thing.

℟. **Taste and see the goodness of the Lord.**

3.

Psalm 78:3 and 4bc, 23-24, 25, 54

℟. (24b) **The Lord gave them bread from heaven.**

What we have heard and know,
   and what our fathers have declared to us,
   we will declare to the generation to come
The glorious deeds of the LORD **and his strength**
   and the wonders that he wrought.

℟. **The Lord gave them bread from heaven.**

Yet he commanded the skies above
   and the doors of heaven he opened;
He rained manna upon them for food
   and gave them heavenly bread.

℟. **The Lord gave them bread from heaven.**

Man ate the bread of angels,
   food he sent them in abundance.

℟. **The Lord gave them bread from heaven.**

He brought them to his holy land,
   to the mountain his right hand had won.

℟. **The Lord gave them bread from heaven.**

4.

Psalm 110:1bc, 2, 3, 4

R̕. (4b) **You are a priest for ever, in the line of Melchizedek.**

The LORD said to my Lord: "Sit at my right hand
    till I make your enemies your footstool."

R̕. **You are a priest for ever, in the line of Melchizedek.**

The scepter of your power the LORD will stretch forth from Zion:
    "Rule in the midst of your enemies."

R̕. **You are a priest for ever, in the line of Melchizedek.**

"Yours is princely power in the day of your birth, in holy splendor;
    before the daystar, like the dew, I have begotten you."

R̕. **You are a priest for ever, in the line of Melchizedek.**

The LORD has sworn, and he will not repent:
    "You are a priest forever, according to the order of Melchizedek."

R̕. **You are a priest for ever, in the line of Melchizedek.**

5.

Psalm 116:12-13, 15 and 16bc, 17-18

R̕. (13) **I will take the cup of salvation and call on the name of the Lord.**

How shall I make a return to the LORD
    for all the good he has done for me?
The cup of salvation I will take up,
    and I will call upon the name of the LORD.

R̕. **I will take the cup of salvation and call on the name of the Lord.**

Precious in the eyes of the LORD
    is the death of his faithful ones.
I am your servant, the son of your handmaid;
    you have loosed my bonds.

R̕. **I will take the cup of salvation and call on the name of the Lord.**

To you will I offer sacrifice of thanksgiving,
   and I will call upon the name of the LORD.
My vows to the LORD I will pay
   in the presence of all his people.

℞. **I will take the cup of salvation and call on the name of the Lord.**

6.

Psalm 145:10-11, 15-16, 17-18

℞. (see 16) **You open your hand to feed us, Lord; you answer all our needs.**

Let all your works give you thanks, O LORD,
   and let your faithful ones bless you.
Let them discourse of the glory of your Kingdom
   and speak of your might.

℞. **You open your hand to feed us, Lord; you answer all our needs.**

The eyes of all look hopefully to you and
   you give them their food in due season;
You open your hand
   and satisfy the desire of every living thing.

℞. **You open your hand to feed us, Lord; you answer all our needs.**

The LORD is just in all his ways
   and holy in all his works.
The LORD is near to all who call upon him,
   to all who call upon him in truth.

℞. **You open your hand to feed us, Lord; you answer all our needs.**

7.

Psalm 147:12-13, 14-15, 19-20

℟. (John 6:58c) **Whoever eats this bread will live forever.**

Glorify the Lord, O Jerusalem;
  praise your God, O Zion.
For he has strengthened the bars of your gates;
  he has blessed your children within you.

℟. **Whoever eats this bread will live forever.**

He has granted peace in your borders;
  with the best of wheat he fills you.
He sends forth his command to the earth;
  swiftly runs his word!

℟. **Whoever eats this bread will live forever.**

He has proclaimed his word to Jacob,
  his statutes and ordinances to Israel.
He has not done thus for any other nation;
  his ordinances he has not made known to them. Alleluia.

℟. **Whoever eats this bread will live forever.**

788 ALLELUIA VERSE AND VERSE BEFORE THE GOSPEL

1.

John 6:35

**I am the bread of life, says the Lord;
whoever comes to me will never hunger,
and whoever believes in me will never thirst.**

2.

John 6:51

**I am the living bread that came down from heaven,
says the Lord;
whoever eats this bread will live forever.**

3.

John 6:56

**Whoever eats my Flesh and drinks my Blood
remains in me and I in him, says the Lord.**

4.

John 6:57

**Just as the living Father sent me and I have life because of the Father,
so also the one who feeds on me will have life because of me.**

789 GOSPEL

1.

Mark 14:12-16, 22-26   This is my Body. This is my Blood.

✠ **A reading from the holy Gospel according to Mark**

On the first day of the Feast of Unleavened Bread,
   when they sacrificed the Passover Lamb,
   his disciples said to him,
   "Where do you want us to go
   and prepare for you to eat the Passover?"
He sent two of his disciples and said to them,
   "Go into the city and a man will meet you,
   carrying a jar of water.
Follow him.
Wherever he enters, say to the master of the house,
   'The Teacher says, "Where is my guest room
   where I may eat the Passover with my disciples?"'
Then he will show you a large upper room furnished and ready.
Make the preparations for us there."
The disciples then went off, entered the city,
   and found it just as he had told them;
   and they prepared the Passover.

While they were eating,
   he took bread, said the blessing,
   broke it, and gave it to them, and said,
   "Take it; this is my Body."
Then he took a cup, gave thanks, and gave it to them,
   and they all drank from it.
He said to them,
   "This is my Blood of the covenant,
   which will be shed for many.
Amen, I say to you,
   I shall not drink again the fruit of the vine
   until the day when I drink it new in the Kingdom of God."
Then, after singing a hymn,
   they went out to the Mount of Olives.

The Gospel of the Lord.

2.

Luke 9:11b-17   They all ate and were satisfied.

☩ **A reading from the holy Gospel according to Luke**

Jesus spoke to the crowds about the Kingdom of God,
   and he healed those who needed to be cured.
As the day was drawing to a close,
   the Twelve approached him and said, "Dismiss the crowd
   so that they can go to the surrounding villages and farms
   and find lodging and provisions;
   for we are in a deserted place here."
He said to them, "Give them some food yourselves."
They replied, "Five loaves and two fish are all we have,
   unless we ourselves go and buy food for all these people."
Now the men there numbered about five thousand.
Then he said to his disciples,
   "Have them sit down in groups of about fifty."
They did so and made them all sit down.
Then taking the five loaves and the two fish,
   and looking up to heaven,
   he said the blessing over them, broke them,
   and gave them to the disciples to set before the crowd.
They all ate and were satisfied.
And when the leftover fragments were picked up,
   they filled twelve wicker baskets.

The Gospel of the Lord.

3.

Luke 24:13-35   He was made known to them in the breaking of the bread.

✠   **A reading from the holy Gospel according to Luke**

Two of the disciples of Jesus were going
    to a village called Emmaus, seven miles from Jerusalem,
    and they were conversing about all the things that had occurred.
And it happened that while they were conversing and debating,
    Jesus himself drew near and walked with them,
    but their eyes were prevented from recognizing him.
He asked them,
    "What are you discussing as you walk along?"
They stopped, looking downcast.
One of them, named Cleopas, said to him in reply,
    "Are you the only visitor to Jerusalem
    who does not know of the things
    that have taken place there in these days?"
And he replied to them, "What sort of things?"
They said to him,
    "The things that happened to Jesus the Nazarene,
    who was a prophet mighty in deed and word
    before God and all the people,
    how our chief priests and rulers both handed him over
    to a sentence of death and crucified him.
But we were hoping that he would be the one to redeem Israel;
    and besides all this,
    it is now the third day since this took place.
Some women from our group, however, have astounded us:
    they were at the tomb early in the morning
    and did not find his Body;
    they came back and reported
    that they had indeed seen a vision of angels
    who announced that he was alive.
Then some of those with us went to the tomb
    and found things just as the women had described,
    but him they did not see."
And he said to them, "Oh, how foolish you are!
How slow of heart to believe all that the prophets spoke!
Was it not necessary that the Christ should suffer these things
    and enter into his glory?"

Then beginning with Moses and all the prophets,
    he interpreted to them what referred to him
    in all the Scriptures.
As they approached the village to which they were going,
    he gave the impression that he was going on farther.
But they urged him, "Stay with us,
    for it is nearly evening and the day is almost over."
So he went in to stay with them.
And it happened that, while he was with them at table,
    he took bread, said the blessing,
    broke it, and gave it to them.
With that their eyes were opened and they recognized him,
    but he vanished from their sight.
Then they said to each other,
    "Were not our hearts burning within us
    while he spoke to us on the way and opened the Scriptures to us?"
So they set out at once and returned to Jerusalem
    where they found gathered together
    the Eleven and those with them who were saying,
    "The Lord has truly been raised and has appeared to Simon!"
Then the two recounted what had taken place on the way
    and how he was made known to them in the breaking of the bread.

The Gospel of the Lord.

4.

John 6:1-15   Jesus distributed to those who were reclining, as much as they wanted.

✠ **A reading from the holy Gospel according to John**

**Jesus went across the Sea of Galilee.
A large crowd followed him,
   because they saw the signs he was performing on the sick.
Jesus went up on the mountain,
   and there he sat down with his disciples.
The Jewish feast of Passover was near.
When Jesus raised his eyes
   and saw that a large crowd was coming to him,
   he said to Philip,
   "Where can we buy enough food for them to eat?"
He said this to test him,
   because he himself knew what he was going to do.
Philip answered him,
   "Two hundred days' wages worth of food would not be enough
   for each of them to have a little bit."
One of his disciples,
   Andrew, the brother of Simon Peter, said to him,
   "There is a boy here who has five barley loaves and two fish;
   but what good are these for so many?"
Jesus said, "Have the people recline."
Now there was a great deal of grass in that place.
So the men reclined, about five thousand in number.
Then Jesus took the loaves, gave thanks,
   and distributed them to those who were reclining,
   and also as much of the fish as they wanted.
When they had their fill, he said to his disciples,
   "Gather the fragments left over,
   so that nothing will be wasted."
So they collected them,
   and filled twelve wicker baskets
   with fragments from the five barley loaves
   that had been more than they could eat.
When the people saw the sign he had done, they said,
   "This is truly the Prophet, the one who is to come into the world."**

**Since Jesus knew that they were going to come
   and carry him off to make him king,
   he withdrew again to the mountain alone.**

The Gospel of the Lord.

5.

John 6:24-35   Whoever comes to me will never hunger, and whoever believes in me will never thirst.

☩   **A reading from the holy Gospel according to John**

When the crowd saw that neither Jesus nor his disciples were there,
they themselves got into boats
and came to Capernaum looking for Jesus.
And when they found him across the sea they said to him,
"Rabbi, when did you get here?"
Jesus answered them and said,
"Amen, amen, I say to you,
you are looking for me not because you saw signs
but because you ate the loaves and were filled.
Do not work for food that perishes
but for the food that endures for eternal life,
which the Son of Man will give you.
For on him the Father, God, has set his seal."
So they said to him,
"What can we do to accomplish the works of God?"
Jesus answered and said to them,
"This is the work of God, that you believe in the one he sent."
So they said to him,
"What sign can you do, that we may see and believe in you?
What can you do?
Our ancestors ate manna in the desert, as it is written:

He gave them bread from heaven to eat."

So Jesus said to them,
"Amen, amen, I say to you,
it was not Moses who gave the bread from heaven;
my Father gives you the true bread from heaven.
For the bread of God is that which comes down from heaven
and gives life to the world."

So they said to him,
"Sir, give us this bread always."
Jesus said to them,
"I am the bread of life;
whoever comes to me will never hunger,
and whoever believes in me will never thirst."

The Gospel of the Lord.

6.

John 6:41-51   I am the living bread that came down from heaven.

✝ **A reading from the holy Gospel according to John**

The Jews murmured about Jesus because he said,
  "I am the bread that came down from heaven,"
  and they said,
  "Is this not Jesus, the son of Joseph?
Do we not know his father and mother?
Then how can he say,
  'I have come down from heaven'?"
Jesus answered and said to them,
  "Stop murmuring among yourselves.
No one can come to me unless the Father who sent me draw him,
  and I will raise him on the last day.
It is written in the prophets:

> ***They shall all be taught by God.***

Everyone who listens to my Father and learns from him comes to me.
Not that anyone has seen the Father
  except the one who is from God;
  he has seen the Father.
Amen, amen, I say to you,
  whoever believes has eternal life.
I am the bread of life.
Your ancestors ate the manna in the desert, but they died;
  this is the bread that comes down from heaven
  so that one may eat it and not die.
I am the living bread that came down from heaven;
  whoever eats this bread will live forever;
  and the bread that I will give is my Flesh for the life of the world."

The Gospel of the Lord.

7.

John 6:51-59   My Flesh is true food and my Blood true drink.

✠   **A reading from the holy Gospel according to John**

Jesus said to the crowds of Jews:
"I am the living bread that came down from heaven;
 whoever eats this bread will live forever;
 and the bread that I will give
is my Flesh for the life of the world."

The Jews quarreled among themselves, saying,
 "How can this man give us his Flesh to eat?"
Jesus said to them,
 "Amen, amen, I say to you,
 unless you eat the Flesh of the Son of Man and drink his Blood,
 you do not have life within you.
Whoever eats my Flesh and drinks my Blood
 has eternal life,
 and I will raise him on the last day.
For my Flesh is true food,
 and my Blood is true drink.
Whoever eats my Flesh and drinks my Blood
 remains in me and I in him.
Just as the living Father sent me
 and I have life because of the Father,
 so also the one who feeds on me
 will have life because of me.
This is the bread that came down from heaven.
Unlike your ancestors who ate and still died,
 whoever eats this bread will live forever."
These things he said while teaching in the synagogue in Capernaum.

The Gospel of the Lord.

8.

John 21:1-14   Jesus took the bread and gave it to them.

✠   **A reading from the holy Gospel according to John**

Jesus revealed himself again to his disciples at the Sea of Tiberias.
He revealed himself in this way.

Together were Simon Peter, Thomas called Didymus,
    Nathanael from Cana in Galilee,
    Zebedee's sons, and two others of his disciples.
Simon Peter said to them, "I am going fishing."
They said to him, "We also will come with you."
So they went out and got into the boat,
    but that night they caught nothing.
When it was already dawn, Jesus was standing on the shore;
    but the disciples did not realize that it was Jesus.
Jesus said to them, "Children, have you caught anything to eat?"
They answered him, "No."
So he said to them, "Cast the net over the right side of the boat
    and you will find something."
So they cast it, and were not able to pull it in
    because of the number of fish.
So the disciple whom Jesus loved said to Peter, "It is the Lord."
When Simon Peter heard that it was the Lord,
    he tucked in his garment, for he was lightly clad,
    and jumped into the sea.
The other disciples came in the boat,
    for they were not far from shore, only about a hundred yards,
    dragging the net with the fish.
When they climbed out on shore,
    they saw a charcoal fire with fish on it and bread.
Jesus said to them, "Bring some of the fish you just caught."
So Simon Peter went over and dragged the net ashore
    full of one hundred fifty-three large fish.
Even though there were so many, the net was not torn.
Jesus said to them, "Come, have breakfast."
And none of the disciples dared to ask him, "Who are you?"
    because they realized it was the Lord.
Jesus came over and took the bread and gave it to them,
    and in like manner the fish.
This was now the third time Jesus was revealed to his disciples
    after being raised from the dead.

The Gospel of the Lord.

V. FOR THE PASTORAL CARE OF THE SICK AND THE DYING

1. ANOINTING OF THE SICK

790 READING FROM THE OLD TESTAMENT

1.

1 Kings 19:1-8   Elijah, tired from the journey, is comforted by God.

A reading from the first Book of Kings

Ahab told Jezebel all that Elijah had done—
that he had put all the prophets to the sword.
Jezebel then sent a messenger to Elijah and said,
"May the gods do thus and so to me
if by this time tomorrow
I have not done with your life what was done to each of them."
Elijah was afraid and fled for his life,
going to Beer-sheba of Judah.
He left his servant there and went a day's journey into the desert,
until he came to a broom tree and sat beneath it.
He prayed for death:
"This is enough, O Lord!
Take my life, for I am no better than my fathers."
He lay down and fell asleep under the broom tree,
but then an angel touched him and ordered him to get up and eat.
He looked and there at his head was a hearth cake
and a jug of water.
After he ate and drank, he lay down again,
but the angel of the Lord came back a second time,
touched him, and ordered, "Get up and eat,
else the journey will be too long for you!"
He got up, ate, and drank;
then strengthened by that food,
he walked forty days and forty nights to the mountain of God, Horeb.

The word of the Lord.

2.

Job 3:1-3, 11-17, 20-23   Why is light given to the toilers?

A reading from the Book of Job

Job opened his mouth and cursed his day.
He spoke out and said:

> **Perish the day on which I was born,**
> > **the night when they said, "The child is a boy!"**

> **Why did I not perish at birth,**
> > **come forth from the womb and expire?**
> **Or why was I not buried away like an untimely birth,**
> > **like babes that have never seen the light?**
> **Wherefore did the knees receive me?**
> > **or why did I suck at the breasts?**

> **For then I should have lain down and been tranquil;**
> > **had I slept, I should then have been at rest**
> **With kings and counselors of the earth**
> > **who built where now there are ruins**
> **Or with princes who had gold**
> > **and filled their houses with silver.**
> **There the wicked cease from troubling,**
> > **there the weary are at rest.**
> **Why is light given to the toilers,**
> > **and life to the bitter in spirit?**
> **They wait for death and it comes not;**
> > **they search for it rather than for hidden treasures,**
> **Rejoice in it exultingly,**
> > **and are glad when they reach the grave:**
> **Men whose path is hidden from them,**
> > **and whom God has hemmed in!**

The word of the Lord.

3.

Job 7:1-4, 6-11   Remember that my life is like the wind.

A reading from the Book of Job

Job spoke, saying:
Is not man's life on earth a drudgery?
Are not his days those of a hireling?
He is a slave who longs for the shade,
a hireling who waits for his wages.
So I have been assigned months of misery,
and troubled nights have been allotted to me.

If in bed I say, "When shall I arise?"
Then the night drags on;
I am filled with restlessness until the dawn.
My days are swifter than a weaver's shuttle;
they come to an end without hope.
Remember that my life is like the wind;
I shall not see happiness again.
The eye that now sees me shall no more behold me;
as you look at me, I shall be gone.
As a cloud dissolves and vanishes,
so he who goes down to the nether world shall come up no more.
He shall not again return to his house;
his place shall know him no more.

My own utterance I will not restrain;
I will speak in the anguish of my spirit;
I will complain in the bitterness of my soul.

The word of the Lord.

4.

Job 7:12-21   What is man that you make much of him?

A reading from the Book of Job

Job spoke, saying:
Am I the sea, or a monster of the deep,
that you place a watch over me?
Why have you set me up as an object of attack?
or why should I be a target for you?

When I say, "My bed shall comfort me,
   my couch shall ease my complaint,"
Then you affright me with dreams
   and with visions terrify me,
So that I should prefer choking
   and death rather than my pains.
I waste away: I cannot live forever;
   let me alone, for my days are but a breath.
What is man, that you make much of him,
   or pay him any heed?
You observe him with each new day
   and try him at every moment!
How long will it be before you look away from me,
   and let me alone long enough to swallow my spittle?
Though I have sinned, what can I do to you,
   O watcher of men?
Why do you not pardon my offense,
   or take away my guilt?
For soon I shall lie down in the dust;
   and should you seek me I shall then be gone.

The word of the Lord.

5. (For the Dying)

Job 19:23-27a   I know that my Vindicator lives.

A reading from the Book of Job

Job spoke, saying:
Oh, would that my words were written down!
   Would that they were inscribed in a record:
That with an iron chisel and with lead
   they were cut in the rock forever!
But as for me, I know that my Vindicator lives,
   and that he will at last stand forth upon the dust;
Whom I myself shall see.

The word of the Lord.

6.

Wisdom 9:9-11, 13-18   Who ever knew your counsel, except you had given Wisdom?

A reading from the Book of Wisdom

[O Lord of mercy,] with you is Wisdom, who knows your works
  and was present when you made the world;
Who understands what is pleasing in your eyes
  and what is conformable with your commands.
Send her forth from your holy heavens
  and from your glorious throne dispatch her
That she may be with me and work with me,
  that I may know what is your pleasure.
For she knows and understands all things,
  and will guide me discreetly in my affairs
  and safeguard me by her glory.
For what man knows God's counsel,
  or who can conceive what the LORD intends?
For the deliberations of mortals are timid,
  and unsure are our plans.
For the corruptible body burdens the soul
  and the earthen shelter weighs down the mind that has many concerns.
And scarce do we guess the things on earth,
  and what is within our grasp we find with difficulty;
  but when things are in heaven, who can search them out?
Or who ever knew your counsel, except you had given Wisdom
  and sent your Holy Spirit from on high?
And thus were the paths of those on earth made straight,
  and men learned what was your pleasure,
  and were saved by Wisdom.

The word of the Lord.

7.

Isaiah 35:1-10   Strengthen the hands that are feeble.

A reading from the Book of the Prophet Isaiah

In those days:
The desert and the parched land will exult;
  the steppe will rejoice and bloom.

They will bloom with abundant flowers,
    and rejoice with joyful song.
The glory of Lebanon will be given to them,
    the splendor of Carmel and Sharon;
They will see the glory of the LORD,
    the splendor of our God.
Strengthen the hands that are feeble,
    make firm the knees that are weak,
Say to those whose hearts are frightened:
    Be strong, fear not!
Here is your God,
    he comes with vindication;
With divine recompense
    he comes to save you.
Then will the eyes of the blind be opened,
    the ears of the deaf be cleared;
Then will the lame leap like a stag,
    then the tongue of the mute will sing.
Streams will burst forth in the desert,
    and rivers in the steppe.
The burning sands will become pools,
    and the thirsty ground, springs of water;
The abode where jackals lurk
    will be a marsh for the reed and papyrus.
A highway will be there,
    called the holy way;
No one unclean may pass over it,
    nor fools go astray on it.
No lion will be there,
    nor beast of prey go up to be met upon it.
It is for those with a journey to make,
    and on it the redeemed will walk.
Those whom the LORD has ransomed will return
    and enter Zion singing,
    crowned with everlasting joy;
They will meet with joy and gladness,
    sorrow and mourning will flee.

The word of the Lord.

8.

Isaiah 52:13–53:12   Our sufferings he endured.

A reading from the Book of the Prophet Isaiah

See, my servant shall prosper,
  he shall be raised high and greatly exalted.
Even as many were amazed at him—
  so marred was his look beyond human semblance
  and his appearance beyond that of the sons of man—
So shall he startle many nations,
  because of him kings shall stand speechless;
For those who have not been told shall see,
  those who have not heard shall ponder it.

Who would believe what we have heard?
  To whom has the arm of the LORD been revealed?
He grew up like a sapling before him,
  like a shoot from the parched earth;
There was in him no stately bearing to make us look at him,
  nor appearance that would attract us to him.
He was spurned and avoided by people,
  a man of suffering, accustomed to infirmity,
One of those from whom men hide their faces,
  spurned, and we held him in no esteem.

Yet it was our infirmities that he bore,
  our sufferings that he endured,
While we thought of him as stricken,
  as one smitten by God and afflicted.
But he was pierced for our offenses,
  crushed for our sins;
Upon him was the chastisement that makes us whole,
  by his stripes we were healed.
We had all gone astray like sheep,
  each following his own way;
But the LORD laid upon him
  the guilt of us all.

Though he was harshly treated, he submitted
  and opened not his mouth;
Like a lamb led to the slaughter
  or a sheep before the shearers,
  he was silent and opened not his mouth.
Oppressed and condemned, he was taken away,
  and who would have thought any more of his destiny?
When he was cut off from the land of the living,
  and smitten for the sin of his people,
A grave was assigned him among the wicked
  and a burial place with evildoers,
Though he had done no wrong
  nor spoken any falsehood.
But the Lord was pleased
  to crush him in infirmity.

If he gives his life as an offering for sin,
  he shall see his descendants in a long life,
  and the will of the Lord shall be accomplished through him.
Because of his affliction
  he shall see the light in fullness of days;
Through his suffering, my servant shall justify many,
  and their guilt he shall bear.
Therefore I will give him his portion among the great,
  and he shall divide the spoils with the mighty,
Because he surrendered himself to death
  and was counted among the wicked;
And he shall take away the sins of many,
  and win pardon for their offenses.

The word of the Lord.

9.

Isaiah 61:1-3abcd   The Spirit of the Lord has sent me to comfort all who mourn.

A reading from the Book of the Prophet Isaiah

The Spirit of the Lord God is upon me,
   because the Lord has anointed me;
He has sent me to bring glad tidings to the lowly,
   to heal the brokenhearted,
To proclaim liberty to the captives
   and release to the prisoners,
To announce a year of favor from the Lord
   and a day of vindication by our God,
   to comfort all who mourn;
To place on those who mourn in Zion
   a diadem instead of ashes,
To give them oil of gladness in place of mourning,
   a glorious mantle instead of a listless spirit.

The word of the Lord.

791 READING FROM THE NEW TESTAMENT DURING THE SEASON OF EASTER

First Option

Acts 3:1-10   In the name of Jesus Christ the Nazorean, rise!

A reading from the Acts of the Apostles

Peter and John were going up to the temple area
   for the three o'clock hour of prayer.
And a man crippled from birth
   was carried and placed
   at the gate of the temple called "the Beautiful Gate"
   every day to beg for alms from the people who entered the temple.
When he saw Peter and John about to go into the temple,
   he asked for alms.
But Peter looked intently at him, as did John,
   and said, "Look at us."
He paid attention to them,
   expecting to receive something from them.
Peter said, "I have neither silver nor gold, but what I do have I give you:
   in the name of Jesus Christ the Nazorean, rise and walk."
Then Peter took him by the right hand and raised him up,
   and immediately his feet and ankles grew strong.
He leaped up, stood, and walked around,
   and went into the temple with them,
   walking and jumping and praising God.
When all the people saw him walking and praising God,
   they recognized him as the one
   who used to sit begging at the Beautiful Gate of the temple,
   and they were filled with amazement and astonishment
   at what had happened to him.

The word of the Lord.

422 For the Pastoral Care of the Sick and the Dying

Acts 3:11-16   Faith in the risen Jesus has given him perfect health.

A reading from the Acts of the Apostles

As the beggar who had been cured clung to Peter and John,
all the people hurried in amazement toward them
in the portico called "Solomon's Portico."
When Peter saw this, he addressed the people,
"You children of Israel, why are you amazed at this,
and why do you look so intently at us
as if we had made him walk by our own power or piety?
The God of Abraham, the God of Isaac, and the God of Jacob,
the God of our ancestors, has glorified his servant Jesus
whom you handed over and denied in Pilate's presence,
when he had decided to release him.
You denied the Holy and Righteous One
and asked that a murderer be released to you.
The author of life you put to death,
but God raised him from the dead; of this we are witnesses.
And by faith in his name,
this man, whom you see and know, his name has made strong,
and the faith that comes through it
has given him perfect health,
in the presence of all of you."

The word of the Lord.

Third Option

Acts 4:8-12   Nor is there any other name by which we are to be saved.

A reading from the Acts of the Apostles

Peter, filled with the Holy Spirit, said:
"Leaders of the people and elders:
If we are being examined today
about a good deed done to a cripple,
namely, by what means he was saved,
then all of you and all the people of Israel should know
that it was in the name of Jesus Christ the Nazorean
whom you crucified, whom God raised from the dead;
in his name this man stands before you healed.

He is *the stone rejected by you, the builders,*
    which has become the cornerstone.
There is no salvation through anyone else,
    nor is there any other name under heaven
    given to the human race by which we are to be saved."

The word of the Lord.

Fourth Option

Acts 13:32-39   The one whom God raised up did not see corruption.

A reading from the Acts of the Apostles

Paul said:
"We ourselves are proclaiming this good news to you
    that what God promised our fathers
    he has brought to fulfillment for us, their children,
    by raising up Jesus,
    as it is written in the second psalm,
    You are my Son; this day I have begotten you.
And that he raised him from the dead never to return to corruption
    he declared in this way,
    I shall give you the benefits assured to David.
That is why he also says in another psalm,
    You will not suffer your holy one to see corruption.
Now David, after he had served the will of God in his lifetime,
    fell asleep, was gathered to his fathers, and did see corruption.
But the one whom God raised up did not see corruption.
You must know, my brothers,
    that through him forgiveness of sins is being proclaimed to you,
    and in regard to everything from which you could not be justified under
        the law of Moses,
    in him every believer is justified."

The word of the Lord.

792 READING FROM THE NEW TESTAMENT DURING OTHER SEASONS

1.

Romans 8:14-17   If only we suffer with him, we will also be glorified with him.

A reading from the Letter of Saint Paul to the Romans

Brothers and sisters:
For those who are led by the Spirit of God are sons of God.
For you did not receive a spirit of slavery to fall back into fear,
  but you received a spirit of adoption,
  through which we cry, "*Abba*, Father!"
The Spirit himself bears witness with our spirit
  that we are children of God,
  and if children, then heirs,
  heirs of God and joint heirs with Christ,
  if only we suffer with him
  so that we may also be glorified with him.

The word of the Lord.

2.

Romans 8:18-27   We also groan as we wait for the redemption of our bodies.

A reading from the Letter of Saint Paul to the Romans

Brothers and sisters:
I consider that the sufferings of this present time are as nothing
  compared with the glory to be revealed for us.
For creation awaits with eager expectation
  the revelation of the children of God;
  for creation was made subject to futility,
  not of its own accord but because of the one who subjected it,
  in hope that creation itself
  would be set free from slavery to corruption
  and share in the glorious freedom of the children of God.
We know that all creation is groaning in labor pains even until now;
  and not only that, but we ourselves,
  who have the firstfruits of the Spirit,
  we also groan within ourselves
  as we wait for adoption, the redemption of our bodies.

For in hope we were saved.
Now hope that sees for itself is not hope.
For who hopes for what one sees?
But if we hope for what we do not see, we wait with endurance.

In the same way, the Spirit too comes to the aid of our weakness;
   for we do not know how to pray as we ought,
   but the Spirit himself intercedes with inexpressible groanings.
And the one who searches hearts
   knows what is the intention of the Spirit,
   because it intercedes for the holy ones
   according to God's will.

The word of the Lord.

3.

Romans 8:31b-35, 37-39   Who will separate us from the love of Christ?

A reading from the Letter of Saint Paul to the Romans

Brothers and sisters:
If God is for us, who can be against us?
He who did not spare his own Son
   but handed him over for us all,
   how will he not also give us everything else along with him?
Who will bring a charge against God's chosen ones?
It is God who acquits us.
Who will condemn?
It is Christ Jesus who died, rather, was raised,
   who also is at the right hand of God,
   who indeed intercedes for us.
What will separate us from the love of Christ?
Will anguish, or distress or persecution, or famine,
   or nakedness, or peril, or the sword?

No, in all these things, we conquer overwhelmingly
   through him who loved us.
For I am convinced that neither death, nor life,
   nor angels, nor principalities,
   nor present things, nor future things,
   nor powers, nor height, nor depth,
   nor any other creature will be able to separate us
   from the love of God in Christ Jesus our Lord.

The word of the Lord.

4.

1 Corinthians 1:18-25   The weakness of God is stronger than
human wisdom.

A reading from the first Letter of Saint Paul to the Corinthians

Brothers and sisters:
The message of the cross is foolishness to those who are perishing,
but to us who are being saved it is the power of God.
For it is written:

> *I will destroy the wisdom of the wise,*
> *and the learning of the learned I will set aside.*

Where is the wise one?
Where is the scribe?
Where is the debater of this age?
Has not God made the wisdom of the world foolish?
For since in the wisdom of God
the world did not come to know God through wisdom,
it was the will of God through the foolishness of the proclamation
to save those who have faith.
For Jews demand signs and Greeks look for wisdom,
but we proclaim Christ crucified,
a stumbling block to Jews and foolishness to Gentiles,
but to those who are called, Jews and Greeks alike,
Christ the power of God and the wisdom of God.
For the foolishness of God is wiser than human wisdom,
and the weakness of God is stronger than human strength.

The word of the Lord.

5. (For the Dying)

1 Corinthians 12:12-22, 24b-27   If one part suffers, all the parts suffer with it.

A reading from the first Letter of Saint Paul to the Corinthians

Brothers and sisters:
As a body is one though it has many parts,
  and all the parts of the body, though many, are one body, so also Christ.
For in one Spirit we were all baptized into one Body,
  whether Jews or Greeks, slaves or free persons,
  and we were all given to drink of one Spirit.

Now the body is not a single part, but many.
If a foot should say,
  "Because I am not a hand I do not belong to the body,"
  it does not for this reason belong any less to the body.
Or if an ear should say,
  "Because I am not an eye I do not belong to the body,"
  it does not for this reason belong any less to the body.
If the whole body were an eye, where would the hearing be?
If the whole body were hearing, where would the sense of smell be?
But as it is, God placed the parts,
  each one of them, in the body as he intended.
If they were all one part, where would the body be?
But as it is, there are many parts, yet one body.
The eye cannot say to the hand, "I do not need you,"
  nor again the head to the feet, "I do not need you."
Indeed, the parts of the body that seem to be weaker
  are all the more necessary.
But God has so constructed the body
  as to give greater honor to a part that is without it,
  so that there may be no division in the body,
  but that the parts may have the same concern for one another.
If one part suffers, all the parts suffer with it;
  if one part is honored, all the parts share its joy.

Now you are Christ's Body, and individually parts of it.

The word of the Lord.

6. (For the Dying)

1 Corinthians 15:12-20   If there is no resurrection of the dead, then neither has Christ been raised.

A reading from the first Letter of Saint Paul to the Corinthians

Brothers and sisters:
If Christ is preached as raised from the dead,
  how can some among you say there is no resurrection of the dead?
If there is no resurrection of the dead,
  then neither has Christ been raised.
And if Christ has not been raised, then empty too is our preaching;
  empty, too, your faith.
Then we are also false witnesses to God,
  because we testified against God that he raised Christ,
  whom he did not raise if in fact the dead are not raised.
For if the dead are not raised, neither has Christ been raised,
  and if Christ has not been raised, your faith is vain;
  you are still in your sins.
Then those who have fallen asleep in Christ have perished.
If for this life only we have hoped in Christ,
  we are the most pitiable people of all.

But now Christ has been raised from the dead,
  the firstfruits of those who have fallen asleep.

The word of the Lord.

7.

2 Corinthians 4:16-18   Our inner self is being renewed day by day.

A reading from the second Letter of Saint Paul to the Corinthians

Brothers and sisters:
We are not discouraged;
  rather, although our outer self is wasting away,
  our inner self is being renewed day by day.
For this momentary light affliction
  is producing for us an eternal weight of glory beyond all comparison,
  as we look not to what is seen but to what is unseen;
  for what is seen is transitory, but what is unseen is eternal.

The word of the Lord.

8. (For the Dying)

2 Corinthians 5:1, 6-10   We have an eternal dwelling in heaven.

A reading from the second Letter of Saint Paul to the Corinthians

Brothers and sisters:
We know that if our earthly dwelling, a tent,
   should be destroyed,
   we have a building from God,
   a dwelling not made with hands,
   eternal in heaven.

So we are always courageous,
   although we know that while we are at home in the body
   we are away from the Lord,
   for we walk by faith, not by sight.
Yet we are courageous,
   and we would rather leave the body and go home to the Lord.
Therefore, we aspire to please him,
   whether we are at home or away.
For we must all appear before the judgment seat of Christ,
   so that each may receive recompense,
   according to what he did in the body, whether good or evil.

The word of the Lord.

9.

Galatians 4:12-19   Because of a physical illness I originally preached the Gospel to you.

A reading from the Letter of Saint Paul to the Galatians

I implore you, brothers and sisters,
  be as I am,
  because I have also become as you are.
You did me no wrong;
  you know that it was because of a physical illness
  that I originally preached the Gospel to you,
  and you did not show disdain or contempt
  because of the trial caused you by my physical condition,
  but rather you received me as an angel of God,
  as Christ Jesus.
Where now is that blessedness of yours?
Indeed, I can testify to you that,
  if it had been possible,
  you would have torn out your eyes and given them to me.
So now have I become your enemy
  by telling you the truth?
They show interest in you,
  but not in a good way;
  they want to isolate you,
  so that you may show interest in them.
Now it is good to be shown interest
  for good reason at all times,
  and not only when I am with you.
My children,
  for whom I am again in labor
  until Christ be formed in you!

The word of the Lord.

10.

Philippians 2:25-30   He was indeed ill, but God had mercy on him.

A reading from the Letter of Saint Paul to the Philippians

Brothers and sisters:
With regard to Epaphroditus,
   my brother and co-worker and fellow soldier,
   your messenger and minister in my need,
   I consider it necessary to send him to you.
For he has been longing for all of you
   and was distressed because you heard that he was ill.
He was indeed ill, close to death;
   but God had mercy on him,
   not just on him but also on me,
   so that I might not have sorrow upon sorrow.
I send him therefore with the greater eagerness,
   so that, on seeing him,
   you may rejoice again,
   and I may have less anxiety.
Welcome him then in the Lord with all joy
   and hold such people in esteem,
   because for the sake of the work of Christ
   he came close to death,
   risking his life to make up for those services to me
   that you could not perform.

The word of the Lord.

11.

Colossians 1:22-29   In my flesh I am filling up what is lacking in the afflictions of Christ.

A reading from the Letter of Saint Paul to the Colossians

Brothers and sisters:
Christ Jesus has now reconciled you
   in his fleshly Body through his death,
   to present you holy, without blemish,
   and irreproachable before him,
   provided that you persevere in the faith,
   firmly grounded, stable,
   and not shifting from the hope of the Gospel that you heard,
   which has been preached to every creature under heaven,
   of which I, Paul, am a minister.

Now I rejoice in my sufferings for your sake,
   and in my flesh I am filling up
   what is lacking in the afflictions of Christ
   on behalf of his Body, which is the Church,
   of which I am a minister
   in accordance with God's stewardship given to me
   to bring to completion for you the word of God,
   the mystery hidden from ages and from generations past.
But now it has been manifested to his holy ones,
   to whom God chose to make known the riches of the glory
   of this mystery among the Gentiles;
   it is Christ in you, the hope for glory.
It is he whom we proclaim,
   admonishing everyone and teaching everyone with all wisdom,
   that we may present everyone perfect in Christ.
For this I labor and struggle,
   in accord with the exercise of his power working within me.

The word of the Lord.

12.

Hebrews 4:14-16; 5:7-9   We do not have a high priest who is unable to sympathize with our weaknesses.

A reading from the Letter to the Hebrews

Brothers and sisters:
Since we have a great high priest who has passed through the heavens,
   Jesus, the Son of God,
     let us hold fast to our confession.
For we do not have a high priest
     who is unable to sympathize with our weaknesses,
     but one who has similarly been tested in every way,
     yet without sin.
So let us confidently approach the throne of grace
     to receive mercy and to find grace for timely help.

In the days when he was in the flesh,
     he offered prayers and supplications with loud cries and tears
     to the one who was able to save him from death,
     and he was heard because of his reverence.
Son though he was, he learned obedience from what he suffered;
     and when he was made perfect,
     he became the source of eternal salvation for all who obey him.

The word of the Lord.

13.

James 5:13-16   The prayer of faith will save the sick person.

A reading from the Letter of James

Beloved:
Is anyone among you suffering?
He should pray.
Is anyone in good spirits?
He should sing praise.
Is anyone among you sick?
He should summon the presbyters of the Church,
  and they should pray over him
  and anoint him with oil in the name of the Lord,
  and the prayer of faith will save the sick person
  and the Lord will raise him up.
If he has committed any sins, he will be forgiven.

Therefore, confess your sins to one another
  and pray for one another, that you may be healed.
The fervent prayer of a righteous person is very powerful.

The word of the Lord.

14.

1 Peter 1:3-9   You rejoice, although now for a little while you may have
to suffer.

A reading from the first Letter of Saint Peter

Blessed be the God and Father of our Lord Jesus Christ,
  who in his great mercy gave us a new birth to a living hope
  through the resurrection of Jesus Christ from the dead,
  to an inheritance that is imperishable, undefiled, and unfading,
  kept in heaven for you
  who by the power of God are safeguarded through faith,
  to a salvation that is ready to be revealed in the final time.
In this you rejoice, although now for a little while
  you may have to suffer through various trials,
  so that the genuineness of your faith,
  more precious than gold that is perishable even though tested by fire,
  may prove to be for praise, glory, and honor
  at the revelation of Jesus Christ.

Although you have not seen him you love him;
even though you do not see him now yet believe in him,
you rejoice with an indescribable and glorious joy,
as you attain the goal of your faith, the salvation of your souls.

The word of the Lord.

15.

1 John 3:1-2   What we shall be has not yet been revealed.

A reading from the first Letter of Saint John

Beloved:
See what love the Father has bestowed on us
that we may be called the children of God.
Yet so we are.
The reason the world does not know us
is that it did not know him.
Beloved, we are God's children now;
what we shall be has not yet been revealed.
We do know that when it is revealed we shall be like him,
for we shall see him as he is.

The word of the Lord.

16.

Revelation 21:1-7   There shall be no more death or mourning, wailing or pain.

A reading from the Book of Revelation

I, John, saw a new heaven and a new earth.
The former heaven and the former earth had passed away,
  and the sea was no more.
I also saw the holy city, a new Jerusalem,
  coming down out of heaven from God,
  prepared as a bride adorned for her husband.
I heard a loud voice from the throne saying,
  "Behold, God's dwelling is with the human race.
He will dwell with them and they will be his people
  and God himself will always be with them as their God.
He will wipe every tear from their eyes,
  and there shall be no more death or mourning, wailing or pain,
  for the old order has passed away."

The one who sat on the throne said,
  "Behold, I make all things new."
Then he said, "Write these words down,
  for they are trustworthy and true."
He said to me, "They are accomplished.
I am the Alpha and the Omega,
  the beginning and the end.
To the thirsty I will give a gift
  from the spring of life-giving water.
The victor will inherit these gifts,
  and I shall be his God,
  and he will be my son."

The word of the Lord.

17. (For the Dying)

Revelation 22:17, 20-21   Come, Lord Jesus!

A reading from the Book of Revelation

The Spirit and the bride say, "Come."
Let the hearer say, "Come."
Let the one who thirsts come forward,
   and the one who wants it receive the gift of life-giving water.

The one who gives this testimony says,
   "Yes, I am coming soon."
Amen! Come, Lord Jesus!

The grace of the Lord Jesus be with you all.

The word of the Lord.

793 RESPONSORIAL PSALM

1.

Isaiah 38:10, 11, 12abcd, 16

℟. (see 17b) **You saved my life, O Lord; I shall not die.**

Once I said,
"In the noontime of life I must depart!
To the gates of the nether world I shall be consigned
for the rest of my years."

℟. **You saved my life, O Lord; I shall not die.**

I said, "I shall see the LORD no more
in the land of the living.
No longer shall I behold my fellow men
among those who dwell in the world."

℟. **You saved my life, O Lord; I shall not die.**

My dwelling, like a shepherd's tent,
is struck down and borne away from me;
You have folded up my life, like a weaver
who severs the last thread.

℟. **You saved my life, O Lord; I shall not die.**

Those live whom the LORD protects;
yours the life of my spirit.
You have given me health and life.

℟. **You saved my life, O Lord; I shall not die.**

2.

Psalm 6:2-4a, 4b-6, 9-10

℟. (3a) **Have mercy on me, Lord; my strength is gone.**

O L ORD, reprove me not in your anger,
   nor chastise me in your wrath.
Have mercy on me, O L ORD, for my strength is gone;
   heal me, O L ORD, for my body is in terror;
My soul, too, is utterly terrified.

℟. **Have mercy on me, Lord; my strength is gone.**

But you, O L ORD, how long?
Return, O L ORD, save my life;
   rescue me because of your kindness,
For among the dead no one remembers you;
   in the nether world who gives you thanks?

℟. **Have mercy on me, Lord; my strength is gone.**

Depart from me, all evildoers,
   for the L ORD has heard the sound of my weeping;
The L ORD has heard my plea;
   the L ORD has accepted my prayer.

℟. **Have mercy on me, Lord; my strength is gone.**

3.

Psalm 25:4-5ab, 6 and 7bc, 8-9, 10 and 14, 15-16

℟. (1) **To you, O Lord, I lift my soul.**

Your ways, O Lord, make known to me;
 teach me your paths,
Guide me in your truth and teach me,
 for you are God my savior.

℟. **To you, O Lord, I lift my soul.**

Remember that your compassion, O Lord,
 and your kindness are from of old.
In your kindness remember me,
 because of your goodness, O Lord.

℟. **To you, O Lord, I lift my soul.**

Good and upright is the Lord;
 thus he shows sinners the way.
He guides the humble to justice,
 he teaches the humble his way.

℟. **To you, O Lord, I lift my soul.**

All the paths of the Lord are kindness and constancy
 toward those who keep his covenant and his decrees.
The friendship of the Lord is with those who fear him,
 and his covenant, for their instruction.

℟. **To you, O Lord, I lift my soul.**

My eyes are ever toward the Lord,
 for he will free my feet from the snare.
Look toward me, and have pity on me,
 for I am alone and afflicted.

℟. **To you, O Lord, I lift my soul.**

4.

Psalm 27:1bcde, 4, 5, 7-8a, 8b-9ab, 9cd-10

℞. (14) **Put your hope in the Lord; take courage and be strong.**

The LORD is my light and salvation;
  whom should I fear?
The LORD is my life's refuge;
  of whom should I be afraid?

℞. **Put your hope in the Lord; take courage and be strong.**

One thing I ask of the LORD;
  this I seek:
To dwell in the house of the LORD
  all the days of my life,
That I may gaze on the loveliness of the LORD
  and contemplate his temple.

℞. **Put your hope in the Lord; take courage and be strong.**

For he will hide me in his abode
  in the day of trouble;
He will conceal me in the shelter of his tent,
  he will set me high upon a rock.

℞. **Put your hope in the Lord; take courage and be strong.**

Hear, O LORD, the sound of my call;
  have pity on me, and answer me.
Of you my heart speaks; you my glance seeks.

℞. **Put your hope in the Lord; take courage and be strong.**

Your presence, O LORD, I seek.
Hide not your face from me;
  do not in anger repel your servant.

℞. **Put your hope in the Lord; take courage and be strong.**

You are my helper: cast me not off;
  forsake me not, O God my savior.
Though my father and mother forsake me,
  yet will the LORD receive me.

℞. **Put your hope in the Lord; take courage and be strong.**

5.

Psalm 34:2-3, 4-5, 6-7, 10-11, 12-13, 17 and 19

℟. (19a) **The Lord is close to the brokenhearted.**
    or:
℟. (9a) **Taste and see the goodness of the Lord.**

I will bless the LORD **at all times;**
    his praise shall be ever in my mouth.
Let my soul glory in the LORD**;**
    the lowly will hear me and be glad.

℟. **The Lord is close to the brokenhearted.**
    or:
℟. **Taste and see the goodness of the Lord.**

Glorify the LORD **with me,**
    let us together extol his name.
I sought the LORD**, and he answered me**
    and delivered me from all my fears.

℟. **The Lord is close to the brokenhearted.**
    or:
℟. **Taste and see the goodness of the Lord.**

Look to him that you may be radiant with joy,
    and your faces may not blush with shame.
When the poor one called out, the LORD **heard,**
    and from all his distress he saved him.

℟. **The Lord is close to the brokenhearted.**
    or:
℟. **Taste and see the goodness of the Lord.**

Fear the LORD**, you his holy ones,**
    for nought is lacking to those who fear him.
The great grow poor and hungry;
    but those who seek the LORD **want for no good thing.**

℟. **The Lord is close to the brokenhearted.**
    or:
℟. **Taste and see the goodness of the Lord.**

Come children, hear me;
    I will teach you the fear of the LORD.
Which of you desires life,
    and takes delight in prosperous days?

R℣. The Lord is close to the brokenhearted.
    or:
R℣. Taste and see the goodness of the Lord.

The LORD confronts the evildoers,
    to destroy remembrance of them from the earth.
The LORD is close to the brokenhearted;
    and those who are crushed in spirit he saves.

R℣. The LORD is close to the brokenhearted.
    or:
R℣. Taste and see the goodness of the Lord.

6.

Psalm 42:3, 5cde; 43:3, 4

R℣. (42:2) Like a deer that longs for running streams, my soul longs for you, my God.

Athirst is my soul for God, the living God.
    When shall I go and behold the face of God?

R℣. Like a deer that longs for running streams, my soul longs for you, my God.

I went with the throng
    and led them in procession to the house of God,
Amid loud cries of joy and thanksgiving.

R℣. Like a deer that longs for running streams, my soul longs for you, my God.

Send forth your light and your fidelity;
    they shall lead me on
And bring me to your holy mountain,
    to your dwelling-place.

R℣. Like a deer that longs for running streams, my soul longs for you, my God.

Then will I go to the altar of God,
    the God of my gladness and joy;
Then will I give you thanks upon the harp,
    O God, my God!

R℣. Like a deer that longs for running streams, my soul longs for you, my God.

7.

Psalm 63:2-3, 4-6, 7-9

℟. (2b) **My soul is thirsting for you, O Lord my God.**

O God, you are my God whom I seek;
  for you my flesh pines and my soul thirsts
  like the earth, parched, lifeless and without water.
Thus have I gazed toward you in the sanctuary
  to see your power and your glory.

℟. **My soul is thirsting for you, O Lord my God.**

For your kindness is a greater good than life;
  my lips shall glorify you.
Thus will I bless you while I live;
  lifting up my hands, I will call upon your name.
As with the riches of a banquet shall my soul be satisfied,
  and with exultant lips my mouth shall praise you.

℟. **My soul is thirsting for you, O Lord my God.**

I will remember you upon my couch,
  and through the night-watches I will meditate on you:
That you are my help,
  and in the shadow of your wings I shout for joy.
My soul clings to you;
  your right hand upholds me.

℟. **My soul is thirsting for you, O Lord my God.**

8.

Psalm 71:1-2, 5-6ab, 8-9, 14-15

℟. (12b) **My God, come quickly to help me.**
  or:
℟. (23) **My lips, my very soul will shout for joy: you have redeemed me!**

In you, O LORD, I take refuge;
  let me never be put to shame.
In your justice rescue me, and deliver me;
  incline your ear to me, and save me.

℟. **My God, come quickly to help me.**
  or:
℟. **My lips, my very soul will shout for joy: you have redeemed me!**

For you are my hope, O Lord;
   my trust, O God, from my youth.
On you I depend from birth;
   from my mother's womb you are my strength.

℟. **My God, come quickly to help me.**
   or:
℟. **My lips, my very soul will shout for joy: you have redeemed me!**

My mouth shall be filled with your praise,
   with your glory day by day.
Cast me not off in my old age;
   as my strength fails, forsake me not.

℟. **My God, come quickly to help me.**
   or:
℟. **My lips, my very soul will shout for joy: you have redeemed me!**

But I will always hope
   and praise you ever more and more.
My mouth shall declare your justice,
   day by day your salvation,
      though I know not their extent.

℟. **My God, come quickly to help me.**
   or:
℟. **My lips, my very soul will shout for joy: you have redeemed me!**

   9.

Psalm 86:1-2, 3-4, 5-6, 11, 12-13, 15-16ab

℟. (1a) **Incline your ear, O Lord, and answer me.**
   or:
℟. (15a and 16a) **God, you are merciful and gracious; turn to me and have mercy.**

Incline your ear, O Lord; answer me,
   for I am afflicted and poor.
Keep my life, for I am devoted to you;
   save your servant who trusts in you.
You are my God.

(cont.)

℞. Incline your ear, O Lord, and answer me.
  or:
℞. God, you are merciful and gracious; turn to me and have mercy.

Have mercy on me, O Lord,
  for to you I call all the day.
Gladden the soul of your servant,
  for to you, O Lord, I lift up my soul.

℞. Incline your ear, O Lord, and answer me.
  or:
℞. God, you are merciful and gracious; turn to me and have mercy.

For you, O Lord, are good and forgiving,
  abounding in kindness to all who call upon you.
Hearken, O LORD, to my prayer
  and attend to the sound of my pleading.

℞. Incline your ear, O Lord, and answer me.
  or:
℞. God, you are merciful and gracious; turn to me and have mercy.

Teach me, O Lord, your way
  that I may walk in your truth;
  direct my heart that I may fear your name.

℞. Incline your ear, O Lord, and answer me.
  or:
℞. God, you are merciful and gracious; turn to me and have mercy.

I will give thanks to you, O Lord my God,
  with all my heart,
  and I will glorify your name forever.
Great has been your kindness toward me;
  you have rescued me from the depths of the nether world.

℞. Incline your ear, O Lord, and answer me.
  or:
℞. God, you are merciful and gracious; turn to me and have mercy.

But you, O Lord, are a God merciful and gracious,
  slow to anger, abounding in kindness and fidelity.
Turn toward me, and have pity on me;
  give your strength to your servant.

R̘. Incline your ear, O Lord, and answer me.
  or:
R̘. God, you are merciful and gracious; turn to me and have mercy.

  10.

Psalm 90:2, 3-4, 5-6, 10, 12, 14 and 16

R̘. (1) In every age, O Lord, you have been our refuge.

Before the mountains were begotten
  and the earth and the world were brought forth,
  from everlasting to everlasting you are God.

R̘. In every age, O Lord, you have been our refuge.

You turn man back to dust,
  saying, "Return, O children of men."
For a thousand years in your sight
  are as yesterday, now that it is past,
  or as a watch of the night.

R̘. In every age, O Lord, you have been our refuge.

You make an end of them in their sleep;
  the next morning they are like the changing grass,
Which at dawn springs up anew,
  but by evening wilts and fades.

R̘. In every age, O Lord, you have been our refuge.

Seventy is the sum of our years,
  or eighty, if we are strong,
And most of them are fruitless toil,
  for they pass quickly and we drift away.

R̘. In every age, O Lord, you have been our refuge.

Fill us at daybreak with your kindness,
  that we may shout for joy and gladness all our days.
Let your work be seen by your servants
  and your glory by their children.

R̘. In every age, O Lord, you have been our refuge.

11.

Psalm 102:2-3, 24-25, 26-28, 19-21

℟. (2) **O Lord, hear my prayer and let my cry come to you.**

O Lᴏʀᴅ, hear my prayer,
  and let my cry come to you.
Hide not your face from me
  in the day of my distress.
Incline your ear to me;
  in the day when I call, answer me speedily.

℟. **O Lord, hear my prayer and let my cry come to you.**

He has broken down my strength in the way;
  he has cut short my days.
    I say: O my God,
Take me not hence in the midst of my days;
  through all generations your years endure.

℟. **O Lord, hear my prayer and let my cry come to you.**

Of old you established the earth,
  and the heavens are the work of your hands.
They shall perish, but you remain
  though all of them grow old like a garment.
Like clothing you change them, and they are changed,
  but you are the same, and your years have no end.

℟. **O Lord, hear my prayer and let my cry come to you.**

Let this be written for the generation to come,
  and let his future creatures praise the Lᴏʀᴅ:
"The Lᴏʀᴅ looked down from his holy height,
  from heaven he beheld the earth,
To hear the groaning of the prisoners,
  to release those doomed to die."

℟. **O Lord, hear my prayer and let my cry come to you.**

12.

Psalm 103:1bc-2, 3-4, 11-12, 13-14, 15-16, 17-18

℞. (1) **O bless the Lord, my soul!**
   or:
℞. (8) **The Lord is kind and merciful; slow to anger and rich in compassion.**

Bless the LORD, O my soul;
   and all my being, bless his holy name.
Bless the LORD, O my soul,
   and forget not all his benefits.

℞. **O bless the Lord, my soul!**
   or:
℞. **The Lord is kind and merciful; slow to anger and rich in compassion.**

He pardons all your iniquities,
   he heals all your ills.
He redeems your life from destruction,
   he crowns you with kindness and compassion.

℞. **O bless the Lord, my soul!**
   or:
℞. **The Lord is kind and merciful; slow to anger and rich in compassion.**

For as the heavens are high above the earth,
   so surpassing is his kindness toward those who fear him.
As far as the east is from the west,
   so far has he put our transgressions from us.

℞. **O bless the Lord, my soul!**
   or:
℞. **The Lord is kind and merciful; slow to anger and rich in compassion.**

As a father has compassion on his children,
   so the LORD has compassion on those who fear him,
For he knows how we are formed;
   he remembers that we are dust.

(cont.)

℟. **O bless the Lord, my soul!**
   or:
℟. **The Lord is kind and merciful; slow to anger and rich in compassion.**

Man's days are like those of grass;
   like a flower of the field he blooms;
The wind sweeps over him and he is gone,
   and his place knows him no more.

℟. **O bless the Lord, my soul!**
   or:
℟. **The Lord is kind and merciful; slow to anger and rich in compassion.**

But the kindness of the Lord is from eternity
   to eternity toward those who fear him,
And his justice toward children's children
   among those who keep his covenant.

℟. **O bless the Lord, my soul!**
   or:
℟. **The Lord is kind and merciful; slow to anger and rich in compassion.**

13.

Psalm 123:1-2ab, 2cdef

℟. (2cd) **Our eyes are fixed on the Lord, pleading for mercy.**

To you I lift up my eyes
   who are enthroned in heaven.
Behold, as the eyes of servants
   are on the hands of their masters.

℟. **Our eyes are fixed on the Lord, pleading for mercy.**

As the eyes of a maid
   are on the hands of her mistress,
So are our eyes on the Lord, our God,
   till he have pity on us.

℟. **Our eyes are fixed on the Lord, pleading for mercy.**

14.

Psalm 143:1bcd-2, 5-6, 10

R̸. (1b) **O Lord, hear my prayer.**
or:
R̸. (11a) **For the sake of your name, O Lord, save my life.**

O LORD, hear my prayer;
hearken to my pleading in your faithfulness;
in your justice answer me.
And enter not into judgment with your servant,
for before you no living man is just.

R̸. **O Lord, hear my prayer.**
or:
R̸. **For the sake of your name, O Lord, save my life.**

I remember the days of old;
I meditate on all your doings,
the works of your hands I ponder.
I stretch out my hands to you;
my soul thirsts for you like parched land.

R̸. **O Lord, hear my prayer.**
or:
R̸. **For the sake of your name, O Lord, save my life.**

Teach me to do your will,
for you are my God.
May your good spirit guide me
on level ground.

R̸. **O Lord, hear my prayer.**
or:
R̸. **For the sake of your name, O Lord, save my life.**

794 ALLELUIA VERSE AND VERSE BEFORE THE GOSPEL

1.

Psalm 33:22

**May your kindness, O LORD, be upon us
who have put our hope in you.**

2.

Matthew 5:4

**Blessed are they who mourn,
for they will be comforted.**

3.

Matthew 8:17

**Christ took away our infirmities
and bore our diseases.**

4.

Matthew 11:28

**Come to me, all you who labor and are burdened,
and I will give you rest, says the Lord.**

5.

2 Corinthians 1:3b-4a

**Blessed be the Father of compassion and God of all encouragement,
who encourages us in our every affliction.**

6.

Ephesians 1:3

**Blessed be the God and Father of our Lord Jesus Christ,
who has blessed us in Christ with every spiritual blessing.**

7.

James 1:12

**Blessed is the man who perseveres in temptation,
for when he has been proved he will receive the crown of life.**

795 GOSPEL

1.

Matthew 5:1-12a   Rejoice and be glad, for your reward will be great in heaven.

✟ **A reading from the holy Gospel according to Matthew**

When Jesus saw the crowds, he went up the mountain,
  and after he had sat down, his disciples came to him.
He began to teach them, saying:

  "Blessed are the poor in spirit,
    for theirs is the Kingdom of heaven.
  Blessed are they who mourn,
    for they will be comforted.
  Blessed are the meek,
    for they will inherit the land.
  Blessed are they who hunger and thirst for righteousness,
    for they will be satisfied.
  Blessed are the merciful,
    for they will be shown mercy.
  Blessed are the clean of heart,
    for they will see God.
  Blessed are the peacemakers,
    for they will be called children of God.
  Blessed are they who are persecuted for the sake of righteousness,
    for theirs is the Kingdom of heaven.
  Blessed are you when they insult you and persecute you
    and utter every kind of evil against you falsely because of me.
  Rejoice and be glad,
    for your reward will be great in heaven."

The Gospel of the Lord.

2.

Matthew 8:1-4   Lord, if you wish, you can make me clean.

✠ **A reading from the holy Gospel according to Matthew**

When Jesus came down from the mountain, great crowds followed him.
And then a leper approached, did him homage, and said,
   "Lord, if you wish, you can make me clean."
Jesus stretched out his hand, touched him and said,
   "I will do it. Be made clean."
His leprosy was cleansed immediately.
Then Jesus said to him, "See that you tell no one,
   but go show yourself to the priest,
   and offer the gift that Moses prescribed;
   that will be proof for them."

The Gospel of the Lord.

3.

Long Form

Matthew 8:5-17   He bore our diseases.

✠ **A reading from the holy Gospel according to Matthew**

When Jesus entered Capernaum,
   a centurion approached him and appealed to him, saying,
   "Lord, my servant is lying at home paralyzed, suffering dreadfully."
He said to him, "I will come and cure him."
The centurion said in reply,
   "Lord, I am not worthy to have you enter under my roof;
   only say the word and my servant will be healed.
For I too am a man subject to authority,
   with soldiers subject to me.
And I say to one, 'Go,' and he goes;
   and to another, 'Come here,' and he comes;
   and to my slave, 'Do this,' and he does it."
When Jesus heard this, he was amazed and said to those following him,
   "Amen, I say to you, in no one in Israel have I found such faith.
I say to you, many will come from the east and the west,
   and will recline with Abraham, Isaac, and Jacob
   at the banquet in the Kingdom of heaven,
   but the children of the Kingdom

will be driven out into the outer darkness,
   where there will be wailing and grinding of teeth."
And Jesus said to the centurion,
   "You may go; as you have believed, let it be done for you."
And at that very hour his servant was healed.

Jesus entered the house of Peter,
   and saw Peter's mother-in-law lying in bed with a fever.
Jesus touched her hand, the fever left her,
   and she rose and waited on him.

When it was evening, they brought him many
   who were possessed by demons,
   and he drove out the spirits by a word and cured all the sick,
   to fulfill what had been said by Isaiah the prophet:

> *He took away our infirmities*
>   *and bore our diseases.*

The Gospel of the Lord.

OR Short Form

Matthew 8:5-13   He bore our diseases.

✠ **A reading from the holy Gospel according to Matthew**

When Jesus entered Capernaum,
    a centurion approached him and appealed to him, saying,
    "Lord, my servant is lying at home paralyzed, suffering dreadfully."
He said to him, "I will come and cure him."
The centurion said in reply,
    "Lord, I am not worthy to have you enter under my roof;
    only say the word and my servant will be healed.
For I too am a man subject to authority,
    with soldiers subject to me.
And I say to one, 'Go,' and he goes;
    and to another, 'Come here,' and he comes;
    and to my slave, 'Do this,' and he does it."
When Jesus heard this, he was amazed and said to those following him,
    "Amen, I say to you, in no one in Israel have I found such faith.
I say to you, many will come from the east and the west,
    and will recline with Abraham, Isaac, and Jacob
    at the banquet in the Kingdom of heaven,
    but the children of the Kingdom
    will be driven out into the outer darkness,
    where there will be wailing and grinding of teeth."
And Jesus said to the centurion,
    "You may go; as you have believed, let it be done for you."
And at that very hour his servant was healed.

The Gospel of the Lord.

OR Shortest Form

Matthew 8:14-17   He bore our diseases.

✝   **A reading from the holy Gospel according to Matthew**

Jesus entered the house of Peter,
   and saw Peter's mother-in-law lying in bed with a fever.
Jesus touched her hand, the fever left her,
   and she rose and waited on him.

When it was evening, they brought him many
   who were possessed by demons,
   and he drove out the spirits by a word and cured all the sick,
   to fulfill what had been said by Isaiah the prophet:

> *He took away our infirmities*
> *and bore our diseases.*

The Gospel of the Lord.

4.

Matthew 11:25-30   Come to me, all you who labor.

✝   **A reading from the holy Gospel according to Matthew**

At that time Jesus answered:
"I give praise to you, Father, Lord of heaven and earth,
   for although you have hidden these things
   from the wise and the learned
   you have revealed them to the childlike.
Yes, Father, such has been your gracious will.
All things have been handed over to me by my Father.
No one knows the Son except the Father,
   and no one knows the Father except the Son
   and anyone to whom the Son wishes to reveal him.

"Come to me, all you who labor and are burdened,
   and I will give you rest.
Take my yoke upon you and learn from me,
   for I am meek and humble of heart;
   and you will find rest for yourselves.
For my yoke is easy, and my burden light."

The Gospel of the Lord.

5.

Matthew 15:29-31   Jesus healed many.

✠   **A reading from the holy Gospel according to Matthew**

Jesus walked by the Sea of Galilee,
  went up on the mountain, and sat down there.
Great crowds came to him,
  having with them the lame, the blind, the deformed, the mute,
  and many others.
They placed them at his feet, and he cured them.
The crowds were amazed when they saw the mute speaking,
  the deformed made whole,
  the lame walking,
  and the blind able to see,
  and they glorified the God of Israel.

The Gospel of the Lord.

6.

Matthew 25:31-40   Whatever you did for one of these least brothers of mine you did for me.

☩ **A reading from the holy Gospel according to Matthew**

Jesus said to his disciples:
"When the Son of Man comes in his glory,
    and all the angels with him,
    he will sit upon his glorious throne,
    and all the nations will be assembled before him.
And he will separate them one from another,
    as a shepherd separates the sheep from the goats.
He will place the sheep on his right and the goats on his left.
Then the king will say to those on his right,
    'Come, you who are blessed by my Father.
Inherit the kingdom prepared for you from the foundation of the world.
For I was hungry and you gave me food,
    I was thirsty and you gave me drink,
    a stranger and you welcomed me,
    naked and you clothed me,
    ill and you cared for me,
    in prison and you visited me.'
Then the righteous will answer him and say,
    'Lord, when did we see you hungry and feed you,
    or thirsty and give you drink?
When did we see you a stranger and welcome you,
    or naked and clothe you?
When did we see you ill or in prison, and visit you?'
And the king will say to them in reply,
    'Amen, I say to you, whatever you did
    for one of these least brothers of mine, you did for me.'"

The Gospel of the Lord.

7.

Mark 2:1-12   When Jesus saw their faith, he said: "Child, your sins are forgiven."

✝ **A reading from the holy Gospel according to Mark**

When Jesus returned to Capernaum after some days,
  it became known that he was at home.
Many gathered together so that there was no longer room for them,
  not even around the door,
  and he preached the word to them.
They came bringing to him a paralytic carried by four men.
Unable to get near Jesus because of the crowd,
  they opened up the roof above him.
After they had broken through,
  they let down the mat on which the paralytic was lying.
When Jesus saw their faith, he said to the paralytic,
  "Child, your sins are forgiven."
Now some of the scribes were sitting there asking themselves,
  "Why does this man speak that way? He is blaspheming.
Who but God alone can forgive sins?"
Jesus immediately knew in his mind
what they were thinking to themselves,
  so he said, "Why are you thinking such things in your hearts?
Which is easier, to say to the paralytic,
  'Your sins are forgiven,'
  or to say, 'Rise, pick up your mat and walk'?
But that you may know
  that the Son of Man has authority to forgive sins on earth"—
  he said to the paralytic,
  "I say to you, rise, pick up your mat, and go home."
He rose, picked up his mat at once,
  and went away in the sight of everyone.
They were all astounded
  and glorified God, saying, "We have never seen anything like this."

The Gospel of the Lord.

8.

Mark 4:35-41   Why are you terrified? Do you not have faith?

☩ **A reading from the holy Gospel according to Mark**

One day, as evening drew on, Jesus said to his disciples:
"Let us cross to the other side."
Leaving the crowd, they took him with them in the boat just as he was.
And other boats were with him.
A violent squall came up and waves were breaking over the boat,
   so that it was already filling up.
Jesus was in the stern, asleep on a cushion.
They woke him and said to him,
   "Teacher, do you not care that we are perishing?"
He woke up,
   rebuked the wind, and said to the sea, "Quiet! Be still!"
The wind ceased and there was great calm.
Then he asked them, "Why are you terrified?
Do you not yet have faith?"
They were filled with great awe and said to one another,
   "Who then is this whom even wind and sea obey?"

The Gospel of the Lord.

9.

Mark 10:46-52   Jesus, Son of David, have pity on me.

☩ **A reading from the holy Gospel according to Mark**

As Jesus was leaving Jericho with his disciples and a sizable crowd,
  Bartimaeus, a blind man, the son of Timaeus,
    sat by the roadside begging.
On hearing that it was Jesus of Nazareth,
  he began to cry out and say,
  "Jesus, Son of David, have pity on me."
And many rebuked him, telling him to be silent.
But he kept calling out all the more,
  "Son of David, have pity on me."
Jesus stopped and said, "Call him."
So they called the blind man, saying to him,
  "Take courage; get up, he is calling you."
He threw aside his cloak, sprang up, and came to Jesus.
Jesus said to him in reply,
  "What do you want me to do for you?"
The blind man replied to him,
  "Master, I want to see."
Jesus told him,
  "Go your way; your faith has saved you."
Immediately he received his sight
  and followed him on the way.

The Gospel of the Lord.

10.

Mark 16:15-20   They will lay their hands on the sick, and they
will recover.

☩ **A reading from the holy Gospel according to Mark**

Jesus appeared to the Eleven and said to them:
"Go into the whole world
  and proclaim the Gospel to every creature.
Whoever believes and is baptized will be saved;
  whoever does not believe will be condemned.
These signs will accompany those who believe:
  in my name they will drive out demons,
  they will speak new languages.

They will pick up serpents with their hands,
   and if they drink any deadly thing, it will not harm them.
They will lay hands on the sick, and they will recover."

Then the Lord Jesus, after he spoke to them,
   was taken up into heaven
   and took his seat at the right hand of God.
But they went forth and preached everywhere,
   while the Lord worked with them
   and confirmed the word through accompanying signs.

The Gospel of the Lord.

11.

Luke 7:18b-23   Go and tell John what you have seen and heard.

✠   **A reading from the holy Gospel according to Luke**

John summoned two of his disciples and sent them to the Lord to ask,
   "Are you the one who is to come, or should we look for another?"
When the men came to the Lord, they said,
   "John the Baptist has sent us to you to ask,
   'Are you the one who is to come, or should we look for another?'"
At that time
   he cured many of their diseases, sufferings, and evil spirits;
   he also granted sight to many who were blind.
And he said to them in reply,
   "Go and tell John what you have seen and heard:
   the blind regain their sight,
   the lame walk,
   lepers are cleansed,
   the deaf hear, the dead are raised,
   the poor have the good news proclaimed to them.
And blessed is the one who takes no offense at me."

The Gospel of the Lord.

12.

Luke 10:5-6, 8-9   Cure the sick.

☩   **A reading from the holy Gospel according to Luke**

Jesus said to his disciples:
"Into whatever house you enter, first say,
   'Peace to this household.'
If a peaceful person lives there,
   your peace will rest on him;
   but if not, it will return to you.
Whatever town you enter and they welcome you,
   eat what is set before you,
   cure the sick in it and say to them,
   'The Kingdom of God is at hand for you.'"

The Gospel of the Lord.

13.

Luke 10:25-37   Who is my neighbor?

☩   **A reading from the holy Gospel according to Luke**

There was a scholar of the law who stood up to test Jesus and said,
   "Teacher, what must I do to inherit eternal life?"
Jesus said to him, "What is written in the law?
How do you read it?"
He said in reply,
   "You shall love the Lord, your God,
   with all your heart,
   with all your being,
   with all your strength,
   and with all your mind,
   and your neighbor as yourself."
He replied to him, "You have answered correctly;
   do this and you will live."

But because he wished to justify himself, he said to Jesus,
   "And who is my neighbor?"
Jesus replied,
   "A man fell victim to robbers
   as he went down from Jerusalem to Jericho.
They stripped and beat him and went off leaving him half-dead.

A priest happened to be going down that road,
  but when he saw him, he passed by on the opposite side.
Likewise a Levite came to the place,
  and when he saw him, he passed by on the opposite side.
But a Samaritan traveler who came upon him
  was moved with compassion at the sight.
He approached the victim,
  poured oil and wine over his wounds and bandaged them.
Then he lifted him up on his own animal,
  took him to an inn and cared for him.
The next day he took out two silver coins
  and gave them to the innkeeper with the instruction,
  'Take care of him.
If you spend more than what I have given you,
  I shall repay you on my way back.'
Which of these three, in your opinion,
  was neighbor to the robbers' victim?"
He answered, "The one who treated him with mercy."
Jesus said to him, "Go and do likewise."

The Gospel of the Lord.

14.

Luke 11:5-13   Ask and you will receive.

✠ **A reading from the holy Gospel according to Luke**

Jesus said to his disciples:
"Suppose one of you has a friend
  to whom he goes at midnight and says,
  'Friend, lend me three loaves of bread,
  for a friend of mine has arrived at my house from a journey
  and I have nothing to offer him,'
  and he says in reply from within,
  'Do not bother me; the door has already been locked
  and my children and I are already in bed.
I cannot get up to give you anything.'
I tell you, if he does not get up to give him the loaves
  because of their friendship,
  he will get up to give him whatever he needs
  because of his persistence.

"And I tell you, ask and you will receive;
  seek and you will find;
  knock and the door will be opened to you.
For everyone who asks, receives;
  and the one who seeks, finds;
  and to the one who knocks, the door will be opened.
What father among you would hand his son a snake
  when he asks for a fish?
Or hand him a scorpion when he asks for an egg?
If you then, who are wicked,
  know how to give good gifts to your children,
  how much more will the Father in heaven give the Holy Spirit
  to those who ask him?"

The Gospel of the Lord.

15.

Luke 12:35-44   Blessed those servants whom the master finds vigilant on his arrival.

☩ **A reading from the holy Gospel according to Luke**

Jesus said to his disciples:
"Gird your loins and light your lamps
    and be like servants who await their master's return from a wedding,
    ready to open immediately when he comes and knocks.
Blessed are those servants
    whom the master finds vigilant on his arrival.
Amen, I say to you, he will gird himself,
    have them recline at table, and proceed to wait on them.
And should he come in the second or third watch
    and find them prepared in this way,
    blessed are those servants.
Be sure of this:
    if the master of the house had known the hour
    when the thief was coming,
    he would not have let his house be broken into.
You also must be prepared, for at an hour you do not expect,
    the Son of Man will come."

Then Peter said,
    "Lord, is this parable meant for us or for everyone?"
And the Lord replied,
    "Who, then, is the faithful and prudent steward
    whom the master will put in charge of his servants
    to distribute the food allowance at the proper time?
Blessed is that servant whom his master on arrival finds doing so.
Truly, I say to you, he will put him in charge of all his property."

The Gospel of the Lord.

16.

Luke 18:9-14   O God, be merciful to me, a sinner.

✠   **A reading from the holy Gospel according to Luke**

Jesus addressed this parable
   to those who were convinced of their own righteousness
   and despised everyone else.
"Two people went up to the temple area to pray;
   one was a Pharisee and the other was a tax collector.
The Pharisee took up his position and spoke this prayer to himself,
   'O God, I thank you that I am not like the rest of humanity—
   greedy, dishonest, adulterous—even like this tax collector.
I fast twice a week, and I pay tithes on my whole income.'
But the tax collector stood off at a distance
   and would not even raise his eyes to heaven
   but beat his breast and prayed,
   'O God, be merciful to me a sinner.'
I tell you, the latter went home justified, not the former;
   for everyone who exalts himself will be humbled,
   and the one who humbles himself will be exalted."

The Gospel of the Lord.

17. (For the Dying)

John 6:35-40   This is the will of my Father, that I should not lose anything
of what he gave me.

✠   **A reading from the holy Gospel according to John**

Jesus said to the crowds:
"I am the bread of life;
   whoever comes to me will never hunger,
   and whoever believes in me will never thirst.
But I told you that although you have seen me,
   you do not believe.
Everything that the Father gives me will come to me,
   and I will not reject anyone who comes to me,
   because I came down from heaven not to do my own will
   but the will of the one who sent me.
And this is the will of the one who sent me,
   that I should not lose anything of what he gave me,
   but that I should raise it on the last day.

For this is the will of my Father,
   that everyone who sees the Son and believes in him
   may have eternal life,
   and I shall raise him on the last day."

The Gospel of the Lord.

18. (For the Dying)

John 6:53-58   Whoever eats this bread will live forever.

✟ **A reading from the holy Gospel according to John**

Jesus said to the crowds:
"Amen, amen, I say to you,
   unless you eat the Flesh of the Son of Man and drink his Blood,
   you do not have life within you.
Whoever eats my Flesh and drinks my Blood
   has eternal life,
   and I will raise him on the last day.
For my Flesh is true food,
   and my Blood is true drink.
Whoever eats my Flesh and drinks my Blood
   remains in me and I in him.
Just as the living Father sent me
   and I have life because of the Father,
   so also the one who feeds on me will have life because of me.
This is the bread that came down from heaven.
Unlike your ancestors who ate and still died,
   whoever eats this bread will live forever."

The Gospel of the Lord.

19.

John 9:1-7   Neither he nor his parents sinned; he was born blind so that the works of God might be made visible through him.

☩ **A reading from the holy Gospel according to John**

As Jesus passed by he saw a man blind from birth.
His disciples asked him,
  "Rabbi, who sinned, this man or his parents,
  that he was born blind?"
Jesus answered,
  "Neither he nor his parents sinned;
  it is so that the works of God might be made visible through him.
We have to do the works of the one who sent me while it is day.
Night is coming when no one can work.
While I am in the world, I am the light of the world."
When he had said this, he spat on the ground
  and made clay with the saliva,
  and smeared the clay on his eyes, and said to him,
  "Go wash in the Pool of Siloam" (which means Sent).
So he went and washed, and came back able to see.

The Gospel of the Lord.

20.

John 10:11-18   A good shepherd lays down his life for his sheep.

✠ **A reading from the holy Gospel according to John**

Jesus said:
"I am the good shepherd.
A good shepherd lays down his life for the sheep.
A hired man, who is not a shepherd
  and whose sheep are not his own,
  sees a wolf coming and leaves the sheep and runs away,
  and the wolf catches and scatters them.
This is because he works for pay and has no concern for the sheep.
I am the good shepherd,
  and I know mine and mine know me,
  just as the Father knows me and I know the Father;
  and I will lay down my life for the sheep.
I have other sheep that do not belong to this fold.
These also I must lead, and they will hear my voice,
  and there will be one flock, one shepherd.
This is why the Father loves me,
  because I lay down my life in order to take it up again.
No one takes it from me, but I lay it down on my own.
I have power to lay it down, and power to take it up again.
This command I have received from my Father."

The Gospel of the Lord.

2. VIATICUM

796 READING FROM THE OLD TESTAMENT

First Option

1 Kings 19:4-8   Strengthened by that food, he walked to the mountain of the Lord.

A reading from the first Book of Kings

Elijah went a day's journey into the desert,
   until he came to a broom tree and sat beneath it.
He prayed for death:
   "This is enough, O LORD!
Take my life, for I am no better than my fathers."
He lay down and fell asleep under the broom tree,
   but then an angel touched him and ordered him to get up and eat.
He looked and there at his head was a hearth cake
   and a jug of water.
After he ate and drank, he lay down again,
   but the angel of the LORD came back a second time,
   touched him, and ordered,
   "Get up and eat, else the journey will be too long for you!"
He got up, ate, and drank;
   then strengthened by that food,
   he walked forty days and forty nights to the mountain of God, Horeb.

The word of the Lord.

Second Option

Job 19:23-27a   I know that my Vindicator lives.

A reading from the Book of Job

Job spoke, saying:
Oh, would that my words were written down!
   Would that they were inscribed in a record:
That with an iron chisel and with lead
   they were cut in the rock forever!
But as for me, I know that my Vindicator lives,
   and that he will at last stand forth upon the dust;
Whom I myself shall see.

The word of the Lord.

797 READING FROM THE NEW TESTAMENT

First Option

1 Corinthians 10:16-17   We, though many, are one bread, one Body.

A reading from the first Letter of Saint Paul to the Corinthians

Brothers and sisters:
The cup of blessing that we bless,
   is it not a participation in the Blood of Christ?
The bread that we break,
   is it not a participation in the Body of Christ?
Because the loaf of bread is one,
   we, though many, are one Body,
   for we all partake of the one loaf.

The word of the Lord.

Second Option

1 Corinthians 11:23-26   As often as you eat this bread and drink the cup,
you proclaim the death of the Lord until he comes.

A reading from the first Letter of Saint Paul to the Corinthians

Brothers and sisters:
I received from the Lord what I also handed on to you,
   that the Lord Jesus, on the night he was handed over,
   took bread, and, after he had given thanks,
   broke it and said, "This is my Body that is for you.
Do this in remembrance of me."
In the same way also, the cup, after supper, saying,
   "This cup is the new covenant in my Blood.
Do this, as often as you drink it, in remembrance of me."
For as often as you eat this bread and drink the cup,
   you proclaim the death of the Lord until he comes.

The word of the Lord.

Third Option

Revelation 3:14b, 20-22　　I will dine with him and he with me.

A reading from the Book of Revelation

**""The Amen, the faithful and true witness,
the source of God's creation, says this:**

**"" Behold, I stand at the door and knock.
If anyone hears my voice and opens the door,
then I will enter his house and dine with him,
and he with me.
I will give the victor the right to sit with me on my throne,
as I myself first won the victory
and sit with my Father on his throne.**

**""Whoever has ears ought to hear
what the Spirit says to the churches."""**

The word of the Lord.

Fourth Option

Revelation 22:17, 20-21　　Come, Lord Jesus!

A reading from the Book of Revelation

**The Spirit and the bride say, "Come."
Let the hearer say, "Come."
Let the one who thirsts come forward,
and the one who wants it receive the gift of life-giving water.**

**The one who gives this testimony says,
"Yes, I am coming soon."
Amen! Come, Lord Jesus!**

The grace of the Lord Jesus be with all.

The word of the Lord.

798 RESPONSORIAL PSALM

1.

Psalm 23:1-3, 4, 5, 6

R︎︎. (4ab) **Though I walk in the valley of darkness I fear no evil, for you are with me.**
     or:
R︎︎. (1) **The Lord is my shepherd; there is nothing I shall want.**

The LORD is my shepherd; I shall not want.
     In verdant pastures he gives me repose;
Beside restful waters he leads me;
     he refreshes my soul.
He guides me in right paths
     for his name's sake.

R︎︎. **Though I walk in the valley of darkness I fear no evil, for you are with me.**
     or:
R︎︎. **The Lord is my shepherd; there is nothing I shall want.**

Even though I walk in the dark valley
     I fear no evil; for you are at my side
With your rod and your staff
     that give me courage.

R︎︎. **Though I walk in the valley of darkness I fear no evil, for you are with me.**
     or:
R︎︎. **The Lord is my shepherd; there is nothing I shall want.**

You spread the table before me
     in the sight of my foes;
You anoint my head with oil;
     my cup overflows.

R︎︎. **Though I walk in the valley of darkness I fear no evil, for you are with me.**
     or:
R︎︎. **The Lord is my shepherd; there is nothing I shall want.**

Only goodness and kindness follow me
     all the days of my life;
And I shall dwell in the house of the LORD
     for years to come.

(cont.)

℞. Though I walk in the valley of darkness I fear no evil, for you are with me.
or:

℞. The Lord is my shepherd; there is nothing I shall want.

2.

Psalm 34:2-3, 4-5, 6-7, 10-11

℞. (9a) Taste and see the goodness of the Lord.

I will bless the LORD at all times;
his praise shall be ever in my mouth.
Let my soul glory in the LORD;
the lowly will hear me and be glad.

℞. Taste and see the goodness of the Lord.

Glorify the LORD with me,
let us together extol his name.
I sought the LORD, and he answered me
and delivered me from all my fears.

℞. Taste and see the goodness of the Lord.

Look to him that you may be radiant with joy,
and your faces may not blush with shame.
When the poor one called out, the LORD heard,
and from all his distress he saved him.

℞. Taste and see the goodness of the Lord.

Fear the LORD, you his holy ones,
for nought is lacking to those who fear him.
The great grow poor and hungry;
but those who seek the LORD want for no good thing.

℞. Taste and see the goodness of the Lord.

3.

Psalm 42:2, 3, 5cdef; 43:3, 4, 5

℞. (42:3) **My soul is thirsting for the living God: when shall I see him face to face?**

As the hind longs for the running waters,
   so my soul longs for you, O God.

℞. **My soul is thirsting for the living God: when shall I see him face to face?**

Athirst is my soul for God, the living God.
   When shall I go and behold the face of God?

℞. **My soul is thirsting for the living God: when shall I see him face to face?**

I went with the throng
   and led them in procession to the house of God,
Amid loud cries of joy and thanksgiving,
   with the multitude keeping festival.

℞. **My soul is thirsting for the living God: when shall I see him face to face?**

Send forth your light and your fidelity;
   they shall lead me on
And bring me to your holy mountain,
   to your dwelling-place.

℞. **My soul is thirsting for the living God: when shall I see him face to face?**

Then will I go in to the altar of God,
   the God of my gladness and joy;
Then will I give you thanks upon the harp,
   O God, my God!

℞. **My soul is thirsting for the living God: when shall I see him face to face?**

Why are you so downcast, O my soul?
   Why do you sigh within me?
Hope on God! For I shall again be thanking him,
   in the presence of my savior and my God.

℞. **My soul is thirsting for the living God: when shall I see him face to face?**

4.

Psalm 116:12-13, 15 and 16bc, 17-18

℟. (9) **I will walk in the presence of the Lord in the land of the living.**
or:

℟. (13) **I will take the cup of salvation, and call on the name of the Lord.**
or:

℟. **Alleluia.**

How shall I make a return to the Lord
for all the good he has done for me?
The cup of salvation I will take up,
and I will call upon the name of the Lord.

℟. **I will walk in the presence of the Lord in the land of the living.**
or:

℟. **I will take the cup of salvation, and call on the name of the Lord.**
or:

℟. **Alleluia.**

Precious in the eyes of the Lord
is the death of his faithful ones.
I am your servant, the son of your handmaid;
you have loosed my bonds.

℟. **I will walk in the presence of the Lord in the land of the living.**
or:

℟. **I will take the cup of salvation, and call on the name of the Lord.**
or:

℟. **Alleluia.**

To you will I offer a sacrifice of thanksgiving,
and I will call upon the name of the Lord.
My vows to the Lord I will pay
in the presence of all his people.

℟. **I will walk in the presence of the Lord in the land of the living.**
or:

℟. **I will take the cup of salvation, and call on the name of the Lord.**
or:

℟. **Alleluia.**

5.

Psalm 145:10 and 14, 15-16, 17-18

℟. (18a) **The Lord is near to all who call upon him.**

Let all your works give you thanks, O LORD,
    and let your faithful ones bless you.
The LORD lifts up all who are falling
    and raises up all who are bowed down.

℟. **The Lord is near to all who call upon him.**

The eyes of all look hopefully to you
    and you give them their food in due season;
You open your hand
    and satisfy the desire of every living thing.

℟. **The Lord is near to all who call upon him.**

The LORD is just in all his ways
    and holy in all his works.
The LORD is near to all who call upon him,
    to all who call upon him in truth.

℟. **The Lord is near to all who call upon him.**

799 ALLELUIA VERSE AND VERSE BEFORE THE GOSPEL

1.

John 6:51

**I am the living bread that came down from heaven,
says the Lord;
whoever eats this bread will live forever.**

2.

John 6:54

**Whoever eats my Flesh and drinks my Blood
remains in me and I in him,
says the Lord.**

3.

John 10:9

**I am the gate, says the Lord;
whoever enters through me will be saved and find pasture.**

4.

John 11:25; 14:6

**I am the resurrection and the life, says the Lord;
no one comes to the Father except through me.**

800 GOSPEL

First Option

John 6:41-51   I am the living bread that came down from heaven.

✝ **A reading from the holy Gospel according to John**

The Jews murmured about Jesus because he said,
   "I am the bread that came down from heaven,"
and they said,
   "Is this not Jesus, the son of Joseph?
Do we not know his father and mother?
Then how can he say,
   'I have come down from heaven'?"
Jesus answered and said to them,
   "Stop murmuring among yourselves.
No one can come to me unless the Father who sent me draw him,
   and I will raise him on the last day.
It is written in the prophets:

   They shall all be taught by God.

Everyone who listens to my Father and learns from him comes to me.
Not that anyone has seen the Father
   except the one who is from God;
   he has seen the Father.
Amen, amen, I say to you,
   whoever believes has eternal life.
I am the bread of life.
Your ancestors ate the manna in the desert, but they died;
   this is the bread that comes down from heaven
   so that one may eat it and not die.
I am the living bread that came down from heaven;
   whoever eats this bread will live forever;
   and the bread that I will give is my Flesh
   for the life of the world."

The Gospel of the Lord.

Second Option

John 6:51-58   Whoever eats my Flesh has eternal life, and I will raise him up on the last day.

✠   **A reading from the holy Gospel according to John**

Jesus said to the crowds:
"I am the living bread that came down from heaven;
whoever eats this bread will live forever;
and the bread that I will give
is my Flesh for the life of the world."

They quarreled among themselves, saying,
"How can this man give us his Flesh to eat?"
Jesus said to them,
"Amen, amen, I say to you,
unless you eat the Flesh of the Son of Man and drink his Blood,
you do not have life within you.
Whoever eats my Flesh and drinks my Blood has eternal life,
and I will raise him on the last day.
For my Flesh is true food, and my Blood is true drink.
Whoever eats my Flesh and drinks my Blood
remains in me and I in him.
Just as the living Father sent me
and I have life because of the Father,
so also the one who feeds on me
will have life because of me.
This is the bread that came down from heaven.
Unlike your ancestors who ate and still died,
whoever eats this bread will live forever."

The Gospel of the Lord.

VI. FOR THE CONFERRAL OF THE SACRAMENT OF MARRIAGE

Whenever marriage anniversaries are celebrated on a day when Masses "For Various Needs and Occasions" are permitted, the same readings may be used as below in the celebration of marriage; the readings may also be taken from the Mass of Thanksgiving (nos. 943–947).

801 READING FROM THE OLD TESTAMENT

1.

Genesis 1:26-28, 31a   Male and female he created them.

A reading from the Book of Genesis

Then God said:
"Let us make man in our image, after our likeness.
Let them have dominion over the fish of the sea,
    the birds of the air, and the cattle,
    and over all the wild animals
    and all the creatures that crawl on the ground."

God created man in his image;
    in the image of God he created him;
    male and female he created them.

God blessed them, saying:
    "Be fertile and multiply;
    fill the earth and subdue it.
Have dominion over the fish of the sea, the birds of the air,
    and all the living things that move on the earth."
God looked at everything he had made, and he found it very good.

The word of the Lord.

2.

Genesis 2:18-24　The two of them become one body.

A reading from the Book of Genesis

**The Lord God said: "It is not good for the man to be alone.
I will make a suitable partner for him."
So the Lord God formed out of the ground
　　various wild animals and various birds of the air,
　　and he brought them to the man to see what he would call them;
　　whatever the man called each of them would be its name.
The man gave names to all the cattle,
　　all the birds of the air, and all wild animals;
　　but none proved to be the suitable partner for the man.**

**So the Lord God cast a deep sleep on the man,
　　and while he was asleep,
　　he took out one of his ribs and closed up its place with flesh.
The Lord God then built up into a woman the rib
　　that he had taken from the man.
When he brought her to the man, the man said:**

**　　"This one, at last, is bone of my bones
　　　　and flesh of my flesh;
　　This one shall be called 'woman,'
　　　　for out of 'her man' this one has been taken."**

**That is why a man leaves his father and mother
　　and clings to his wife,
　　and the two of them become one body.**

The word of the Lord.

3.

Genesis 24:48-51, 58-67　In his love for Rebekah, Isaac found solace after the death of his mother.

A reading from the Book of Genesis

**The servant of Abraham said to Laban:
"I bowed down in worship to the Lord,
　　blessing the Lord, the God of my master Abraham,
　　who had led me on the right road
　　to obtain the daughter of my master's kinsman for his son.**

If, therefore, you have in mind to show true loyalty to my master,
    let me know;
    but if not, let me know that, too.
I can then proceed accordingly."

Laban and his household said in reply:
    "This thing comes from the LORD;
    we can say nothing to you either for or against it.
Here is Rebekah, ready for you;
    take her with you,
    that she may become the wife of your master's son,
    as the LORD has said."

So they called Rebekah and asked her,
    "Do you wish to go with this man?"
She answered, "I do."
At this they allowed their sister Rebekah and her nurse to take leave,
    along with Abraham's servant and his men.
Invoking a blessing on Rebekah, they said:

    "Sister, may you grow
        into thousands of myriads;
    And may your descendants gain possession
        of the gates of their enemies!"

Then Rebekah and her maids started out;
    they mounted their camels and followed the man.
So the servant took Rebekah and went on his way.

Meanwhile Isaac had gone from Beer-lahai-roi
    and was living in the region of the Negeb.
One day toward evening he went out . . . in the field,
    and as he looked around, he noticed that camels were approaching.
Rebekah, too, was looking about, and when she saw him,
    she alighted from her camel and asked the servant,
    "Who is the man out there, walking through the fields toward us?"
"That is my master," replied the servant.
Then she covered herself with her veil.

The servant recounted to Isaac all the things he had done.
Then Isaac took Rebekah into his tent;
    he married her, and thus she became his wife.
In his love for her Isaac found solace
    after the death of his mother Sarah.

The word of the Lord.

4.

Tobit 7:6-14   May the Lord of heaven prosper you both. May he grant
you mercy and peace.

A reading from the Book of Tobit

**Raphael and Tobiah entered the house of Raguel and greeted him.
Raguel sprang up and kissed Tobiah, shedding tears of joy.
But when he heard that Tobit had lost his eyesight,
     he was grieved and wept aloud.
He said to Tobiah:
     "My child, God bless you!
You are the son of a noble and good father.
But what a terrible misfortune
     that such a righteous and charitable man
     should be afflicted with blindness!"
He continued to weep in the arms of his kinsman Tobiah.
His wife Edna also wept for Tobit;
     and even their daughter Sarah began to weep.**

**Afterward, Raguel slaughtered a ram from the flock
     and gave them a cordial reception.
When they had bathed and reclined to eat,
     Tobiah said to Raphael, "Brother Azariah,
     ask Raguel to let me marry my kinswoman Sarah."
Raguel overheard the words;
     so he said to the boy:
     "Eat and drink and be merry tonight,
     for no man is more entitled to marry my daughter Sarah
     than you, brother.
Besides, not even I have the right to give her to anyone but you,
     because you are my closest relative.
But I will explain the situation to you very frankly.
I have given her in marriage to seven men,
     all of whom were kinsmen of ours,
     and all died on the very night they approached her.
But now, son, eat and drink.
I am sure the Lord will look after you both."
Tobiah answered, "I will eat or drink nothing
     until you set aside what belongs to me."**

Raguel said to him: "I will do it.
She is yours according to the decree of the Book of Moses.
Your marriage to her has been decided in heaven!
Take your kinswoman;
    from now on you are her love,
    and she is your beloved.
She is yours today and ever after.
And tonight, son, may the Lord of heaven prosper you both.
May he grant you mercy and peace."
Then Raguel called his daughter Sarah, and she came to him.
He took her by the hand and gave her to Tobiah with the words:
    "Take her according to the law.
According to the decree written in the Book of Moses she is your wife.
Take her and bring her back safely to your father.
And may the God of heaven grant both of you peace and prosperity."
He then called her mother and told her to bring a scroll,
    so that he might draw up a marriage contract
    stating that he gave Sarah to Tobiah as his wife
    according to the decree of the Mosaic law.
Her mother brought the scroll,
    and he drew up the contract,
    to which they affixed their seals.
Afterward they began to eat and drink.

The word of the Lord.

5.

Tobit 8:4b-8   Allow us to live together to a happy old age.

A reading from the Book of Tobit

On their wedding night Tobiah arose from bed and said to his wife,
   "Sister, get up. Let us pray and beg our Lord
   to have mercy on us and to grant us deliverance."
Sarah got up, and they started to pray
   and beg that deliverance might be theirs.
They began with these words:

   "Blessed are you, O God of our fathers;
      praised be your name forever and ever.
   Let the heavens and all your creation
      praise you forever.
   You made Adam and you gave him his wife Eve
      to be his help and support;
      and from these two the human race descended.
   You said, 'It is not good for the man to be alone;
      let us make him a partner like himself.'
   Now, Lord, you know that I take this wife of mine
      not because of lust,
      but for a noble purpose.
   Call down your mercy on me and on her,
      and allow us to live together to a happy old age."

They said together, "Amen, amen."

The word of the Lord.

6.

Proverbs 31:10-13, 19-20, 30-31   The woman who fears the Lord is to be praised.

A reading from the Book of Proverbs

When one finds a worthy wife,
   her value is far beyond pearls.
Her husband, entrusting his heart to her,
   has an unfailing prize.
She brings him good, and not evil,
   all the days of her life.
She obtains wool and flax
   and makes cloth with skillful hands.
She puts her hands to the distaff,
   and her fingers ply the spindle.
She reaches out her hands to the poor,
   and extends her arms to the needy.
Charm is deceptive and beauty fleeting;
   the woman who fears the Lord is to be praised.
Give her a reward of her labors,
   and let her works praise her at the city gates.

The word of the Lord.

7.

Song of Songs 2:8-10, 14, 16a; 8:6-7a   Stern as death is love.

A reading from the Song of Songs

Hark! my lover—here he comes
  springing across the mountains,
  leaping across the hills.
My lover is like a gazelle
  or a young stag.
Here he stands behind our wall,
  gazing through the windows,
  peering through the lattices.
My lover speaks; he says to me,
  "Arise, my beloved, my dove, my beautiful one, and come!

"O my dove in the clefts of the rock,
  in the secret recesses of the cliff,
Let me see you,
  let me hear your voice,
For your voice is sweet,
  and you are lovely."

My lover belongs to me and I to him.
  He says to me:

"Set me as a seal on your heart,
  as a seal on your arm;
For stern as death is love,
  relentless as the nether-world is devotion;
  its flames are a blazing fire.
Deep waters cannot quench love,
  nor floods sweep it away."

The word of the Lord.

8.

Sirach 26:1-4, 13-16   Like the sun rising in the LORD's heavens, the beauty
of a virtuous wife is the radiance of her home.

A reading from the Book of Sirach

Blessed the husband of a good wife,
  twice-lengthened are his days;
A worthy wife brings joy to her husband,
  peaceful and full is his life.
A good wife is a generous gift
  bestowed upon him who fears the LORD;
Be he rich or poor, his heart is content,
  and a smile is ever on his face.

A gracious wife delights her husband,
  her thoughtfulness puts flesh on his bones;
A gift from the LORD is her governed speech,
  and her firm virtue is of surpassing worth.
Choicest of blessings is a modest wife,
  priceless her chaste soul.
A holy and decent woman adds grace upon grace;
  indeed, no price is worthy of her temperate soul.
Like the sun rising in the LORD's heavens,
  the beauty of a virtuous wife is the radiance of her home.

The word of the Lord.

9.

Jeremiah 31:31-32a, 33-34a   I will make a new covenant with the house of Israel and the house of Judah.

A reading from the Book of the Prophet Jeremiah

The days are coming, says the L**ORD****,**
when I will make a new covenant with the house of Israel
and the house of Judah.
It will not be like the covenant I made with their fathers:
the day I took them by the hand
to lead them forth from the land of Egypt.
But this is the covenant which I will make
with the house of Israel after those days, says the L**ORD****.**
I will place my law within them, and write it upon their hearts;
I will be their God, and they shall be my people.
No longer will they have need to teach their friends and relatives
how to know the L**ORD****.**
All, from least to greatest, shall know me, says the L**ORD****.**

The word of the Lord.

802 READING FROM THE NEW TESTAMENT

1.

Romans 8:31b-35, 37-39   What will separate us from the love of Christ?

A reading from the Letter of Saint Paul to the Romans

Brothers and sisters:
If God is for us, who can be against us?
He did not spare his own Son
 but handed him over for us all,
 will he not also give us everything else along with him?
Who will bring a charge against God's chosen ones?
It is God who acquits us.
Who will condemn?
It is Christ Jesus who died, rather, was raised,
 who also is at the right hand of God,
 who indeed intercedes for us.
What will separate us from the love of Christ?
Will anguish, or distress, or persecution, or famine,
 or nakedness, or peril, or the sword?

No, in all these things, we conquer overwhelmingly
 through him who loved us.
For I am convinced that neither death, nor life,
 nor angels, nor principalities,
 nor present things, nor future things,
 nor powers, nor height, nor depth,
 nor any other creature will be able to separate us
 from the love of God in Christ Jesus our Lord.

The word of the Lord.

2.

Long Form

Romans 12:1-2, 9-18   Offer your bodies as a living sacrifice, holy and pleasing to God.

A reading from the Letter of Saint Paul to the Romans

I urge you, brothers and sisters, by the mercies of God,
   to offer your bodies as a living sacrifice,
   holy and pleasing to God, your spiritual worship.
Do not conform yourselves to this age
   but be transformed by the renewal of your mind,
   that you may discern what is the will of God,
   what is good and pleasing and perfect.

Let love be sincere;
   hate what is evil,
   hold on to what is good;
   love one another with mutual affection;
   anticipate one another in showing honor.
Do not grow slack in zeal,
   be fervent in spirit,
   serve the Lord.
Rejoice in hope,
   endure in affliction,
   persevere in prayer.
Contribute to the needs of the holy ones,
   exercise hospitality.
Bless those who persecute you,
   bless and do not curse them.
Rejoice with those who rejoice,
   weep with those who weep.
Have the same regard for one another;
   do not be haughty but associate with the lowly;
   do not be wise in your own estimation.
Do not repay anyone evil for evil;
   be concerned for what is noble in the sight of all.
If possible, on your part, live at peace with all.

The word of the Lord.

OR Short Form

Romans 12:1-2, 9-13   Offer your bodies as a living sacrifice, holy and pleasing to God.

A reading from the Letter of Saint Paul to the Romans

I urge you, brothers and sisters, by the mercies of God,
   to offer your bodies as a living sacrifice,
      holy and pleasing to God, your spiritual worship.
Do not conform yourselves to this age
   but be transformed by the renewal of your mind,
   that you may discern what is the will of God,
   what is good and pleasing and perfect.

Let love be sincere;
   hate what is evil,
   hold on to what is good;
   love one another with mutual affection;
   anticipate one another in showing honor.
Do not grow slack in zeal,
   be fervent in spirit,
   serve the Lord.
Rejoice in hope,
   endure in affliction,
   persevere in prayer.
Contribute to the needs of the holy ones,
   exercise hospitality.

The word of the Lord.

3.

Romans 15:1b-3a, 5-7, 13   Welcome one another as Christ welcomed you.

A reading from the Letter of Saint Paul to the Romans

Brothers and sisters:
We ought to put up with the failings of the weak and not to please ourselves;
   let each of us please our neighbor for the good,
   for building up.
For Christ did not please himself.
May the God of endurance and encouragement
   grant you to think in harmony with one another,
   in keeping with Christ Jesus,
   that with one accord you may with one voice
   glorify the God and Father of our Lord Jesus Christ.

Welcome one another, then, as Christ welcomed you,
   for the glory of God.
May the God of hope fill you with all joy and peace in believing,
   so that you may abound in hope by the power of the Holy Spirit.

The word of the Lord.

4.

1 Corinthians 6:13c-15a, 17-20   Your body is a temple of the Spirit.

A reading from the first Letter of Saint Paul to the Corinthians

Brothers and sisters:
The body is not for immorality, but for the Lord,
   and the Lord is for the body;
   God raised the Lord and will also raise us by his power.

Do you not know that your bodies are members of Christ?
Whoever is joined to the Lord becomes one spirit with him.
Avoid immorality.
Every other sin a person commits is outside the body,
   but the immoral person sins against his own body.
Do you not know that your body
   is a temple of the Holy Spirit within you,
   whom you have from God, and that you are not your own?
For you have been purchased at a price.
Therefore glorify God in your body.

The word of the Lord.

5.

1 Corinthians 12:31—13:8a   If I do not have love, I gain nothing.

A reading from the first Letter of Saint Paul to the Corinthians

Brothers and sisters:
Strive eagerly for the greatest spiritual gifts.

But I shall show you a still more excellent way.

If I speak in human and angelic tongues
   but do not have love,
   I am a resounding gong or a clashing cymbal.
And if I have the gift of prophecy
   and comprehend all mysteries and all knowledge;
   if I have all faith so as to move mountains,
   but do not have love, I am nothing.
If I give away everything I own,
   and if I hand my body over so that I may boast
   but do not have love, I gain nothing.

Love is patient, love is kind.
It is not jealous, is not pompous,
   it is not inflated, it is not rude,
   it does not seek its own interests,
   it is not quick-tempered, it does not brood over injury, it does not rejoice
      over wrongdoing
   but rejoices with the truth.
It bears all things, believes all things,
   hopes all things, endures all things.

Love never fails.

The word of the Lord.

6.

Long Form

Ephesians 5:2a, 21-33   This is a great mystery, but I speak in reference to Christ and the Church.

A reading from the Letter of Saint Paul to the Ephesians

Brothers and sisters:
Live in love, as Christ loved us
  and handed himself over for us.

Be subordinate to one another out of reverence for Christ.
Wives should be subordinate to their husbands as to the Lord.
For the husband is head of his wife
  just as Christ is head of the Church,
  he himself the savior of the body.
As the Church is subordinate to Christ,
  so wives should be subordinate to their husbands in everything.
Husbands, love your wives,
  even as Christ loved the Church
  and handed himself over for her to sanctify her,
  cleansing her by the bath of water with the word,
  that he might present to himself the Church in splendor,
  without spot or wrinkle or any such thing,
  that she might be holy and without blemish.
So also husbands should love their wives as their own bodies.
He who loves his wife loves himself.
For no one hates his own flesh
  but rather nourishes and cherishes it,
  even as Christ does the Church,
  because we are members of his Body.

  For this reason a man shall leave his father and his mother
    and be joined to his wife,
  and the two shall become one flesh.

This is a great mystery,
  but I speak in reference to Christ and the Church.
In any case, each one of you should love his wife as himself,
  and the wife should respect her husband.

The word of the Lord.

OR Short Form

Ephesians 5:2a, 25-32   This is a great mystery, but I speak in reference to Christ and the Church.

A reading from the Letter of Saint Paul to the Ephesians

Brothers and sisters:
Live in love, as Christ loved us
   and handed himself over for us.

Husbands, love your wives,
   even as Christ loved the Church
   and handed himself over for her to sanctify her,
   cleansing her by the bath of water with the word,
   that he might present to himself the Church in splendor,
   without spot or wrinkle or any such thing,
   that she might be holy and without blemish.
So also husbands should love their wives as their own bodies.
He who loves his wife loves himself.
For no one hates his own flesh
   but rather nourishes and cherishes it,
   even as Christ does the Church,
   because we are members of his Body.

   For this reason a man shall leave his father and his mother
      and be joined to his wife,
   and the two shall become one flesh.

This is a great mystery,
   but I speak in reference to Christ and the Church.

The word of the Lord.

7.

Philippians 4:4-9   The God of peace will be with you.

A reading from the Letter of Saint Paul to the Philippians

Brothers and sisters:
Rejoice in the Lord always.
I shall say it again: rejoice!
Your kindness should be known to all.
The Lord is near.
Have no anxiety at all, but in everything,
   by prayer and petition, with thanksgiving,
   make your requests known to God.
Then the peace of God that surpasses all understanding
   will guard your hearts and minds in Christ Jesus.

Finally, brothers and sisters,
   whatever is true, whatever is honorable,
   whatever is just, whatever is pure,
   whatever is lovely, whatever is gracious,
   if there is any excellence
   and if there is anything worthy of praise,
   think about these things.
Keep on doing what you have learned and received
   and heard and seen in me.
Then the God of peace will be with you.

The word of the Lord.

8.

Colossians 3:12-17   And over all these put on love, that is, the bond of perfection.

A reading from the Letter of Saint Paul to the Colossians

Brothers and sisters:
Put on, as God's chosen ones, holy and beloved,
   heartfelt compassion, kindness, humility, gentleness, and patience,
   bearing with one another and forgiving one another,
   if one has a grievance against another;
   as the Lord has forgiven you, so must you also do.
And over all these put on love,
   that is, the bond of perfection.

And let the peace of Christ control your hearts,
   the peace into which you were also called in one Body.
And be thankful.
Let the word of Christ dwell in you richly,
   as in all wisdom you teach and admonish one another,
   singing psalms, hymns, and spiritual songs
   with gratitude in your hearts to God.
And whatever you do, in word or in deed,
   do everything in the name of the Lord Jesus,
   giving thanks to God the Father through him.

The word of the Lord.

9.

Hebrews 13:1-4a, 5-6b   Let marriage be held in honor by all.

A reading from the Letter to the Hebrews

Brothers and sisters:
Let mutual love continue.
Do not neglect hospitality,
   for through it some have unknowingly entertained angels.
Be mindful of prisoners as if sharing their imprisonment,
   and of the ill-treated as of yourselves,
   for you also are in the body.
Let marriage be honored among all
   and the marriage bed be kept undefiled.
Let your life be free from love of money
   but be content with what you have,
   for he has said, *I will never forsake you or abandon you.*
Thus we may say with confidence:

   The Lord is my helper,
   and I will not be afraid.

The word of the Lord.

10.

1 Peter 3:1-9   Be of one mind, sympathetic, loving toward one another.

A reading from the first Letter of Saint Peter

Beloved:
You wives should be subordinate to your husbands so that,
   even if some disobey the word,
   they may be won over without a word by their wives' conduct
   when they observe your reverent and chaste behavior.
Your adornment should not be an external one:
   braiding the hair, wearing gold jewelry, or dressing in fine clothes,
   but rather the hidden character of the heart,
   expressed in the imperishable beauty
   of a gentle and calm disposition,
   which is precious in the sight of God.
For this is also how the holy women who hoped in God
   once used to adorn themselves
   and were subordinate to their husbands;
   thus Sarah obeyed Abraham, calling him "lord."
You are her children when you do what is good
   and fear no intimidation.

Likewise, you husbands should live with your wives in understanding,
   showing honor to the weaker female sex,
   since we are joint heirs of the gift of life,
   so that your prayers may not be hindered.

Finally, all of you, be of one mind, sympathetic,
   loving toward one another, compassionate, humble.
Do not return evil for evil, or insult for insult;
   but, on the contrary, a blessing, because to this you were called,
   that you might inherit a blessing.

The word of the Lord.

11.

1 John 3:18-24   Love in deed and in truth

A reading from the first Letter of Saint John

Children, let us love not in word or speech
   but in deed and truth.

Now this is how we shall know that we belong to the truth
  and reassure our hearts before him
  in whatever our hearts condemn,
  for God is greater than our hearts and knows everything.
Beloved, if our hearts do not condemn us,
  we have confidence in God
  and receive from him whatever we ask,
  because we keep his commandments and do what pleases him.
And his commandment is this:
  we should believe in the name of his Son, Jesus Christ,
  and love one another just as he commanded us.
Those who keep his commandments remain in him, and he in them,
  and the way we know that he remains in us
  is from the Spirit that he gave us.

The word of the Lord.

12.

1 John 4:7-12   God is love.

A reading from the first Letter of Saint John

Beloved, let us love one another,
  because love is of God;
  everyone who loves is begotten by God and knows God.
Whoever is without love does not know God, for God is love.
In this way the love of God was revealed to us:
  God sent his only-begotten Son into the world
  so that we might have life through him.
In this is love:
  not that we have loved God, but that he loved us
  and sent his Son as expiation for our sins.
Beloved, if God so loved us,
  we also must love one another.
No one has ever seen God.
Yet, if we love one another, God remains in us,
  and his love is brought to perfection in us.

The word of the Lord.

13.

Revelation 19:1, 5-9a   Blessed are those who have been called to the wedding feast of the Lamb.

A reading from the Book of Revelation

I, John, heard what sounded like the loud voice
  of a great multitude in heaven, saying:

  "Alleluia!
Salvation, glory, and might belong to our God."

A voice coming from the throne said:

  "Praise our God, all you his servants,
    and you who revere him, small and great."

Then I heard something like the sound of a great multitude
  or the sound of rushing water or mighty peals of thunder,
  as they said:
    "Alleluia!
The Lord has established his reign,
    our God, the almighty.
Let us rejoice and be glad
    and give him glory.
For the wedding day of the Lamb has come,
    his bride has made herself ready.
She was allowed to wear
    a bright, clean linen garment."
(The linen represents the righteous deeds of the holy ones.)

Then the angel said to me,
  "Write this:
  Blessed are those who have been called
  to the wedding feast of the Lamb."

The word of the Lord.

803 RESPONSORIAL PSALM

1.

Psalm 33:12 and 18, 20-21, 22

℟. (5b) **The earth is full of the goodness of the Lord.**

Blessed the nation whose God is the LORD,
 the people he has chosen for his own inheritance.
But see, the eyes of the LORD are upon those who fear him,
 upon those who hope for his kindness.

℟. **The earth is full of the goodness of the Lord.**

Our soul waits for the LORD,
 who is our help and our shield,
For in him our hearts rejoice;
 in his holy name we trust.

℟. **The earth is full of the goodness of the Lord.**

May your kindness, O LORD, be upon us
 who have put our hope in you.

℟. **The earth is full of the goodness of the Lord.**

2.

Psalm 34:2-3, 4-5, 6-7, 8-9

℟. (2a) **I will bless the Lord at all times.**
   or:
℟. (9a) **Taste and see the goodness of the Lord.**

I will bless the LORD at all times;
   his praise shall be ever in my mouth.
Let my soul glory in the LORD;
   the lowly will hear me and be glad.

℟. **I will bless the Lord at all times.**
   or:
℟. **Taste and see the goodness of the Lord.**

Glorify the LORD with me,
   let us together extol his name.
I sought the LORD, and he answered me
   and delivered me from all my fears.

℟. **I will bless the Lord at all times.**
   or:
℟. **Taste and see the goodness of the Lord.**

Look to him that you may be radiant with joy,
   and your faces may not blush with shame.
When the poor one called out, the LORD heard,
   and from all his distress he saved him.

℟. **I will bless the Lord at all times.**
   or:
℟. **Taste and see the goodness of the Lord.**

The angel of the LORD encamps
   around those who fear him, and delivers them.
Taste and see how good the LORD is;
   blessed the man who takes refuge in him.

℟. **I will bless the Lord at all times.**
   or:
℟. **Taste and see the goodness of the Lord.**

3.

Psalm 103:1-2, 8 and 13, 17-18a

℟. (8a) **The Lord is kind and merciful.**
    or:
℟. (see 17) **The Lord's kindness is everlasting to those who fear him.**

Bless the LORD, O my soul;
    and all my being, bless his holy name.
Bless the LORD, O my soul,
    and forget not all his benefits.

℟. **The Lord is kind and merciful.**
    or:
℟. **The Lord's kindness is everlasting to those who fear him.**

Merciful and gracious is the LORD,
    slow to anger and abounding in kindness.
As a father has compassion on his children,
    so the LORD has compassion on those who fear him.

℟. **The Lord is kind and merciful.**
    or:
℟. **The Lord's kindness is everlasting to those who fear him.**

But the kindness of the LORD is from eternity
    to eternity toward those who fear him,
And his justice towards children's children
    among those who keep his covenant.

℟. **The Lord is kind and merciful.**
    or:
℟. **The Lord's kindness is everlasting to those who fear him.**

4.

Psalm 112:1bc-2, 3-4, 5-7a, 7b-8, 9

R̸. (see 1) **Blessed the man who greatly delights in the Lord's commands.**
    or:
R̸. **Alleluia.**

Blessed the man who fears the LORD,
   who greatly delights in his commands.
His posterity shall be mighty upon the earth;
   the upright generation shall be blessed.

R̸. **Blessed the man who greatly delights in the Lord's commands.**
    or:
R̸. **Alleluia.**

Wealth and riches shall be in his house;
   his generosity shall endure forever.
Light shines through the darkness for the upright;
   he is gracious and merciful and just.

R̸. **Blessed the man who greatly delights in the Lord's commands.**
    or:
R̸. **Alleluia.**

Well for the man who is gracious and lends,
   who conducts his affairs with justice;
He shall never be moved;
   the just one shall be in everlasting remembrance.
An evil report he shall not fear.

R̸. **Blessed the man who greatly delights in the Lord's commands.**
    or:
R̸. **Alleluia.**

His heart is firm, trusting in the LORD.
His heart is steadfast; he shall not fear
   till he looks down upon his foes.

R̸. **Blessed the man who greatly delights in the Lord's commands.**
    or:
R̸. **Alleluia.**

Lavishly he gives to the poor;
  his generosity shall endure forever;
  his horn shall be exalted in glory.

R℟. **Blessed the man who greatly delights in the Lord's commands.**
  or:
R℟. **Alleluia.**

5.

Psalm 128:1-2, 3, 4-5

R℟. (see 1a) **Blessed are those who fear the Lord.**
  or:
R℟. (4) **See how the Lord blesses those who fear him.**

Blessed are you who fear the LORD,
  who walk in his ways!
For you shall eat the fruit of your handiwork;
  blessed shall you be, and favored.

R℟. **Blessed are those who fear the Lord.**
  or:
R℟. **See how the Lord blesses those who fear him.**

Your wife shall be like a fruitful vine
  in the recesses of your home;
Your children like olive plants
  around your table.

R℟. **Blessed are those who fear the Lord.**
  or:
R℟. **See how the Lord blesses those who fear him.**

Behold, thus is the man blessed
  who fears the LORD.
The LORD bless you from Zion:
  may you see the prosperity of Jerusalem
  all the days of your life.

R℟. **Blessed are those who fear the Lord.**
  or:
R℟. **See how the Lord blesses those who fear him.**

6.

Psalm 145:8-9, 10 and 15, 17-18

R℣. (9a) **The Lord is compassionate toward all his works.**

The LORD is gracious and merciful,
   slow to anger and of great kindness.
The LORD is good to all
   and compassionate toward all his works.

R℣. **The Lord is compassionate toward all his works.**

Let all your works give you thanks, O LORD,
   and let your faithful ones bless you.
The eyes of all look hopefully to you
   and you give them their food in due season.

R℣. **The Lord is compassionate toward all his works.**

The LORD is just in all his ways
   and holy in all his works.
The LORD is near to all who call upon him,
   to all who call upon him in truth.

R℣. **The Lord is compassionate toward all his works.**

7.

Psalm 148:1-2, 3-4, 9-10, 11-13a, 13c-14a

R℣. (13a) **Let all praise the name of the Lord.**
   or:
R℣. **Alleluia.**

Alleluia.
Praise the LORD from the heavens,
   praise him in the heights;
Praise him, all you his angels,
   praise him, all you his hosts.

R℣. **Let all praise the name of the Lord.**
   or:
R℣. **Alleluia.**

Praise him, sun and moon;
  praise him, all you shining stars.
Praise him, you highest heavens,
  and you waters above the heavens.

℟. Let all praise the name of the Lord.
  or:
℟. Alleluia.

You mountains and all you hills,
  you fruit trees and all you cedars;
You wild beasts and all tame animals,
  you creeping things and winged fowl.

℟. Let all praise the name of the Lord.
  or:
℟. Alleluia.

Let the kings of the earth and all peoples,
  the princes and all the judges of the earth,
Young men too, and maidens,
  old men and boys,
Praise the name of the LORD,
  for his name alone is exalted.

℟. Let all praise the name of the Lord.
  or:
℟. Alleluia.

His majesty is above earth and heaven,
  and he has lifted his horn above the people.

℟. Let all praise the name of the Lord.
  or:
℟. Alleluia.

804   ALLELUIA VERSE AND VERSE BEFORE THE GOSPEL

1.

1 John 4:7b

Everyone who loves is begotten of God and knows God.

2.

1 John 4:8b, 11

God is love.
If God loved us, we also must love one another.

3.

1 John 4:12

If we love one another,
God remains in us
and his love is brought to perfection in us.

4.

1 John 4:16

Whoever remains in love,
remains in God and God in him.

805 GOSPEL

1.

Matthew 5:1-12a   Rejoice and be glad, for your reward will be great in heaven.

✠ **A reading from the holy Gospel according to Matthew**

When Jesus saw the crowds, he went up the mountain,
**   and after he had sat down, his disciples came to him.**
He began to teach them, saying:

> **"Blessed are the poor in spirit,**
> **   for theirs is the Kingdom of heaven.**
> **Blessed are they who mourn,**
> **   for they will be comforted.**
> **Blessed are the meek,**
> **   for they will inherit the land.**
> **Blessed are they who hunger and thirst for righteousness,**
> **   for they will be satisfied.**
> **Blessed are the merciful,**
> **   for they will be shown mercy.**
> **Blessed are the clean of heart,**
> **   for they will see God.**
> **Blessed are the peacemakers,**
> **   for they will be called children of God.**
> **Blessed are they who are persecuted for the sake of righteousness,**
> **   for theirs is the Kingdom of heaven.**
> **Blessed are you when they insult you and persecute you**
> **   and utter every kind of evil against you falsely because of me.**
> **Rejoice and be glad,**
> **   for your reward will be great in heaven."**

The Gospel of the Lord.

2.

Matthew 5:13-16   You are the light of the world.

✠   **A reading from the holy Gospel according to Matthew**

Jesus said to his disciples:
"You are the salt of the earth.
But if salt loses its taste, with what can it be seasoned?
It is no longer good for anything
  but to be thrown out and trampled underfoot.
You are the light of the world.
A city set on a mountain cannot be hidden.
Nor do they light a lamp and then put it under a bushel basket;
  it is set on a lamp stand,
  where it gives light to all in the house.
Just so, your light must shine before others,
  that they may see your good deeds
  and glorify your heavenly Father."

The Gospel of the Lord.

3.

Long Form

Matthew 7:21, 24-29   A wise man built his house on rock.

✠   **A reading from the holy Gospel according to Matthew**

Jesus said to his disciples:
"Not everyone who says to me, 'Lord, Lord,'
  will enter the Kingdom of heaven,
  but only the one who does the will of my Father in heaven.

"Everyone who listens to these words of mine and acts on them
  will be like a wise man who built his house on rock.
The rain fell, the floods came,
  and the winds blew and buffeted the house.
But it did not collapse; it had been set solidly on rock.
And everyone who listens to these words of mine
  but does not act on them
  will be like a fool who built his house on sand.
The rain fell, the floods came,
  and the winds blew and buffeted the house.
And it collapsed and was completely ruined."

When Jesus finished these words,
   the crowds were astonished at his teaching,
   for he taught them as one having authority,
   and not as their scribes.

The Gospel of the Lord.

OR Short Form

Matthew 7:21, 24-25   A wise man built his house on rock.

☩   **A reading from the holy Gospel according to Matthew**

Jesus said to his disciples:
"Not everyone who says to me, 'Lord, Lord,'
   will enter the Kingdom of heaven,
   but only the one who does the will of my Father in heaven.

"Everyone who listens to these words of mine and acts on them
   will be like a wise man who built his house on rock.
The rain fell, the floods came,
   and the winds blew and buffeted the house.
But it did not collapse;
   it had been set solidly on rock."

The Gospel of the Lord.

4.

Matthew 19:3-6   What God has united, man must not separate.

☩   **A reading from the holy Gospel according to Matthew**

Some Pharisees approached Jesus, and tested him, saying,
   "Is it lawful for a man to divorce his wife for any cause whatever?"
He said in reply, "Have you not read that from the beginning
   the Creator *made them male and female* and said,
   For this reason a man shall leave his father and mother
   and be joined to his wife, and the two shall become one flesh?
So they are no longer two, but one flesh.
Therefore, what God has joined together, man must not separate."

The Gospel of the Lord.

5.

Matthew 22:35-40   This is the greatest and the first commandment. The second is like it.

✠   **A reading from the holy Gospel according to Matthew**

One of the Pharisees, a scholar of the law, tested Jesus by asking,
   "Teacher, which commandment in the law is the greatest?"
He said to him,
   "You shall love the Lord, your God,
   with all your heart,
   with all your soul,
   and with all your mind.
This is the greatest and the first commandment.
The second is like it:
   You shall love your neighbor as yourself.
The whole law and the prophets depend on these two commandments."

The Gospel of the Lord.

6.

Mark 10:6-9   They are no longer two, but one flesh.

✠   **A reading from the holy Gospel according to Mark**

Jesus said:
"From the beginning of creation,
   God made them male and female.
For this reason a man shall leave his father and mother
   and be joined to his wife,
   and the two shall become one flesh.
So they are no longer two but one flesh.
Therefore what God has joined together,
   no human being must separate."

The Gospel of the Lord.

7.

John 2:1-11   Jesus did this as the beginning of his signs in Cana in Galilee.

✠ **A reading from the holy Gospel according to John**

There was a wedding in Cana in Galilee,
   and the mother of Jesus was there.
Jesus and his disciples were also invited to the wedding.
When the wine ran short,
   the mother of Jesus said to him,
   "They have no wine."
And Jesus said to her,
   "Woman, how does your concern affect me?
My hour has not yet come."
His mother said to the servers,
   "Do whatever he tells you."
Now there were six stone water jars there for Jewish ceremonial washings,
   each holding twenty to thirty gallons.
Jesus told them,
   "Fill the jars with water."
So they filled them to the brim.
Then he told them,
   "Draw some out now and take it to the headwaiter."
So they took it.
And when the headwaiter tasted the water that had become wine,
   without knowing where it came from
   (although the servants who had drawn the water knew),
   the headwaiter called the bridegroom and said to him,
   "Everyone serves good wine first,
   and then when people have drunk freely, an inferior one;
   but you have kept the good wine until now."
Jesus did this as the beginning of his signs in Cana in Galilee
   and so revealed his glory,
   and his disciples began to believe in him.

The Gospel of the Lord.

8.

John 15:9-12   Remain in my love.

✠   **A reading from the holy Gospel according to John**

Jesus said to his disciples:
"As the Father loves me, so I also love you.
Remain in my love.
If you keep my commandments, you will remain in my love,
  just as I have kept my Father's commandments
  and remain in his love.

"I have told you this so that my joy might be in you
  and your joy might be complete.
This is my commandment: love one another as I love you."

The Gospel of the Lord.

9.

John 15:12-16   This is my commandment: love one another.

✠   **A reading from the holy Gospel according to John**

Jesus said to his disciples:
"This is my commandment: love one another as I love you.
No one has greater love than this,
  to lay down one's life for one's friends.
You are my friends if you do what I command you.
I no longer call you slaves,
  because a slave does not know what his master is doing.
I have called you friends,
  because I have told you everything I have heard from my Father.
It was not you who chose me, but I who chose you
  and appointed you to go and bear fruit that will remain,
  so that whatever you ask the Father in my name he may give you."

The Gospel of the Lord.

10.

Long Form

John 17:20-26   That they may be brought to perfection as one.

✠   **A reading from the holy Gospel according to John**

Jesus raised his eyes to heaven and said:
"I pray not only for my disciples,
> **but also for those who will believe in me through their word,**
> **so that they may all be one,**
> **as you, Father, are in me and I in you,**
> **that they also may be in us,**
> **that the world may believe that you sent me.**

And I have given them the glory you gave me,
> **so that they may be one, as we are one,**
> **I in them and you in me,**
> **that they may be brought to perfection as one,**
> **that the world may know that you sent me,**
> **and that you loved them even as you loved me.**

Father, they are your gift to me.
I wish that where I am they also may be with me,
> **that they may see my glory that you gave me,**
> **because you loved me before the foundation of the world.**

Righteous Father, the world also does not know you,
> **but I know you, and they know that you sent me.**

I made known to them your name and I will make it known,
> **that the love with which you loved me**
> **may be in them and I in them."**

The Gospel of the Lord.

OR Short Form

John 17:20-23   That they may be brought to perfection as one.

✠ **A reading from the holy Gospel according to John**

Jesus raised his eyes to heaven and said:
"Holy Father, I pray not only for these,
> **but also for those who will believe in me through their word,**
> **so that they may all be one,**
> **as you, Father, are in me and I in you,**
> **that they also may be in us,**
> **that the world may believe that you sent me.**

And I have given them the glory you gave me,
> **so that they may be one, as we are one,**
> **I in them and you in me,**
> **that they may be brought to perfection as one,**
> **that the world may know that you sent me,**
> **and that you loved them even as you loved me."**

The Gospel of the Lord.

VII. FOR THE BLESSING OF ABBOTS AND ABBESSES

806 READING FROM THE OLD TESTAMENT

First Option

Proverbs 2:1-9   Inclining your heart to understanding.

A reading from the Book of Proverbs

**My son, if you receive my words
  and treasure my commands,
Turning your ear to wisdom,
  inclining your heart to understanding;
Yes, if you call to intelligence,
  and to understanding raise your voice;
If you seek her like silver,
  and like hidden treasures search her out:**

**Then will you understand the fear of the LORD;
  the knowledge of God you will find;
For the LORD gives wisdom,
  from his mouth come knowledge and understanding;
He has counsel in store for the upright,
  he is the shield of those who walk honestly,
Guarding the paths of justice,
  protecting the way of his pious ones.**

**Then you will understand rectitude and justice,
  honesty, every good path.**

The word of the Lord.

Second Option

Proverbs 4:7-13   Go the way of wisdom I direct you.

A reading from the Book of Proverbs

"The beginning of wisdom is: get wisdom;
   at the cost of all you have, get understanding.
Extol her, and she will exalt you;
   she will bring you honors if you embrace her;
She will put on your head a graceful diadem;
   a glorious crown will she bestow on you."

Hear, my son, and receive my words,
   and the years of your life shall be many.
On the way of wisdom I direct you,
   I lead you on straightforward paths.
When you walk, your step will not be impeded,
   and should you run, you will not stumble.
Hold fast to instruction, never let her go;
   keep her, for she is your life.

The word of the Lord.

807 READING FROM THE NEW TESTAMENT

1.

Acts 2:42-47   All those who believed were together and had everything in common.

A reading from the Acts of the Apostles

The disciples devoted themselves
   to the teaching of the Apostles and to the communal life,
   to the breaking of the bread and to the prayers.
Awe came upon everyone,
   and many wonders and signs were done through the Apostles.
All who believed were together and had all things in common;
   they would sell their property and possessions
   and divide them among all according to each one's need.
Every day they devoted themselves
   to meeting together in the temple area
   and to breaking bread in their homes.
They ate their meals with exultation and sincerity of heart,
   praising God and enjoying favor with all the people.
And every day the Lord added to their number those who were being saved.

The word of the Lord.

2.

Ephesians 4:1-6   Striving to preserve the unity of the Spirit through the bond of peace.

A reading from the Letter of Saint Paul to the Ephesians

Brothers and sisters:
I, a prisoner for the Lord,
   urge you to live in a manner worthy of the call you have received,
   with all humility and gentleness, with patience,
   bearing with one another through love,
   striving to preserve the unity of the Spirit
   through the bond of peace: one Body and one Spirit,
   as you were also called to the one hope of your call;
   one Lord, one faith, one baptism;
   one God and Father of all,
   who is over all and through all and in all.

The word of the Lord.

3.

Colossians 3:12-17   Over all these put on love, that is, the bond
of perfection.

A reading from the Letter of Saint Paul to the Colossians

Brothers and sisters:
Put on, as God's chosen ones, holy and beloved,
  heartfelt compassion, kindness, humility, gentleness, and patience,
  bearing with one another and forgiving one another,
  if one has a grievance against another;
  as the Lord has forgiven you, so must you also do.
And over all these put on love,
  that is, the bond of perfection.
And let the peace of Christ control your hearts,
  the peace into which you were also called in one Body.
And be thankful.
Let the word of Christ dwell in you richly,
  as in all wisdom you teach and admonish one another,
  singing psalms, hymns, and spiritual songs
  with gratitude in your hearts to God.
And whatever you do, in word or in deed,
  do everything in the name of the Lord Jesus,
  giving thanks to God the Father through him.

The word of the Lord.

4.

Hebrews 13:1-2, 7-8, 17-18   Obey your leaders. Pray for us.

A reading from the Letter to the Hebrews

Brothers and sisters:
Let mutual love continue.
Do not neglect hospitality,
  for through it some have unknowingly entertained angels.

Remember your leaders who spoke the word of God to you.
Consider the outcome of their way of life
  and imitate their faith.
Jesus Christ is the same yesterday, today, and forever.

Obey your leaders and defer to them,
    for they keep watch over you and will have to give an account,
    that they may fulfill their task with joy and not with sorrow,
    for that would be of no advantage to you.

Pray for us, for we are confident that we have a clear conscience,
    wishing to act rightly in every respect.

The word of the Lord.

5.

1 Peter 5:1-4   Be examples to the flock.

A reading from the first Letter of Saint Peter

Beloved:
I exhort the presbyters among you,
    as a fellow presbyter and witness to the sufferings of Christ
    and one who has a share in the glory to be revealed.
Tend the flock of God in your midst,
    overseeing it not by constraint but willingly,
    as God would have it, not for shameful profit but eagerly.
Do not lord it over those assigned to you,
    but be examples to the flock.
And when the chief Shepherd is revealed,
    you will receive the unfading crown of glory.

The word of the Lord.

808 RESPONSORIAL PSALM

First Option

Psalm 1:1-2, 3, 4 and 6

R̷. (Psalm 40:5a) **Blessed are they who hope in the Lord.**

Blessed the man who follows not
   the counsel of the wicked
Nor walks in the way of sinners,
   nor sits in the company of the insolent,
But delights in the law of the LORD
   and meditates on his law day and night.

R̷. **Blessed are they who hope in the Lord.**

He is like a tree
   planted near running water,
That yields its fruit in due season,
   and whose leaves never fade.
   Whatever he does, prospers.

R̷. **Blessed are they who hope in the Lord.**

Not so are the wicked, not so;
   they are like chaff which the wind drives away.
For the LORD watches over the way of the just,
   but the way of the wicked vanishes.

R̷. **Blessed are they who hope in the Lord.**

Second Option

Psalm 34:2-3, 4-5, 10-11, 12-13

℟. (12) **Come, children, hear me: I will teach you the fear of the Lord.**

I will bless the LORD at all times;
   his praise shall ever be in my mouth.
Let my soul glory in the LORD;
   the lowly will hear me and be glad.

℟. Come, children, hear me: I will teach you the fear of the Lord.

Glorify the LORD with me,
   let us together extol his name.
I sought the LORD, and he answered me
   and delivered me from all my fears.

℟. Come, children, hear me: I will teach you the fear of the Lord.

Fear the LORD, you his holy ones,
   for nought is lacking to those who fear him.
The great grow poor and hungry;
   but those who seek the LORD want for no good thing.

℟. Come, children, hear me: I will teach you the fear of the Lord.

Come, children, hear me;
   I will teach you the fear of the LORD.
Which of you desires life,
   and takes delight in prosperous days?

℟. Come, children, hear me: I will teach you the fear of the Lord.

Third Option

Psalm 92:2-3, 5-6, 13-14, 15-16

R℣. (see 2a) **Lord, it is good to give thanks to you.**

It is good to give thanks to the LORD,
to sing praise to your name, Most High,
To proclaim your kindness at dawn
and your faithfulness throughout the night.

R℣. **Lord, it is good to give thanks to you.**

For you make me glad, O LORD, by your deeds;
at the works of your hands I rejoice.
How great are your works, O LORD!
How very deep are your thoughts!

R℣. **Lord, it is good to give thanks to you.**

The just man shall flourish like the palm tree,
like a cedar of Lebanon shall he grow.
They that are planted in the house of the LORD
shall flourish in the courts of our God.

R℣. **Lord, it is good to give thanks to you.**

They shall bear fruit even in old age,
vigorous and sturdy shall they be,
Declaring how just is the LORD,
my Rock, in whom there is no wrong.

R℣. **Lord, it is good to give thanks to you.**

809 ALLELUIA VERSE AND VERSE BEFORE THE GOSPEL

1.

Matthew 23:9b, 10b

**You have but one Father in heaven;
you have but one master, the Christ.**

2.

Colossians 3:15

**Let the peace of Christ control your hearts,
the peace to which you were called in one Body.**

810　GOSPEL

First Option

Matthew 23:8-12　The greatest among you must be your servant.

☩　**A reading from the holy Gospel according to Matthew**

Jesus spoke to the crowds and to his disciples:
"Do not be called 'Rabbi.'
You have but one teacher, and you are all brothers.
Call no one on earth your father;
　you have but one Father in heaven.
Do not be called 'Master';
　you have but one master, the Christ.
The greatest among you must be your servant.
Whoever exalts himself will be humbled;
　but whoever humbles himself will be exalted."

The Gospel of the Lord.

Second Option

Luke 12:35-44　The master will put him in charge of his servants.

☩　**A reading from the holy Gospel according to Luke**

Jesus said to his disciples:
"Gird your loins and light your lamps
　and be like servants who await their master's return from a wedding,
　ready to open immediately when he comes and knocks.
Blessed are those servants
　whom the master finds vigilant on his arrival.
Amen, I say to you, he will gird himself,
　have them recline at table, and proceed to wait on them.
And should he come in the second or third watch
　and find them prepared in this way,
　blessed are those servants.
Be sure of this:
　if the master of the house had known the hour
　when the thief was coming,
　he would not have let his house be broken into.
You also must be prepared, for at an hour you do not expect,
　the Son of Man will come."

Then Peter said,
   "Lord, is this parable meant for us or for everyone?"
And the Lord replied,
   "Who, then, is the faithful and prudent steward
   whom the master will put in charge of his servants
   to distribute the food allowance at the proper time?
Blessed is that servant whom his master on arrival finds doing so.
Truly, I say to you, he will put him in charge of all his property."

The Gospel of the Lord.

Third Option

Luke 22:24-27   I am among you as one who serves.

☩ **A reading from the holy Gospel according to Luke**

An argument broke out among the disciples
   about which of them should be regarded as the greatest.
Jesus said to them,
   "The kings of the Gentiles lord it over them
   and those in authority over them are addressed as 'Benefactors';
   but among you it shall not be so.
Rather, let the greatest among you be as the youngest,
   and the leader as the servant.
For who is greater:
   the one seated at table or the one who serves?
Is it not the one seated at table?
I am among you as the one who serves."

The Gospel of the Lord.

VIII. FOR THE CONSECRATION OF VIRGINS AND RELIGIOUS PROFESSION

811 READING FROM THE OLD TESTAMENT

1.

Genesis 12:1-4a   Go forth from the land of your kinsfolk and from your father's home.

A reading from the Book of Genesis

The LORD said to Abram:
"Go forth from the land of your kinsfolk
  and from your father's house to a land that I will show you.

  "I will make of you a great nation,
    and I will bless you;
  I will make your name great,
    so that you will be a blessing.
  I will bless those who bless you
    and curse those who curse you.
  All the communities of the earth
    shall find blessing in you."

Abram went as the LORD directed him.

The word of the Lord.

2.

A reading from the first Book of Samuel

During the time young Samuel was minister to the LORD** under Eli,**
  a revelation of the LORD** was uncommon and vision infrequent.**
One day Eli was asleep in his usual place.
His eyes had lately grown so weak that he could not see.
The lamp of God was not yet extinguished,
  and Samuel was sleeping in the temple of the LORD
  where the ark of God was.
The LORD** called to Samuel, who answered, "Here I am."**
He ran to Eli and said, "Here I am. You called me."
"I did not call you," Eli said.
"Go back to sleep."
So he went back to sleep.
Again the LORD** called Samuel, who rose and went to Eli.**
"Here I am," he said. "You called me."
But Eli answered, "I did not call you, my son.
Go back to sleep."

At that time Samuel was not familiar with the LORD**,**
  because the LORD** had not revealed anything to him as yet.**
The LORD** called Samuel again, for the third time.**
Getting up and going to Eli, he said, "Here I am. You called me."
Then Eli understood that the LORD** was calling the youth.**
So Eli said to Samuel, "Go to sleep, and if you are called, reply,
  'Speak, LORD**, for your servant is listening.'"**
When Samuel went to sleep in his place,
  the LORD** came and revealed his presence,**
  calling out as before, "Samuel, Samuel!"
Samuel answered, "Speak, for your servant is listening."

The word of the Lord.

3.

1 Kings 19:4-9a, 11-15a   Go out and stand on the mountain before
the Lord.

A reading from the first Book of Kings

Elijah went a day's journey into the desert,
until he came to a broom tree and sat beneath it.
He prayed for death saying:
"This is enough, O Lord!
Take my life, for I am no better than my fathers."
He lay down and fell asleep under the broom tree,
but then an angel touched him and ordered him to get up and eat.
He looked and there at his head was a hearth cake
and a jug of water.
After he ate and drank, he lay down again,
but the angel of the Lord came back a second time,
touched him, and ordered,
"Get up and eat, else the journey will be too long for you!"
He got up, ate, and drank;
then strengthened by that food,
he walked forty days and forty nights to the mountain of God, Horeb.

There he came to a cave, where he took shelter.
Then the Lord said,
"Go outside and stand on the mountain before the Lord;
the Lord will be passing by."
A strong and heavy wind was rending the mountains
and crushing rocks before the Lord—
but the Lord was not in the wind.
After the wind there was an earthquake—
but the Lord was not in the earthquake.
After the earthquake there was fire—
but the Lord was not in the fire.
After the fire there was a tiny whispering sound.
When he heard this,
Elijah hid his face in his cloak
and went and stood at the entrance of the cave.
A voice said to him, "Elijah, why are you here?"
He replied, "I have been most zealous for the Lord, the God of hosts.
But the children of Israel have forsaken your covenant,
torn down your altars, and put your prophets to the sword.

I alone am left, and they seek to take my life."
The LORD said to him,
    "Go, take the road back to the desert near Damascus."

The word of the Lord.

4.

1 Kings 19:16b, 19-21   Then he left and followed Elijah as his attendant.

A reading from the first Book of Kings

The LORD said to Elijah:
"You shall anoint Elisha, son of Shaphat of Abel-meholah,
    as prophet to succeed you."

Elijah set out and came upon Elisha, son of Shaphat,
    as he was plowing with twelve yoke of oxen;
    he was following the twelfth.
Elijah went over to him and threw his cloak over him.
Elisha left the oxen, ran after Elijah, and said,
    "Please, let me kiss my father and mother goodbye,
    and I will follow you."
Elijah answered, "Go back!
Have I done anything to you?"
Elisha left him and taking the yoke of oxen, slaughtered them;
    he used the plowing equipment for fuel to boil their flesh,
    and gave it to his people to eat.
Then he left and followed Elijah as his attendant.

The word of the Lord.

5.

Song of Songs 2:8-14   Arise, my beloved, my beautiful one, and come!

A reading from the Song of Songs

Hark! my lover—here he comes
  springing across the mountains,
  leaping across the hills.
My lover is like a gazelle
  or a young stag.
Here he stands behind our wall,
  gazing through the windows,
  peering through the lattices.
My lover speaks; he says to me,
  "Arise, my beloved, my dove, my beautiful one,
  and come!

"For see, the winter is past,
  the rains are over and gone.
The flowers appear on the earth,
  the time of pruning the vines has come,
  and the song of the dove is heard in our land.
The fig tree puts forth its figs,
  and the vines, in bloom, give forth fragrance.
Arise, my beloved, my beautiful one,
  and come!

"O my dove in the clefts of the rock
  in the secret recesses of the cliff,
Let me see you,
  let me hear your voice,
For your voice is sweet,
  and you are lovely."

The word of the Lord.

6.

Song of Songs 8:6-7   Stern as death is love.

A reading from the Song of Songs

Set me as a seal upon your heart,
  as a seal on your arm;
For stern as death is love,
  relentless as the nether world is devotion;
  its flames are a blazing fire.
Deep waters cannot quench love,
  nor floods sweep it away.
Were one to offer all he owns to purchase love,
  he would be roundly mocked.

The word of the Lord.

7.

Isaiah 44:1-5   One shall say, "I am the LORD's."

A reading from the Book of the Prophet Isaiah

Hear then, O Jacob, my servant,
  Israel, whom I have chosen.
Thus says the LORD who made you,
  your help, who formed you from the womb:
Fear not, O Jacob, my servant,
  the darling whom I have chosen.
I will pour out water upon the thirsty ground,
  and streams upon the dry land;
I will pour out my spirit upon your offspring,
  and my blessing upon your descendants.
They shall spring up amid the verdure
  like poplars beside the flowing waters.
One shall say, "I am the LORD's,"
  another shall be named after Jacob,
and this one shall write on his hand, "The LORD's,"
  and Israel shall be his surname.

The word of the Lord.

8.

Isaiah 61:9-11   I rejoice heartily in the LORD.

A reading from the Book of the Prophet Isaiah

Thus says the LORD:
Their descendants shall be renowned among the nations,
** and their offspring among the peoples;**
All who see them shall acknowledge them
** as a race the LORD has blessed.**

I rejoice heartily in the LORD,
** in my God is the joy of my soul;**
For he has clothed me with a robe of salvation
** and wrapped me in a mantle of justice,**
Like a bridegroom adorned with a diadem,
** like a bride bedecked with her jewels.**
As the earth brings forth its plants,
** and a garden makes its growth spring up,**
So will the Lord GOD make justice and praise
** spring up before all the nations.**

The word of the Lord.

9.

Jeremiah 31:31-37   A new covenant.

A reading from the Book of the Prophet Jeremiah

The days are coming, says the LORD,
** when I will make a new covenant with the house of Israel**
** and the house of Judah.**
It will not be like the covenant I made with their fathers
** the day I took them by the hand**
** to lead them forth from the land of Egypt;**
** for they broke my covenant**
** and I had to show myself their master, says the LORD.**
But this is the covenant which I will make
** with the house of Israel after those days, says the LORD.**
I will place my law within them, and write it upon their hearts;
** I will be their God, and they shall be my people.**
No longer will they have need to teach their friends and relatives
** how to know the LORD.**

All, from least to greatest, shall know me, says the LORD,
    for I will forgive their evildoing and remember their sin no more.

    Thus says the LORD,
He who gives the sun to light the day,
    moon and stars to light the night;
Who stirs up the sea till its waves roar,
    whose name is LORD of hosts:
If ever these natural laws give way
    in spite of me, says the LORD,
Then shall the race of Israel cease
    as a nation before me forever.
      Thus says the LORD:
If the heavens on high can be measured,
    or the foundations below the earth be sounded,
Then will I cast off the whole race of Israel
    because of all they have done, says the LORD.

The word of the Lord.

10.

Hosea 2:16, 21-22   I will espouse you to me forever.

A reading from the Book of the Prophet Hosea

Thus says the LORD:
I will allure her;
    I will lead her into the desert
    and speak to her heart.

I will espouse you to me forever:
    I will espouse you in right and in justice,
    in love and in mercy;
I will espouse you in fidelity,
    and you shall know the LORD.

The word of the Lord.

812 READING FROM THE NEW TESTAMENT

1.

Acts 2:42-47   All who believed were together and had all things in common.

A reading from the Acts of the Apostles

The brothers and sisters devoted themselves
   to the teaching of the Apostles and to the communal life,
   to the breaking of the bread and to the prayers.
Awe came upon everyone,
   and many wonders and signs were done through the Apostles.
All who believed were together and had all things in common;
   they would sell their property and possessions
   and divide them among all according to each one's need.
Every day they devoted themselves
   to meeting together in the temple area
   and to breaking bread in their homes.
They ate their meals with exultation and sincerity of heart,
   praising God and enjoying favor with all the people.
And every day the Lord added to their number those who were being saved.

The word of the Lord.

2.

Acts 4:32-35   The community of believers was of one heart and mind.

A reading from the Acts of the Apostles

The community of believers was of one heart and mind,
   and no one claimed that any of his possessions was his own,
   but they had everything in common.
With great power the Apostles bore witness
   to the resurrection of the Lord Jesus,
   and great favor was accorded them all.
There was no needy person among them,
   for those who owned property or houses would sell them,
   bring the proceeds of the sale,
   and put them at the feet of the Apostles,
   and they were distributed to each according to need.

The word of the Lord.

3.

Romans 6:3-11   So that we too might live in newness of life.

A reading from the Letter of Saint Paul to the Romans

Brothers and sisters:
Are you unaware that we who were baptized into Christ Jesus
  were baptized into his death?
We were indeed buried with him through baptism into death,
  so that, just as Christ was raised from the dead
  by the glory of the Father,
  we too might live in newness of life.

For if we have grown into union with him through a death like his,
  we shall also be united with him in the resurrection.
We know that our old self was crucified with him,
  so that our sinful body might be done away with,
  that we might no longer be in slavery to sin.
For a dead person has been absolved from sin.
If, then, we have died with Christ,
  we believe that we shall also live with him.
We know that Christ, raised from the dead, dies no more;
  death no longer has power over him.
As to his death, he died to sin once and for all;
  as to his life, he lives for God.
Consequently, you too must think of yourselves as being dead to sin
  and living for God in Christ Jesus.

The word of the Lord.

4.

Romans 12:1-13   Offer your bodies as a living sacrifice, holy and pleasing to God.

A reading from the Letter of Saint Paul to the Romans

I urge you, brothers and sisters, by the mercies of God,
  to offer your bodies as a living sacrifice,
  holy and pleasing to God, your spiritual worship.
Do not conform yourselves to this age
  but be transformed by the renewal of your mind,
  that you may discern what is the will of God,
  what is good and pleasing and perfect.

For by the grace given to me I tell everyone among you
  not to think of himself more highly than one ought to think,
  but to think soberly,
  each according to the measure of faith that God has apportioned.
For as in one body we have many parts,
  and all the parts do not have the same function,
  so we, though many, are one Body in Christ
  and individually parts of one another.
Since we have gifts that differ according to the grace given to us,
  let us exercise them:
  if prophecy, in proportion to the faith;
  if ministry, in ministering;
  if one is a teacher, in teaching;
  if one exhorts, in exhortation;
  if one contributes, in generosity;
  if one is over others, with diligence;
  if one does acts of mercy, with cheerfulness.

Let love be sincere;
  hate what is evil,
  hold on to what is good;
  love one another with mutual affection;
  anticipate one another in showing honor.
Do not grow slack in zeal,
  be fervent in spirit,
  serve the Lord.

Rejoice in hope,
  endure in affliction,
  persevere in prayer.
Contribute to the needs of the holy ones,
  exercise hospitality.

The word of the Lord.

5.

1 Corinthians 1:22-31   We proclaim Christ crucified.

A reading from the first Letter of Saint Paul to the Corinthians

Brothers and sisters:
Jews demand signs and Greeks look for wisdom,
  but we proclaim Christ crucified,
  a stumbling block to Jews and foolishness to Gentiles,
  but to those who are called, Jews and Greeks alike,
  Christ the power of God and the wisdom of God.
For the foolishness of God is wiser than human wisdom,
  and the weakness of God is stronger than human strength.

Consider your own calling, brothers and sisters.
Not many of you were wise by human standards,
  not many were powerful,
  not many were of noble birth.
Rather, God chose the foolish of the world to shame the wise,
  and God chose the weak of the world to shame the strong,
  and God chose the lowly and despised of the world,
  those who count for nothing,
  to reduce to nothing those who are something,
  so that no human being might boast before God.
It is due to him that you are in Christ Jesus,
  who became for us wisdom from God,
  as well as righteousness, sanctification, and redemption,
  so that, as it is written,
  Whoever boasts, should boast in the Lord.

The word of the Lord.

6.

1 Corinthians 7:25-35   A virgin is anxious about the things of the Lord.

A reading from the first Letter of Saint Paul to the Corinthians

In regard to virgins, I have no commandment from the Lord,
  but I give my opinion as one who by the Lord's mercy is trustworthy.
So this is what I think best because of the present distress:
  that it is a good thing for a person to remain as he is.
Are you bound to a wife? Do not seek a separation.
Are you free of a wife? Then do not look for a wife.
If you marry, however, you do not sin,
  nor does an unmarried woman sin if she marries;
  but such people will experience affliction in their earthly life,
  and I would like to spare you that.

I tell you, brothers and sisters, the time is running out.
From now on, let those having wives act as not having them,
  those weeping as not weeping,
  those rejoicing as not rejoicing,
  those buying as not owning,
  those using the world as not using it fully.
For the world in its present form is passing away.

I should like you to be free of anxieties.
An unmarried man is anxious about the things of the Lord,
  how he may please the Lord.
But a married man is anxious about the things of the world,
  how he may please his wife, and he is divided.
An unmarried woman or a virgin is anxious about the things of the Lord,
  so that she may be holy in both body and spirit.
A married woman, on the other hand,
  is anxious about the things of the world,
  how she may please her husband.
I am telling you this for your own benefit,
  not to impose a restraint upon you,
  but for the sake of propriety
  and adherence to the Lord without distraction.

The word of the Lord.

7.

Ephesians 1:3-14   God chose us in Christ to be holy and without blemish before him in love.

A reading from the Letter of Saint Paul to the Ephesians

Blessed be the God and Father of our Lord Jesus Christ,
who has blessed us in Christ
with every spiritual blessing in the heavens,
as he chose us in him, before the foundation of the world,
to be holy and without blemish before him.
In love he destined us for adoption to himself through Jesus Christ,
in accord with the favor of his will,
for the praise of the glory of his grace
that he granted us in the beloved.

In him we have redemption by his Blood,
the forgiveness of transgressions,
in accord with the riches of his grace that he lavished upon us.
In all wisdom and insight, he has made known to us
the mystery of his will in accord with his favor
that he set forth in him as a plan for the fullness of times,
to sum up all things in Christ, in heaven and on earth.

In him we were also chosen,
destined in accord with the purpose of the One
who accomplishes all things according to the intention of his will,
so that we might exist for the praise of his glory,
we who first hoped in Christ.
In him you also, who have heard the word of truth,
the Gospel of your salvation, and have believed in him,
were sealed with the promised Holy Spirit,
which is the first installment of our inheritance
toward redemption as God's possession, to the praise of his glory.

The word of the Lord.

8.

Philippians 2:1-4   Being of the same mind, with the same love.

A reading from the Letter of Saint Paul to the Philippians

Brothers and sisters:
If there is any encouragement in Christ,
   any solace in love,
   any participation in the Spirit,
   any compassion and mercy,
   complete my joy by being of the same mind, with the same love,
   united in heart, thinking one thing.
Do nothing out of selfishness or out of vainglory;
   rather, humbly regard others as more important than yourselves,
   each looking out not for his own interests,
   but also everyone for those of others.

The word of the Lord.

9.

Philippians 3:8-14   I consider them so much rubbish, that I may gain Christ.

A reading from the Letter of Saint Paul to the Philippians

Brothers and sisters:
I consider everything as a loss
   because of the supreme good of knowing Christ Jesus my Lord.
For his sake I have accepted the loss of all things
   and I consider them so much rubbish,
   that I may gain Christ and be found in him,
   not having any righteousness of my own based on the law
   but that which comes through faith in Christ,
   the righteousness from God,
   depending on faith to know him and the power of his resurrection
   and the sharing of his sufferings by being conformed to his death,
   if somehow I may attain the resurrection from the dead.

It is not that I have already taken hold of it
   or have already attained perfect maturity,
   but I continue my pursuit in hope that I may possess it,
   since I have indeed been taken possession of by Christ Jesus.

Brothers and sisters, I for my part
    do not consider myself to have taken possession.
Just one thing: forgetting what lies behind
    but straining forward to what lies ahead,
    I continue my pursuit toward the goal,
    the prize of God's upward calling, in Christ Jesus.

The word of the Lord.

10.

Colossians 3:1-4   Think of what is above, not of what is on earth.

A reading from the Letter of Saint Paul to the Colossians

Brothers and sisters:
If you were raised with Christ, seek what is above,
    where Christ is seated at the right hand of God.
Think of what is above, not of what is on earth.
For you have died, and your life is hidden with Christ in God.
When Christ your life appears,
    then you too will appear with him in glory.

The word of the Lord.

11.

Colossians 3:12-17   Over all these put on love, that is, the bond
of perfection.

A reading from the Letter of Saint Paul to the Colossians

Brothers and sisters:
Put on, as God's chosen ones, holy and beloved,
    heartfelt compassion, kindness, humility, gentleness, and patience,
    bearing with one another and forgiving one another,
    if one has a grievance against another;
    as the Lord has forgiven you, so must you also do.
And over all these put on love,
    that is, the bond of perfection.
And let the peace of Christ control your hearts,
    the peace into which you were also called in one Body.
And be thankful.
Let the word of Christ dwell in you richly,
    as in all wisdom you teach and admonish one another,
    singing psalms, hymns, and spiritual songs
    with gratitude in your hearts to God.
And whatever you do, in word or in deed,
    do everything in the name of the Lord Jesus,
    giving thanks to God the Father through him.

The word of the Lord.

12.

1 Thessalonians 4:1-3, 7-12   This is the will of God, your holiness.

A reading from the first Letter of Saint Paul to the Thessalonians

Brothers and sisters,
    we earnestly ask and exhort you in the Lord Jesus that,
    as you received from us
    how you should conduct yourselves to please God—
    and as you are conducting yourselves—
    you do so even more.
For you know what instructions we gave you through the Lord Jesus.

This is the will of God, your holiness:
    that you refrain from immorality.
For God did not call us to impurity but to holiness.

Therefore, whoever disregards this,
  disregards not a human being but God,
  who also gives his Holy Spirit to you.

On the subject of mutual charity
  you have no need for anyone to write you,
  for you yourselves have been taught by God to love one another.
Indeed, you do this for all the brothers throughout Macedonia.
Nevertheless we urge you, brothers and sisters, to progress even more,
  and to aspire to live a tranquil life,
  to mind your own affairs,
  and to work with your own hands,
  as we instructed you,
  that you may conduct yourselves properly toward outsiders
  and not depend on anyone.

The word of the Lord.

13.

1 Peter 1:3-9   Although you have not seen him you love him.

A reading from the first Letter of Saint Peter

Blessed be the God and Father of our Lord Jesus Christ,
  who in his great mercy gave us a new birth to a living hope
  through the resurrection of Jesus Christ from the dead,
  to an inheritance that is imperishable, undefiled, and unfading,
  kept in heaven for you
  who by the power of God are safeguarded through faith,
  to a salvation that is ready to be revealed in the final time.
In this you rejoice, although now for a little while
  you may have to suffer through various trials,
  so that the genuineness of your faith,
  more precious than gold that is perishable even though tested by fire,
  may prove to be for praise, glory, and honor
  at the revelation of Jesus Christ.
Although you have not seen him you love him;
  even though you do not see him now yet you believe in him,
  you rejoice with an indescribable and glorious joy,
  as you attain the goal of your faith, the salvation of your souls.

The word of the Lord.

14.

1 John 4:7-16   If we love one another, God remains in us.

A reading from the first Letter of Saint John

Beloved, let us love one another,
   because love is of God;
   everyone who loves is begotten by God and knows God.
Whoever is without love does not know God, for God is love.
In this way the love of God was revealed to us:
   God sent his only-begotten Son into the world
   so that we might have life through him.
In this is love:
   not that we have loved God, but that he loved us
   and sent his Son as expiation for our sins.
Beloved, if God so loved us,
   we also must love one another.
No one has ever seen God.
Yet, if we love one another, God remains in us,
   and his love is brought to perfection in us.

This is how we know that we remain in him and he in us,
   that he has given us of his Spirit.
Moreover, we have seen and testify
   that the Father sent his Son as savior of the world.
Whoever acknowledges that Jesus is the Son of God,
   God remains in him and he in God.
We have come to know and to believe in the love God has for us.

God is love, and whoever remains in love
   remains in God and God in him.

The word of the Lord.

15.

Revelation 3:14b, 20-22   I will dine with him and he with me.

A reading from the Book of Revelation

""The Amen, the faithful and true witness,
   the source of God's creation, says this:

""Behold, I stand at the door and knock.
If anyone hears my voice and opens the door,
    then I will enter his house and dine with him,
    and he with me.
I will give the victor the right to sit with me on my throne,
    as I myself first won the victory
    and sit with my Father on his throne.

""Whoever has ears ought to hear
    what the Spirit says to the churches.""

The word of the Lord.

16.

Revelation 22:12-14, 16-17, 20   Come, Lord Jesus!

A reading from the Book of Revelation

I, John, heard a voice saying to me:
    "Behold, I am coming soon.
I bring with me the recompense I will give to each
    according to his deeds.
I am the Alpha and the Omega, the first and the last,
    the beginning and the end."

Blessed are they who wash their robes
    so as to have the right to the tree of life
    and enter the city through its gates.

"I, Jesus, sent my angel to give you this testimony for the churches.
I am the root and offspring of David,
    the bright morning star."

The Spirit and the bride say, "Come."
Let the hearer say, "Come."
Let the one who thirsts come forward,
    and the one who wants it receive the gift of life-giving water.

The one who gives this testimony says, "Yes, I am coming soon."
Amen! Come, Lord Jesus!

The word of the Lord.

813 RESPONSORIAL PSALM

1.

Psalm 24:1bc-2, 3-4ab, 5-6

R̷. (see 6) **Lord, this is the people that longs to see your face.**

The LORD's are the earth and its fullness;
    the world and those who dwell in it.
For he founded it upon the seas
    and established it upon the rivers.

R̷. Lord, this is the people that longs to see your face.

Who can ascend the mountain of the LORD?
    or who may stand in his holy place?
He whose hands are sinless, whose heart is clean,
    who desires not what is vain.

R̷. Lord, this is the people that longs to see your face.

He shall receive a blessing from the LORD,
    a reward from God his savior.
Such is the race that seeks for him,
    that seeks the face of the God of Jacob.

R̷. Lord, this is the people that longs to see your face.

2.

Psalm 27:1, 4, 5, 8-9abc, 11

℟. (8b) **I long to see your face, O Lord.**

The LORD is my light and my salvation;
  whom should I fear?
The LORD is my life's refuge;
  of whom should I be afraid?

℟. **I long to see your face, O Lord.**

One thing I ask of the LORD; this I seek:
To dwell in the house of the LORD
  all the days of my life,
That I may gaze on the loveliness of the LORD
  and contemplate his temple.

℟. **I long to see your face, O Lord.**

For he will hide me in his abode
  in the day of trouble;
He will conceal me in the shelter of his tent,
  he will set me high upon a rock.

℟. **I long to see your face, O Lord.**

You my glance seeks;
  your presence, O LORD, I seek.
Hide not your face from me;
  do not in anger repel your servant.
You are my helper: cast me not off.

℟. **I long to see your face, O Lord.**

Show me, O LORD, your way and lead me on a level path,
  because of my adversaries.

℟. **I long to see your face, O Lord.**

3.

Psalm 33:2-3, 4-5, 11-12, 13-14, 18-19, 20-21

℟. (12) **Blessed the people the Lord has chosen to be his own.**

Give thanks to the LORD **on the harp;**
   with the ten-stringed lyre chant his praises.
Sing to him a new song;
   pluck the strings skillfully, with shouts of gladness.

℟. **Blessed the people the Lord has chosen to be his own.**

For upright is the word of the LORD**,**
   and all his works are trustworthy.
He loves justice and right;
   of the kindness of the LORD **the earth is full.**

℟. **Blessed the people the Lord has chosen to be his own.**

But the plan of the LORD **stands forever;**
   the design of his heart, through all generations.
Blessed the nation whose God is the LORD**,**
   the people he has chosen for his own inheritance.

℟. **Blessed the people the Lord has chosen to be his own.**

From heaven the LORD **looks down;**
   he sees all mankind.
From his fixed throne he beholds
   all who dwell on earth.

℟. **Blessed the people the Lord has chosen to be his own.**

But see, the eyes of the LORD **are upon those who fear him,**
   upon those who hope for his kindness,
To deliver them from death
   and preserve them in spite of famine.

℟. **Blessed the people the Lord has chosen to be his own.**

Our soul waits for the LORD**,**
   who is our help and our shield,
For in him our hearts rejoice;
   in his holy name we trust.

℟. **Blessed the people the Lord has chosen to be his own.**

4.

Psalm 34:2-3, 4-5, 6-7, 8-9

℟. (2a) **I will bless the Lord at all times.**
    or:
℟. (9a) **Taste and see the goodness of the Lord.**

I will bless the LORD at all times;
    his praise shall be ever in my mouth.
Let my soul glory in the LORD;
    the lowly will hear me and be glad.

℟. **I will bless the Lord at all times.**
    or:
℟. **Taste and see the goodness of the Lord.**

Glorify the LORD with me,
    let us together extol his name.
I sought the LORD, and he answered me
    and delivered me from all my fears.

℟. **I will bless the Lord at all times.**
    or:
℟. **Taste and see the goodness of the Lord.**

Look to him that you may be radiant with joy,
    and your faces may not blush with shame.
When the poor one called out, the LORD heard,
    and from all his distress he saved him.

℟. **I will bless the Lord at all times.**
    or:
℟. **Taste and see the goodness of the Lord.**

The angel of the LORD encamps
    around those who fear him, and delivers them.
Taste and see how good the LORD is;
    blessed the man who takes refuge in him.

℟. **I will bless the Lord at all times.**
    or:
℟. **Taste and see the goodness of the Lord.**

5.

Psalm 34:10-11, 12-13, 14-15, 17 and 19

℟. (2a) **I will bless the Lord at all times.**
   or:
℟. (9a) **Taste and see the goodness of the Lord.**

Fear the LORD, you his holy ones,
   for nought is lacking to those who fear him.
The great grow poor and hungry;
   but those who seek the LORD want for no good thing.

℟. **I will bless the Lord at all times.**
   or:
℟. **Taste and see the goodness of the Lord.**

Come children, hear me;
   I will teach you the fear of the LORD.
Which of you desires life,
   and takes delight in prosperous days?

℟. **I will bless the Lord at all times.**
   or:
℟. **Taste and see the goodness of the Lord.**

Keep your tongue from evil
   and your lips from speaking guile;
Turn from evil, and do good;
   seek peace, and follow after it.

℟. **I will bless the Lord at all times.**
   or:
℟. **Taste and see the goodness of the Lord.**

The LORD confronts the evildoers,
   to destroy remembrance of them from the earth.
The LORD is close to the brokenhearted;
   and those who are crushed in spirit he saves.

℟. **I will bless the Lord at all times.**
   or:
℟. **Taste and see the goodness of the Lord.**

6.

Psalm 40:2 and 4ab, 7-8a, 8b-9, 10, 12

℟. (8a and 9a) **Here I am, Lord: I come to do your will.**

I have waited, waited for the Lord;
    and he stooped toward me and he heard my cry
And he put a new song into my mouth,
    a hymn to our God.

℟. **Here I am, Lord: I come to do your will.**

Sacrifice or oblation you wished not,
    but ears open to obedience you gave me.
Burnt offerings or sin-offerings you sought not;
    then said I, "Behold I come."

℟. **Here I am, Lord: I come to do your will.**

"In the written scroll it is prescribed for me,
To do your will, O my God, is my delight,
    and your law is within my heart!"

℟. **Here I am, Lord: I come to do your will.**

I announced your justice in the vast assembly;
    I did not restrain my lips, as you, O Lord, know.

℟. **Here I am, Lord: I come to do your will.**

Withhold not, O Lord, your compassion from me;
    may your mercy and your truth ever preserve me.

℟. **Here I am, Lord: I come to do your will.**

7.

Psalm 45:11-12, 14-15, 16-17

R̞. (see Matthew 25:6) **The bridegroom is here; let us go out to meet Christ the Lord.**

Hear, O daughter, and see; turn your ear,
    forget your people and your father's house.
So shall the king desire your beauty;
    for he is your lord, and you must worship him.

R̞. **The bridegroom is here; let us go out to meet Christ the Lord.**

All glorious is the king's daughter as she enters;
    her raiment is threaded with spun gold.
In embroidered apparel she is borne in to the king;
    behind her the virgins of her train are brought to you.

R̞. **The bridegroom is here; let us go out to meet Christ the Lord.**

They are borne in with gladness and joy;
    they enter the palace of the king.
The place of your fathers your sons shall have;
    you shall make them princes through all the land.

R̞. **The bridegroom is here; let us go out to meet Christ the Lord.**

8.

Psalm 63:2, 3-4, 5-6, 8-9

℟. (2b) **My soul is thirsting for you, O Lord my God.**

O God, you are my God whom I seek;
for you my flesh pines and my soul thirsts
like the earth, parched, lifeless and without water.

℟. **My soul is thirsting for you, O Lord my God.**

Thus have I gazed toward you in the sanctuary
to see your power and your glory,
For your kindness is a greater good than life;
my lips shall glorify you.

℟. **My soul is thirsting for you, O Lord my God.**

Thus will I bless you while I live;
lifting up my hands, I will call upon your name.
As with the riches of a banquet shall my soul be satisfied,
and with exultant lips my mouth shall praise you.

℟. **My soul is thirsting for you, O Lord my God.**

That you are my help,
and in the shadow of your wings I shout for joy.
My soul clings to you;
your right hand upholds me.

℟. **My soul is thirsting for you, O Lord my God.**

9.

Psalm 84:3, 4, 5-6a and 8, 11, 12

R̸. (2) **How lovely is your dwelling place, Lord, mighty God!**

My soul yearns and pines
    for the courts of the Lord.
My heart and my flesh
    cry out for the living God.

R̸. How lovely is your dwelling place, Lord, mighty God!

Even the sparrow finds a home,
    and the swallow a nest
    in which she puts her young—
Your altars, O Lord of hosts,
    my king and my God!

R̸. How lovely is your dwelling place, Lord, mighty God!

Blessed they who dwell in your house!
    continually they praise you.
Blessed the men whose strength you are!
They go from strength to strength;
    they shall see the God of gods in Zion.

R̸. How lovely is your dwelling place, Lord, mighty God!

I had rather one day in your courts
    than a thousand elsewhere;
I had rather lie at the threshold of the house of my God
    than dwell in the tents of the wicked.

R̸. How lovely is your dwelling place, Lord, mighty God!

For a sun and a shield is the Lord God;
    grace and glory he bestows;
The Lord withholds no good thing
    from those who walk in sincerity.

R̸. How lovely is your dwelling place, Lord, mighty God!

10.

Psalm 100:1b-2, 3, 4, 5

℟. (2b) **Come with joy into the presence of the Lord.**

Sing joyfully to the L ORD **, all you lands;**
serve the L ORD **with gladness;**
come before him with joyful song.

℟. **Come with joy into the presence of the Lord.**

Know that the L ORD **is God;**
he made us, his we are;
his people, the flock he tends.

℟. **Come with joy into the presence of the Lord.**

Enter his gates with thanksgiving,
his courts with praise;
Give thanks to him; bless his name.

℟. **Come with joy into the presence of the Lord.**

For he is good:
the L ORD **, whose kindness endures forever,**
and his faithfulness, to all generations.

℟. **Come with joy into the presence of the Lord.**

814 ALLELUIA VERSE AND VERSE
BEFORE THE GOSPEL

1.

Psalm 133:1

**Behold, how good it is, and how pleasant,
when brothers and sisters dwell as one!**

2.

See Matthew 11:25

**Blessed are you, Father, Lord of heaven and earth;
you have revealed to little ones the mysteries of the Kingdom.**

3.

Luke 11:28

**Blessed are those who hear the word of God
and observe it.**

4.

John 13:34

**I give you a new commandment:
love one another as I have loved you.**

5.

John 15:5

**I am the vine, you are the branches, says the Lord:
whoever remains in me and I in him will bear much fruit.**

6.

2 Corinthians 8:9

**Jesus Christ became poor although he was rich,
so that by his poverty you might become rich.**

7.

Galatians 6:14

**May I never boast except in the cross of our Lord Jesus Christ,
through which the world has been crucified to me and I to the world.**

8.

Philippians 3:8-9

**I consider all things so much rubbish
that I may gain Christ and be found in him.**

815 GOSPEL

1.

Matthew 5:1-12a   Blessed are you . . . rejoice and be glad.

✠   **A reading from the holy Gospel according to Matthew**

When Jesus saw the crowds, he went up the mountain,
** and after he had sat down, his disciples came to him.**
He began to teach them, saying:

"Blessed are the poor in spirit,
** for theirs is the Kingdom of heaven.**
Blessed are they who mourn,
** for they will be comforted.**
Blessed are the meek,
** for they will inherit the land.**
Blessed are they who hunger and thirst for righteousness,
** for they will be satisfied.**
Blessed are the merciful,
** for they will be shown mercy.**
Blessed are the clean of heart,
** for they will see God.**
Blessed are the peacemakers,
** for they will be called children of God.**
Blessed are they who are persecuted for the sake of righteousness,
** for theirs is the Kingdom of heaven.**
Blessed are you when they insult you and persecute you
** and utter every kind of evil against you falsely because of me.**
Rejoice and be glad,
** for your reward will be great in heaven."**

The Gospel of the Lord.

2.

Matthew 11:25-30   You have hidden these things from the wise and the learned and you have revealed them to the childlike.

✠ **A reading from the holy Gospel according to Matthew**

At that time Jesus answered:
"I give praise to you, Father, Lord of heaven and earth,
    for although you have hidden these things
    from the wise and the learned
    you have revealed them to the childlike.
Yes, Father, such has been your gracious will.
All things have been handed over to me by my Father.
No one knows the Son except the Father,
    and no one knows the Father except the Son
    and anyone to whom the Son wishes to reveal him.

"Come to me, all you who labor and are burdened,
    and I will give you rest.
Take my yoke upon you and learn from me,
    for I am meek and humble of heart;
    and you will find rest for yourselves.
For my yoke is easy, and my burden light."

The Gospel of the Lord.

3.

Matthew 16:24-27   Whoever loses his life for my sake will find it.

✠ **A reading from the holy Gospel according to Matthew**

Jesus said to his disciples,
    "Whoever wishes to come after me must deny himself,
    take up his cross, and follow me.
For whoever wishes to save his life will lose it,
    but whoever loses his life for my sake will find it.
What profit would there be for one to gain the whole world
    and forfeit his life?
Or what can one give in exchange for his life?
For the Son of Man will come with his angels in his Father's glory,
    and then he will repay each one according to his conduct."

The Gospel of the Lord.

4.

Matthew 19:3-12   For the sake of the Kingdom of heaven.

✠ **A reading from the holy Gospel according to Matthew**

Some Pharisees approached Jesus, and tested him, saying,
  "Is it lawful for a man to divorce his wife for any cause whatever?"
He said in reply,
  "Have you not read that from the beginning
  the Creator *made them male and female* and said,
  For this reason a man shall leave his father and mother
  and be joined to his wife, and the two shall become one flesh?
So they are no longer two, but one flesh.
Therefore, what God has joined together, man must not separate."
They said to him, "Then why did Moses command
  that the man give the woman a bill of divorce and dismiss her?"
He said to them, "Because of the hardness of your hearts
  Moses allowed you to divorce your wives,
  but from the beginning it was not so.
I say to you, whoever divorces his wife
  unless the marriage is unlawful
  and marries another commits adultery."
His disciples said to him,
  "If that is the case of a man with his wife,
  it is better not to marry."
He answered,
  "Not all can accept this word,
  but only those to whom that is granted.
Some are incapable of marriage because they were born so;
  some, because they were made so by others;
  some, because they have renounced marriage
  for the sake of the Kingdom of heaven.
Whoever can accept this ought to accept it."

The Gospel of the Lord.

5.

Matthew 19:16-26   If you wish to be perfect, go sell what you have and
follow me.

✠ **A reading from the holy Gospel according to Matthew**

A young man approached Jesus and said,
  "Teacher, what good must I do to gain eternal life?"
He answered him,
  "Why do you ask me about the good?
There is only One who is good.
If you wish to enter into life, keep the commandments."
He asked him, "Which ones?"
And Jesus replied, "*You shall not kill;*
  you shall not commit adultery; you shall not steal;
  you shall not bear false witness; honor your father and your mother;
  and *you shall love your neighbor as yourself."*
The young man said to him,
  "All of these I have observed. What do I still lack?"
Jesus said to him, "If you wish to be perfect,
  go, sell what you have and give to the poor,
  and you will have treasure in heaven.
Then come, follow me."
When the young man heard this statement, he went away sad,
  for he had many possessions.
Then Jesus said to his disciples, "Amen, I say to you,
  it will be hard for one who is rich to enter the Kingdom of heaven.
Again I say to you,
  it is easier for a camel to pass through the eye of a needle
  than for one who is rich to enter the Kingdom of God."
When the disciples heard this, they were greatly astonished and said,
  "Who then can be saved?"
Jesus looked at them and said,
  "For men this is impossible,
  but for God all things are possible."

The Gospel of the Lord.

6.

Matthew 25:1-13   Behold the bridegroom! Come out to meet him!

✠ **A reading from the holy Gospel according to Matthew**

Jesus told his disciples this parable:
"The Kingdom of heaven will be like ten virgins
   who took their lamps and went out to meet the bridegroom.
Five of them were foolish and five were wise.
The foolish ones, when taking their lamps,
   brought no oil with them,
   but the wise brought flasks of oil with their lamps.
Since the bridegroom was long delayed,
   they all became drowsy and fell asleep.
At midnight, there was a cry,
   'Behold, the bridegroom! Come out to meet him!'
Then all those virgins got up and trimmed their lamps.
The foolish ones said to the wise,
   'Give us some of your oil,
   for our lamps are going out.'
But the wise ones replied,
   'No, for there may not be enough for us and you.
Go instead to the merchants and buy some for yourselves.'
While they went off to buy it,
   the bridegroom came
   and those who were ready went into the wedding feast with him.
Then the door was locked.
Afterwards the other virgins came and said,
   'Lord, Lord, open the door for us!'
But he said in reply,
   'Amen, I say to you, I do not know you.'
Therefore, stay awake,
   for you know neither the day nor the hour."

The Gospel of the Lord.

7.

Mark 3:31-35   Whoever does the will of God is my brother and sister and mother.

✠ **A reading from the holy Gospel according to Mark**
The mother of Jesus and his brothers arrived at the house.
Standing outside they sent word to him and called him.
A crowd seated around him told him,
   "Your mother and your brothers and your sisters
   are outside asking for you."
But he said to them in reply,
   "Who are my mother and my brothers?"
And looking around at those seated in the circle he said,
   "Here are my mother and my brothers.
For whoever does the will of God
   is my brother and sister and mother."

The Gospel of the Lord.

8.

Mark 10:24b-30   We have given up everything and followed you.

✠ **A reading from the holy Gospel according to Mark**

Jesus said to his disciples:
"Children, how hard it is to enter the Kingdom of God!
It is easier for a camel to pass through the eye of a needle
than for one who is rich to enter the Kingdom of God."
They were exceedingly astonished and said among themselves,
"Then who can be saved?"
Jesus looked at them and said,
"For men it is impossible, but not for God.
All things are possible for God."
Peter began to say to him,
"We have given up everything and followed you."
Jesus said, "Amen, I say to you,
there is no one who has given up house or brothers or sisters
or mother or father or children or lands for my sake
and for the sake of the Gospel
who will not receive a hundred times more now in this present age:
houses and brothers and sisters and mothers and children and lands,
with persecutions, and eternal life in the age to come."

The Gospel of the Lord.

9.

Luke 1:26-38   "Behold, I am the handmaid of the Lord."

✠ **A reading from the holy Gospel according to Luke**

The angel Gabriel was sent from God
    to a town of Galilee called Nazareth,
    to a virgin betrothed to a man named Joseph,
    of the house of David,
    and the virgin's name was Mary.
And coming to her, he said,
    "Hail, full of grace! The Lord is with you."
But she was greatly troubled at what was said
    and pondered what sort of greeting this might be.
Then the angel said to her,
    "Do not be afraid, Mary,
    for you have found favor with God.
Behold, you will conceive in your womb and bear a son,
    and you shall name him Jesus.
He will be great and will be called Son of the Most High,
    and the Lord God will give him the throne of David his father,
    and he will rule over the house of Jacob forever,
    and of his Kingdom there will be no end."
But Mary said to the angel,
    "How can this be,
    since I have no relations with a man?"
And the angel said to her in reply,
    "The Holy Spirit will come upon you,
    and the power of the Most High will overshadow you.
Therefore the child to be born
    will be called holy, the Son of God.
And behold, Elizabeth, your relative,
    has also conceived a son in her old age,
    and this is the sixth month for her who was called barren;
    for nothing will be impossible for God."
Mary said, "Behold, I am the handmaid of the Lord.
May it be done to me according to your word."
Then the angel departed from her.

The Gospel of the Lord.

10.

Luke 9:57-62   No one who sets a hand to the plow and looks to what was left behind is fit for the Kingdom of God.

☩ **A reading from the holy Gospel according to Luke**

As Jesus and his disciples were proceeding on their journey
   someone said to him, "I will follow you wherever you go."
Jesus answered him,
   "Foxes have dens and birds of the sky have nests,
   but the Son of Man has nowhere to rest his head."
And to another he said, "Follow me."
But he replied, "Lord, let me go first and bury my father."
But he answered him, "Let the dead bury their dead.
But you, go and proclaim the Kingdom of God."
And another said, "I will follow you, Lord,
   but first let me say farewell to my family at home."
Jesus said, "No one who sets a hand to the plow
   and looks to what was left behind is fit for the Kingdom of God."

The Gospel of the Lord.

11.

Luke 10:38-42   Martha welcomed him. Mary has chosen the better part.

☩ **A reading from the holy Gospel according to Luke**

Jesus entered a village
   where a woman whose name was Martha welcomed him.
She had a sister named Mary
   who sat beside the Lord at his feet listening to him speak.
Martha, burdened with much serving, came to him and said,
   "Lord, do you not care
   that my sister has left me by myself to do the serving?
Tell her to help me."
The Lord said to her in reply,
   "Martha, Martha, you are anxious and worried about many things.
There is need of only one thing.
Mary has chosen the better part
   and it will not be taken from her."

The Gospel of the Lord.

12.

Luke 11:27-28   Blessed are those who hear the word of God and observe it.

✝ **A reading from the holy Gospel according to Luke**

While Jesus was speaking,
   a woman from the crowd called out and said to him,
   "Blessed is the womb that carried you
and the breasts at which you nursed."
He replied, "Rather, blessed are those
   who hear the word of God and observe it."

The Gospel of the Lord.

13.

John 12:24-26   If a grain of wheat dies, it produces much fruit.

✝ **A reading from the holy Gospel according to John**

Jesus said to his disciples:
"Amen, amen, I say to you,
   unless a grain of wheat falls to the ground and dies,
   it remains just a grain of wheat;
   but if it dies, it produces much fruit.
Whoever loves his life loses it,
   and whoever hates his life in this world
   will preserve it for eternal life.
Whoever serves me must follow me,
   and where I am, there also will my servant be.
The Father will honor whoever serves me."

The Gospel of the Lord.

14.

John 15:1-8   Remain in me, as I remain in you.

✝ **A reading from the holy Gospel according to John**

Jesus said to his disciples:
"I am the true vine, and my Father is the vine grower.
He takes away every branch in me that does not bear fruit,
    and everyone that does he prunes so that it bears more fruit.
You are already pruned because of the word that I spoke to you.
Remain in me, as I remain in you.
Just as a branch cannot bear fruit on its own
    unless it remains on the vine,
    so neither can you unless you remain in me.
I am the vine, you are the branches.
Whoever remains in me and I in him will bear much fruit,
    because without me you can do nothing.
Anyone who does not remain in me
    will be thrown out like a branch and wither;
    people will gather them and throw them into a fire and they will be burned.
If you remain in me and my words remain in you,
    ask for whatever you want and it will be done for you.
By this is my Father glorified,
    that you bear much fruit and become my disciples."

The Gospel of the Lord.

15.

John 15:9-17   You are my friends if you do what I command you.

✝ **A reading from the holy Gospel according to John**

Jesus said to his disciples:
"As the Father loves me, so I also love you.
Remain in my love.
If you keep my commandments, you will remain in my love,
    just as I have kept my Father's commandments
    and remain in his love.

"I have told you this so that my joy might be in you
    and your joy might be complete.
This is my commandment: love one another as I love you.
No one has greater love than this,
    to lay down one's life for one's friends.

You are my friends if you do what I command you.
I no longer call you slaves,
  because a slave does not know what his master is doing.
I have called you friends,
  because I have told you everything I have heard from my Father.
It was not you who chose me, but I who chose you
  and appointed you to go and bear fruit that will remain,
  so that whatever you ask the Father in my name he may give you.
This I command you: love one another."

The Gospel of the Lord.

  16.

John 17:20-26   I wish that where I am, they also may be with me.

✠ **A reading from the holy Gospel according to John**

Jesus raised his eyes to heaven and said:
"Holy Father, I pray not only for these,
  but also for those who will believe in me through their word,
  so that they may all be one,
  as you, Father, are in me and I in you,
  that they also may be in us,
  that the world may believe that you sent me.
And I have given them the glory you gave me,
  so that they may be one, as we are one,
  I in them and you in me,
  that they may be brought to perfection as one,
  that the world may know that you sent me,
  and that you loved them even as you loved me.
Father, they are your gift to me.
I wish that where I am they also may be with me,
  that they may see my glory that you gave me,
  because you loved me before the foundation of the world.
Righteous Father, the world also does not know you,
  but I know you, and they know that you sent me.
I made known to them your name and I will make it known,
  that the love with which you loved me
  may be in them and I in them."

The Gospel of the Lord.

IX. FOR THE DEDICATION OR BLESSING OF A CHURCH OR AN ALTAR

816   1. DEDICATION OF A CHURCH

FIRST READING

Nehemiah 8:2-4a, 5-6, 8-10   Ezra read plainly from the book of the law of God, interpreting it.

A reading from the Book of Nehemiah

Ezra the priest brought the law before the assembly,
   which consisted of men, women,
   and those children old enough to understand.
Standing at one end of the open place that was before the Water Gate,
   he read out of the book from daybreak till midday,
   in the presence of the men, the women,
   and those children old enough to understand;
   and all the people listened attentively to the book of the law.
Ezra the scribe stood on a wooden platform
   that had been made for the occasion.
He opened the scroll
   so that all the people might see it
   (for he was standing higher up than any of the people);
   and, as he opened it, all the people rose.
Ezra blessed the LORD, the great God,
   and all the people, their hands raised high, answered,
   "Amen, amen!"
Then they bowed down and prostrated themselves before the LORD,
   their faces to the ground.
Ezra read plainly from the book of the law of God,
   interpreting it so that all could understand what was read.
Then Nehemiah, that is, His Excellency, and Ezra the priest-scribe
   and the Levites who were instructing the people
   said to all the people:
   "Today is holy to the LORD your God.
Do not be sad, and do not weep"—
   for all the people were weeping as they heard the words of the law.
He said further: "Go, eat rich foods and drink sweet drinks,
   and allot portions to those who had nothing prepared;
   for today is holy to our LORD.

Do not be saddened this day,
for rejoicing in the LORD must be your strength!"

The word of the Lord.

RESPONSORIAL PSALM

Psalm 19:8-9, 10, 15

℟. (see John 6:63c) **Your words, Lord, are Spirit and life.**

The law of the LORD is perfect,
refreshing the soul;
The decree of the LORD is trustworthy,
giving wisdom to the simple.
The precepts of the LORD are right,
rejoicing the heart;
The command of the LORD is clear,
enlightening the eye.

℟. Your words, Lord, are Spirit and life.

The fear of the LORD is pure,
enduring forever;
The ordinances of the LORD are true,
all of them just.

℟. Your words, Lord, are Spirit and life.

Let the words of my mouth and the thought of my heart
find favor before you,
O LORD, my rock and my redeemer.

℟. Your words, Lord, are Spirit and life.

SECOND READING

See the anniversary of the dedication of a church, no. 704.

During the season of Easter one can choose Revelation 21:1-5 or Revelation 21:9-14 as indicated for the first reading of the anniversary of the dedication of a church, no. 702.

ALLELUIA VERSE AND VERSE BEFORE THE GOSPEL

See the anniversary of the dedication of a church, no. 705.

GOSPEL

See the anniversary of the dedication of a church, no. 706.

2. DEDICATION OF AN ALTAR

817 READING I FROM THE OLD TESTAMENT

First Option

Genesis 28:11-18   Early the next morning Jacob took the stone that he had put under his head, set it up as a memorial stone, and poured oil on top of it.

A reading from the Book of Genesis

When Jacob came upon a certain shrine, as the sun had already set,
   he stopped there for the night.
Taking one of the stones at the shrine, he put it under his head
   and lay down to sleep at that spot.
Then he had a dream: a stairway rested on the ground,
   with its top reaching to the heavens;
   and God's messengers were going up and down on it.
And there was the LORD standing beside him and saying:
   "I, the LORD, am the God of your forefather Abraham
   and the God of Isaac;
   the land on which you are lying
   I will give to you and your descendants.
These shall be as plentiful as the dust of the earth,
   and through them you shall spread out east and west, north and south.
In you and your descendants
   all the nations of the earth shall find blessing.
Know that I am with you;
   I will protect you wherever you go,
   and bring you back to this land.
I will never leave you until I have done what I promised you."

When Jacob awoke from his sleep, he exclaimed,
   "Truly, the LORD is in this spot, although I did not know it!"
In solemn wonder he cried out: "How awesome is this shrine!
This is nothing else but an abode of God,
   and that is the gateway to heaven!"
Early the next morning Jacob took the stone
   that he had put under his head,
   set it up as a memorial stone, and poured oil on top of it.

The word of the Lord.

Second Option

Joshua 8:30-35   Joshua built an altar to the Lord.

A reading from the Book of Joshua

Joshua built an altar to the LORD, the God of Israel, on Mount Ebal,
of unhewn stones on which no iron tool had been used,
in keeping with the command to the children of Israel of Moses,
the servant of the LORD, as recorded in the book of the law.
On this altar they offered burnt offerings and peace offerings to the LORD.
There, in the presence of the children of Israel,
Joshua inscribed upon the stones a copy of the law written by Moses.
And all Israel, stranger and native alike,
with their elders, officers, and judges,
stood on either side of the ark facing the levitical priests
who were carrying the ark of the covenant of the LORD.
Half of them were facing Mount Gerizim and half Mount Ebal,
thus carrying out the instructions of Moses, the servant of the LORD,
for the blessing of the people of Israel on this first occasion.
Then were read aloud all the words of the law,
the blessings and the curses,
exactly as written in the book of the law.
Every single word that Moses had commanded, Joshua read aloud
to the entire community, including the women and children,
and the strangers who had accompanied Israel.

The word of the Lord.

Third Option

1 Maccabees 4:52-59   They celebrated the dedication of the altar and there was great joy among the people.

A reading from the first Book of Maccabees

Early in the morning on the twenty-fifth day of the ninth month,
  that is, the month of Chislev,
  in the year one hundred and forty-eight,
  they arose and offered sacrifice according to the law
  on the new altar of burnt offerings that they had made.
On the anniversary of the day on which the Gentiles had defiled it,
  on that very day it was reconsecrated
  with songs, harps, flutes, and cymbals.
All the people prostrated themselves and adored and praised Heaven,
  who had given them success.

For eight days they celebrated the dedication of the altar
  and joyfully offered burnt offerings and sacrifices
  of deliverance and praise.
They ornamented the façade of the temple with gold crowns and shields;
  they repaired the gates and the priests' chambers
  and furnished them with doors.
There was great joy among the people
  now that the disgrace of the Gentiles was removed.
Then Judas and his brothers and the entire congregation of Israel
  decreed that the days of the dedication of the altar
  should be observed with joy and gladness
  on the anniversary every year for eight days,
  from the twenty-fifth day of the month Chislev.

The word of the Lord.

818 READING I FROM THE NEW TESTAMENT DURING THE SEASON OF EASTER

First Option

Acts 2:42-47　The believers devoted themselves to the communal life and to the breaking of the bread.

A reading from the Acts of the Apostles

The brothers and sisters devoted themselves
**　to the teaching of the Apostles and to the communal life,**
**　to the breaking of the bread and to the prayers.**
Awe came upon everyone,
**　and many wonders and signs were done through the Apostles.**
All who believed were together and had all things in common;
**　they would sell their property and possessions**
**　and divide them among all according to each one's need.**
Every day they devoted themselves
**　to meeting together in the temple area**
**　and to breaking bread in their homes.**
They ate their meals with exultation and sincerity of heart,
**　praising God and enjoying favor with all the people.**
And every day the Lord added to their number those who were being saved.

The word of the Lord.

Second Option

Revelation 8:3-4　An angel came and stood at the altar.

A reading from the Book of Revelation

I, John, saw:
Another angel came and stood at the altar, holding a gold censer.
He was given a great quantity of incense to offer,
**　along with the prayers of all the holy ones,**
**　on the gold altar that was before the throne.**
The smoke of the incense along with the prayers of the holy ones
**　went up before God from the hand of the angel.**

The word of the Lord.

819 RESPONSORIAL PSALM

1.

Psalm 84:3, 4, 5-6a and 8a, 11

R̷. (2) **How lovely is your dwelling place, Lord, mighty God!**
   or:
R̷. (Rev 21:3b) **Here God lives among his people.**
   or:
R̷. (Rev 21:3b) **God who is with them will be their God.**

My soul yearns and pines
   for the courts of the L<small>ORD</small>**.**
My heart and my flesh
   cry out for the living God.

R̷. **How lovely is your dwelling place, Lord, mighty God!**
   or:
R̷. **Here God lives among his people.**
   or:
R̷. **God who is with them will be their God.**

Even the sparrow finds a home,
   and the swallow a nest
   in which she puts her young—
Your altars, O L<small>ORD</small> **of hosts,**
   my king and my God!

R̷. **How lovely is your dwelling place, Lord, mighty God.**
   or:
R̷. **Here God lives among his people.**
   or:
R̷. **God who is with them will be their God.**

Blessed they who dwell in your house!
   continually they praise you.
Blessed the men whose strength you are!
They go from strength to strength.

(cont.)

℟. How lovely is your dwelling place, Lord, mighty God.
> or:

℟. Here God lives among his people.
> or:

℟. God who is with them will be their God.

I had rather one day in your courts
>   than a thousand elsewhere;
I had rather lie at the threshold of the house of my God
>   than dwell in the tents of the wicked.

℟. How lovely is your dwelling place, Lord, mighty God!
> or:

℟. Here God lives among his people.
> or:

℟. God who is with them will be their God.

2.

Psalm 95:1-2, 3-5, 6-7ab

℟. (see 2a) Let us come before the Lord and praise him.

Come, let us sing joyfully to the LORD;
>   let us acclaim the Rock of our salvation.
Let us come into his presence with thanksgiving;
>   let us joyfully sing psalms to him.

℟. Let us come before the Lord and praise him.

For the LORD is a great God,
>   and a great king above all gods;
In his hands are the depths of the earth,
>   and the tops of the mountains are his.
His is the sea, for he has made it,
>   and the dry land, which his hands have formed.

℟. Let us come before the Lord and praise him.

Come, let us bow down in worship;
>   let us kneel before the LORD who made us.
For he is our God,
>   and we are the people he shepherds, the flock he guides.

℟. Let us come before the Lord and praise him.

3.

Psalm 118:15ab-16, 19-20, 22-23, 27

℟. (1) **Give thanks for the Lord is good; his love is everlasting.**

The joyful shout of victory
  in the tents of the just:
"The right hand of the Lord is exalted;
  the right hand of the Lord has struck with power."

℟. **Give thanks for the Lord is good; his love is everlasting.**

Open to me the gates of justice;
  I will enter them and give thanks to the Lord.
This is the gate of the Lord;
  the just shall enter it.

℟. **Give thanks for the Lord is good; his love is everlasting.**

The stone which the builders rejected
  has become the cornerstone.
By the Lord has this been done;
  it is wonderful in our eyes.

℟. **Give thanks for the Lord is good; his love is everlasting.**

The Lord is God, and he has given us light.
Join in the procession with leafy boughs
  up to the horns of the altar.

℟. **Give thanks for the Lord is good; his love is everlasting.**

4.

Psalm 119:129, 130, 133, 135, 144

℟. (105a) **Your word, O Lord, is a lamp for my feet.**

Wonderful are your decrees;
   therefore I observe them.

℟. **Your word, O Lord, is a lamp for my feet.**

The revelation of your words sheds light,
   giving understanding to the simple.

℟. **Your word, O Lord, is a lamp for my feet.**

Steady my footsteps according to your promise,
   and let no iniquity rule over me.

℟. **Your word, O Lord, is a lamp for my feet.**

Let your countenance shine upon your servant
   and teach me your statutes.

℟. **Your word, O Lord, is a lamp for my feet.**

Your decrees are forever just;
   give me discernment that I may live.

℟. **Your word, O Lord, is a lamp for my feet.**

5.

Psalm 122:1-2, 3-4, 8-9

℟. (see 1) **Let us go rejoicing to the house of the Lord.**

I rejoiced because they said to me,
  "We will go up to the house of the Lord."
And now we have set foot
  within your gates, O Jerusalem.

℟. **Let us go rejoicing to the house of the Lord.**

Jerusalem, built as a city
  with compact unity.
To it the tribes go up,
  the tribes of the Lord.
According to the decree for Israel,
  to give thanks to the name of the Lord.

℟. **Let us go rejoicing to the house of the Lord.**

Because of my relatives and friends
  I will say, "Peace be within you!"
Because of the house of the Lord, our God,
  I will pray for your good.

℟. **Let us go rejoicing to the house of the Lord.**

820 READING II FROM THE NEW TESTAMENT

First Option

1 Corinthians 10:16-21   You cannot partake of the table of the Lord and the table of demons.

A reading from the first Letter of Saint Paul to the Corinthians

Brothers and sisters:
The cup of blessing that we bless,
   is it not a participation in the Blood of Christ?
The bread that we break,
   is it not a participation in the Body of Christ?
Because the loaf of bread is one,
    we, though many, are one Body,
    for we all partake of the one loaf.

Look at Israel according to the flesh;
   are not those who eat the sacrifices participants in the altar?
So what am I saying?
That meat sacrificed to idols is anything?
Or that an idol is anything?
No, I mean that what they sacrifice,
   they sacrifice to demons, not to God,
   and I do not want you to become participants with demons.
You cannot drink the chalice of the Lord and also the chalice of demons.
You cannot partake of the table of the Lord
   and the table of demons.

The word of the Lord.

Second Option

Hebrews 13:8-15   We have an altar from which those who serve the
tabernacle have no right to eat.

A reading from the Letter to the Hebrews

Jesus Christ is the same yesterday, today, and forever.

Do not be carried away by all kinds of strange teaching.
It is good to have our hearts strengthened by grace and not by foods,
  which do not benefit those who live by them.
We have an altar from which those who serve the tabernacle
  have no right to eat.
The bodies of the animals whose blood
  the high priest brings into the sanctuary as a sin offering
  are burned outside the camp.
Therefore, Jesus also suffered outside the gate,
  to consecrate the people by his own Blood.
Let us then go to him outside the camp,
  bearing the reproach that he bore.
For here we have no lasting city,
  but we seek the one that is to come.
Through him then let us continually offer God a sacrifice of praise,
  that is, the fruit of lips that confess his name.

The word of the Lord.

821   ALLELUIA VERSE AND VERSE BEFORE THE GOSPEL

1.

Ezekiel 37:27

My dwelling shall be with them, says the Lord;
I will be their God, and they shall be my people.

2.

See John 4:23, 24

The Father seeks true worshipers
who worship him in Spirit and truth.

3.

Hebrews 13:8

Jesus Christ is the same yesterday, today, and forever.

822 GOSPEL

First Option

Matthew 5:23-24   Go first and be reconciled with your brother, and then come and offer your gift.

✠ **A reading from the holy Gospel according to Matthew**

Jesus said to his disciples:
"If you bring your gift to the altar,
  and there recall that your brother
  has anything against you,
  leave your gift there at the altar,
  go first and be reconciled with your brother,
  and then come and offer your gift."

The Gospel of the Lord.

Second Option

John 4:19-24   True worshipers will worship the Father in Spirit and in truth.

✠ **A reading from the holy Gospel according to John**

The Samaritan woman said to Jesus,
  "Sir, I can see that you are a prophet.
Our ancestors worshiped on this mountain;
  but you people say that the place to worship is in Jerusalem."
Jesus said to her,
  "Believe me, woman, the hour is coming
  when you will worship the Father
  neither on this mountain nor in Jerusalem.
You people worship what you do not understand;
  we worship what we understand,
  because salvation is from the Jews.
But the hour is coming, and is now here,
  when true worshipers will worship the Father in Spirit and truth;
  and indeed the Father seeks such people to worship him.
God is Spirit, and those who worship him
  must worship in Spirit and truth."

The Gospel of the Lord.

Third Option

John 12:31-36a   When I am lifted up from the earth I will draw everyone to myself.

✝ **A reading from the holy Gospel according to John**

Jesus said to the crowd:
"Now is the time of judgment on this world;
  now the ruler of this world will be driven out.
And when I am lifted up from the earth,
  I will draw everyone to myself."
He said this indicating the kind of death he would die.
So the crowd answered him,
  "We have heard from the law that the Christ remains forever.
Then how can you say that the Son of Man must be lifted up?
Who is this Son of Man?"
Jesus said to them,
  "The light will be among you only a little while.
Walk while you have the light,
  so that darkness may not overcome you.
Whoever walks in the dark does not know where he is going.
While you have the light, believe in the light,
  so that you may become children of the light."

The Gospel of the Lord.

3. BLESSING OF A CHALICE AND PATEN

823   READING FROM THE NEW TESTAMENT

First Option

1 Corinthians 10:14-22a   The cup of blessing that we bless, is it not a participation in the Blood of Christ?

A reading from the first Letter of Saint Paul to the Corinthians

My beloved, avoid idolatry.
I am speaking as to sensible people;
  judge for yourselves what I am saying.
The cup of blessing that we bless,
  is it not a participation in the Blood of Christ?
The bread that we break,
  is it not a participation in the Body of Christ?
Because the loaf of bread is one,
  we, though many, are one Body, for we all partake of the one loaf.

Look at Israel according to the flesh;
  are not those who eat the sacrifices participants in the altar?
So what am I saying?
That meat sacrificed to idols is anything?
Or that an idol is anything?
No, I mean that what they sacrifice, they sacrifice to demons, not to God,
  and I do not want you to become participants with demons.
You cannot drink the chalice of the Lord and also the chalice of demons.
You cannot partake of the table of the Lord and of the table of demons.
Or are we provoking the Lord to jealous anger?

The word of the Lord.

Second Option

1 Corinthians 11:23-26   This cup is the new covenant in my Blood.

A reading from the first Letter of Saint Paul to the Corinthians

Brothers and sisters:
I received from the Lord what I also handed on to you,
that the Lord Jesus, on the night he was handed over,
took bread, and, after he had given thanks,
broke it and said, "This is my Body that is for you.
Do this in remembrance of me."
In the same way also the cup, after supper, saying,
"This cup is the new covenant in my Blood.
Do this, as often as you drink it, in remembrance of me."
For as often as you eat this bread and drink the cup,
you proclaim the death of the Lord until he comes.

The word of the Lord.

824 RESPONSORIAL PSALM

1.

Psalm 16:5 and 8, 9-10, 11

R̶. (5a) **The Lord is my inheritance and my cup.**

O LORD, **my allotted portion and my cup,**
  you it is who hold fast my lot.
I set the LORD ever before me;
  with him at my right hand I shall not be disturbed.

R̶. **The Lord is my inheritance and my cup.**

Therefore my heart is glad and my soul rejoices,
  my body, too, abides in confidence;
Because you will not abandon my soul to the nether world,
  nor will you suffer your faithful one to undergo corruption.

R̶. **The Lord is my inheritance and my cup.**

You will show me the path to life,
  fullness of joys in your presence,
  the delights at your right hand forever.

R̶. **The Lord is my inheritance and my cup.**

2.

Psalm 23:1-3a, 3b-4, 5, 6

℟. (5a, 5d) **You prepared a banquet before me; my cup overflows.**

The Lord is my shepherd; I shall not want.
  In verdant pastures he gives me repose;
Beside restful waters he leads me;
  he refreshes my soul.

℟. **You prepared a banquet before me; my cup overflows.**

He guides me in right paths
  for his name's sake.
Even though I walk in the dark valley
  I fear no evil; for you are at my side
With your rod and your staff
  that give me courage.

℟. **You prepared a banquet before me; my cup overflows.**

You spread the table before me
  in the sight of my foes;
You anoint my head with oil;
  my cup overflows.

℟. **You prepared a banquet before me; my cup overflows.**

Only goodness and kindness follow me
  all the days of my life;
And I shall dwell in the house of the Lord
  for years to come.

℟. **You prepared a banquet before me; my cup overflows.**

825 ALLELUIA VERSE AND VERSE BEFORE THE GOSPEL

1.

John 6:56

**Whoever eats my Flesh and drinks my Blood
remains in me and I in him, says the Lord.**

2.

John 6:57

**Just as the living Father sent me and I have life because of the Father,
so also the one who feeds on me will have life because of me.**

826 GOSPEL

First Option

Matthew 20:20-28   My chalice you will indeed drink.

✠ **A reading from the holy Gospel according to Matthew**

The mother of the sons of Zebedee
   approached Jesus with her sons and did him homage,
   wishing to ask him for something.
He said to her,
   "What do you wish?"
She answered him,
   "Command that these two sons of mine sit,
   one at your right and the other at your left, in your Kingdom."
Jesus said in reply,
   "You do not know what you are asking.
Can you drink the chalice that I am going to drink?"
They said to him, "We can."
He replied,
   "My chalice you will indeed drink,
   but to sit at my right and at my left,
   this is not mine to give
   but is for those for whom it has been prepared by my Father."
When the ten heard this,
   they became indignant at the two brothers.
But Jesus summoned them and said,
   "You know that the rulers of the Gentiles lord it over them,
   and the great ones make their authority over them felt.
But it shall not be so among you.
Rather, whoever wishes to be great among you shall be your servant;
   whoever wishes to be first among you shall be your slave.
Just so, the Son of Man did not come to be served
   but to serve and to give his life as a ransom for many."

The Gospel of the Lord.

Second Option

Mark 14:12-16, 22-26   Then he took a cup, gave thanks and gave it to them, and they all drank from it.

☩ **A reading from the holy Gospel according to Mark**

On the first day of the Feast of Unleavened Bread,
   when they sacrificed the Passover Lamb,
   the disciples of Jesus said to him,
   "Where do you want us to go
   and prepare for you to eat the Passover?"
He sent two of his disciples and said to them,
   "Go into the city and a man will meet you,
   carrying a jar of water.
Follow him.
Wherever he enters, say to the master of the house,
   'The Teacher says, "Where is my guest room
   where I may eat the Passover with my disciples?"'
Then he will show you a large upper room furnished and ready.
Make the preparations for us there."
The disciples then went off, entered the city,
   and found it just as he had told them;
   and they prepared the Passover.

While they were eating,
   he took bread, said the blessing,
   broke it and gave it to them, and said,
   "Take it; this is my Body."
Then he took a cup, gave thanks, and gave it to them,
   and they all drank from it.
He said to them,
   "This is my Blood of the covenant,
   which will be shed for many.
Amen, I say to you,
   I shall not drink again the fruit of the vine
   until the day when I drink it new in the Kingdom of God."
Then, after singing a hymn,
   they went out to the Mount of Olives.

The Gospel of the Lord.

MASSES FOR VARIOUS NEEDS
AND OCCASIONS

I. FOR THE HOLY CHURCH

1. FOR THE CHURCH

827 READING FROM THE OLD TESTAMENT

1.

Isaiah 56:1, 6-7   My house shall be called a house of prayer for all peoples.

A reading from the Book of the Prophet Isaiah

Thus says the LORD:
Observe what is right, do what is just;
  for my salvation is about to come,
  my justice, about to be revealed.

The foreigners who join themselves to the LORD,
  ministering to him,
Loving the name of the LORD,
  and becoming his servants—
All who keep the sabbath free from profanation
  and hold to my covenant,
Them I will bring to my holy mountain
  and make joyful in my house of prayer;
Their burnt offerings and sacrifices
  will be acceptable on my altar,
For my house shall be called
  a house of prayer for all peoples.

The word of the Lord.

2.

Isaiah 60:1-6   Nations shall walk by your light.

A reading from the Book of the Prophet Isaiah

Rise up in splendor, Jerusalem! Your light has come,
  the glory of the LORD **shines upon you.**
See, darkness covers the earth,
  and thick clouds cover the peoples;
But upon you the LORD **shines,**
  and over you appears his glory.
Nations shall walk by your light,
  and kings by your shining radiance.
Raise your eyes and look about;
  they all gather and come to you:
Your sons come from afar,
  and your daughters in the arms of their nurses.

Then you shall be radiant at what you see,
  your heart shall throb and overflow,
For the riches of the sea shall be emptied out before you,
  the wealth of nations shall be brought to you.
Caravans of camels shall fill you,
  dromedaries from Midian and Ephah;
All from Sheba shall come
    bearing gold and frankincense,
    and proclaiming the praises of the LORD**.**

The word of the Lord.

3.

Ezekiel 34:11-16   As a shepherd tends his flock, so will I tend my sheep.

A reading from the Book of the Prophet Ezekiel

Thus says the Lord GOD**:**
I myself will look after and tend my sheep.
As a shepherd tends his flock
  when he finds himself among his scattered sheep,
  so will I tend my sheep.
I will rescue them from every place where they were scattered
  when it was cloudy and dark.

I will lead them out from among the peoples
  and gather them from the foreign lands;
  I will bring them back to their own country
  and pasture them upon the mountains of Israel
  in the land's ravines and all its inhabited places.
In good pastures will I pasture them,
  and on the mountain heights of Israel
  shall be their grazing ground.
There they shall lie down on good grazing ground,
  and in rich pastures shall they be pastured
  on the mountains of Israel.
I myself will pasture my sheep;
  I myself will give them rest, says the Lord GOD.
The lost I will seek out,
  the strayed I will bring back,
  the injured I will bind up,
  the sick I will heal
  but the sleek and the strong I will destroy,
  shepherding them rightly.

The word of the Lord.

4.

Hosea 2:16b, 17b, 21-22   I will espouse you to me forever.

A reading from the Book of the Prophet Hosea

Thus says the LORD:
  I will lead her into the desert
    and speak to her heart.
  She shall respond there as in the days of her youth,
    when she came up from the land of Egypt.

  I will espouse you to me forever:
    I will espouse you in right and in justice,
    in love and in mercy;
  I will espouse you in fidelity,
    and you shall know the LORD.

The word of the Lord.

5.

Zephaniah 3:14-18a   The King of Israel, the Lord, is in your midst.

A reading from the Book of the Prophet Zephaniah

Shout for joy, O daughter Zion!
   sing joyfully, O Israel!
Be glad and exult with all your heart,
   O daughter Jerusalem!
The LORD has removed the judgment against you,
   he turned away your enemies;
The King of Israel, the LORD, is in your midst,
   you have no further misfortune to fear.
On that day, it shall be said to Jerusalem:
   Fear not, O Zion, be not discouraged!
The LORD, your God, is in your midst,
   a mighty savior;
He will rejoice over you with gladness,
   and renew you in his love,
He will sing joyfully because of you,
   as one sings at festivals.

The word of the Lord.

828 READING FROM THE NEW TESTAMENT

1.

Acts 2:42-47 All who believed were together and had all things in common.

A reading from the Acts of the Apostles

The brothers and sisters devoted themselves
   to the teaching of the Apostles and to the communal life,
   to the breaking of the bread and to the prayers.
Awe came upon everyone,
   and many wonders and signs were done through the Apostles.
All who believed were together and had all things in common;
   they would sell their property and possessions
   and divide them among all according to each one's need.
Every day they devoted themselves
   to meeting together in the temple area
   and to breaking bread in their homes.
They ate their meals with exultation and sincerity of heart,
   praising God and enjoying favor with all the people.
And every day the Lord added to their number those who were being saved.

The word of the Lord.

2.

1 Corinthians 3:9c-11, 16-17   For the temple of God, which you are, is holy.

A reading from the first Letter of Saint Paul to the Corinthians

Brothers and sisters:
You are God's building.

According to the grace of God given to me,
** like a wise master builder I laid a foundation,**
** and another is building upon it.**
But each one must be careful how he builds upon it,
** for no one can lay a foundation other than the one that is there,**
** namely, Jesus Christ.**
Do you not know that you are the temple of God,
** and that the Spirit of God dwells in you?**
If anyone destroys God's temple,
** God will destroy that person;**
** for the temple of God, which you are, is holy.**

The word of the Lord.

3.

1 Corinthians 12:3b-7, 12-13   In the one Spirit we were all baptized into
one Body.

A reading from the first Letter of Saint Paul to the Corinthians

Brothers and sisters:
No one can say, "Jesus is Lord," except by the Holy Spirit.

There are different kinds of spiritual gifts but the same Spirit;
** there are different forms of service but the same Lord;**
** there are different workings but the same God**
** who produces all of them in everyone.**
To each individual the manifestation of the Spirit
** is given for some benefit.**
As a body is one though it has many parts,
** and all the parts of the body, though many, are one body,**
** so also Christ.**
For in one Spirit we were all baptized into one Body,
** whether Jews or Greeks, slaves or free persons,**
** and we were all given to drink of one Spirit.**

The word of the Lord.

4.

Ephesians 1:3-14   God chose us in Christ, before the foundation of the world.

A reading from the Letter of Saint Paul to the Ephesians

Blessed be the God and Father of our Lord Jesus Christ,
who has blessed us in Christ
with every spiritual blessing in the heavens,
as he chose us in him, before the foundation of the world,
to be holy and without blemish before him.
In love he destined us for adoption to himself through Jesus Christ,
in accord with the favor of his will,
for the praise of the glory of his grace
that he granted us in the beloved.

In him we have redemption by his Blood,
the forgiveness of transgressions,
in accord with the riches of his grace that he lavished upon us.
In all wisdom and insight, he has made known to us
the mystery of his will in accord with his favor
that he set forth in him as a plan for the fullness of times,
to sum up all things in Christ, in heaven and on earth.

In him we were also chosen,
destined in accord with the purpose of the One
who accomplishes all things according to the intention of his will,
so that we might exist for the praise of his glory,
we who first hoped in Christ.
In him you also, who have heard the word of truth,
the Gospel of your salvation, and have believed in him,
were sealed with the promised Holy Spirit,
which is the first installment of our inheritance
toward redemption as God's possession, to the praise of his glory.

The word of the Lord.

5.

Ephesians 2:19-22   The whole structure grows into a temple, sacred to the Lord.

A reading from the Letter of Saint Paul to the Ephesians

Brothers and sisters:
You are no longer strangers and sojourners,
**   but you are fellow citizens with the holy ones**
**   and members of the household of God,**
**   built upon the foundation of the Apostles and prophets,**
**   with Christ Jesus himself as the capstone.**
Through him the whole structure is held together
**   and grows into a temple sacred in the Lord;**
**   in him you also are being built together**
**   into a dwelling place of God in the Spirit.**

The word of the Lord.

6.

1 Peter 2:4-9   Like living stones, let yourselves be built into a
spiritual house.

A reading from the first Letter of Saint Peter

Beloved:
Come to the Lord, a living stone, rejected by human beings
  but chosen and precious in the sight of God,
  and, like living stones,
  let yourselves be built into a spiritual house
  to be a holy priesthood to offer spiritual sacrifices
  acceptable to God through Jesus Christ.
For it says in Scripture:

  Behold, I am laying a stone in Zion,
    a cornerstone, chosen and precious,
  and whoever believes in it shall not be put to shame.

Therefore, its value is for you who have faith,
  but for those without faith:

  The stone which the builders rejected
    has become the cornerstone,

  and

  A stone that will make people stumble,
    and a rock that will make them fall.

They stumble by disobeying the word, as is their destiny.

You are "a chosen race, a royal priesthood,
  a holy nation, a people of his own,
  so that you may announce the praises" of him
  who called you out of darkness into his wonderful light.

The word of the Lord.

7.

Revelation 7:2-4, 9-14   I, John, had a vision of a great multitude, which no one could count, from every nation, race, people, and tongue.

A reading from the Book of Revelation

I, John, saw another angel come up from the East,
  holding the seal of the living God.
He cried out in a loud voice to the four angels
  who were given power to damage the land and the sea,
  "Do not damage the land or the sea or the trees
  until we put the seal on the foreheads of the servants of our God."
I heard the number of those who had been marked with the seal,
  one hundred and forty-four thousand marked
  from every tribe of the children of Israel.

After this I had a vision of a great multitude,
  which no one could count,
  from every nation, race, people, and tongue.
They stood before the throne and before the Lamb,
  wearing white robes and holding palm branches in their hands.
They cried out in a loud voice:

  "Salvation comes from our God, who is seated on the throne,
    and from the Lamb."

All the angels stood around the throne
  and around the elders and the four living creatures.
They prostrated themselves before the throne,
  worshiped God, and exclaimed:

  "Amen. Blessing and glory, wisdom and thanksgiving,
    honor, power, and might
    be to our God forever and ever. Amen."

Then one of the elders spoke up and said to me,
  "Who are these wearing white robes, and where did they come from?"
I said to him, "My lord, you are the one who knows."
He said to me,
  "These are the ones who have survived the time of great distress;
  they have washed their robes
  and made them white in the Blood of the Lamb."

The word of the Lord.

8.

Revelation 21:1-5a   Behold, God's dwelling with the human race.

A reading from the Book of Revelation

I, John, saw a new heaven and a new earth.
The former heaven and the former earth had passed away,
    and the sea was no more.
I also saw the holy city, a new Jerusalem,
    coming down out of heaven from God,
    prepared as a bride adorned for her husband.
I heard a loud voice from the throne saying,
    "Behold, God's dwelling is with the human race.
He will dwell with them and they will be his people
    and God himself will always be with them as their God.
He will wipe every tear from their eyes,
    and there shall be no more death or mourning, wailing or pain,
    for the old order has passed away."

The One who sat on the throne said,
    "Behold, I make all things new."

The word of the Lord.

9.

Revelation 21:9-14   I will show you the bride, the wife of the Lamb.

A reading from the Book of Revelation

The angel spoke to me, saying:
"Come here. I will show you the bride, the wife of the Lamb."
He took me in spirit to a great, high mountain
    and showed me the holy city Jerusalem
    coming down out of heaven from God.
It gleamed with the splendor of God.
Its radiance was like that of a precious stone,
    like jasper, clear as crystal.
It had a massive, high wall,
    with twelve gates where twelve angels were stationed
    and on which names were inscribed,
    the names of the twelve tribes of the children of Israel.
There were three gates facing east,
    three north, three south, and three west.
The wall of the city had twelve courses of stones as its foundation,
    on which were inscribed the twelve names
    of the twelve Apostles of the Lamb.

The word of the Lord.

829 RESPONSORIAL PSALM

1.

Psalm 19:2-3, 4-5ab, 5c-7

℟. (5a) **Their message goes out through all the earth.**

The heavens declare the glory of God,
   and the firmament proclaims his handiwork.
Day pours out the word to day,
   and night to night imparts knowledge.

℟. **Their message goes out through all the earth.**

Not a word nor a discourse
   whose voice is not heard;
Through all the earth their voice resounds,
   and to the ends of the world, their message.

℟. **Their message goes out through all the earth.**

He has pitched a tent there for the sun,
   which comes forth like the groom from his bridal chamber
   and, like a giant, joyfully runs its course.
At one end of the heavens it comes forth,
   and its course is to their other end;
   nothing escapes its heat.

℟. **Their message goes out through all the earth.**

2.

Psalm 25:4-5ab, 6-7, 8-9, 10, 14

℟. (6a) **Remember your mercies, O Lord.**

Your ways, O Lord, make known to me;
   teach me your paths,
Guide me in your truth and teach me,
   for you are God my savior.

(cont.)

℞. Remember your mercies, O Lord.

Remember that your compassion, O Lord,
   and your kindness are from of old.
The sins of my youth and my frailties remember not;
   in your kindness remember me,
   because of your goodness, O Lord.

℞. Remember your mercies, O Lord.

Good and upright is the Lord;
   thus he shows sinners the way.
He guides the humble to justice,
   he teaches the humble his way.

℞. Remember your mercies, O Lord.

All the paths of the Lord are kindness and constancy
   toward those who keep his covenant and his decrees.

℞. Remember your mercies, O Lord.

The friendship of the Lord is with those who fear him,
   and his covenant, for their instruction.

℞. Remember your mercies, O Lord.

3.

Psalm 27:1, 2, 3, 5

℞. (see 9d) Do not abandon me, O God my Savior.

The Lord is my light and my salvation;
   whom should I fear?
The Lord is my life's refuge;
   of whom should I be afraid?

℞. Do not abandon me, O God my Savior.

When evildoers come at me
   to devour my flesh,
My foes and my enemies
   themselves stumble and fall.

℟. **Do not abandon me, O God my Savior.**

**Though an army encamp against me
    my heart will not fear;
Though war be waged upon me,
    even then will I trust.**

℟. **Do not abandon me, O God my Savior.**

**For he will hide me in his abode
    in the day of trouble;
He will conceal me in the shelter of his tent,
    he will set me high upon a rock.**

℟. **Do not abandon me, O God my Savior.**

4.

Psalm 67:2-3, 5, 7-8

℟. (4) **O God, let all the nations praise you!**

**May God have pity on us and bless us;
    may he let his face shine upon us.
So may your way be known upon earth;
    among all nations, your salvation.**

℟. **O God, let all the nations praise you!**

**May the nations be glad and exult
    because you rule the peoples in equity;
    the nations on the earth you guide.**

℟. **O God, let all the nations praise you!**

**The earth has yielded its fruits;
    God, our God, has blessed us.
May God bless us,
    and may all the ends of the earth fear him!**

℟. **O God, let all the nations praise you!**

5.

Psalm 96:1-2a, 2b-3, 7-8a, 9-10a

R℣. (3) **Proclaim God's marvelous deeds to all the nations.**
   or:
R℣. (see Matthew 28:19) **Go out to the world and teach all nations, alleluia.**

Sing to the LORD a new song;
   sing to the LORD, all you lands;
Sing to the LORD; bless his name.

R℣. **Proclaim God's marvelous deeds to all the nations.**
   or:
R℣. **Go out to the world and teach all nations, alleluia.**

Announce his salvation, day after day.
Tell his glory among the nations;
   among all peoples, his wondrous deeds.

R℣. **Proclaim God's marvelous deeds to all the nations.**
   or:
R℣. **Go out to the world and teach all nations, alleluia.**

Give to the LORD, you families of nations,
   give to the LORD glory and praise;
   give to the LORD the glory due his name!

R℣. **Proclaim God's marvelous deeds to all the nations.**
   or:
R℣. **Go out to the world and teach all nations, alleluia.**

Worship the LORD in holy attire.
Tremble before him all the earth;
   say among the nations: The LORD is king.

R℣. **Proclaim God's marvelous deeds to all the nations.**
   or:
R℣. **Go out to the world and teach all nations, alleluia.**

6.

Psalm 98:1, 2-3ab, 3cd-4, 5-6

℟. (see 2b) **The Lord has revealed to the nations his saving power.**

Sing to the LORD a new song,
   for he has done wondrous deeds;
His right hand has won victory for him,
   his holy arm.

℟. **The Lord has revealed to the nations his saving power.**

The LORD has made his salvation known:
   in the sight of the nations he has revealed his justice.
He has remembered his kindness and his faithfulness
   toward the house of Israel.

℟. **The Lord has revealed to the nations his saving power.**

All the ends of the earth have seen
   the salvation by our God.
Sing joyfully to the LORD, all you lands;
   break into song; sing praise.

℟. **The Lord has revealed to the nations his saving power.**

Sing praise to the LORD with the harp,
   with the harp and melodious song.
With trumpets and the sound of the horn
   sing joyfully before the King, the LORD.

℟. **The Lord has revealed to the nations his saving power.**

7.

Psalm 110:1bc, 2, 3, 4

℟. (4b) **You are a priest for ever, in the line of Melchizedek.**

The LORD said to my Lord: "Sit at my right hand
   till I make your enemies your footstool."

℟. **You are a priest for ever, in the line of Melchizedek.**

The scepter of your power the LORD will stretch forth from Zion:
   "Rule in the midst of your enemies."

(cont.)

℟. **You are a priest for ever, in the line of Melchizedek.**

**"Yours is princely power in the day of your birth, in holy splendor;
    before the daystar, like the dew, I have begotten you."**

℟. **You are a priest for ever, in the line of Melchizedek.**

**The LORD has sworn, and he will not repent:
    "You are a priest forever, according to the order of Melchizedek."**

℟. **You are a priest for ever, in the line of Melchizedek.**

8.

Psalm 117:1bc, 2

℟. (Mark 16:15) **Go out to all the world and tell the Good News.**

**Praise the LORD, all you nations,
    glorify him, all you peoples!**

℟. **Go out to all the world and tell the Good News.**

**For steadfast is his kindness toward us,
    and the fidelity of the LORD endures forever.**

℟. **Go out to all the world and tell the Good News.**

9.

Psalm 123:1bc, 2

℟. (2cd) **Our eyes are fixed on the Lord, pleading for his mercy.**

**To you I lift up my eyes
    who are enthroned in heaven.**

℟. **Our eyes are fixed on the Lord, pleading for his mercy.**

**Behold, as the eyes of servants
    are on the hands of their masters,
As the eyes of a maid
    are on the hands of her mistress,
So are our eyes on the LORD, our God,
    till he have pity on us.**

℟. **Our eyes are fixed on the Lord, pleading for his mercy.**

830 ALLELUIA VERSE AND VERSE BEFORE THE GOSPEL

1.

Psalm 133:1

**Behold, how good it is and how pleasant,
when brothers and sisters dwell as one!**

2.

Matthew 16:18

**You are Peter, and upon this rock I will build my Church
and the gates of the netherworld shall not prevail against it.**

3.

Matthew 28:19a, 20b

**Go and teach all nations, says the Lord;
I am with you always, until the end of the world.**

4.

John 10:11

**I am the good shepherd, says the Lord;
the good shepherd gives his life for the sheep.**

5.

John 10:14

**I am the good shepherd, says the Lord;
I know my sheep, and mine know me.**

6.

John 15:4a, 5b

**Remain in me, as I remain in you, says the Lord;
whoever remains in me will bear much fruit.**

831   GOSPEL

1.

Matthew 16:13-19   You are Peter, and upon this rock I will build my Church.

✠   **A reading from the holy Gospel according to Matthew**

When Jesus went into the region of Caesarea Philippi
he asked his disciples,
"Who do people say that the Son of Man is?"
They replied, "Some say John the Baptist, others Elijah,
still others Jeremiah or one of the prophets."
He said to them, "But who do you say that I am?"
Simon Peter said in reply,
"You are the Christ, the Son of the living God."
Jesus said to him in reply, "Blessed are you, Simon son of Jonah.
For flesh and blood has not revealed this to you, but my heavenly Father.
And so I say to you, you are Peter,
and upon this rock I will build my Church,
and the gates of the netherworld shall not prevail against it.
I will give you the keys to the Kingdom of heaven.
Whatever you bind on earth shall be bound in heaven;
and whatever you loose on earth shall be loosed in heaven."

The Gospel of the Lord.

2.

Matthew 18:15-20   If he listens to you, you will have won over your brother.

✠   **A reading from the holy Gospel according to Matthew**

Jesus said to his disciples:
"If your brother sins against you,
go and tell him his fault between you and him alone.
If he listens to you, you have won over your brother.
If he does not listen,
take one or two others along with you,
so that 'every fact may be established
on the testimony of two or three witnesses.'
If he refuses to listen to them, tell the Church.

If he refuses to listen even to the Church,
>   then treat him as you would a Gentile or a tax collector.
Amen, I say to you,
>   whatever you bind on earth shall be bound in heaven,
>   and whatever you loose on earth shall be loosed in heaven.
Again, amen, I say to you,
>   if two of you agree on earth
>   about anything for which they are to pray,
>   it shall be granted to them by my heavenly Father.
For where two or three are gathered together in my name,
>   there am I in the midst of them."

The Gospel of the Lord.

3.

Matthew 28:16-20   Go, therefore, and make disciples of all nations.

✠ **A reading from the holy Gospel according to Matthew**

The Eleven disciples went to Galilee,
>   to the mountain to which Jesus had ordered them.
When they saw him, they worshiped, but they doubted.
Then Jesus approached and said to them,
>   "All power in heaven and on earth has been given to me.
Go, therefore, and make disciples of all nations,
>   baptizing them in the name of the Father,
>   and of the Son, and of the Holy Spirit,
>   teaching them to observe all that I have commanded you.
And behold, I am with you always, until the end of the age."

The Gospel of the Lord.

4.

John 15:1-8   Whoever remains in me and I in him will bear much fruit.

✠   **A reading from the holy Gospel according to John**

Jesus said to his disciples:
"I am the true vine, and my Father is the vine grower.
He takes away every branch in me that does not bear fruit,
  and every one that does he prunes so that it bears more fruit.
You are already pruned because of the word that I spoke to you.
Remain in me, as I remain in you.
Just as a branch cannot bear fruit on its own
  unless it remains on the vine,
  so neither can you unless you remain in me.
I am the vine, you are the branches.
Whoever remains in me and I in him will bear much fruit,
  because without me you can do nothing.
Anyone who does not remain in me
  will be thrown out like a branch and wither;
  people will gather them and throw them into a fire
  and they will be burned.
If you remain in me and my words remain in you,
  ask for whatever you want and it will be done for you.
By this is my Father glorified,
  that you bear much fruit and become my disciples."

The Gospel of the Lord.

5.

John 17:11b, 17-23   As you sent me into the world, so I have sent them
into the world.

✠   **A reading from the holy Gospel according to John**

Jesus raised his eyes toward heaven and prayed, saying:
"Holy Father, keep them in your name that you have given me,
  so that they may be one just as we are one.
Consecrate them in the truth.
Your word is truth.
As you sent me into the world,
  so I sent them into the world.
And I consecrate myself for them,
  so that they also may be consecrated in truth.

"I pray not only for them,
   but also for those who will believe in me through their word,
   so that they may all be one,
   as you, Father, are in me and I in you,
   that they also may be in us,
   that the world may believe that you sent me.
And I have given them the glory you gave me,
   so that they may be one, as we are one,
   I in them and you in me,
   that they may be brought to perfection as one,
   that the world may know that you sent me,
   and that you loved them even as you loved me."

The Gospel of the Lord.

6.

John 21:15-17   Feed my lambs, feed my sheep.

☩ **A reading from the holy Gospel according to John**

After Jesus had revealed himself to his disciples
   and eaten breakfast with them, he said to Simon Peter,
   "Simon, son of John, do you love me more than these?"
Simon Peter answered him, "Yes, Lord, you know that I love you."
Jesus said to him, "Feed my lambs."
He then said to Simon Peter a second time,
   "Simon, son of John, do you love me?"
Simon Peter answered him, "Yes, Lord, you know that I love you."
He said to him, "Tend my sheep."
He said to him the third time,
   "Simon, son of John, do you love me?"
Peter was distressed that he had said to him a third time,
   "Do you love me?" and he said to him,
   "Lord, you know everything; you know that I love you."
Jesus said to him, "Feed my sheep."

The Gospel of the Lord.

832   2. FOR THE POPE OR A BISHOP, ESPECIALLY ON THEIR ANNIVERSARIES

Appropriate texts may be taken from the Common of Pastors, nos. 719–724.

3. FOR THE ELECTION OF A POPE OR A BISHOP

833 READING FROM THE OLD TESTAMENT

Isaiah 61:1-3a   The Lord has anointed me; he has sent me to bring glad tidings to the lowly.

A reading from the Book of the Prophet Isaiah

> **The Spirit of the Lord GOD is upon me,**
>> **because the LORD has anointed me;**
> **He has sent me to bring glad tidings to the lowly,**
>> **to heal the brokenhearted,**
> **To proclaim liberty to the captives**
>> **and release to the prisoners,**
> **To announce a year of favor from the LORD**
>> **and a day of vindication by our God,**
>> **to comfort all who mourn;**
> **To place on those who mourn in Zion**
>> **a diadem instead of ashes.**

The word of the Lord.

834 READING FROM THE NEW TESTAMENT

First Option

Ephesians 4:11-16   Bringing about the body's growth, building it up in love.

A reading from the Letter of Saint Paul to the Ephesians

Brothers and sisters:
Christ gave some as Apostles, others as prophets,
others as evangelists, others as pastors and teachers,
to equip the holy ones for the work of ministry,
for building up the Body of Christ,
until we all attain to the unity of faith
and knowledge of the Son of God, to mature manhood,
to the extent of the full stature of Christ,
so that we may no longer be infants,
tossed by waves and swept along by every wind of teaching
arising from human trickery,
from their cunning in the interests of deceitful scheming.
Rather, living the truth in love,
we should grow in every way into him who is the head,
Christ, from whom the whole Body,
joined and held together by every supporting ligament,
with the proper functioning of each part,
brings about the Body's growth and builds itself up in love.

The word of the Lord.

Second Option

Hebrews 5:1-10   Christ was acclaimed by God as high priest, in the line of Melchizedek.

A reading from the Letter to the Hebrews

Every high priest is taken from among men
    and made their representative before God,
      to offer gifts and sacrifices for sins.
He is able to deal patiently with the ignorant and erring,
    for he himself is beset by weakness
    and so, for this reason, must make sin offerings for himself
    as well as for the people.
No one takes this honor upon himself
    but only when called by God,
    just as Aaron was.
In the same way,
    it was not Christ who glorified himself in becoming high priest,
    but rather the one who said to him:

    You are my Son:
    this day I have begotten you;

    just as he says in another place:

    You are a priest forever
    according to the order of Melchizedek.

In the days when he was in the flesh,
    he offered prayers and supplications with loud cries and tears
    to the one who was able to save him from death,
    and he was heard because of his reverence.
Son though he was, he learned obedience from what he suffered;
    and when he was made perfect,
    he became the source of eternal salvation for all who obey him,
    declared by God high priest according to the order of Melchizedek.

The word of the Lord.

835   RESPONSORIAL PSALM

Psalm 89:4-5, 21-22, 25 and 27

R̸. (2a) **For ever I will sing the goodness of the Lord.**

"I have made a covenant with my chosen one;
  I have sworn to David my servant:
Forever will I confirm your posterity
  and establish your throne for all generations."

R̸. **For ever I will sing the goodness of the Lord.**

"I have found David, my servant;
  with my holy oil I have anointed him,
That my hand may be always with him,
  and that my arm may make him strong."

R̸. **For ever I will sing the goodness of the Lord.**

"My faithfulness and my mercy shall be with him,
  and through my name shall his horn be exalted.
He shall say of me, 'You are my father,
  my God, the Rock, my savior.'"

R̸. **For ever I will sing the goodness of the Lord.**

836 ALLELUIA VERSE AND VERSE BEFORE THE GOSPEL

John 10:11

**I am the good shepherd, says the Lord;
a good shepherd lays down his life for the sheep.**

837   GOSPEL

First Option

John 15:9-17   I chose you and appointed you to go and bear fruit that will remain.

✠   **A reading from the holy Gospel according to John**

Jesus said to his disciples:
"As the Father loves me, so I also love you.
Remain in my love.
If you keep my commandments, you will remain in my love,
   just as I have kept my Father's commandments
   and remain in his love.

"I have told you this so that my joy might be in you
   and your joy might be complete.
This is my commandment: love one another as I love you.
No one has greater love than this,
   to lay down one's life for one's friends.
You are my friends if you do what I command you.
I no longer call you slaves,
   because a slave does not know what his master is doing.
I have called you friends,
   because I have told you everything I have heard from my Father.
It was not you who chose me, but I who chose you
   and appointed you to go and bear fruit that will remain,
   so that whatever you ask the Father in my name he may give you.
This I command you: love one another."

The Gospel of the Lord.

Second Option

John 17:11b, 17-23   As you sent me into the world, so I have sent them into the world.

✠ **A reading from the holy Gospel according to John**

Jesus raised his eyes toward heaven and prayed, saying:
"Holy Father, keep them in your name that you have given me,
  so that they may be one just as we are one.
Consecrate them in the truth.
Your word is truth.
As you sent me into the world,
  so I sent them into the world.
And I consecrate myself for them,
  so that they also may be consecrated in truth.

"I pray not only for them,
  but also for those who will believe in me through their word,
  so that they may all be one,
  as you, Father, are in me and I in you,
  that they also may be in us,
  that the world may believe that you sent me.
And I have given them the glory you gave me,
  so that they may be one, as we are one,
  I in them and you in me,
  that they may be brought to perfection as one,
  that the world may know that you sent me,
  and that you loved them even as you loved me."

The Gospel of the Lord.

4. FOR A COUNCIL OR SYNOD OR FOR A SPIRITUAL OR PASTORAL MEETING

838   READING FROM THE OLD TESTAMENT

Deuteronomy 30:10-14   My command is something very near to you; you have only to carry it out.

A reading from the Book of Deuteronomy

Moses said to the people:
"Heed the voice of the LORD, your God,
    and keep his commandments and statutes
    that are written in this book of the law,
    when you return to the LORD, your God,
    with all your heart and all your soul.

"For this command which I enjoin on you today
    is not too mysterious and remote for you.
It is not up in the sky, that you should say,
    'Who will go up in the sky to get it for us
    and tell us of it, that we may carry it out?'
Nor is it across the sea, that you should say,
    'Who will cross the sea to get it for us
    and tell us of it, that we may carry it out?'
No, it is something very near to you,
    already in your mouths and in your hearts;
    you have only to carry it out."

The word of the Lord.

839 READING FROM THE NEW TESTAMENT

Philippians 2:1-4   Being of the same mind, with the same love.

A reading from the Letter of Saint Paul to the Philippians

Brothers and sisters:
If there is any encouragement in Christ,
  any solace in love,
  any participation in the Spirit,
  any compassion and mercy,
  complete my joy by being of the same mind, with the same love,
  united in heart, thinking one thing.
Do nothing out of selfishness or out of vainglory;
  rather, humbly regard others as more important than yourselves,
  each looking out not for his own interests,
  but also everyone for those of others.

The word of the Lord.

840 RESPONSORIAL PSALM

Psalm 19:8, 9, 10, 11

R̸. (John 6:68c) **Lord, you have the words of everlasting life.**

The law of the Lord is perfect,
    refreshing the soul;
The decree of the Lord is trustworthy,
    giving wisdom to the simple.

R̸. **Lord, you have the words of everlasting life.**

The precepts of the Lord are right,
    rejoicing the heart;
The command of the Lord is clear,
    enlightening the eye.

R̸. **Lord, you have the words of everlasting life.**

The fear of the Lord is pure,
    enduring forever;
The ordinances of the Lord are true,
    all of them just.

R̸. **Lord, you have the words of everlasting life.**

They are more precious than gold,
    than a heap of purest gold;
Sweeter also than syrup
    or honey from the comb.

R̸. **Lord, you have the words of everlasting life.**

841 ALLELUIA VERSE AND VERSE BEFORE THE GOSPEL

1.

Psalm 133:1

**Behold, how good it is and how pleasant,
where brothers and sisters dwell as one!**

2.

John 16:13a; 14:26d

**When the Spirit of truth comes,
he will guide you to all truth
and remind you of all I told you.**

842   GOSPEL

First Option

Matthew 18:15-20   Where two or three are gathered together in my name, there I am in their midst.

✠   **A reading from the holy Gospel according to Matthew**

Jesus said to his disciples:
"If your brother sins against you,
   go and tell him his fault between you and him alone.
If he listens to you, you have won over your brother.
If he does not listen,
   take one or two others along with you,
   so that 'every fact may be established
   on the testimony of two or three witnesses.'
If he refuses to listen to them, tell the Church.
If he refuses to listen even to the Church,
   then treat him as you would a Gentile or a tax collector.
Amen, I say to you,
   whatever you bind on earth shall be bound in heaven,
   and whatever you loose on earth shall be loosed in heaven.
Again, amen, I say to you,
   if two of you agree on earth
   about anything for which they are to pray,
   it shall be granted to them by my heavenly Father.
For where two or three are gathered together in my name,
   there am I in the midst of them."

The Gospel of the Lord.

Second Option

Mark 6:30-34   Come away by yourselves to a deserted place and rest a while.

✠   **A reading from the holy Gospel according to Mark**

The Apostles gathered together with Jesus
   and reported all they had done and taught.
He said to them,
   "Come away by yourselves to a deserted place and rest a while."
People were coming and going in great numbers,
   and they had no opportunity even to eat.

So they went off in the boat by themselves to a deserted place.
People saw them leaving and many came to know about it.
They hastened there on foot from all the towns
   and arrived at the place before them.

When he disembarked and saw the vast crowd,
   his heart was moved with pity for them,
   for they were like sheep without a shepherd;
   and he began to teach them many things.

The Gospel of the Lord.

Third Option

John 14:23-29   The Advocate, the Holy Spirit, will teach you everything.

✠ **A reading from the holy Gospel according to John**

Jesus said to his disciples:
"Whoever loves me will keep my word,
   and my Father will love him,
   and we will come to him and make our dwelling with him.
Whoever does not love me does not keep my words;
   yet the word you hear is not mine
   but that of the Father who sent me.

"I have told you this while I am with you.
The Advocate, the Holy Spirit
   whom the Father will send in my name,
   will teach you everything
   and remind you of all that I told you.
Peace I leave with you; my peace I give to you.
Not as the world gives do I give it to you.
Do not let your hearts be troubled or afraid.
You heard me tell you,
   'I am going away and I will come back to you.'
If you loved me,
   you would rejoice that I am going to the Father;
   for the Father is greater than I.
And now I have told you this before it happens,
   so that when it happens you may believe."

The Gospel of the Lord.

5. FOR PRIESTS

843 READING FROM THE OLD TESTAMENT

First Option

Isaiah 61:1-3a   The Lord has anointed me; he has sent me to bring glad tidings to the lowly.

A reading from the Book of the Prophet Isaiah

The Spirit of the Lord G**OD**** is upon me,
    because the L****ORD**** has anointed me;
He has sent me to bring glad tidings to the lowly,
    to heal the brokenhearted,
To proclaim liberty to the captives
    and release to the prisoners,
To announce a year of favor from the L****ORD****
    and a day of vindication by our God,
    to comfort all who mourn;
To place on those who mourn in Zion
    a diadem instead of ashes,
To give them oil of gladness in place of mourning,
    a glorious mantle instead of a listless spirit.**

The word of the Lord.

Second Option

Jeremiah 1:4-9   To whomever I send you, you shall go.

A reading from the Book of the Prophet Jeremiah

The word of the LORD **came to me thus:**

> **Before I formed you in the womb I knew you,**
>> **before you were born I dedicated you,**
>> **a prophet to the nations I appointed you.**

> **"Ah, Lord G**OD**!" I said,**
> **"I know not how to speak; I am too young."**

> **But the L**ORD **answered me,**

> **Say not, "I am too young."**
>> **To whomever I send you, you shall go;**
>> **whatever I command you, you shall speak.**
> **Have no fear before them,**
>> **because I am with you to deliver you, says the L**ORD**.**

Then the LORD **extended his hand and touched my mouth, saying,**

> **See, I place my words in your mouth!**

The word of the Lord.

844 READING FROM THE NEW TESTAMENT

1.

1 Corinthians 11:23-26   For as often as you eat this bread and drink the cup, you proclaim the death of the Lord until he comes.

A reading from the first Letter of Saint Paul to the Corinthians

Brothers and sisters:
I received from the Lord what I also handed on to you,
   that the Lord Jesus, on the night he was handed over,
   took bread, and, after he had given thanks,
   broke it and said, "This is my Body that is for you.
Do this in remembrance of me."
In the same way also the cup, after supper, saying,
   "This cup is the new covenant in my Blood.
Do this, as often as you drink it, in remembrance of me."
For as often as you eat this bread and drink the cup,
   you proclaim the death of the Lord until he comes.

The word of the Lord.

2.

2 Corinthians 4:1-2, 5-7   We do not preach ourselves but Jesus Christ as Lord, and ourselves as your slaves for the sake of Jesus.

A reading from the second Letter of Saint Paul to the Corinthians

Brothers and sisters:
Since we have this ministry through the mercy shown us,
   we are not discouraged.
Rather, we have renounced shameful, hidden things;
   not acting deceitfully or falsifying the word of God,
   but by the open declaration of the truth
   we commend ourselves to everyone's conscience in the sight of God.
For we do not preach ourselves but Jesus Christ as Lord,
   and ourselves as your slaves for the sake of Jesus.
For God who said, "Let light shine out of darkness,"
   has shone in our hearts to bring to light
   the knowledge of the glory of God on the face of Jesus Christ.

But we hold this treasure in earthen vessels,
   that the surpassing power may be of God and not from us.

The word of the Lord.

3.

2 Corinthians 5:14-20   He entrusted to us the ministry of reconciliation.

A reading from the second Letter of Saint Paul to the Corinthians

Brothers and sisters:
The love of Christ impels us,
> **once we have come to the conviction that one died for all;**
> **therefore, all have died.**

He indeed died for all,
> **so that those who live might no longer live for themselves**
> **but for him who for their sake died and was raised.**

Consequently, from now on we regard no one according to the flesh;
> **even if we once knew Christ according to the flesh,**
> **yet now we know him so no longer.**

So whoever is in Christ is a new creation:
> **the old things have passed away;**
> **behold, new things have come.**

And all this is from God,
> **who has reconciled us to himself through Christ**
> **and given us the ministry of reconciliation,**
> **namely, God was reconciling the world to himself in Christ,**
> **not counting their trespasses against them**
> **and entrusting to us the message of reconciliation.**

So we are ambassadors for Christ,
> **as if God were appealing through us.**

We implore you on behalf of Christ,
> **be reconciled to God.**

The word of the Lord.

4.

Ephesians 4:1-7, 11-13   In the work of ministry, in building up the Body of Christ.

A reading from the Letter of Saint Paul to the Ephesians

I, a prisoner for the Lord,
    urge you to live in a manner worthy of the call you have received,
    with all humility and gentleness, with patience,
    bearing with one another through love,
    striving to preserve the unity of the Spirit
    through the bond of peace:
    one Body and one Spirit,
    as you were also called to the one hope of your call;
    one Lord, one faith, one baptism;
    one God and Father of all,
    who is over all and through all and in all.

But grace was given to each of us
    according to the measure of Christ's gift.

And he gave some as Apostles, others as prophets,
    others as evangelists, others as pastors and teachers,
    to equip the holy ones for the work of ministry,
    for building up the Body of Christ,
    until we all attain to the unity of faith
    and knowledge of the Son of God, to mature manhood,
    to the extent of the full stature of Christ.

The word of the Lord.

5.

Colossians 1:24-29   The Church, of which I am a minister, in accordance with God's stewardship.

A reading from the Letter of Saint Paul to the Colossians

Brothers and sisters:
I rejoice in my sufferings for your sake,
    and in my flesh I am filling up
    what is lacking in the afflictions of Christ
    on behalf of his Body, which is the Church,
    of which I am a minister
    in accordance with God's stewardship given to me

to bring to completion for you the word of God,
  the mystery hidden from ages and from generations past.
But now it has been manifested to his holy ones,
  to whom God chose to make known the riches of the glory
  of this mystery among the Gentiles;
  it is Christ in you, the hope for glory.
It is him whom we proclaim,
  admonishing everyone and teaching everyone with all wisdom,
  that we may present everyone perfect in Christ.
For this I labor and struggle,
  in accord with the exercise of his power working within me.

The word of the Lord.

6.

1 Thessalonians 2:2b-8   We were determined to share with you not only
the Gospel of God, but our very selves as well.

A reading from the first Letter of Saint Paul to the Thessalonians

Brothers and sisters:
We drew courage through our God
  to speak to you the Gospel of God with much struggle.
Our exhortation was not from delusion or impure motives,
  nor did it work through deception.
But as we were judged worthy by God to be entrusted with the Gospel,
  that is how we speak,
  not as trying to please men,
  but rather God, who judges our hearts.
Nor, indeed, did we ever appear with flattering speech, as you know,
  or with a pretext for greed—
  God is witness—
  nor did we seek praise from men,
  either from you or from others,
  although we were able to impose our weight as Apostles of Christ.
Rather, we were gentle among you,
  as a nursing mother cares for her children.
With such affection for you,
  we were determined to share with you not only the Gospel of God,
  but our very selves as well,
  so dearly beloved had you become to us.

The word of the Lord.

845 RESPONSORIAL PSALM

1.

Psalm 16:1-2a and 5, 7-8, 11

R̸. (see 5a) **You are my inheritance, O Lord.**

Keep me, O God, for in you I take refuge;
 I say to the LORD, "My Lord are you."
O LORD, my allotted portion and my cup,
 you it is who hold fast my lot.

R̸. **You are my inheritance, O Lord.**

I bless the LORD who counsels me;
 even in the night my heart exhorts me.
I set the LORD ever before me;
 with him at my right hand I shall not be disturbed.

R̸. **You are my inheritance, O Lord.**

You will show me the path to life,
 fullness of joys in your presence,
 the delights at your right hand forever.

R̸. **You are my inheritance, O Lord.**

2.

Psalm 19:2-3, 4-5ab, 5c-7

R̸. (5a) **Their message goes out through all the earth.**

The heavens declare the glory of God,
 and the firmament proclaims his handiwork.
Day pours out the word to day,
 and night to night imparts knowledge.

R̸. **Their message goes out through all the earth.**

Not a word nor a discourse
 whose voice is not heard;
Through all the earth their voice resounds,
 and to the ends of the world, their message.

R̸. **Their message goes out through all the earth.**

He has pitched a tent there for the sun,
    which comes forth like the groom from his bridal chamber
    and, like a giant, joyfully runs its course.
At one end of the heavens it comes forth,
    and its course is to their other end;
    nothing escapes its heat.

R̈. Their message goes out through all the earth.

3.

Psalm 27:1, 4, 5, 8-9b, 9c-11

R̈. (8b) **I long to see your face, O Lord.**

The Lord is my light and my salvation;
    whom should I fear?
The Lord is my life's refuge;
    of whom should I be afraid?

R̈. I long to see your face, O Lord.

One thing I ask of the Lord;
    this I seek:
To dwell in the house of the Lord
    all the days of my life,
That I may gaze on the loveliness of the Lord
    and contemplate his temple.

R̈. I long to see your face, O Lord.

For he will hide me in his abode
    in the day of trouble;
He will conceal me in the shelter of his tent,
    he will set me high upon a rock.

R̈. I long to see your face, O Lord.

Of you my heart speaks; you my glance seeks;
    your presence, O Lord, I seek.
Hide not your face from me;
    do not in anger repel your servant.

(cont.)

R℣. I long to see your face, O Lord.

You are my helper: cast me not off.
Show me, O LORD, your way and lead me on a level path,
    because of my adversaries.

R℣. I long to see your face, O Lord.

4.

Psalm 84:3, 4, 5, 6a and 8, 11

R℣. (5a) **Blessed are they who dwell in your house, O Lord.**

My soul yearns and pines
    for the courts of the LORD.
My heart and my flesh
    cry out for the living God.

R℣. **Blessed are they who dwell in your house, O Lord.**

Even the sparrow finds a home,
    and the swallow a nest,
    in which she puts her young—
Your altars, O Lord of hosts,
    my king and my God!

R℣. **Blessed are they who dwell in your house, O Lord.**

Blessed they who dwell in your house!
    continually they praise you.

R℣. **Blessed are they who dwell in your house, O Lord.**

Blessed the men whose strength you are!
They go from strength to strength.

R℣. **Blessed are they who dwell in your house, O Lord.**

I had rather one day in your courts
    than a thousand elsewhere;
I had rather lie at the threshold of the house of my God
    than dwell in the tents of the wicked.

R℣. **Blessed are they who dwell in your house, O Lord.**

5.

Psalm 110:1, 2, 3, 4

R℟. (4b) **You are a priest for ever, in the line of Melchizedek.**

The LORD said to my Lord: "Sit at my right hand
  till I make your enemies your footstool."

R℟. **You are a priest for ever, in the line of Melchizedek.**

The scepter of your power the LORD will stretch forth from Zion;
  "Rule in the midst of all your foes."

R℟. **You are a priest for ever, in the line of Melchizedek.**

"Yours is princely power in the day of your birth, in holy splendor;
  before the daystar, like the dew, I have begotten you."

R℟. **You are a priest for ever, in the line of Melchizedek.**

The LORD has sworn, and he will not repent:
  "You are a priest forever, according to the order of Melchizedek."

R℟. **You are a priest forever, in the line of Melchizedek.**

846 ALLELUIA VERSE AND VERSE BEFORE THE GOSPEL

1.

Matthew 28:19a, 20b

**Go and teach all nations, says the Lord,
I am with you always, until the end of the world.**

2.

John 10:14

**I am the good shepherd, says the Lord;
I know my sheep, and mine know me.**

3.

John 12:26

**Whoever serves me must follow me, says the Lord;
and where I am, there also will my servant be.**

4.

John 15:9

**As the Father loves me, so I also love you.
Remain in my love.**

5.

See John 15:16

**I chose you from the world
to go and bear fruit that will last, says the Lord.**

847 GOSPEL

1.

Matthew 20:20-28   My chalice you will indeed drink.

✠ **A reading from the holy Gospel according to Matthew**

**The mother of the sons of Zebedee approached Jesus with her sons
and did him homage, wishing to ask him for something.
He said to her,
"What do you wish?"
She answered him,
"Command that these two sons of mine sit,
one at your right and the other at your left, in your Kingdom."
Jesus said in reply,
"You do not know what you are asking.
Can you drink the chalice that I am going to drink?"
They said to him, "We can."
He replied,
"My chalice you will indeed drink,
but to sit at my right and at my left,
this is not mine to give
but is for those for whom it has been prepared by my Father."
When the ten heard this,
they became indignant at the two brothers.
But Jesus summoned them and said,
"You know that the rulers of the Gentiles lord it over them,
and the great ones make their authority over them felt.
But it shall not be so among you.
Rather, whoever wishes to be great among you shall be your servant;
whoever wishes to be first among you shall be your slave.
Just so, the Son of Man did not come to be served
but to serve and to give his life as a ransom for many."**

The Gospel of the Lord.

2.

Matthew 28:16-20   Go and make disciples of all nations.

✛ **A reading from the holy Gospel according to Matthew**

The Eleven disciples went to Galilee,
   to the mountain to which Jesus had ordered them.
When they saw him, they worshiped, but they doubted.
Then Jesus approached and said to them,
   "All power in heaven and on earth has been given to me.
Go, therefore, and make disciples of all nations,
   baptizing them in the name of the Father,
   and of the Son, and of the Holy Spirit,
   teaching them to observe all that I have commanded you.
And behold, I am with you always, until the end of the age."

The Gospel of the Lord.

3.

Luke 10:1-9   The harvest is abundant but the laborers are few.

✛ **A reading from the holy Gospel according to Luke**

The Lord Jesus appointed seventy-two other disciples
   whom he sent ahead of him in pairs
   to every town and place he intended to visit.
He said to them,
   "The harvest is abundant but the laborers are few;
   so ask the master of the harvest
   to send out laborers for his harvest.
Go on your way;
   behold, I am sending you like lambs among wolves.
Carry no money bag, no sack, no sandals;
   and greet no one along the way.
Into whatever house you enter,
   first say, 'Peace to this household.'
If a peaceful person lives there,
   your peace will rest on him;
   but if not, it will return to you.
Stay in the same house and eat and drink what is offered to you,
   for the laborer deserves payment.
Do not move about from one house to another.

Whatever town you enter and they welcome you,
   eat what is set before you,
   cure the sick in it and say to them,
   'The Kingdom of God is at hand for you.'"

The Gospel of the Lord.

4.

Luke 22:24-30   I confer a kingdom on you, just as my Father has conferred one on me.

☩ **A reading from the holy Gospel according to Luke**

An argument broke out among the Apostles
   about which of them should be regarded as the greatest.
Jesus said to them,
   "The kings of the Gentiles lord it over them
   and those in authority over them are addressed as 'Benefactors';
   but among you it shall not be so.
Rather, let the greatest among you be as the youngest,
   and the leader as the servant.
For who is greater:
   the one seated at table or the one who serves?
Is it not the one seated at table?
I am among you as the one who serves.
It is you who have stood by me in my trials;
   and I confer a Kingdom on you,
   just as my Father has conferred one on me,
   that you may eat and drink at my table in my Kingdom;
   and you will sit on thrones
   judging the twelve tribes of Israel."

The Gospel of the Lord.

5.

John 10:11-16   A good shepherd lays down his life for the sheep.

☩ **A reading from the holy Gospel according to John**

Jesus said:
"I am the good shepherd.
A good shepherd lays down his life for the sheep.
A hired man, who is not a shepherd
 and whose sheep are not his own,
  sees a wolf coming and leaves the sheep and runs away,
  and the wolf catches and scatters them.
This is because he works for pay and has no concern for the sheep.
I am the good shepherd,
 and I know mine and mine know me,
  just as the Father knows me and I know the Father;
  and I will lay down my life for the sheep.
I have other sheep that do not belong to this fold.
These also I must lead, and they will hear my voice,
 and there will be one flock, one shepherd."

The Gospel of the Lord.

6.

John 15:9-17   I no longer call you slaves; I have called you friends.

☩ **A reading from the holy Gospel according to John**

Jesus said to his disciples:
"As the Father loves me, so I also love you.
Remain in my love.
If you keep my commandments, you will remain in my love,
 just as I have kept my Father's commandments
 and remain in his love.

"I have told you this so that my joy might be in you
 and your joy might be complete.
This is my commandment: love one another as I love you.
No one has greater love than this,
 to lay down one's life for one's friends.
You are my friends if you do what I command you.
I no longer call you slaves,
 because a slave does not know what his master is doing.

I have called you friends,
   because I have told you everything I have heard from my Father.
It was not you who chose me, but I who chose you
   and appointed you to go and bear fruit that will remain,
   so that whatever you ask the Father in my name he may give you.
This I command you: love one another."

The Gospel of the Lord.

7.

John 21:15-17   Feed my lambs, feed my sheep.

✠ **A reading from the holy Gospel according to John**

After Jesus had revealed himself to his disciples
   and eaten breakfast with them, he said to Simon Peter,
   "Simon, son of John, do you love me more than these?"
Simon Peter answered him, "Yes, Lord, you know that I love you."
Jesus said to him, "Feed my lambs."
He then said to Simon Peter a second time,
   "Simon, son of John, do you love me?"
Simon Peter answered him, "Yes, Lord, you know that I love you."
He said to him, "Tend my sheep."
He said to him the third time,
   "Simon, son of John, do you love me?"
Peter was distressed that he had said to him a third time,
   "Do you love me?" and he said to him,
   "Lord, you know everything; you know that I love you."
Jesus said to him, "Feed my sheep."

The Gospel of the Lord.

6. FOR MINISTERS OF THE CHURCH

848 READING FROM THE NEW TESTAMENT

1.

1 Corinthians 9:16-19, 22-23   Punishment will come to me if I do not
preach the Gospel.

A reading from the first Letter of Saint Paul to the Corinthians

Brothers and sisters:
If I preach the Gospel, this is no reason for me to boast,
    for an obligation has been imposed on me,
    and woe to me if I do not preach it!
If I do so willingly, I have a recompense,
    but if unwillingly, then I have been entrusted with a stewardship.
What then is my recompense?
That, when I preach,
    I offer the Gospel free of charge
    so as not to make full use of my right in the Gospel.

Although I am free in regard to all,
    I have made myself a slave to all
    so as to win over as many as possible.
To the weak I became weak, to win over the weak.
I have become all things to all, to save at least some.
All this I do for the sake of the Gospel,
    so that I too may have a share in it.

The word of the Lord.

2.

1 Corinthians 12:3b-7, 12-13   In the one Spirit we were all baptized into one Body.

A reading from the first Letter of Saint Paul to the Corinthians

Brothers and sisters:
No one can say, "Jesus is Lord," except by the Holy Spirit.

There are different kinds of spiritual gifts but the same Spirit;
**   there are different forms of service but the same Lord;**
**   there are different workings but the same God**
**   who produces all of them in everyone.**
To each individual the manifestation of the Spirit
**   is given for some benefit.**

As a body is one though it has many parts,
**   and all the parts of the body, though many, are one body,**
**   so also Christ.**
For in one Spirit we were all baptized into one Body,
**   whether Jews or Greeks, slaves or free persons,**
**   and we were all given to drink of one Spirit.**

The word of the Lord.

3.

Ephesians 4:1-7, 11-13   In the work of ministry, in building up the Body of Christ.

A reading from the Letter of Saint Paul to the Ephesians

Brothers and sisters:
I, a prisoner for the Lord,
   urge you to live in a manner worthy of the call you have received,
   with all humility and gentleness, with patience,
   bearing with one another through love,
   striving to preserve the unity of the Spirit
   through the bond of peace:
   one Body and one Spirit,
   as you were also called to the one hope of your call;
   one Lord, one faith, one baptism;
   one God and Father of all,
   who is over all and through all and in all.

But grace was given to each of us
   according to the measure of Christ's gift.

And he gave some as Apostles, others as prophets,
   others as evangelists, others as pastors and teachers,
   to equip the holy ones for the work of ministry,
   for building up the Body of Christ,
   until we all attain to the unity of faith
   and knowledge of the Son of God, to maturity,
   to the extent of the full stature of Christ.

The word of the Lord.

4.

Colossians 1:24-29   I became the servant of the Church when God made me responsible for delivering his message to you.

A reading from the Letter of Saint Paul to the Colossians

Brothers and sisters:
I rejoice in my sufferings for your sake,
  and in my flesh I am filling up
  what is lacking in the afflictions of Christ
  on behalf of his Body, which is the Church,
  of which I am a minister
  in accordance with God's stewardship given to me
  to bring to completion for you the word of God,
  the mystery hidden from ages and from generations past.
But now it has been manifested to his holy ones,
  to whom God chose to make known the riches of the glory
  of this mystery among the Gentiles;
  it is Christ in you, the hope for glory.
It is he whom we proclaim,
  admonishing everyone and teaching everyone with all wisdom,
  that we may present everyone perfect in Christ.
For this I labor and struggle,
  in accord with the exercise of his power working within me.

The word of the Lord.

5.

2 Timothy 4:1-5   Perform the work of an evangelist; fulfill your ministry.

A reading from the second Letter of Saint Paul to Timothy

Beloved:
I charge you in the presence of God and of Christ Jesus,
   who will judge the living and the dead,
   and by his appearing and his kingly power:
   proclaim the word;
   be persistent whether it is convenient or inconvenient;
   convince, reprimand, encourage through all patience and teaching.
For the time will come when people will not tolerate sound doctrine
   but, following their own desires and insatiable curiosity,
   will accumulate teachers and will stop listening to the truth
   and will be diverted to myths.
But you, be self-possessed in all circumstances;
   put up with hardship;
   perform the work of an evangelist;
   fulfill your ministry.

The word of the Lord.

849 RESPONSORIAL PSALM

First Option

Psalm 19:8, 9, 10, 11

℟. (10cd) **The judgments of the Lord are true, and all of them are just.**

**The law of the LORD is perfect,
refreshing the soul;
The decree of the LORD is trustworthy,
giving wisdom to the simple.**

℟. **The judgments of the Lord are true, and all of them are just.**

**The precepts of the LORD are right,
rejoicing the heart;
The command of the LORD is clear,
enlightening the eye.**

℟. **The judgments of the Lord are true, and all of them are just.**

**The fear of the LORD is pure,
enduring forever;
The ordinances of the LORD are true,
all of them just.**

℟. **The judgments of the Lord are true, and all of them are just.**

**They are more precious than gold,
than a heap of purest gold;
Sweeter also than syrup
or honey from the comb.**

℟. **The judgments of the Lord are true, and all of them are just.**

Second Option

Psalm 34:2-3, 4-5, 6-7, 8-9, 10-11

℞. (2a) **I will bless the Lord at all times.**

I will bless the LORD **at all times;**
   his praise shall be ever in my mouth.
Let my soul glory in the LORD**;**
   the lowly will hear me and be glad.

℞. I will bless the Lord at all times.

Glorify the LORD **with me,**
   let us together extol his name.
I sought the LORD**, and he answered me**
   and delivered me from all my fears.

℞. I will bless the Lord at all times.

Look to him that you may be radiant with joy,
   and your faces may not blush with shame.
When the poor one called out, the LORD **heard,**
   and from all his distress he saved him.

℞. I will bless the Lord at all times.

The angel of the LORD **encamps**
   around those who fear him, and delivers them.
Taste and see how good the LORD **is;**
   blessed the man who takes refuge in him.

℞. I will bless the Lord at all times.

Fear the LORD**, you his holy ones,**
   for nought is lacking to those who fear him.
The great grow poor and hungry;
   but those who seek the LORD **want for no good thing.**

℞. I will bless the Lord at all times.

Third Option

Psalm 96:1-2a, 2b-3, 7-8a, 10

℞. (3) **Proclaim his marvelous deeds to all the nations.**

Sing to the LORD a new song;
  sing to the LORD, all you lands.
Sing to the LORD; bless his name.

℞. **Proclaim his marvelous deeds to all the nations.**

Announce his salvation, day after day.
Tell his glory among the nations;
  among all peoples, his wondrous deeds.

℞. **Proclaim his marvelous deeds to all the nations.**

Give to the LORD, you families of nations,
  give to the LORD glory and praise;
  give to the LORD the glory due his name!

℞. **Proclaim his marvelous deeds to all the nations.**

Say among the nations: The LORD is king.
  He has made the world firm, not to be moved;
  he governs the people with equity.

℞. **Proclaim his marvelous deeds to all the nations.**

850 ALLELUIA VERSE AND VERSE BEFORE THE GOSPEL

1.

Matthew 28:19a, 20b

Go and teach all nations, says the Lord:
I am with you always, until the end of the world.

2.

See John 15:16

I chose you from the world,
to go and bear fruit that will last, says the Lord.

3.

1 Corinthians 1:23-24

We proclaim Christ crucified,
he is the power of God and the wisdom of God.

851 GOSPEL

First Option

Matthew 20:20-28   You shall indeed drink my chalice.

☩ **A reading from the holy Gospel according to Matthew**

The mother of the sons of Zebedee approached Jesus with her sons
    and did him homage, wishing to ask him for something.
He said to her,
    "What do you wish?"
She answered him,
    "Command that these two sons of mine sit,
    one at your right and the other at your left, in your Kingdom."
Jesus said in reply,
    "You do not know what you are asking.
Can you drink the chalice that I am going to drink?"
They said to him, "We can."
He replied,
    "My chalice you will indeed drink,
    but to sit at my right and at my left,
    this is not mine to give
    but is for those for whom it has been prepared by my Father."
When the ten heard this,
    they became indignant at the two brothers.
But Jesus summoned them and said,
    "You know that the rulers of the Gentiles lord it over them,
    and the great ones make their authority over them felt.
But it shall not be so among you.
Rather, whoever wishes to be great among you shall be your servant;
    whoever wishes to be first among you shall be your slave.
Just so, the Son of Man did not come to be served
    but to serve and to give his life as a ransom for many."

The Gospel of the Lord.

Second Option

Mark 16:15-20　Go into the whole world and proclaim the Gospel.

✠ **A reading from the holy Gospel according to Mark**

Jesus appeared to the Eleven and said to them:
"Go into the whole world
　　and proclaim the Gospel to every creature.
Whoever believes and is baptized will be saved;
　　whoever does not believe will be condemned.
These signs will accompany those who believe:
　　in my name they will drive out demons,
　　they will speak new languages.
They will pick up serpents with their hands,
　　and if they drink any deadly thing, it will not harm them.
They will lay hands on the sick, and they will recover."

Then the Lord Jesus, after he spoke to them,
　　was taken up into heaven
　　and took his seat at the right hand of God.
But they went forth and preached everywhere,
　　while the Lord worked with them
　　and confirmed the word through accompanying signs.

The Gospel of the Lord.

Third Option

Luke 10:1-9   The harvest is abundant but the laborers are few.

A reading from the holy Gospel according to Luke

The Lord Jesus appointed seventy-two other disciples
   whom he sent ahead of him in pairs
   to every town and place he intended to visit.
He said to them,
   "The harvest is abundant but the laborers are few;
   so ask the master of the harvest
   to send out laborers for his harvest.
Go on your way;
   behold, I am sending you like lambs among wolves.
Carry no money bag, no sack, no sandals;
   and greet no one along the way.
Into whatever house you enter,
   first say, 'Peace to this household.'
If a peaceful person lives there,
   your peace will rest on him;
   but if not, it will return to you.
Stay in the same house and eat and drink what is offered to you,
   for the laborer deserves his payment.
Do not move about from one house to another.
Whatever town you enter and they welcome you,
   eat what is set before you,
   cure the sick in it and say to them,
   'The Kingdom of God is at hand for you.'"

The Gospel of the Lord.

7. FOR RELIGIOUS

852 READING FROM THE OLD TESTAMENT

First Option

1 Kings 19:4-9a, 11-15a   Go out and stand on the mountain before the
L ORD God.

A reading from the first Book of Kings

Elijah went a day's journey into the desert,
 until he came to a broom tree and sat beneath it.
He prayed for death saying:
 "This is enough, O L ORD!
Take my life, for I am no better than my fathers."
He lay down and fell asleep under the broom tree,
 but then an angel touched him and ordered him to get up and eat.
He looked and there at his head was a hearth cake
 and a jug of water.
After he ate and drank, he lay down again,
 but the angel of the L ORD came back a second time,
 touched him, and ordered,
 "Get up and eat, else the journey will be too long for you!"
He got up, ate, and drank;
 then strengthened by that food,
 he walked forty days and forty nights to the mountain of God, Horeb.

There he came to a cave, where he took shelter.
Then the L ORD said,
 "Go outside and stand on the mountain before the L ORD;
 the L ORD will be passing by."
A strong and heavy wind was rending the mountains
 and crushing rocks before the L ORD—
 but the L ORD was not in the wind.
After the wind there was an earthquake—
 but the L ORD was not in the earthquake.
After the earthquake there was fire—
 but the L ORD was not in the fire.
After the fire there was a tiny whispering sound.
When he heard this,
 Elijah hid his face in his cloak
 and went and stood at the entrance of the cave.

A voice said to him, "Elijah, why are you here?"
He replied, "I have been most zealous for the LORD, the God of hosts.
But the children of Israel have forsaken your covenant,
   torn down your altars, and put your prophets to the sword.
   I alone am left, and they seek to take my life."
The LORD said to him,
   "Go, take the road back to the desert near Damascus."

The word of the Lord.

Second Option

Song of Songs 8:6-7   As stern as death is love.

A reading from the Song of Songs

Set me as a seal on your heart,
   as a seal on your arm;
For stern as death is love,
   relentless as the nether world is devotion;
   its flames are a blazing fire.
Deep waters cannot quench love,
   nor floods sweep it away.
Were one to offer all he owns to purchase love,
   he would be roundly mocked.

The word of the Lord.

Third Option

Isaiah 61:9-11   I rejoice heartily in the LORD.

A reading from the Book of the Prophet Isaiah

The LORD says:
The descendants of my people shall be renowned among the nations,
   and their offspring among the peoples;
All who see them shall acknowledge them
   as a race the LORD has blessed.

I rejoice heartily in the LORD,
   in my God is the joy of my soul;
For he has clothed me with a robe of salvation,
   and wrapped me in a mantle of justice,
Like a bridegroom adorned with a diadem,
   like a bride bedecked with her jewels.
As the earth brings forth its plants,
   and a garden makes its growth spring up,
So will the Lord GOD make justice and praise
   spring up before all the nations.

The word of the Lord.

Fourth Option

Hosea 2:16, 21-22   I will espouse you to myself forever.

A reading from the Book of the Prophet Hosea

Thus says the LORD:
I will allure her;
   I will lead her into the desert
   and speak to her heart.

I will espouse you to me forever:
   I will espouse you in right and in justice,
   in love and in mercy;
I will espouse you in fidelity,
   and you shall know the LORD.

The word of the Lord.

853 READING FROM THE NEW TESTAMENT

1.

Acts 2:42-47   All devoted themselves to the teaching of the Apostles and to the communal life.

A reading from the Acts of the Apostles

**The brothers and sisters devoted themselves
   to the teaching of the Apostles and to the communal life,
   to the breaking of the bread and to the prayers.
Awe came upon everyone,
   and many wonders and signs were done through the Apostles.
All who believed were together and had all things in common;
   they would sell their property and possessions
   and divide them among all according to each one's need.
Every day they devoted themselves
   to meeting together in the temple area
   and to breaking bread in their homes.
They ate their meals with exultation and sincerity of heart,
   praising God and enjoying favor with all the people.
And every day the Lord added to their number those who were being
      saved.**

The word of the Lord.

2.

1 Corinthians 1:22-31   We proclaim Christ crucified.

A reading from the first Letter of Saint Paul to the Corinthians

Brothers and sisters:
Jews demand signs and Greeks look for wisdom,
but we proclaim Christ crucified,
a stumbling block to Jews and foolishness to Gentiles,
but to those who are called, Jews and Greeks alike,
Christ the power of God and the wisdom of God.
For the foolishness of God is wiser than human wisdom,
and the weakness of God is stronger than human strength.

Consider your own calling, brothers and sisters.
Not many of you were wise by human standards,
not many were powerful,
not many were of noble birth.
Rather, God chose the foolish of the world to shame the wise,
and God chose the weak of the world to shame the strong,
and God chose the lowly and despised of the world,
those who count for nothing,
to reduce to nothing those who are something,
so that no human being might boast before God.
It is due to him that you are in Christ Jesus,
who became for us wisdom from God,
as well as righteousness, sanctification, and redemption,
so that, as it is written,
Whoever boasts, should boast in the Lord.

The word of the Lord.

3.

1 Corinthians 7:25-35   A virgin is anxious about the things of the Lord.

A reading from the first Letter of Saint Paul to the Corinthians

Brothers and sisters:
In regard to virgins, I have no commandment from the Lord,
   but I give my opinion as one who by the Lord's mercy is trustworthy.
So this is what I think best because of the present distress:
   that it is a good thing for a person to remain as he is.
Are you bound to a wife? Do not seek a separation.
Are you free of a wife? Then do not look for a wife.
If you marry, however, you do not sin,
   nor does an unmarried woman sin if she marries;
   but such people will experience affliction in their earthly life,
   and I would like to spare you that.

I tell you, brothers and sisters, the time is running out.
From now on, let those having wives act as not having them,
   those weeping as not weeping,
   those rejoicing as not rejoicing,
   those buying as not owning,
   those using the world as not using it fully.
For the world in its present form is passing away.

I should like you to be free of anxieties.
An unmarried man is anxious about the things of the Lord,
   how he may please the Lord.
But a married man is anxious about the things of the world,
   how he may please his wife, and he is divided.
An unmarried woman or a virgin is anxious about the things of the Lord,
   so that she may be holy in both body and spirit.
A married woman, on the other hand,
   is anxious about the things of the world,
   how she may please her husband.
I am telling you this for your own benefit,
   not to impose a restraint upon you,
   but for the sake of propriety
   and adherence to the Lord without distraction.

The word of the Lord.

4.

Philippians 2:1-4   Be of the same mind, with the same love.

A reading from the Letter of Saint Paul to the Philippians

Brothers and sisters:
If there is any encouragement in Christ,
    any solace in love,
    any participation in the Spirit,
    any compassion and mercy,
    complete my joy by being of the same mind, with the same love,
    united in heart, thinking one thing.
Do nothing out of selfishness or out of vainglory;
    rather, humbly regard others as more important than yourselves,
    each looking out not for his own interests,
    but also everyone for those of others.

The word of the Lord.

5.

1 Peter 1:3-9   Although you have not seen Jesus Christ you love him.

A reading from the first Letter of Saint Peter

Blessed be the God and Father of our Lord Jesus Christ,
    who in his great mercy gave us a new birth to a living hope
    through the resurrection of Jesus Christ from the dead,
    to an inheritance that is imperishable, undefiled, and unfading,
    kept in heaven for you
    who by the power of God are safeguarded through faith,
    to a salvation that is ready to be revealed in the final time.
In this you rejoice, although now for a little while
    you may have to suffer through various trials,
    so that the genuineness of your faith,
    more precious than gold that is perishable even though tested by fire,
    may prove to be for praise, glory, and honor
    at the revelation of Jesus Christ.
Although you have not seen him you love him;
    even though you do not see him now yet believe in him,
    you rejoice with an indescribable and glorious joy,
    as you attain the goal of your faith, the salvation of your souls.

The word of the Lord.

6.

Revelation 3:14b, 20-22   I will dine with him and he with me.

A reading from the Book of Revelation

"The Amen, the faithful and true witness,
  the source of God's creation, says this:

""Behold, I stand at the door and knock.
If anyone hears my voice and opens the door,
  then I will enter his house and dine with him,
  and he with me.
I will give the victor the right to sit with me on my throne,
  as I myself first won the victory
  and sit with my Father on his throne.

""Whoever has ears ought to hear
  what the Spirit says to the churches."""

The word of the Lord.

854 RESPONSORIAL PSALM

1.

Psalm 19:9, 10, 11

℟. (John 6:63b) **Your words, Lord, are Spirit and life.**

**The precepts of the LORD are right,
  rejoicing the heart;
The command of the LORD is clear,
  enlightening the eye.**

℟. **Your words, Lord, are Spirit and life.**

**The fear of the LORD is pure,
  enduring forever;
The ordinances of the LORD are true,
  all of them just.**

℟. **Your words, Lord, are Spirit and life.**

**They are more precious than gold,
  than a heap of purest gold;
Sweeter also than syrup
  or honey from the comb.**

℟. **Your words, Lord, are Spirit and life.**

2.

Psalm 27:1, 2, 3, 5

℟. (see 9d) **Do not abandon me, O God my Savior.**

**The LORD is my light and my salvation;
  whom should I fear?
The LORD is my life's refuge;
  of whom should I be afraid?**

℟. **Do not abandon me, O God my Savior.**

**When evildoers come at me
  to devour my flesh,
My foes and my enemies
  themselves stumble and fall.**

℟. **Do not abandon me, O God my Savior.**

Though an army encamp against me,
  my heart will not fear;
Though war be waged upon me,
  even then will I trust.

℟. Do not abandon me, O God my Savior.

For he will hide me in his abode
  in the day of trouble;
He will conceal me in the shelter of his tent,
  he will set me high upon a rock.

℟. Do not abandon me, O God my Savior.

3.

Psalm 45:11-12, 14-15, 16-17

℟. (11) **Listen to me, daughter; see and bend your ear.**
  or:
℟. (see Matthew 25:6) **The bridegroom is here; let us go out to meet Christ the Lord.**

Hear, O daughter, and see; turn your ear,
  forget your people and your father's house.
So shall the king desire your beauty;
  for he is your lord, and you must worship him.

℟. **Listen to me, daughter; see and bend your ear.**
  or:
℟. **The bridegroom is here; let us go out to meet Christ the Lord.**

All glorious is the king's daughter as she enters;
  her raiment is threaded with spun gold.
In embroidered apparel she is borne in to the king;
  behind her the virgins of her train are brought to you.

℟. **Listen to me, daughter; see and bend your ear.**
  or:
℟. **The bridegroom is here; let us go out to meet Christ the Lord.**

They are borne in with gladness and joy;
  they enter the palace of the king.
The place of your fathers your sons shall have;
  you shall make them princes through all the land.

℟. **Listen to me, daughter; see and bend your ear.**
  or:
℟. **The bridegroom is here; let us go out to meet Christ the Lord.**

4.

Psalm 112:1-2, 3-4, 5-6, 7-8, 9

℟. (1b) **Blessed are they who fear the Lord.**

Blessed the man who fears the LORD**,**
   who greatly delights in his commands.
His posterity shall be mighty upon the earth;
   the upright generation shall be blessed.

℟. **Blessed are they who fear the Lord.**

Wealth and riches shall be in his house;
   his generosity shall endure forever.
Light shines through the darkness for the upright;
   he is gracious and merciful and just.

℟. **Blessed are they who fear the Lord.**

Well for the man who is gracious and lends,
   who conducts his affairs with justice;
He shall never be moved;
   the just one shall be in everlasting remembrance.

℟. **Blessed are they who fear the Lord.**

An evil report he shall not fear;
   his heart is firm, trusting in the LORD**.**
His heart is steadfast; he shall not fear
   till he looks down upon his foes.

℟. **Blessed are they who fear the Lord.**

Lavishly he gives to the poor;
   his generosity shall endure forever;
   his horn shall be exalted in glory.

℟. **Blessed are they who fear the Lord.**

5.

Psalm 123:1-2ab, 2bcdef

℞. (2ef) **Our eyes are fixed on the Lord, pleading for his mercy.**

To you I lift up my eyes
  who are enthroned in heaven.
Behold, as the eyes of servants
  are on the hands of their masters.

℞. **Our eyes are fixed on the Lord, pleading for his mercy.**

As the eyes of a maid
  are on the hands of her mistress,
So are our eyes on the LORD, our God,
  till he have pity on us.

℞. **Our eyes are fixed on the Lord, pleading for his mercy.**

6.

Psalm 148:1-2, 11-13a, 13c-14

℞. (see 12a and 13a) **Young men and women, praise the name of the Lord.**

Praise the LORD from the heavens,
  praise him in the heights;
Praise him, all you his angels,
  praise him, all you his hosts.

℞. **Young men and women, praise the name of the Lord.**

Let the kings of the earth and all peoples,
  the princes and all the judges of the earth,
Young men too, and maidens,
  old men and boys,
Praise the name of the LORD,
  for his name alone is exalted.

℞. **Young men and women, praise the name of the Lord.**

His majesty is above earth and heaven,
  and he has lifted up the horn of his people.
Be this his praise from all his faithful ones,
  from the children of Israel, the people close to him. Alleluia.

℞. **Young men and women, praise the name of the Lord.**

855   ALLELUIA VERSE AND VERSE BEFORE THE GOSPEL

1.

Matthew 5:6

**Blessed are those who hunger and thirst for righteousness,
for they will be satisfied.**

2.

See Matthew 11:25

**Blessed are you, Father, Lord of heaven and earth;
you have revealed to little ones the mysteries of the Kingdom.**

3.

John 8:31b-32

**If you remain in my word, you will truly be my disciples,
and you will know the truth, says the Lord.**

4.

John 14:23

**Whoever loves me will keep my word,
and my Father will love him,
and we will come to him.**

5.

John 15:9b, 5b

**Remain in my love, says the Lord;
whoever remains in me and I in him will bear much fruit.**

856 GOSPEL

1.

Matthew 11:25-30   Though you have hidden these things from the wise and the learned you have revealed them to the childlike.

✠ **A reading from the holy Gospel according to Matthew**

At that time Jesus answered:
"I give praise to you, Father, Lord of heaven and earth,
   for although you have hidden these things
   from the wise and the learned
   you have revealed them to the childlike.
Yes, Father, such has been your gracious will.
All things have been handed over to me by my Father.
No one knows the Son except the Father,
   and no one knows the Father except the Son
   and anyone to whom the Son wishes to reveal him.

"Come to me, all you who labor and are burdened,
   and I will give you rest.
Take my yoke upon you and learn from me,
   for I am meek and humble of heart;
   and you will find rest for yourselves.
For my yoke is easy, and my burden light."

The Gospel of the Lord.

2.

Matthew 16:24-27   Whoever loses his life for my sake will save it.

✠ **A reading from the holy Gospel according to Matthew**

Jesus said to all,
  "Whoever wishes to come after me, he must deny himself
    and take up his cross and follow me.
For whoever wishes to save his life will lose it,
    but whoever loses his life for my sake will save it.
What profit would there be for one to gain the whole world
    and forfeit his life?
Or what can one give in exchange for his life?
    For the Son of Man will come with his angels in his Father's glory,
    and then he will repay each one according to his conduct."

The Gospel of the Lord.

3.

Matthew 19:3-12   Some have renounced marriage for the sake of the Kingdom of heaven.

✝ **A reading from the holy Gospel according to Matthew**

Some Pharisees approached Jesus, and tested him, saying,
 "Is it lawful for a man to divorce his wife for any cause whatever?"
He said in reply,
 "Have you not read that from the beginning
 the Creator *made them male and female* and said,
 For this reason a man shall leave his father and mother
 ***and be joined to his wife, and the two shall become one flesh*?**
So they are no longer two, but one flesh.
Therefore, what God has joined together, man must not separate."
They said to him,
 "Then why did Moses command that the man give the woman
 a bill of divorce and dismiss her?"
He said to them,
 "Because of the hardness of your hearts
 Moses allowed you to divorce your wives,
 but from the beginning it was not so.
I say to you, whoever divorces his wife
 (unless the marriage is unlawful)
 and marries another commits adultery."
His disciples said to him,
 "If that is the case of a man with his wife,
 it is better not to marry."
He answered, "Not all can accept this word,
 but only those to whom that is granted.
Some are incapable of marriage because they were born so;
 some, because they were made so by others;
 some, because they have renounced marriage
 for the sake of the Kingdom of heaven.
Whoever can accept this ought to accept it."

The Gospel of the Lord.

4.

Mark 3:31-35   Whoever does the will of God is my brother and sister and mother.

✠ **A reading from the holy Gospel according to Mark**

The mother of Jesus and his brothers arrived at the house.
Standing outside they sent word to Jesus and called him.
A crowd seated around him told him,
  "Your mother and your brothers and your sisters
  are outside asking for you."
But he said to them in reply,
  "Who are my mother and my brothers?"
And looking around at those seated in the circle he said,
  "Here are my mother and my brothers.
For whoever does the will of God
  is my brother and sister and mother."

The Gospel of the Lord.

5.

Luke 10:38-42   Martha welcomed him. Mary has chosen the better part.

✠ **A reading from the holy Gospel according to Luke**

Jesus entered a village
  where a woman whose name was Martha welcomed him.
She had a sister named Mary
  who sat beside the Lord at his feet listening to him speak.
Martha, burdened with much serving, came to him and said,
  "Lord, do you not care
  that my sister has left me by myself to do the serving?
Tell her to help me."
The Lord said to her in reply,
  "Martha, Martha, you are anxious and worried about many things.
There is need of only one thing.
Mary has chosen the better part
  and it will not be taken from her."

The Gospel of the Lord.

6.

John 15:1-8   Whoever remains in me, and I in him, will bear much fruit.

☩ **A reading from the holy Gospel according to John**

Jesus said to his disciples:
"I am the true vine, and my Father is the vine grower.
He takes away every branch in me that does not bear fruit,
   and everyone that does he prunes so that it bears more fruit.
You are already pruned because of the word that I spoke to you.
Remain in me, as I remain in you.
Just as a branch cannot bear fruit on its own
   unless it remains on the vine,
   so neither can you unless you remain in me.
I am the vine, you are the branches.
Whoever remains in me and I in him will bear much fruit,
   because without me you can do nothing.
Whoever does not remain in me
   will be thrown out like a branch and wither;
   people will gather them and throw them into a fire
   and they will be burned.
If you remain in me and my words remain in you,
   ask for whatever you want and it will be done for you.
By this is my Father glorified,
   that you bear much fruit and become my disciples."

The Gospel of the Lord.

8. FOR VOCATIONS TO HOLY ORDERS OR RELIGIOUS LIFE

857 READING FROM THE OLD TESTAMENT

1.

Genesis 12:1-4a   Go forth from the land of your kinsfolk, and come.

A reading from the Book of Genesis

The LORD said to Abram:
"Go forth from the land of your kinsfolk
   and from your father's house to a land that I will show you.

   "I will make of you a great nation,
     and I will bless you;
I will make your name great,
     so that you will be a blessing.
I will bless those who bless you
     and curse those who curse you.
All the communities of the earth
     shall find blessing in you."

Abram went as the LORD directed him.

The word of the Lord.

2.

Exodus 3:1-6, 9-12   I will be with you.

A reading from the Book of Exodus

Moses was tending the flock of his father-in-law Jethro,
   the priest of Midian.
Leading the flock across the desert, he came to Horeb,
   the mountain of God.
There an angel of the LORD appeared to him in fire
   flaming out of a bush.
As he looked on, he was surprised to see that the bush,
   though on fire, was not consumed.
So Moses decided,
   "I must go over to look at this remarkable sight,
   and see why the bush is not burned."

When the L<small>ORD</small> saw him coming over to look at it more closely,
> God called out to him from the bush, "Moses! Moses!"

He answered, "Here I am."

God said, "Come no nearer!

Remove the sandals from your feet,
> for the place where you stand is holy ground.

I am the God of your father," he continued,
> "the God of Abraham, the God of Isaac, the God of Jacob."

Moses hid his face, for he was afraid to look at God.

But the L<small>ORD</small> said,
> "I have witnessed the affliction of my people in Egypt
>
> and have heard their cry of complaint against their slave drivers,
>
> so I know well what they are suffering.

Therefore, I have come down to rescue them
> from the hands of the Egyptians,
>
> and lead them out of that land into a good and spacious land,
>
> a land flowing with milk and honey,
>
> the country of the Canaanites, Hittites, Amorites, Perizites, Hivites and
>> Jebusites.

So indeed the cry of the children of Israel has reached me,
> and I have truly noted that the Egyptians are oppressing them.

Come, now! I will send you to Pharaoh to lead my people,
> the children of Israel, out of Egypt."

But Moses said to God,
> "Who am I that I should go to Pharaoh
>
> and lead the children of Israel out of Egypt?"

He answered, "I will be with you;
> and this shall be your proof that it is I who have sent you:
>
> when you bring my people out of Egypt,
>
> you will worship God on this very mountain."

The word of the Lord.

3.

1 Samuel 3:1-10   Speak, LORD, for your servant is listening.

A reading from the first Book of Samuel

During the time young Samuel was minister to the LORD under Eli,
 a revelation of the LORD was uncommon and vision infrequent.
One day Eli was asleep in his usual place.
His eyes had lately grown so weak that he could not see.
The lamp of God was not yet extinguished,
 and Samuel was sleeping in the temple of the LORD
  where the ark of God was.
The LORD called to Samuel, who answered, "Here I am."
Samuel ran to Eli and said, "Here I am. You called me."
"I did not call you," Eli said. "Go back to sleep."
So he went back to sleep.
Again the LORD called Samuel, who rose and went to Eli.
"Here I am," he said. "You called me."
But Eli answered, "I did not call you, my son. Go back to sleep."

At that time Samuel was not familiar with the LORD,
 because the LORD had not revealed anything to him as yet.
The LORD called Samuel again, for the third time.
Getting up and going to Eli, he said, "Here I am. You called me."
Then Eli understood that the LORD was calling the youth.
So he said to Samuel, "Go to sleep, and if you are called, reply,
 'Speak, LORD, for your servant is listening.'"
When Samuel went to sleep in his place,
 the LORD came and revealed his presence,
  calling out as before, "Samuel, Samuel!"
Samuel answered, "Speak, for your servant is listening."

The word of the Lord.

4.

1 Kings 19:16b, 19-21   Elisha left and followed Elijah.

A reading from the first Book of Kings

The Lord said to Elijah:
"You shall anoint Elisha, son of Shaphat of Abelmeholah,
  as prophet to succeed you."

Elijah set out and came upon Elisha, son of Shaphat,
  as he was plowing with twelve yoke of oxen;
  he was following the twelfth.
Elijah went over to him and threw his cloak over him.
Elisha left the oxen, ran after Elijah, and said,
  "Please, let me kiss my father and mother goodbye,
  and I will follow you."
Elijah answered, "Go back!
Have I done anything to you?"
Elisha left him, and taking the yoke of oxen, slaughtered them;
  he used the plowing equipment for fuel to boil their flesh,
  and gave it to his people to eat.
Then Elisha left and followed Elijah as his attendant.

The word of the Lord.

5.

Isaiah 6:1, 6-8   Whom shall I send? Who will go for us?

A reading from the Book of the Prophet Isaiah

In the year King Uzziah died,
  I saw the LORD seated on a high and lofty throne,
  with the train of his garment filling the temple.

One of the seraphim flew to me,
  holding an ember which he had taken with tongs from the altar.

He touched my mouth with it and said,
  "See, now that this has touched your lips,
  your wickedness is removed, your sin purged."

Then I heard the voice of the LORD saying,
  "Whom shall I send? Who will go for us?"
"Here I am," I said; "send me!"

The word of the Lord.

6.

Jeremiah 1:4-9   To whomever I send you, you shall go.

A reading from the Book of the Prophet Jeremiah

The word of the LORD came to me thus:

> **Before I formed you in the womb I knew you,**
>> **before you were born I dedicated you,**
>> **a prophet to the nations I appointed you.**

> **"Ah, Lord GOD!" I said,**
>> **"I know not how to speak; I am too young."**

But the LORD answered me,

> **Say not, "I am too young."**
>> **To whomever I send you, you shall go;**
>> **whatever I command you, you shall speak.**
> **Have no fear before them,**
>> **because I am with you to deliver you, says the LORD.**

Then the LORD extended his hand and touched my mouth, saying,

> **See, I place my words in your mouth!**

The word of the Lord.

7.

Jeremiah 20:7-9   The desire to speak the word of the Lord becomes like fire burning in my heart.

A reading from the Book of the Prophet Jeremiah

> **You duped me, O LORD, and I let myself be duped;**
>> **you were too strong for me, and you triumphed.**
> **All the day I am an object of laughter;**
>> **everyone mocks me.**
> **Whenever I speak, I must cry out,**
>> **violence and outrage is my message;**
> **The word of the LORD has brought me**
>> **derision and reproach all the day.**
> **I say to myself, I will not mention him,**
>> **I will speak in his name no more.**
> **But then it becomes like fire burning in my heart,**
>> **imprisoned in my bones;**
> **I grow weary holding it in,**
>> **I cannot endure it.**

The word of the Lord.

858 READING FROM THE NEW TESTAMENT

First Option (For Priestly Vocations)

2 Corinthians 5:14-20   Christ has given us the ministry of reconciliation.

A reading from the second Letter of Saint Paul to the Corinthians

Brothers and sisters:
The love of Christ impels us,
>**once we have come to the conviction that one died for all;**
>**therefore, all have died.**
He indeed died for all,
>**so that those who live might no longer live for themselves**
>**but for him who for their sake died and was raised.**

Consequently, from now on we regard no one according to the flesh;
>**even if we once knew Christ according to the flesh,**
>**yet now we know him so no longer.**
So whoever is in Christ is a new creation:
>**the old things have passed away;**
>**behold, new things have come.**
And all this is from God,
>**who has reconciled us to himself through Christ**
>**and given us the ministry of reconciliation,**
>**namely, God was reconciling the world to himself in Christ,**
>**not counting their trespasses against them**
>**and entrusting to us the message of reconciliation.**
So we are ambassadors for Christ,
>**as if God were appealing through us.**
We implore you on behalf of Christ,
>**be reconciled to God.**

The word of the Lord.

Second Option

Philippians 3:8-14   I consider all things so much rubbish, that I may gain Christ.

A reading from the Letter of Saint Paul to the Philippians

Brothers and sisters:
I consider everything as a loss
   because of the supreme good of knowing Christ Jesus my Lord.
For his sake I have accepted the loss of all things
   and I consider them so much rubbish,
   that I may gain Christ and be found in him,
   not having any righteousness of my own based on the law
   but that which comes through faith in Christ,
   the righteousness from God,
   depending on faith to know him and the power of his resurrection
   and the sharing of his sufferings by being conformed to his death,
   if somehow I may attain the resurrection from the dead.

It is not that I have already taken hold of it
   or have already attained perfect maturity,
   but I continue my pursuit in hope that I may possess it,
   since I have indeed been taken possession of by Christ Jesus.
Brothers and sisters, I for my part
   do not consider myself to have taken possession.
Just one thing: forgetting what lies behind
   but straining forward to what lies ahead,
   I continue my pursuit toward the goal,
   the prize of God's upward calling, in Christ Jesus.

The word of the Lord.

Third Option (For Priestly Vocations)

Hebrews 5:1-9   Christ was acclaimed by God as high priest, in the line of Melchizedek.

A reading from the Letter to the Hebrews

Every high priest is taken from among men
and made their representative before God,
to offer gifts and sacrifices for sins.
He is able to deal patiently with the ignorant and erring,
for he himself is beset by weakness
and so, for this reason, must make sin offerings for himself
as well as for the people.
No one takes this honor upon himself
but only when called by God,
just as Aaron was.
In the same way,
it was not Christ who glorified himself in becoming high priest,
but rather the one who said to him:

> *You are my Son:*
> *this day I have begotten you.*

just as he says in another place:

> *You are a priest forever*
> *according to the order of Melchizedek.*

In the days when he was in the flesh,
he offered prayers and supplications with loud cries and tears
to the one who was able to save him from death,
and he was heard because of his reverence.
Son though he was, he learned obedience from what he suffered;
and when he was made perfect,
he became the source of eternal salvation for all who obey him,
declared by God high priest according to the order of Melchizedek.

The word of the Lord.

859 RESPONSORIAL PSALM

First Option

Psalm 16:1-2a and 5, 7-8, 11

R℣. (see 5a) **You are my inheritance, O Lord.**

Keep me, O God, for in you I take refuge;
  I say to the Lord, "My Lord are you."
O Lord, my allotted portion and my cup,
  you it is who hold fast my lot.

R℣. **You are my inheritance, O Lord.**

I bless the Lord who counsels me;
  even in the night my heart exhorts me.
I set the Lord ever before me;
  with him at my right hand I shall not be disturbed.

R℣. **You are my inheritance, O Lord.**

You will show me the path to life,
  fullness of joys in your presence,
  the delights at your right hand forever.

R℣. **You are my inheritance, O Lord.**

Second Option

Psalm 27:1, 4, 5, 8b-9ab, 9cd and 11

R℣. (8b) **I long to see your face, O Lord.**

The Lord is my light and my salvation;
  whom should I fear?
The Lord is my life's refuge;
  of whom should I be afraid?

R℣. **I long to see your face, O Lord.**

One thing I ask of the Lord;
  this I seek:
To dwell in the house of the Lord
  all the days of my life,
That I may gaze on the loveliness of the Lord
  and contemplate his temple.

℟. I long to see your face, O Lord.

For he will hide me in his abode
 in the day of trouble;
He will conceal me in the shelter of his tent,
 he will set me high upon a rock.

℟. I long to see your face, O Lord.

Your presence, O Lord, I seek.
Hide not your face from me;
 do not in anger repel your servant.

℟. I long to see your face, O Lord.

You are my helper: cast me not off;
 forsake me not, O God my savior.
Show me, O Lord, your way, and lead me on a level path,
 because of my adversaries.

℟. I long to see your face, O Lord.

Third Option

Psalm 40:2 and 4ab, 7-8a, 8b-9, 10, 12

℟. (see 8a and 9a) Here I am, Lord; I come to do your will.

I have waited, waited for the Lord,
 and he stooped toward me and heard my cry.
And he put a new song into my mouth,
 a hymn to our God.

℟. Here I am, Lord; I come to do your will.

Sacrifice or oblation you wished not,
 but ears open to obedience you gave me.
Burnt offerings or sin-offerings you sought not;
 then said I, "Behold I come."

℟. Here I am, Lord; I come to do your will.

"In the written scroll it is prescribed for me.
To do your will is my delight;
 my God, your law is in my heart!"

(cont.)

℟. Here I am, Lord; I come to do your will.

I announced your justice in the vast assembly;
  I did not restrain my lips, as you, O LORD, know.

℟. Here I am, Lord; I come to do your will.

Withhold not, O LORD, your compassion from me;
  may your mercy and your truth ever preserve me.

℟. Here I am, Lord; I come to do your will.

Fourth Option

Psalm 84:3-4, 6 and 8a, 11

℟. (5a) **Blessed are they who dwell in your house, O Lord.**

My soul yearns and pines
  for the courts of the LORD.
My heart and my flesh
  cry out for the living God.
Even the sparrow finds a home,
  and the swallow a nest
  in which she puts her young—
Your altars, O LORD of hosts,
  my king and my God!

℟. Blessed are they who dwell in your house, O Lord.

Blessed the men whose strength you are!
  their hearts are set upon the pilgrimage.
They go from strength to strength.

℟. Blessed are they who dwell in your house, O Lord.

I had rather one day in your courts
  than a thousand elsewhere;
I had rather lie at the threshold of the house of my God
  than dwell in the tents of the wicked.

℟. Blessed are they who dwell in your house, O Lord.

860 ALLELUIA VERSE AND VERSE BEFORE THE GOSPEL

1.

Mark 1:17

**Come after me, says the Lord,
and I will make you fishers of men.**

2.

John 15:5

**I am the vine, you are the branches, says the Lord:
whoever remains in me and I in him will bear much fruit.**

3.

See John 15:16

**I chose you from the world,
go and bear fruit that will last, says the Lord.**

4.

Philippians 3:8-9

**I consider all things so much rubbish,
that I may gain Christ and be found in him.**

861 GOSPEL

1.

Matthew 9:35-38   The harvest is abundant but the laborers are few.

A reading from the holy Gospel according to Matthew

Jesus went around to all the towns and villages,
teaching in their synagogues,
proclaiming the Gospel of the Kingdom,
and curing every disease and illness.
At the sight of the crowds, his heart was moved with pity for them
because they were troubled and abandoned,
like sheep without a shepherd.
Then he said to his disciples,
"The harvest is abundant but the laborers are few;
so ask the master of the harvest
to send out laborers for his harvest."

The Gospel of the Lord.

2.

Mark 10:17-27   Go, sell what you have, and follow me.

✟ **A reading from the holy Gospel according to Mark**

As Jesus was setting out on a journey,
a man ran up, knelt down before him, and asked him,
"Good teacher, what must I do to inherit eternal life?"
Jesus answered him, "Why do you call me good?
No one is good but God alone.
You know the commandments:
You shall not kill;
you shall not commit adultery;
you shall not steal;
you shall not bear false witness;
you shall not defraud;
honor your father and your mother."
He replied and said to him,
"Teacher, all of these I have observed from my youth."
Jesus, looking at him, loved him and said to him,
"You are lacking in one thing.

Go, sell what you have, and give to the poor
and you will have treasure in heaven; then come, follow me."
At that statement his face fell,
and he went away sad, for he had many possessions.

Jesus looked around and said to his disciples,
"How hard it is for those who have wealth
to enter the Kingdom of God!"
The disciples were amazed at his words.
So Jesus again said to them in reply,
"Children, how hard it is to enter the Kingdom of God!
It is easier for a camel to pass through the eye of a needle
than for one who is rich to enter the Kingdom of God."
They were exceedingly astonished
and said among themselves, "Then who can be saved?"
Jesus looked at them and said,
"For men it is impossible, but not for God.
All things are possible for God."

The Gospel of the Lord.

3.

Mark 10:28-30   You will not be without persecutions but you will be repaid a hundred times over in this life and eternal life in the age to come.

☩ **A reading from the holy Gospel according to Mark**

Peter said to Jesus:
"We have given up everything and followed you."
Jesus said, "Amen, I say to you,
there is no one who has given up house or brothers or sisters
or mother or father or children or lands
for my sake and for the sake of the Gospel
who will not receive a hundred times more now in this present age:
houses and brothers and sisters and mothers and children and lands,
with persecutions, and eternal life in the age to come."

The Gospel of the Lord.

4. (For Vocations to Holy Orders)

Luke 5:1-11   From this moment on, you will be fishers of men.

☩ **A reading from the holy Gospel according to Luke**

While the crowd was pressing in on Jesus and listening to the word of God,
  he was standing by the Lake of Gennesaret.
He saw two boats there alongside the lake;
  the fishermen had disembarked and were washing their nets.
Getting into one of the boats, the one belonging to Simon,
  he asked him to put out a short distance from the shore.
Then he sat down and taught the crowds from the boat.
After he had finished speaking, he said to Simon,
  "Put out into deep water and lower your nets for a catch."
Simon said in reply,
  "Master, we have worked hard all night and have caught nothing,
  but at your command I will lower the nets."
When they had done this, they caught a great number of fish
  and their nets were tearing.
They signaled to their partners in the other boat
  to come to help them.
They came and filled both boats
  so that they were in danger of sinking.
When Simon Peter saw this, he fell at the knees of Jesus and said,
  "Depart from me, Lord, for I am a sinful man."
For astonishment at the catch of fish they had made seized him
  and all those with him,
  and likewise James and John, the sons of Zebedee,
  who were partners of Simon.
Jesus said to Simon, "Do not be afraid;
  from now on you will be catching men."
When they brought their boats to the shore,
  they left everything and followed him.

The Gospel of the Lord.

5.

Luke 9:57-62   No one who sets a hand to the plow and looks to what was left behind is fit for the Kingdom of God.

✠   **A reading from the holy Gospel according to Luke**

As Jesus and his disciples were proceeding
  on their journey,
  someone said to him, "I will follow you wherever you go."
Jesus answered him,
  "Foxes have dens and birds of the sky have nests,
  but the Son of Man has nowhere to rest his head."
And to another he said, "Follow me."
But he replied, "Lord, let me go first and bury my father."
But he answered him, "Let the dead bury their dead.
But you, go and proclaim the Kingdom of God."
And another said, "I will follow you, Lord,
  but first let me say farewell to my family at home."
Jesus said, "No one who sets a hand to the plow
  and looks to what was left behind is fit for the Kingdom of God."

The Gospel of the Lord.

6.

Luke 14:25-33   Whoever does not carry his cross and come after me cannot be my disciple.

✝ **A reading from the holy Gospel according to Luke**

Great crowds were traveling with Jesus,
   and he turned and addressed them,
   "If anyone comes to me without hating his father and mother,
   wife and children, brothers and sisters,
   and even his own life,
   he cannot be my disciple.
Whoever does not carry his own cross and come after me
   cannot be my disciple.
Which of you wishing to construct a tower
   does not first sit down and calculate the cost
   to see if there is enough for its completion?
Otherwise, after laying the foundation
   and finding himself unable to finish the work
   the onlookers should laugh at him and say,
   'This one began to build but did not have the resources to finish.'
Or what king marching into battle would not first sit down
   and decide whether with ten thousand troops
   he can successfully oppose another king
   advancing upon him with twenty thousand troops?
But if not, while he is still far away,
   he will send a delegation to ask for peace terms.
In the same way,
   everyone of you who does not renounce all his possessions
   cannot be my disciple."

The Gospel of the Lord.

7.

Long Form

John 1:35-51   Follow me.

✝ **A reading from the holy Gospel according to John**

John was standing with two of his disciples,
   and as he watched Jesus walk by, he said,
   "Behold, the Lamb of God."

The two disciples heard what he said and followed Jesus.
Jesus turned and saw them following him and said to them,
   "What are you looking for?"
They said to him, "Rabbi" (which translated means Teacher),
   "where are you staying?"
He said to them, "Come, and you will see."
So they went and saw where he was staying,
   and they stayed with him that day.
It was about four in the afternoon.
Andrew, the brother of Simon Peter,
   was one of the two who heard John and followed Jesus.
He first found his own brother Simon and told him,
   "We have found the Messiah" (which is translated Christ).
Then he brought him to Jesus.
Jesus looked at him and said,
   "You are Simon the son of John;
   you will be called Cephas" (which is translated Peter).

The next day he decided to go to Galilee, and he found Philip.
And Jesus said to him, "Follow me."
Now Philip was from Bethsaida, the town of Andrew and Peter.
Philip found Nathanael and told him,
   "We have found the one about whom Moses wrote in the law,
   and also the prophets, Jesus, son of Joseph, from Nazareth."
But Nathanael said to him, "Can anything good come from Nazareth?"
Philip said to him, "Come and see."
Jesus saw Nathanael coming toward him and said of him,
   "Here is a true child of Israel. There is no duplicity in him."
Nathanael said to him, "How do you know me?"
Jesus answered and said to him,
   "Before Philip called you, I saw you under the fig tree."
Nathanael answered him, "Rabbi, you are the Son of God;
   you are the King of Israel."
Jesus answered and said to him,
   "Do you believe because I told you that
   I saw you under the fig tree?
You will see greater things than this."
And he said to him, "Amen, amen, I say to you,
   you will see the sky opened
   and the angels of God ascending and descending on the Son of Man."

The Gospel of the Lord.

OR Short Form

John 1:35-42   Follow me.

☩ **A reading from the holy Gospel according to John**

John was standing with two of his disciples,
    and as he watched Jesus walk by, he said,
    "Behold, the Lamb of God."
The two disciples heard what he said and followed Jesus.
Jesus turned and saw them following him and said to them,
    "What are you looking for?"
They said to him, "Rabbi" (which translated means Teacher),
    "where are you staying?"
He said to them, "Come, and you will see."
So they went and saw where he was staying,
    and they stayed with him that day.
It was about four in the afternoon.
Andrew, the brother of Simon Peter,
    was one of the two who heard John and followed Jesus.
He first found his own brother Simon and told him,
    "We have found the Messiah" (which is translated Christ).
Then he brought him to Jesus.
Jesus looked at him and said,
    "You are Simon the son of John;
    you will be called Cephas" (which is translated Peter).

The Gospel of the Lord.

8.

John 15:9-17   It was not you who chose me, but I who chose you.

✠ **A reading from the holy Gospel according to John**

Jesus said to his disciples:
"As the Father loves me, so I also love you.
Remain in my love.
If you keep my commandments, you will remain in my love,
 just as I have kept my Father's commandments
 and remain in his love.

"I have told you this so that my joy might be in you
 and your joy might be complete.
This is my commandment: love one another as I love you.
No one has greater love than this,
 to lay down one's life for one's friends.
You are my friends if you do what I command you.
I no longer call you slaves,
 because a slave does not know what his master is doing.
I have called you friends,
 because I have told you everything I have heard from my Father.
It was not you who chose me, but I who chose you
 and appointed you to go and bear fruit that will remain,
 so that whatever you ask the Father in my name he may give you.
This I command you: love one another."

The Gospel of the Lord.

9. FOR THE LAITY

862 READING FROM THE OLD TESTAMENT

First Option

Ezekiel 36:24-28   I will take you away from among the nations. I will give you a new heart.

A reading from the Book of the Prophet Ezekiel

Thus says the Lord GOD:
I will take you away from among the nations,
   gather you from all the foreign lands,
   and bring you back to your own land.
I will sprinkle clean water upon you
   to cleanse you from all your impurities,
   and from all your idols I will cleanse you.
I will give you a new heart and place a new spirit within you,
   taking from your bodies your stony hearts
   and giving you natural hearts.
I will put my spirit within you and make you live by my statutes,
   careful to observe my decrees.
You shall live in the land I gave your ancestors;
   you shall be my people, and I will be your God.

The word of the Lord.

Second Option

Joel 3:1a-5   I will pour out my Spirit on all flesh.

A reading from the Book of the Prophet Joel

Thus says the LORD:
    I will pour out
        my Spirit upon all flesh.
    Your sons and daughters shall prophesy,
        your old men shall dream dreams,
        your young men shall see visions;
    Even upon the servants and the handmaids,
        in those days, I will pour out my Spirit.
    And I will work wonders in the heavens and on the earth,
        blood, fire, and columns of smoke;
    The sun will be turned to darkness,
        and the moon to blood,
    At the coming of the day of the LORD,
        the great and terrible day.
    Then everyone shall be rescued
        who calls upon the name of the LORD;
    For on Mount Zion there shall be a remnant,
        as the LORD has said,
    And in Jerusalem survivors
        whom the LORD shall call.

The word of the Lord.

863 READING FROM THE NEW TESTAMENT

1.

Acts 2:1-11   They were all filled with the Holy Spirit and began to speak in different tongues.

A reading from the Acts of the Apostles

When the time for Pentecost was fulfilled,
  they were all in one place together.
And suddenly there came from the sky
  a noise like a strong driving wind,
  and it filled the entire house in which they were.
Then there appeared to them tongues as of fire,
  which parted and came to rest on each one of them.
And they were all filled with the Holy Spirit
  and began to speak in different tongues,
  as the Spirit enabled them to proclaim.

Now there were devout Jews
  from every nation under heaven staying in Jerusalem.
At this sound, they gathered in a large crowd,
  but they were confused
  because each one heard them speaking in his own language.
They were astounded, and in amazement they asked,
  "Are not all these people who are speaking Galileans?
Then how does each of us hear them in his own native language?
We are Parthians, Medes, and Elamites,
  inhabitants of Mesopotamia, Judea and Cappadocia,
  Pontus and Asia, Phrygia and Pamphylia,
  Egypt and the districts of Libya near Cyrene,
  as well as travelers from Rome,
  both Jews and converts to Judaism, Cretans and Arabs,
  yet we hear them speaking in our own tongues
  of the mighty acts of God."

The word of the Lord.

2.

Romans 6:2-4, 12-14   Consider yourselves dead to sin but alive to God.

A reading from the Letter of Saint Paul to the Romans

Brothers and sisters:
How can we who died to sin yet live in it?
Or are you unaware that we who were baptized into Christ Jesus
 were baptized into his death?
We were indeed buried with him through baptism into death,
 so that, just as Christ was raised from the dead
 by the glory of the Father,
 we too might live in newness of life.

Therefore, sin must not reign over your mortal bodies
 so that you obey their desires.
And do not present the parts of your bodies to sin
 as weapons for wickedness,
 but present yourselves to God as raised from the dead to life
 and the parts of your bodies to God as weapons for righteousness.
For sin is not to have any power over you,
 since you are not under the law but under grace.

The word of the Lord.

3.

Romans 8:31b-39   Neither death nor life will be able to ever separate us from the love of Christ.

A reading from the Letter of Saint Paul to the Romans

Brothers and sisters:
If God is for us, who can be against us?
He who did not spare his own Son
   but handed him over for us all,
   how will he not also give us everything else along with him?
Who will bring a charge against God's chosen ones?
It is God who acquits us.
Who will condemn?
It is Christ Jesus who died, rather, was raised,
   who also is at the right hand of God,
   who indeed intercedes for us.
What will separate us from the love of Christ?
Will anguish, or distress, or persecution, or famine,
   or nakedness, or peril, or the sword?
As it is written:

   For your sake we are being slain all the day;
      we are looked upon as sheep to be slaughtered.

No, in all these things we conquer overwhelmingly
   through him who loved us.
For I am convinced that neither death, nor life,
   nor angels, nor principalities,
   nor present things, nor future things,
   nor powers, nor height, nor depth,
   nor any other creature will be able to separate us
   from the love of God in Christ Jesus our Lord.

The word of the Lord.

4.

Romans 12:1-13   Offer your bodies as a living sacrifice, holy and pleasing to God.

A reading from the Letter of Saint Paul to the Romans

I urge you, brothers and sisters, by the mercies of God,
   to offer your bodies as a living sacrifice,
   holy and pleasing to God, your spiritual worship.

Do not conform yourselves to this age
   but be transformed by the renewal of your mind,
   that you may discern what is the will of God,
   what is good and pleasing and perfect.

For by the grace given to me I tell everyone among you
   not to think of himself more highly than one ought to think,
   but to think soberly,
   each according to the measure of faith that God has apportioned.
For as in one body we have many parts,
   and all the parts do not have the same function,
   so we, though many, are one Body in Christ
   and individually parts of one another.
Since we have gifts that differ according to the grace given to us,
   let us exercise them:
   if prophecy, in proportion to the faith;
   if ministry, in ministering;
   if one is a teacher, in teaching;
   if one exhorts, in exhortation;
   if one contributes, in generosity;
   if one is over others, with diligence;
   if one does acts of mercy, with cheerfulness.

Let love be sincere;
   hate what is evil,
   hold on to what is good;
   love one another with mutual affection;
   anticipate one another in showing honor.
Do not grow slack in zeal,
   be fervent in spirit,
   serve the Lord.
Rejoice in hope,
   endure in affliction,
   persevere in prayer.
Contribute to the needs of the holy ones,
   exercise hospitality.

The word of the Lord.

5.

1 Corinthians 12:3b-7, 12-13   In the one Spirit we were all baptized into one Body.

A reading from the first Letter of Saint Paul to the Corinthians

Brothers and sisters:
No one can say, "Jesus is Lord," except by the Holy Spirit.

There are different kinds of spiritual gifts but the same Spirit;
   there are different forms of service but the same Lord;
   there are different workings but the same God
   who produces all of them in everyone.
To each individual the manifestation of the Spirit
   is given for some benefit.

As a body is one though it has many parts,
   and all the parts of the body, though many, are one body,
   so also Christ.
For in one Spirit we were all baptized into one Body,
   whether Jews or Greeks, slaves or free persons,
   and we were all given to drink of one Spirit.

The word of the Lord.

6.

Ephesians 1:3-14   The Father chose us in Christ to be holy and without blemish before him.

A reading from the Letter of Saint Paul to the Ephesians

Blessed be the God and Father of our Lord Jesus Christ,
   who has blessed us in Christ
   with every spiritual blessing in the heavens,
   as he chose us in him, before the foundation of the world,
   to be holy and without blemish before him.
In love he destined us for adoption to himself through Jesus Christ,
   in accord with the favor of his will,
   for the praise of the glory of his grace
   that he granted us in the beloved.

In him we have redemption by his Blood,
   the forgiveness of transgressions,
   in accord with the riches of his grace that he lavished upon us.
In all wisdom and insight, he has made known to us
   the mystery of his will in accord with his favor
   that he set forth in him as a plan for the fullness of times,
   to sum up all things in Christ, in heaven and on earth.

In him we were also chosen,
   destined in accord with the purpose of the One
   who accomplishes all things according to the intention of his will,
   so that we might exist for the praise of his glory,
   we who first hoped in Christ.
In him you also, who have heard the word of truth,
   the Gospel of your salvation, and have believed in him,
   were sealed with the promised Holy Spirit,
   which is the first installment of our inheritance
   toward redemption as God's possession, to the praise of his glory.

The word of the Lord.

7.

Ephesians 4:1-6   There is one Lord, one faith, one baptism.

A reading from the Letter of Saint Paul to the Ephesians

Brothers and sisters:
I, a prisoner for the Lord,
   urge you to live in a manner worthy of the call you have received,
   with all humility and gentleness, with patience,
   bearing with one another through love,
   striving to preserve the unity of the spirit
   through the bond of peace:
   one Body and one Spirit,
   as you were also called to the one hope of your call;
   one Lord, one faith, one baptism;
   one God and Father of all,
   who is over all and through all and in all.

The word of the Lord.

8.

1 Peter 2:4-10   As living stones, you will be built into a spiritual temple.

A reading from the first Letter of Saint Peter

Beloved:
Come to the Lord, a living stone, rejected by human beings
>   **but chosen and precious in the sight of God,**
>   **and, like living stones,**
>   **let yourselves be built into a spiritual house**
>   **to be a holy priesthood to offer spiritual sacrifices**
>   **acceptable to God through Jesus Christ.**
For it says in Scripture:

>   *Behold, I am laying a stone in Zion,*
>   *a cornerstone, chosen and precious,*
>   *and whoever believes in it shall not be put to shame.*

Therefore, its value is for you who have faith,
>   **but for those without faith:**
>   *The stone which the builders rejected*
>   *has become the cornerstone,*

and

>   *A stone that will make people stumble,*
>   *and a rock that will make them fall.*

They stumble by disobeying the word, as is their destiny.

You are *a chosen race, a royal priesthood,*
>   *a holy nation, a people of his own,*
>   *so that you may announce the praises* **of him**
>   **who called you out of darkness into his wonderful light.**

>   **Once you were *no people***
>   **but now you are God's people;**
>   **you *had not received mercy***
>   **but now you have received mercy.**

The word of the Lord.

864 RESPONSORIAL PSALM

First Option

Psalm 85:2-4, 5-6, 7-8

R̸. (8) **Lord, show us your mercy and love, and grant us your salvation.**

You have favored, O LORD, your land;
  you have brought back the captives of Jacob.
You have forgiven the guilt of your people;
  you have covered all their sins.
You have withdrawn all your wrath;
  you have revoked your burning anger.

R̸. **Lord, show us your mercy and love, and grant us your salvation.**

Restore us, O God our savior,
  and abandon your displeasure against us.
Will you be ever angry with us,
  prolonging your anger to all generations?

R̸. **Lord, show us your mercy and love, and grant us your salvation.**

Will you not instead give us life;
  and shall not your people rejoice in you?
Show us, O LORD, your kindness,
  and grant us your salvation.

R̸. **Lord, show us your mercy and love, and grant us your salvation.**

Second Option

Psalm 100:1b-2, 3, 4, 5

R̸. (3c) **We are his people: the sheep of his flock.**

Sing joyfully to the LORD, all you lands;
  serve the LORD with gladness;
  come before him with joyful song.

R̸. **We are his people: the sheep of his flock.**

Know that the LORD is God;
  he made us, his we are;
  his people, the flock he tends.

(cont.)

℟. **We are his people: the sheep of his flock.**

Enter his gates with thanksgiving,
   his courts with praise;
Give thanks to him; bless his name.

℟. **We are his people: the sheep of his flock.**

For he is good:
   the LORD, whose kindness endures forever,
   and his faithfulness, to all generations.

℟. **We are his people: the sheep of his flock.**

Third Option

Psalm 103:1-2, 3-4, 8-9, 11-12

℟. (10a) **Lord, do not deal with us as our sins deserve.**
   or:
℟. (8a) **The Lord is kind and merciful.**

Bless the LORD, O my soul;
   and all my being, bless his holy name.
Bless the LORD, O my soul,
   and forget not all his benefits.

℟. **Lord, do not deal with us as our sins deserve.**
   or:
℟. **The Lord is kind and merciful.**

He pardons all your iniquities,
   he heals all your ills.
He redeems your life from destruction,
   he crowns you with kindness and compassion.

℟. **Lord, do not deal with us as our sins deserve.**
   or:
℟. **The Lord is kind and merciful.**

Merciful and gracious is the LORD,
  slow to anger and abounding in kindness.
He will not always chide,
  nor does he keep his wrath forever.

R̸. Lord, do not deal with us as our sins deserve.
  or:
R̸. The Lord is kind and merciful.

For as the heavens are high above the earth,
  so surpassing is his kindness toward those who fear him.
As far as the east is from the west,
  so far has he put our transgressions from us.

R̸. Lord, do not deal with us as our sins deserve.
  or:
R̸. The Lord is kind and merciful.

Fourth Option

Psalm 113:1-3, 4-6, 7-8

R̸. (see 2) Blessed be the name of the Lord for ever.

Praise, you servants of the LORD,
  praise the name of the LORD.
Blessed be the name of the LORD
  both now and forever.
From the rising to the setting of the sun
  is the name of the Lord to be praised.

R̸. Blessed be the name of the Lord for ever.

High above all nations is the LORD;
  above the heavens is his glory.
Who is like the LORD, our God, who is enthroned on high
  and looks upon the heavens and the earth below?

R̸. Blessed be the name of the Lord for ever.

He raises up the lowly from the dust;
  from the dunghill he lifts up the poor
To seat them with princes,
  with the princes of his own people.

R̸. Blessed be the name of the Lord for ever.

865 ALLELUIA VERSE AND VERSE BEFORE THE GOSPEL

1.

Matthew 5:9

**Blessed are the peacemakers;
they shall be called children of God.**

2.

John 8:12

**I am the light of the world, says the Lord;
whoever follows me will have the light of life.**

3.

John 15:4a, 5b

**Remain in me, as I remain in you, says the Lord;
whoever remains in me will bear much fruit.**

4.

See John 15:16

**I chose you from the world,
to go and bear fruit that will last, says the Lord.**

5.

James 1:12

**Blessed is the man who perseveres in temptation,
for when he has been proved he will receive the crown of life.**

6.

**The seed is the word of God, Christ is the sower;
all who come to him will live for ever.**

866 GOSPEL

1.

Matthew 5:1-12a   Rejoice and be glad, for your reward will be great in heaven.

✠ **A reading from the holy Gospel according to Matthew**

When Jesus saw the crowds, he went up the mountain,
   and after he had sat down, his disciples came to him.
He began to teach them, saying:

   "Blessed are the poor in spirit,
      for theirs is the Kingdom of heaven.
   Blessed are they who mourn,
      for they will be comforted.
   Blessed are the meek,
      for they will inherit the land.
   Blessed are they who hunger and thirst for righteousness,
      for they will be satisfied.
   Blessed are the merciful,
      for they will be shown mercy.
   Blessed are the clean of heart,
      for they will see God.
   Blessed are the peacemakers,
      for they will be called children of God.
   Blessed are they who are persecuted for the sake of righteousness,
      for theirs is the Kingdom of heaven.
   Blessed are you when they insult you and persecute you
      and utter every kind of evil against you falsely because of me.
   Rejoice and be glad,
      for your reward will be great in heaven."

The Gospel of the Lord.

2.

Matthew 16:24-27   Whoever loses his life for my sake will save it.

✠ **A reading from the holy Gospel according to Matthew**

Jesus said to all,
  "Whoever wishes to come after me, he must deny himself
  and take up his cross and follow me.
For whoever wishes to save his life will lose it,
  but whoever loses his life for my sake will save it.
What profit would there be for one to gain the whole world
  and forfeit his life?
Or what can one give in exchange for his life?
For the Son of Man will come with his angels in his Father's glory,
  and then he will repay each one according to his conduct."

The Gospel of the Lord.

3.

Matthew 25:14-30   Since you were faithful in small matters, come, share your master's joy.

✠ **A reading from the holy Gospel according to Matthew**

Jesus told his disciples this parable:
"A man going on a journey called in his servants
  and entrusted his possessions to them.
To one he gave five talents;
  to another, two; to a third, one—
  to each according to his ability.
Then he went away.
Immediately the one who received five talents went and traded with them,
  and made another five.
Likewise, the one who received two made another two.
But the man who received one went off and dug a hole in the ground
  and buried his master's money.
After a long time
  the master of those servants came back
  and settled accounts with them.
The one who had received five talents
  came forward bringing the additional five.
He said, 'Master, you gave me five talents.
See, I have made five more.'

His master said to him, 'Well done, my good and faithful servant.
Since you were faithful in small matters,
    I will give you great responsibilities.
Come, share your master's joy.'
Then the one who had received two talents also came forward and said,
    'Master, you gave me two talents.
See, I have made two more.'
His master said to him, 'Well done, my good and faithful servant.
Since you were faithful in small matters,
    I will give you great responsibilities.
Come, share your master's joy.'
Then the one who had received the one talent came forward and said,
    'Master, I knew you were a demanding person,
    harvesting where you did not plant
    and gathering where you did not scatter;
    so out of fear I went off and buried your talent in the ground.
Here it is back.'
His master said to him in reply, 'You wicked, lazy servant!
So you knew that I harvest where I did not plant
    and gather where I did not scatter?
Should you not then have put my money in the bank
    so that I could have got it back with interest on my return?
Now then! Take the talent from him and give it to the one with ten.
For to everyone who has,
    more will be given and he will grow rich;
    but from the one who has not,
    even what he has will be taken away.
And throw this useless servant into the darkness outside,
    where there will be wailing and grinding of teeth.'"

The Gospel of the Lord.

4.

Mark 3:31-35   Whoever does the will of God is my brother and sister and mother.

✝ **A reading from the holy Gospel according to Mark**

The mother of Jesus and his brothers arrived at the house.
Standing outside they sent word to him and called him.
A crowd seated around him told him,
   "Your mother and your brothers and your sisters
   are outside asking for you."
But he said to them in reply,
   "Who are my mother and my brothers?"
And looking around at those seated in the circle he said,
   "Here are my mother and my brothers.
For whoever does the will of God
   is my brother and sister and mother."

The Gospel of the Lord.

5.

Mark 4:1-9   A sower went out to sow.

✝ **A reading from the holy Gospel according to Mark**

On another occasion, Jesus began to teach by the sea.
A very large crowd gathered around him
   so that he got into a boat on the sea and sat down.
And the whole crowd was beside the sea on land.
And he taught them at length in parables,
   and in the course of his instruction he said to them,
   "Hear this! A sower went out to sow.
And as he sowed, some seed fell on the path,
   and the birds came and ate it up.
Other seed fell on rocky ground where it had little soil.
It sprang up at once because the soil was not deep.
And when the sun rose, it was scorched
   and it withered for lack of roots.
Some seed fell among thorns,
   and the thorns grew up and choked it
   and it produced no grain.

And some seed fell on rich soil and produced fruit.
It came up and grew and yielded thirty, sixty, and a hundredfold."
He added, "Whoever has ears to hear ought to hear."

The Gospel of the Lord.

6.

John 15:1-8   Whoever remains in me and I in him will bear much fruit.

✝ **A reading from the holy Gospel according to John**

Jesus said to his disciples:
"I am the true vine, and my Father is the vine grower.
He takes away every branch in me that does not bear fruit,
   and everyone that does he prunes so that it bears more fruit.
You are already pruned because of the word that I spoke to you.
Remain in me, as I remain in you.
Just as a branch cannot bear fruit on its own
   unless it remains on the vine,
   so neither can you unless you remain in me.
I am the vine, you are the branches.
Whoever remains in me and I in him will bear much fruit,
   because without me you can do nothing.
Whoever does not remain in me
   will be thrown out like a branch and wither;
   people will gather them and throw them into a fire
   and they will be burned.
If you remain in me and my words remain in you,
   ask for whatever you want and it will be done for you.
By this is my Father glorified,
   that you bear much fruit and become my disciples."

The Gospel of the Lord.

7.

John 15:18-21   If they have persecuted me, they will also persecute you.

✠ **A reading from the holy Gospel according to John**

Jesus said to his disciples:
"If the world hates you, realize that it hated me first.
If you belonged to the world, the world would love its own;
    but because you do not belong to the world,
    and I have chosen you out of the world,
    the world hates you.
Remember the word I spoke to you,
    'No slave is greater than his master.'
If they persecuted me, they will also persecute you.
If they kept my word, they will also keep yours.
And they will do all these things to you on account of my name,
    because they do not know the one who sent me."

The Gospel of the Lord.

10. FOR THE UNITY OF CHRISTIANS

867 READING FROM THE OLD TESTAMENT

First Option

Deuteronomy 30:1-4   The Lord, your God, will gather you from all
the nations.

A reading from the Book of Deuteronomy

Moses told the people:
"When all these things which I have set before you,
the blessings and the curses, are fulfilled in you,
and from among whatever nations
the LORD, your God, may have dispersed you,
you ponder them in your heart:
then, provided that you and your children return to the LORD, your God,
and heed his voice with all your heart and all your soul,
just as I now command you,
the LORD, your God, will change your lot;
and taking pity on you,
he will again gather you from all the nations
wherein he has scattered you.
Though you may have been driven to the farthest corner of the world,
even from there will the LORD, your God, gather you;
even from there will he bring you back."

The word of the Lord.

Second Option

Ezekiel 36:24-28   I will take you away from among the nations and give you natural hearts.

A reading from the Book of the Prophet Ezekiel

Thus says the Lord GOD:
I will take you away from among the nations,
  gather you from all the foreign lands,
  and bring you back to your own land.
I will sprinkle clean water upon you
  to cleanse you from all your impurities,
  and from all your idols I will cleanse you.
I will give you a new heart and place a new spirit within you,
  taking from your bodies your stony hearts
  and giving you natural hearts.
I will put my spirit within you and make you live by my statutes,
  careful to observe my decrees.
You shall live in the land I gave your fathers;
  you shall be my people and I will be your God.

The word of the Lord.

Third Option

Ezekiel 37:15-19, 21b-22, 26-28   Never again shall they be two nations.

A reading from the Book of the Prophet Ezekiel

Thus the word of the Lord came to me:
Now, son of man, take a single stick, and write on it:
    Judah and those children of Israel who are associated with him.
Then take another stick and write on it:
    Joseph the stick of Ephraim
    and all the house of Israel associated with him.
Then join the two sticks together,
    so that they form one stick in your hand.
When your countrymen ask you,
    "Will you not tell us what you mean by all this?"
    answer them: Thus says the Lord God:
    I will take the stick of Joseph, which is in the hand of Ephraim,
    and of the tribes of Israel associated with him,
    and I will join to it the stick of Judah,
    making them a single stick; they shall be one in my hand.
I will take the children of Israel from among the nations
    to which they have come,
    and gather them from all sides
    to bring them back to their land.
I will make them one nation upon the land,
    in the mountains of Israel,
    and there shall be one prince for them all.
Never again shall they be two nations,
    and never again shall they be divided into two kingdoms.

I will make with them a covenant of peace;
    it shall be an everlasting covenant with them,
    and I will multiply them, and put my sanctuary among them forever.
My dwelling shall be with them;
    I will be their God, and they shall be my people.
Thus the nations shall know that it is I, the Lord,
    who make Israel holy,
    when my sanctuary shall be set up among them forever.

The word of the Lord.

Fourth Option

Zephaniah 3:16b-20   At that time, I will gather you.

A reading from the Book of the Prophet Zephaniah

Fear not, O Zion, be not discouraged!
The Lord, your God, is in your midst,
  a mighty savior;
He will rejoice over you with gladness,
  and renew you in his love,
He will sing joyfully because of you,
  as one sings at festivals.
I will remove disaster from among you,
  so that none may recount your disgrace.
Yes, at that time I will deal
  with all who oppress you:
I will save the lame,
  and assemble the outcasts;
I will give them praise and renown
  in all the earth, when I bring about their restoration.

At that time I will bring you home,
  and at that time I will gather you;
For I will give you renown and praise,
  among all the peoples of the earth,
When I bring about your restoration
  before your very eyes, says the Lord.

The word of the Lord.

868 READING FROM THE NEW TESTAMENT

1.

1 Corinthians 1:10-13   There should be no serious divisions among you. Is Christ divided?

A reading from the first Letter of Saint Paul to the Corinthians

I urge you, brothers and sisters, in the name of our Lord Jesus Christ,
  that all of you agree in what you say,
  and that there be no divisions among you,
  but that you be united in the same mind and in the same purpose.
For it has been reported to me about you, my brothers and sisters,
  by Chloe's people, that there are rivalries among you.
I mean that each of you is saying,
  "I belong to Paul," or "I belong to Apollos,"
  or "I belong to Cephas," or "I belong to Christ."
Is Christ divided?
Was Paul crucified for you?
Or were you baptized in the name of Paul?

The word of the Lord.

2.

Ephesians 2:19-22   You are members of a household built upon the foundation of the Apostles and prophets with Christ Jesus himself as the capstone.

A reading from the Letter of Saint Paul to the Ephesians

Brothers and sisters:
You are no longer strangers and sojourners,
  but you are fellow citizens with the holy ones
  and members of the household of God,
  built upon the foundation of the Apostles and prophets,
  with Christ Jesus himself as the capstone.
Through him the whole structure is held together
  and grows into a temple sacred in the Lord;
  in him you also are being built together
  into a dwelling place of God in the Spirit.

The word of the Lord.

3.

Ephesians 4:1-6   Do all you can to preserve the unity of the Spirit through the bond of peace.

A reading from the Letter of Saint Paul to the Ephesians

Brothers and sisters:
I, a prisoner for the Lord,
   urge you to live in a manner worthy of the call you have received,
   with all humility and gentleness, with patience,
   bearing with one another through love,
   striving to preserve the unity of the Spirit
   through the bond of peace: one Body and one Spirit,
   as you were also called to the one hope of your call;
   one Lord, one faith, one baptism;
   one God and Father of all,
   who is over all and through all and in all.

The word of the Lord.

4.

Ephesians 4:30–5:2   Forgive one another as God has forgiven you in Christ.

A reading from the Letter of Saint Paul to the Ephesians

Brothers and sisters:
Do not grieve the Holy Spirit of God,
   with which you were sealed for the day of redemption.
All bitterness, fury, anger, shouting, and reviling
   must be removed from you, along with all malice.
And be kind to one another, compassionate,
   forgiving one another as God has forgiven you in Christ.

So be imitators of God, as beloved children,
   and live in love, as Christ loved us
   and handed himself over for us as a sacrificial offering to God
   for a fragrant aroma.

The word of the Lord.

5.

Philippians 2:1-13   Have among yourselves the same attitude.

A reading from the Letter of Saint Paul to the Philippians

Brothers and sisters:
If there is any encouragement in Christ,
   any solace in love,
   any participation in the Spirit,
   any compassion and mercy,
   complete my joy by being of the same mind, with the same love,
   united in heart, thinking one thing.
Do nothing out of selfishness or out of vainglory;
   rather, humbly regard others as more important than yourselves,
   each looking out not for his own interests,
   but also for those of others.

Have among yourselves the same attitude
   that is also yours in Christ Jesus,

   Who, though he was in the form of God,
      did not regard equality with God something to be grasped.
      Rather, he emptied himself,
      taking the form of a slave,
      coming in human likeness;
      and found human in appearance,
      he humbled himself,
      becoming obedient to death,
         even death on a cross.
   Because of this, God greatly exalted him
      and bestowed on him the name
      that is above every name,
      that at the name of Jesus
      every knee should bend,
      of those in heaven and on earth and under the earth,
      and every tongue confess that
      Jesus Christ is Lord,
      to the glory of God the Father.

So then, my beloved, obedient as you have always been,
   not only when I am present
   but all the more now when I am absent,
   work out your salvation with fear and trembling.
For God is the one who, for his good purpose,
   works in you both to desire and to work.

The word of the Lord.

6.

Colossians 3:9b-17   You have been called together into the unity of one Body.

A reading from the Letter of Saint Paul to the Colossians

Brothers and sisters:
You have taken off the old self with its practices
   and have put on the new self,
   which is being renewed, for knowledge,
   in the image of its creator.
   Here there is not Greek and Jew,
   circumcision and uncircumcision,
   barbarian, Scythian, slave, free;
   but Christ is all and in all.

Put on then, as God's chosen ones, holy and beloved,
   heartfelt compassion, kindness, humility, gentleness, and patience,
   bearing with one another and forgiving one another,
   if one has a grievance against another;
   as the Lord has forgiven you, so must you also do.
And over all these put on love,
   that is, the bond of perfection.
And let the peace of Christ control your hearts,
   the peace into which you were also called in one Body.
And be thankful.
Let the word of Christ dwell in you richly,
   as in all wisdom you teach and admonish one another,
   singing psalms, hymns, and spiritual songs
   with gratitude in your hearts to God.
And whatever you do, in word or in deed,
   do everything in the name of the Lord Jesus,
   giving thanks to God the Father through him.

The word of the Lord.

7.

1 Timothy 2:5-8   There is only one mediator between God and the human race, Christ Jesus, himself human.

A reading from the first Letter of Saint Paul to Timothy

Beloved:
   There is one God.

There is also one mediator between God and men,
the man Christ Jesus,
who gave himself as ransom for all.

This was the testimony at the proper time.
For this I was appointed preacher and Apostle
(I am speaking the truth, I am not lying),
teacher of the Gentiles in faith and truth.

It is my wish, then, that in every place the men should pray,
lifting up holy hands, without anger or argument.

The word of the Lord.

8.

1 John 4:9-15   If God so loved us, we also must love one another.

A reading from the first Letter of Saint John

Beloved:
The love of God was revealed to us in this way:
God sent his only-begotten Son into the world
so that we might have life through him.
In this is love:
not that we have loved God, but that he loved us
and sent his Son as expiation for our sins.
Beloved, if God so loved us,
we also must love one another.
No one has ever seen God.
Yet, if we love one another, God remains in us,
and his love is brought to perfection in us.

This is how we know that we remain in him and he in us,
that he has given us of his Spirit.
Moreover, we have seen and testify
that the Father sent his Son as savior of the world.
Whoever acknowledges that Jesus is the Son of God,
God remains in him and he in God.

The word of the Lord.

869 RESPONSORIAL PSALM

1.

Jeremiah 31:10, 11-12ab, 13-14

R̷. (see 10c) **Lord, gather your scattered people.**

Hear the word of the LORD, O nations,
   proclaim it on distant isles, and say:
He who scattered Israel, now gathers them together,
   he guards them as a shepherd his flock.

R̷. **Lord, gather your scattered people.**

The LORD shall ransom Jacob,
   he shall redeem him from the hand of his conqueror.
Shouting, they shall mount the heights of Zion,
   they shall come streaming to the LORD's blessings.

R̷. **Lord, gather your scattered people.**

Then the virgins shall make merry and dance,
   and young men and old as well.
I will turn their mourning into joy,
   I will console and gladden them after their sorrows.
I will lavish choice portions upon the priests,
   and my people shall be filled with my blessings,
      says the LORD.

R̷. **Lord, gather your scattered people.**

2.

Psalm 23:1-3, 4, 5, 6

R̷. (1b) **The Lord is my shepherd; there is nothing I shall want.**

The LORD is my shepherd; I shall not want.
   In verdant pastures he gives me repose;
Beside restful waters he leads me;
   he refreshes my soul.
He guides me in right paths
   for his name's sake.

R̷. **The Lord is my shepherd; there is nothing I shall want.**

Even though I walk in the dark valley
 I fear no evil; for you are at my side
With your rod and your staff
 that give me courage.

℟. The Lord is my shepherd; there is nothing I shall want.

You spread the table before me
 in the sight of my foes;
You anoint my head with oil;
 my cup overflows.

℟. The Lord is my shepherd; there is nothing I shall want.

Only goodness and kindness follow me
 all the days of my life;
And I shall dwell in the house of the Lord
 for years to come.

℟. The Lord is my shepherd; there is nothing I shall want.

 3.

Psalm 100:1b-2, 3, 4, 5

℟. (3c) We are his people: the sheep of his flock.
 or:
℟. (2b) Come with joy into the presence of the Lord.

Sing joyfully to the Lord, all you lands;
 serve the Lord with gladness;
 come before him with joyful song.

℟. We are his people: the sheep of his flock.
 or:
℟. Come with joy into the presence of the Lord.

Know that the Lord is God;
 he made us, his we are;
 his people, the flock he tends.

(cont.)

℟. We are his people: the sheep of his flock.
   or:
℟. Come with joy into the presence of the Lord.

Enter his gates with thanksgiving,
   his courts with praise;
Give thanks to him; bless his name.

℟. We are his people: the sheep of his flock.
   or:
℟. Come with joy into the presence of the Lord.

For he is good:
   the LORD, whose kindness endures forever,
   and his faithfulness, to all generations.

℟. We are his people: the sheep of his flock.
   or:
℟. Come with joy into the presence of the Lord.

4.

Psalm 118:22-23, 25-26, 28

℟. (22) The stone rejected by the builders has become the cornerstone.
   or:
℟. Alleluia.

The stone which the builders rejected
   has become the cornerstone.
By the LORD has this been done;
   it is wonderful in our eyes.

℟. The stone rejected by the builders has become the cornerstone.
   or:
℟. Alleluia.

O LORD, grant salvation!
   O LORD, grant prosperity!
Blessed is he who comes in the name of the LORD;
   we bless you from the house of the LORD.

℟. The stone rejected by the builders has become the cornerstone.
   or:
℟. Alleluia.

You are my God, and I give thanks to you;
 O my God, I extol you.

℟. **The stone rejected by the builders has become the cornerstone.**
 or:
℟. **Alleluia.**

5.

Psalm 122:1-2, 4-5, 6-7, 8-9

℟. (1) **I rejoiced when I heard them say: let us go to the house of the Lord.**
 or:
℟. (see 1) **Let us go rejoicing to the house of the Lord.**
 or:
℟. (Isaiah 66:10) **Rejoice with Jerusalem, and be glad.**

I rejoiced because they said to me,
 "We will go up to the house of the Lord."
And now we have set foot
 within your gates, O Jerusalem.

℟. **I rejoiced when I heard them say: let us go to the house of the Lord.**
 or:
℟. **Let us go rejoicing to the house of the Lord.**
 or:
℟. **Rejoice with Jerusalem, and be glad.**

To it the tribes go up,
 the tribes of the LORD,
According to the decree for Israel,
 to give thanks to the name of the LORD.
In it are set up judgment seats,
 seats for the house of David.

℟. **I rejoiced when I heard them say: let us go to the house of the Lord.**
 or:
℟. **Let us go rejoicing to the house of the Lord.**
 or:
℟. **Rejoice with Jerusalem, and be glad.**

(cont.)

Pray for the peace of Jerusalem!
  May those who love you prosper!
May peace be within your walls,
  prosperity in your buildings.

R⁊. I rejoiced when I heard them say: let us go to the house of the Lord.
  or:
R⁊. Let us go rejoicing to the house of the Lord.
  or:
R⁊. Rejoice with Jerusalem, and be glad.

Because of my relatives and friends
  I will say, "Peace be within you!"
Because of the house of the LORD, our God,
  I will pray for your good.

R⁊. I rejoiced when I heard them say: let us go to the house of the Lord.
  or:
R⁊. Let us go rejoicing to the house of the Lord.
  or:
R⁊. Rejoice with Jerusalem, and be glad.

870 ALLELUIA VERSE AND VERSE BEFORE THE GOSPEL

1.

John 17:21

May they all be one as you, Father, are in me and I in you,
that the world may believe that you sent me, says the Lord.

2.

Ephesians 4:5-6a

There is one Lord, one faith, one baptism,
one God and Father of all.

3.

Colossians 3:15

Let the peace of Christ control your hearts,
the peace into which you were called in one Body.

4.

Lord, let your Church be gathered from the ends of the earth into your
**   Kingdom,**
for glory and power are yours through Jesus Christ forever.

5.

The Church of the Lord is a single light;
it shines everywhere, yet the Church is not divided.

871　GOSPEL

1.

Matthew 18:19-22　Where two or three are gathered together in my name, there I am in their midst.

✠　**A reading from the holy Gospel according to Matthew**

**Jesus said to his disciples:
"If two of you agree on earth
　about anything for which they are to pray,
　it shall be granted to them by my heavenly Father.
For where two or three are gathered together in my name,
　there I am in the midst of them."**

**Then Peter approaching asked him,
　"Lord, if my brother sins against me,
　how often must I forgive him?
As many as seven times?"
Jesus answered, "I say to you,
　not seven times but seventy-seven times."**

The Gospel of the Lord.

2.

Luke 9:49-56　Whoever is not against you is for you.

✠　**A reading from the holy Gospel according to Luke**

**John said to Jesus:
"Master, we saw someone casting out demons in your name
　and we tried to prevent him
　because he does not follow in our company."
Jesus said to him,
　"Do not prevent him, for whoever is not against you is for you."**

**When the days for his being taken up were fulfilled,
　he resolutely determined to journey to Jerusalem,
　and he sent messengers ahead of him.
On the way they entered a Samaritan village
　to prepare for his reception there,
　but they would not welcome him
　because the destination of his journey was Jerusalem.**

When the disciples James and John saw this they asked,
  "Lord, do you want us to call down fire from heaven
  to consume them?"
Jesus turned and rebuked them,
  and they journeyed to another village.

The Gospel of the Lord.

3.

John 10:11-16   There will be one flock, one shepherd.

✝ **A reading from the holy Gospel according to John**

Jesus said:
"I am the good shepherd.
A good shepherd lays down his life for the sheep.
A hired man, who is not a shepherd
  and whose sheep are not his own,
  sees a wolf coming and leaves the sheep and runs away,
  and the wolf catches and scatters them.
This is because he works for pay and has no concern for the sheep.
I am the good shepherd,
  and I know mine and mine know me,
  just as the Father knows me and I know the Father;
  and I will lay down my life for the sheep.
I have other sheep that do not belong to this fold.
These also I must lead, and they will hear my voice,
  and there will be one flock, one shepherd."

The Gospel of the Lord.

4.

John 11:45-52   Jesus was going to die to gather together into one the dispersed children of God.

✝ **A reading from the holy Gospel according to John**

Many of the Jews who had come to Mary and Martha,
   the sisters of Lazarus,
   and seen what Jesus had done began to believe in him.
But some of them went to the Pharisees
   and told them what Jesus had done.
So the chief priests and the Pharisees
   convened the Sanhedrin and said,
   "What are we going to do?
This man is performing many signs.
If we leave him alone, all will believe in him,
   and the Romans will come
   and take away both our land and our nation."
But one of them, Caiaphas,
   who was high priest that year, said to them,
   "You know nothing,
   nor do you consider that it is better for you
   that one man should die instead of the people,
   so that the whole nation may not perish."
He did not say this on his own,
   but since he was high priest for that year,
   he prophesied that Jesus was going to die for the nation,
   and not only for the nation,
   but also to gather into one the dispersed children of God.

The Gospel of the Lord.

5.

John 13:1-15   I have given you an example to follow, so that as I have done for you, you should also do.

✝ **A reading from the holy Gospel according to John**

Before the feast of Passover, Jesus knew that his hour had come
   to pass from this world to the Father.
He loved his own in the world and he loved them to the end.
The Devil had already induced Judas, son of Simon the Iscariot,
   to hand him over.

So, during supper,

    fully aware that the Father had put everything into his power

    and that he had come from God and was returning to God,

    he rose from supper and took off his outer garments.

He took a towel and tied it around his waist.

Then he poured water into a basin

    and began to wash the disciples' feet

    and dry them with the towel around his waist.

He came to Simon Peter, who said to him,

    "Master, are you going to wash my feet?"

Jesus answered and said to him,

    "What I am doing, you do not understand now,

    but you will understand later."

Peter said to him, "You will never wash my feet."

Jesus answered him,

    "Unless I wash you, you will have no inheritance with me."

Simon Peter said to him,

    "Master, then not only my feet, but my hands and head as well."

Jesus said to him,

    "Whoever has bathed has no need except to have his feet washed,

    for he is clean all over;

    so you are clean, but not all."

For he knew who would betray him;

    for this reason, he said, "Not all of you are clean."

So when he had washed their feet

    and put his garments back on and reclined at table again,

    he said to them, "Do you realize what I have done for you?

You call me 'teacher' and 'master,'

    and rightly so, for indeed I am.

If I, therefore, the master and teacher, have washed your feet,

    you ought to wash one another's feet.

I have given you an example to follow,

    so that as I have done for you, you should also do."

The Gospel of the Lord.

6.

John 17:1-11a   They belonged to you, and you gave them to me, and they have kept your word.

☩   **A reading from the holy Gospel according to John**

Jesus raised his eyes to heaven and said,
  "Father, the hour has come.
Give glory to your Son, so that your Son may glorify you,
  just as you gave him authority over all people,
  so that your Son may give eternal life to all you gave him.
Now this is eternal life,
  that they should know you, the only true God,
  and the one whom you sent, Jesus Christ.
I glorified you on earth
  by accomplishing the work that you gave me to do.
Now glorify me, Father, with you,
  with the glory that I had with you before the world began.

"I revealed your name to those whom you gave me out of the world.
They belonged to you, and you gave them to me,
  and they have kept your word.
Now they know that everything you gave me is from you,
  because the words you gave to me I have given to them,
  and they accepted them and truly understood that I came from you,
  and they have believed that you sent me.
I pray for them.
I do not pray for the world but for the ones you have given me,
  because they are yours, and everything of mine is yours
  and everything of yours is mine,
  and I have been glorified in them.
And now I will no longer be in the world,
  but they are in the world, while I am coming to you."

The Gospel of the Lord.

7.

John 17:11b-19   May they be one just as we are.

✠ **A reading from the holy Gospel according to John**

Jesus raised his eyes to heaven and prayed, saying:
"Holy Father, keep them in your name that you have given me,
   so that they may be one just as we are one.
When I was with them
   I protected them in your name that you gave me,
   and I guarded them, and none of them was lost
   except the son of destruction,
   in order that the Scripture might be fulfilled.
But now I am coming to you.
I speak this in the world
   so that they may share my joy completely.
I gave them your word, and the world hated them,
   because they do not belong to the world
   any more than I belong to the world.
I do not ask that you take them out of the world
   but that you keep them from the Evil One.
They do not belong to the world
   any more than I belong to the world.
Consecrate them in the truth.
Your word is truth.
As you sent me into the world,
   so I sent them into the world.
And I consecrate myself for them,
   so that they also may be consecrated in truth."

The Gospel of the Lord.

8.

John 17:20-26   May they be one!

✠ **A reading from the holy Gospel according to John**

Jesus raised his eyes to heaven and said:
"Holy Father, I pray not only for these,
   but also for those who will believe in me through their word,
   so that they may all be one,
   as you, Father, are in me and I in you,
   that they also may be in us,
   that the world may believe that you sent me.
And I have given them the glory you gave me,
   so that they may be one, as we are one,
   I in them and you in me,
   that they may be brought to perfection as one,
   that the world may know that you sent me,
   and that you loved them even as you loved me.
Father, they are your gift to me.
I wish that where I am they also may be with me,
   that they may see my glory that you gave me,
   because you loved me before the foundation of the world.
Righteous Father, the world also does not know you,
   but I know you, and they know that you sent me.
I made known to them your name and I will make it known,
   that the love with which you loved me
   may be in them and I in them."

The Gospel of the Lord.

11. FOR THE EVANGELIZATION OF PEOPLES

872 READING FROM THE OLD TESTAMENT

1.

Isaiah 2:1-5   All the nations shall stream to the mountain of the Lord.

A reading from the Book of the Prophet Isaiah

This is what Isaiah, son of Amoz,
saw concerning Judah and Jerusalem.

In days to come,
The mountain of the LORD's house
shall be established as the highest mountain
and raised above the hills.
All nations shall stream toward it;
many peoples shall come and say:
"Come, let us climb the LORD's mountain,
to the house of the God of Jacob,
That he may instruct us in his ways,
and we may walk in his paths."
For from Zion shall go forth instruction,
and the word of the LORD from Jerusalem.
He shall judge between the nations,
and impose terms on many peoples.
They shall beat their swords into plowshares
and their spears into pruning hooks;
One nation shall not raise the sword against another,
nor shall they train for war again.
O house of Jacob, come,
let us walk in the light of the LORD!

The word of the Lord.

2.

Isaiah 56:1, 6-7   My house shall be called a house of prayer for all peoples.

A reading from the Book of the Prophet Isaiah

Thus says the LORD:
Observe what is right, do what is just;
for my salvation is about to come,
my justice, about to be revealed.

And the foreigners who join themselves to the LORD,
ministering to him,
Loving the name of the LORD,
and becoming his servants—
All who keep the sabbath free from profanation
and hold to my covenant,
Them I will bring to my holy mountain
and make joyful in my house of prayer;
Their burnt offerings and sacrifices
will be acceptable on my altar,
For my house shall be called
a house of prayer for all peoples.

The word of the Lord.

3.

Isaiah 60:1-6　All nations shall walk by your light.

A reading from the Book of the Prophet Isaiah

Rise up in splendor, Jerusalem! Your light has come,
　the glory of the Lord shines upon you.
See, darkness covers the earth,
　and thick clouds cover the peoples;
But upon you the Lord shines,
　and over you appears his glory.
Nations shall walk by your light,
　and kings by your shining radiance.
Raise your eyes and look about;
　they all gather and come to you:
Your sons come from afar,
　and your daughters in the arms of their nurses.

Then you shall be radiant at what you see,
　your heart shall throb and overflow,
For the riches of the sea shall be emptied out before you,
　the wealth of nations shall be brought to you.
Caravans of camels shall fill you,
　dromedaries from Midian and Ephah;
All from Sheba shall come
　bearing gold and frankincense,
　and proclaiming the praises of the LORD.

The word of the Lord.

4.

Jonah 3:10–4:11   Should I not show mercy to Nineveh?

A reading from the Book of the Prophet Jonah

When God saw by their actions
    how the Ninevites turned from their evil way,
    he repented of the evil that he had threatened to do to them;
    he did not carry it out.

But this was greatly displeasing to Jonah, and he became angry.
"I beseech you, Lord," he prayed,
    "is not this what I said while I was still in my own country?
This is why I fled at first to Tarshish.
I knew that you are a gracious and merciful God,
    slow to anger, rich in clemency, loathe to punish.
And now, Lord, please take my life from me;
    for it is better for me to die than to live."
But the Lord asked, "Have you reason to be angry?"

Jonah then left the city for a place to the east of it,
    where he built himself a hut and waited under it in the shade,
    to see what would happen to the city.
And when the Lord God provided a gourd plant
    that grew up over Jonah's head,
    giving shade that relieved him of any discomfort,
    Jonah was very happy over the plant.
But the next morning at dawn God sent a worm which attacked the plant,
    so that it withered.
And when the sun arose, God sent a burning east wind;
    and the sun beat upon Jonah's head till he became faint.
Then he asked for death, saying, "I would be better off dead than alive."

But God said to Jonah, "Have you reason to be angry over the plant?"
Jonah answered, "I have reason to be angry, angry enough to die."
Then the Lord said,
    "You are concerned over the plant which cost you no labor
    and which you did not raise;
    it came up in one night and in one night it perished.
And should I not be concerned over Nineveh, the great city,
    in which there are more than a hundred and twenty thousand persons
    who cannot distinguish their right hand from their left,
    not to mention the many cattle?"

The word of the Lord.

5.

Zechariah 8:20-23   Many strong nations shall come to seek the Lord of hosts in Jerusalem.

A reading from the Book of the Prophet Zechariah

Thus says the LORD **of hosts:**
There shall yet come peoples,
   the inhabitants of many cities;
   and the inhabitants of one city shall approach those of another,
   and say, "Come! let us go to implore the favor of the LORD**";**
   and, "I too will go to seek the LORD**."**
Many peoples and strong nations shall come
   to seek the LORD **of hosts in Jerusalem**
   and to implore the favor of the LORD**.**
Thus says the LORD **of hosts:**
   In those days ten men of every nationality,
   speaking different tongues, shall take hold,
   yes, take hold of every Jew by the edge of his garment and say,
   "Let us go with you, for we have heard that God is with you."

The word of the Lord.

873   READING FROM THE NEW TESTAMENT

1.

Acts 1:3-8   You will be my witnesses to the ends of the earth.

A reading from the Acts of the Apostles

Jesus showed the Apostles that he was alive
  by many proofs after he had suffered,
  appearing to them during forty days
  and speaking about the Kingdom of God.
While meeting with them,
  he enjoined them not to depart from Jerusalem,
  but to wait for "the promise of the Father
  about which you have heard me speak;
  for John baptized with water,
  but in a few days you will be baptized with the Holy Spirit."

When they had gathered together they asked him,
  "Lord, are you at this time going to restore the kingdom to Israel?"
He answered them, "It is not for you to know the times or seasons
  that the Father has established by his own authority.
But you will receive power when the Holy Spirit comes upon you,
  and you will be my witnesses in Jerusalem,
  throughout Judea and Samaria,
  and to the ends of the earth."

The word of the Lord.

2.

Acts 11:19-26   The disciples preached to the Greeks, proclaiming the Good News of the Lord Jesus.

A reading from the Acts of the Apostles

Those who had been scattered by the persecution
  that arose because of Stephen
  went as far as Phoenicia, Cyprus, and Antioch,
  preaching the word to no one but Jews.
There were some Cypriots and Cyrenians among them, however,
  who came to Antioch and began to speak to the Greeks as well,
  proclaiming the Lord Jesus.
The hand of the Lord was with them
  and a great number who believed turned to the Lord.

The news about them reached the ears of the Church in Jerusalem,
   and they sent Barnabas to go to Antioch.
When he arrived and saw the grace of God,
   he rejoiced and encouraged them all to remain faithful to the Lord
   in firmness of heart,
   for he was a good man, filled with the Holy Spirit and faith.
And a large number of people was added to the Lord.
Then he went to Tarsus to look for Saul,
   and when he had found him he brought him to Antioch.
For a whole year they met with the Church
   and taught a large number of people,
   and it was in Antioch that the disciples were first called Christians.

The word of the Lord.

3.

Acts 13:46-49   We now turn to the Gentiles.

A reading from the Acts of the Apostles

Paul and Barnabas spoke out boldly and said,
   "It was necessary that the word of God be spoken to you first,
   but since you reject it
   and condemn yourselves as unworthy of eternal life,
   we now turn to the Gentiles.
For so the Lord has commanded us,
   I have made you a light to the Gentiles,
   that you may be an instrument of salvation
   to the ends of the earth."

The Gentiles were delighted when they heard this
   and glorified the word of the Lord.
All who were destined for eternal life came to believe,
   and the word of the Lord continued to spread
   through the whole region.

The word of the Lord.

4.

Romans 10:9-18   How can they hear without someone to preach? How can people preach unless they are sent?

A reading from the Letter of Saint Paul to the Romans

Brothers and sisters:
If you confess with your mouth that Jesus is Lord
  and believe in your heart that God raised him from the dead,
  you will be saved.
For one believes with the heart and so is justified,
  and one confesses with the mouth and so is saved.
For the Scripture says,
  No one who believes in him will be put to shame.
For there is no distinction between Jew and Greek;
  the same Lord is Lord of all,
  enriching all who call upon him.
For *everyone who calls on the name of the Lord will be saved.*

But how can they call on him in whom they have not believed?
And how can they believe in him of whom they have not heard?
And how can they hear without someone to preach?
And how can people preach unless they are sent?
As it is written,
  How beautiful are the feet of those who bring the good news!
But not everyone has heeded the good news;
  for Isaiah says, *Lord, who has believed what was heard from us?*
Thus faith comes from what is heard,
  and what is heard comes through the word of Christ.
But I ask, did they not hear?
Certainly they did; for

  Their voice has gone forth to all the earth,
    and their words to the ends of the world.

The word of the Lord.

5.

Ephesians 3:2-12   The mystery of Christ was made known to me by revelation; the Gentiles are coheirs in the promise.

A reading from the Letter of Saint Paul to the Ephesians

Brothers and sisters:
You have heard of the stewardship of God's grace
  that was given to me for your benefit,
    namely, that the mystery was made known to me by revelation,
  as I have written briefly earlier.
When you read this
  you can understand my insight into the mystery of Christ,
    which was not made known to human beings in other generations
  as it has now been revealed
  to his holy Apostles and prophets by the Spirit,
    that the Gentiles are coheirs, members of the same Body,
  and copartners in the promise in Christ Jesus through the Gospel.

Of this I became a minister by the gift of God's grace
  that was granted me in accord with the exercise of his power.
To me, the very least of all the holy ones, this grace was given,
  to preach to the Gentiles the inscrutable riches of Christ,
  and to bring to light for all what is the plan of the mystery
  hidden from ages past in God who created all things,
  so that the manifold wisdom of God
  might now be made known through the Church
  to the principalities and authorities in the heavens.
This was according to the eternal purpose
  that he accomplished in Christ Jesus our Lord,
  in whom we have boldness of speech
  and confidence of access through faith in him.

The word of the Lord.

6.

1 Timothy 2:1-8   God wants all to be saved.

A reading from the first Letter of Saint Paul to Timothy

Beloved:
First of all, I ask that supplications, prayers,
   petitions, and thanksgivings be offered for everyone,
   for kings and for all in authority,
   that we may lead a quiet and tranquil life
   in all devotion and dignity.
This is good and pleasing to God our savior,
   who wills everyone to be saved
   and to come to knowledge of the truth.

   For there is one God.
   There is also one mediator between God and men,
   the man Christ Jesus,
   who gave himself as ransom for all.

This was the testimony at the proper time.
For this I was appointed preacher and Apostle
   (I am speaking the truth, I am not lying),
   teacher of the Gentiles in faith and truth.

It is my wish, then, that in every place the men should pray,
   lifting up holy hands, without anger or argument.

The word of the Lord.

874 RESPONSORIAL PSALM

1.

Psalm 19:2-3, 4-5

R̰. (5a) **Their message goes out through all the earth.**

The heavens declare the glory of God,
  and the firmament proclaims his handiwork.
Day pours out the word to day,
  and night to night imparts knowledge.

R̰. **Their message goes out through all the earth.**

Not a word nor a discourse
  whose voice is not heard;
Through all the earth their voice resounds,
  and to the ends of the world, their message.

R̰. **Their message goes out through all the earth.**

2.

Psalm 67:2-3, 5, 7-8

R̰. (4) **O God, let all the nations praise you!**
  or:
R̰. (3) **Let all the nations know your saving power.**

May God have pity on us and bless us;
  may he let his face shine upon us.
So may your way be known upon earth;
  among all nations, your salvation.

R̰. **O God, let all the nations praise you!**
  or:
R̰. **Let all the nations know your saving power.**

May the nations be glad and exult
  because you rule the peoples in equity;
  the nations on the earth you guide.

R̰. **O God, let all the nations praise you!**
  or:
R̰. **Let all the nations know your saving power.**

(cont.)

The earth has yielded its fruits;
    God, our God, has blessed us.
May God bless us,
    and may all the ends of the earth fear him!

℟. O God, let all the nations praise you!
    or:
℟. Let all the nations know your saving power.

3.

Psalm 96:1-2a, 2b-3, 7-8a, 9-10a

℟. (3) **Proclaim God's marvelous deeds to all the nations.**
    or:
℟. (see Matthew 28:19) **Go out to the world and teach all nations, alleluia.**

Sing to the LORD a new song;
    sing to the LORD, all you lands.
Sing to the LORD; bless his name.

℟. Proclaim God's marvelous deeds to all the nations.
    or:
℟. Go out to the world and teach all nations, alleluia.

Announce his salvation, day after day.
Tell his glory among the nations;
    Among all peoples, his wondrous deeds.

℟. Proclaim God's marvelous deeds to all the nations.
    or:
℟. Go out to the world and teach all nations, alleluia.

Give to the LORD, you families of nations,
    give to the LORD glory and praise;
    give to the LORD the glory due his name!

℟. Proclaim God's marvelous deeds to all the nations.
    or:
℟. Go out to the world and teach all nations, alleluia.

Worship the LORD in holy attire.
Tremble before him, all the earth;
    say among the nations: The LORD is king.

℟. Proclaim God's marvelous deeds to all the nations.
    or:
℟. Go out to the world and teach all nations, alleluia.

4.

Psalm 98:1, 2-3ab, 3cd-4, 5-6

℟. (see 2b) **The Lord has revealed to the nations his saving power.**
   or:
℟. (3cd) **All the ends of the earth have seen the saving power of God.**

Sing to the Lᴏʀᴅ a new song,
   for he has done wondrous deeds;
His right hand has won victory for him,
   his holy arm.

℟. **The Lord has revealed to the nations his saving power.**
   or:
℟. **All the ends of the earth have seen the saving power of God.**

The Lᴏʀᴅ has made his salvation known:
   in the sight of the nations he has revealed his justice.
He has remembered his kindness and his faithfulness
   toward the house of Israel.

℟. **The Lord has revealed to the nations his saving power.**
   or:
℟. **All the ends of the earth have seen the saving power of God.**

All the ends of the earth have seen
   the salvation by our God.
Sing joyfully to the Lᴏʀᴅ, all you lands;
   break into song; sing praise.

℟. **The Lord has revealed to the nations his saving power.**
   or:
℟. **All the ends of the earth have seen the saving power of God.**

Sing praise to the Lᴏʀᴅ with the harp,
   with the harp and melodious song.
With trumpets and the sound of the horn
   sing joyfully before the King, the Lᴏʀᴅ.

℟. **The Lord has revealed to the nations his saving power.**
   or:
℟. **All the ends of the earth have seen the saving power of God.**

5.

Psalm 117:1bc, 2

℟. (Mark 16:15) **Go out to all the world and tell the Good News.**

Praise the LORD, all you nations;
    glorify him, all you peoples!

℟. **Go out to all the world and tell the Good News.**

For steadfast is his kindness toward us,
    and the fidelity of the LORD endures forever.

℟. **Go out to all the world and tell the Good News.**

875 ALLELUIA VERSE AND VERSE BEFORE THE GOSPEL

1.

Matthew 28:19a, 20b

**Go and teach all nations, says the Lord;
I am with you always, until the end of the world.**

2.

Mark 16:15

**Go into the whole world
and proclaim the Gospel.**

3.

John 3:16

**God so loved the world that he gave his only-begotten Son,
so that everyone who believes in him might have eternal life.**

876 GOSPEL

1.

Matthew 28:16-20   Go and makes disciples of all nations.

✠ **A reading from the holy Gospel according to Matthew**

The Eleven disciples went to Galilee,
  to the mountain to which Jesus had ordered them.
When they saw him, they worshiped, but they doubted.
Then Jesus approached and said to them,
  "All power in heaven and on earth has been given to me.
Go, therefore, and make disciples of all nations,
  baptizing them in the name of the Father,
  and of the Son, and of the Holy Spirit,
  teaching them to observe all that I have commanded you.
And behold, I am with you always, until the end of the age."

The Gospel of the Lord.

2.

Mark 16:15-20   Go into the whole world and proclaim the Gospel.

✠ **A reading from the holy Gospel according to Mark**

Jesus appeared to the Eleven and said to them:
"Go into the whole world
  and proclaim the Gospel to every creature.
Whoever believes and is baptized will be saved;
  whoever does not believe will be condemned.
These signs will accompany those who believe:
  in my name they will drive out demons,
  they will speak new languages.
They will pick up serpents with their hands,
  and if they drink any deadly thing, it will not harm them.
They will lay hands on the sick, and they will recover."

So then the Lord Jesus, after he spoke to them,
  was taken up into heaven
  and took his seat at the right hand of God.
But they went forth and preached everywhere,
  while the Lord worked with them
  and confirmed the word through accompanying signs.

The Gospel of the Lord.

3.

Luke 24:44-53   In the name of Jesus, repentance for the forgiveness of
sins will be preached to all the nations.

✠ **A reading from the holy Gospel according to Luke**

Jesus said to his disciples:
"These are my words that I spoke to you while I was still with you,
  that everything written about me in the law of Moses
  and in the prophets and psalms must be fulfilled."
Then he opened their minds to understand the Scriptures.
And Jesus said to them,
  "Thus it is written that the Christ would suffer
  and rise from the dead on the third day
  and that repentance, for the forgiveness of sins,
  would be preached in his name
  to all the nations, beginning from Jerusalem.
You are witnesses of these things.
And behold I am sending the promise of my Father upon you;
  but stay in the city
  until you are clothed with power from on high."

Then he led them out as far as Bethany,
  raised his hands, and blessed them.
As he blessed them he parted from them
  and was taken up to heaven.
They did him homage
  and then returned to Jerusalem with great joy,
  and they were continually in the temple praising God.

The Gospel of the Lord.

4.

John 11:45-52   Jesus was going to die to gather into one the dispersed children of God.

✠   **A reading from the holy Gospel according to John**

Many of the Jews who had come to Mary and Martha,
    the sisters of Lazarus,
    and had seen what Jesus had done began to believe in him.
But some of them went to the Pharisees
    and told them what Jesus had done.
So the chief priests and the Pharisees
    convened the Sanhedrin and said,
    "What are we going to do?
This man is performing many signs.
If we leave him alone, all will believe in him,
    and the Romans will come
    and take away both our land and our nation."
But one of them, Caiaphas,
    who was high priest that year, said to them,
    "You know nothing,
    nor do you consider that it is better for you
    that one man should die instead of the people,
    so that the whole nation may not perish."
He did not say this on his own,
    but since he was high priest for that year,
    he prophesied that Jesus was going to die for the nation,
    and not only for the nation,
    but also to gather into one the dispersed children of God.

The Gospel of the Lord.

5.

John 17:11, 17-23   As you sent me into the world, so I have sent them into the world.

✠ **A reading from the holy Gospel according to John**

**Jesus raised his eyes toward heaven and prayed, saying:
"Holy Father, keep them in your name that you have given me,
  so that they may be one just as we are one.
Consecrate them in the truth.
Your word is truth.
As you sent me into the world,
  so I sent them into the world.
And I consecrate myself for them,
  so that they also may be consecrated in truth.**

**"I pray not only for them,
  but also for those who will believe in me through their word,
  so that they may all be one,
  as you, Father, are in me and I in you,
  that they also may be in us,
  that the world may believe that you sent me.
And I have given them the glory you gave me,
  so that they may be one, as we are one,
  I in them and you in me,
  that they may be brought to perfection as one,
  that the world may know that you sent me,
  and that you loved them even as you loved me."**

The Gospel of the Lord.

12. FOR PERSECUTED CHRISTIANS

877 READING FROM THE OLD TESTAMENT

First Option

Esther C:1-4, 8-10   Spare your people; some are bent upon destroying
our inheritance.

A reading from the Book of Esther

Mordecai, recalling all that the LORD had done,
  prayed to him and said:
  "O God of Abraham, God of Isaac, God of Jacob, blessed are you;
  O Lord God, almighty King, all things are in your power,
  and there is no one to oppose you in your will to save Israel.
You made heaven and earth
  and every wonderful thing under the heavens.
You are LORD of all,
  and there is no one to resist you.
And now, LORD God, King, God of Abraham,
  God of Isaac and God of Jacob,
  spare your people,
  for our enemies plan our ruin
  and are bent upon destroying your inheritance.
Do not spurn your portion,
  which you redeemed for yourself out of Egypt.
Hear my prayer; have pity on your inheritance
  and turn our sorrow into joy:
  thus we shall live to sing praise to your name, O LORD.
Do not silence those who praise you."

The word of the Lord.

Second Option

1 Maccabees 2:49-52, 57-64   None who hope in the Lord shall fail in strength.

A reading from the first Book of Maccabees

When the time came for Mattathias to die, he said to his sons:
"Arrogance and scorn have now grown strong;
   it is a time of disaster and violent anger.
Therefore, my sons, be zealous for the law
   and give your lives for the covenant of our fathers.

   "Remember the deeds that our fathers did in their times,
      and you shall win great glory and an everlasting name.
   Was not Abraham found faithful in trial,
      and it was reputed to him as uprightness?
   David, for his piety,
      received as a heritage a throne of everlasting royalty.
   Elijah, for his burning zeal for the law,
      was taken up to heaven.
   Hananiah, Azariah, and Mishael, for their faith,
      were saved from the fire.
   Daniel, for his innocence,
      was delivered from the jaws of lions.
   And so, consider this from generation to generation,
      that none who hope in him shall fail in strength.
   Do not fear the words of a sinful man,
      for his glory ends in corruption and worms.
   Today he is exalted, and tomorrow he is not to be found,
      because he has returned to his dust,
      and his schemes have perished.
   Children! be courageous and strong in keeping the law,
      for by it you shall be glorified."

The word of the Lord.

Third Option

Isaiah 41:8-10, 13-14   You are my servant whom I have chosen, whom I
will not cast off.

A reading from the Book of the Prophet Isaiah

Thus said the Lord GOD:
>   You, Israel, my servant,
>   Jacob, whom I have chosen,
>   offspring of Abraham my friend—
>   You whom I have taken from the ends of the earth
>   and summoned from its far-off places,
>   You whom I have called my servant,
>   whom I have chosen and will not cast off—
>   Fear not, I am with you;
>   be not dismayed; I am your God.
>   I will strengthen you, and help you,
>   and uphold you with my right hand of justice.
>
>   For I am the LORD, your God,
>   who grasp your right hand;
>   It is I who say to you, "Fear not,
>   I will help you."
>   Fear not, O worm Jacob,
>   O maggot Israel;
>   I will help you, says the LORD;
>   your redeemer is the Holy One of Israel.

The word of the Lord.

Fourth Option

Daniel 3:25, 34-43   For your name's sake, do not deliver us up forever.

A reading from the Book of the Prophet Daniel

Azariah stood up in the fire and prayed aloud:

> **"For your name's sake, O Lord, do not deliver us up forever,**
>> **or make void your covenant.**
> **Do not take away your mercy from us,**
>> **for the sake of Abraham, your beloved,**
>> **Isaac your servant, and Israel your holy one,**
> **To whom you promised to multiply their offspring**
>> **like the stars of heaven,**
>> **or the sand on the shore of the sea.**
> **For we are reduced, O Lord, beyond any other nation,**
>> **brought low everywhere in the world this day**
>> **because of our sins.**
> **We have in our day no prince, prophet, or leader,**
>> **no burnt offering, sacrifice, oblation, or incense,**
>> **no place to offer first fruits, to find favor with you.**
> **But with contrite heart and humble spirit**
>> **let us be received;**
> **As though it were burnt offerings of rams and bullocks,**
>> **or thousands of fat lambs,**
> **So let our sacrifice be in your presence today**
>> **as we follow you unreservedly;**
>> **for those who trust in you cannot be put to shame.**
> **And now we follow you with our whole heart,**
>> **we fear you and we pray to you.**
> **Do not let us be put to shame,**
>> **but deal with us in your kindness and great mercy.**
> **Deliver us by your wonders,**
>> **and bring glory to your name, O Lord."**

The word of the Lord.

878 READING FROM THE NEW TESTAMENT

1.

Acts 4:1-5, 18-21   It is impossible for us not to speak about what we have
seen and heard.

A reading from the Acts of the Apostles

While Peter and John were still speaking to the people,
   the priests, the captain of the temple guard,
   and the Sadducees confronted them,
   disturbed that they were teaching the people
   and proclaiming in Jesus the resurrection of the dead.
They laid hands on them
   and put them in custody until the next day,
   since it was already evening.
But many of those who heard the word came to believe
   and the number of men grew to about five thousand.

On the next day, their leaders, elders, and scribes
   were assembled in Jerusalem.

So they called them back
   and ordered them not to speak or teach at all in the name of Jesus.
Peter and John, however, said to them in reply,
   "Whether it is right in the sight of God
   for us to obey you rather than God,
   you be the judges.
It is impossible for us not to speak about what we have seen and heard."
After threatening them further, they released them,
   finding no way to punish them,
   on account of the people who were all praising God for what had
      happened.

The word of the Lord.

2.

Acts 4:23-31   Now, Lord, take note of their threats.

A reading from the Acts of the Apostles

After their release Peter and John went back to their own people
and reported what the chief priests and elders had told them.
And when they heard it,
  they raised their voices to God with one accord and said,
  "Sovereign Lord, maker of heaven and earth
  and the sea and all that is in them,
  you said by the Holy Spirit
  through the mouth of our father David, your servant:

Why did the Gentiles rage
  and the peoples entertain folly?
The kings of the earth took their stand
  and the princes gathered together
    against the Lord and against his anointed.

"Indeed they gathered in this city
  against your holy servant Jesus whom you anointed,
  Herod and Pontius Pilate,
  together with the Gentiles and the peoples of Israel,
  to do what your hand and your will
  had long ago planned to take place.
And now, Lord, take note of their threats,
  and enable your servants to speak your word with all boldness,
  as you stretch forth your hand to heal,
  and signs and wonders are done
  through the name of your holy servant Jesus."
As they prayed, the place where they were gathered shook,
  and they were all filled with the Holy Spirit
  and continued to speak the word of God with boldness.

The word of the Lord.

3.

Acts 5:27b-32, 40b-42   They rejoiced that they had been found worthy to suffer dishonor for the sake of Jesus' name.

A reading from the Acts of the Apostles

When the court officers had brought the Apostles in
    and made them stand before the Sanhedrin,
    the high priest questioned them,
    "We gave you strict orders, did we not?
    to stop teaching in that name.
Yet you have filled Jerusalem with your teaching
    and want to bring this man's Blood upon us."
But Peter and the Apostles said in reply,
    "We must obey God rather than men.
The God of our ancestors raised Jesus,
    though you had him killed by hanging him on a tree.
God exalted him at his right hand as leader and savior
    to grant Israel repentance and forgiveness of sins.
We are witnesses of these things,
    as is the Holy Spirit that God has given to those who obey him."

After recalling the Apostles, they had them flogged,
    ordered them to stop speaking in the name of Jesus,
    and dismissed them.
So they left the presence of the Sanhedrin,
    rejoicing that they had been found worthy
    to suffer dishonor for the sake of the name.
And all day long, both at the temple and in their homes,
    they did not stop teaching and proclaiming the Christ, Jesus.

The word of the Lord.

4.

Philippians 1:27-30   God granted you the privilege not only to believe in him, but also to suffer for him.

A reading from the Letter of Saint Paul to the Philippians

Brothers and sisters:
Conduct yourselves in a way worthy of the Gospel of Christ,
   so that, whether I come and see you or am absent,
   I may hear news of you,
   that you are standing firm in one spirit,
   with one mind struggling together for the faith of the Gospel,
   not intimidated in any way by your opponents.
This is proof to them of destruction, but of your salvation.
And this is God's doing.
For to you has been granted, for the sake of Christ,
   not only to believe in him but also to suffer for him.
Yours is the same struggle as you saw in me
   and now hear about me.

The word of the Lord.

5.

Hebrews 12:2-13   What son is there whom his father does not discipline?

A reading from the Letter to the Hebrews

Brothers and sisters:
Let us keep our eyes fixed on Jesus,
    the leader and perfecter of faith.
For the sake of the joy that lay before him
    He endured the cross, despising its shame,
    and has taken his seat at the right of the throne of God.
Consider how he endured such opposition from sinners,
    in order that you may not grow weary and lose heart.
In your struggle against sin you have not yet resisted
    to the point of shedding blood.
You have also forgotten the exhortation addressed to you as sons:

    My son, do not disdain the discipline of the Lord
        or lose heart when reproved by him;
    for whom the Lord loves, he disciplines;
        he scourges every son he acknowledges.

Endure your trials as "discipline";
    God treats you as sons.
For what "son" is there whom his father does not discipline?
If you are without discipline, in which all have shared,
    you are not sons but bastards.
Besides this, we have had our earthly fathers to discipline us,
    and we respected them.
Should we not then submit all the more to the Father of spirits and live?
They disciplined us for a short time as seemed right to them,
    but he does so for our benefit,
    in order that we may share his holiness.
At the time, all discipline seems a cause not for joy but for pain,
    yet later it brings the peaceful fruit of righteousness
    to those who are trained by it.

So strengthen your drooping hands and your weak knees.
Make straight paths for your feet,
    that what is lame may not be dislocated but healed.

The word of the Lord.

6.

1 Peter 1:3-9   You rejoice, although now for a little while you may have to suffer through various trials.

A reading from the first Letter of Saint Peter

Blessed be the God and Father of our Lord Jesus Christ,
    who in his great mercy gave us a new birth to a living hope
    through the resurrection of Jesus Christ from the dead,
    to an inheritance that is imperishable, undefiled, and unfading,
    kept in heaven for you
    who by the power of God are safeguarded through faith,
    to a salvation that is ready to be revealed in the final time.
In this you rejoice, although now for a little while
    you may have to suffer through various trials,
    so that the genuineness of your faith,
    more precious than gold that is perishable even though tested by fire,
    may prove to be for praise, glory, and honor
    at the revelation of Jesus Christ.
Although you have not seen him you love him;
    even though you do not see him now yet believe in him,
    you rejoice with an indescribable and glorious joy,
    as you attain the goal, the salvation of your souls.

The word of the Lord.

7.

Revelation 7:9-10, 14b-17   These are the ones who have survived the time of great distress.

A reading from the Book of Revelation

I, John, had a vision of a great multitude,
  which no one could count,
    from every nation, race, people, and tongue.
They stood before the throne and before the Lamb,
  wearing white robes and holding palm branches in their hands.
They cried out in a loud voice:

  "Salvation comes from our God, who is seated on the throne,
    and from the Lamb.

  "These are the ones who have survived the time of great distress;
  they have washed their robes
  and made them white in the Blood of the Lamb.

  "For this reason they stand before God's throne
    and worship him day and night in his temple.
    The One who sits on the throne will shelter them.
  They will not hunger or thirst anymore,
    nor will the sun or any heat strike them.
  For the Lamb who is in the center of the throne will shepherd them
    and lead them to springs of life-giving water,
      and God will wipe away every tear from their eyes."

  The word of the Lord.

879 RESPONSORIAL PSALM

First Option

Psalm 2:1-3, 4-6, 10-12a

℞. (11e) **Blessed are all who put their trust in the Lord.**

Why do the nations rage
  and the peoples utter folly?
The kings of the earth rise up,
  and the princes conspire together
  against the LORD and against his anointed:
"Let us break their fetters
  and cast their bonds from us!"

℞. **Blessed are all who put their trust in the Lord.**

He who is throned in heaven laughs;
  the LORD derides them.
Then in anger he speaks to them;
  he terrifies them in his wrath:
"I myself have set up my king
  on Zion, my holy mountain."

℞. **Blessed are all who put their trust in the Lord.**

And now, O kings, give heed;
  take warning, you rulers of the earth.
Serve the LORD with fear, and rejoice before him;
  with trembling pay homage to him.

℞. **Blessed are all who put their trust in the Lord.**

Second Option

Psalm 27:1, 2, 3, 5

R℣. (see 9d) **Do not abandon me, O God my Savior.**
 or:
R℣. (1b) **The Lord is my light and my salvation.**

The LORD is my light and my salvation;
 whom should I fear?
The LORD is my life's refuge;
 of whom should I be afraid?

R℣. **Do not abandon me, O God my Savior.**
 or:
R℣. **The Lord is my light and my salvation.**

When evildoers come at me
 to devour my flesh,
My foes and my enemies
 themselves stumble and fall.

R℣. **Do not abandon me, O God my Savior.**
 or:
R℣. **The Lord is my light and my salvation.**

Though an army encamp against me,
 my heart will not fear;
Though war be waged upon me,
 even then will I trust.

R℣. **Do not abandon me, O God my Savior.**
 or:
R℣. **The Lord is my light and my salvation.**

For he will hide me in his abode
 in the day of trouble;
He will conceal me in the shelter of his tent,
 he will set me high upon a rock.

R℣. **Do not abandon me, O God my Savior.**
 or:
R℣. **The Lord is my light and my salvation.**

Third Option

Psalm 123:1, 2

℞. (3a) **Have mercy on us, Lord, have mercy.**
   or:
℞. (2ef) **Our eyes are fixed on the Lord, pleading for his mercy.**

To you I lift up my eyes
   who are enthroned in heaven.

℞. **Have mercy on us, Lord, have mercy.**
   or:
℞. **Our eyes are fixed on the Lord, pleading for his mercy.**

Behold, as the eyes of servants
   are on the hands of their masters,
As the eyes of a maid
   are on the hands of her mistress,
So are the eyes on the LORD, our God,
   till he have pity on us.

℞. **Have mercy on us, Lord, have mercy.**
   or:
℞. **Our eyes are fixed on the Lord, pleading for his mercy.**

Fourth Option

Psalm 124:2-3, 4-5, 7c-8

℟. (7ab) **Our soul has been rescued like a bird from the fowler's snare.**

Had not the LORD **been with us—**
When men rose up against us,
    then would they have swallowed us alive,
When their fury was inflamed against us.

℟. **Our soul has been rescued like a bird from the fowler's snare.**

Then would the waters have overwhelmed us;
The torrent would have swept over us;
    over us then would have swept
    the raging waters.

℟. **Our soul has been rescued like a bird from the fowler's snare.**

Broken was the snare,
    and we were freed.
Our help is in the name of the LORD**,**
    who made heaven and earth.

℟. **Our soul has been rescued like a bird from the fowler's snare.**

880 ALLELUIA VERSE AND VERSE
BEFORE THE GOSPEL

1.

Matthew 5:10

**Blessed are those who are persecuted for the sake of righteousness,
for theirs is the Kingdom of heaven.**

2.

2 Corinthians 1:3b-4a

**Blessed be the Father of compassion and the God of all encouragement,
who encourages us in our every affliction.**

3.

James 1:12

**Blessed is the man who perseveres in temptation,
for when he has been proved he will receive the crown of life.**

4.

1 Peter 4:14

**If you are insulted for the name of Christ, blessed are you,
for the Spirit of God rests upon you.**

881 GOSPEL

1.

Matthew 5:1-12a   Blessed are you when they insult you and persecute you and utter every kind of evil against you falsely because of me.

✠ **A reading from the holy Gospel according to Matthew**

**When Jesus saw the crowds, he went up the mountain,
  and after he had sat down, his disciples came to him.
He began to teach them, saying:**

**"Blessed are the poor in spirit,
  for theirs is the Kingdom of heaven.
Blessed are they who mourn,
  for they will be comforted.
Blessed are the meek,
  for they will inherit the land.
Blessed are they who hunger and thirst for righteousness,
  for they will be satisfied.
Blessed are the merciful,
  for they will be shown mercy.
Blessed are the clean of heart,
  for they will see God.
Blessed are the peacemakers,
  for they will be called children of God.
Blessed are they who are persecuted for the sake of righteousness,
  for theirs is the Kingdom of heaven.
Blessed are you when they insult you and persecute you
  and utter every kind of evil against you falsely because of me.
Rejoice and be glad,
  for your reward will be great in heaven."**

The Gospel of the Lord.

2.

Matthew 10:17-22   If they persecuted me, they will also persecute you.

✠ **A reading from the holy Gospel according to Matthew**

**Jesus said to the Twelve:
"Beware of men, for they will hand you over to courts
  and scourge you in their synagogues,**

and you will be led before governors and kings for my sake
   as a witness before them and the pagans.
When they hand you over,
   do not worry about how you are to speak
   or what you are to say.
You will be given at that moment what you are to say.
For it will not be you who speak
   but the Spirit of your Father speaking through you.
Brother will hand over brother to death,
   and the father his child;
   children will rise up against parents and have them put to death.
You will be hated by all because of my name,
   but whoever endures to the end will be saved."

The Gospel of the Lord.

3.

Matthew 10:26-33   Do not be afraid of those who kill the body.

✠   A reading from the holy Gospel according to Matthew

Jesus said to his Apostles:
"Do not be afraid of those who hate you.
Nothing is concealed that will not be revealed,
   nor secret that will not be known.
What I say to you in the darkness, speak in the light;
   what you hear whispered, proclaim on the housetops.
And do not be afraid of those who kill the body but cannot kill the soul;
   rather, be afraid of the one who can destroy
   both soul and body in Gehenna.
Are not two sparrows sold for a small coin?
Yet not one of them falls to the ground without your Father's knowledge.
Even all the hairs of your head are counted.
So do not be afraid; you are worth more than many sparrows.
Everyone who acknowledges me before others
   I will acknowledge before my heavenly Father.
But whoever denies me before others,
   I will deny before my heavenly Father."

The Gospel of the Lord.

4.

John 15:18-21, 26–16:4   If they persecuted me, they will also persecute you.

✝ **A reading from the holy Gospel according to John**

Jesus said to his disciples:
"If the world hates you, realize that it hated me first.
If you belonged to the world, the world would love its own;
 but because you do not belong to the world,
 and I have chosen you out of the world,
 the world hates you.
Remember the word I spoke to you,
 'No slave is greater than his master.'
If they persecuted me, they will also persecute you.
If they kept my word, they will also keep yours.
And they will do all these things to you on account of my name,
 because they do not know the one who sent me.

"When the Advocate comes whom I will send you from the Father,
 the Spirit of truth that proceeds from the Father,
 he will testify to me.
And you also testify,
 because you have been with me from the beginning.

"I have told you this so that you may not fall away.
They will expel you from the synagogues;
 in fact, the hour is coming when everyone who kills you
 will think he is offering worship to God.
They will do this because they have not known either the Father or me.
I have told you this so that when their hour comes
 you may remember that I told you."

The Gospel of the Lord.

5.

John 17:11b-19   The world hated them.

✝ **A reading from the holy Gospel according to John**

Jesus raised his eyes to heaven and prayed, saying:
"Holy Father, keep them in your name that you have given me,
 so that they may be one just as we are one.
When I was with them I protected them in your name that you gave me,
 and I guarded them, and none of them was lost
 except the son of destruction,
 in order that the Scripture might be fulfilled.
But now I am coming to you.
I speak this in the world
 so that they may share my joy completely.
I gave them your word, and the world hated them,
 because they do not belong to the world
 any more than I belong to the world.
I do not ask that you take them out of the world
 but that you keep them from the Evil One.
They do not belong to the world
 any more than I belong to the world.
Consecrate them in the truth.
Your word is truth.
As you sent me into the world,
 so I sent them into the world.
And I consecrate myself for them,
 so that they also may be consecrated in truth."

The Gospel of the Lord.

II. FOR PUBLIC NEEDS

13. FOR THE COUNTRY OR A CITY OR FOR THOSE WHO SERVE IN PUBLIC OFFICE OR FOR THE CONGRESS OR FOR THE PRESIDENT OR FOR THE PROGRESS OF PEOPLES

882 READING FROM THE OLD TESTAMENT

1.

Genesis 1:26—2:3   Fill the earth and subdue it.

A reading from the Book of Genesis

**God said:
"Let us make man in our image, after our likeness.
Let them have dominion over the fish of the sea,
the birds of the air, and the cattle,
and over all the wild animals
and all the creatures that crawl on the ground."**

**God created man in his image;
in the divine image he created him;
male and female he created them.**

**God blessed them, saying:
"Be fertile and multiply;
fill the earth and subdue it.
Have dominion over the fish of the sea, the birds of the air,
and all the living things that move on the earth."
God also said:
"See, I give you every seed-bearing plant all over the earth
and every tree that has seed-bearing fruit on it to be your food;
and to all the animals of the land, all the birds of the air,
and all the living creatures that crawl on the ground,
I give all the green plants for food."
And so it happened.
God looked at everything he had made, and he found it very good.
Evening came, and morning followed—the sixth day.**

Thus the heavens and the earth and all their array were completed.
Since on the seventh day God was finished with the work he had been
    doing,
    he rested on the seventh day from all the work he had undertaken.
So God blessed the seventh day and made it holy,
    because on it he rested from all the work he had done in creation.

The word of the Lord.

    2.

Genesis 2:4b-9, 15   God took Adam and placed him in the garden of Eden
to cultivate and care for it.

A reading from the Book of Genesis

At the time when the Lord God made the earth and the heavens—
    while as yet there was no field shrub on earth
    and no grass of the field had sprouted,
    for the Lord God had sent no rain upon the earth
    and there was no man to till the soil,
    but a stream was welling up out of the earth
    and was watering all the surface of the ground—
    the Lord God formed man out of the clay of the ground
    and blew into his nostrils the breath of life,
    and so man became a living being.

Then the Lord God planted a garden in Eden, in the east,
    and he placed there the man whom he had formed.
Out of the ground the Lord God made various trees grow
    that were delightful to look at and good for food,
    with the tree of life in the middle of the garden
    and the tree of the knowledge of good and evil.

The Lord God then took the man
    and settled him in the garden of Eden,
    to cultivate and care for it.

The word of the Lord.

3.

Genesis 4:3-10   Cain attacked his brother Abel and killed him.

A reading from the Book of Genesis

Cain brought an offering to the LORD **from the fruit of the soil,**
    while Abel, for his part,
    brought one of the best firstlings of his flock.
The LORD **looked with favor on Abel and his offering,**
    but on Cain and his offering he did not.
Cain greatly resented this and was crestfallen.
So the LORD **said to Cain:**
    "Why are you so resentful and crestfallen?
If you do well, you can hold up your head;
    but if not, sin is a demon lurking at the door:
    his urge is toward you, yet you can be his master."

Cain said to his brother Abel, "Let us go out in the field."
When they were in the field,
    Cain attacked his brother Abel and killed him.
Then the LORD **asked Cain, "Where is your brother Abel?"**
He answered, "I do not know.
Am I my brother's keeper?"
The LORD **then said: "What have you done!**
Listen: Your brother's blood cries out to me from the soil!"

The word of the Lord.

4.

Numbers 6:22-27   They will invoke my name upon the children of Israel and I will bless them.

A reading from the Book of Numbers

The LORD said to Moses:
"Speak to Aaron and his sons and tell them:
  This is how you shall bless the children of Israel.
Say to them:

  The LORD bless you and keep you!
  The LORD let his face shine upon you, and be gracious to you!
  The LORD look upon you kindly and give you peace!

So shall they invoke my name upon the children of Israel,
  and I will bless them."

The word of the Lord.

5.

1 Kings 3:11-14   I give you a heart wise and understanding.

A reading from the first Book of Kings

The LORD said to Solomon:
"Because you have not asked for a long life for yourself,
  nor for riches, nor for the life of your enemies,
    but for understanding so that you may know what is right—
  I do as you requested.
I give you a heart so wise and understanding
  that there has never been anyone like you up to now,
  and after you there will come no one to equal you.
In addition, I give you what you have not asked for,
  such riches and glory that among kings there is not your like.
And if you follow me by keeping my statutes and commandments,
  as your father David did,
  I will give you a long life."

The word of the Lord.

6.

Esther C:1-4, 8-10   Turn our sorrow into joy.

A reading from the Book of Esther

Mordecai prayed to the LORD and said:
"God of Abraham, God of Isaac and God of Jacob,
  O Lord God, almighty King, all things are in your power,
    and there is no one to oppose you in your will to save Israel.
You made heaven and earth
    and every wonderful thing under the heavens.
You are LORD of all,
    and there is no one who can resist you, LORD.
And now, LORD God, King,
    God of Abraham, God of Isaac and God of Jacob,
    spare your people,
    for our enemies plan our ruin
    and are bent upon destroying your inheritance.
Do not spurn your portion,
    which you redeemed for yourself out of Egypt.
Hear my prayer; have pity on your inheritance
    and turn our sorrow into joy:
    thus we shall live to sing praise to your name, O LORD.
Do not silence those who praise you."

The word of the Lord.

7.

Job 31:16-20, 24-25, 31-32   If I have eaten my portion alone and have not given a share of it to the fatherless.

A reading from the Book of Job

If I have denied anything to the poor,
  or allowed the eyes of the widow to languish
While I ate my portion alone,
  with no share in it for the fatherless,
Though like a father God has reared me from my youth,
  guiding me even from my mother's womb—
If I have seen a wanderer without clothing,
  or a poor man without covering,

Whose limbs have not blessed me
   when warmed with the fleece of my sheep;
Had I put my trust in gold
   or called fine gold my security;
Or had I rejoiced that my wealth was great,
   or that my hand had acquired abundance—

Had not the men of my tent exclaimed,
   "Who has not been fed with this meat!"
Because no stranger lodged in the street,
   but I opened my door to wayfarers.

The word of the Lord.

8.

Isaiah 32:15-18   Justice will bring about peace.

A reading from the Book of the Prophet Isaiah

In those days:
The spirit from on high
   will be poured out on us.

Then will the desert become an orchard
   and the orchard be regarded as a forest.
Right will dwell in the desert
   and justice abide in the orchard.
Justice will bring about peace;
   right will produce calm and security.
My people will live in peaceful country,
   in secure dwellings and quiet resting places.

The word of the Lord.

9.

Isaiah 58:6-11   Share your bread with the hungry.

A reading from the Book of the Prophet Isaiah

Thus says the LORD:
This is the fasting that I wish:
  releasing those bound unjustly,
  untying the thongs of the yoke;
Setting free the oppressed,
  breaking every yoke;
Sharing your bread with the hungry,
  sheltering the oppressed and the homeless;
Clothing the naked when you see them,
  and not turning your back on your own.
Then your light shall break forth like the dawn,
  and your wound shall quickly be healed;
Your vindication shall go before you,
  and the glory of the LORD shall be your rear guard.
Then you shall call, and the LORD will answer,
  you shall cry for help, and he will say: Here I am!
If you remove from your midst oppression,
  false accusation and malicious speech;
If you bestow your bread on the hungry
  and satisfy the afflicted;
Then light shall rise for you in the darkness,
  and the gloom shall become for you like midday;
Then the LORD will guide you always
  and give you plenty even on the parched land.
He will renew your strength,
  and you shall be like a watered garden,
  like a spring whose water never fails.

The word of the Lord.

10.

Ezekiel 3:17-21   I have appointed you a watchman for the house of Israel.

A reading from the Book of the Prophet Ezekiel

The word of the LORD came to me:
Son of man, I have appointed you a watchman
for the house of Israel.
When you hear a word from my mouth,
you shall warn them for me.

If I say to the wicked man,
You shall surely die;
and you do not warn him or speak out
to dissuade him from his wicked conduct so that he may live:
the wicked man shall die for his sins,
but I will hold you responsible for his death.
If, on the other hand, you have warned the wicked man,
yet he has not turned away from his evil
nor from his wicked conduct,
then he shall die for his sins,
but you shall save your life.

If a virtuous man turns away from virtue and does wrong
when I place a stumbling block before him, he shall die.
He shall die for his sins,
and his virtuous deeds shall not be remembered;
but I will hold you responsible for his death
if you did not warn him.
When, on the other hand, you have warned a virtuous man not to sin,
and he has in fact not sinned,
he shall surely live because of the warning,
and you shall save your own life.

The word of the Lord.

883 READING FROM THE NEW TESTAMENT

1.

Acts 11:27-30   The disciples determined that each should send relief to the brothers who lived in Jerusalem.

A reading from the Acts of the Apostles

In those days some prophets came down from Jerusalem to Antioch,
> **and one of them named Agabus stood up and predicted by the Spirit**
> **that there would be a severe famine all over the world,**
> **and it happened under Claudius.**

So the disciples determined that, according to ability,
> **each should send relief to the brothers**
> **who lived in Judea.**

This they did, sending it to the presbyters in care of Barnabas and Saul.

The word of the Lord.

2.

Romans 8:18-30   All things work for good for those who love God.

A reading from the Letter of Saint Paul to the Romans

Brothers and sisters:
I consider that the sufferings of this present time are as nothing
> **compared with the glory to be revealed for us.**

For creation awaits with eager expectation
> **the revelation of the children of God;**
> **for creation was made subject to futility,**
> **not of its own accord but because of the one who subjected it,**
> **in hope that creation itself**
> **would be set free from slavery to corruption**
> **and share in the glorious freedom of the children of God.**

We know that all creation is groaning in labor pains even until now;
> **and not only that, but we ourselves,**
> **who have the first fruits of the Spirit,**
> **we also groan within ourselves**
> **as we wait for adoption, the redemption of our bodies.**

For in hope we were saved.

Now hope that sees for itself is not hope.

For who hopes for what one sees?

But if we hope for what we do not see, we wait with endurance.

In the same way, the Spirit too comes to the aid of our weakness;
    for we do not know how to pray as we ought,
    but the Spirit himself intercedes with inexpressible groanings.
And the one who searches hearts
    knows what is the intention of the Spirit,
    because he intercedes for the holy ones
    according to God's will.

We know that all things work for good for those who love God,
    who are called according to his purpose.
For those he foreknew he also predestined
    to be conformed to the image of his Son,
    so that he might be the firstborn
    among many brothers and sisters.
And those he predestined he also called;
    and those he called he also justified;
    and those he justified he also glorified.

The word of the Lord.

3.

2 Corinthians 8:1-5, 9-15   Your abundance must supply their wants.

A reading from the second Letter of Saint Paul to the Corinthians

We want you to know, brothers and sisters,
  of the grace of God that has been given to the churches of Macedonia,
  for in a severe test of affliction,
  the abundance of their joy and their profound poverty
  overflowed in a wealth of generosity on their part.
For according to their means, I can testify,
  and beyond their means, spontaneously, they begged us insistently
  for the favor of taking part in the service to the holy ones,
  and this, not as we expected,
  but they gave themselves first to the Lord and to us
  through the will of God.

For you know the gracious act of our Lord Jesus Christ,
  that for your sake he became poor although he was rich,
  so that by his poverty you might become rich.
And I am giving counsel in this matter,
  for it is appropriate for you who began not only to act
  but to act willingly last year:
  complete it now, so that your eager willingness may be matched
  by your completion of it out of what you have.
For if the eagerness is there,
  it is acceptable according to what one has,
  not according to what one does not have;
  not that others should have relief while you are burdened,
  but that as a matter of equality your surplus at the present time
  should supply their needs,
  so that their surplus may also supply your needs,
  that there may be equality.
As it is written:

  Whoever had much did not have more,
    and whoever had little did not have less.

The word of the Lord.

4.

2 Corinthians 9:6-15   Each must give from his heart without sadness or compulsion.

A reading from the second Letter of Saint Paul to the Corinthians

Brothers and sisters:
Whoever sows sparingly will also reap sparingly,
  and whoever sows bountifully will also reap bountifully.
Each must do as already determined, without sadness or compulsion,
  for God loves a cheerful giver.
Moreover, God is able to make every grace abundant for you,
  so that in all things, always having all you need,
  you may have an abundance for every good work.
As it is written:

  He scatters abroad, he gives to the poor;
    his righteousness endures forever.

The one who supplies seed to the sower and bread for food
  will supply and multiply your seed
  and increase the harvest of your righteousness.
You are being enriched in every way for all generosity,
  which through us produces thanksgiving to God,
  for the administration of this public service
  is not only supplying the needs of the holy ones
  but is also overflowing in many acts of thanksgiving to God.
Through the evidence of this service, you are glorifying God
  for your obedient confession of the Gospel of Christ
  and the generosity of your contribution to them and to all others,
  while in prayer on your behalf they long for you,
  because of the surpassing grace of God upon you.
Thanks be to God for his indescribable gift!

The word of the Lord.

5.

Galatians 5:17-26   The works of the flesh are obvious: hatreds, rivalry, jealousy, outbursts of fury and dissensions.

A reading from the Letter of Saint Paul to the Galatians

Brothers and sisters:
The flesh has desires against the Spirit,
    and the Spirit against the flesh;
    these are opposed to each other,
    so that you may not do what you want.
But if you are guided by the Spirit, you are not under the law.
Now the works of the flesh are obvious:
    immorality, impurity, licentiousness, idolatry,
    sorcery, hatreds, rivalry, jealousy,
    outbursts of fury, acts of selfishness,
    dissensions, factions, occasions of envy,
    drinking bouts, orgies, and the like.
I warn you, as I warned you before,
    that those who do such things will not inherit the Kingdom of God.
In contrast, the fruit of the Spirit is love, joy, peace,
    patience, kindness, generosity,
    faithfulness, gentleness, self-control.
Against such there is no law.
Now those who belong to Christ Jesus have crucified their flesh
    with its passions and desires.
If we live in the Spirit, let us also follow the Spirit.
Let us not be conceited, provoking one another, envious of one another.

The word of the Lord.

6.

Ephesians 4:30–5:2   All bitterness, fury, anger, shouting, and reviling must be removed from you, along with all malice.

A reading from the Letter of Saint Paul to the Ephesians

Brothers and sisters:
Do not grieve the Holy Spirit of God,
    with which you were sealed for the day of redemption.
All bitterness, fury, anger, shouting, and reviling
    must be removed from you, along with all malice.

And be kind to one another, compassionate,
   forgiving one another as God has forgiven you in Christ.

So be imitators of God, as beloved children, and live in love,
   as Christ loved us and handed himself over for us
   as a sacrificial offering to God for a fragrant aroma.

The word of the Lord.

   7.

Colossians 3:9b-17   You have been called together into one Body.

A reading from the Letter of Saint Paul to the Colossians

Brothers and sisters:
You have taken off the old self with its practices
   and have put on the new self,
   which is being renewed, for knowledge,
   in the image of its creator.
   Here there is not Greek and Jew,
   circumcision and uncircumcision,
   barbarian, Scythian, slave, free;
   but Christ is all and in all.

Put on then, as God's chosen ones, holy and beloved,
   heartfelt compassion, kindness, humility, gentleness, and patience,
   bearing with one another and forgiving one another,
   if one has a grievance against another;
   as the Lord has forgiven you, so must you also do.
And over all these put on love,
   that is, the bond of perfection.
And let the peace of Christ control your hearts,
   the peace into which you were also called in one Body.
And be thankful.
Let the word of Christ dwell in you richly,
   as in all wisdom you teach and admonish one another,
   singing psalms, hymns, and spiritual songs
   with gratitude in your hearts to God.
And whatever you do, in word or in deed,
   do everything in the name of the Lord Jesus,
   giving thanks to God the Father through him.

The word of the Lord.

8.

1 Timothy 6:6-11, 17-19   Tell the rich not to rely on so uncertain a thing as wealth.

A reading from the first Letter of Saint Paul to Timothy

Beloved:
Religion with contentment is a great gain.
For we brought nothing into the world,
   just as we shall not be able to take anything out of it.
If we have food and clothing, we shall be content with that.
Those who want to be rich are falling into temptation and into a trap
   and into many foolish and harmful desires,
   which plunge them into ruin and destruction.
For the love of money is the root of all evils,
   and some people in their desire for it have strayed from the faith
   and have pierced themselves with many pains.

But you, man of God, avoid all this.
Instead, pursue righteousness, devotion, faith,
   love, patience, and gentleness.

Tell the rich in the present age not to be proud
   and not to rely on so uncertain a thing as wealth
   but rather on God, who richly provides us with all things
   for our enjoyment.
Tell them to do good, to be rich in good works,
   to be generous, ready to share,
   thus accumulating as treasure a good foundation for the future,
   so as to win the life that is true life.

The word of the Lord.

9.

James 3:13-18   The fruit of righteousness is sown in peace for those who cultivate peace.

A reading from the Letter of James

Beloved:
Who among you is wise and understanding?
Let him show his works by a good life
    in the humility that comes from wisdom.
But if you have bitter jealousy and selfish ambition in your hearts,
    do not boast and be false to the truth.
Wisdom of this kind does not come down from above
    but is earthly, unspiritual, demonic.
For where jealousy and selfish ambition exist,
    there is disorder and every foul practice.
But the wisdom from above is first of all pure,
    then peaceable, gentle, compliant,
    full of mercy and good fruits,
    without inconstancy or insincerity.
And the fruit of righteousness is sown in peace
    for those who cultivate peace.

The word of the Lord.

10.

James 4:1-10   Where do the wars and where do the conflicts among you come from?

A reading from the Letter of James

Beloved:
Where do the wars and where do the conflicts among you come from?
Is it not from your passions that make war within your members?
You covet but do not possess.
You kill and envy but you cannot obtain;
   you fight and wage war.
You do not possess because you do not ask.
You ask but do not receive, because you ask wrongly,
   to spend it on your passions.
Adulterers!
Do you not know that to be a lover of the world
   means enmity with God?
Therefore, whoever wants to be a lover of the world
   makes himself an enemy of God.
Or do you suppose that the Scripture speaks without meaning when it says,
   The spirit that he has made to dwell in us tends toward jealousy?
But he bestows a greater grace; therefore, it says:

   God resists the proud,
      but gives grace to the humble.

So submit yourselves to God.
Resist the Devil, and he will flee from you.
Draw near to God, and he will draw near to you.
Cleanse your hands, you sinners,
   and purify your hearts, you of two minds.
Begin to lament, to mourn, to weep.
Let your laughter be turned into mourning
   and your joy into dejection.
Humble yourselves before the Lord and he will exalt you.

The word of the Lord.

884 RESPONSORIAL PSALM

1.

Psalm 8:4-5, 6-7a, 7b-9

℟. (2ab) **O Lord, our God, how wonderful your name in all the earth!**

When I behold your heavens, the work of your fingers,
 the moon and the stars which you have set in place—
What is man that you should be mindful of him,
 or the son of man that you should care for him?

℟. **O Lord, our God, how wonderful your name in all the earth!**

Yet you have made him little less than the angels,
 and crowned him with glory and honor.
You have given him rule over the works of your hands.

℟. **O Lord, our God, how wonderful your name in all the earth!**

Putting all things under his feet:
All sheep and oxen,
 yes, and the beasts of the field,
The birds of the air, the fishes of the sea,
 and whatever swims the paths of the seas.

℟. **O Lord, our God, how wonderful your name in all the earth!**

2.

Psalm 80:2ac and 3b, 5-7

℟. (4b) **Let us see your face, Lord, and we shall be saved.**

O shepherd of Israel, hearken,
From your throne upon the cherubim, shine forth,
Rouse your power.

℟. **Let us see your face, Lord, and we shall be saved.**

O LORD of hosts, how long will you burn with anger
 while your people pray?
You have fed them with the bread of tears,
 and give them tears to drink in ample measure.
You have left us to be fought over by our neighbors;
 our enemies mock us.

℟. **Let us see your face, Lord, and we shall be saved.**

3.

Psalm 85:9ab-10, 11-12, 13-14

R̂. (see 9b) **The Lord speaks of peace to his people.**

I will hear what God proclaims;
    the LORD—for he proclaims peace.
Near indeed is his salvation to those who fear him,
    glory dwelling in our land.

R̂. **The Lord speaks of peace to his people.**

Kindness and truth shall meet;
    justice and peace shall kiss.
Truth shall spring out of the earth,
    and justice shall look down from heaven.

R̂. **The Lord speaks of peace to his people.**

The LORD himself will give his benefits;
    our land shall yield its increase.
Justice shall walk before him,
    and salvation, along the way of his steps.

R̂. **The Lord speaks of peace to his people.**

4

Psalm 100:1b-2, 3, 4, 5

R̂. (3c) **We are his people: the sheep of his flock.**

Sing joyfully to the LORD, all you lands;
    serve the LORD with gladness;
    come before him with joyful song.

R̂. **We are his people: the sheep of his flock.**

Know that the LORD is God;
    he made us, his we are;
    his people, the flock he tends.

R̂. **We are his people: the sheep of his flock.**

Enter his gates with thanksgiving,
  his courts with praise;
Give thanks to him; bless his name.

℟. We are his people: the sheep of his flock.

For he is good:
  the LORD, whose kindness endures forever,
  and his faithfulness, to all generations.

℟. We are his people: the sheep of his flock.

5.

Psalm 107:2-3, 4-5, 6-7, 8-9

℟. (1) Give thanks to the Lord, his love is everlasting.

Thus let the redeemed of the LORD say,
  those whom he has redeemed from the hand of the foe
And gathered from the lands,
  from the east and the west, from the north and the south.

℟. Give thanks to the Lord, his love is everlasting.

They went astray in the desert wilderness;
  the way to an inhabited city they did not find.
Hungry and thirsty,
  their life was wasting away within them.

℟. Give thanks to the Lord, his love is everlasting.

They cried to the LORD in their distress;
  from their straits he rescued them.
And he led them by a direct way
  to reach an inhabited city.

℟. Give thanks to the Lord, his love is everlasting.

Let them give thanks to the LORD for his mercy
  and his wondrous deeds to the children of men,
Because he satisfied the longing soul
  and filled the hungry soul with good things.

℟. Give thanks to the Lord, his love is everlasting.

6.

Psalm 112:1bc-2, 3-4, 5-7a, 7b-8, 9

R̸. (see 1a and 9a) **Blessed the man who gives to the poor.**

Blessed the man who fears the Lord,
　who greatly delights in his commands.
His posterity shall be mighty upon the earth;
　the upright generation shall be blessed.

R̸. Blessed the man who gives to the poor.

Wealth and riches shall be in his house;
　his generosity shall endure forever.
Light shines through the darkness for the upright;
　he is gracious and merciful and just.

R̸. Blessed the man who gives to the poor.

Well for the man who is gracious and lends,
　who conducts his affairs with justice;
He shall never be moved;
　the just one shall be in everlasting remembrance.
An evil report he shall not fear.

R̸. Blessed the man who gives to the poor.

His heart is firm, trusting in the Lord.
His heart is steadfast; he shall not fear
　till he looks down upon his foes.

R̸. Blessed the man who gives to the poor.

Lavishly he gives to the poor;
　his generosity shall endure forever;
　his horn shall be exalted in glory.

R̸. Blessed the man who gives to the poor.

7.

Psalm 122:1-2, 4-5, 6-7, 8-9

℟. (see Sirach 36:15) **Give peace, O Lord, to those who wait for you.**

I rejoiced because they said to me,
  "We will go up to the house of the LORD."
And now we have set foot
  within your gates, O Jerusalem.

℟. **Give peace, O Lord, to those who wait for you.**

To it the tribes go up,
  the tribes of the LORD,
According to the decree for Israel,
  to give thanks to the name of the LORD.
In it are set up judgment seats,
  seats for the house of David.

℟. **Give peace, O Lord, to those who wait for you.**

"Pray for the peace of Jerusalem!
  May those who love you prosper!
May peace be within your walls,
  prosperity in your buildings."

℟. **Give peace, O Lord, to those who wait for you.**

Because of my relatives and friends
  I will say, "Peace be within you!"
Because of the house of the LORD, our God,
  I will pray for your good.

℟. **Give peace, O Lord, to those who wait for you.**

8.

Psalm 123:1-2ab, 2cdef

℟. (2ef) **Our eyes are fixed on the Lord, pleading for his mercy.**
  or:
℟. (3a) **Have mercy on us, Lord, have mercy.**

To you I lift up my eyes
  who are enthroned in heaven.
Behold, as the eyes of servants
  are on the hands of their masters.

℟. **Our eyes are fixed on the Lord, pleading for his mercy.**
  or:
℟. **Have mercy on us, Lord, have mercy.**

As the eyes of a maid
  are on the hands of her mistress,
So are our eyes on the LORD, our God,
  till he have pity on us.

℟. **Our eyes are fixed on the Lord, pleading for his mercy.**
  or:
℟. **Have mercy on us, Lord, have mercy.**

9.

Psalm 127:1, 2

℟. (see 1) **The Lord will build a house for us and guard our city.**

Unless the LORD build the house,
  they labor in vain who build it.
Unless the LORD guard the city,
  in vain does the guard keep vigil.

℟. **The Lord will build a house for us and guard our city.**

It is vain for you to rise early
  or put off your rest,
You that eat hard-earned bread,
  for he gives to his beloved in sleep.

℟. **The Lord will build a house for us and guard our city.**

885 ALLELUIA VERSE AND VERSE
BEFORE THE GOSPEL

1.

1 Chronicles 29:10b, 11b

Blessed are you, O LORD **our God;
all things in heaven and on earth are yours.**

2.

Psalm 126:5

**Those who sow in tears
shall reap with shouts of joy.**

3.

Matthew 5:9

**Blessed are the peacemakers;
they shall be called children of God.**

4.

Matthew 25:34

**Come, you who are blessed by my Father, says the Lord;
inherit the kingdom prepared for you from the foundation of the world.**

5.

Luke 21:36

**Be vigilant at all times and pray,
that you may have strength to stand before the Son of Man.**

6.

John 8:12

**I am the light of the world, says the Lord;
whoever follows me will have the light of life.**

7.

John 12:26

**Whoever serves me must follow me, says the Lord;
and where I am, there also will my servant be.**

8.

John 13:34

**I give you a new commandment:
love one another as I have loved you.**

9.

2 Corinthians 8:9

**Jesus Christ became poor although he was rich,
so that by his poverty you might become rich.**

886 GOSPEL

1.

Matthew 5:1-12a   Blessed are the peacemakers, for they will be called children of God.

✠ **A reading from the holy Gospel according to Matthew**

When Jesus saw the crowds, he went up the mountain,
  and after he had sat down, his disciples came to him.
He began to teach them, saying:

  "Blessed are the poor in spirit,
    for theirs is the Kingdom of heaven.
  Blessed are they who mourn,
    for they will be comforted.
  Blessed are the meek,
    for they will inherit the land.
  Blessed are they who hunger and thirst for righteousness,
    for they will be satisfied.
  Blessed are the merciful,
    for they will be shown mercy.
  Blessed are the clean of heart,
    for they will see God.
  Blessed are the peacemakers,
    for they will be called children of God.
  Blessed are they who are persecuted for the sake of righteousness,
    for theirs is the Kingdom of heaven.
  Blessed are you when they insult you and persecute you
    and utter every kind of evil against you falsely because of me.
  Rejoice and be glad,
    for your reward will be great in heaven."

The Gospel of the Lord.

2.

Matthew 5:20-24   Whoever is angry with his brother will be liable to judgment.

✠ **A reading from the holy Gospel according to Matthew**

Jesus said to his disciples:
"I tell you, unless your righteousness surpasses that of the scribes and
    Pharisees,
    you will not enter into the Kingdom of heaven.

"You have heard that it was said to your ancestors,
    You shall not kill; and whoever kills will be liable to judgment.
But I say to you, whoever is angry with his brother
    will be liable to judgment,
    and whoever says to his brother, 'Raqa,'
      will be answerable to the Sanhedrin,
    and whoever says, 'You fool,' will be liable to fiery Gehenna.
Therefore, if you bring your gift to the altar,
    and there recall that your brother
    has anything against you,
    leave your gift there at the altar,
    go first and be reconciled with your brother,
    and then come and offer your gift."

The Gospel of the Lord.

3.

Matthew 5:38-48   I say to you, offer no resistance to one who is evil.

✠ **A reading from the holy Gospel according to Matthew**

Jesus said to his disciples:
"You have heard that it was said,
    An eye for an eye and a tooth for a tooth.
But I say to you, offer no resistance to one who is evil.
When someone strikes you on your right cheek,
    turn the other to him as well.
If anyone wants to go to law with you over your tunic,
    hand him your cloak as well.
Should anyone press you into service for one mile,
    go with him two miles.
Give to the one who asks of you,
    and do not turn your back on one who wants to borrow.

"You have heard that it was said,
   You shall love your neighbor and hate your enemy.
But I say to you, love your enemies,
   and pray for those who persecute you,
   that you may be children of your heavenly Father,
   for he makes his sun rise on the bad and the good,
   and causes rain to fall on the just and the unjust.
For if you love those who love you, what recompense will you have?
Do not the tax collectors do the same?
And if you greet your brothers only,
   what is unusual about that?
Do not the pagans do the same?
So be perfect, just as your heavenly Father is perfect."

The Gospel of the Lord.

   4.

Matthew 22:15-21   Repay to Caesar what belongs to Caesar and to God
what belongs to God.

✝ **A reading from the holy Gospel according to Matthew**

The Pharisees went off and plotted how they might entrap Jesus in speech.
They sent their disciples to him, with the Herodians, saying,
   "Teacher, we know that you are a truthful man
   and that you teach the way of God in accordance with the truth.
And you are not concerned with anyone's opinion,
   for you do not regard a person's status.
Tell us, then, what is your opinion:
   Is it lawful to pay the census tax to Caesar or not?"
Knowing their malice, Jesus said,
   "Why are you testing me, you hypocrites?
Show me the coin that pays the census tax."
Then they handed him the Roman coin.
He said to them, "Whose image is this and whose inscription?"
They replied, "Caesar's."
At that he said to them,
   "Then repay to Caesar what belongs to Caesar
   and to God what belongs to God."

The Gospel of the Lord.

5.

Matthew 25:14-30   Since you were faithful in small matters, come, share
your master's joy.

☩ **A reading from the holy Gospel according to Matthew**

Jesus told his disciples this parable:
"A man going on a journey
   called in his servants
   and entrusted his possessions to them.
To one he gave five talents;
   to another, two; to a third, one—
   to each according to his ability.
Then he went away.
Immediately the one who received five talents went and traded with them,
   and made another five.
Likewise, the one who received two made another two.
But the man who received one went off and dug a hole in the ground
   and buried his master's money.
After a long time
   the master of those servants came back
   and settled accounts with them.
The one who had received five talents
   came forward bringing the additional five.
He said, 'Master, you gave me five talents.
See, I have made five more.'
His master said to him, 'Well done, my good and faithful servant.
Since you were faithful in small matters,
   I will give you great responsibilities.
Come, share your master's joy.'
Then the one who had received two talents also came forward and said,
   'Master, you gave me two talents.
See, I have made two more.'
His master said to him, 'Well done, my good and faithful servant.
Since you were faithful in small matters,
   I will give you great responsibilities.
Come, share your master's joy.'

Then the one who had received the one talent came forward and said,
  'Master, I knew you were a demanding person,
  harvesting where you did not plant
  and gathering where you did not scatter;
  so out of fear I went off and buried your talent in the ground.
Here it is back.'
His master said to him in reply, 'You wicked, lazy servant!
So you knew that I harvest where I did not plant
  and gather where I did not scatter?
Should you not then have put my money in the bank
  so that I could have got it back with interest on my return?
Now then! Take the talent from him and give it to the one with ten.
For to the one who has,
  more will be given and he will grow rich;
  but from the one who has not,
  even what he has will be taken away.
And throw this useless servant into the darkness outside,
  where there will be wailing and grinding of teeth.'"

The Gospel of the Lord.

6.

Matthew 25:31-46   Whatever you did for these least brothers of mine, you did for me.

✟ **A reading from the holy Gospel according to Matthew**

Jesus said to his disciples:
"When the Son of Man comes in his glory,
   and all the angels with him,
   he will sit upon his glorious throne,
   and all the nations will be assembled before him.
And he will separate them one from another,
   as a shepherd separates the sheep from the goats.
He will place the sheep on his right and the goats on his left.
Then the king will say to those on his right,
   'Come, you who are blessed by my Father.
Inherit the kingdom prepared for you from the foundation of the world.
For I was hungry and you gave me food,
   I was thirsty and you gave me drink,
   a stranger and you welcomed me,
   naked and you clothed me,
   ill and you cared for me,
   in prison and you visited me.'
Then the righteous will answer him and say,
   'Lord, when did we see you hungry and feed you,
   or thirsty and give you drink?
When did we see you a stranger and welcome you,
   or naked and clothe you?
When did we see you ill or in prison, and visit you?'
And the king will say to them in reply,
   'Amen, I say to you, whatever you did
   for the least brothers of mine, you did for me.'
Then he will say to those on his left,
   'Depart from me, you accursed,
   into the eternal fire prepared for the Devil and his angels.
For I was hungry and you gave me no food,
   I was thirsty and you gave me no drink,
   a stranger and you gave me no welcome,
   naked and you gave me no clothing,
   ill and in prison, and you did not care for me.'

Then they will answer and say,
   'Lord, when did we see you hungry or thirsty
   or a stranger or naked or ill or in prison,
   and not minister to your needs?'
He will answer them, 'Amen, I say to you,
   what you did not do for one of these least ones,
   you did not do for me.'
And these will go off to eternal punishment,
   but the righteous to eternal life."

The Gospel of the Lord.

7.

Luke 12:15-21   Though one may be rich, one's life does not consist
of possessions.

✠ **A reading from the holy Gospel according to Luke**

Jesus said to the crowd,
   "Take care to guard against all greed,
   for though one may be rich,
   one's life does not consist of possessions."

Then he told them a parable.
"There was a rich man whose land produced a bountiful harvest.
He asked himself,
   'What shall I do, for I do not have space to store my harvest?'
And he said, 'This is what I shall do:
   I shall tear down my barns and build larger ones.
There I shall store all my grain and other goods
   and I shall say to myself,
   "Now as for you, you have so many good things
   stored up for many years,
   rest, eat, drink, be merry!"'
But God said to him, 'You fool,
   this night your life will be demanded of you;
   and the things you have prepared, to whom will they belong?'
Thus will it be for the one who stores up treasure for himself
   but is not rich in what matters to God."

The Gospel of the Lord.

8.

Luke 12:35-40   Be prepared.

✠ **A reading from the holy Gospel according to Luke**

Jesus said to his disciples:
"Gird your loins and light your lamps
    and be like servants who await their master's return from a wedding,
    ready to open immediately when he comes and knocks.
Blessed are those servants
    whom the master finds vigilant on his arrival.
Amen, I say to you, he will gird himself,
    have them recline at table, and proceed to wait on them.
And should he come in the second or third watch
    and find them prepared in this way,
    blessed are those servants.
Be sure of this:
    if the master of the house had known the hour
    when the thief was coming,
    he would not have let his house be broken into.
You also must be prepared, for at an hour you do not expect,
    the Son of Man will come."

The Gospel of the Lord.

9.

Luke 14:12-14   When you hold a banquet, invite the poor.

✠ **A reading from the holy Gospel according to Luke**

On a sabbath Jesus went to dine
    at the home of one of the leading Pharisees.
He said to the host who invited him,
    "When you hold a lunch or a dinner,
    do not invite your friends or your brothers
    or your relatives or your wealthy neighbors,
    in case they may invite you back and you have repayment.
Rather, when you hold a banquet,
    invite the poor, the crippled, the lame, or the blind;
    blessed indeed will you be because of their inability to repay you.
For you will be repaid at the resurrection of the righteous."

The Gospel of the Lord.

10.

Luke 16:19-31   There was a poor man named Lazarus.

✠ **A reading from the holy Gospel according to Luke**

Jesus said to the Pharisees:
"There was a rich man who dressed in purple garments and fine linen
   and dined sumptuously each day.
And lying at his door was a poor man named Lazarus, covered with sores,
   who would gladly have eaten his fill of the scraps
   that fell from the rich man's table.
Dogs even used to come and lick his sores.
When the poor man died,
   he was carried away by angels to the bosom of Abraham.
The rich man also died and was buried,
   and from the netherworld, where he was in torment,
   he raised his eyes and saw Abraham far off
   and Lazarus at his side.
And he cried out, 'Father Abraham, have pity on me.
Send Lazarus to dip the tip of his finger in water and cool my tongue,
   for I am suffering torment in these flames.'
Abraham replied,
   'My child, remember that you received
   what was good during your lifetime
   while Lazarus likewise received what was bad;
   but now he is comforted here, whereas you are tormented.
Moreover, between us and you a great chasm is established
   to prevent anyone from crossing who might wish to go
   from our side to yours or from your side to ours.'
He said, 'Then I beg you, father,
   send him to my father's house, for I have five brothers,
   so that he may warn them,
   lest they too come to this place of torment.'
But Abraham replied, 'They have Moses and the prophets.
Let them listen to them.'
He said, 'Oh no, father Abraham,
   but if someone from the dead goes to them, they will repent.'
Then Abraham said, 'If they will not listen to Moses and the prophets,
   neither will they be persuaded if someone should rise from the dead.'"

The Gospel of the Lord.

11.

Luke 22:24-30   I confer a Kingdom on you, just as my Father has conferred one on me.

✛ **A reading from the holy Gospel according to Luke**

An argument broke out among the Apostles
  about which of them should be regarded as the greatest.
Jesus said to them,
  "The kings of the Gentiles lord it over them
  and those in authority over them are addressed as 'Benefactors';
  but among you it shall not be so.
Rather, let the greatest among you be as the youngest,
  and the leader as the servant.
For who is greater:
  the one seated at table or the one who serves?
Is it not the one seated at table?
I am among you as the one who serves.
It is you who have stood by me in my trials;
  and I confer a Kingdom on you,
  just as my Father has conferred one on me,
  that you may eat and drink at my table in my Kingdom;
  and you will sit on thrones
  judging the twelve tribes of Israel."

The Gospel of the Lord.

12.

John 15:9-12   This is my commandment: love one another as I love you.

✛ **A reading from the holy Gospel according to John**

Jesus said to his disciples:
"As the Father loves me, so I also love you.
Remain in my love.
If you keep my commandments, you will remain in my love,
  just as I have kept my Father's commandments
  and remain in his love.

"I have told you this so that my joy might be in you
  and your joy might be complete.
This is my commandment: love one another as I love you."

The Gospel of the Lord.

14. FOR PEACE AND JUSTICE

887 READING FROM THE OLD TESTAMENT

First Option

Isaiah 9:1-6   His dominion is vast and forever peaceful.

A reading from the Book of the Prophet Isaiah

**The people who walked in darkness
   have seen a great light;
Upon those who dwelt in the land of gloom
   a light has shone.
You have brought them abundant joy
   and great rejoicing,
As they rejoice before you as at the harvest,
   as people make merry when dividing spoils.
For the yoke that burdened them,
   the pole on their shoulder,
And the rod of their taskmaster
   you have smashed, as on the day of Midian.
For every boot that tramped in battle,
   every cloak rolled in blood,
   will be burned as fuel for flames.
For a child is born to us, a son is given us;
   upon his shoulder dominion rests.
They name him Wonder-Counselor, God-Hero,
   Father-Forever, Prince of Peace.
His dominion is vast
   and forever peaceful,
From David's throne, and over his kingdom,
   which he confirms and sustains
By judgment and justice,
   both now and forever.
The zeal of the LORD of hosts will do this!**

The word of the Lord.

Second Option

Isaiah 32:15-18   Justice will bring about peace.

A reading from the Book of the Prophet Isaiah

In those days:
The spirit from on high
    will be poured out on us.
Then will the desert become an orchard
    and the orchard be regarded as a forest.

Right will dwell in the desert
    and justice abide in the orchard.
Justice will bring about peace;
    right will produce calm and security.
My people will live in peaceful country,
    in secure dwellings and quiet resting places.

The word of the Lord.

Third Option

Isaiah 57:15-19   Peace, peace for all, both far and near.

A reading from the Book of the Prophet Isaiah

Thus says he who is high and exalted,
**   living eternally, whose name is the Holy One:**
On high I dwell, and in holiness,
**   and with the crushed and dejected in spirit,**
To revive the spirits of the dejected,
**   to revive the hearts of the crushed.**
I will not accuse forever,
**   nor always be angry;**
For their spirits would faint before me,
**   the souls that I have made.**
Because of their wicked avarice I was angry,
**   and struck them, hiding myself in wrath,**
**   as they went their own rebellious way.**
I saw their ways,
**   but I will heal them and lead them;**
I will give full comfort
**   to them and to those who mourn for them,**
**   I, the Creator, who gave them life.**

Peace, peace to the far and the near,
**   says the LORD; and I will heal them.**

The word of the Lord.

888 READING FROM THE NEW TESTAMENT

First Option

Philippians 4:6-9   The peace of God will guard your hearts and minds.

A reading from the Letter of Saint Paul to the Philippians

Brothers and sisters:
Have no anxiety at all, but in everything,
    by prayer and petition, with thanksgiving,
    make your requests known to God.
Then the peace of God that surpasses all understanding
    will guard your hearts and minds in Christ Jesus.

Finally, brothers and sisters,
    whatever is true, whatever is honorable,
    whatever is just, whatever is pure,
    whatever is lovely, whatever is gracious,
    if there is any excellence
    and if there is anything worthy of praise,
    think about these things.
Keep on doing what you have learned and received
    and heard and seen in me.
Then the God of peace will be with you.

The word of the Lord.

Second Option

Colossians 3:12-15   Let the peace of Christ control your hearts.

A reading from the Letter of Saint Paul to the Colossians

Brothers and sisters:
Put on, as God's chosen ones, holy and beloved,
    heartfelt compassion, kindness, humility, gentleness, and patience,
    bearing with one another and forgiving one another,
    if one has a grievance against another;
    as the Lord has forgiven you, so must you also do.
And over all these put on love,
    that is, the bond of perfection.
And let the peace of Christ control your hearts,
    the peace into which you were also called in one Body.
And be thankful.

The word of the Lord.

Third Option

James 3:13-18   The fruit of righteousness is sown in peace for those who cultivate peace.

A reading from the Letter of James

Beloved:
Who among you is wise and understanding?
Let him show his works by a good life
    in the humility that comes from wisdom.
But if you have bitter jealousy and selfish ambition in your hearts,
    do not boast and be false to the truth.
Wisdom of this kind does not come down from above
    but is earthly, unspiritual, demonic.
For where jealousy and selfish ambition exist,
    there is disorder and every foul practice.
But the wisdom from above is first of all pure,
    then peaceable, gentle, compliant,
    full of mercy and good fruits,
    without inconstancy or insincerity.
And the fruit of righteousness is sown in peace
    for those who cultivate peace.

The word of the Lord.

889 RESPONSORIAL PSALM

First Option

Psalm 72:2, 3-4ab, 7-8, 11-12, 13-14

℞. (see 7) **Justice shall flourish in his time, and fullness of peace forever.**

O God, with your judgment endow the king,
and with your justice, the king's son;
He shall govern your people with justice
and your afflicted ones with judgment.

℞. **Justice shall flourish in his time, and fullness of peace forever.**

The mountains shall yield peace for the people,
and the hills justice.
He shall defend the afflicted among the people,
save the children of the poor.

℞. **Justice shall flourish in his time, and fullness of peace forever.**

Justice shall flower in his days,
and profound peace, till the moon be no more.
May he rule from sea to sea,
and from the River to the ends of the earth.

℞. **Justice shall flourish in his time, and fullness of peace forever.**

All kings shall pay him homage,
all nations shall serve him,
For he shall rescue the poor one when he cries out,
and the afflicted when he has no one to help him.

℞. **Justice shall flourish in his time, and fullness of peace forever.**

He shall have pity for the lowly and the poor;
the lives of the poor he shall save.
From fraud and violence he shall redeem them,
and precious shall their blood be in his sight.

℞. **Justice shall flourish in his time, and fullness of peace forever.**

Second Option

Psalm 85:9 and 10, 11-12, 13-14

℟. (9b) **The Lord speaks of peace to his people.**

I will hear what God proclaims;
the LORD**—for he proclaims peace.**
Near indeed is his salvation to those who fear him,
glory dwelling in our land.

℟. **The Lord speaks of peace to his people.**

Kindness and truth shall meet;
justice and peace shall kiss.
Truth shall spring out of the earth,
and justice shall look down from heaven.

℟. **The Lord speaks of peace to his people.**

The LORD **himself will give his benefits;**
our land shall yield its increase.
Justice shall walk before him,
and salvation, along the way of his steps.

℟. **The Lord speaks of peace to his people.**

Third Option

Psalm 122:1-2, 4-5, 6-7, 8-9

R⁓. (see Sirach 36:15) **Give peace, O Lord, to those who wait for you.**

I rejoiced because they said to me,
  "We will go up to the house of the LORD."
And now we have set foot
  within your gates, O Jerusalem.

R⁓. **Give peace, O Lord, to those who wait for you.**

To it the tribes go up,
  the tribes of the LORD,
According to the decree for Israel,
  to give thanks to the name of the LORD.
In it are set up judgment seats,
  seats for the house of David.

R⁓. **Give peace, O Lord, to those who wait for you.**

Pray for the peace of Jerusalem!
  May those who love you prosper!
May peace be within your walls,
  prosperity in your buildings.

R⁓. **Give peace, O Lord, to those who wait for you.**

Because of my relatives and friends
  I will say, "Peace be within you!"
Because of the house of the LORD, our God,
  I will pray for your good.

R⁓. **Give peace, O Lord, to those who wait for you.**

890 ALLELUIA VERSE AND VERSE BEFORE THE GOSPEL

1.

Matthew 5:9

**Blessed are the peacemakers;
they shall be called children of God.**

2.

John 14:27

**Peace I leave with you, says the Lord,
my peace I give to you.**

891 GOSPEL

First Option

Matthew 5:1-12a   Blessed are the peacemakers, for they will be called children of God.

✠ **A reading from the holy Gospel according to Matthew**

When Jesus saw the crowds, he went up the mountain,
   and after he had sat down, his disciples came to him.
He began to teach them, saying:

   "Blessed are the poor in spirit,
      for theirs is the Kingdom of heaven.
   Blessed are they who mourn,
      for they will be comforted.
   Blessed are the meek,
      for they will inherit the land.
   Blessed are they who hunger and thirst for righteousness,
      for they will be satisfied.
   Blessed are the merciful,
      for they will be shown mercy.
   Blessed are the clean of heart,
      for they will see God.
   Blessed are the peacemakers,
      for they will be called children of God.
   Blessed are they who are persecuted for the sake of righteousness,
      for theirs is the Kingdom of heaven.
   Blessed are you when they insult you and persecute you
      and utter every kind of evil against you falsely because of me.
   Rejoice and be glad,
      for your reward will be great in heaven."

The Gospel of the Lord.

Second Option

Matthew 5:38-48   I say this to you: offer no resistance to one who is evil.

✠ **A reading from the holy Gospel according to Matthew**

Jesus said to his disciples:
"You have heard that it was said,
   An eye for an eye and a tooth for a tooth.
But I say to you, offer no resistance to one who is evil.
When someone strikes you on your right cheek,
   turn the other to him as well.
If anyone wants to go to law with you over your tunic,
   hand him your cloak as well.
Should anyone press you into service for one mile,
   go with him two miles.
Give to the one who asks of you,
   and do not turn your back on one who wants to borrow.

"You have heard that it was said,
   You shall love your neighbor and hate your enemy.
But I say to you, love your enemies
   and pray for those who persecute you,
   that you may be children of your heavenly Father,
   for he makes his sun rise on the bad and the good,
   and causes rain to fall on the just and the unjust.
For if you love those who love you, what recompense will you have?
Do not the tax collectors do the same?
And if you greet your brothers only,
   what is unusual about that?
Do not the pagans do the same?
So be perfect, just as your heavenly Father is perfect."

The Gospel of the Lord.

Third Option

John 14:23-29   My peace I give to you.

☩ **A reading from the holy Gospel according to John**

Jesus said to his disciple, Jude:
"Whoever loves me will keep my word,
   and my Father will love him,
   and we will come to him and make our dwelling with him.
Whoever does not love me does not keep my words;
   yet the word you hear is not mine
   but that of the Father who sent me.

"I have told you this while I am with you.
The Advocate, the Holy Spirit—
   that the Father will send in my name—
   he will teach you everything
   and remind you of all that I told you.
Peace I leave with you; my peace I give to you.
Not as the world gives do I give it to you.
Do not let your hearts be troubled or afraid.
You heard me tell you,
   'I am going away and I will come back to you.'
If you loved me,
   you would rejoice that I am going to the Father;
   for the Father is greater than I.
And now I have told you this before it happens,
   so that when it happens you may believe."

The Gospel of the Lord.

Fourth Option

John 20:19-23   Peace be with you.

✠ **A reading from the holy Gospel according to John**

On the evening of that first day of the week,
   when the doors were locked, where the disciples were, for fear of the
      Jews,
   Jesus came and stood in their midst
   and said to them, "Peace be with you."
When he had said this, he showed them his hands and his side.
The disciples rejoiced when they saw the Lord.
Jesus said to them again, "Peace be with you.
As the Father has sent me, so I send you."
And when he had said this, he breathed on them and said to them,
   "Receive the Holy Spirit.
Whose sins you forgive are forgiven them,
   and whose sins you retain are retained."

The Gospel of the Lord.

15. FOR RECONCILIATION

892 READING FROM THE OLD TESTAMENT

First Option

Isaiah 55:1-3, 6-9   Seek the Lord.

A reading from the Book of the Prophet Isaiah

Thus says the LORD:
All you who are thirsty,
    come to the water!
You who have no money,
    come, receive grain and eat;
Come, without paying and without cost,
    drink wine and milk!
Why spend your money for what is not bread,
    your wages for what fails to satisfy?
Heed me, and you shall eat well,
    you shall delight in rich fare.
Come to me heedfully;
    listen, that you may have life.
I will renew with you the everlasting covenant,
    the benefits assured to David.

Seek the LORD while he may be found,
    call him while he is near.
Let the scoundrel forsake his ways,
    and the wicked man his thoughts;
Let him turn to the LORD for mercy;
    to our God, who is generous in forgiving.
For my thoughts are not your thoughts,
    nor are your ways my ways, says the LORD.
As high as the heavens are above the earth,
    so high are my ways above your ways
    and my thoughts above your thoughts.

The word of the Lord.

Second Option

Jeremiah 31:31-34   I will forgive their evildoing.

A reading from the Book of the Prophet Jeremiah

The days are coming, says the Lord,
> **when I will make a new covenant with the house of Israel**
> **and the house of Judah.**

It will not be like the covenant I made with their fathers,
> **the day I took them by the hand**
> **to lead them forth from the land of Egypt;**
> **for they broke my covenant**
> **and I had to show myself their master, says the Lord.**

But this is the covenant which I will make
> **with the house of Israel after those days, says the Lord.**

I will place my law within them and write it upon their hearts;
> **I will be their God, and they shall be my people.**

No longer will they have need to teach their friends and relatives
> **how to know the Lord.**

All, from least to greatest, shall know me, says the Lord,
> **for I will forgive their evildoing and remember their sin no more.**

The word of the Lord.

Third Option

Amos 5:4, 14-15, 21-24   Seek good that you may live.

A reading from the Book of the Prophet Amos

Thus says the Lord GOD:
Seek me, that you may live.

Seek good and not evil,
   that you may live;
Then truly will the LORD, the God of hosts,
   be with you as you claim!
Hate evil and love good,
   and let justice prevail at the gate;
Then it may be that the LORD, the God of hosts,
   will have pity on the remnant of Joseph.

I hate, I spurn your feasts,
   I take no pleasure in your solemnities;
Your cereal offerings I will not accept,
   nor consider your stall-fed peace offerings.
Away with your noisy songs!
   I will not listen to the melodies of your harps.
But if you would offer me burnt offerings,
      then let justice surge like water,
      and goodness like an unfailing stream.

The word of the Lord.

893 READING FROM THE NEW TESTAMENT

First Option

Acts 3:13-15, 17-19   Repent, therefore, and be converted.

A reading from the Acts of the Apostles

**Peter said to the people:
"The God of Abraham,
   the God of Isaac, and the God of Jacob,
   the God of our fathers, has glorified his servant Jesus
   whom you handed over and denied in Pilate's presence,
   when he had decided to release him.
You denied the Holy and Righteous One
   and asked that a murderer be released to you.
The author of life you put to death,
   but God raised him from the dead;
   of this we are witnesses.
Now I know, brothers,
   that you acted out of ignorance, just as your leaders did;
   but God has thus brought to fulfillment
   what he had announced beforehand
   through the mouth of all the prophets,
   that his Christ would suffer.
Repent, therefore, and be converted, that your sins may be wiped away."**

The word of the Lord.

Second Option

2 Corinthians 5:17–6:2   Be reconciled to God.

A reading from the second Letter of Saint Paul to the Corinthians

Brothers and sisters:
Whoever is in Christ is a new creation:
the old things have passed away;
behold, new things have come.
And all this is from God,
who has reconciled us to himself through Christ
and given us the ministry of reconciliation,
namely, God was reconciling the world to himself in Christ,
not counting their trespasses against them
and entrusting to us the message of reconciliation.
So we are ambassadors for Christ,
as if God were appealing through us.
We implore you on behalf of Christ,
be reconciled to God.
For our sake he made him to be sin who did not know sin,
so that we might become the righteousness of God in him.

Working together, then,
we appeal to you not to receive the grace of God in vain.
For he says:
In an acceptable time I heard you,
and on the day of salvation I helped you.
Behold, now is a very acceptable time;
behold, now is the day of salvation.

The word of the Lord.

Third Option

1 John 2:1-5a   Jesus Christ is the expiation for our sins.

A reading from the first Letter of Saint John

My children,
  I am writing this to you
  so that you may not commit sin.
But if anyone does sin, we have an Advocate with the Father,
  Jesus Christ the righteous one.
He is expiation for our sins,
  and not for our sins only but for those of the whole world.
The way we may be sure that we know him
  is to keep his commandments.
Whoever says, "I know him"
  but does not keep his commandments is a liar,
  and the truth is not in him.
But whoever keeps his word,
  the love of God is truly perfected in him.

The word of the Lord.

894 RESPONSORIAL PSALM

First Option

Psalm 51:3-4, 12-13, 14-15

℟. (12a) **Create a clean heart in me, O God.**

Have mercy on me, O God, in your goodness;
 in the greatness of your compassion wipe out my offense.
Thoroughly wash me from my guilt
 and of my sin cleanse me.

℟. **Create a clean heart in me, O God.**

A clean heart create for me, O God,
 and a steadfast spirit renew within me.
Cast me not out from your presence,
 and your Holy Spirit take not from me.

℟. **Create a clean heart in me, O God.**

Give me back the joy of your salvation,
 and a willing spirit sustain in me.
I will teach transgressors your ways,
 and sinners shall return to you.

℟. **Create a clean heart in me, O God.**

Second Option

Psalm 130:1-2, 3-4, 5-6ab, 6c-8

R̶. (7bc) **With the Lord there is mercy, and fullness of redemption.**

Out of the depths I cry to you, O LORD;
  LORD, hear my voice!
Let your ears be attentive
  to my voice in supplication.

R̶. **With the Lord there is mercy, and fullness of redemption.**

If you, O LORD, mark iniquities,
  LORD, who can stand?
But with you is forgiveness,
  that you may be revered.

R̶. **With the Lord there is mercy, and fullness of redemption.**

I trust in the LORD;
  my soul trusts in his word.
My soul waits for the LORD
  more than sentinels wait for the dawn.

R̶. **With the Lord there is mercy, and fullness of redemption.**

More than sentinels for the dawn,
  let Israel wait for the LORD,
For with the LORD is kindness
  and with him is plenteous redemption;
And he will redeem Israel
  from all their iniquities.

R̶. **With the Lord there is mercy, and fullness of redemption.**

895 ALLELUIA VERSE AND VERSE BEFORE THE GOSPEL

1.

Ezekiel 33:11

**I take no pleasure in the death of the wicked man, says the Lord,
but rather in his conversion, that he may live.**

2.

Matthew 5:9

**Blessed are the peacemakers,
they shall be called children of God.**

3.

Mark 1:15

**The Kingdom of God is at hand:
repent and believe in the Gospel!**

896 GOSPEL

First Option

Matthew 5:1-12a   Rejoice and be glad.

✠ **A reading from the holy Gospel according to Matthew**

When Jesus saw the crowds, he went up the mountain,
   and after he had sat down, his disciples came to him.
He began to teach them, saying:

   "Blessed are the poor in spirit,
      for theirs is the Kingdom of heaven.
   Blessed are they who mourn,
      for they will be comforted.
   Blessed are the meek,
      for they will inherit the land.
   Blessed are they who hunger and thirst for righteousness,
      for they will be satisfied.
   Blessed are the merciful,
      for they will be shown mercy.
   Blessed are the clean of heart,
      for they will see God.
   Blessed are the peacemakers,
      for they will be called children of God.
   Blessed are they who are persecuted for the sake of righteousness,
      for theirs is the Kingdom of heaven.
   Blessed are you when they insult you and persecute you
      and utter every kind of evil against you falsely because of me.
   Rejoice and be glad,
      for your reward will be great in heaven."

The Gospel of the Lord.

Second Option

Luke 3:7-18   What, then, should we do?

✠ **A reading from the holy Gospel according to Luke**

John the Baptist said to the crowds who came out to be baptized by him,
  "You brood of vipers!
Who warned you to flee from the coming wrath?
Produce good fruits as evidence of your repentance;
  and do not begin to say to yourselves,
  'We have Abraham as our father,'
  for I tell you, God can raise up children to Abraham
  from these stones.
Even now the ax lies at the root of the trees.
Therefore every tree that does not produce good fruit
  will be cut down and thrown into the fire."

And the crowds asked him,
  "What then should we do?"
He said to them in reply,
  "Whoever has two cloaks
  should share with the person who has none.
And whoever has food should do likewise."
Even tax collectors came to be baptized and they said to him,
  "Teacher, what should we do?"
He answered them,
  "Stop collecting more than what is prescribed."
Soldiers also asked him,
  "And what is it that we should do?"
He told them,
  "Do not practice extortion,
  do not falsely accuse anyone,
  and be satisfied with your wages."

Now the people were filled with expectation,
  and all were asking in their hearts
  whether John might be the Christ.
John answered them all, saying,
  "I am baptizing you with water,
  but one mightier than I is coming.
I am not worthy to loosen the thongs of his sandals.
He will baptize you with the Holy Spirit and fire.

His winnowing fan is in his hand to clear his threshing floor
   and to gather the wheat into his barn,
   but the chaff he will burn with unquenchable fire."
Exhorting them in many other ways,
   he preached good news to the people.

The Gospel of the Lord.

Third Option

Luke 15:1-3, 11-32   Father, I have sinned.

✠ **A reading from the holy Gospel according to Luke**

Tax collectors and sinners were all drawing near to listen to Jesus,
   but the Pharisees and scribes began to complain, saying,
   "This man welcomes sinners and eats with them."

So Jesus addressed this parable to them.
"A man had two sons, and the younger son said to his father,
   'Father give me the share of your estate that should come to me.'
So the father divided the property between them.
After a few days, the younger son collected all his belongings
   and set off to a distant country
   where he squandered his inheritance on a life of dissipation.
When he had freely spent everything,
   a severe famine struck that country,
   and he found himself in dire need.
So he hired himself out to one of the local citizens
   who sent him to his farm to tend the swine.
And he longed to eat his fill of the pods on which the swine fed,
   but nobody gave him any.
Coming to his senses he thought,
   'How many of my father's hired workers
   have more than enough food to eat,
   but here am I, dying from hunger.
I shall get up and go to my father and I shall say to him,
   "Father, I have sinned against heaven and against you.
I no longer deserve to be called your son;
   treat me as you would treat one of your hired workers."'
So he got up and went back to his father.
While he was still a long way off,
   his father caught sight of him, and was filled with compassion.
He ran to his son, embraced him and kissed him.
His son said to him,
   'Father, I have sinned against heaven and against you;
   I no longer deserve to be called your son.'
But his father ordered his servants,
   'Quickly bring the finest robe and put it on him;
   put a ring on his finger and sandals on his feet.
Take the fattened calf and slaughter it.

Then let us celebrate with a feast,

> because this son of mine was dead, and has come to life again;
>
> he was lost, and has been found.'

Then the celebration began.

Now the older son had been out in the field

> and, on his way back, as he neared the house,
>
> he heard the sound of music and dancing.

He called one of the servants and asked what this might mean.

The servant said to him,

> 'Your brother has returned
>
> and your father has slaughtered the fattened calf
>
> because he has him back safe and sound.'

He became angry,

> and when he refused to enter the house,
>
> his father came out and pleaded with him.

He said to his father in reply,

> 'Look, all these years I served you
>
> and not once did I disobey your orders;
>
> yet you never gave me even a young goat to feast on with my friends.

But when your son returns

> who swallowed up your property with prostitutes,
>
> for him you slaughter the fattened calf.'

He said to him,

> 'My son, you are here with me always;
>
> everything I have is yours.

But now we must celebrate and rejoice,

> because your brother was dead and has come to life again;
>
> he was lost and has been found.'"

The Gospel of the Lord.

16. IN TIME OF WAR OR CIVIL DISTURBANCE

Readings from the Mass for Peace and Justice may also be used, nos. 887–891.

897 READING FROM THE OLD TESTAMENT

First Option

Genesis 4:3-10   Cain attacked his brother Abel and killed him.

A reading from the Book of Genesis

Cain brought an offering to the LORD from the fruit of the soil,
> **while Abel, for his part,**
> **brought one of the best firstlings of his flock.**
The LORD looked with favor on Abel and his offering,
> **but on Cain and his offering he did not.**
Cain greatly resented this and was crestfallen.
So the LORD said to Cain:
> **"Why are you so resentful and crestfallen?**
If you do well, you can hold up your head;
> **but if not, sin is a demon lurking at the door:**
> **his urge is toward you, yet you can be his master."**

Cain said to his brother Abel,
> **"Let us go out in the field."**
When they were in the field,
> **Cain attacked his brother Abel and killed him.**
Then the LORD asked Cain, "Where is your brother Abel?"
He answered, "I do not know.
Am I my brother's keeper?"
The LORD then said: "What have you done!
Listen: your brother's blood cries out to me from the soil!"

The word of the Lord.

Second Option

Micah 4:1-4   They shall not train for war again.

A reading from the Book of the Prophet Micah

In days to come
    the mount of the LORD**'s house**
Shall be established higher than the mountains;
    it shall rise high above the hills,
And peoples shall stream to it:
    many nations shall come, and say,
"Come, let us climb the mount of the LORD**,**
    to the house of the God of Jacob,
That he may instruct us in his ways,
    that we may walk in his paths."
For from Zion shall go forth instruction,
    and the word of the LORD **from Jerusalem.**
He shall judge between many peoples
    and impose terms on strong and distant nations;
They shall beat their swords into plowshares,
    and their spears into pruning hooks;
One nation shall not raise the sword against another,
    nor shall they train for war again.
Every man shall sit under his own vine
    or under his own fig tree, undisturbed;
    for the mouth of the LORD **of hosts has spoken.**

The word of the Lord.

Third Option

Zechariah 9:9-10   The weapons of war will be banished.

A reading from the Book of the Prophet Zechariah

Thus says the Lord:
Rejoice heartily, O daughter Zion,
   shout for joy, O daughter Jerusalem!
See, your king shall come to you;
   a just savior is he,
Meek, and riding on an ass,
   on a colt, the foal of an ass.
He shall banish the chariot from Ephraim,
   and the horse from Jerusalem;
The warrior's bow shall be banished,
   and he shall proclaim peace to the nations.
His dominion shall be from sea to sea,
   and from the River to the ends of the earth.

The word of the Lord.

898 READING FROM THE NEW TESTAMENT

First Option

Galatians 5:17-26　The works of the flesh are obvious: hatreds, rivalry, jealousy, outbursts of fury and dissensions.

A reading from the Letter of Saint Paul to the Galatians

Brothers and sisters:
The flesh has desires against the Spirit,
**　and the Spirit against the flesh;**
**　these are opposed to each other,**
**　so that you may not do what you want.**
But if you are guided by the Spirit,
**　you are not under the law.**
Now the works of the flesh are obvious:
**　immorality, impurity, licentiousness, idolatry,**
**　sorcery, hatreds, rivalry, jealousy,**
**　outbursts of fury, acts of selfishness,**
**　dissensions, factions, occasions of envy,**
**　drinking bouts, orgies, and the like.**
I warn you, as I warned you before,
**　that those who do such things will not inherit the Kingdom of God.**
In contrast, the fruit of the Spirit is love, joy, peace,
**　patience, kindness, generosity,**
**　faithfulness, gentleness, self-control.**
Against such there is no law.
Now those who belong to Christ Jesus
**　have crucified their flesh with its passions and desires.**
If we live in the Spirit, let us also follow the Spirit.
Let us not be conceited, provoking one another, envious of one another.

The word of the Lord.

Second Option

Ephesians 4:30–5:2   All bitterness, fury, anger, shouting, and reviling must be removed from you, along with all malice.

A reading from the Letter of Saint Paul to the Ephesians

Brothers and sisters:
Do not grieve the Holy Spirit of God,
** with which you were sealed for the day of redemption.**
All bitterness, fury, anger, shouting, and reviling
** must be removed from you, along with all malice.**
And be kind to one another, compassionate,
** forgiving one another as God has forgiven you in Christ.**

Be imitators of God, as beloved children,
** and live in love, as Christ loved us**
** and handed himself over for us as a sacrificial offering to God**
** for a fragrant aroma.**

The word of the Lord.

Third Option

James 4:1-10   Where do the wars and where do the conflicts among you come from?

A reading from the Letter of James

Beloved:
Where do the wars and where do the conflicts among you come from?
Is it not from your passions that make war within your members?
You covet but do not possess.
You kill and envy but you cannot obtain;
   you fight and wage war.
You do not possess because you do not ask.
You ask but do not receive, because you ask wrongly,
   to spend it on your passions.
Adulterers!
Do you not know that to be a lover of the world
   means enmity with God?
Therefore, whoever wants to be a lover of the world
   makes himself an enemy of God.
Or do you suppose that the Scripture speaks without meaning when it says,
   The spirit that he has made to dwell in us tends toward jealousy?
But he bestows a greater grace; therefore, it says:

   God resists the proud,
      but gives grace to the humble.

So submit yourselves to God.
Resist the Devil, and he will flee from you.
Draw near to God, and he will draw near to you.
Cleanse your hands, you sinners,
   and purify your hearts, you of two minds.
Begin to lament, to mourn, to weep.
Let your laughter be turned into mourning
   and your joy into dejection.
Humble yourselves before the Lord and he will exalt you.

The word of the Lord.

899 RESPONSORIAL PSALM

First Option

Psalm 72:1bc-2, 3-4, 7-8, 12-13, 18

R̸. (see 7) **Justice shall flourish in his time, and fullness of peace forever.**

O God, with your judgment endow the king,
  and with your justice, the king's son;
He shall govern your people with justice
  and your afflicted ones with judgment.

R̸. **Justice shall flourish in his time, and fullness of peace forever.**

The mountains shall yield peace for the people,
  and the hills justice.
He shall defend the afflicted among the people,
  save the children of the poor and crush the oppressor.

R̸. **Justice shall flourish in his time, and fullness of peace forever.**

Justice shall flower in his days,
  and profound peace, till the moon be no more.
May he rule from sea to sea,
  and from the River to the ends of the earth.

R̸. **Justice shall flourish in his time, and fullness of peace forever.**

For he shall rescue the poor one when he cries out,
  and the afflicted when he has no one to help him.
He shall have pity for the lowly and the poor;
  the lives of the poor he shall save.

R̸. **Justice shall flourish in his time, and fullness of peace forever.**

Blessed be the LORD, the God of Israel,
  who alone does wondrous deeds.
And blessed forever be his glorious name;
  may the whole earth be filled with his glory.

R̸. **Justice shall flourish in his time, and fullness of peace forever.**

Second Option

Psalm 85:9ab and 10, 11-12, 13-14

℟. (see 9b) **The Lord speaks of peace to his people.**

I will hear what God proclaims;
   the LORD—for he proclaims peace.
Near indeed is his salvation to those who fear him,
   glory dwelling in our land.

℟. **The Lord speaks of peace to his people.**

Kindness and truth shall meet;
   justice and peace shall kiss.
Truth shall spring out of the earth,
   and justice shall look down from heaven.

℟. **The Lord speaks of peace to his people.**

The LORD himself will give his benefits;
   our land shall yield its increase.
Justice shall walk before him,
   and salvation, along the way of his steps.

℟. **The Lord speaks of peace to his people.**

900 ALLELUIA VERSE AND VERSE BEFORE THE GOSPEL

1.

Matthew 5:9

**Blessed are the peacemakers;
they shall be called children of God.**

2.

2 Corinthians 1:3b-4a

**Blessed be the Father of compassion and God of all encouragement,
who encourages us in our every affliction.**

3.

John 13:34

**I give you a new commandment:
love one another as I have loved you.**

901 GOSPEL

First Option

Matthew 5:20-24   Whoever is angry with his brother will be liable to judgment.

☩ A reading from the holy Gospel according to Matthew

Jesus said to his disciples:
"I tell you, unless your righteousness surpasses that
    of the scribes and Pharisees,
    you will not enter into the Kingdom of heaven.

"You have heard that it was said to your ancestors,
    You shall not kill; and whoever kills will be liable to judgment.
But I say to you, whoever is angry with his brother
    will be liable to judgment,
    and whoever says to his brother, 'Raqa,'
        will be answerable to the Sanhedrin
    and whoever says, 'You fool,' will be liable to fiery Gehenna.
Therefore, if you bring your gift to the altar,
    and there recall that your brother
    has anything against you,
    leave your gift there at the altar,
    go first and be reconciled with your brother,
    and then come and offer your gift."

The Gospel of the Lord.

Second Option

John 15:9-12   This is my commandment: love one another as I love you.

✠ **A reading from the holy Gospel according to John**

Jesus said to his disciples:
"As the Father loves me, so I also love you.
Remain in my love.
If you keep my commandments, you will remain in my love,
   just as I have kept my Father's commandments
   and remain in his love.

"I have told you this so that my joy might be in you
   and your joy might be complete.
This is my commandment: love one another as I love you."

The Gospel of the Lord.

III. IN VARIOUS PUBLIC CIRCUMSTANCES
17. FOR THE BEGINNING OF THE CIVIL YEAR

902 READING FROM THE OLD TESTAMENT

First Option

Genesis 1:14-18   Let there be lights to mark the fixed times, the days and
the years.

A reading from the Book of Genesis

God said:
"Let there be lights in the dome of the sky,
   to separate day from night.
Let them mark the fixed times, the days and the years,
   and serve as luminaries in the dome of the sky,
   to shed light upon the earth."
And so it happened:
   God made the two great lights,
   the greater one to govern the day,
   and the lesser one to govern the night;
   and he made the stars.
God set them in the dome of the sky,
   to shed light upon the earth,
   to govern the day and the night,
   and to separate the light from the darkness.
God saw how good it was.

The word of the Lord.

Second Option

Numbers 6:22-27   They shall invoke my name upon the children of Israel, and I will bless them.

A reading from the Book of Numbers

The LORD said to Moses:
"Speak to Aaron and his sons and tell them:
   This is how you shall bless the children of Israel.
Say to them:
   The LORD bless you and keep you!
   The LORD let his face shine upon you, and be gracious to you!
   The LORD look upon you kindly and give you peace!

So shall they invoke my name upon the children of Israel,
   and I will bless them."

The word of the Lord.

903 READING FROM THE NEW TESTAMENT

First Option

1 Corinthians 7:29-31   For the world in its present form is passing away.

A reading from the first Letter of Saint Paul to the Corinthians

I tell you, brothers, the time is running out.
From now on, let those having wives act as not having them,
those weeping as not weeping,
those rejoicing as not rejoicing,
those buying as not owning,
those using the world as not using it fully.
For the world in its present form is passing away.

The word of the Lord.

Second Option

James 4:13-15   You have no idea what your life will be like tomorrow.

A reading from the Letter of James

Beloved:
Come now, you who say,
"Today or tomorrow we shall go into such and such a town,
spend a year there doing business, and make a profit"—
you have no idea what your life will be like tomorrow.
You are a puff of smoke that appears briefly and then disappears.
Instead you should say,
"If the Lord wills it, we shall live to do this or that."

The word of the Lord.

904 RESPONSORIAL PSALM

First Option

Psalm 8:4-5, 6-7, 8-9

R̸. (2ab) **O Lord, our God, how wonderful your name in all the earth!**

When I behold your heavens, the work of your fingers,
   the moon and the stars which you set in place—
What is man that you should be mindful of him,
   or the son of man that you should care for him?

R̸. **O Lord, our God, how wonderful your name in all the earth!**

You have made him little less than the angels,
   and crowned him with glory and honor.
You have given him rule over the works of your hands,
   putting all things under his feet.

R̸. **O Lord, our God, how wonderful your name in all the earth!**

All sheep and oxen,
   yes, and the beasts of the field,
The birds of the air, the fishes of the sea,
   and whatever swims the paths of the seas.

R̸. **O Lord, our God, how wonderful your name in all the earth!**

Second Option

Psalm 49:2-3, 6-7, 8-10, 11, 17-18

R̸. (Matthew 5:3) **Blessed are the poor in spirit; the Kingdom of heaven is**
      theirs!
   or:
R̸. (Matthew 6:33a) **Seek first the Kingdom of God and his holiness.**

Hear this, all you peoples;
   hearken, all who dwell in the world,
Of lowly birth or high degree,
   rich and poor alike.

R̸. **Blessed are the poor in spirit; the Kingdom of heaven is theirs!**
   or:
R̸. **Seek first the Kingdom of God and his holiness.**

Why should I fear in evil days
   when my wicked ensnares ring me round?
They trust in their wealth;
   the abundance of their riches is their boast.

R̸. **Blessed are the poor in spirit; the Kingdom of heaven is theirs!**
   or:
R̸. **Seek first the Kingdom of God and his holiness.**

Yet in no way can a man redeem himself,
   or pay his own ransom to God;
Too high is the price to redeem one's life; he would never have enough
   to remain alive always and not see destruction.

R̸. **Blessed are the poor in spirit; the Kingdom of heaven is theirs!**
   or:
R̸. **Seek first the Kingdom of God and his holiness.**

For he can see that wise men die,
   and likewise the senseless and the stupid pass away,
   leaving to others their wealth.

R̸. **Blessed are the poor in spirit; the Kingdom of heaven is theirs!**
   or:
R̸. **Seek first the Kingdom of God and his holiness.**

Fear not when a man grows rich,
   when the wealth of his house becomes great,
For when he dies, he shall take none of it;
   his wealth shall not follow him down.

R̸. **Blessed are the poor in spirit; the Kingdom of heaven is theirs!**
   or:
R̸. **Seek first the Kingdom of God and his holiness.**

Third Option

Psalm 90:2, 3-4, 5-6, 12-13, 14 and 16

℟. (see 17b) **Lord, give success to the work of our hands.**

Before the mountains were begotten
   and the earth and the world were brought forth,
   from everlasting to everlasting you are God.

℟. **Lord, give success to the work of our hands.**

You turn man back to dust,
   saying, "Return, O children of men."
For a thousand years in your sight
   are as yesterday, now that it is past,
   or as a watch of the night.

℟. **Lord, give success to the work of our hands.**

You make an end of them in their sleep;
   the next morning they are like the changing grass,
Which at dawn springs up anew,
   but by evening wilts and fades.

℟. **Lord, give success to the work of our hands.**

Teach us to number our days aright,
   that we may gain wisdom of heart.
Return, O LORD! How long?
   Have pity on your servants.

℟. **Lord, give success to the work of our hands.**

Fill us at daybreak with your kindness,
   that we may shout for joy and gladness all of our days.
Let your work be seen by your servants
   and your glory by their children.

℟. **Lord, give success to the work of our hands.**

905 ALLELUIA VERSE AND VERSE
BEFORE THE GOSPEL

1.

1 Chronicles 29:10b, 11b

Blessed are you, O LORD our God;
all things in heaven and earth are yours.

2.

Day after day we bless you;
we praise your name without ceasing.

906 GOSPEL

First Option

Matthew 6:31-34   Do not worry about tomorrow.

✠   **A reading from the holy Gospel according to Matthew**

Jesus said to his disciples:
"Do not worry and say, 'What are we to eat?'
  or 'What are we to drink?' or 'What are we to wear?'
All these things the pagans seek.
Your heavenly Father knows that you need them all.
But seek first the Kingdom of God and his righteousness,
  and all these things will be given you besides.
Do not worry about tomorrow; tomorrow will take care of itself.
Sufficient for a day is its own evil."

The Gospel of the Lord.

Second Option

Luke 12:35-40   Be prepared.

✠   **A reading from the holy Gospel according to Luke**

Jesus said to his disciples:
"Gird your loins and light your lamps
  and be like servants who await their master's return from a wedding,
  ready to open immediately when he comes and knocks.
Blessed are those servants
  whom the master finds vigilant on his arrival.
Amen, I say to you, he will gird himself,
  have them recline at table, and proceed to wait on them.
And should he come in the second or third watch
  and find them prepared in this way,
  blessed are those servants.
Be sure of this:
  if the master of the house had known the hour
  when the thief was coming,
  he would not have let his house be broken into.
You also must be prepared, for at an hour you do not expect,
  the Son of Man will come."

The Gospel of the Lord.

18. FOR THE BLESSING OF HUMAN LABOR

907 READING FROM THE OLD TESTAMENT

First Option

Genesis 1:26–2:3   Fill the earth and subdue it.

A reading from the Book of Genesis

God said:
"Let us make man in our image, after our likeness.
Let them have dominion over the fish of the sea,
   the birds of the air, and the cattle,
   and over all the wild animals
   and all the creatures that crawl on the ground."

God created man in his image;
   in the divine image he created him;
   male and female he created them.

God blessed them, saying:
   "Be fertile and multiply;
   fill the earth and subdue it.
Have dominion over the fish of the sea, the birds of the air,
   and all the living things that move on the earth."
God also said:
   "See, I give you every seed-bearing plant all over the earth
   and every tree that has seed-bearing fruit on it to be your food;
   and to all the animals of the land, all the birds of the air,
   and all the living creatures that crawl on the ground,
   I give all the green plants for food."
And so it happened.
God looked at everything he had made, and he found it very good.
Evening came, and morning followed—the sixth day.

Thus the heavens and the earth and all their array were completed.
Since on the seventh day God was finished with the work he had been doing,
   he rested on the seventh day from all the work he had undertaken.
So God blessed the seventh day and made it holy,
   because on it he rested from all the work he had done in creation.

The word of the Lord.

Second Option

Genesis 2:4b-9, 15   God took the man and settled him in the garden of Eden to cultivate and care for it.

A reading from the Book of Genesis

At the time when the LORD God made the earth and the heavens—
while as yet there was no field shrub on earth
and no grass of the field had sprouted,
for the LORD God had sent no rain upon the earth
and there was no man to till the soil,
but a stream was welling up out of the earth
and was watering all the surface of the ground—
the LORD God formed man out of the clay of the ground
and blew into his nostrils the breath of life,
and so man became a living being.

Then the LORD God planted a garden in Eden, in the east,
and placed there the man whom he had formed.
Out of the ground the LORD God made various trees grow
that were delightful to look at and good for food,
with the tree of life in the middle of the garden
and the tree of the knowledge of good and evil.

The LORD God then took the man
and settled him in the garden of Eden,
to cultivate and care for it.

The word of the Lord.

908 READING FROM THE NEW TESTAMENT

First Option

1 Thessalonians 4:1b-2, 9-12   Work with your own hands that you may conduct yourselves properly.

A reading from the first Letter of Saint Paul to the Thessalonians

Brothers and sisters,
    we earnestly ask and exhort you in the Lord Jesus that,
    as you received from us
    how you should conduct yourselves to please God—
    and as you are conducting yourselves—
    you do so even more.
For you know what instructions we gave you through the Lord Jesus.

On the subject of mutual charity
    you have no need for anyone to write you,
    for you yourselves have been taught by God to love one another.
Indeed, you do this for all the brothers throughout Macedonia.
Nevertheless, we urge you, brothers, to progress even more,
    and to aspire to live a tranquil life,
    to mind your own affairs,
    and to work with your own hands,
    as we instructed you,
    that you may conduct yourselves properly toward outsiders
    and not depend on anyone.

The word of the Lord.

Second Option

2 Thessalonians 3:6-12, 16   If anyone was unwilling to work, neither should that one eat.

A reading from the second Letter of Saint Paul to the Thessalonians

We instruct you, brothers and sisters,
  in the name of our Lord Jesus Christ,
  to shun any brother who walks in a disorderly way
  and not according to the tradition they received from us.
For you know how one must imitate us.
For we did not act in a disorderly way among you,
  nor did we eat food received free from anyone.
On the contrary, in toil and drudgery, night and day
  we worked, so as not to burden any of you.
Not that we do not have the right.
Rather, we wanted to present ourselves as a model for you,
  so that you might imitate us.
In fact, when we were with you,
  we instructed you that if anyone was unwilling to work,
  neither should that one eat.
We hear that some are conducting themselves among you in a disorderly way,
  by not keeping busy but minding the business of others.
Such people we instruct and urge in the Lord Jesus Christ to work quietly
  and to eat their own food.
May the Lord of peace himself give you peace at all times
  and in every way.
The Lord be with all of you.

The word of the Lord.

909 RESPONSORIAL PSALM

1.

Psalm 90:2, 3-5a, 12-13, 14 and 16

℟. (see 17b) **Lord, give success to the work of our hands.**

Before the mountains were begotten,
and the earth and the world were brought forth,
from everlasting to everlasting you are God.

℟. **Lord, give success to the work of our hands.**

You turn man back to dust,
saying, "Return, O children of men."
For a thousand years in your sight
are as yesterday, now that it is past,
or as a watch of the night.
You make an end of them in their sleep.

℟. **Lord, give success to the work of our hands.**

Teach us to number our days aright,
that we may gain wisdom of heart.
Return, O LORD! How long?
Have pity on your servants!

℟. **Lord, give success to the work of our hands.**

Fill us at daybreak with your kindness,
that we may shout for joy and gladness all of our days.
Let your work be seen by your servants
and your glory by their children.

℟. **Lord, give success to the work of our hands.**

2.

Psalm 127:1, 2

℟. (see 1) **The Lord will build a house for us and guard our city.**

Unless the L<small>ORD</small> **build the house,**
   they labor in vain who build.
Unless the L<small>ORD</small> **guard the city,**
   in vain does the guard keep vigil.

℟. **The Lord will build a house for us and guard our city.**

It is vain for you to rise early
   or put off your rest,
You that eat hard-earned bread,
   for he gives to his beloved in sleep.

℟. **The Lord will build a house for us and guard our city.**

910 ALLELUIA VERSE AND VERSE BEFORE THE GOSPEL

1.

Psalm 68:20

Blessed be the Lord day by day,
God, our salvation, who bears our burdens.

2.

Matthew 11:28

Come to me, all you who labor and are burdened,
and I will give you rest, says the Lord.

911 GOSPEL

First Option

Matthew 6:31-34   Do not worry about tomorrow.

☩ A reading from the holy Gospel according to Matthew

Jesus said to his disciples:
"Do not worry and say, 'What are we to eat?'
  or 'What are we to drink?' or 'What are we to wear?'
All these things the pagans seek.
Your heavenly Father knows that you need them all.
But seek first the Kingdom of God and his righteousness,
  and all these things will be given you besides.
Do not worry about tomorrow; tomorrow will take care of itself.
Sufficient for a day is its own evil."

The Gospel of the Lord.

Second Option

Matthew 25:14-30   Since you were faithful in small matters, come, share
your master's joy.

☩ A reading from the holy Gospel according to Matthew

Jesus told his disciples this parable:
"A man going on a journey
  called in his servants
  and entrusted his possessions to them.
To one he gave five talents; to another, two; to a third, one—
  to each according to his ability.
Then he went away.
Immediately the one who received five talents went and traded with them,
  and made another five.
Likewise, the one who received two made another two.
But the one who received one went off and dug a hole in the ground
  and buried his master's money.
After a long time
  the master of those servants came back and settled accounts with them.
The one who had received five talents
  came forward bringing the additional five.
He said, 'Master, you gave me five talents.
See, I have made five more.'

His master said to him, 'Well done, my good and faithful servant.
Since you were faithful in small matters,
   I will give you great responsibilities.
Come, share your master's joy.'
Then the one who had received two talents also came forward and said,
   'Master, you gave me two talents.
See, I have made two more.'
His master said to him, 'Well done, my good and faithful servant.
Since you were faithful in small matters,
   I will give you great responsibilities.
Come, share your master's joy.'
Then the one who had received the one talent came forward and said,
   'Master, I knew you were a demanding person,
   harvesting where you did not plant
   and gathering where you did not scatter;
   so out of fear I went off and buried your talent in the ground.
Here it is back.'
His master said to him in reply, 'You wicked, lazy servant!
So you knew that I harvest where I did not plant
   and gather where I did not scatter?
Should you not then have put my money in the bank
   so that I could have got it back with interest on my return?
Now then! Take the talent from him and give it to the one with ten.
For to everyone who has
   more will be given and he will grow rich;
   but from the one who has not,
   even what he has will be taken away.
And throw this useless servant into the darkness outside,
   where there will be wailing and grinding of teeth.'"

The Gospel of the Lord.

19. FOR PRODUCTIVE LAND

Readings from the Mass for the Blessing of Human Labor may also be used, above, nos. 907–911.

912 READING FROM THE OLD TESTAMENT

First Option

Genesis 1:11-12   Let the earth bring forth vegetation: Every kind of plant that bears seed.

A reading from the Book of Genesis

God said, "Let the earth bring forth vegetation:
  every kind of plant that bears seed
  and every kind of fruit tree on earth
  that bears fruit with its seed in it."
And so it happened:
  the earth brought forth every kind of plant that bears seed
  and every kind of fruit tree on earth
  that bears fruit with its seed in it.
God saw how good it was.

The word of the Lord.

Second Option

Isaiah 55:6-13   Giving seed to the one who sows and bread to the one
who eats.

A reading from the Book of the Prophet Isaiah

Seek the LORD while he may be found,
  call him while he is near.
Let the scoundrel forsake his ways,
  and the wicked his thoughts;
Let him turn to the LORD for mercy;
  to our God, who is generous in forgiving.
For my thoughts are not your thoughts,
  nor are your ways my ways, says the LORD.
As high as the heavens are above the earth,
  so high are my ways above your ways
  and my thoughts above your thoughts.

For just as from the heavens
  the rain and snow come down
And do not return there
  till they have watered the earth,
  making it fertile and fruitful,
Giving seed to the one who sows
  and bread to the one who eats,
So shall my word be
  that goes forth from my mouth;
My word shall not return to me void,
  but shall do my will,
  achieving the end for which I sent it.

Yes, in joy you shall depart,
  in peace you shall be brought back;
Mountains and hills shall break out in song before you,
  and all the trees of the countryside shall clap their hands.
In place of the thornbush, the cypress shall grow,
  instead of nettles, the myrtle.
This shall be to the LORD's renown,
  an everlasting imperishable sign.

The word of the Lord.

913 READING FROM THE NEW TESTAMENT

First Option

2 Corinthians 9:8-11   God will provide bread to eat.

A reading from the second Letter of Saint Paul to the Corinthians

Brothers and sisters:
God is able to make every grace abundant for you,
    so that in all things, always having all you need,
    you may have an abundance for every good work.
As it is written:

> *He scatters abroad, he gives to the poor;*
>   *his righteousness endures forever.*

The one who supplies seed to the sower and bread for food
    will supply and multiply your seed
    and increase the harvest of your righteousness.

You are being enriched in every way for all generosity,
    which through us produces thanksgiving to God.

The word of the Lord.

Second Option

James 5:7-8, 16c-18   The farmer waits for the precious fruit of the earth.

A reading from the Letter of Saint James

Be patient, brothers and sisters,
    until the coming of the Lord.
See how the farmer waits for the precious fruit of the earth,
    being patient with it
    until it receives the early and the late rains.
You too must be patient.
Make your hearts firm,
    because the coming of the Lord is at hand.

The fervent prayer of a righteous person is very powerful.
Elijah was a man like us;
    yet he prayed earnestly that it might not rain,
    and for three years and six months it did not rain upon the land.
Then he prayed again, and the sky gave rain
    and the earth produced its fruit.

The word of the Lord.

914 RESPONSORIAL PSALM

First Option

Psalm 65:10, 11-12, 13-14

℞. (6) **Hear us, O saving God.**

You have visited the land and watered it;
   greatly have you enriched it.
God's watercourses are filled;
   you have prepared the grain.

℞. **Hear us, O saving God.**

Thus have you prepared the land:
   drenching its furrows, breaking up its clods,
Softening it with showers,
   blessing its yield.
You have crowned the year with your bounty,
   and your paths overflow with a rich harvest.

℞. **Hear us, O saving God.**

The untilled meadows overflow with it,
   and rejoicing clothes the hills.
The fields are garmented with flocks
   and the valleys blanketed with grain.
   They shout and sing for joy.

℞. **Hear us, O saving God.**

Second Option

Psalm 104:1-2a, 14-15, 24, 27-28

℞. (24c) **The earth is full of your riches, O Lord.**

Bless the LORD, O my soul!
   O LORD, my God, you are great indeed!
You are clothed with majesty and glory,
   robed in light as with a cloak.

℞. **The earth is full of your riches, O Lord.**

(cont.)

You raise grass for the cattle,
  and vegetation for men's use,
Producing bread from the earth,
  and wine to gladden men's hearts,
So that their faces gleam with oil,
  and bread fortifies the hearts of men.

℟. The earth is full of your riches, O Lord.

How manifold are your works, O Lord!
  In wisdom you have wrought them all—
  the earth is full of your creatures.

℟. The earth is full of your riches, O Lord.

They all look to you
  to give them food in due time.
When you give it to them, they gather it;
  when you open your hand, they are filled with good things.

℟. The earth is full of your riches, O Lord.

Third Option

Psalm 107:35-36, 37-38, 41-42

℟. (1b) Give thanks to the Lord, for he is good.

He changed the desert into pools of water,
  waterless land into water springs.
And there he settled the hungry,
  and they built a city to dwell in.

℟. Give thanks to the Lord, for he is good.

They sowed fields and planted vineyards,
  and they obtained a fruitful yield.
He blessed them, and they became very many;
  nor did he suffer their cattle to decrease.

℟. Give thanks to the Lord, for he is good.

Lifted up the needy out of misery
  and made the families numerous like flocks.
The upright see this and rejoice,
  and all wickedness closes its mouth.

℟. Give thanks to the Lord, for he is good.

915 ALLELUIA VERSE AND VERSE BEFORE THE GOSPEL

1.

Psalm 85:13

**The Lord himself will give his benefits;
our land shall yield its increase.**

2.

Psalm 126:5

**Those who sow in tears
shall reap rejoicing.**

916 GOSPEL

First Option

Matthew 13:1-9   A sower went out to sow seed.

✠ **A reading from the holy Gospel according to Matthew**

**One day, Jesus went out of the house and sat down by the sea.
Such large crowds gathered around him**
    that he got into a boat and sat down,
    and the whole crowd stood along the shore.
And he spoke to them at length in parables, saying:
    "A sower went out to sow.
And as he sowed, some seed fell on the path,
    and birds came and ate it up.
Some fell on rocky ground, where it had little soil.
It sprang up at once because the soil was not deep,
    and when the sun rose it was scorched,
    and it withered for lack of roots.
Some seed fell among thorns, and the thorns grew up and choked it.
But some seed fell on rich soil, and produced fruit,
    a hundred or sixty or thirtyfold.
Whoever has ears ought to hear."

The Gospel of the Lord.

Second Option

Mark 4:26-29   A man scatters seed and while he sleeps it grows even though he does not know how.

☩ **A reading from the holy Gospel according to Mark**

Jesus said to the crowd:
"This is how it is with the Kingdom of God;
    it is as if a man were to scatter seed on the land
    and would sleep and rise night and day
    and the seed would sprout and grow, he knows not how.
Of its own accord the land yields fruit,
    first the blade, then the ear, then the full grain in the ear.
And when the grain is ripe, he wields the sickle at once,
    for the harvest has come."

The Gospel of the Lord.

20. AFTER THE HARVEST

Readings from the Mass in Thanksgiving may also be used, nos. 943–947.

917 READING FROM THE OLD TESTAMENT

First Option

Deuteronomy 8:7-18   Be mindful of the LORD your God, how he showed you his favor.

A reading from the Book of Deuteronomy

Moses spoke to the people, and said:
"The LORD, your God, is bringing you into a good country,
   a land with streams of water,
   with springs and fountains welling up in the hills and valleys,
   a land of wheat and barley,
   of vines and fig trees and pomegranates,
   of olive trees and of honey,
   a land where you can eat bread without stint
   and where you will lack nothing,
   a land whose stones contain iron
   and in whose hills you can mine copper.
But when you have eaten your fill, you must bless the LORD, your God,
   for the good country he has given you.
Be careful not to forget the LORD, your God,
   by neglecting his commandments and decrees and statutes
   which I enjoin on you today:
   lest, when you have eaten your fill,
   and have built fine houses and lived in them,
   and have increased your herds and flocks,
   your silver and gold, and all your property,
   you then become haughty of heart and unmindful of the LORD, your God,
   who brought you out of the land of Egypt,
   that place of slavery;
   who guided you through the vast and terrible desert
   with its saraph serpents and scorpions,
   its parched and waterless ground;
   who brought forth water for you from the flinty rock
   and fed you in the desert with manna,
   a food unknown to your fathers,

that he might afflict you and test you,
   but also make you prosperous in the end.
Otherwise, you might say to yourselves,
   'It is my own power and the strength of my own hand
   that has obtained for me this wealth.'
Remember then, it is the LORD, your God,
   who gives you the power to acquire wealth,
   by fulfilling, as he has now done,
   the covenant that he swore to your fathers."

The word of the Lord.

Second Option

Joel 2:21-24, 26-27   They shall be filled with the fruit of the threshing floor.

A reading from the Book of the Prophet Joel

Fear not, O land!
   exult and rejoice!
   for the LORD has done great things.
Fear not, beasts of the field!
   for the pastures of the plain are green;
The tree bears its fruit,
   the fig tree and the vine give their yield.

O children of Zion, exult
   and rejoice in the LORD, your God!
He has given you the teacher of justice:
   he has made the rain come down for you,
   the early and the late rain as before.
The threshing floors shall be full of grain
   and the vats shall overflow with wine and oil.

You shall eat and be filled,
   and shall praise the name of the LORD, your God,
Because he has dealt wondrously with you;
   my people shall nevermore be put to shame.
And you shall know that I am in the midst of Israel;
   I am the LORD, your God, and there is no other;
   my people shall nevermore be put to shame.

The word of the Lord.

918 READING FROM THE NEW TESTAMENT

First Option

1 Corinthians 3:6-10   God caused the growth.

A reading from the first Letter of Saint Paul to the Corinthians

Brothers and sisters:
I planted, Apollos watered, but God caused the growth.
Therefore, neither the one who plants nor the one who waters is anything,
   but only God, who causes the growth.
He who plants and he who waters are one,
   and each will receive wages in proportion to his labor.
For we are God's coworkers;
   you are God's field, God's building.

According to the grace of God given to me,
   like a wise master builder I laid a foundation,
   and another is building upon it.
But each one must be careful how he builds upon it.

The word of the Lord.

Second Option

1 Timothy 6:6-11, 17-19   Tell the rich not to rely on so uncertain a thing as wealth.

A reading from the first Letter of Saint Paul to Timothy

Beloved:
Religion with contentment is a great gain.
For we brought nothing into the world,
   just as we shall not be able to take anything out of it.
If we have food and clothing, we shall be content with that.
Those who want to be rich are falling into temptation and into a trap
   and into many foolish and harmful desires,
   which plunge them into ruin and destruction.
For the love of money is the root of all evils,
   and some people in their desire for it have strayed from the faith
   and have pierced themselves with many pains.

But you, avoid all this.
Instead, pursue righteousness, devotion, faith,
   love, patience, and gentleness.

Tell the rich in the present age not to be proud
   and not to rely on so uncertain a thing as wealth
   but rather on God, who richly provides us with all things
   for our enjoyment.
Tell them to do good, to be rich in good works,
   to be generous, ready to share,
   thus accumulating as treasure a good foundation for the future,
   so as to win the life that is true life.

The word of the Lord.

919 RESPONSORIAL PSALM

1.

Psalm 67:2-3, 5, 7-8

R̊. (7) **The earth has yielded its fruit, the Lord our God has blessed us.**
    or:
R̊. (4) **O God, let all the nations praise you!**

May God have pity on us and bless us;
    may he let his face shine upon us.
So may your way be known upon earth;
    among all nations, your salvation.

R̊. **The earth has yielded its fruit, the Lord our God has blessed us.**
    or:
R̊. **O God, let all the nations praise you!**

May the nations be glad and exult
    because you rule the peoples in equity;
    the nations on the earth you guide.

R̊. **The earth has yielded its fruit, the Lord our God has blessed us.**
    or:
R̊. **O God, let all the nations praise you!**

The earth has yielded its fruits;
    God, our God, has blessed us.
May God bless us,
    and may all the ends of the earth fear him!

R̊. **The earth has yielded its fruit, the Lord our God has blessed us.**
    or:
R̊. **O God, let all the nations praise you!**

2.

Psalm 126:2b-3, 4-5, 6-7

℟. (3a) **The Lord has done great things for us.**

Then they said among the nations,
    "The LORD has done great things for them."
The LORD has done great things for us;
    we are glad indeed.

℟. **The Lord has done great things for us.**

Restore our fortunes, O LORD,
    like the torrents in the southern desert.
Those who sow in tears
    shall reap rejoicing.

℟. **The Lord has done great things for us.**

Although they go forth weeping,
    carrying the seed to be sown,
They shall come back rejoicing,
    carrying their sheaves.

℟. **The Lord has done great things for us.**

920 ALLELUIA VERSE AND VERSE BEFORE THE GOSPEL

Psalm 126:5

**Those who sow in tears
shall reap rejoicing.**

921 GOSPEL

First Option

Luke 12:15-21   Though one may be rich, one's life does not consist of possessions.

✠ **A reading from the holy Gospel according to Luke**

Jesus said to the crowd,
   "Take care to guard against all greed,
   for though one may be rich,
   one's life does not consist of possessions."

Then he told them a parable.
"There was a rich man whose land produced a bountiful harvest.
He asked himself,
   'What shall I do, for I do not have space to store my harvest?'
And he said, 'This is what I shall do:
   I shall tear down my barns and build larger ones.
There I shall store all my grain and other goods
   and I shall say to myself,
   "Now as for you, you have so many good things
   stored up for many years,
   rest, eat, drink, be merry!"'
But God said to him, 'You fool,
   this night your life will be demanded of you;
   and the things you have prepared, to whom will they belong?'
Thus will it be for the one who stores up treasure for himself
   but is not rich in what matters to God."

The Gospel of the Lord.

Second Option

Luke 17:11-19   He fell at the feet of Jesus and thanked him.

✚ **A reading from the holy Gospel according to Luke**

As Jesus continued his journey to Jerusalem,
** he traveled through Samaria and Galilee.**
As he was entering a village, ten persons with leprosy met him.
They stood at a distance from him and raised their voices, saying,
** "Jesus, Master! Have pity on us!"**
And when he saw them, he said,
** "Go show yourselves to the priests."**
As they were going they were cleansed.
And one of them, realizing he had been healed,
** returned, glorifying God in a loud voice;**
** and he fell at the feet of Jesus and thanked him.**
He was a Samaritan.
Jesus said in reply,
** "Ten were cleansed, were they not?**
Where are the other nine?
Has none but this foreigner returned to give thanks to God?"
Then he said to him, "Stand up and go;
** your faith has saved you."**

The Gospel of the Lord.

21. IN TIME OF FAMINE OR FOR THOSE WHO SUFFER FROM FAMINE

922 READING FROM THE OLD TESTAMENT

First Option

Deuteronomy 24:17-22 Let what remains be for the alien, the orphan, and the widow.

A reading from the Book of Deuteronomy

Moses spoke to the people, and said:
"You shall not violate the rights of the alien or of the orphan,
  nor take the clothing of a widow as a pledge.
For, remember, you were once slaves in Egypt,
  and the LORD**, your God, ransomed you from there;**
  that is why I command you to observe this rule.

"When you reap the harvest in your field and overlook a sheaf there,
  you shall not go back to get it;
  let it be for the alien, the orphan, or the widow,
  that the LORD**, your God, may bless you in all your undertakings.**
When you knock down the fruit of your olive trees,
  you shall not go over the branches a second time;
  let what remains be for the alien, the orphan, and the widow.
When you pick your grapes,
  you shall not go over the vineyard a second time;
  let what remains be for the alien, the orphan, and the widow.
For remember that you were once slaves in Egypt;
  that is why I command you to observe this rule."

The word of the Lord.

Second Option

Job 31:16-20, 24-25, 31-32   While I ate my portion alone with no share in it for the fatherless.

A reading from the Book of Job

If I have denied anything to the poor,
  or allowed the eyes of the widow to languish
While I ate my portion alone,
  with no share in it for the fatherless,
Though like a father God has reared me from my youth,
  guiding me even from my mother's womb—

If I have seen a wanderer without clothing,
  or a poor person without covering,
Whose limbs have not blessed me
  when warmed with the fleece of my sheep;

Had I put my trust in gold
  or called fine gold my security;
Or had I rejoiced that my wealth was great,
  or that my hand had acquired abundance—

Had not the men of my tent exclaimed,
  "Who has not been fed with his meat!"
Because no stranger lodged in the street,
  but I opened my door to wayfarers.

The word of the Lord.

Third Option

Isaiah 58:6-11   Share your bread with the hungry.

A reading from the Book of the Prophet Isaiah

Thus says the Lord:
This is the fasting that I wish:
    releasing those bound unjustly,
    untying the thongs of the yoke;
Setting free the oppressed,
    breaking every yoke;
Sharing your bread with the hungry,
    sheltering the oppressed and the homeless;
Clothing the naked when you see them,
    and not turning your back on your own.

Then your light shall break forth like the dawn,
    and your wound shall quickly be healed;
Your vindication shall go before you,
    and the glory of the Lord shall be your rear guard.
Then you shall call, and the Lord will answer,
    you shall cry for help, and he will say: Here I am!
If you remove from your midst oppression,
    false accusation and malicious speech;
If you bestow your bread on the hungry
    and satisfy the afflicted;
Then light shall rise for you in darkness,
    and the gloom shall become for you like midday;
Then the Lord will guide you always
    and give you plenty even on the parched land.
He will renew your strength,
    and you shall be like a watered garden,
    like a spring whose water never fails.

The word of the Lord.

923   READING FROM THE NEW TESTAMENT

First Option

Acts 11:27-30   The disciples determined that, according to ability, each should send relief to the brothers who lived in Judea.

A reading from the Acts of the Apostles

Some prophets came down from Jerusalem to Antioch,
  and one of them named Agabus stood up and predicted by the Spirit
  that there would be a severe famine all over the world,
  and it happened under Claudius.
So the disciples determined that, according to ability,
  each should send relief to the brothers
    who lived in Judea.
This they did, sending it to the presbyters in care of Barnabas and Saul.

The word of the Lord.

Second Option

2 Corinthians 8:1-5, 9-15   Your abundance should supply their needs.

A reading from the second Letter of Saint Paul to the Corinthians

We want you to know, brothers and sisters,
  of the grace of God that has been given to the churches of Macedonia,
  for in a severe test of affliction,
  the abundance of their joy and their profound poverty
  overflowed in a wealth of generosity on their part.
For according to their means, I can testify,
  and beyond their means, spontaneously, they begged us insistently
  for the favor of taking part in the service to the holy ones,
  and this, not as we expected,
  but they gave themselves first to the Lord
  and to us through the will of God.

For you know the gracious act of our Lord Jesus Christ,
  that for your sake he became poor although he was rich,
  so that by his poverty you might become rich.
And I am giving counsel in this matter,
  for it is appropriate for you who began not only to act
  but to act willingly last year:
  complete it now, so that your eager willingness may be matched
  by your completion of it out of what you have.
For if the eagerness is there,
  it is acceptable according to what one has,
  not according to what one does not have;
  not that others should have relief while you are burdened,
  but that as a matter of equality
  your surplus at the present time should supply their needs,
  so that their surplus may also supply your needs,
  that there may be equality.
As it is written:
  Whoever had much did not have more,
    and whoever had little did not have less.

The word of the Lord.

Third Option

2 Corinthians 9:6-15   Each must do as already determined, without sadness or compulsion, for God loves a cheerful giver.

A reading from the second Letter of Saint Paul to the Corinthians

Brothers and sisters:
Whoever sows sparingly will also reap sparingly,
and whoever sows bountifully will also reap bountifully.
Each must do as already determined,
without sadness or compulsion,
for God loves a cheerful giver.
Moreover, God is able to make every grace abundant for you,
so that in all things, always having all you need,
you may have an abundance for every good work.
As it is written:

> *He scatters abroad, he gives to the poor;*
> *his righteousness endures forever.*

The one who supplies seed to the sower and bread for food
will supply and multiply your seed
and increase the harvest of your righteousness.

You are being enriched in every way for all generosity,
which through us produces thanksgiving to God,
for the administration of this public service
is not only supplying the needs of the holy ones
but is also overflowing in many acts of thanksgiving to God.
Through the evidence of this service,
you are glorifying God for your obedient confession
of the Gospel of Christ
and the generosity of your contribution to them and to all others,
while in prayer on your behalf they long for you,
because of the surpassing grace of God upon you.
Thanks be to God for his indescribable gift!

The word of the Lord.

924 RESPONSORIAL PSALM

1.

Psalm 22:23-24, 26-27, 28 and 31-32

℞. (27a) **The poor shall eat and shall have their fill.**

I will proclaim your name to my brothers and sisters;
  in the midst of the assembly I will praise you:
"You who fear the LORD, praise him;
  all descendants of Jacob, give glory to him;
  revere him, all you descendants of Israel!"

℞. **The poor shall eat and shall have their fill.**

By your gift will I utter praise in the vast assembly;
  I will fulfill my vows before those who fear him.
The lowly shall eat their fill;
  they who seek the LORD shall praise him:
  "May your hearts be ever merry!"

℞. **The poor shall eat and shall have their fill.**

All the ends of the earth
  shall remember and turn to the Lord;
All the families of the nations
  shall bow down before him.
My descendants shall serve him.
Let the coming generation be told of the Lord
  that they may proclaim to a people yet to be born
  the justice he has shown.

℞. **The poor shall eat and shall have their fill.**

2.

Psalm 107:2-3, 4-5, 6-7, 8-9

℟. (1) **Give thanks to the Lord, his love is everlasting.**
    or:
℟. **Alleluia.**

Let the redeemed of the L<small>ORD</small> say,
    those whom he has redeemed from the hand of the foe
And gathered from the lands,
    from the east and the west, from the north and the south.

℟. **Give thanks to the Lord, his love is everlasting.**
    or:
℟. **Alleluia.**

They went astray in the desert wilderness;
    the way to an inhabited city they did not find.
Hungry and thirsty,
    their life was wasting away within them.

℟. **Give thanks to the Lord, his love is everlasting.**
    or:
℟. **Alleluia.**

They cried to the L<small>ORD</small> in their distress;
    from their straits he rescued them.
And he led them by a direct way
    to reach an inhabited city.

℟. **Give thanks to the Lord, his love is everlasting.**
    or:
℟. **Alleluia.**

Let them give thanks to the L<small>ORD</small> for his mercy
    and his wondrous deeds to the children of men,
Because he satisfied the longing soul
    and filled the hungry soul with good things.

℟. **Give thanks to the Lord, his love is everlasting.**
    or:
℟. **Alleluia.**

3.

Psalm 112:1-2, 3-4, 5-6, 7-8, 9

℟. (see 1a and 9a) **Blessed the one who gives to the poor.**
   or:
℟. **Alleluia.**

Blessed the man who fears the Lord,
   who greatly delights in his commands.
His posterity shall be mighty upon the earth;
   the upright generation shall be blessed.

℟. **Blessed the one who gives to the poor.**
   or:
℟. **Alleluia.**

Wealth and riches shall be in his house;
   his generosity shall endure forever.
Light shines through the darkness for the upright;
   he is gracious and merciful and just.

℟. **Blessed the one who gives to the poor.**
   or:
℟. **Alleluia.**

Well for the man who is gracious and lends,
   who conducts his affairs with justice;
He shall never be moved;
   the just one shall be in everlasting remembrance.

℟. **Blessed the one who gives to the poor.**
   or:
℟. **Alleluia.**

An evil report he shall not fear;
   his heart is firm, trusting in the Lord.
His heart is steadfast; he shall not fear
   till he looks down upon his foes.

(cont.)

℞. **Blessed the one who gives to the poor.**

or:

℞. **Alleluia.**

Lavishly he gives to the poor;
    his generosity shall endure forever;
    his horn shall be exalted in glory.

℞. **Blessed the one who gives to the poor.**

or:

℞. **Alleluia.**

925 ALLELUIA VERSE AND VERSE
BEFORE THE GOSPEL

1.

Matthew 25:34

Come, you who are blessed by my Father, says the Lord;
inherit the kingdom prepared for you from the foundation of the world.

2.

2 Corinthians 8:9

Jesus Christ became poor although he was rich,
so that by his poverty you might become rich.

926 GOSPEL

First Option

Matthew 25:31-46   I was hungry and you gave me food.

✠   **A reading from the holy Gospel according to Matthew**

Jesus said to his disciples:
"When the Son of Man comes in his glory,
   and all the angels with him,
   he will sit upon his glorious throne,
   and all the nations will be assembled before him.
And he will separate them one from another,
   as a shepherd separates the sheep from the goats.
He will place the sheep on his right and the goats on his left.
Then the king will say to those on his right,
   'Come, you who are blessed by my Father.
Inherit the kingdom prepared for you from the foundation of the world.
For I was hungry and you gave me food,
   I was thirsty and you gave me drink,
   a stranger and you welcomed me,
   naked and you clothed me,
   ill and you cared for me,
   in prison and you visited me.'
Then the righteous will answer him and say,
   'Lord, when did we see you hungry and feed you,
   or thirsty and give you drink?
When did we see you a stranger and welcome you,
   or naked and clothe you?
When did we see you ill or in prison, and visit you?'
And the king will say to them in reply,
   'Amen, I say to you, whatever you did
   for one of the least brothers of mine, you did for me.'
Then he will say to those on his left,
   'Depart from me, you accursed,
   into the eternal fire prepared for the Devil and his angels.
For I was hungry and you gave me no food,
   I was thirsty and you gave me no drink,
   a stranger and you gave me no welcome,
   naked and you gave me no clothing,
   ill and in prison, and you did not care for me.'

Then they will answer and say,
    'Lord, when did we see you hungry or thirsty
    or a stranger or naked or ill or in prison,
    and not minister to your needs?'
He will answer them, 'Amen, I say to you,
    what you did not do for one of these least ones,
    you did not do for me.'
And these will go off to eternal punishment,
    but the righteous to eternal life."

The Gospel of the Lord.

Second Option

Mark 6:34-44   Give them some food yourselves.

☩ **A reading from the holy Gospel according to Mark**

When Jesus saw the vast crowd, his heart was moved with pity for them,
for they were like sheep without a shepherd;
and he began to teach them many things.
By now it was already late and his disciples approached him and said,
"This is a deserted place and it is already very late.
Dismiss them so that they can go to
the surrounding farms and villages
and buy themselves something to eat."
He said to them in reply,
"Give them some food yourselves."
But they said to him,
"Are we to buy two hundred days' wages worth of food
and give it to them to eat?"
He asked them, "How many loaves do you have? Go and see."
And when they had found out they said,
"Five loaves and two fish."
So he gave orders to have them sit down in groups on the green grass.
The people took their places in rows by hundreds and by fifties.
Then, taking the five loaves and the two fish and looking up to heaven,
he said the blessing, broke the loaves, and gave them to his disciples
to set before the people;
he also divided the two fish among them all.
They all ate and were satisfied.
And they picked up twelve wicker baskets full of fragments
and what was left of the fish.
Those who ate of the loaves were five thousand men.

The Gospel of the Lord.

Third Option

Luke 14:12-14   When you have a banquet, invite the poor.

✠ **A reading from the holy Gospel according to Luke**

On a sabbath Jesus went to dine
   at the home of one of the leading Pharisees.
He said to the host who invited him,
   "When you hold a lunch or a dinner,
   do not invite your friends or your brothers
   or your relatives or your wealthy neighbors,
   in case they may invite you back and you have repayment.
Rather, when you hold a banquet,
   invite the poor, the crippled, the lame, and the blind;
   blessed indeed will you be because of their inability to repay you.
For you will be repaid at the resurrection of the righteous."

The Gospel of the Lord.

Fourth Option

Luke 16:19-31   There was a poor man named Lazarus.

✠ **A reading from the holy Gospel according to Luke**

Jesus said to the Pharisees:
"There was a rich man who dressed in purple garments and fine linen
    and dined sumptuously each day.
And lying at his door was a poor man named Lazarus, covered with sores,
    who would gladly have eaten his fill of the scraps
    that fell from the rich man's table.
Dogs even used to come and lick his sores.
When the poor man died,
    he was carried away by angels to the bosom of Abraham.
The rich man also died and was buried,
    and from the netherworld, where he was in torment,
    he raised his eyes and saw Abraham far off
    and Lazarus at his side.
And he cried out, 'Father Abraham, have pity on me.
Send Lazarus to dip the tip of his finger in water and cool my tongue,
    for I am suffering torment in these flames.'
Abraham replied,
    'My child, remember that you received
    what was good during your lifetime
    while Lazarus likewise received what was bad;
    but now he is comforted here, whereas you are tormented.
Moreover, between us and you a great chasm is established
    to prevent anyone from crossing who might wish to go
    from our side to yours or from your side to ours.'
He said, 'Then I beg you, father,
    send him to my father's house, for I have five brothers,
    so that he may warn them,
    lest they too come to this place of torment.'
But Abraham replied, 'They have Moses and the prophets.
Let them listen to them.'
He said, 'Oh no, father Abraham,
    but if someone from the dead goes to them, they will repent.'
Then Abraham said, 'If they will not listen to Moses and the prophets,
    neither will they be persuaded if someone should rise from the dead.'"

The Gospel of the Lord.

22. FOR REFUGEES AND EXILES

927 READING FROM THE OLD TESTAMENT

First Option

Deuteronomy 10:17-19   The Lord God befriends the alien, giving him food and clothing him.

A reading from the Book of Deuteronomy

Moses told the people:
"The LORD, your God, is the God of gods,
  the LORD of lords, the great God, mighty and awesome,
  who has no favorites, accepts no bribes;
  who executes justice for the orphan and the widow,
  and befriends the alien, feeding and clothing them.
So you too must befriend the alien,
  for you were once aliens yourselves in the land of Egypt."

The word of the Lord.

Second Option

Deuteronomy 24:17-22   Let what remains be for the alien, the orphan, and the widow.

A reading from the Book of Deuteronomy

Moses spoke to the people, and said:
"You shall not violate the rights of the alien or of the orphan,
    nor take the clothing of a widow as a pledge.
For, remember, you were once slaves in Egypt,
    and the LORD, your God, ransomed you from there;
    that is why I command you to observe this rule.

"When you reap the harvest in your field and overlook a sheaf there,
    you shall not go back to get it;
    let it be for the alien, the orphan, or the widow,
    that the LORD, your God, may bless you in all your undertakings.
When you knock down the fruit of your olive trees,
    you shall not go over the branches a second time;
    let what remains be for the alien, the orphan, and the widow.
When you pick your grapes,
    you shall not go over the vineyard a second time;
    let what remains be for the alien, the orphan, and the widow.
For remember that you were once slaves in Egypt;
    that is why I command you to observe this rule."

The word of the Lord.

928 READING FROM THE NEW TESTAMENT

First Option

Romans 12:9-16b   Exercise hospitality.

A reading from the Letter of Saint Paul to the Romans

**Brothers and sisters:
Let love be sincere;
  hate what is evil,
  hold on to what is good;
  love one another with mutual affection;
  anticipate one another in showing honor.
Do not grow slack in zeal,
  be fervent in spirit,
  serve the Lord.
Rejoice in hope,
  endure in affliction,
  persevere in prayer.
Contribute to the needs of the holy ones,
  exercise hospitality.
Bless those who persecute you,
  bless and do not curse them.
Rejoice with those who rejoice,
  weep with those who weep.
Have the same regard for one another;
  do not be haughty but associate with the lowly;
  do not be wise in your own estimation.

The word of the Lord.**

Second Option

Hebrews 11:13-16   Those who speak thus show that they are seeking a homeland.

A reading from the Letter to the Hebrews

Brothers and sisters:
All the ancients died in faith.
They did not receive what had been promised
    but saw it and greeted it from afar
      and acknowledged themselves to be strangers and aliens on earth,
      for those who speak thus show that they are seeking a homeland.
If they had been thinking of the land from which they had come,
    they would have had opportunity to return.
But now they desire a better homeland, a heavenly one.
Therefore, God is not ashamed to be called their God,
    for he has prepared a city for them.

The word of the Lord.

Third Option

Hebrews 13:1-3, 14-16   Do not neglect hospitality.

A reading from the Letter to the Hebrews

Brothers and sisters:
Let mutual love continue.
Do not neglect hospitality,
    for through it some have unknowingly entertained angels.
Be mindful of prisoners as if sharing their imprisonment,
    and of the ill-treated as of yourselves,
    for you also are in the body.

For here we have no lasting city,
    but we seek the one that is to come.
Through him then let us continually offer God a sacrifice of praise,
    that is, the fruit of lips that confess his name.
Do not neglect to do good and to share what you have;
    God is pleased by sacrifices of that kind.

The word of the Lord.

929 RESPONSORIAL PSALM

1.

Tobit 13:2, 3-4, 6, 7, 8

R̸. (1b) **Blessed be God, who lives for ever.**

He scourges and then has mercy;
he casts down to the depths of the nether world,
and he brings up from the great abyss.
No one can escape his hand.

R̸. **Blessed be God, who lives for ever.**

Praise him, you children of Israel, before the Gentiles,
for though he has scattered you among them,
he has shown you his greatness even there.
Exalt him before every living being,
because he is the Lord our God,
our Father and God forever.

R̸. **Blessed be God, who lives for ever.**

When you turn back to him with all your heart,
to do what is right before him,
Then he will turn back to you,
and no longer hide his face from you.

R̸. **Blessed be God, who lives for ever.**

So now consider what he has done for you,
and praise him with full voice.
Bless the LORD of righteousness,
and exalt the King of the ages.

R̸. **Blessed be God, who lives for ever.**

In the land of my exile I praise him,
and show his power and majesty to a sinful nation.

R̸. **Blessed be God, who lives for ever.**

Bless the Lord, all you his chosen ones,
and may all of you praise his majesty.
Celebrate days of gladness, and give him praise.

R̸. **Blessed be God, who lives for ever.**

2.

Psalm 107:33-34, 35-36, 41-42

R℣. (1) **Give thanks to the Lord; his love is everlasting.**
   or:
R℣. **Alleluia.**

He changed rivers into desert,
   water springs into thirsty ground,
Fruitful land into salt marshes,
   because of the wickedness of its inhabitants.

R℣. **Give thanks to the Lord; his love is everlasting.**
   or:
R℣. **Alleluia.**

He changed the desert into pools of water,
   waterless lands into water spring.
And there he settled the hungry,
   and they built a city to dwell in.

R℣. **Give thanks to the Lord; his love is everlasting.**
   or:
R℣. **Alleluia.**

Lifted up the needy out of misery
   and made the families numerous like flocks.
The upright see this and rejoice,
   and all wickedness closes its mouth.

R℣. **Give thanks to the Lord; his love is everlasting.**
   or:
R℣. **Alleluia.**

3.

Psalm 121:1bc-2, 3-4, 5-6, 7-8

R̝. (2) **Our help is from the Lord, who made heaven and earth.**

I lift up my eyes toward the mountains;
    whence shall help come to me?
My help is from the LORD,
    who made heaven and earth.

R̝. **Our help is from the Lord, who made heaven and earth.**

May he not suffer your foot to slip;
    may he slumber not who guards you:
Indeed he neither slumbers nor sleeps,
    the guardian of Israel.

R̝. **Our help is from the Lord, who made heaven and earth.**

The LORD is your guardian; the LORD is your shade;
    he is beside you at your right hand.
The sun shall not harm you by day,
    nor the moon by night.

R̝. **Our help is from the Lord, who made heaven and earth.**

The LORD will guard you from all evil;
    he will guard your life.
The LORD will guard your coming and your going,
    both now and forever.

R̝. **Our help is from the Lord, who made heaven and earth.**

930 ALLELUIA VERSE AND VERSE BEFORE THE GOSPEL

1.

2 Corinthians 1:3b-4a

**Blessed be the Father of compassion and God of all encouragement,
who encourages us in our every affliction.**

2.

Hebrews 13:14

**For here we have no lasting city,
but we seek the one that is to come.**

931 GOSPEL

First Option

Matthew 2:13-15, 19-23   Take the child and his mother, and flee to Egypt.

☩ **A reading from the holy Gospel according to Matthew**

When the magi had departed, behold,
the angel of the Lord appeared to Joseph in a dream and said,
"Rise, take the child and his mother, flee to Egypt,
and stay there until I tell you.
Herod is going to search for the child to destroy him."
Joseph rose and took the child and his mother by night
and departed for Egypt.
He stayed there until the death of Herod,
that what the Lord had said through the prophet might be fulfilled,
Out of Egypt I called my son.

When Herod had died, behold,
the angel of the Lord appeared in a dream
to Joseph in Egypt and said,
"Rise, take the child and his mother and go to the land of Israel,
for those who sought the child's life are dead."
He rose, took the child and his mother,
and went to the land of Israel.
But when he heard that Archelaus was ruling over Judea
in place of his father Herod,
he was afraid to go back there.
And because he had been warned in a dream,
he departed for the region of Galilee.
He went and dwelt in a town called Nazareth,
so that what had been spoken through the prophets might be fulfilled,
He shall be called a Nazorean.

The Gospel of the Lord.

Second Option

Matthew 25:31-46   Whatever you did for one of the least brothers of mine you did for me.

✠ **A reading from the holy Gospel according to Matthew**

Jesus said to his disciples:
"When the Son of Man comes in his glory,
   and all the angels with him,
   he will sit upon his glorious throne,
   and all the nations will be assembled before him.
And he will separate them one from another,
   as a shepherd separates the sheep from the goats.
He will place the sheep on his right and the goats on his left.
Then the king will say to those on his right,
   'Come, you who are blessed by my Father.
Inherit the kingdom prepared for you from the foundation of the world.
For I was hungry and you gave me food,
   I was thirsty and you gave me drink,
   a stranger and you welcomed me,
   naked and you clothed me,
   ill and you cared for me,
   in prison and you visited me.'
Then the righteous will answer him and say,
   'Lord, when did we see you hungry and feed you,
   or thirsty and give you drink?
When did we see you a stranger and welcome you,
   or naked and clothe you?
When did we see you ill or in prison, and visit you?'
And the king will say to them in reply,
   'Amen, I say to you, whatever you did
   for one of the least brothers of mine, you did for me.'
Then he will say to those on his left,
   'Depart from me, you accursed,
   into the eternal fire prepared for the Devil and his angels.
For I was hungry and you gave me no food,
   I was thirsty and you gave me no drink,
   a stranger and you gave me no welcome,
   naked and you gave me no clothing,
   ill and in prison, and you did not care for me.'

Then they will answer and say,
  'Lord, when did we see you hungry or thirsty
  or a stranger or naked or ill or in prison,
  and not minister to your needs?'
He will answer them, 'Amen, I say to you,
  what you did not do for one of these least ones,
  you did not do for me.'
And these will go off to eternal punishment,
  but the righteous to eternal life."

The Gospel of the Lord.

Third Option

Luke 10:25-37   Who is my neighbor?

✠ **A reading from the holy Gospel according to Luke**

A scholar of the law stood up to test Jesus and said,
  "Teacher, what must I do to inherit eternal life?"
Jesus said to him, "What is written in the law?
How do you read it?"
He said in reply,
  "You shall love the Lord, your God,
  with all your heart,
  with all your being,
  with all your strength,
  and with all your mind,
  and your neighbor as yourself."
He replied to him, "You have answered correctly;
  do this and you will live."

But because he wished to justify himself, he said to Jesus,
  "And who is my neighbor?"
Jesus replied,
  "A man fell victim to robbers
  as he went down from Jerusalem to Jericho.
They stripped and beat him and went off leaving him half-dead.
A priest happened to be going down that road,
  but when he saw him, he passed by on the opposite side.
Likewise a Levite came to the place,
  and when he saw him, he passed by on the opposite side.
But a Samaritan traveler who came upon
  him was moved with compassion at the sight.
He approached the victim,
  poured oil and wine over his wounds and bandaged them.
Then he lifted him up on his own animal,
  took him to an inn, and cared for him.
The next day he took out two silver coins
  and gave them to the innkeeper with the instruction,
  'Take care of him.
If you spend more than what I have given you,
  I shall repay you on my way back.'
Which of these three, in your opinion,
  was neighbor to the robbers' victim?"

He answered, "The one who treated him with mercy."
Jesus said to him, "Go and do likewise."

The Gospel of the Lord.

23. FOR THOSE HELD CAPTIVE

Readings from the Mass for Any Need may also be used, nos. 938–942, with the Gospel.

932 GOSPEL

Matthew 25:31-46   I was in prison and you visited me.

✠ **A reading from the holy Gospel according to Matthew**

Jesus said to his disciples:
"When the Son of Man comes in his glory,
   and all the angels with him,
   he will sit upon his glorious throne,
   and all the nations will be assembled before him.
And he will separate them one from another,
   as a shepherd separates the sheep from the goats.
He will place the sheep on his right and the goats on his left.
Then the king will say to those on his right,
   'Come, you who are blessed by my Father.
Inherit the kingdom prepared for you from the foundation of the world.
For I was hungry and you gave me food,
   I was thirsty and you gave me drink,
   a stranger and you welcomed me,
   naked and you clothed me,
   ill and you cared for me,
   in prison and you visited me.'
Then the righteous will answer him and say,
   'Lord, when did we see you hungry and feed you,
   or thirsty and give you drink?
When did we see you a stranger and welcome you,
   or naked and clothe you?
When did we see you ill or in prison, and visit you?'
And the king will say to them in reply,
   'Amen, I say to you, whatever you did
   for one of the least brothers of mine, you did for me.'
Then he will say to those on his left,
   'Depart from me, you accursed,
   into the eternal fire prepared for the Devil and his angels.
For I was hungry and you gave me no food,
   I was thirsty and you gave me no drink,

a stranger and you gave me no welcome,
naked and you gave me no clothing,
ill and in prison, and you did not care for me.'
Then they will answer and say,
'Lord, when did we see you hungry or thirsty
or a stranger or naked or ill or in prison,
and not minister to your needs?'
He will answer them, 'Amen, I say to you,
what you did not do for one of these least ones,
you did not do for me.'
And these will go off to eternal punishment,
but the righteous to eternal life."

The Gospel of the Lord.

24. FOR THE SICK

For the dying, readings for the Pastoral Care of the Sick and Dying may be used, nos. 790–800.

933 READING FROM THE OLD TESTAMENT

First Option

2 Kings 20:1-6   I have seen your tears, and I will heal you.

A reading from the second Book of Kings

**In those days, when Hezekiah was mortally ill,
the prophet Isaiah, son of Amoz, came and said to him:
"Thus says the Lord: 'Put your house in order,
for you are about to die; you shall not recover.'"
He turned his face to the wall and prayed to the Lord:
"O Lord, remember how faithfully and wholeheartedly
I conducted myself in your presence,
doing what was pleasing to you!"
And Hezekiah wept bitterly.**

**Before Isaiah had left the central courtyard,
the word of the Lord came to him:
"Go back and tell Hezekiah, the leader of my people:
'Thus says the Lord, the God of your forefather David:
I have heard your prayer and seen your tears.
I will heal you.
In three days you shall go up to the Lord's temple;
I will add fifteen years to your life.
I will rescue you and this city from the hand of the king of Assyria;
I will be a shield to this city for my own sake,
and for the sake of my servant David.'"**

The word of the Lord.

Second Option

Isaiah 53:1-5, 10-11   It was our sufferings that he endured.

A reading from the Book of the Prophet Isaiah

Who would believe what we have heard?
 To whom has the arm of the Lord been revealed?
He grew up like a sapling before him,
 like a shoot from the parched earth;
There was in him no stately bearing to make us look at him,
 nor appearance that would attract us to him.
He was spurned and avoided by people,
 a man of suffering, accustomed to infirmity,
One of those from whom people hide their faces,
 spurned, and we held him in no esteem.

Yet it was our infirmities that he bore,
 our sufferings that he endured,
While we thought of him as stricken,
 as one smitten by God and afflicted.
But he was pierced for our offenses,
 crushed for our sins,
Upon him was the chastisement that makes us whole,
 by his stripes we were healed.

But the Lord was pleased
 to crush him in infirmity.
If he gives his life as an offering for sin,
 he shall see his descendants in a long life,
 and the will of the Lord shall be accomplished through him.

Because of his affliction
 he shall see the light in fullness of days;
Through his suffering, my servant shall justify many,
 and their guilt he shall bear.

The word of the Lord.

934   READING FROM THE NEW TESTAMENT

First Option

Acts 28:7-10   The rest of the sick on the island came to Paul and were cured.

A reading from the Acts of the Apostles

**In that place there were lands belonging to a man named Publius,
    the chief of the island [of Malta].
He welcomed us and received us cordially as his guests for three days.
It so happened that the father of Publius was sick
    with a fever and dysentery.
Paul visited him and, after praying,
    laid his hands on him and healed him.
After this had taken place,
    the rest of the sick on the island came to Paul and were cured.
They paid us great honor and when we eventually set sail
    they brought us the provisions we needed.**

The word of the Lord.

Second Option

2 Corinthians 4:10-18   We are constantly being given up to death for the sake of Jesus.

A reading from the second Letter of Saint Paul to the Corinthians

**Brothers and sisters:
We always carry about in the body the dying of Jesus,
    so that the life of Jesus may also be manifested in our body.
For we who live are constantly being given up to death
    for the sake of Jesus,
    so that the life of Jesus may be manifested in our mortal flesh.**

**So death is at work in us, but life in you.
Since, then, we have the same spirit of faith,
    according to what is written, "I believed, therefore I spoke,"
    we too believe and therefore we speak,
    knowing that the one who raised the Lord Jesus
    will raise us also with Jesus and place us with you in his presence.
Everything indeed is for you,
    so that the grace bestowed in abundance on more and more people
    may cause the thanksgiving to overflow for the glory of God.**

Therefore, we are not discouraged;
　　rather, although our outer self is wasting away,
　　our inner self is being renewed day by day.
For this momentary light affliction is producing for us
　　an eternal weight of glory beyond all comparison,
　　as we look not to what is seen but to what is unseen;
　　for what is seen is transitory,
　　but what is unseen is eternal.

The word of the Lord.

Third Option

2 Corinthians 12:7b-10　My grace is sufficient for you; for my power is made perfect in weakness.

A reading from the second Letter of Saint Paul to the Corinthians

Brothers and sisters:
A thorn in the flesh was given to me, an angel of Satan,
　　to beat me, to keep me from being too elated.
Three times I begged the Lord about this, that it might leave me,
　　but the Lord said to me, "My grace is sufficient for you,
　　for power is made perfect in weakness."
I will rather boast most gladly of my weaknesses,
　　in order that the power of Christ may dwell with me.
Therefore, I am content with weaknesses, insults,
　　hardships, persecutions, and constraints,
　　for the sake of Christ;
　　for when I am weak, then I am strong.

The word of the Lord.

Fourth Option

James 5:13-16   The prayer of faith will save the sick.

A reading from the Letter of James

Beloved:
Is anyone among you suffering?
He should pray.
Is anyone in good spirits?
He should sing a song of praise.
Is anyone among you sick?
He should summon the presbyters of the Church,
  and they should pray over him
  and anoint him with oil in the name of the Lord,
  and the prayer of faith will save the sick person,
  and the Lord will raise him up.
If he has committed any sins, he will be forgiven.

Therefore, confess your sins to one another
  and pray for one another, that you may be healed.
The fervent prayer of a righteous person is very powerful.

The word of the Lord.

935 RESPONSORIAL PSALM

1.

Isaiah 38:10, 11, 12abcd, 16

℟. (see 17b) **You saved my life, O Lord; I shall not die.**

Once I said, "In the noontime of life I must depart!
    To the gates of the nether world I shall be consigned
    for the rest of my years."

℟. **You saved my life, O Lord; I shall not die.**

I said, "I shall see the LORD no more
    in the land of the living.
No longer shall I behold my fellow men
    among those who dwell in the world."

℟. **You saved my life, O Lord; I shall not die.**

My dwelling, like a shepherd's tent,
    is struck down and borne away from me;
You have folded up my life, like a weaver
    who severs the last thread.

℟. **You saved my life, O Lord; I shall not die.**

Those live whom the LORD protects;
    yours is the life of my spirit.
You have given me health and life.

℟. **You saved my life, O Lord; I shall not die.**

2.

Psalm 102:2-3, 24-25, 19-21

℟. (2) **O Lord, hear my prayer, and let my cry come to you.**

O Lord, hear my prayer,
  and let my cry come to you.
Hide not your face from me
  in the day of my distress.
Incline your ear to me;
  in the day when I call, answer me speedily.

℟. **O Lord, hear my prayer, and let my cry come to you.**

He has broken down my strength in the way;
  he has cut short my days.
    I say: O my God,
Take me not hence in the midst of my days;
  through all generations for years to come.

℟. **O Lord, hear my prayer, and let my cry come to you.**

Let this be written for the generation to come,
  and let his future creatures praise the Lord:
"The Lord looked down from his holy height,
  from heaven he beheld the earth,
To hear the groaning of the prisoners,
  to release those doomed to die."

℟. **O Lord, hear my prayer, and let my cry come to you.**

936 ALLELUIA VERSE AND VERSE BEFORE THE GOSPEL

1.

Matthew 8:17

**Christ took away our infirmities,
and bore our diseases.**

2.

2 Corinthians 1:3b-4a

**Blessed be the Father of compassion and God of all encouragement,
who encourages us in our every affliction.**

3.

Colossians 1:24

**In my flesh I am filling up what is lacking in the afflictions of Christ
on behalf of his Body, which is the Church.**

937 GOSPEL

First Option

Matthew 8:14-17   Christ bore our diseases.

☩ **A reading from the holy Gospel according to Matthew**

Jesus entered the house of Peter,
and saw Peter's mother-in-law lying in bed with a fever.
Jesus touched her hand, the fever left her,
and she rose and waited on him.

When it was evening, people brought Jesus many
who were possessed by demons,
and he drove out the spirits by a word and cured all the sick,
to fulfill what had been said by Isaiah the prophet:

> *He took away our infirmities*
> *and bore our diseases.*

The Gospel of the Lord.

Second Option

Mark 16:15-20   They will lay hands on the sick and they will recover.

☩ **A reading from the holy Gospel according to Mark**

Jesus appeared to the Eleven and said to them:
"Go into the whole world
  and proclaim the Gospel to every creature.
Whoever believes and is baptized will be saved;
  whoever does not believe will be condemned.
These signs will accompany those who believe:
  in my name they will drive out demons,
  they will speak new languages.
They will pick up serpents with their hands,
  and if they drink any deadly thing, it will not harm them.
They will lay hands on the sick, and they will recover."

Then the Lord Jesus, after he spoke to them,
  was taken up into heaven
  and took his seat at the right hand of God.
But they went forth and preached everywhere,
  while the Lord worked with them
  and confirmed the word through accompanying signs.

The Gospel of the Lord.

Third Option

Luke 22:39-43   Father, not my will but yours be done.

☩ **A reading from the holy Gospel according to Luke**

Jesus went, as was his custom, to the Mount of Olives,
  and the disciples followed him.
When he arrived at the place he said to them,
  "Pray that you may not undergo the test."
After withdrawing about a stone's throw from them and kneeling,
  he prayed, saying, "Father, if you are willing,
    take this cup away from me;
  still, not my will but yours be done."
And to strengthen him an angel from heaven appeared to him.

The Gospel of the Lord.

Fourth Option

John 15:1-8   Every branch that bears fruit he prunes so that it bears more fruit.

✢ **A reading from the holy Gospel according to John**

Jesus said to his disciples:
"I am the true vine, and my Father is the vine grower.
He takes away every branch in me that does not bear fruit,
   and everyone that does he prunes so that it bears more fruit.
You are already pruned because of the word that I spoke to you.
Remain in me, as I remain in you.
Just as a branch cannot bear fruit on its own
   unless it remains on the vine,
   so neither can you unless you remain in me.
I am the vine, you are the branches.
Whoever remains in me and I in him will bear much fruit,
   because without me you can do nothing.
Anyone who does not remain in me
   will be thrown out like a branch and wither;
   people will gather them and throw them into a fire
   and they will be burned.
If you remain in me and my words remain in you,
   ask for whatever you want and it will be done for you.
By this is my Father glorified,
   that you bear much fruit and become my disciples."

The Gospel of the Lord.

25. IN TIME OF EARTHQUAKE OR FOR RAIN OR FOR GOOD WEATHER OR TO AVERT STORMS OR FOR ANY NEED

938 READING FROM THE OLD TESTAMENT

First Option

Esther C:1-4, 8-10   Turn our sorrow into joy.

A reading from the Book of Esther

Mordecai prayed to the LORD and said:
"O God of Abraham, God of Isaac and God of Jacob,
  O Lord God, almighty King, all things are in your power,
  and there is no one to oppose you in your will to save Israel.
You made heaven and earth
  and every wonderful thing under the heavens.
You are LORD of all,
  and there is no one to resist you, LORD.
And now, LORD God, King,
  God of Abraham, God of Isaac and God of Jacob,
  spare your people,
  for our enemies plan our ruin
  and are bent upon destroying your inheritance
Do not spurn your portion,
  which you redeemed for yourself out of Egypt.
Hear my prayer; have pity on your inheritance
  and turn our sorrow into joy:
  thus we shall live to sing praise to your name, O LORD.
Do not silence those who praise you."

The word of the Lord.

Second Option

Lamentations 3:17-26   It is good to hope in silence for the saving help of
the Lord.

A reading from the Book of Lamentations

My soul is deprived of peace,
** I have forgotten what happiness is;**
I tell myself my future is lost,
** all that I hoped for from the LORD.**
The thought of my homeless poverty
** is wormwood and gall;**
Remembering it over and over
** leaves my soul downcast within me.**
But I will call this to mind,
** as my reason to have hope:**

The favors of the LORD are not exhausted,
** his mercies are not spent;**
They are renewed each morning,
** so great is his faithfulness.**
My portion is the LORD, says my soul;
** therefore will I hope in him.**

Good is the LORD to one who waits for him,
** to the soul that seeks him;**
It is good to hope in silence
** for the saving help of the LORD.**

The word of the Lord.

Third Option

Daniel 3:25, 34-43   Deliver us by your wonders.

A reading from the Book of the Prophet Daniel

**Azariah stood up in the fire and prayed aloud:
"For your name's sake, O Lord, do not deliver us up forever,
    or make void your covenant.
Do not take away your mercy from us,
    for the sake of Abraham, your beloved,
    Isaac your servant, and Israel your holy one,
To whom you promised to multiply their offspring
    like the stars of heaven,
    or the sand on the shore of the sea.
For we are reduced, O Lord, beyond any other nation,
    brought low everywhere in the world this day
    because of our sins.
We have in our day no prince, prophet, or leader,
    no burnt offering, sacrifice, oblation, or incense,
    no place to offer firstfruits, to find favor with you.
But with contrite heart and humble spirit
    let us be received;
As though it were burnt offerings of rams and bullocks,
    or thousands of fat lambs,
So let our sacrifice be in your presence today
    as we follow you unreservedly;
    for those who trust in you cannot be put to shame.
And now we follow you with our whole heart,
    we fear you and we pray to you.
Do not let us be put to shame,
    but deal with us in your kindness and great mercy.
Deliver us by your wonders,
    and bring glory to your name, O Lord."**

The word of the Lord.

939 READING FROM THE NEW TESTAMENT

First Option

Romans 8:18-30   All things work for good for those who love God.

A reading from the Letter of Saint Paul to the Romans

Brothers and sisters:
I consider that the sufferings of this present time are as nothing
    compared with the glory to be revealed for us.
For creation awaits with eager expectation
    the revelation of the children of God;
    for creation was made subject to futility,
    not of its own accord but because of the one who subjected it,
    in hope that creation itself
    would be set free from slavery to corruption
    and share in the glorious freedom of the children of God.
We know that all creation is groaning in labor pains even until now;
    and not only that, but we ourselves,
    who have the firstfruits of the Spirit,
    we also groan within ourselves
    as we wait for adoption, the redemption of our bodies.
For in hope we were saved.
Now hope that sees is not hope.
For who hopes for what one sees?
But if we hope for what we do not see, we wait with endurance.

In the same way, the Spirit too comes to the aid of our weakness;
    for we do not know how to pray as we ought,
    but the Spirit himself intercedes with inexpressible groanings.
And the one who searches hearts
    knows what is the intention of the Spirit,
    because he intercedes for the holy ones
    according to God's will.

We know that all things work for good for those who love God,
    who are called according to his purpose.
For those he foreknew he also predestined
    to be conformed to the image of his Son,
    so that he might be the firstborn
    among many brothers.

And those he predestined he also called;
  and those he called he also justified;
  and those he justified he also glorified.

The word of the Lord.

Second Option

Romans 8:31b-39   Neither death nor life will be able to separate us from the love of God.

A reading from the Letter of Saint Paul to the Romans

Brothers and sisters:
If God is for us, who can be against us?
He did not spare his own Son
  but handed him over for us all,
  will he not also give us everything else along with him?
Who will bring a charge against God's chosen ones?
It is God who acquits us.
Who will condemn?
It is Christ Jesus who died, rather, was raised,
  who also is at the right hand of God,
  who indeed intercedes for us.
What will separate us from the love of Christ?
Will anguish, or distress, or persecution, or famine,
  or nakedness, or peril, or the sword?
As it is written:
  For your sake we are being slain all the day;
    we are looked upon as sheep to be slaughtered.
No, in all these things we conquer overwhelmingly
  through him who loved us.
For I am convinced that neither death, nor life,
  nor angels, nor principalities,
  nor present things, nor future things,
  nor powers, nor height, nor depth,
  nor any other creature will be able to separate us
  from the love of God in Christ Jesus our Lord.

The word of the Lord.

Third Option

James 1:2-4, 12   Blessed is the man who perseveres in temptation.

A reading from the Letter of James

Consider it all joy, my brothers and sisters,
 when you encounter various trials,
 for you know that the testing of your faith produces perseverance.
And let perseverance be perfect,
 so that you may be perfect and complete, lacking in nothing.

Blessed is the man who perseveres in temptation,
 for when he has been proved he will receive the crown of life
 that he promised to those who love him.

The word of the Lord.

Fourth Option

Revelation 21:1-5a, 6b-7   There shall be no more death or mourning, wailing or pain.

A reading from the Book of Revelation

I, John, saw a new heaven and a new earth.
The former heaven and the former earth had passed away,
    and the sea was no more.
I also saw the holy city, a new Jerusalem,
    coming down out of heaven from God,
      prepared as a bride adorned for her husband.
I heard a loud voice from the throne saying,
    "Behold, God's dwelling is with the human race.
He will dwell with them and they will be his people
    and God himself will always be with them as their God.
He will wipe every tear from their eyes,
    and there shall be no more death or mourning, wailing or pain,
    for the old order has passed away."

The One who sat on the throne said,
    "Behold, I make all things new.
I am the Alpha and the Omega,
    the beginning and the end.
To the thirsty I will give a gift
    from the spring of life-giving water.
The victor will inherit these gifts,
    and I shall be his God,
    and he will be my son."

The word of the Lord.

940 RESPONSORIAL PSALM

1.

Psalm 80:2ac and 3b, 5-7

R⁷. (4b) **Let us see your face, Lord, and we shall be saved.**

O shepherd of Israel, hearken,
From your throne upon the cherubim, shine forth.
Rouse your power.

R⁷. **Let us see your face, Lord, and we shall be saved.**

O LORD of hosts, how long will you burn with anger
    while your people pray?
You have fed them with the bread of tears
    and given them tears to drink in ample measure.
You have left us to be fought over by our neighbors,
    and our enemies mock us.

R⁷. **Let us see your face, Lord, and we shall be saved.**

2.

Psalm 85:2-4, 5-6, 7-8

R⁷. (8) **Lord, show us your mercy and love, and grant us your salvation.**

You have favored, O LORD, your land;
    you have brought back the captives of Jacob.
You have forgiven the guilt of your people;
    you have covered all their sins.
You have withdrawn all your wrath;
    you have revoked your burning anger.

R⁷. **Lord, show us your mercy and love, and grant us your salvation.**

Restore us, O God our savior,
    and abandon your displeasure against us.
Will you be ever angry with us,
    prolonging your anger to all generations?

℟. **Lord, show us your mercy and love, and grant us your salvation.**

Will you not instead give us life;
    and shall not your people rejoice in you?
Show us, O LORD, your kindness,
    and grant us your salvation.

℟. **Lord, show us your mercy and love, and grant us your salvation.**

   3.

Psalm 123:1-2ab, 2cdef

℟. (3a) **Have mercy on us, Lord, have mercy.**
    or:
℟. (2ef) **Our eyes are fixed on the Lord, pleading for his mercy.**

To you I lift up my eyes
    who are enthroned in heaven.
Behold, as the eyes of servants
    are on the hands of their masters.

℟. **Have mercy on us, Lord, have mercy.**
    or:
℟. **Our eyes are fixed on the Lord, pleading for his mercy.**

As the eyes of a maid
    are on the hands of her mistress,
So are our eyes on the LORD, our God,
    till he have pity on us.

℟. **Have mercy on us, Lord, have mercy.**
    or:
℟. **Our eyes are fixed on the Lord, pleading for his mercy.**

941 ALLELUIA VERSE AND VERSE BEFORE THE GOSPEL

1.

Psalm 33:22

**May your kindness, O Lord, be upon us,
who have put our hope in you.**

2.

2 Corinthians 1:3b-4a

**Blessed be the Father of compassion and God of all encouragement,
who encourages us in our every affliction.**

3.

James 1:12

**Blessed is the man who perseveres in temptation,
for when he has been proved he will receive the crown of life.**

942 GOSPEL

First Option

Matthew 7:7-11 Everyone who asks, receives.

✠ **A reading from the holy Gospel according to Matthew**

Jesus said to his disciples:
"Ask and it will be given to you; seek and you will find;
  knock and the door will be opened to you.
For everyone who asks, receives; and the one who seeks, finds;
  and to the one who knocks, the door will be opened.
Which one of you would hand his son a stone
  when he asks for a loaf of bread,
  or a snake when he asks for a fish?
If you then, who are wicked,
  know how to give good gifts to your children,
  how much more will your heavenly Father give good things
  to those who ask him."

The Gospel of the Lord.

Second Option

Mark 4:35-41   Who then is this whom even wind and sea obey?

✠ **A reading from the holy Gospel according to Mark**

One day, as evening drew on, Jesus said to his disciples:
"Let us cross to the other side."
Leaving the crowd, they took Jesus with them in the boat just as he was.
And other boats were with him.
A violent squall came up and waves were breaking over the boat,
   so that it was already filling up.
Jesus was in the stern, asleep on a cushion.
They woke Jesus and said to him,
   "Teacher, do you not care that we are perishing?"
He woke up,
   rebuked the wind, and said to the sea, "Quiet! Be still!"
The wind ceased and there was great calm.
Then he asked them, "Why are you terrified?
Do you not yet have faith?"
They were filled with great awe and said to one another,
   "Who then is this whom even wind and sea obey?"

The Gospel of the Lord.

Third Option

Luke 18:1-8   God will secure the rights of his chosen ones who call out to him day and night.

✠ **A reading from the holy Gospel according to Luke**

Jesus told his disciples a parable
  about the necessity for them to pray always without becoming weary.
He said, "There was a judge in a certain town
  who neither feared God nor respected any human being.
And a widow in that town used to come to him and say,
  'Render a just decision for me against my adversary.'
For a long time the judge was unwilling, but eventually he thought,
  'While it is true that I neither fear God nor respect any human being,
  because this widow keeps bothering me
  I shall deliver a just decision for her
  lest she finally come and strike me.'"
The Lord said, "Pay attention to what the dishonest judge says.
Will not God then secure the rights of his chosen ones
  who call out to him day and night?
Will he be slow to answer them?
I tell you, he will see to it that justice is done for them speedily.
But when the Son of Man comes, will he find faith on earth?"

The Gospel of the Lord.

26. IN THANKSGIVING TO GOD

943 READING FROM THE OLD TESTAMENT

First Option

1 Kings 8:55-61   Blessed is the LORD God who has granted rest to his people.

A reading from the first Book of Kings

King Solomon stood and blessed the whole congregation of Israel,
     saying in a loud voice:
     "Blessed be the LORD who has given rest to his people Israel,
     just as he promised.
Not a single word has gone unfulfilled
     of the entire generous promise he made through his servant Moses.
May the LORD, our God, be with us as he was with our fathers
     and may he not forsake us nor cast us off.
May he draw our hearts to himself,
     that we may follow him in everything
     and keep the commands, statutes, and ordinances
     which he enjoined on our fathers.
May this prayer I have offered to the LORD, our God,
     be present to him day and night,
     that he may uphold the cause of his servant and of his people Israel
     as each day requires,
     that all the peoples of the earth may know the LORD is God
     and there is no other.
You must be wholly devoted to the LORD, our God,
     observing his statutes and keeping his commandments, as on this day."

The word of the Lord.

Second Option

Sirach 50:22-24   God has done wondrous things on earth.

A reading from the Book of Sirach

And now, bless the God of all,
  who has done wondrous things on earth;
Who fosters people's growth from their mother's womb,
  and fashions them according to his will!
May he grant you joy of heart
  and may peace abide among you;
May his goodness toward us endure in Israel
  to deliver us in our days.

The word of the Lord.

Third Option

Isaiah 63:7-9   The favors of the Lord I will recall, for he is good to the house of Israel.

A reading from the Book of the Prophet Isaiah

The favors of the Lord I will recall,
  the glorious deeds of the Lord,
Because of all he has done for us;
  for he is good to the house of Israel,
He has favored us according to his mercy
  and his great kindness.
The Lord said: They are indeed my people,
  children who are not disloyal;
So he became their savior
  in their every affliction.
It was not a messenger or an angel,
  but he himself who saved them.
Because of his love and pity
  he himself redeemed them,
Lifting them and carrying them
  all the days of old.

The word of the Lord.

Fourth Option

Zephaniah 3:14-15   The King of Israel, the Lord is in your midst.

A reading from the Book of the Prophet Zephaniah

Shout for joy, O daughter Zion!
  Sing joyfully, O Israel!
Be glad and exult with all your heart,
  O daughter Jerusalem!
The LORD has removed the judgment against you
  and turned away your enemies;
The King of Israel, the LORD, is in your midst,
  you have no further misfortune to fear.

The word of the Lord.

944 READING FROM THE NEW TESTAMENT

First Option

1 Corinthians 1:3-9   I give thanks to my God always on your account.

A reading from the first Letter of Saint Paul to the Corinthians

Brothers and sisters:
Grace to you and peace from God our Father
  and the Lord Jesus Christ.

I give thanks to my God always on your account
  for the grace of God bestowed on you in Christ Jesus,
  that in him you were enriched in every way,
  with all discourse and all knowledge,
  as the testimony to Christ was confirmed among you,
  so that you are not lacking in any spiritual gift
  as you wait for the revelation of our Lord Jesus Christ.
He will keep you firm to the end,
  irreproachable on the day of our Lord Jesus Christ.
God is faithful,
  and by him you were called to fellowship with his Son, Jesus Christ
    our Lord.

The word of the Lord.

Second Option

Ephesians 1:3-14   For the praise of the glory of his grace.

A reading from the Letter of Saint Paul to the Ephesians

Blessed be the God and Father of our Lord Jesus Christ,
   who has blessed us in Christ
   with every spiritual blessing in the heavens,
   as he chose us in him, before the foundation of the world,
   to be holy and without blemish before him.
In love he destined us for adoption to himself through Jesus Christ,
   in accord with the favor of his will,
   for the praise of the glory of his grace
   that he granted us in the beloved.

In him we have redemption by his Blood,
   the forgiveness of transgressions,
   in accord with the riches of his grace that he lavished upon us.
In all wisdom and insight, he has made known to us
   the mystery of his will in accord with his favor
   that he set forth in him as a plan for the fullness of times,
   to sum up all things in Christ, in heaven and on earth.

In him we were also chosen,
   destined in accord with the purpose of the One
   who accomplishes all things according to the intention of his will,
   so that we might exist for the praise of his glory,
   we who first hoped in Christ.
In him you also, who have heard the word of truth,
   the Gospel of your salvation, and have believed in him,
   were sealed with the promised Holy Spirit,
   which is the first installment of our inheritance
   toward redemption as his possession, to the praise of his glory.

The word of the Lord.

Third Option

Colossians 3:12-17   Give thanks to God the Father through Christ.

A reading from the Letter of Saint Paul to the Colossians

Brothers and sisters:
Put on, as God's chosen ones, holy and beloved,
    heartfelt compassion, kindness, humility, gentleness, and patience,
    bearing with one another and forgiving one another,
    if one has a grievance against another;
    as the Lord has forgiven you, so must you also do.
And over all these put on love,
    that is, the bond of perfection.
And let the peace of Christ control your hearts,
    the peace into which you were also called in one Body.
And be thankful.
Let the word of Christ dwell in you richly,
    as in all wisdom you teach and admonish one another,
    singing psalms, hymns, and spiritual songs
    with gratitude in your hearts to God.
And whatever you do, in word or in deed,
    do everything in the name of the Lord Jesus,
    giving thanks to God the Father through him.

The word of the Lord.

945 RESPONSORIAL PSALM

1.

1 Chronicles 29:10bc, 11, 12

℞. (13b) **We praise your glorious name, O mighty God.**

"Blessed may you be, O LORD,
  God of Israel our father,
  from eternity to eternity."

℞. **We praise your glorious name, O mighty God.**

"Yours, O LORD, are grandeur and power,
  majesty, splendor, and glory.
For all in heaven and on earth is yours;
  yours, O LORD, is the sovereignty;
  you are exalted as head over all."

℞. **We praise your glorious name, O mighty God.**

"Riches and honor are from you,
  and you have dominion over all.
In your hand are power and might;
  it is yours to give grandeur and strength to all."

℞. **We praise your glorious name, O mighty God.**

2.

Psalm 113:1-2, 3-4, 5-6, 7-8

℞. (see 2) **Blessed be the name of the Lord for ever.**
  or:
℞. **Alleluia.**

Praise, you servants of the LORD,
  praise the name of the LORD.
Blessed be the name of the LORD
  both now and forever.

℞. **Blessed be the name of the Lord for ever.**
  or:
℞. **Alleluia.**

From the rising to the setting of the sun
  is the name of the LORD to be praised.
High above all nations is the Lord;
  above the heavens is his glory.

℟. **Blessed be the name of the Lord for ever.**
  or:
℟. **Alleluia.**

Who is like the LORD, our God, who is enthroned on high
  and looks upon the heavens and the earth below?

℟. **Blessed be the name of the Lord for ever.**
  or:
℟. **Alleluia.**

He raises up the lowly from the dust;
  from the dunghill he lifts up the poor.
To seat them with princes,
  with the princes of his own people.

℟. **Blessed be the name of the Lord for ever.**
  or:
℟. **Alleluia.**

  3.

Psalm 138:1-2a, 2bc-3, 4-5

℟. (2bc) **Lord, I thank you for your faithfulness and love.**

I will give thanks to you, O LORD, with all of my heart,
  for you have heard the words of my mouth;
  in the presence of the angels I will sing your praise;
I will worship at your holy temple.

℟. **Lord, I thank you for your faithfulness and love.**

I will give thanks to your name,
Because of your kindness and your truth.
When I called, you answered me;
  you built up strength within me.

℟. **Lord, I thank you for your faithfulness and love.**

(cont.)

All the kings of the earth shall give thanks to you, O Lᴏʀᴅ,
  when they hear the words of your mouth;
And they shall sing of the ways of the Lᴏʀᴅ:
  "Great is the glory of the Lᴏʀᴅ."

R̷. Lord, I thank you for your faithfulness and love.

4.

Psalm 145:2-3, 4-5, 6-7, 8-9, 10-11

R̷. (see 1) I will praise your name for ever, Lord.

Every day will I bless you,
  and I will praise your name forever and ever.
Great is the Lᴏʀᴅ and highly to be praised;
  his greatness is unsearchable.

R̷. I will praise your name for ever, Lord.

Generation after generation praises your works
  and proclaims your might.
They speak of the splendor of your glorious majesty
  and tell of your wondrous works.

R̷. I will praise your name for ever, Lord.

They discourse of the power of your terrible deeds
  and declare your greatness.
They publish the fame of your abundant goodness
  and joyfully sing of your justice.

R̷. I will praise your name for ever, Lord.

The Lᴏʀᴅ is gracious and merciful,
  slow to anger and of great kindness.
The Lᴏʀᴅ is good to all
  and compassionate toward all his works.

R̷. I will praise your name for ever, Lord.

Let all your works give you thanks, O Lᴏʀᴅ,
  and let your faithful ones bless you.
Let them discourse of the glory of your Kingdom
  and speak of your might.

R̷. I will praise your name for ever, Lord.

946 ALLELUIA VERSE AND VERSE BEFORE THE GOSPEL

1.

Psalm 66:16

**Hear now, all you who fear God,
while I declare what he has done for me.**

2.

Psalm 138:1bc

**I will give thanks to you, O LORD, with all my heart,
for you have heard the words of my mouth.**

3.

See Matthew 11:25

**Blessed are you, Father, Lord of heaven and earth;
you have revealed to little ones the mysteries of the Kingdom.**

4.

Luke 1:49

**The Mighty One has done great things for me,
and holy is his Name.**

5.

John 15:11

**I have told you this, says the Lord,
that my joy might be in you,
and that your joy might be complete.**

6.

Ephesians 1:3

**Blessed be the God and Father of our Lord Jesus Christ,
who has blessed us in Christ with every spiritual blessing.**

7.

1 Thessalonians 5:18

**In all circumstances, give thanks,
for this is the will of God for you in Christ Jesus.**

8.

See *Te Deum*

**We praise you, O God,
we acclaim you as Lord;
throughout the world the holy Church acclaims you.**

947 GOSPEL

1.

Matthew 7:7-11   Anyone who asks, receives.

✠ **A reading from the holy Gospel according to Matthew**

Jesus said to his disciples:
"Ask and it will be given to you; seek and you will find;
  knock and the door will be opened to you.
For everyone who asks, receives; and the one who seeks, finds;
  and to the one who knocks, the door will be opened.
Which one of you would hand his son a stone
  when he asks for a loaf of bread,
  or a snake when he asks for a fish?
If you then, who are wicked, know how to give good gifts to your children,
  how much more will your heavenly Father give good things
  to those who ask him."

The Gospel of the Lord.

2.

Matthew 11:25-30   You have hidden these things from the wise and the learned, you have revealed them to little ones.

✠ **A reading from the holy Gospel according to Matthew**

At that time Jesus answered:
"I give praise to you, Father, Lord of heaven and earth,
    for although you have hidden these things
    from the wise and the learned
    you have revealed them to little ones.
Yes, Father, such has been your gracious will.
All things have been handed over to me by my Father.
No one knows the Son except the Father,
    and no one knows the Father except the Son
    and anyone to whom the Son wishes to reveal him.

"Come to me, all you who labor and are burdened,
    and I will give you rest.
Take my yoke upon you and learn from me,
    for I am meek and humble of heart;
    and you will find rest for yourselves.
For my yoke is easy, and my burden light."

The Gospel of the Lord.

3.

Mark 5:18-20   Announce all that the Lord has done for you.

✝ **A reading from the holy Gospel according to Mark**

As Jesus was getting into the boat,
  the man who had been possessed pleaded to remain with him.
But he would not permit him but told him instead,
  "Go home to your family and announce to them
  all that the Lord in his pity has done for you."
Then the man went off and began to proclaim in the Decapolis
  what Jesus had done for him;
  and all were amazed.

The Gospel of the Lord.

4.

Luke 1:39-55   My soul proclaims the greatness of the Lord.

☩ **A reading from the holy Gospel according to Luke**

Mary set out
 and traveled to the hill country in haste
 to a town of Judah,
 where she entered the house of Zechariah
 and greeted Elizabeth.
When Elizabeth heard Mary's greeting,
 the infant leaped in her womb,
 and Elizabeth, filled with the Holy Spirit,
 cried out in a loud voice and said,
 "Blessed are you among women,
 and blessed is the fruit of your womb.
And how does this happen to me,
 that the mother of my Lord should come to me?
For at the moment the sound of your greeting reached my ears,
 the infant in my womb leaped for joy.
Blessed are you who believed
 that what was spoken to you by the Lord
 would be fulfilled."

And Mary said:

 "My soul proclaims the greatness of the Lord;
  my spirit rejoices in God my savior,
  for he has looked upon his lowly servant.

 From this day all generations will call me blessed:
  the Almighty has done great things for me,
  and holy is his Name.

 He has mercy on those who fear him
  in every generation.

 He has shown the strength of his arm,
  and has scattered the proud in their conceit.

 He has cast down the mighty from their thrones
  and has lifted up the lowly.

 He has filled the hungry with good things,
  and the rich he has sent away empty.

He has come to the help of his servant Israel
  for he remembered his promise of mercy,
  the promise he made to our fathers,
  to Abraham and his children for ever."

The Gospel of the Lord.

5.

Luke 10:17-24   Rejoice because your names are written in heaven.

✝ **A reading from the holy Gospel according to Luke**

The seventy-two returned rejoicing and said to Jesus,
  "Lord, even the demons are subject to us because of your name."
Jesus said, "I have observed Satan fall like lightning from the sky.
Behold, I have given you the power
  'to tread upon serpents' and scorpions
  and upon the full force of the enemy
  and nothing will harm you.
Nevertheless, do not rejoice because the spirits are subject to you,
  but rejoice because your names are written in heaven."

At that very moment he rejoiced in the Holy Spirit and said,
  "I give you praise, Father, Lord of heaven and earth,
  for although you have hidden these things
  from the wise and the learned
  you have revealed them to the childlike.
Yes, Father, such has been your gracious will.
All things have been handed over to me by my Father.
No one knows who the Son is except the Father,
  and who the Father is except the Son
  and anyone to whom the Son wishes to reveal him."

Turning to the disciples in private he said,
  "Blessed are the eyes that see what you see.
For I say to you,
  many prophets and kings desired to see what you see,
  but did not see it,
  and to hear what you hear, but did not hear it."

The Gospel of the Lord.

6.

Luke 17:11-19   He fell at the feet of Jesus and thanked him.

✠ **A reading from the holy Gospel according to Luke**

As Jesus continued his journey to Jerusalem,
  he traveled through Samaria and Galilee.
As he was entering a village, ten persons with leprosy met him.
They stood at a distance from him and raised their voices, saying,
  "Jesus, Master! Have pity on us!"
And when he saw them, he said,
  "Go show yourselves to the priests."
As they were going they were cleansed.
And one of them, realizing he had been healed,
  returned, glorifying God in a loud voice;
  and he fell at the feet of Jesus and thanked him.
He was a Samaritan.
Jesus said in reply,
  "Ten were cleansed, were they not?
Where are the other nine?
Has none but this foreigner returned to give thanks to God?"
Then he said to him, "Stand up and go;
  your faith has saved you."

The Gospel of the Lord.

7.

John 15:9-17   This I command you: love one another.

✠ **A reading from the holy Gospel according to John**

Jesus said to his disciples:
"As the Father loves me, so I also love you.
Remain in my love.
If you keep my commandments, you will remain in my love,
  just as I have kept my Father's commandments
  and remain in his love.

"I have told you this so that my joy may be in you
  and your joy may be complete.
This is my commandment: love one another as I love you.
No one has greater love than this,
  to lay down one's life for one's friends.

You are my friends if you do what I command you.
I no longer call you slaves,
   because a slave does not know what his master is doing.
I have called you friends,
   because I have told you everything I have heard from my Father.
It was not you who chose me, but I who chose you
   and appointed you to go and bear fruit that will remain,
   so that whatever you ask the Father in my name he may give you.
This I command you: love one another."

The Gospel of the Lord.

8.

John 16:20-22   No one will take your joy away from you.

✠ **A reading from the holy Gospel according to John**

Jesus said to his disciples:
"Amen, amen, I say to you, you will weep and mourn,
   while the world rejoices;
   you will grieve, but your grief will become joy.
When a woman is in labor, she is in anguish
   because her hour has arrived;
   but when she has given birth to a child,
   she no longer remembers the pain because of her joy
   that a child has been born into the world.
So you also are now in anguish.
But I will see you again, and your hearts will rejoice,
   and no one will take your joy away from you."

The Gospel of the Lord.

IV. FOR VARIOUS NEEDS

27. FOR THE REMISSION OF SINS

948 READING FROM THE OLD TESTAMENT

First Option

Isaiah 55:6-9   Let him turn to the Lord who is generous in forgiving.

A reading from the Book of the Prophet Isaiah

**Seek the Lord while he may be found,
   call him while he is near.
Let the scoundrel forsake his ways
   and the wicked his thoughts;
Let him turn to the Lord for mercy;
   to our God, who is generous in forgiving.
For my thoughts are not your thoughts,
   nor are your ways my ways, says the Lord.
As high as the heavens are above the earth,
   so high are my ways above your ways
   and my thoughts above your thoughts.**

The word of the Lord.

Second Option

Ezekiel 18:21-23, 30-32   Turn and be converted from all your crimes.

A reading from the Book of the Prophet Ezekiel

Thus says the LORD:
If the wicked man turns away from all the sins he has committed,
  if he keeps all my statutes and does what is right and just,
  he shall surely live, he shall not die.
None of the crimes he committed shall be remembered against him;
  he shall live because of the virtue he has practiced.
Do I indeed derive any pleasure from the death of the wicked?
  says the Lord GOD.
Do I not rather rejoice when he turns from his evil way
  that he may live?

Therefore I will judge you, house of Israel,
  each one according to his ways, says the Lord GOD.
Turn and be converted from all your crimes,
  that there may be no cause of guilt for you.
Cast away from you all the crimes you have committed,
  and make for yourselves a new heart and a new spirit.
Why should you die, O house of Israel?
For I have no pleasure in the death of anyone who dies,
  says the Lord GOD.
Return and live!

The word of the Lord.

Third Option

Joel 2:12-18   Rend your hearts, not your garments.

A reading from the Book of the Prophet Joel

Even now, says the LORD,
   return to me with your whole heart,
   with fasting, and weeping, and mourning;
Rend your hearts, not your garments,
   and return to the LORD your God.
For gracious and merciful is he,
   slow to anger, rich in kindness,
   and relenting in punishment.
Perhaps he will again relent
   and leave behind him a blessing,
Offerings and libations
   for the LORD, your God.

Blow the trumpet in Zion!
   proclaim a fast,
   call an assembly;
Gather the people,
   notify the congregation;
Assemble the elders,
   gather the children
   and the infants at the breast;
Let the bridegroom quit his room,
   and the bride her chamber.
Between the porch and the altar
   let the priests, the ministers of the LORD, weep,
And say, "Spare, O LORD, your people,
   and make not your heritage a reproach,
   with the nations ruling over them!
Why should they say among the peoples,
   'Where is their God?'"

Then the LORD was stirred to concern for his land
   and took pity on his people.

The word of the Lord.

Fourth Option

Jonah 3:1-10   The Ninevites turned from their evil ways.

A reading from the Book of the Prophet Jonah

The word of the LORD came to Jonah a second time:
"Set out for the great city of Nineveh,
   and announce to it the message that I will tell you."
So Jonah made ready and went to Nineveh,
   according to the LORD's bidding.
Now Nineveh was an enormously large city;
   it took three days to go through it.
Jonah began his journey through the city,
   and had gone but a single day's walk announcing,
   "Forty days more and Nineveh shall be destroyed,"
   when the people of Nineveh believed God;
   they proclaimed a fast
   and all of them, great and small,
   put on sackcloth.

When the news reached the king of Nineveh,
   he rose from his throne, laid aside his robe,
   covered himself with sackcloth, and sat in the ashes.
Then he had this proclaimed throughout Nineveh,
   by decree of the king and his nobles:
   "Neither man nor beast, neither cattle nor sheep,
   shall taste anything;
   they shall not eat, nor shall they drink water.
Man and beast shall be covered with sackcloth
   and call loudly to God;
   every man shall turn from his evil way
   and from the violence he has in hand.
Who knows, God may relent and forgive,
   and withhold his blazing wrath,
   so that we shall not perish."
When God saw by their actions how they turned from their evil way,
   he repented of the evil that he had threatened to do to them;
   he did not carry it out.

The word of the Lord.

949 READING FROM THE NEW TESTAMENT

First Option

Romans 6:2-14   Consequently, you too must think of yourselves as being dead to sin and living for God.

A reading from the Letter of Saint Paul to the Romans

Brothers and sisters:
How can we who died to sin yet live in it?
Are you unaware that we who were baptized into Christ Jesus
  were baptized into his death?
We were indeed buried with him through baptism into death,
  so that, just as Christ was raised from the dead
  by the glory of the Father,
  we too might live in newness of life.

For if we have grown into union with him through a death like his,
  we shall also be united with him in the resurrection.
We know that our old self was crucified with him,
  so that our sinful body might be done away with,
  that we might no longer be in slavery to sin.
For a dead person has been absolved from sin.
If, then, we have died with Christ,
  we believe that we shall also live with him.
We know that Christ, raised from the dead, dies no more;
  death no longer has power over him.
As to his death, he died to sin once and for all;
  as to his life, he lives for God.
Consequently, you too must think of yourselves as being dead to sin
  and living for God in Christ Jesus.

Therefore, sin must not reign over your mortal bodies
  so that you obey their desires.
And do not present the parts of your bodies to sin
  as weapons for wickedness,
    but present yourselves to God as raised from the dead to life
    and the parts of your bodies to God as weapons for righteousness.
For sin is not to have any power over you,
  since you are not under the law but under grace.

The word of the Lord.

Second Option

1 John 1:5–2:2   The Blood of Jesus Christ cleanses us from all sin.

A reading from the first Letter of Saint John

Beloved:
This is the message that we have heard from Jesus Christ
    and proclaim to you: God is light,
    and in him there is no darkness at all.
If we say, "We have fellowship with God,"
    while we continue to walk in darkness,
    we lie and do not act in truth.
But if we walk in the light as he is in the light,
    then we have fellowship with one another,
    and the Blood of his Son Jesus cleanses us from all sin.
If we say, "We are without sin," we deceive ourselves,
    and the truth is not in us.
If we acknowledge our sins, he is faithful and just
    and will forgive our sins and cleanse us from every wrongdoing.
If we say, "We have not sinned," we make him a liar,
    and his word is not in us.

My children, I am writing this to you so that you may not commit sin.
But if anyone does sin, we have an Advocate with the Father,
    Jesus Christ the righteous one.
He is expiation for our sins,
    and not for our sins only but for those of the whole world.

The word of the Lord.

950 RESPONSORIAL PSALM

First Option

Psalm 51:3-4, 5-6, 12-13, 14 and 17

R̸. (see 3a) **Be merciful, O Lord, for we have sinned.**

Have mercy on me, O God, in your goodness;
 in the greatness of your compassion wipe out my offense.
Thoroughly wash me from my guilt
 and of my sin cleanse me.

R̸. **Be merciful, O Lord, for we have sinned.**

For I acknowledge my offense,
 and my sin is before me always:
"Against you only have I sinned,
 and done what is evil in your sight."

R̸. **Be merciful, O Lord, for we have sinned.**

A clean heart create for me, O God,
 and a steadfast spirit renew within me.
Cast me not out from your presence,
 and your Holy Spirit take not from me.

R̸. **Be merciful, O Lord, for we have sinned.**

Give me back the joy of your salvation,
 and a willing spirit sustain in me.
O Lord, open my lips,
 and my mouth shall proclaim your praise.

R̸. **Be merciful, O Lord, for we have sinned.**

Second Option

Psalm 103:1-2, 3-4, 8-9, 11-12

R̸. (10a) **Lord, do not deal with us as our sins deserve.**
 or:
R̸. (8a) **The Lord is kind and merciful.**

Bless the LORD, O my soul;
 and all my being, bless his holy name.
Bless the LORD, O my soul,
 and forget not all his benefits.

R℣. **Lord, do not deal with us as our sins deserve.**
  or:
R℣. **The Lord is kind and merciful.**

He pardons all your iniquities,
  he heals all your ills.
He redeems your life from destruction,
  he crowns you with kindness and compassion.

R℣. **Lord, do not deal with us as our sins deserve.**
  or:
R℣. **The Lord is kind and merciful.**

Merciful and gracious is the LORD,
  slow to anger and abounding in kindness.
He will not always chide,
  nor does he keep his wrath forever.

R℣. **Lord, do not deal with us as our sins deserve.**
  or:
R℣. **The Lord is kind and merciful.**

For as the heavens are high above the earth,
  so surpassing is his kindness toward those who fear him.
As far as the east is from the west,
  so far has he put our transgressions from us.

R℣. **Lord, do not deal with us as our sins deserve.**
  or:
R℣. **The Lord is kind and merciful.**

Third Option

Psalm 130:1-2, 3-4, 5-6ab, 6c-7, 8

R̷. (3) **If you, O Lord, laid bare our guilt, who could endure it?**

Out of the depths I cry to you, O LORD;
    LORD, hear my voice!
Let your ears be attentive
    to my voice in supplication.

R̷. **If you, O Lord, laid bare our guilt, who could endure it?**

If you, O LORD, mark iniquities,
    LORD, who can stand?
But with you is forgiveness,
    that you may be revered.

R̷. **If you, O Lord, laid bare our guilt, who could endure it?**

I trust in the LORD;
    my soul trusts in his word.
My soul waits for the LORD
    more than sentinels wait for the dawn.

R̷. **If you, O Lord, laid bare our guilt, who could endure it?**

More than sentinels for the dawn,
    let Israel wait for the LORD,
For with the LORD is kindness,
    and with him is plenteous redemption.

R̷. **If you, O Lord, laid bare our guilt, who could endure it?**

And he will redeem Israel
    from all their iniquities.

R̷. **If you, O Lord, laid bare our guilt, who could endure it?**

951 ALLELUIA VERSE AND VERSE BEFORE THE GOSPEL

1.

Ezekiel 33:11

**I take no pleasure in the death of the wicked man, says the Lord,
but rather in his conversion, that he may live.**

2.

Mark 1:15

**The Kingdom of God is at hand;
repent, and believe in the Gospel!**

3.

See Revelation 1:5ab

**Jesus Christ, you are the faithful witness,
the firstborn of the dead;
you have loved us and freed us from our sins by your Blood.**

952 GOSPEL

1.

Matthew 9:1-8   They glorified God who had given such authority to men.

✠ **A reading from the holy Gospel according to Matthew**

Jesus entered a boat, made the crossing, and came into his own town.
And there people brought to him a paralytic,
  lying on a stretcher.
When Jesus saw their faith, he said to the paralytic,
  "Courage, child, your sins are forgiven."
At that, some of the scribes said to themselves,
  "This man is blaspheming."
Jesus knew what the scribes were thinking, and said,
  "Why do you harbor evil thoughts?
Which is easier, to say, 'Your sins are forgiven,'
  or to say, 'Rise and walk'?
But that you may know that the Son of Man
  has authority on earth to forgive sins"—
  he then said to the paralytic,
  "Rise, pick up your stretcher, and go home."
He rose and went home.
When the crowds saw this they were struck with awe
  and glorified God who had given such authority to men.

The Gospel of the Lord.

2.

Mark 1:1-8, 14-15   Repent and believe in the Gospel.

✢ **A reading from the beginning of the holy Gospel according to Mark**

The beginning of the Gospel of Jesus Christ the Son of God.

As it is written in Isaiah the prophet:

> *Behold, I am sending my messenger ahead of you;*
>> *he will prepare your way.*
> *A voice of one crying out in the desert:*
>> *"Prepare the way of the Lord,*
>> *make straight his paths."*

John the Baptist appeared in the desert
proclaiming a baptism of repentance for the forgiveness of sins.
People of the whole Judean countryside
and all the inhabitants of Jerusalem
were going out to him
and were being baptized by him in the Jordan River
as they acknowledged their sins.
John was clothed in camel's hair,
with a leather belt around his waist.
He fed on locusts and wild honey.
And this is what he proclaimed:
"One mightier than I is coming after me.
I am not worthy to stoop and loosen the thongs of his sandals.
I have baptized you with water;
he will baptize you with the Holy Spirit."

After John had been arrested,
Jesus came to Galilee proclaiming the Gospel of God:
"This is the time of fulfillment.
The Kingdom of God is at hand.
Repent, and believe in the Gospel."

The Gospel of the Lord.

3.

Luke 7:36-50   *Her many sins have been forgiven because she has shown great love.*

✠ **A reading from the holy Gospel according to Luke**

A Pharisee invited Jesus to dine with him,
  and Jesus entered the Pharisee's house and reclined at table.
Now there was a sinful woman in the city
  who learned that he was at table in the house of the Pharisee.
Bringing an alabaster flask of ointment,
  she stood behind him at his feet weeping
  and began to bathe his feet with her tears.
Then she wiped them with her hair,
  kissed them, and anointed them with the ointment.
When the Pharisee who had invited him saw this he said to himself,
  "If this man were a prophet,
  he would know who and what sort of woman this is who is touching him,
  that she is a sinner."
Jesus said to him in reply,
  "Simon, I have something to say to you."
"Tell me, teacher," he said.
"Two people were in debt to a certain creditor;
  one owed five hundred days' wages and the other owed fifty.
Since they were unable to repay the debt, he forgave it for both.
Which of them will love him more?"
Simon said in reply,
  "The one, I suppose, whose larger debt was forgiven."
He said to him, "You have judged rightly."
Then he turned to the woman and said to Simon,
  "Do you see this woman?
When I entered your house, you did not give me water for my feet,
  but she has bathed them with her tears
  and wiped them with her hair.
You did not give me a kiss,
  but she has not ceased kissing my feet since the time I entered.
You did not anoint my head with oil,
  but she anointed my feet with ointment.
So I tell you, her many sins have been forgiven;
  hence, she has shown great love.
But the one to whom little is forgiven, loves little."

He said to her, "Your sins are forgiven."
The others at table said to themselves,
   "Who is this who even forgives sins?"
But he said to the woman,
   "Your faith has saved you; go in peace."

The Gospel of the Lord.

4.

Luke 15:1-3, 11-32   But now we must celebrate and rejoice, because your brother was dead and has come to life again.

☩   **A reading from the holy Gospel according to Luke**

Tax collectors and sinners were all drawing near to listen to Jesus,
  but the Pharisees and scribes began to complain, saying,
  "This man welcomes sinners and eats with them."
So he addressed to them this parable.

"A man had two sons, and the younger son said to his father,
  'Father, give me the share of your estate that should come to me.'
So the father divided the property between them.
After a few days, the younger son collected all his belongings
  and set off to a distant country
  where he squandered his inheritance on a life of dissipation.
When he had freely spent everything,
  a severe famine struck that country,
  and he found himself in dire need.
So he hired himself out to one of the local citizens
  who sent him to his farm to tend the swine.
And he longed to eat his fill of the pods on which the swine fed,
  but nobody gave him any.
Coming to his senses he thought,
  'How many of my father's hired workers
  have more than enough food to eat,
  but here am I, dying from hunger.
I shall get up and go to my father and I shall say to him,
  "Father, I have sinned against heaven and against you.
I no longer deserve to be called your son;
  treat me as you would treat one of your hired workers."'
So he got up and went back to his father.
While he was still a long way off,
  his father caught sight of him, and was filled with compassion.
He ran to his son, embraced him and kissed him.
His son said to him,
  'Father, I have sinned against heaven and against you;
  I no longer deserve to be called your son.'
But his father ordered his servants,
  'Quickly bring the finest robe and put it on him;
  put a ring on his finger and sandals on his feet.

Take the fattened calf and slaughter it.

Then let us celebrate with a feast,

    because this son of mine was dead, and has come to life again;

    he was lost, and has been found.'

Then the celebration began.

Now the older son had been out in the field

    and, on his way back, as he neared the house,

    he heard the sound of music and dancing.

He called one of the servants and asked what this might mean.

The servant said to him,

    'Your brother has returned

    and your father has slaughtered the fattened calf

    because he has him back safe and sound.'

He became angry,

    and when he refused to enter the house,

    his father came out and pleaded with him.

He said to his father in reply,

    'Look, all these years I served you

    and not once did I disobey your orders;

    yet you never gave me even a young goat to feast on with my friends.

But when your son returns

    who swallowed up your property with prostitutes,

    for him you slaughter the fattened calf.'

He said to him,

    'My son, you are here with me always;

    everything I have is yours.

But now we must celebrate and rejoice,

    because your brother was dead and has come to life again;

    he was lost and has been found.'"

The Gospel of the Lord.

5.

Luke 24:46-48   Jesus sent the Apostles to preach repentance for the forgiveness of sins.

☩ **A reading from the holy Gospel according to Luke**

Jesus said to his disciples,
    "Thus it is written that the Christ would suffer
    and rise from the dead on the third day
    and that repentance, for the forgiveness of sins,
    would be preached in his name
    to all the nations, beginning from Jerusalem.
You are witnesses of these things."

The Gospel of the Lord.

28. FOR THE PROMOTION OF CHARITY OR TO FOSTER HARMONY OR FOR FAMILY AND FRIENDS

953 READING FROM THE NEW TESTAMENT

First Option

Romans 12:3-13   We have gifts that differ according to the grace given to us.

A reading from the Letter of Saint Paul to the Romans

Brothers and sisters:
By the grace given to me I tell everyone among you
   not to think of himself more highly than one ought to think,
   but to think soberly,
   each according to the measure of faith that God has apportioned.
For as in one body we have many parts,
   and all the parts do not have the same function,
   so we, though many, are one Body in Christ
   and individually parts of one another.
Since we have gifts that differ according to the grace given to us,
   let us exercise them:
   if prophecy, in proportion to the faith;
   if ministry, in ministering;
   if one is a teacher, in teaching;
   if one exhorts, in exhortation;
   if one contributes, in generosity;
   if one is over others, with diligence;
   if one does acts of mercy, with cheerfulness.

Let love be sincere;
   hate what is evil,
   hold on to what is good;
   love one another with mutual affection;
   anticipate one another in showing honor.
Do not grow slack in zeal,
   be fervent in spirit,
   serve the Lord.
Rejoice in hope,
   endure in affliction,
   persevere in prayer.
Contribute to the needs of the holy ones,
   exercise hospitality.

The word of the Lord.

Second Option

1 Corinthians 12:31–13:13   So faith, hope, and love remain, these three; but the greatest of these is love.

A reading from the first Letter of Saint Paul to the Corinthians

Brothers and sisters:
Strive eagerly for the greatest spiritual gifts.

But I shall show you a still more excellent way.

If I speak in human and angelic tongues,
 but do not have love,
 I am a resounding gong or a clashing cymbal.
And if I have the gift of prophecy,
 and comprehend all mysteries and all knowledge;
 if I have all faith so as to move mountains,
 but do not have love, I am nothing.
If I give away everything I own,
 and if I hand my body over so that I may boast,
 but do not have love, I gain nothing.

Love is patient, love is kind.
It is not jealous, it is not pompous,
 it is not inflated, it is not rude,
 it does not seek its own interests,
 it is not quick-tempered, it does not brood over injury, it does not rejoice
  over wrongdoing
 but rejoices with the truth.
It bears all things, believes all things,
 hopes all things, endures all things.

Love never fails.
If there are prophecies, they will be brought to nothing;
 if tongues, they will cease;
 if knowledge, it will be brought to nothing.
For we know partially and we prophesy partially,
 but when the perfect comes, the partial will pass away.
When I was a child, I used to talk as a child,
 think as a child, reason as a child;
 when I became a man, I put aside childish things.
At present we see indistinctly, as in a mirror,
 but then face to face.

At present I know partially;
  then I shall know fully, as I am fully known.
So faith, hope, love remain, these three;
  but the greatest of these is love.

The word of the Lord.

Third Option

1 John 3:14-18   We ought to lay down our lives for our brothers.

A reading from the first Letter of Saint John

Beloved:
We know that we have passed from death to life
  because we love our brothers.
Whoever does not love remains in death.
Everyone who hates his brother is a murderer,
  and you know that anyone who is a murderer
  does not have eternal life remaining in him.
The way we came to know love
  was that he laid down his life for us;
  so we ought to lay down our lives for our brothers.
If someone who has worldly means
  sees a brother in need and refuses him compassion,
  how can the love of God remain in him?
Children, let us love not in word or speech
  but in deed and truth.

The word of the Lord.

954 RESPONSORIAL PSALM

1.

Psalm 85:7-8, 9, 11-12

R℣. (see 9b) **The Lord speaks of peace to his people.**

Will you not instead give us life;
and shall not your people rejoice in you?
Show us, O LORD, your kindness,
and grant us your salvation.

R℣. **The Lord speaks of peace to his people.**

I will hear what God proclaims;
the LORD—for he proclaims peace.
To his people, and to his faithful ones,
and to those who put in him their hope.

R℣. **The Lord speaks of peace to his people.**

Kindness and truth shall meet;
justice and peace shall kiss.
Truth shall spring out of the earth,
and justice shall look down from heaven.

R℣. **The Lord speaks of peace to his people.**

2.

Psalm 100:1b-2, 3, 4, 5

℟. (3c) **We are his people: the sheep of his flock.**

Sing joyfully to the LORD, all you lands;
   serve the LORD with gladness;
   come before him with joyful song.

℟. **We are his people: the sheep of his flock.**

Know that the LORD is God,
   he made us, his we are;
   his people, the flock he tends.

℟. **We are his people: the sheep of his flock.**

Enter his gates with thanksgiving,
   his courts with praise;
   give thanks to him; bless his name.

℟. **We are his people: the sheep of his flock.**

The LORD is good:
   his kindness endures forever,
   and his faithfulness, to all generations.

℟. **We are his people: the sheep of his flock.**

955 ALLELUIA VERSE AND VERSE BEFORE THE GOSPEL

1.

Psalm 133:1

**Behold how good it is, and how pleasant,
where brothers and sisters dwell as one!**

2.

John 15:12

**This is my commandment:
love one another as I love you.**

956 GOSPEL

First Option

Matthew 18:15-20   For where two or three are gathered together in my name, there am I in the midst of them.

✝ **A reading from the holy Gospel according to Matthew**

Jesus said to his disciples:
"If your brother sins against you,
   go and tell him his fault between you and him alone.
If he listens to you, you have won over your brother.
If he does not listen,
   take one or two others along with you,
   so that 'every fact may be established
   on the testimony of two or three witnesses.'
If he refuses to listen to them, tell the Church.
If he refuses to listen even to the Church,
   then treat him as you would a Gentile or a tax collector.
Amen, I say to you,
   whatever you bind on earth shall be bound in heaven,
   and whatever you loose on earth shall be loosed in heaven.
Again, amen, I say to you,
   if two of you agree on earth
   about anything for which they are to pray,
   it shall be granted to them by my heavenly Father.
For where two or three are gathered together in my name,
   there am I in the midst of them."

The Gospel of the Lord.

Second Option

John 15:12-17   This I command you: love one another.

✠ **A reading from the holy Gospel according to John**

Jesus said to his disciples:
"This is my commandment: love one another as I love you.
No one has greater love than this,
   to lay down one's life for one's friends.
You are my friends if you do what I command you.
I no longer call you slaves,
   because a slave does not know what his master is doing.
I have called you friends,
   because I have told you everything I have heard from my Father.
It was not you who chose me, but I who chose you
   and appointed you to go and bear fruit that will remain,
   so that whatever you ask the Father in my name he may give you.
This I command you: love one another."

The Gospel of the Lord.

29. FOR THE FAMILY

957

Readings from the Mass of the feast of the Holy Family, no. 17, or from the Mass for Family and Friends, nos. 953–956, may be used.

30. FOR OUR OPPRESSORS

958   READING FROM THE OLD TESTAMENT

First Option

1 Samuel 26:2, 7-9, 12-13, 22-23   Though the Lord delivered you into my grasp, I would not harm the Lord's anointed.

A reading from the first Book of Samuel

Saul went down to the desert of Ziph
  with three thousand picked men of Israel,
  to search for David in the desert of Ziph.
So David and Abishai went among Saul's soldiers by night
  and found Saul lying asleep within the barricade,
  with his spear thrust into the ground at his head
  and Abner and his men sleeping around him.

Abishai whispered to David:
  "God has delivered your enemy into your grasp this day.
Let me nail him to the ground with one thrust of the spear;
  I will not need a second thrust!"
But David said to Abishai, "Do not harm him,
  for who can lay hands on the Lord's anointed and remain unpunished?"
So David took the spear and the water jug from their place at Saul's head,
  and they got away without anyone's seeing or knowing or awakening.
All remained asleep,
  because the Lord had put them into a deep slumber.

Going across to an opposite slope,
  David stood on a remote hilltop
  at a great distance from Abner, son of Ner, and the troops.

He shouted: "Here is the king's spear.
Let an attendant come over to get it.
The Lord will reward each man for his justice and faithfulness.
Today, though the Lord delivered you into my grasp,
  I would not harm the Lord's anointed."

The word of the Lord.

Second Option

Isaiah 50:4-9a   My face I did not shield from buffets and spitting.

A reading from the Book of the Prophet Isaiah

The Lord GOD has given me
  a well-trained tongue,
That I might know how to speak to the weary
  a word that will rouse them.
Morning after morning
  he opens my ear that I may hear;
And I have not rebelled,
  have not turned back.
I gave my back to those who beat me,
  my cheeks to those who plucked my beard;
My face I did not shield
  from buffets and spitting.

The Lord GOD is my help,
  therefore I am not disgraced;
I have set my face like flint,
  knowing that I shall not be put to shame.
He is near who upholds my right;
  if anyone wishes to oppose me,
  let us appear together.
Who disputes my right?
  Let him confront me.
See, the Lord GOD is my help;
  who will prove me wrong?

The word of the Lord.

959 READING FROM THE NEW TESTAMENT

First Option

Acts 7:55-60   Lord, do not hold this sin against them.

A reading from the Acts of the Apostles

Stephen, filled with the Holy Spirit,
  looked up intently to heaven and saw the glory of God
  and Jesus standing at the right hand of God,
  and he said, "Behold, I see the heavens opened
  and the Son of Man standing at the right hand of God."
But they cried out in a loud voice,
  covered their ears, and rushed upon him together.
They threw him out of the city, and began to stone him.
The witnesses laid down their cloaks
  at the feet of a young man named Saul.
As they were stoning Stephen, he called out,
  "Lord Jesus, receive my spirit."
Then he fell to his knees and cried out in a loud voice,
  "Lord, do not hold this sin against them";
  and when he said this, he fell asleep.

The word of the Lord.

Second Option

Colossians 3:12-15   Let the peace of Christ control your hearts.

A reading from the Letter of Saint Paul to the Colossians

Brothers and sisters:
Put on, as God's chosen ones, holy and beloved,
  heartfelt compassion, kindness, humility, gentleness, and patience,
  bearing with one another and forgiving one another,
  if one has a grievance against another;
  as the Lord has forgiven you, so must you also do.
And over all these put on love,
  that is, the bond of perfection.
And let the peace of Christ control your hearts,
  the peace into which you were also called in one Body.
And be thankful.

The word of the Lord.

960 RESPONSORIAL PSALM

1.

Psalm 86:1-2, 3-4, 5-6, 14, 17

℟. (6b) **Listen, O Lord, to my pleading.**

Incline your ear, O LORD; answer me,
  for I am afflicted and poor.
Keep my life, for I am devoted to you;
  save your servant who trusts in you.
You are my God.

℟. **Listen, O Lord, to my pleading.**

Have mercy on me, O LORD,
  for to you I call all the day.
Gladden the soul of your servant,
  for to you, O Lord, I lift up my soul.

℟. **Listen, O Lord, to my pleading.**

For you, O Lord, are good and forgiving,
  abounding in kindness to all who call upon you.
Hearken, O LORD, to my prayer
  and attend to the sound of my pleading.

℟. **Listen, O Lord, to my pleading.**

O God, the haughty have risen up against me,
  and the company of fierce men seeks my life,
  nor do they set you before their eyes.

℟. **Listen, O Lord, to my pleading.**

Grant me a proof of your favor,
  that my enemies may see, to their confusion,
  that you, O LORD, have helped and comforted me.

℟. **Listen, O Lord, to my pleading.**

2.

Psalm 103:1-2, 3-4, 8-9, 11-12

℟. (8a) **The Lord is kind and merciful.**

Bless the LORD, O my soul;
   and all my being, bless his holy name.
Bless the LORD, O my soul,
   and forget not all his benefits.

℟. **The Lord is kind and merciful.**

He pardons all your iniquities,
   he heals all your ills.
He redeems your life from destruction,
   he crowns you with kindness and compassion.

℟. **The Lord is kind and merciful.**

Merciful and gracious is the LORD,
   slow to anger and abounding in kindness.
He will not always chide,
   nor does he keep his wrath forever.

℟. **The Lord is kind and merciful.**

For as the heavens are high above the earth,
   so surpassing is his kindness toward those who fear him.
As far as the east is from the west,
   so far has he put our transgressions from us.

℟. **The Lord is kind and merciful.**

961 ALLELUIA VERSE AND VERSE BEFORE THE GOSPEL

1.

Matthew 5:9

**Blessed are the peacemakers;
for they will be called children of God.**

2.

John 13:34

**I give you a new commandment:
love one another as I have loved you.**

962 GOSPEL

First Option

Matthew 5:38-48   Love your enemies.

✠ **A reading from the holy Gospel according to Matthew**

Jesus said to his disciples:
"You have heard that it was said,
  An eye for an eye and a tooth for a tooth.
But I say to you, offer no resistance to one who is evil.
When someone strikes you on your right cheek,
  turn the other one as well.
If anyone wants to go to law with you over your tunic,
  hand over your cloak as well.
Should anyone press you into service for one mile,
  go for two miles.
Give to the one who asks of you,
  and do not turn your back on one who wants to borrow.

"You have heard that it was said,
  You shall love your neighbor and hate your enemy.
But I say to you, love your enemies
  and pray for those who persecute you,
    that you may be children of your heavenly Father,
    for he makes his sun rise on the bad and the good,
    and causes rain to fall on the just and the unjust.
For if you love those who love you, what recompense will you have?
Do not the tax collectors do the same?
And if you greet your brothers and sisters only,
  what is unusual about that?
Do not the pagans do the same?
So be perfect, just as your heavenly Father is perfect."

The Gospel of the Lord.

Second Option

Luke 6:27-38   Be merciful, just as your Father is merciful.

✠ **A reading from the holy Gospel according to Luke**

Jesus said to his disciples:
"To you who hear I say,
love your enemies, do good to those who hate you,
bless those who curse you, pray for those who mistreat you.
To the person who strikes you on one cheek,
offer the other one as well,
and from the person who takes your cloak,
do not withhold even your tunic.
Give to everyone who asks of you,
and from the one who takes what is yours do not demand it back.
Do to others as you would have them do to you.
For if you love those who love you,
what credit is that to you?
Even sinners love those who love them.
And if you do good to those who do good to you,
what credit is that to you?
Even sinners do the same.
If you lend money to those from whom you expect repayment,
what credit is that to you?
Even sinners lend to sinners,
and get back the same amount.
But rather, love your enemies and do good to them,
and lend expecting nothing back;
then your reward will be great
and you will be children of the Most High,
for he himself is kind to the ungrateful and the wicked.
Be merciful, just as your Father is merciful.

"Stop judging and you will not be judged.
Stop condemning and you will not be condemned.
Forgive and you will be forgiven.
Give and gifts will be given to you;
a good measure, packed together, shaken down, and overflowing,
will be poured into your lap.
For the measure with which you measure
will in return be measured out to you."

The Gospel of the Lord.

31. FOR THE GRACE OF A HAPPY DEATH

963 READING FROM THE OLD TESTAMENT

Isaiah 25:6-10a   He will destroy death forever.

A reading from the Book of the Prophet Isaiah

On this mountain the LORD of hosts
  will provide for all peoples
A feast of rich food and choice wines,
  juicy, rich food and pure, choice wines.
On this mountain he will destroy
  the veil that veils all peoples,
The web that is woven over all nations;
  he will destroy death forever.
The Lord GOD will wipe away
  the tears from all faces;
The reproach of his people he will remove
  from the whole earth; for the LORD has spoken.

  On that day it will be said:
"Behold our God, to whom we looked to save us!
  This is the LORD for whom we looked;
  let us rejoice and be glad that he has saved us!"
For the hand of the LORD will rest on this mountain.

The word of the Lord.

964 READING FROM THE NEW TESTAMENT

Romans 14:7-9, 10c-12   Whether we live or die, we are the Lord's.

A reading from the Letter of Saint Paul to the Romans

Brothers and sisters:
No one lives for oneself, and no one dies for oneself.
For if we live, we live for the Lord,
and if we die, we die for the Lord;
so then, whether we live or die, we are the Lord's.
For this is why Christ died and came to life,
that he might be Lord of both the dead and the living.
Why then do you judge your brother?
Or you, why do you look down on your brother?
For we shall all stand before the judgment seat of God;
for it is written:

As I live, says the Lord, every knee
shall bend before me,
and every tongue shall give praise to God.

So then each of us shall give an account of himself to God.

The word of the Lord.

For Various Needs

965 RESPONSORIAL PSALM

Psalm 31:2 and 6, 8bc-9, 15-16, 17 and 25

℞. (Luke 23:46) **Father, into your hands I commend my spirit.**

In you, O Lord**, I take refuge;**
   let me never be put to shame.
In your justice rescue me.
Into your hands, I commend my spirit;
   you will redeem me, O Lord**, O faithful God.**

℞. **Father, into your hands I commend my spirit.**

When you have seen my affliction
   and watched over me in my distress,
Not shutting me up in the grip of the enemy
   but enabling me to move about at large.

℞. **Father, into your hands I commend my spirit.**

But my trust is in you, O Lord**;**
   I say, "You are my God."
In your hands is my destiny;
   rescue me from the clutches of my enemies and my persecutors.

℞. **Father, into your hands I commend my spirit.**

Let your face shine on your servant;
   save me in your kindness.
Take courage and be stouthearted,
   all you who hope in the Lord**.**

℞. **Father, into your hands I commend my spirit.**

966 ALLELUIA VERSE AND VERSE BEFORE THE GOSPEL

1.

Matthew 24:42a, 44

Stay awake and be prepared!
For you do not know when the Son of Man will come.

2.

Luke 21:36

Be vigilant at all times and pray
that you may have the strength to stand before the Son of Man.

3.

John 13:1

Jesus knew that his hour had come to pass from this world to the Father.
He loved his own in the world and he loved them to the end.

4.

Revelation 2:10c

Remain faithful until death,
and I will give you the crown of life.

967 GOSPEL

First Option

Matthew 25:1-13   Behold the bridegroom! Come out to meet him.

✢ **A reading from the holy Gospel according to Matthew**

Jesus told his disciples this parable:
"The Kingdom of heaven will be like ten virgins
   who took their lamps and went out to meet the bridegroom.
Five of them were foolish and five were wise.
The foolish ones, when taking their lamps,
   brought no oil with them,
   but the wise brought flasks of oil with their lamps.
Since the bridegroom was long delayed,
   they all became drowsy and fell asleep.
At midnight, there was a cry,
   'Behold, the bridegroom! Come out to meet him!'
Then all those virgins got up and trimmed their lamps.
The foolish ones said to the wise,
   'Give us some of your oil,
   for our lamps are going out.'
But the wise ones replied,
   'No, for there may not be enough for us and you.
Go instead to the merchants and buy some for yourselves.'
While they went off to buy it,
   the bridegroom came
   and those who were ready went into the wedding feast with him.
Then the door was locked.
Afterwards the other virgins came and said,
   'Lord, Lord, open the door for us!'
But he said in reply,
   'Amen, I say to you, I do not know you.'
Therefore, stay awake,
   for you know neither the day nor the hour."

The Gospel of the Lord.

Second Option

Luke 12:35-40   At the hour you do not expect, the Son of Man will come.

✠ **A reading from the holy Gospel according to Luke**

Jesus said to his disciples:
"Gird your loins and light your lamps
   and be like servants who await their master's return from a wedding,
   ready to open immediately when he comes and knocks.
Blessed are those servants
   whom the master finds vigilant on his arrival.
Amen, I say to you, he will gird himself,
   have them recline at table, and proceed to wait on them.
And should he come in the second or third watch
   and find them prepared in this way,
   blessed are those servants.
Be sure of this:
   if the master of the house had known the hour
   when the thief was coming,
   he would not have let his house be broken into.
You also must be prepared, for at an hour you do not expect,
   the Son of Man will come."

The Gospel of the Lord.

Third Option

Luke 21:34-36   Be vigilant at all times and pray.

✠ **A reading from the holy Gospel according to Luke**

Jesus said to his disciples:
"Beware that your hearts do not become drowsy
   from carousing and drunkenness
   and the anxieties of daily life,
   and that day catch you by surprise like a trap.
For that day will assault everyone
   who lives on the face of the earth.
Be vigilant at all times
   and pray that you have the strength
   to escape the tribulations that are imminent
   and to stand before the Son of Man."

The Gospel of the Lord.

Fourth Option

Luke 23:39-46   Father, into your hands I commend my spirit.

✠   **A reading from the holy Gospel according to Luke**

**One of the criminals hanging in crucifixion
    reviled Jesus, saying,
    "Are you not the Christ?
    Save yourself and us."
The other man however, rebuking him, said in reply,
    "Have you no fear of God,
    for you are subject to the same condemnation?
And indeed, we have been condemned justly,
    for the sentence we received corresponds to our crimes,
    but he has done nothing criminal."
Then he said,
    "Jesus, remember me when you come into your Kingdom."
He replied to him,
    "Amen, I say to you,
    today you will be with me in Paradise."**

**It was now about noon and darkness came over the whole land
    until three in the afternoon
    because of an eclipse of the sun.
Then the veil of the temple was torn down the middle.
Jesus cried out in a loud voice,
    "Father, into your hands I commend my spirit";
    and when he had said this he breathed his last.**

The Gospel of the Lord.

VOTIVE MASSES

First readings assigned to the season of Easter are used when votive
Masses are celebrated during the season of Easter in accord with no. 333
in the General Instruction of the Roman Missal.

968 THE MOST HOLY TRINITY

The readings are taken from the solemnity of the Holy Trinity, the first
Sunday after Pentecost, nos. 164–166.

THE MYSTERY OF THE HOLY CROSS

969 READING I FROM THE OLD TESTAMENT

1.

Exodus 12:1-8, 11-14   The law regarding the Passover meal.

A reading from the Book of Exodus

The Lord said to Moses and Aaron in the land of Egypt,
  "This month shall stand at the head of your calendar;
  you shall reckon it the first month of the year.
Tell the whole community of Israel:
  On the tenth of this month every one of your families
  must procure for itself a lamb, one apiece for each household.
If a family is too small for a whole lamb,
  it shall join the nearest household in procuring one
  and shall share in the lamb
  in proportion to the number of persons who partake of it.
The lamb must be a year-old male and without blemish.
You may take it from either the sheep or the goats.
You shall keep it until the fourteenth day of this month,
  and then, with the whole assembly of Israel present,
  it shall be slaughtered during the evening twilight.
They shall take some of its blood
  and apply it to the two doorposts and the lintel
  of every house in which they partake of the lamb.
That same night they shall eat its roasted flesh
  with unleavened bread and bitter herbs.

"This is how you are to eat it:
  with your loins girt, sandals on your feet and your staff in hand,
  you shall eat like those who are in flight.
It is the Passover of the Lord.
For on this same night I will go through Egypt,
  striking down every firstborn of the land, both man and beast,
  and executing judgment on all the gods of Egypt—I, the Lord!
But the blood will mark the houses where you are.
Seeing the blood, I will pass over you;
  thus, when I strike the land of Egypt,
  no destructive blow will come upon you.

"This day shall be a memorial feast for you,
 which all your generations shall celebrate
 with pilgrimage to the LORD, as a perpetual institution."

The word of the Lord.

2.

Wisdom 2:1a, 12-22   Let us condemn him to a shameful death.

A reading from the Book of Wisdom

The wicked said among themselves, thinking not aright:
"Let us beset the just one, because he is obnoxious to us;
   he sets himself against our doings,
Reproaches us for transgressions of the law
   and charges us with violations of our training.
He professes to have knowledge of God
   and styles himself a child of the Lord.
To us he is the censure of our thoughts;
   merely to see him is a hardship for us.
Because his life is not like that of others,
   and different are his ways.
He judges us debased;
   he holds aloof from our paths as from things impure.
He calls blest the destiny of the just
   and boasts that God is his Father.
Let us see whether his words be true;
   let us find out what will happen to him.
For if the just one be the son of God, he will defend him
   and deliver him from the hand of his foes.
With revilement and torture let us put the just one to the test
   that we may have proof of his gentleness
   and try his patience.
Let us condemn him to a shameful death;
   for according to his own words, God will take care of him."
These were their thoughts, but they erred;
   for their wickedness blinded them,
And they knew not the hidden counsels of God;
   neither did they count on a recompense of holiness
   nor discern the innocent souls' reward.

The word of the Lord.

3.

Isaiah 50:4-9a   My face I did not shield from buffets and spitting.

A reading from the Book of the Prophet Isaiah

The Lord G od has given me
  a well-trained tongue,
That I might know how to speak to the weary
  a word that will rouse them.
Morning after morning
  he opens my ear that I may hear;
And I have not rebelled,
  have not turned back.
I gave my back to those who beat me,
  my cheeks to those who plucked my beard;
My face I did not shield
  from buffets and spitting.

The Lord G od is my help,
  therefore I am not disgraced;
I have set my face like flint,
  knowing that I shall not be put to shame.
He is near who upholds my right;
  if anyone wishes to oppose me,
  let us appear together.
Who disputes my right?
  Let him confront me.
See, the Lord G od is my help;
  who will prove me wrong?

The word of the Lord.

4.

Isaiah 52:13–53:12   He was pierced for our offenses.

A reading from the Book of the Prophet Isaiah

The LORD says:
See, my servant shall prosper,
    he shall be raised high and greatly exalted.
Even as many were amazed at him—
    so marred was his look beyond human semblance
    and his appearance beyond that of the sons of man—
So shall he startle many nations,
    because of him kings shall stand speechless;
For those who have not been told shall see,
    those who have not heard shall ponder it.

Who would believe what we have heard?
    To whom has the arm of the LORD been revealed?
He grew up like a sapling before him,
    like a shoot from the parched earth;
There was in him no stately bearing to make us look at him,
    nor appearance that would attract us to him.
He was spurned and avoided by people,
    a man of suffering, accustomed to infirmity,
One of those from whom people hide their faces,
    spurned, and we held him in no esteem.

Yet it was our infirmities that he bore,
    our sufferings that he endured,
While we thought of him as stricken,
    as one smitten by God and afflicted.
But he was pierced for our offenses,
    crushed for our sins;
Upon him was the chastisement that makes us whole,
    by his stripes we were healed.
We had all gone astray like sheep,
    each following his own way;
But the LORD laid upon him
    the guilt of us all.

Though he was harshly treated, he submitted
    and opened not his mouth;

Like a lamb led to the slaughter
 or a sheep before the shearers,
 he was silent and opened not his mouth.
Oppressed and condemned, he was taken away,
 and who would have thought any more of his destiny?
When he was cut off from the land of the living,
 and smitten for the sin of his people,
A grave was assigned him among the wicked
 and a burial place with evildoers,
Though he had done no wrong
 nor spoken any falsehood.
But the LORD was pleased
 to crush him in infirmity.

If he gives his life as an offering for sin,
 he shall see his descendants in a long life,
 and the will of the LORD shall be accomplished through him.

Because of his affliction
 he shall see the light in fullness of days;
Through his suffering, my servant shall justify many,
 and their guilt he shall bear.
Therefore I will give him his portion among the great,
 and he shall divide the spoils with the mighty,
Because he surrendered himself to death
 and was counted among the wicked;
And he shall take away the sins of many,
 and win pardon for their offenses.

The word of the Lord.

5.

Zechariah 12:10-11; 13:6-7   They shall look on him whom they have pierced.

A reading from the Book of the Prophet Zechariah

Thus says the LORD:
I will pour out on the house of David
    and on the inhabitants of Jerusalem
    a Spirit of grace and petition;
    and they shall look on him whom they have thrust through,
    and they shall mourn for him as one mourns for an only son,
    and they shall grieve over him as one grieves over a firstborn.

On that day the mourning in Jerusalem shall be as great
    as the mourning of Hadadrimmon, in the plain of Megiddo.

And if anyone asks him,
    "What are these wounds on your chest?" he shall answer,
    "With these I was wounded in the house of my dear ones."

    Awake, O sword, against my shepherd,
        against the man who is my associate,
        says the LORD of hosts.
    Strike the shepherd
        that the sheep may be dispersed,
        and I will turn my hand against the little ones.

The word of the Lord.

970 READING I FROM THE NEW TESTAMENT DURING THE SEASON OF EASTER

First Option

Acts 10:34-43   They put him to death by hanging him on a tree. This man God raised on the third day.

A reading from the Acts of the Apostles

Peter proceeded to speak, saying:
"In truth, I see that God shows no partiality.
Rather, in every nation whoever fears him and acts uprightly
    is acceptable to him.
You know the word that he sent to the children of Israel
    as he proclaimed peace through Jesus Christ, who is Lord of all,
    what has happened all over Judea,
    beginning in Galilee after the baptism
    that John preached,
    how God anointed Jesus of Nazareth
    with the Holy Spirit and power.
He went about doing good
    and healing all those oppressed by the Devil,
    for God was with him.
We are witnesses of all that he did
    both in the country of the Jews and in Jerusalem.
They put him to death by hanging him on a tree.
This man God raised on the third day and granted that he be visible,
    not to all the people, but to us,
    the witnesses chosen by God in advance,
    who ate and drank with him after he rose from the dead.
He commissioned us to preach to the people
    and testify that he is the one appointed by God
    as judge of the living and the dead.
To him all the prophets bear witness,
    that everyone who believes in him
    will receive forgiveness of sins through his name."

The word of the Lord.

Second Option

Acts 13:26-33   What God promised to our ancestors he has brought to fulfillment for us by raising up Jesus.

A reading from the Acts of the Apostles

**When Paul came to Antioch in Pisidia, he said in the synagogue:
"My brothers, sons of the family of Abraham,
    and those others among you who are God-fearing,
    to us this word of salvation has been sent.
The inhabitants of Jerusalem and their leaders failed to recognize him,
    and by condemning him they fulfilled the oracles of the prophets
    that are read sabbath after sabbath.
For even though they found no grounds for a death sentence,
    they asked Pilate to have him put to death,
    and when they had accomplished all that was written about him,
    they took him down from the tree and placed him in a tomb.
But God raised him from the dead,
    and for many days he appeared to those
    who had come up with him from Galilee to Jerusalem.
These are now his witnesses before the people.
We ourselves are proclaiming this good news to you
    that what God promised our fathers
    he has brought to fulfillment for us, their children, by raising up Jesus,
    as it is written in the second psalm,
    You are my Son; this day I have begotten you."**

The word of the Lord.

Third Option

Revelation 1:5-8   The firstborn of the dead, who loves us and has freed us from our sins by his Blood.

A reading from the Book of Revelation

**Grace to you and peace from Jesus Christ, who is the faithful witness,
    the firstborn of the dead and ruler of the kings of the earth.
To him who loves us and has freed us from our sins by his Blood,
    who has made us into a kingdom, priests for his God and Father,
    to him be glory and power forever and ever. Amen.

    Behold, he is coming amid the clouds,
        and every eye will see him,**

even those who pierced him.
All the peoples of the earth will lament him.
Yes. Amen.

"I am the Alpha and the Omega," says the Lord God,
"the one who is and who was and who is to come, the almighty."

The word of the Lord.

Fourth Option

Revelation 5:6-12   With your Blood you purchased us for God.

A reading from the Book of Revelation

I, John, saw standing in the midst of the throne
and the four living creatures and the elders
a Lamb that seemed to have been slain.
He had seven horns and seven eyes;
these are the seven spirits of God sent out into the whole world.
He came and received the scroll
from the right hand of the One who sat on the throne.
When he took it, the four living creatures and the twenty-four elders
fell down before the Lamb.
Each of the elders held a harp and gold bowls filled with incense,
which are the prayers of the holy ones.
They sang a new hymn:
"Worthy are you to receive the scroll
and to break open its seals,
for you were slain and with your Blood you purchased for God
those from every tribe and tongue, people and nation.
You made them a kingdom and priests for our God,
and they will reign on earth."
I looked again and heard the voices of many angels
who surrounded the throne
and the living creatures and the elders.
They were countless in number, and they cried out in a loud voice:
"Worthy is the Lamb that was slain
to receive power and riches, wisdom and strength,
honor and glory and blessing."

The word of the Lord.

971 RESPONSORIAL PSALM

1.

Psalm 22:8-9, 17-18a, 19-20, 23-24

R︎. (2a) **My God, my God, why have you abandoned me?**
 or:
R︎. (Matthew 26:42) **My Father, your will be done!**

All who see me scoff at me;
 they mock me with parted lips, they wag their heads:
"He relied on the Lord; let him deliver him,
 let him rescue him, if he loves him."

R︎. **My God, my God, why have you abandoned me?**
 or:
R︎. **My Father, your will be done!**

Indeed, many dogs surround me,
 a pack of evildoers closes in upon me;
They have pierced my hands and my feet;
 I can count all of my bones.

R︎. **My God, my God, why have you abandoned me?**
 or:
R︎. **My Father, your will be done!**

They divide my garments among them,
 and for my vesture they cast lots.
But you, O Lord, be not far from me;
 O my help hasten to aid me.

R︎. **My God, my God, why have you abandoned me?**
 or:
R︎. **My Father, your will be done!**

I will proclaim your name to my brothers and sisters;
 in the midst of the assembly I will praise you:
"You who fear the Lord, praise him;
 all you descendants of Jacob, give glory to him;
 revere him, all you descendants of Israel!"

R︎. **My God, my God, why have you abandoned me?**
 or:
R︎. **My Father, your will be done!**

2.

Psalm 31:2 and 6, 12-13, 15-16, 17 and 25

R℟. (Luke 23:46) **Father, into your hands I commend my spirit.**

In you, O Lᴏʀᴅ, I take refuge;
    let me never be put to shame.
In your justice rescue me.
Into your hands I commend my spirit;
    you will redeem me, O Lord, O faithful God.

R℟. **Father, into your hands I commend my spirit.**

For all my foes I am an object of reproach,
    a laughingstock to my neighbors, and a dread to my friends;
    they who see me abroad flee from me.
I am forgotten like the unremembered dead;
    I am like a dish that is broken.

R℟. **Father, into your hands I commend my spirit.**

But my trust is in you, O Lᴏʀᴅ;
    I say, "You are my God."
In your hands is my destiny; rescue me
    from the hands of my enemies and persecutors.

R℟. **Father, into your hands I commend my spirit.**

Let your face shine upon your servant;
    save me in your kindness.
Take courage and be stouthearted,
    all you who hope in the Lᴏʀᴅ.

R℟. **Father, into your hands I commend my spirit.**

3.

Psalm 55:5-6, 13, 14-15, 17-18, 23

℟. (23ab) **Throw your cares on the Lord, and he will support you.**
   or:
℟. **Alleluia.**

My heart quakes within me;
   the terror of death has fallen upon me.
Fear and trembling come upon me,
   and horror overwhelms me.

℟. **Throw your cares on the Lord, and he will support you.**
   or:
℟. **Alleluia.**

If an enemy had reviled me,
   I could have borne it;
If he who hates me had vaunted himself against me,
   I might have hidden from him.

℟. **Throw your cares on the Lord, and he will support you.**
   or:
℟. **Alleluia.**

But you, my other self,
   my companion and my bosom friend!
You, whose comradeship I enjoyed;
   at whose side I walked in procession in the house of God!

℟. **Throw your cares on the Lord, and he will support you.**
   or:
℟. **Alleluia.**

But I will call upon God,
   and the LORD will save me.
In the evening, and at dawn, and at noon,
   I will grieve and moan,
   and he will hear my voice.

℟. **Throw your cares on the Lord, and he will support you.**
   or:
℟. **Alleluia.**

Cast your care upon the LORD,
  and he will support you;
  never will he permit the just man to be disturbed.

R̹. **Throw your cares on the Lord, and he will support you.**
  or:
R̹. **Alleluia.**

  4.

Psalm 69:8-10, 15-16, 17-19, 20-21, 22 and 27, 31 and 33-34

R̹. (14c) **Lord, in your great love, answer me.**
  or:
R̹. (see 21cd) **I looked for sympathy, there was none; for consolers, not one could I find.**

For your sake I bear insult,
  and shame covers my face.
I have become an outcast to my brothers,
  a stranger to my mother's sons,
Because zeal for your house consumes me,
  and the insults of those who blaspheme you fall upon me.

R̹. **Lord, in your great love, answer me.**
  or:
R̹. **I looked for sympathy, there was none; for consolers, not one could I find.**

Rescue me out of the mire; may I not sink!
  may I be rescued from my foes,
  and from the watery depths.
Let not the flood-waters overwhelm me,
  nor the abyss swallow me up,
  nor the pit close its mouth over me.

R̹. **Lord, in your great love, answer me.**
  or:
R̹. **I looked for sympathy, there was none; for consolers, not one could I find.**

(cont.)

Answer me, O Lᴏʀᴅ, for bounteous is your kindness;
  in your great mercy turn toward me.
Hide not your face from your servant;
  in my distress make haste to answer me.
Come and ransom my life;
  as an answer for my enemies, redeem me.

℟. Lord, in your great love, answer me.
  or:
℟. I looked for sympathy, there was none; for consolers, not one could I find.

You know my reproach, my shame and my ignominy:
  before you are all of my foes.
Insult has broken my heart, and I am weak,
  I looked for sympathy, but there was none;
  for consolers, not one could I find.

℟. Lord, in your great love, answer me.
  or:
℟. I looked for sympathy, there was none; for consolers, not one could I find.

Rather they put gall in my food;
  and in my thirst they gave me vinegar to drink.
For they kept after him whom you smote,
  and added to the pain of him you wounded.

℟. Lord, in your great love, answer me.
  or:
℟. I looked for sympathy, there was none; for consolers, not one could I find.

I will praise the name of God in song,
  and I will glorify him with thanksgiving;
"See, you lowly ones, and be glad;
  you who seek God, may your hearts revive!
For the Lᴏʀᴅ hears the poor,
  and his own who are in the bonds he spurns not."

℟. Lord, in your great love, answer me.
  or:
℟. I looked for sympathy, there was none; for consolers, not one could I find.

5.

Psalm 118:5-7, 10-12, 13-15, 16-18, 19-21, 22-24

R℣. (1) **Give thanks to the Lord, for he is good, his love is everlasting.**

In my straits I called upon the LORD;
   the LORD answered me and set me free.
The LORD is with me; I fear not;
   what can man do against me?
The LORD is with me to help me,
   and I shall look down upon my foes.

R℣. Give thanks to the Lord, for he is good, his love is everlasting.

All the nations encompassed me;
   in the name of the LORD I crushed them.
They encompassed me on every side;
   in the name of the LORD I crushed them.
They encompassed me like bees,
   they flared up like fire among thorns;
   in the name of the LORD I crushed them.

R℣. Give thanks to the Lord, for he is good, his love is everlasting.

I was hard pressed and was falling,
   but the LORD helped me.
My strength and my courage is the LORD,
   and he has been my savior.
The joyful shout of victory
   in the tents of the just:
"The right hand of the LORD has struck with power."

R℣. Give thanks to the Lord, for he is good, his love is everlasting.

"The right hand of the LORD I exalted;
   the right hand of the LORD has struck with power."
I shall not die, but live,
   and declare the works of the LORD.
Though the LORD has indeed chastised me,
   yet he has not delivered me to death.

(cont.)

R℣. Give thanks to the Lord, for he is good, his love is everlasting.

Open to me the gates of justice;
    I will enter them and give thanks to the LORD.
This is the gate of the LORD;
    the just shall enter it.
I will give thanks to you, for you have answered me
    and have been my savior.

R℣. Give thanks to the Lord, for he is good, his love is everlasting.

The stone which the builders rejected
    has become the cornerstone.
By the LORD has this been done;
    it is wonderful in our eyes.
This is the day the LORD has made;
    let us be glad and rejoice in it.

R℣. Give thanks to the Lord, for he is good, his love is everlasting.

972 READING II FROM THE NEW TESTAMENT

1.

1 Corinthians 1:18-25   We proclaim Christ crucified.

A reading from the first Letter of Saint Paul to the Corinthians

Brothers and sisters:
The message of the cross is foolishness to those who are perishing,
but to us who are being saved it is the power of God.
For it is written:

I will destroy the wisdom of the wise,
and the learning of the learned I will set aside.

Where is the wise one?
Where is the scribe?
Where is the debater of this age?
Has not God made the wisdom of the world foolish?
For since in the wisdom of God
the world did not come to know God through wisdom,
it was the will of God through the foolishness of the proclamation
to save those who have faith.
For Jews demand signs and Greeks look for wisdom,
but we proclaim Christ crucified,
a stumbling block to Jews and foolishness to Gentiles,
but to those who are called, Jews and Greeks alike,
Christ the power of God and the wisdom of God.
For the foolishness of God is wiser than human wisdom,
and the weakness of God is stronger than human strength.

The word of the Lord.

2.

Ephesians 2:13-18   Christ is our peace, who broke down the dividing wall
of enmity, through his flesh.

A reading from the Letter of Saint Paul to the Ephesians

Brothers and sisters:
In Christ Jesus you who once were far off have become near
    by the Blood of Christ.

For he is our peace,
    he who made both one
    and broke down the dividing wall of enmity, through his flesh,
    abolishing the law with its commandments and legal claims,
    that he might create in himself one new person in place of the two,
    thus establishing peace,
    and might reconcile both with God, in one Body, through the cross,
    putting that enmity to death by it.
He came and preached peace to you who were far off
    and peace to those who were near,
    for through him we both have access in one Spirit to the Father.

The word of the Lord.

3.

Philippians 2:6-11   He humbled himself. Because of this God greatly exalted him.

A reading from the Letter of Saint Paul to the Philippians

Christ Jesus, though he was in the form of God,
    did not regard equality with God
    something to be grasped.
    Rather, he emptied himself,
    taking the form of a slave,
    coming in human likeness;
    and found human in appearance,
    he humbled himself,
    becoming obedient to death,
        even death on a cross.
Because of this, God greatly exalted him
    and bestowed on him the name
    that is above every name,
    that at the name of Jesus
    every knee should bend,
    of those in heaven and on earth and under the earth,
    and every tongue confess that
    Jesus Christ is Lord,
    to the glory of God the Father.

The word of the Lord.

4.

Philippians 3:8-14   To know him and the power of his resurrection and the sharing of his sufferings.

A reading from the Letter of Saint Paul to the Philippians

Brothers and sisters:
I consider everything as a loss
   because of the supreme good of knowing Christ Jesus my Lord.
For his sake I have accepted the loss of all things
   and I consider them so much rubbish,
   that I may gain Christ and be found in him,
   not having any righteousness of my own based on the law
   but that which comes through faith in Christ,
   the righteousness from God,
   depending on faith to know him and the power of his resurrection
   and the sharing of his sufferings by being conformed to his death,
   if somehow I may attain the resurrection from the dead.

It is not that I have already taken hold of it
   or have already attained perfect maturity,
   but I continue my pursuit in hope that I may possess it,
   since I have indeed been taken possession of by Christ Jesus.
Brothers and sisters, I for my part
   do not consider myself to have taken possession.
Just one thing: forgetting what lies behind
   but straining forward to what lies ahead,
   I continue my pursuit toward the goal,
   the prize of God's upward calling, in Christ Jesus.

The word of the Lord.

5.

Hebrews 5:7-9   He learned obedience and became the source of eternal salvation.

A reading from the Letter to the Hebrews

In the days when Christ Jesus was in the flesh,
  he offered prayers and supplications with loud cries and tears
  to the one who was able to save him from death,
  and he was heard because of his reverence.
Son though he was, he learned obedience from what he suffered;
  and when he was made perfect,
  he became the source of eternal salvation for all who obey him.

The word of the Lord.

973 ALLELUIA VERSE AND VERSE BEFORE THE GOSPEL

1.

Philippians 2:8-9

**Christ humbled himself, becoming obedient to death,
even death on a cross.
Because of this God greatly exalted him
and bestowed on him the name that is above every name.**

2.

**We adore you, O Christ, and we bless you,
because by your Cross you have redeemed the world.**

3.

**Through wood we became slaves, and through the holy Cross we were freed;
the fruit of the tree seduced us, the Son of God redeemed us.**

974 GOSPEL

First Option

Mark 8:31-34   The Son of Man must suffer greatly.

☩ **A reading from the holy Gospel according to Mark**

Jesus began to teach his disciples
    that the Son of Man must suffer greatly
    and be rejected by the elders, the chief priests, and the scribes,
    and be killed, and rise after three days.
He spoke this openly.
Then Peter took him aside and began to rebuke him.
At this he turned around and, looking at his disciples,
    rebuked Peter and said, "Get behind me, Satan.
You are thinking not as God does, but as human beings do."

He summoned the crowd with his disciples and said to them,
    "Whoever wishes to come after me must deny himself,
    take up his cross, and follow me."

The Gospel of the Lord.

Second Option

Mark 12:1-12   They seized him and killed him, and threw him out of the vineyard.

✠ **A reading from the holy Gospel according to Mark**

Jesus began to speak to the chief priests, the scribes, and the elders in
  parables.
"A man planted a vineyard, put a hedge around it,
  dug a wine press, and built a tower.
Then he leased it to tenant farmers and left on a journey.
At the proper time he sent a servant to the tenants
  to obtain from them some of the produce of the vineyard.
But they seized him, beat him,
  and sent him away empty-handed.
Again he sent them another servant.
And that one they beat over the head and treated shamefully.
He sent yet another whom they killed.
So, too, many others;
  some they beat, others they killed.
He had one other to send, a beloved son.
He sent him to them last of all, thinking,
  'They will respect my son.'
But those tenants said to one another, 'This is the heir.
Come, let us kill him, and the inheritance will be ours.'
So they seized him and killed him,
  and threw him out of the vineyard.
What then will the owner of the vineyard do?
He will come, put the tenants to death, and give the vineyard to others.
Have you not read this Scripture passage:

> *The stone that the builders rejected*
>   *has become the cornerstone;*
> *by the Lord has this been done,*
>   *and it is wonderful in our eyes?"*

They were seeking to arrest him
  but they feared the crowd,
  for they realized that he had addressed the parable to them.
So they left him and went away.

The Gospel of the Lord.

Third Option

Luke 24:35-48   Look at my hands and my feet.

✠ **A reading from the holy Gospel according to Luke**

The disciples recounted what had taken place along the way,
  and how they had come to recognize Jesus in the breaking of bread.

While they were still speaking about this,
  He stood in their midst and said to them,
  "Peace be with you."
But they were startled and terrified
  and thought that they were seeing a ghost.
Then he said to them, "Why are you troubled?
And why do questions arise in your hearts?
Look at my hands and my feet, that it is I myself.
Touch me and see, because a ghost does not have flesh and bones
  as you can see I have."
And as he said this,
  he showed them his hands and his feet.
While they were still incredulous for joy and were amazed,
  he asked them, "Have you anything here to eat?"
They gave him a piece of baked fish;
  he took it and ate it in front of them.

He said to them,
  "These are my words that I spoke to you while I was still with you,
  that everything written about me in the law of Moses
  and in the prophets and psalms must be fulfilled."
Then he opened their minds to understand the Scriptures.
And he said to them,
  "Thus it is written that the Christ would suffer
  and rise from the dead on the third day
  and that repentance, for the forgiveness of sins,
  would be preached in his name
  to all the nations, beginning from Jerusalem.
You are witnesses of these things."

The Gospel of the Lord.

Fourth Option

John 12:31-36a   When I am lifted up from the earth I will draw everyone to myself.

☩ **A reading from the holy Gospel according to John**

Jesus said to the crowd:
"Now is the time of judgment on this world;
  now the ruler of this world will be driven out.
And when I am lifted up from the earth,
  I will draw everyone to myself."
He said this indicating the kind of death he would die.
So the crowd answered him,
  "We have heard from the law that the Christ remains forever.
Then how can you say that the Son of Man must be lifted up?
Who is this Son of Man?"
Jesus said to them,
  "The light will be among you only a little while.
Walk while you have the light,
  so that darkness may not overcome you.
Whoever walks in the dark does not know where he is going.
While you have the light, believe in the light,
  so that you may become children of the light."

The Gospel of the Lord.

975 READING FROM THE ACCOUNT OF THE LORD'S PASSION

1.

Matthew 26:47-56   Have you come out as against a robber, with swords and clubs to seize me?

✠ A reading from the holy Gospel according to Matthew

While Jesus was still speaking to his disciples,
  Judas, one of the Twelve, arrived,
    accompanied by a large crowd, with swords and clubs,
    who had come from the chief priests and the elders of the people.
His betrayer had arranged a sign with them, saying,
  "The man I shall kiss is the one; arrest him."
Immediately he went over to Jesus and said,
  "Hail, Rabbi!" and kissed him.
Jesus answered him,
  "Friend, do what you have come for."
Then stepping forward they laid hands on Jesus and arrested him.
And behold, one of those who accompanied Jesus
  put his hand to his sword, drew it,
    and struck the high priest's servant, cutting off his ear.
Then Jesus said to him,
  "Put your sword back into its sheath,
    for all who take the sword will perish by the sword.
Do you think that I cannot call upon my Father
  and he will not provide me at this moment
    with more than twelve legions of angels?
But then how would the Scriptures be fulfilled
  which say that it must come to pass in this way?"
At that hour Jesus said to the crowds,
  "Have you come out as against a robber,
    with swords and clubs to seize me?
Day after day I sat teaching in the temple area,
  yet you did not arrest me.
But all this has come to pass
  that the writings of the prophets may be fulfilled."
Then all the disciples left him and fled.

The Gospel of the Lord.

2.

Matthew 27:33-50   Jesus cried out again with a loud voice and gave up his spirit.

✠ **A reading from the holy Gospel according to Matthew**

They came to a place called Golgotha
  (which means Place of the Skull),
  and they gave Jesus wine to drink mixed with gall.
But when he had tasted it, he refused to drink.
After they had crucified him,
  they divided his garments by casting lots;
  then they sat down and kept watch over him there.
And they placed over his head the written charge against him:
  This is Jesus, the King of the Jews.
Two revolutionaries were crucified with him,
  one on his right and the other on his left.
Those passing by reviled him, shaking their heads and saying,
  "You who would destroy the temple and rebuild it in three days,
  save yourself, if you are the Son of God,
  and come down from the cross!"
Likewise the chief priests with the scribes and elders mocked him and said,
  "He saved others; he cannot save himself.
So he is the king of Israel!
Let him come down from the cross now,
  and we will believe in him.
He trusted in God;
  let God deliver him now if he wants him.
For he said, 'I am the Son of God.'"
The revolutionaries who were crucified with him
  also kept abusing him in the same way.

From noon onward, darkness came over the whole land
  until three in the afternoon.
And about three o'clock Jesus cried out in a loud voice,
  "Eli, Eli, lema sabachthani?"
  which means, "My God, my God, why have you forsaken me?"
Some of the bystanders who heard it said,
  "This one is calling for Elijah."
Immediately one of them ran to get a sponge;
  he soaked it in wine, and putting it on a reed,
  gave it to him to drink.

But the rest said,
  "Wait, let us see if Elijah comes to save him."
But Jesus cried out again in a loud voice,
  and gave up his spirit.

The Gospel of the Lord.

3.

Mark 14:32-41   My soul is sorrowful even to death.

✝ **A reading from the holy Gospel according to Mark**

Then they came to a place named Gethsemane,
  and Jesus said to his disciples,
  "Sit here while I pray."
He took with him Peter, James, and John,
  and began to be troubled and distressed.
Then he said to them, "My soul is sorrowful even to death.
Remain here and keep watch."
He advanced a little and fell to the ground and prayed
    that if it were possible the hour might pass by him;
    he said, "Abba, Father, all things are possible to you.
Take this cup away from me,
    but not what I will but what you will."
When he returned he found them asleep.
He said to Peter, "Simon, are you asleep?
Could you not keep watch for one hour?
Watch and pray that you may not undergo the test.
The spirit is willing but the flesh is weak."
Withdrawing again, he prayed, saying the same thing.
Then he returned once more and found them asleep,
    for they could not keep their eyes open
    and did not know what to answer him.
He returned a third time and said to them,
    "Are you still sleeping and taking your rest?
It is enough. The hour has come.
Behold, the Son of Man is to be handed over to sinners."

The Gospel of the Lord.

4.

Mark 14:55-65   They all condemned him as deserving to die.

✠   **A reading from the holy Gospel according to Mark**

The chief priests and the entire Sanhedrin
kept trying to obtain testimony against Jesus
in order to put him to death,
but they found none.
Many gave false witness against him,
but their testimony did not agree.
Some took the stand and testified falsely against him,
alleging, "We heard him say,
'I will destroy this temple made with hands
and within three days I will build another
not made with hands.'"
Even so their testimony did not agree.
The high priest rose before the assembly and questioned Jesus,
saying, "Have you no answer?
What are these men testifying against you?"
But he was silent and answered nothing.
Again the high priest asked him and said to him,
"Are you the Christ, the son of the Blessed One?"
Then Jesus answered, "I am;
and 'you will see the Son of Man
seated at the right hand of the Power
and coming with the clouds of heaven.'"
At that the high priest tore his garments and said,
"What further need have we of witnesses?
You have heard the blasphemy.
What do you think?"
They all condemned him as deserving to die.
Some began to spit on him.
They blindfolded him and struck him and said to him, "Prophesy!"
And the guards greeted him with blows.

The Gospel of the Lord.

5.

Mark 15:1-15   Then what do you want me to do with the man you call the King of the Jews?

☩   **A reading from the holy Gospel according to Mark**

As soon as morning came,
　　the chief priests with the elders and the scribes,
　　that is, the whole Sanhedrin, held a council.
They bound Jesus, led him away, and handed him over to Pilate.
Pilate questioned him,
　　"Are you the King of the Jews?"
He said to him in reply, "You say so."
The chief priests accused him of many things.
Again Pilate questioned him,
　　"Have you no answer?
See how many things they accuse you of."
Jesus gave him no further answer, so that Pilate was amazed.

Now on the occasion of the feast he used to release to them
　　one prisoner whom they requested.
A man called Barabbas was then in prison
　　along with the rebels who had committed murder in a rebellion.
The crowd came forward and began to ask him
　　to do for them as he was accustomed.
Pilate answered,
　　"Do you want me to release to you the King of the Jews?"
For he knew that it was out of envy
　　that the chief priests had handed him over.
But the chief priests stirred up the crowd
　　to have him release Barabbas for them instead.
Pilate again said to them in reply,
　　"Then what do you want me to do
　　with the man you call the King of the Jews?"
They shouted again, "Crucify him."
Pilate said to them, "Why? What evil has he done?"
They only shouted the louder, "Crucify him."
So Pilate, wishing to satisfy the crowd,
　　released Barabbas to them and, after he had Jesus scourged,
　　handed him over to be crucified.

The Gospel of the Lord.

6.

Mark 15:16-20   They clothed him in purple, and weaving a crown of thorns, placed it on him.

✝ **A reading from the holy Gospel according to Mark**

The soldiers led Jesus away inside the palace,
    that is, the praetorium, and assembled the whole cohort.
They clothed him in purple and,
    weaving a crown of thorns, placed it on him.
They began to salute him with, "Hail, King of the Jews!"
    and kept striking his head with a reed and spitting upon him.
They knelt before him in homage.
And when they had mocked him,
    they stripped him of the purple cloak,
    dressed him in his own clothes,
    and led him out to crucify him.

The Gospel of the Lord.

7.

Mark 15:33-39; 16:1-6   *Eloi, Eloi, lema sabachthani.* You seek Jesus of Nazareth, the crucified. He has been raised.

✝ **A reading from the holy Gospel according to Mark**

At noon darkness came over the whole land
    until three in the afternoon.
And at three o'clock Jesus cried out in a loud voice,
    "Eloi, Eloi, lema sabachthani?"
    which is translated,
    "My God, my God, why have you forsaken me?"
Some of the bystanders who heard it said,
    "Look, he is calling Elijah."
One of them ran, soaked a sponge with wine, put it on a reed,
    and gave it to him to drink, saying,
    "Wait, let us see if Elijah comes to take him down."
Jesus gave a loud cry and breathed his last.
The veil of the sanctuary was torn in two from top to bottom.
When the centurion who stood facing him
    saw how he breathed his last he said,
    "Truly this man was the Son of God!"

When the sabbath was over,
  Mary Magdalene, Mary, the mother of James, and Salome
  bought spices so that they might go and anoint him.
Very early when the sun had risen,
  on the first day of the week, they came to the tomb.
They were saying to one another,
  "Who will roll back the stone for us
  from the entrance to the tomb?"
When they looked up,
  they saw that the stone had been rolled back;
  it was very large.
On entering the tomb they saw a young man
  sitting on the right side, clothed in a white robe,
  and they were utterly amazed.
He said to them, "Do not be amazed!
You seek Jesus of Nazareth, the crucified.
He has been raised; he is not here.
Behold the place where they laid him."

The Gospel of the Lord.

8.

Luke 23:33-34, 39-46   Father, into your hands I commend my spirit.

✝   **A reading from the holy Gospel according to Luke**

**When they came to the place called the Skull,
    they crucified him and the criminals there,
    one on his right, the other on his left.
Then Jesus said,
    "Father, forgive them, they know not what they do."
They divided his garments by casting lots.**

**Now one of the criminals hanging there
    reviled Jesus, saying,
    "Are you not the Christ?
Save yourself and us."
The other man, however, rebuking him, said in reply,
    "Have you no fear of God,
    for you are subject to the same condemnation?
And indeed, we have been condemned justly,
    for the sentence we received corresponds to our crimes,
    but this man has done nothing criminal."
Then he said,
    "Jesus, remember me when you come into your Kingdom."
He replied to him,
    "Amen, I say to you,
    today you will be with me in Paradise."**

**It was now about noon and darkness came over the whole land
    until three in the afternoon
    because of an eclipse of the sun.
Then the veil of the temple was torn down the middle.
Jesus cried out in a loud voice,
    "Father, into your hands I commend my spirit";
    and when he had said this he breathed his last.**

The Gospel of the Lord.

9.

John 19:28-37   One soldier thrust his lance into his side, and
immediately Blood and water flowed out.

☩ **A reading from the holy Gospel according to John**

Jesus, aware that everything was now finished,
in order that the Scripture might be fulfilled, said,
"I thirst."
There was a vessel filled with common wine.
So they put a sponge soaked in wine on a sprig of hyssop
and put it up to his mouth.
When Jesus had taken the wine, he said,
"It is finished."
And bowing his head, he handed over the spirit.

Now since it was preparation day,
in order that the bodies might not remain on the cross on the sabbath,
for the sabbath day of that week was a solemn one,
the Jews asked Pilate that their legs be broken
and they be taken down.
So the soldiers came and broke the legs of the first
and then of the other one who was crucified with Jesus.
But when they came to Jesus and saw that he was already dead,
they did not break his legs,
but one soldier thrust his lance into his side,
and immediately Blood and water flowed out.
An eyewitness has testified, and his testimony is true;
he knows that he is speaking the truth,
so that you also may come to believe.
For this happened so that the Scripture passage might be fulfilled:
Not a bone of it will be broken.
And again another passage says:
They will look upon him whom they have pierced.

The Gospel of the Lord.

THE MOST HOLY EUCHARIST

976 READING I FROM THE OLD TESTAMENT

1.

Genesis 14:18-20 Melchizedek brought out bread and wine.

A reading from the Book of Genesis

Melchizedek, king of Salem, brought out bread and wine,
    and being a priest of God Most High,
    he blessed Abram with these words:
    "Blessed be Abram by God Most High,
        the creator of heaven and earth;
    And blessed be God Most High,
        who delivered your foes into your hand."
Then Abram gave him a tenth of everything.

The word of the Lord.

2.

Exodus 12:21-27 Seeing the blood on the lintel and the two doorposts, the Lord will pass over that door.

A reading from the Book of Exodus

Moses called all the elders of the children of Israel and said to them,
    "Go and procure lambs for your families,
    and slaughter them as Passover victims.
Then take a bunch of hyssop,
    and dipping it in the blood that is in the basin,
    sprinkle the lintel and the two doorposts with this blood.
But none of you shall go outdoors until morning.
For the LORD will go by, striking down the Egyptians.
Seeing the blood on the lintel and the two doorposts,
    the LORD will pass over that door
    and not let the destroyer come into your houses to strike you down.

"You shall observe this as a perpetual ordinance
    for yourselves and your descendants.
Thus, you must also observe this rite
    when you have entered the land
    which the LORD will give you as he promised.

When your children ask you,
   'What does this rite of yours mean?' you shall reply,
   'This is the Passover sacrifice of the LORD,
   who passed over the houses of the children of Israel in Egypt;
   when he struck down the Egyptians, he spared our houses.'"

Then the people bowed down in worship.

The word of the Lord.

   3.

Exodus 16:2-4, 12-15   I will now rain down bread from heaven for you.

A reading from the Book of Exodus

The whole congregation of the children of Israel
   grumbled against Moses and Aaron.
The children of Israel said to them,
   "Would that we had died at the LORD's hand in the land of Egypt,
   as we sat by our fleshpots and ate our fill of bread!
But you had to lead us into this desert
   to make the whole community die of famine!"

Then the LORD said to Moses,
   "I will now rain down bread from heaven for you.
Each day the people are to go out and gather their daily portion;
   thus will I test them,
   to see whether they follow my instructions or not.

"I have heard the grumbling of the children of Israel.
Tell them: In the evening twilight you shall eat flesh,
   and in the morning you shall have your fill of bread,
   so that you may know that I, the LORD, am your God."

In the evening quail came up and covered the camp.
In the morning a dew lay all about the camp,
   and when the dew evaporated, there on the surface of the desert
   were fine flakes like hoarfrost on the ground.
On seeing it, the children of Israel asked one another, "What is this?"
   for they did not know what it was.
But Moses told them,
   "This is the bread that the LORD has given you to eat."

The word of the Lord.

4.

Exodus 24:3-8   This is the blood of the covenant that the Lord has made with you.

A reading from the Book of Exodus

When Moses came to the people
    and related all the words and ordinances of the LORD,
    they all answered with one voice,
    "We will do everything that the LORD has told us."
Moses then wrote down all the words of the LORD and,
    rising early the next day,
    he erected at the foot of the mountain an altar
    and twelve pillars for the twelve tribes of Israel.
Then, having sent certain young men of the children of Israel
    to offer burnt offerings and sacrifice young bulls
    as peace offerings to the LORD,
    Moses took half of the blood and put it in large bowls;
    the other half he splashed on the altar.
Taking the book of the covenant, he read it aloud to the people,
    who answered, "All that the LORD has said, we will heed and do."
Then he took the blood and sprinkled it on the people, saying,
    "This is the blood of the covenant
    that the LORD has made with you
    in accordance with all these words of his."

The word of the Lord.

5.

Deuteronomy 8:2-3, 14b-16a   He fed you with manna, a food unknown to you and your fathers.

A reading from the Book of Deuteronomy

Moses said to the people:
"Remember how for forty years now the LORD, your God,
    has directed all your journeying in the desert,
    so as to test you by affliction
    and find out whether or not it was your intention
    to keep his commandments.
He therefore let you be afflicted with hunger,
    and then fed you with manna,
    a food unknown to you and your fathers;

in order to show you that not by bread alone does one live,
but by every word that comes forth from the mouth of the LORD.

"The LORD, your God,
who brought you out of the land of Egypt,
that place of slavery;
who guided you through the vast and terrible desert
with its saraph serpents and scorpions,
its parched and waterless ground;
who brought forth water for you from the flinty rock
and fed you in the desert with manna,
a food unknown to your fathers."

The word of the Lord.

6.

1 Kings 19:4-8   Strengthened by that food, he walked to the mountain of God.

A reading from the first Book of Kings

Elijah went a day's journey into the desert,
until he came to a broom tree and sat beneath it.
He prayed for death saying:
"This is enough, O LORD!
Take my life, for I am no better than my fathers."
He lay down and fell asleep under the broom tree,
but then an angel touched him and ordered him to get up and eat.
Elijah looked and there at his head was a hearth cake
and a jug of water.
After he ate and drank, he lay down again,
but the angel of the LORD came back a second time,
touched him, and ordered,
"Get up and eat, else the journey will be too long for you!"
He got up, ate, and drank;
then, strengthened by that food,
he walked forty days and forty nights to the mountain of God, Horeb.

The word of the Lord.

7.

Proverbs 9:1-6   Come, eat of my food and drink of the wine I have mixed.

A reading from the Book of Proverbs

Wisdom has built her house,
    she has set up her seven columns;
She has dressed her meat, mixed her wine,
    yes, she has spread her table.
She has sent out her maidens; she calls
    from the heights out over the city:
"Let whoever is simple turn in here;
    to the one who lacks understanding, I say,
Come, eat of my food,
    and drink of the wine I have mixed!
Forsake foolishness that you may live;
    advance in the way of understanding."

The word of the Lord.

977 READING I FROM THE NEW TESTAMENT DURING THE SEASON OF EASTER

First Option

Acts 2:42-47   They devoted themselves to meeting together in the temple area and to breaking bread in their homes.

A reading from the Acts of the Apostles

The brothers and sisters devoted themselves
to the teaching of the Apostles and to the communal life,
to the breaking of the bread and to the prayers.
Awe came upon everyone,
and many wonders and signs were done through the Apostles.
All who believed were together and had all things in common;
they would sell their property and possessions
and divide them among all according to each one's need.
Every day they devoted themselves
to meeting together in the temple area
and to breaking bread in their homes.
They ate their meals with exultation and sincerity of heart,
praising God and enjoying favor with all the people.
And every day the Lord added to their number those who were being saved.

The word of the Lord.

Second Option

Acts 10:34a, 37-43   We ate and drank with him after he rose from
the dead.

A reading from the Acts of the Apostles

Peter proceeded to speak, saying:
"You know what has happened all over Judea,
   beginning in Galilee after the baptism
   that John preached,
   how God anointed Jesus of Nazareth
   with the Holy Spirit and power.
He went about doing good
   and healing all those oppressed by the Devil,
   for God was with him.
We are witnesses of all that he did
   both in the country of the Jews and in Jerusalem.
They put him to death by hanging him on a tree.
This man God raised on the third day and granted that he be visible,
   not to all the people, but to us,
   the witnesses chosen by God in advance,
   who ate and drank with him after he rose from the dead.
He commissioned us to preach to the people
   and testify that he is the one appointed by God
   as judge of the living and the dead.
To him all the prophets bear witness,
   that everyone who believes in him
   will receive forgiveness of sins through his name."

The word of the Lord.

Third Option

Revelation 1:5-8   To him who loves us and freed us from our sins by his Blood.

A reading from the Book of Revelation

Grace to you and peace from Jesus Christ, who is the faithful witness,
** the firstborn of the dead and ruler of the kings of the earth.**
To him who loves us and has freed us from our sins by his Blood,
** who has made us into a kingdom, priests for his God and Father,**
** to him be glory and power forever and ever. Amen.**

** Behold, he is coming amid the clouds,**
**   and every eye will see him,**
**   even those who pierced him.**
** All the peoples of the earth will lament him.**
**   Yes. Amen.**
"I am the Alpha and the Omega," says the Lord God,
** "the one who is and who was and who is to come, the almighty."**

The word of the Lord.

Fourth Option

Revelation 7:9-14   They have washed their robes and made them white
in the Blood of the Lamb.

A reading from the Book of Revelation

I, John, had a vision of a great multitude,
  which no one could count,
    from every nation, race, people, and tongue.
They stood before the throne and before the Lamb,
  wearing white robes and holding palm branches in their hands.
They cried out in a loud voice:

  "Salvation comes from our God, who is seated on the throne,
    and from the Lamb."

All the angels stood around the throne
  and around the elders and the four living creatures.
They prostrated themselves before the throne,
  worshiped God, and exclaimed:

  "Amen. Blessing and glory, wisdom and thanksgiving,
    honor, power, and might
    be to our God forever and ever. Amen."

Then one of the elders spoke up and said to me,
  "Who are these wearing white robes, and where did they come from?"
I said to him, "My lord, you are the one who knows."
He said to me,
  "These are the ones who have survived the time of great distress;
  they have washed their robes
  and made them white in the Blood of the Lamb.

  "For this reason they stand before God's throne
    and worship him day and night in his temple.
    The One who sits on the throne will shelter them.
  They will not hunger or thirst anymore,
    nor will the sun or any heat strike them.
  For the Lamb who is in the center of the throne will shepherd them
    and lead them to springs of life-giving water,
    and God will wipe away every tear from their eyes."

The word of the Lord.

978 RESPONSORIAL PSALM

1.

Psalm 23:1-3, 4, 5, 6

℞. (1) **The Lord is my shepherd; there is nothing I shall want.**

The LORD is my shepherd; I shall not want.
  In verdant pastures he gives me repose;
Beside restful waters he leads me;
  he refreshes my soul.
He guides me in right paths
  for his name's sake.

℞. **The Lord is my shepherd; there is nothing I shall want.**

Even though I walk in the dark valley
  I fear no evil; for you are at my side
With your rod and your staff
  that give me courage.

℞. **The Lord is my shepherd; there is nothing I shall want.**

You spread the table before me
  in the sight of my foes;
You anoint my head with oil;
  my cup overflows.

℞. **The Lord is my shepherd; there is nothing I shall want.**

Only goodness and kindness follow me
  all the days of my life;
And I shall dwell in the house of the LORD
  for years to come.

℞. **The Lord is my shepherd; there is nothing I shall want.**

2.

Psalm 34:2-3, 4-5, 6-7, 8-9, 10-11

℞. (9a) **Taste and see the goodness of the Lord.**
  or:
℞. **Alleluia.**

I will bless the LORD at all times;
  his praise shall be ever in my mouth.
Let my soul glory in the LORD;
  the lowly will hear me and be glad.

℞. **Taste and see the goodness of the Lord.**
  or:
℞. **Alleluia.**

Glorify the LORD with me,
  let us together extol his name.
I sought the LORD, and he answered me
  and delivered me from all my fears.

℞. **Taste and see the goodness of the Lord.**
  or:
℞. **Alleluia.**

Look to him that you may be radiant with joy,
  and your faces may not blush with shame.
When the poor one called out, the Lord heard,
  and from all his distress he saved him.

℞. **Taste and see the goodness of the Lord.**
  or:
℞. **Alleluia.**

The angel of the LORD encamps
  around those who fear him, and delivers them.
Taste and see how good the LORD is;
  blessed the one who takes refuge in him.

℟. Taste and see the goodness of the Lord.
   or:
℟. Alleluia.

Fear the LORD, you his holy ones;
   for nought is lacking to those who fear him.
The great grow poor and hungry;
   but those who seek the LORD want for no good thing.

℟. Taste and see the goodness of the Lord.
   or:
℟. Alleluia.

   3.

Psalm 40:2 and 4ab, 7-8a, 8b-9, 10

℟. (8a and 9a) **Here I am, Lord; I come to do your will.**

I have waited, waited for the LORD,
   and he stooped toward me.
And he put a new song in my mouth,
   a hymn to our God.

℟. Here I am, Lord; I come to do your will.

Sacrifice or oblation you wished not,
   but ears open to obedience you gave me.
Burnt offerings or sin-offerings you sought not;
   then said I, "Behold I come."

℟. Here I am, Lord; I come to do your will.

"In the written scroll it is prescribed for me.
To do your will, O my God, is my delight,
   and your law is within my heart!"

℟. Here I am, Lord; I come to do your will.

I announced your justice in the vast assembly;
   I did not restrain my lips, as you, O LORD, know.

℟. Here I am, Lord; I come to do your will.

4.

Psalm 78:3 and 4a and 7ab, 23-24, 25 and 54

℞. (24b) **The Lord gave them bread from heaven.**

What we have heard and know,
   and what our fathers have declared to us,
We will not hide from their sons;
   that they should put their hope in God,
And not forget the deeds of God.

℞. **The Lord gave them bread from heaven.**

Yet he commanded the skies above;
   the doors of heaven he opened.
He rained manna upon them for food;
   and gave them heavenly bread.

℞. **The Lord gave them bread from heaven.**

Man ate the bread of angels,
   food he sent them in abundance.
And he brought them to his holy land,
   to the mountains his right hand had won.

℞. **The Lord gave them bread from heaven.**

5.

Psalm 110:1, 2, 3, 4

℞. **Christ the Lord, a priest for ever in the line of Melchizedek, offered bread and wine.**
   or:
℞. (4b) **You are a priest for ever in the line of Melchizedek.**

The LORD said to my Lord: "Sit at my right hand
   till I make your enemies your footstool."

℞. **Christ the Lord, a priest for ever in the line of Melchizedek, offered bread and wine.**
   or:
℞. **You are a priest for ever in the line of Melchizedek.**

The scepter of your power the Lord will stretch forth from Zion:
  "Rule in the midst of your enemies."

R︎. Christ the Lord, a priest for ever in the line of Melchizedek, offered bread and wine.
  or:
R︎. You are a priest for ever in the line of Melchizedek.

"Yours is princely power in the day of your birth, in holy splendor;
  before the daystar, like the dew, I have begotten you."

R︎. Christ the Lord, a priest for ever in the line of Melchizedek, offered bread and wine.
  or:
R︎. You are a priest for ever in the line of Melchizedek.

The LORD has sworn, and he will not repent:
  "You are a priest forever, according to the order of Melchizedek."

R︎. Christ the Lord, a priest for ever in the line of Melchizedek, offered bread and wine.
  or:
R︎. You are a priest for ever in the line of Melchizedek.

6.

Psalm 116:12-13, 15-16bc, 17-18

R︎. (see 1 Corinthians 10:16) **Our blessing-cup is a communion with the Blood of Christ.**

How shall I make a return to the LORD
  for all the good he has done for me?
The cup of salvation I will take up,
  and I will call upon the name of the LORD.

R︎. Our blessing-cup is a communion with the Blood of Christ.

Precious in the eyes of the LORD
  is the death of his faithful ones.
I am your servant, the son of your handmaid;
  you have loosed my bonds.

(cont.)

℟. **Our blessing-cup is a communion with the Blood of Christ.**

To you will I offer sacrifice of thanksgiving,
   and I will call upon the name of the LORD.
My vows to the LORD I will pay
   in the presence of all his people.

℟. **Our blessing-cup is a communion with the Blood of Christ.**

   7.

Psalm 145:10-11, 15-16, 17-18

℟. (see 16) **You open your hand to feed us, Lord; you answer all our needs.**

Let all your works give you thanks, O LORD,
   and let your faithful ones bless you.
Let them discourse of the glory of your Kingdom
   and speak of your might.

℟. **You open your hand to feed us, Lord; you answer all our needs.**

The eyes of all look hopefully to you;
   and you give them their food in due season;
You open your hand
   and satisfy the desire of every living thing.

℟. **You open your hand to feed us, Lord; you answer all our needs.**

The LORD is just in all his ways
   and holy in all his works.
The LORD is near to all who call upon him,
   to all who call upon him in truth.

℟. **You open your hand to feed us, Lord; you answer all our needs.**

8.

Psalm 147:12-13, 14-15, 19-20

℟. (John 6:58c) **Whoever eats this bread will live for ever.**
   or:
℟. **Alleluia.**

Glorify the Lord, O Jerusalem;
   praise your God, O Zion.
For he has strengthened the bars of your gates;
   he has blessed your children within you.

℟. **Whoever eats this bread will live for ever.**
   or:
℟. **Alleluia.**

He has granted peace in your borders;
   with the best of wheat he fills you.
He sends forth his command to the earth;
   swiftly runs his word!

℟. **Whoever eats this bread will live for ever.**
   or:
℟. **Alleluia.**

He has proclaimed his word to Jacob,
   his statutes and his ordinances to Israel.
He has not done thus for any other nation;
   his ordinances he has not made known to them. Alleluia.

℟. **Whoever eats this bread will live for ever.**
   or:
℟. **Alleluia.**

979 READING II FROM THE NEW TESTAMENT

1.

1 Corinthians 10:16-17   We, though many, are one bread, one Body.

A reading from the first Letter of Saint Paul to the Corinthians

Brothers and sisters:
The cup of blessing that we bless,
** is it not a participation in the Blood of Christ?**
The bread that we break,
** is it not a participation in the Body of Christ?**
Because the loaf of bread is one,
** we, though many, are one Body,**
** for we all partake of the one loaf.**

The word of the Lord.

2.

1 Corinthians 11:23-26   For as often as you eat the bread and drink the cup, you proclaim the death of the Lord.

A reading from the first Letter of Saint Paul to the Corinthians

Brothers and sisters:
I received from the Lord what I also handed on to you,
** that the Lord Jesus, on the night he was handed over,**
** took bread and, after he had given thanks,**
** broke it and said, "This is my Body that is for you.**
Do this in remembrance of me."
In the same way also the cup, after supper, saying,
** "This cup is the new covenant in my Blood.**
Do this, as often as you drink it, in remembrance of me."
For as often as you eat this bread and drink the cup,
** you proclaim the death of the Lord until he comes.**

The word of the Lord.

3.

Hebrews 9:11-15   The Blood of Christ will cleanse our consciences.

A reading from the Letter to the Hebrews

When Christ came as high priest
** of the good things that have come to be,**

passing through the greater and more perfect tabernacle
  not made by hands, that is, not belonging to this creation,
  he entered once for all into the sanctuary,
  not with the blood of goats and calves
  but with his own Blood, thus obtaining eternal redemption.
For if the blood of goats and bulls
  and the sprinkling of a heifer's ashes
  can sanctify those who are defiled
  so that their flesh is cleansed,
  how much more will the Blood of Christ,
  who through the eternal Spirit offered himself unblemished to God,
  cleanse our consciences from dead works to worship the living God.

For this reason he is mediator of a new covenant:
  since a death has taken place for deliverance from transgressions
  under the first covenant,
  those who are called may receive the promised eternal inheritance.

The word of the Lord.

4.

Hebrews 12:18-19, 22-24   You have approached the sprinkled Blood that speaks more eloquently than that of Abel.

A reading from the Letter to the Hebrews

Brothers and sisters:
You have not approached that which could be touched
  and a blazing fire and gloomy darkness
  and storm and a trumpet blast
  and a voice speaking words such that those who heard
  begged that no message be further addressed to them.
No, you have approached Mount Zion
  and the city of the living God, the heavenly Jerusalem,
  and countless angels in festal gathering,
  and the assembly of the firstborn enrolled in heaven,
  and God the judge of all,
  and the spirits of the just made perfect,
  and Jesus, the mediator of a new covenant,
  and the sprinkled Blood that speaks more eloquently
  than that of Abel.

The word of the Lord.

5.

1 Peter 1:17-21   You were ransomed with the precious Blood of Christ, as of a spotless unblemished Lamb.

A reading from the first Letter of Saint Peter

Beloved:
If you invoke as Father him who judges impartially
  according to each one's works,
    conduct yourselves with reverence during the time of your sojourning,
    realizing that you were ransomed from your futile conduct,
    handed on by your ancestors,
    not with perishable things like silver or gold
    but with the precious Blood of Christ
    as of a spotless unblemished Lamb.
He was known before the foundation of the world
  but revealed in the final time for you,
  who through him believe in God
  who raised him from the dead and gave him glory,
    so that your faith and hope are in God.

The word of the Lord.

6.

1 John 5:4-8   So there are three that testify, the Spirit, the water, and the Blood.

A reading from the first Letter of Saint John

Beloved:
Whoever is begotten by God conquers the world.
And the victory that conquers the world is our faith.
Who indeed is the victor over the world
  but the one who believes that Jesus is the Son of God?

This is the one who came through water and Blood, Jesus Christ,
  not by water alone, but by water and Blood.
The Spirit is the one that testifies,
  and the Spirit is truth.
So there are three that testify,
  the Spirit, the water, and the Blood,
  and the three are of one accord.

The word of the Lord.

980 ALLELUIA VERSE AND VERSE BEFORE THE GOSPEL

1.

John 6:51

**I am the living bread that came down from heaven,
says the Lord;
whoever eats this bread will live forever.**

2.

John 6:56

**Whoever eats my Flesh and drinks my Blood
remains in me, and I in him, says the Lord.**

3.

John 6:57

**Just as the living Father sent me and I have life because of the Father,
so also the one who feeds on me will have life because of me.**

4.

See Revelation 1:5ab

**Jesus Christ, you are the faithful witness,
the firstborn of the dead,
you have loved us and freed us from our sins by your Blood.**

5.

Revelation 5:9

**Worthy are you to receive the scroll and to break open its seals,
for you were slain and have redeemed us with your Blood.**

981 GOSPEL

1.

Mark 14:12-16, 22-26   This is my Body. This is my Blood.

☩ **A reading from the holy Gospel according to Mark**

On the first day of the Feast of Unleavened Bread,
  when they sacrificed the Passover Lamb,
  the disciples of Jesus said to him,
  "Where do you want us to go
  and prepare for you to eat the Passover?"
He sent two of his disciples and said to them,
  "Go into the city and a man will meet you,
  carrying a jar of water.
Follow him.
Wherever he enters, say to the master of the house,
  'The Teacher says, "Where is my guest room
  where I may eat the Passover with my disciples?"'
Then he will show you a large upper room furnished and ready.
Make the preparations for us there."
The disciples then went off, entered the city,
  and found it just as he had told them;
  and they prepared the Passover.

While they were eating,
  he took bread, said the blessing,
  broke it, gave it to them, and said,
  "Take it; this is my Body."
Then he took a cup, gave thanks, and gave it to them,
  and they all drank from it.
He said to them,
  "This is my Blood of the covenant,
  which will be shed for many.
Amen, I say to you,
  I shall not drink again the fruit of the vine
  until the day when I drink it new in the Kingdom of God."
Then, after singing a hymn,
  they went out to the Mount of Olives.

The Gospel of the Lord.

2.

Mark 15:16-20   They clothed him in purple and, weaving a crown of thorns, placed it on him.

✛ **A reading from the holy Gospel according to Mark**

The soldiers led Jesus away inside the palace,
   that is, the praetorium, and assembled the whole cohort.
They clothed him in purple and,
   weaving a crown of thorns, placed it on him.
They began to salute him with, "Hail, King of the Jews!"
   and kept striking his head with a reed and spitting upon him.
They knelt before him in homage.
And when they had mocked him,
   they stripped him of the purple cloak,
   dressed him in his own clothes,
   and led him out to crucify him.

The Gospel of the Lord.

3.

Luke 9:11b-17   They all ate and were satisfied.

✠ **A reading from the holy Gospel according to Luke**

Jesus spoke to the crowds about the Kingdom of God,
    and he healed those who needed to be cured.
As the day was drawing to a close,
    the Twelve approached him and said,
    "Dismiss the crowd
    so that they can go to the surrounding villages and farms
    and find lodging and provisions;
    for we are in a deserted place here."
He said to them, "Give them some food yourselves."
They replied, "Five loaves and two fish are all we have,
    unless we ourselves go and buy food for all these people."
Now the men there numbered about five thousand.
Then he said to his disciples,
    "Have them sit down in groups of about fifty."
They did so and made them all sit down.
Then taking the five loaves and the two fish,
    and looking up to heaven,
    he said the blessing over them, broke them,
    and gave them to the disciples to set before the crowd.
They all ate and were satisfied.
And when the leftover fragments were picked up,
    they filled twelve wicker baskets.

The Gospel of the Lord.

4.

Luke 22:39-44   His sweat became like drops of blood, falling on the ground.

✠ **A reading from the holy Gospel according to Luke**

Jesus went, as was his custom, to the Mount of Olives,
  and the disciples followed him.
When he arrived at the place he said to them,
  "Pray that you may not undergo the test."
After withdrawing about a stone's throw from them and kneeling,
  Jesus prayed, saying, "Father, if you are willing,
  take this cup away from me;
  still, not my will but yours be done."
And to strengthen him an angel from heaven appeared to him.
He was in such agony and he prayed so fervently
  that his sweat became like drops of blood
  falling on the ground.

The Gospel of the Lord.

5.

Long Form

Luke 24:13-35   They recognized him in the breaking of bread.

☩ **A reading from the holy Gospel according to Luke**

That very day, the first day of the week,
    two of the disciples of Jesus were going
    to a village called Emmaus, seven miles from Jerusalem,
    and they were conversing about all the things that had occurred.
And it happened that while they were conversing and debating,
    Jesus himself drew near and walked with them,
    but their eyes were prevented from recognizing him.
He asked them,
    "What are you discussing as you walk along?"
They stopped, looking downcast.
One of them, named Cleopas, said to him in reply,
    "Are you the only visitor to Jerusalem
    who does not know of the things
    that have taken place there in these days?"
And he replied to them, "What sort of things?"
They said to him,
    "The things that happened to Jesus the Nazarene,
    who was a prophet mighty in deed and word
    before God and all the people,
    how our chief priests and rulers both handed him over
    to a sentence of death and crucified him.
But we were hoping that he would be the one to redeem Israel;
    and besides all this,
    it is now the third day since this took place.
Some women from our group, however, have astounded us:
    they were at the tomb early in the morning
    and did not find his Body;
    they came back and reported
    that they had indeed seen a vision of angels
    who announced that he was alive.
Then some of those with us went to the tomb
    and found things just as the women had described,
    but him they did not see."
And he said to them, "Oh, how foolish you are!
How slow of heart to believe all that the prophets spoke!

Was it not necessary that the Christ should suffer these things
and enter into his glory?"
Then beginning with Moses and all the prophets,
he interpreted to them what referred to him
in all the Scriptures.
As they approached the village to which they were going,
he gave the impression that he was going on farther.
But they urged him, "Stay with us,
for it is nearly evening and the day is almost over."
So he went in to stay with them.
And it happened that, while he was with them at table,
he took bread, said the blessing,
broke it, and gave it to them.
With that their eyes were opened and they recognized him,
but he vanished from their sight.
Then they said to each other,
"Were not our hearts burning within us
while he spoke to us on the way and opened the Scriptures to us?"
So they set out at once and returned to Jerusalem
where they found gathered together
the Eleven and those with them, who were saying,
"The Lord has truly been raised and has appeared to Simon!"
Then the two recounted
what had taken place on the way
and how he was made known to them in the breaking of bread.

The Gospel of the Lord.

OR Short Form

Luke 24:13-16, 28-35   They recognized him in the breaking of bread.

☩ **A reading from the holy Gospel according to Luke**

That very day, the first day of the week,
two of the disciples of Jesus were going
to a village called Emmaus, seven miles from Jerusalem,
and they were conversing about all the things that had occurred.
And it happened that while they were conversing and debating,
Jesus himself drew near and walked with them,
but their eyes were prevented from recognizing him.
As they approached the village to which they were going,
he gave the impression that he was going on farther.
But they urged him, "Stay with us,
for it is nearly evening and the day is almost over."
So he went in to stay with them.
And it happened that, while he was with them at table,
he took bread, said the blessing,
broke it, and gave it to them.
With that their eyes were opened and they recognized him,
but he vanished from their sight.
Then they said to each other,
"Were not our hearts burning within us
while he spoke to us on the way and opened the Scriptures to us?"
So they set out at once and returned to Jerusalem
where they found gathered together
the Eleven and those with them, who were saying,
"The Lord has truly been raised and has appeared to Simon!"
Then the two recounted
what had taken place on the way
and how he was made known to them in the breaking of bread.

The Gospel of the Lord.

6.

John 6:1-15   He distributed to those who were reclining as much as they wanted.

☩ **A reading from the holy Gospel according to John**

Jesus went across the Sea of Galilee.
A large crowd followed him,
because they saw the signs he was performing on the sick.

Jesus went up on the mountain,
  and there he sat down with his disciples.
The Jewish feast of Passover was near.
When Jesus raised his eyes
  and saw that a large crowd was coming to him,
  he said to Philip,
  "Where can we buy enough food for them to eat?"
He said this to test him,
  because he himself knew what he was going to do.
Philip answered him,
  "Two hundred days' wages worth of food would not be enough
  for each of them to have a little."
One of his disciples,
  Andrew, the brother of Simon Peter, said to him,
  "There is a boy here who has five barley loaves and two fish;
  but what good are these for so many?"
Jesus said, "Have the people recline."
Now there was a great deal of grass in that place.
So the men reclined, about five thousand in number.
Then Jesus took the loaves, gave thanks,
  and distributed them to those who were reclining,
  and also as much of the fish as they wanted.
When they had had their fill, he said to his disciples,
  "Gather the fragments left over,
  so that nothing will be wasted."
So they collected them,
  and filled twelve wicker baskets with fragments
  from the five barley loaves that had been more than they could eat.
When the people saw the sign he had done, they said,
  "This is truly the prophet, the one who is to come into the world."
Since Jesus knew that they were going to come
  and carry him off to make him king,
  he withdrew again to the mountain alone.

The Gospel of the Lord.

7.

John 6:24-35   Whoever comes to me will never hunger, and whoever believes in me will never thirst.

✠   **A reading from the holy Gospel according to John**

When the crowd saw that neither Jesus nor his disciples were there,
    they themselves got into boats
    and came to Capernaum looking for Jesus.
And when they found him across the sea they said to him,
    "Rabbi, when did you get here?"
Jesus answered them and said,
    "Amen, amen, I say to you,
    you are looking for me not because you saw signs
    but because you ate the loaves and were filled.
Do not work for food that perishes
    but for the food that endures for eternal life,
    which the Son of Man will give you.
For on him the Father, God, has set his seal."
So they said to him,
    "What can we do to accomplish the works of God?"
Jesus answered and said to them,
    "This is the work of God, that you believe in the one he sent."
So they said to him,
    "What sign can you do, that we may see and believe in you?
What can you do?
Our ancestors ate manna in the desert, as it is written:
    He gave them bread from heaven to eat."
So Jesus said to them,
    "Amen, amen, I say to you,
    it was not Moses who gave the bread from heaven;
    my Father gives you the true bread from heaven.
For the bread of God is that which comes down from heaven
    and gives life to the world."
So they said to him,
    "Sir, give us this bread always."
Jesus said to them,
    "I am the bread of life;
    whoever comes to me will never hunger,
    and whoever believes in me will never thirst."

The Gospel of the Lord.

8.

John 6:41-51   I am the living bread that came down from heaven.

☩ **A reading from the holy Gospel according to John**

The Jews murmured about Jesus because he said,
  "I am the bread that came down from heaven,"
  and they said,
  "Is this not Jesus, the son of Joseph?
Do we not know his father and mother?
Then how can he say,
  'I have come down from heaven'?"
Jesus answered and said to them,
  "Stop murmuring among yourselves.
No one can come to me unless the Father who sent me draw him,
  and I will raise him on the last day.
It is written in the prophets:
  They shall all be taught by God.
Everyone who listens to my Father and learns from him comes to me.
Not that anyone has seen the Father
  except the one who is from God;
  he has seen the Father.
Amen, amen, I say to you,
  whoever believes has eternal life.
I am the bread of life.
Your ancestors ate the manna in the desert, but they died;
  this is the bread that comes down from heaven
  so that one may eat it and not die.
I am the living bread that came down from heaven;
  whoever eats this bread will live forever;
  and the bread that I will give is my Flesh for the life of the world."

The Gospel of the Lord.

9.

John 6:51-58   My Flesh is true food and my Blood is true drink.

✠ **A reading from the holy Gospel according to John**

**Jesus said to the Jews who were present:
"I am the living bread that came down from heaven;
     whoever eats this bread will live forever;
     and the bread that I will give
     is my Flesh for the life of the world."**

**The Jews quarreled among themselves, saying,
     "How can this man give us his Flesh to eat?"
Jesus said to them,
     "Amen, amen, I say to you,
     unless you eat the Flesh of the Son of Man and drink his Blood,
     you do not have life within you.
Whoever eats my Flesh and drinks my Blood
     has eternal life,
     and I will raise him on the last day.
For my Flesh is true food,
     and my Blood is true drink.
Whoever eats my Flesh and drinks my Blood
     remains in me and I in him
Just as the living Father sent me
     and I have life because of the Father,
     so also the one who feeds on me
     will have life because of me.
This is the bread that came down from heaven.
Unlike your ancestors who ate and still died,
     whoever eats this bread will live forever."**

The Gospel of the Lord.

10.

John 19:31-37   One soldier thrust his lance into his side and immediately
Blood and water flowed out.

✠ **A reading from the holy Gospel according to John**

Since it was preparation day,
   in order that the bodies might not remain on the cross on the sabbath,
   for the sabbath day of that week was a solemn one,
   the Jews asked Pilate that their legs be broken
   and they be taken down.
So the soldiers came and broke the legs of the first
   and then of the other one who was crucified with Jesus.
But when they came to Jesus and saw that he was already dead,
   they did not break his legs,
   but one soldier thrust his lance into his side,
   and immediately Blood and water flowed out.
An eyewitness has testified, and his testimony is true;
   he knows that he is speaking the truth,
   so that you also may come to believe.
For this happened so that the Scripture passage might be fulfilled:
   Not a bone of it will be broken.
And again another passage says:
   They will look upon him whom they have pierced.

The Gospel of the Lord.

11.

John 21:1-14   Jesus came over and took the bread and gave it to them.

☩ **A reading from the holy Gospel according to John**

**Jesus revealed himself again to his disciples at the Sea of Tiberias.
He revealed himself in this way.
Together were Simon Peter, Thomas called Didymus,
    Nathanael from Cana in Galilee,
    Zebedee's sons, and two others of his disciples.
Simon Peter said to them, "I am going fishing."
They said to him, "We also will come with you."
So they went out and got into the boat,
    but that night they caught nothing.
When it was already dawn, Jesus was standing on the shore;
    but the disciples did not realize that it was Jesus.
Jesus said to them, "Children, have you caught anything to eat?"
They answered him, "No."
So he said to them, "Cast the net over the right side of the boat
    and you will find something."
So they cast it, and were not able to pull it in
    because of the number of fish.
So the disciple whom Jesus loved said to Peter, "It is the Lord."
When Simon Peter heard that it was the Lord,
    he tucked in his garment, for he was lightly clad,
    and jumped into the sea.
The other disciples came in the boat,
    for they were not far from shore, only about a hundred yards,
    dragging the net with the fish.
When they climbed out on shore,
    they saw a charcoal fire with fish on it and bread.
Jesus said to them, "Bring some of the fish you just caught."
So Simon Peter went over and dragged the net ashore
    full of one hundred fifty-three large fish.
Even though there were so many, the net was not torn.
Jesus said to them, "Come, have breakfast."
And none of the disciples dared to ask him, "Who are you?"
    because they realized it was the Lord.
Jesus came over and took the bread and gave it to them,
    and in like manner the fish.**

This was now the third time Jesus was revealed to his disciples after being raised from the dead.

The Gospel of the Lord.

982 JESUS CHRIST, THE ETERNAL HIGH PRIEST

The following readings for the votive Mass of Jesus Christ, the High Priest, may also be used in the votive Mass for the Holy Eucharist.

FIRST READING

First Option

Isaiah 52:13–53:1   He was pierced for our offenses.

A reading from the Book of the Prophet Isaiah

The LORD says:
See, my servant shall prosper,
   he shall be raised high and greatly exalted.
Even as many were amazed at him—
   so marred was his look beyond human semblance
   and his appearance beyond that of the sons of man—
So shall he startle many nations,
   because of him kings shall stand speechless;
For those who have not been told shall see,
   those who have not heard shall ponder it.

Who would believe what we have heard?
   To whom has the arm of the LORD been revealed?
He grew up like a sapling before him,
   like a shoot from the parched earth;
There was in him no stately bearing to make us look at him,
   nor appearance that would attract us to him.
He was spurned and avoided by people,
   a man of suffering, accustomed to infirmity,
One of those from whom people hide their faces,
   spurned, and we held him in no esteem.

Yet it was our infirmities that he bore,
   our sufferings that he endured,
While we thought of him as stricken,
   as one smitten by God and afflicted.
But he was pierced for our offenses,
   crushed for our sins;
Upon him was the chastisement that makes us whole,
   by his stripes we were healed.

We had all gone astray like sheep,
  each following his own way;
But the LORD laid upon him the guilt of us all.

Though he was harshly treated, he submitted
  and opened not his mouth;
Like a lamb led to the slaughter
  or a sheep before the shearers,
  he was silent and opened not his mouth.
Oppressed and condemned, he was taken away,
  and who would have thought any more of his destiny?
When he was cut off from the land of the living,
  and smitten for the sin of his people,
A grave was assigned him among the wicked
  and a burial place with evildoers,
Though he had done no wrong
  nor spoken any falsehood.
But the LORD was pleased
  to crush him in infirmity.

If he gives his life as an offering for sin,
  he shall see his descendants in a long life,
  and the will of the LORD shall be accomplished through him.

Because of his affliction
  he shall see the light in fullness of days;
Through his suffering, my servant shall justify many,
  and their guilt he shall bear.
Therefore I will give him his portion among the great,
  and he shall divide the spoils with the mighty,
Because he surrendered himself to death
  and was counted among the wicked;
And he shall take away the sins of many,
  and win pardon for their offenses.

The word of the Lord.

Second Option

Hebrews 10:12-23   By one offering he has made perfect forever those
who are being consecrated.

A reading from the Letter to the Hebrews

Christ offered one sacrifice for sins,
   and took his seat forever at the right hand of God;
   now he waits until his enemies are made his footstool.
For by one offering he has made perfect forever
   those who are being consecrated.
The Holy Spirit also testifies to us, for after saying:

   This is the covenant I will establish
      with them after those days, says the Lord:
   "I will put my laws in their hearts,
      and I will write them upon their minds,"

   he also says:

   Their sins and their evildoing
      I will remember no more.

Where there is forgiveness of these,
   there is no longer offering for sin.

Therefore, brothers and sisters, since through the Blood of Jesus
   we have confidence of entrance into the sanctuary
   by the new and living way he opened up for us through the veil,
   that is, his Flesh,
   and since we have "a great priest over the house of God,"
   let us approach with a sincere heart and in absolute trust,
   with our hearts sprinkled clean from an evil conscience
   and our bodies washed in pure water.
Let us hold unwaveringly to our confession that gives us hope,
   for he who made the promise is trustworthy.

The word of the Lord.

RESPONSORIAL PSALM

Psalm 40:6ab, 9bc, 10, 11ab

℟. (8a and 9a) **Here I am, Lord; I come to do your will.**

How numerous you have made,
  O Lord, my God, your wondrous deeds!
And in your plans for us
  there is none to equal you.

℟. **Here I am, Lord; I come to do your will.**

To do your will, O God, is my delight,
  and your law is within my heart!

℟. **Here I am, Lord; I come to do your will.**

I announced your justice in the vast assembly;
  I did not restrain my lips, as you, O Lord, know.

℟. **Here I am, Lord; I come to do your will.**

Your justice I kept not hid within my heart;
  your faithfulness and salvation I have spoken of.

℟. **Here I am, Lord; I come to do your will.**

ALLELUIA

Isaiah 42:1

℟. **Alleluia, alleluia.**

Here is my chosen one with whom I am pleased,
upon whom I have put my spirit:
he shall bring forth justice to the nations.

℟. **Alleluia, alleluia.**

GOSPEL

Luke 22:14-20   Do this in memory of me.

✠ **A reading from the holy Gospel according to Luke**

When the hour came,
　Jesus took his place at table with the Apostles.
He said to them,
　"I have eagerly desired to eat this Passover with you before I suffer,
　for, I tell you, I shall not eat it again
　until there is fulfillment in the Kingdom of God."
Then he took a cup, gave thanks, and said,
　"Take this and share it among yourselves;
　for I tell you that from this time on
　I shall not drink of the fruit of the vine
　until the Kingdom of God comes."
Then he took the bread, said the blessing,
　broke it, and gave it to them, saying,
　"This is my Body, which will be given for you;
　do this in memory of me."
And likewise the cup after they had eaten, saying,
　"This cup is the new covenant in my Blood,
　which will be shed for you."

The Gospel of the Lord.

THE MOST HOLY NAME OF JESUS

983 READING I FROM THE OLD TESTAMENT

1.

Exodus 3:11-15   I AM WHO AM sent me to you.

A reading from the Book of Exodus

Moses, hearing the voice of the Lord from the burning bush, said to him,
 "Who am I that I should go to Pharaoh
 and lead the children of Israel out of Egypt?"
He answered, "I will be with you;
 and this shall be your proof that it is I who have sent you:
 when you bring my people out of Egypt,
 you will worship God on this very mountain."
Moses said to God, "But when I go to the children of Israel
 and say to them, 'The God of your fathers has sent me to you,'
 if they ask me, 'What is his name?' what am I to tell them?"
God replied, "I am who am."
Then he added, "This is what you shall tell the children of Israel:
 I AM sent me to you."

God spoke further to Moses, "Thus shall you say to the children of Israel:
 The LORD, the God of your fathers,
 the God of Abraham, the God of Isaac, the God of Jacob,
 has sent me to you.

 "This is my name forever;
 this is my title for all generations."

The word of the Lord.

2.

Sirach 51:8-12   I will ever praise your name and be constant in my prayers to you.

A reading from the Book of Sirach

I remembered the mercies of the LORD,
  his kindness through ages past;
For he saves those who take refuge in him,
  and rescues them from every evil.
So I raised my voice from the very earth,
  from the gates of the netherworld, my cry.
I called out: O Lord, you are my father,
  you are my champion and my savior;
Do not abandon me in time of trouble,
  or leave me in the time of the proud without help.
I will ever praise your name
  and be constant in my prayers to you.

Thereupon my prayer was heard
  and you saved me from evil of every kind
  and rescued me from the time of trouble.

For this reason I thank you and I praise you,
  and bless the name of the LORD.

The word of the Lord.

984 READING I FROM THE NEW TESTAMENT DURING THE SEASON OF EASTER

1.

Acts 3:1-10   In the name of Jesus Christ the Nazorean, rise and walk.

A reading from the Acts of the Apostles

Peter and John were going up to the temple area
  for the three o'clock hour of prayer.
And a man crippled from birth was carried
  and placed at the gate of the temple called "the Beautiful Gate"
  every day to beg for alms from the people who entered the temple.
When he saw Peter and John about to go into the temple,
  he asked for alms.
But Peter looked intently at him, as did John,
  and said, "Look at us."
He paid attention to them, expecting to receive something from them.
Peter said, "I have neither silver nor gold,
  but what I do have I give you:
  in the name of Jesus Christ the Nazorean, rise and walk."
Then Peter took him by the right hand and raised him up,
  and immediately his feet and ankles grew strong.
He leaped up, stood, and walked around,
  and went into the temple with them,
  walking and jumping and praising God.
When all the people saw him walking and praising God,
  they recognized him as the one who used to sit begging
  at the Beautiful Gate of the temple,
  and they were filled with amazement and astonishment
  at what had happened to him.

The word of the Lord.

2.

Acts 4:8-12   There is no other salvation through any other name.

A reading from the Acts of the Apostles

Peter, filled with the Holy Spirit, said:
"Leaders of the people and elders:
   If we are being examined today
   about a good deed done to a cripple,
   namely, by what means he was saved,
   then all of you and all the people of Israel should know
   that it was in the name of Jesus Christ the Nazorean
   whom you crucified, whom God raised from the dead;
   in his name this man stands before you healed.
He is the stone rejected by you, the builders,
   which has become the cornerstone.
There is no salvation through anyone else,
   nor is there any other name under heaven
   given to the human race by which we are to be saved."

The word of the Lord.

3.

Acts 5:27-32, 40-42   They left rejoicing that they had been found worthy to suffer dishonor for the sake of the name.

A reading from the Acts of the Apostles

When the court officers had brought the Apostles in
   and made them stand before the Sanhedrin,
   the high priest questioned them,
   "We gave you strict orders, [did we not?],
   to stop teaching in that name.
Yet you have filled Jerusalem with your teaching
   and want to bring this man's Blood upon us."
But Peter and the Apostles said in reply,
   "We must obey God rather than men.
The God of our ancestors raised Jesus,
   though you had him killed by hanging him on a tree.
God exalted him at his right hand as leader and savior
   to grant Israel repentance and forgiveness of sins.
We are witnesses of these things,
   as is the Holy Spirit that God has given to those who obey him."

After recalling the Apostles, the Sanhedrin had them flogged,
   ordered them to stop speaking in the name of Jesus,
   and dismissed them.
So they left the presence of the Sanhedrin,
   rejoicing that they had been found worthy
   to suffer dishonor for the sake of the name.
And all day long, both at the temple and in their homes,
   they did not stop teaching and proclaiming the Christ, Jesus.

The word of the Lord.

985 RESPONSORIAL PSALM

1.

Isaiah 12:2-3, 4bcd, 5-6

℟. (4a) **Praise the Lord and call upon his name.**

God indeed is my savior;
** I am confident and unafraid.**
My strength and my courage is the LORD,
** and he has been my savior.**
With joy you will draw water
** at the fountain of salvation.**

℟. **Praise the Lord and call upon his name.**

Give thanks to the LORD, acclaim his name;
** among the nations make known his deeds,**
** proclaim how exalted is his name.**

℟. **Praise the Lord and call upon his name.**

Sing praise to the LORD for his glorious achievement;
** let this be known throughout all the earth.**
Shout with exultation, O city of Zion,
** for great in your midst**
** is the Holy One of Israel!**

℟. **Praise the Lord and call upon his name.**

2.

Psalm 113:1-2, 3-4, 5-6

℟. (2) **Blessed be the name of the Lord forever.**
   or:
℟. **Alleluia.**

Praise, you servants of the LORD,
   praise the name of the LORD.
Blessed be the name of the LORD
   both now and forever.

℟. **Blessed be the name of the Lord forever.**
   or:
℟. **Alleluia.**

From the rising to the setting of the sun
   is the name of the LORD to be praised.
High above all nations is the LORD;
   above the heavens is his glory.

℟. **Blessed be the name of the Lord forever.**
   or:
℟. **Alleluia.**

Who is like the LORD, our God, who is enthroned on high
   and looks upon the heavens and the earth below?

℟. **Blessed be the name of the Lord forever.**
   or:
℟. **Alleluia.**

986 READING II FROM THE NEW TESTAMENT

1.

1 Corinthians 1:1-3   With all those everywhere who call upon the name of our Lord Jesus Christ.

A reading from the beginning of the first Letter of Saint Paul to the Corinthians

Paul, called to be an Apostle of Christ Jesus by the will of God,
    and Sosthenes our brother,
      to the Church of God that is in Corinth,
      to you who have been sanctified in Christ Jesus, called to be holy,
      with all those everywhere who call upon the name of our Lord Jesus
        Christ, their Lord and ours.
Grace to you and peace from God our Father
    and the Lord Jesus Christ.

The word of the Lord.

2.

Philippians 2:6-11   God bestowed on him the name that is above every name.

A reading from the Letter of Saint Paul to the Philippians

Christ Jesus, though he was in the form of God,
    did not regard equality with God something to be grasped.
    Rather, he emptied himself,
    taking the form of a slave,
    coming in human likeness;
    and found human in appearance,
    he humbled himself,
    becoming obedient to death,
      even death on a cross.
Because of this, God greatly exalted him
    and bestowed on him the name
    that is above every name,
    that at the name of Jesus
    every knee should bend,

of those in heaven and on earth and under the earth,
and every tongue confess that
Jesus Christ is Lord,
to the glory of God the Father.

The word of the Lord.

3.

Colossians 3:12-17   Do everything in the name of the Lord Jesus.

A reading from the Letter of Saint Paul to the Colossians

Brothers and sisters:
Put on, as God's chosen ones, holy and beloved,
heartfelt compassion, kindness, humility, gentleness, and patience,
bearing with one another and forgiving one another,
if one has a grievance against another;
as the Lord has forgiven you, so must you also do.
And over all these put on love,
that is, the bond of perfection.
And let the peace of Christ control your hearts,
the peace into which you were also called in one Body.
And be thankful.
Let the word of Christ dwell in you richly,
as in all wisdom you teach and admonish one another,
singing psalms, hymns, and spiritual songs
with gratitude in your hearts to God.
And whatever you do, in word or in deed,
do everything in the name of the Lord Jesus,
giving thanks to God the Father through him.

The word of the Lord.

987 ALLELUIA VERSE AND VERSE BEFORE THE GOSPEL

1.

Psalm 96:2

**Sing to the Lord and bless his name,
proclaim his salvation day after day.**

2.

Daniel 3:52b

**Praise to your holy and glorious name,
may you be praised forever.**

988 GOSPEL

1.

Matthew 1:18-25   You are to name him Jesus.

✝ **A reading from the holy Gospel according to Matthew**

This is how the birth of Jesus Christ came about.
When his mother Mary was betrothed to Joseph,
   but before they lived together,
   she was found with child through the Holy Spirit.
Joseph her husband, since he was a righteous man,
   yet unwilling to expose her to shame,
   decided to divorce her quietly.
Such was his intention when, behold,
   the angel of the Lord appeared to him in a dream and said,
   "Joseph, son of David,
   do not be afraid to take Mary your wife into your home.
For it is through the Holy Spirit
   that this child has been conceived in her.
She will bear a son and you are to name him Jesus,
   because he will save his people from their sins."
All this took place to fulfill
   what the Lord had said through the prophet:

   Behold, the virgin shall be with child and bear a son,
     and they shall name him Emmanuel,

   which means "God is with us."
When Joseph awoke, he did as the angel of the Lord had commanded him
   and took his wife into his home.
He had no relations with her until she bore a son,
   and he named him Jesus.

The Gospel of the Lord.

2.

Luke 2:16-21   He was named Jesus.

✠ **A reading from the holy Gospel according to Luke**

The shepherds went in haste to Bethlehem and found Mary and Joseph,
and the infant lying in the manger.
When they saw this,
they made known the message
that had been told them about this child.
All who heard it were amazed
by what had been told them by the shepherds.
And Mary kept all these things,
reflecting on them in her heart.
Then the shepherds returned,
glorifying and praising God
for all they had heard and seen,
just as it had been told to them.

When eight days were completed for his circumcision,
he was named Jesus,
the name given him by the angel
before he was conceived in the womb.

The Gospel of the Lord.

3.

John 14:6-14   If you ask anything of me in my name, I will do it.

✝ **A reading from the holy Gospel according to John**

Jesus said to Thomas, "I am the way and the truth and the life.
No one comes to the Father except through me.
If you know me, then you will also know my Father.
From now on you do know the Father and have seen him."
Philip said to him,
    "Master, show us the Father, and that will be enough for us."
Jesus said to him, "Have I been with you for so long a time
    and you still do not know me, Philip?
Whoever has seen me has seen the Father.
How can you say, 'Show us the Father'?
Do you not believe that I am in the Father and the Father is in me?
The words that I speak to you I do not speak on my own.
The Father who dwells in me is doing his works.
Believe me that I am in the Father and the Father is in me,
    or else, believe because of the works themselves.
Amen, amen, I say to you,
    whoever believes in me will do the works that I do,
    and will do greater ones than these,
    because I am going to the Father.
And whatever you ask in my name, I will do,
    so that the Father may be glorified in the Son.
If you ask anything of me in my name, I will do it."

The Gospel of the Lord.

THE MOST PRECIOUS BLOOD OF OUR LORD JESUS CHRIST

989 READING I FROM THE OLD TESTAMENT

1.

Exodus 12:21-27   Seeing the blood on the lintel and the two doorposts, the Lord will pass over that door.

A reading from the Book of Exodus

Moses called all the elders of the children of Israel and said to them,
  "Go and procure lambs for your families,
  and slaughter them as Passover victims.
Then take a bunch of hyssop,
  and dipping it in the blood that is in the basin,
  sprinkle the lintel and the two doorposts with this blood.
But none of you shall go outdoors until morning.
For the LORD will go by, striking down the Egyptians.
Seeing the blood on the lintel and the two doorposts,
  the LORD will pass over that door
  and not let the destroyer come into your houses to strike you down.

"You shall observe this as a perpetual ordinance
  for yourselves and your descendants.
Thus, you must also observe this rite
  when you have entered the land which the LORD will give you
  as he promised.
When your children ask you,
  'What does this rite of yours mean?' you shall reply,
  'This is the Passover sacrifice of the LORD,
  who passed over the houses of the children of Israel in Egypt;
  when he struck down the Egyptians, he spared our houses.'"

Then the people bowed down in worship.

The word of the Lord.

2.

Exodus 24:3-8   This is the blood of the covenant that the Lord has made
with you.

A reading from the Book of Exodus

When Moses came to the people
   and related all the words and ordinances of the LORD,
   they all answered with one voice,
   "We will do everything that the LORD has told us."
Moses then wrote down all the words of the LORD and,
   rising early the next day,
   he erected at the foot of the mountain an altar
   and twelve pillars for the twelve tribes of Israel.
Then, having sent certain young men of the children of Israel
   to offer burnt offerings and sacrifice young bulls
   as peace offerings to the LORD,
   Moses took half of the blood and put it in large bowls;
   the other half he splashed on the altar.
Taking the book of the covenant, he read it aloud to the people,
   who answered, "All that the LORD has said, we will heed and do."
Then he took the blood and sprinkled it on the people, saying,
   "This is the blood of the covenant
   that the LORD has made with you
   in accordance with all these words of his."

The word of the Lord.

990 READING I FROM THE NEW TESTAMENT DURING THE SEASON OF EASTER

1.

Revelation 1:5-8   To him who loves us and has freed us from our sins by his Blood.

A reading from the Book of Revelation

Grace to you and peace from Jesus Christ, who is the faithful witness,
  the firstborn of the dead and ruler of the kings of the earth.
To him who loves us and has freed us from our sins by his Blood,
  who has made us into a kingdom,
    priests for his God and Father,
  to him be glory and power forever and ever. Amen.

  Behold, he is coming amid the clouds,
    and every eye will see him,
      even those who pierced him.
  All the peoples of the earth will lament him.
    Yes. Amen.

"I am the Alpha and the Omega," says the Lord God,
  "the one who is and who was and who is to come, the almighty."

The word of the Lord.

2.

Revelation 7:9-14   They have washed their robes and made them white in the Blood of the Lamb.

A reading from the Book of Revelation

I, John, had a vision of a great multitude,
  which no one could count,
    from every nation, race, people, and tongue.
They stood before the throne and before the Lamb,
  wearing white robes and holding palm branches in their hands.
They cried out in a loud voice:
  "Salvation comes from our God, who is seated on the throne,
    and from the Lamb."
All the angels stood around the throne
  and around the elders and the four living creatures.
They prostrated themselves before the throne,
  worshiped God, and exclaimed:
  "Amen. Blessing and glory, wisdom and thanksgiving,
    honor, power, and might
    be to our God forever and ever. Amen."

Then one of the elders spoke up and said to me,
  "Who are these wearing white robes, and where did they come from?"
I said to him, "My lord, you are the one who knows."
He said to me,
  "These are the ones who have survived the time of great distress;
    they have washed their robes
    and made them white in the Blood of the Lamb."

The word of the Lord.

991 RESPONSORIAL PSALM

1.

Psalm 40:2 and 4ab, 7-8a, 8b-9, 10

℟. (see 8a and 9a)**Here I am, Lord; I come to do your will.**

I have waited, waited for the LORD,
and he stooped toward me.
And he put a new song into my mouth,
a hymn to our God.

℟. **Here I am, Lord; I come to do your will.**

Sacrifice or oblation you wished not,
but ears open to obedience you gave me.
Burnt offerings or sin-offerings you sought not;
then said I, "Behold I come."

℟. **Here I am, Lord; I come to do your will.**

"In the written scroll it is prescribed for me.
To do your will, O my God, is my delight,
and your law is within my heart!"

℟. **Here I am, Lord; I come to do your will.**

I announced your justice in the vast assembly;
I did not restrain my lips, as you, O LORD, know.

℟. **Here I am, Lord; I come to do your will.**

2.

Psalm 116:12-13, 15 and 16bc, 17-18

℟. (1 Corinthians 10:16) **Our blessing-cup is a communion with the Blood of Christ.**

How shall I make a return to the LORD
　for all the good he has done for me?
The cup of salvation I will take up,
　and I will call upon the name of the LORD.

℟. **Our blessing-cup is a communion with the Blood of Christ.**

Precious in the eyes of the LORD
　is the death of his faithful ones.
I am your servant, the son of your handmaid;
　you have loosed my bonds.

℟. **Our blessing-cup is a communion with the Blood of Christ.**

To you will I offer sacrifice of thanksgiving,
　and I will call upon the name of the LORD.
My vows to the LORD I will pay
　in the presence of all his people.

℟. **Our blessing-cup is a communion with the Blood of Christ.**

992 READING II FROM THE NEW TESTAMENT

1.

Hebrews 9:11-15　He entered once for all into the sanctuary with his own Blood.

A reading from the Letter to the Hebrews

When Christ came as high priest
  of the good things that have come to be,
  passing through the greater and more perfect tabernacle
  not made by hands, that is, not belonging to this creation,
  he entered once for all into the sanctuary,
  not with the blood of goats and calves
  but with his own Blood, thus obtaining eternal redemption.
For if the blood of goats and bulls
  and the sprinkling of a heifer's ashes
  can sanctify those who are defiled
  so that their flesh is cleansed,
  how much more will the Blood of Christ,
  who through the eternal spirit offered himself unblemished to God,
  cleanse our consciences from dead works to worship the living God.

For this reason he is mediator of a new covenant:
  since a death has taken place for deliverance from transgressions
  under the first covenant,
    those who are called may receive the promised eternal inheritance.

The word of the Lord.

2.

Hebrews 12:18-19, 22-24　You have approached the sprinkled Blood that speaks more eloquently than that of Abel.

A reading from the Letter to the Hebrews

Brothers and sisters:
You have not approached that which could be touched
  and a blazing fire and gloomy darkness
  and storm and a trumpet blast
  and a voice speaking words such that those who heard
  begged that no message be further addressed to them.

No, you have approached Mount Zion
and the city of the living God, the heavenly Jerusalem,
and countless angels in festal gathering,
and the assembly of the firstborn enrolled in heaven,
and God the judge of all,
and the spirits of the just made perfect,
and Jesus, the mediator of a new covenant,
and the sprinkled Blood that speaks more eloquently
than that of Abel.

The word of the Lord.

3.

1 Peter 1:17-21   You were ransomed with the precious Blood of Christ.

A reading from the first Letter of Saint Peter

Beloved:
If you invoke as Father him who judges impartially
according to each one's works,
conduct yourselves with reverence during the time of your sojourning,
realizing that you were ransomed from your futile conduct,
handed on by your ancestors,
not with perishable things like silver or gold
but with the precious Blood of Christ
as of a spotless unblemished Lamb.
He was known before the foundation of the world
but revealed in the final time for you,
who through him believe in God
who raised him from the dead and gave him glory,
so that your faith and hope are in God.

The word of the Lord.

4.

1 John 5:4-8   So, there are three that testify, the Spirit, the water, and
the Blood.

A reading from the first Letter of Saint John

Beloved:
Whoever is begotten by God conquers the world.
And the victory that conquers the world is our faith.
Who indeed is the victor over the world
  but the one who believes that Jesus is the Son of God?

This is the one who came through water and Blood, Jesus Christ,
  not by water alone, but by water and Blood.
The Spirit is the one that testifies,
  and the Spirit is truth.
So there are three that testify,
  the Spirit, the water, and the Blood,
  and the three are of one accord.

The word of the Lord.

993 ALLELUIA VERSE AND VERSE BEFORE THE GOSPEL

1.

Revelation 1:5ab

**Jesus Christ, you are the faithful witness,
the firstborn of the dead;
you have loved us and freed us from our sins by your Blood.**

2.

Revelation 5:9

**Worthy are you, O Lord, to receive the scroll and to break open its seals,
for you were slain and have redeemed us with your Blood.**

994 GOSPEL

1.

Mark 14:12-16, 22-26   This is my Body. This is my Blood.

✠ **A reading from the holy Gospel according to Mark**

On the first day of the Feast of Unleavened Bread,
    when they sacrificed the Passover Lamb,
    the disciples of Jesus said to him,
    "Where do you want us to go
    and prepare for you to eat the Passover?"
He sent two of his disciples and said to them,
    "Go into the city and a man will meet you,
    carrying a jar of water.
Follow him.
Wherever he enters, say to the master of the house,
    'The Teacher says, "Where is my guest room
    where I may eat the Passover with my disciples?"'
Then he will show you a large upper room furnished and ready.
Make the preparations for us there."
The disciples then went off, entered the city,
    and found it just as he had told them;
    and they prepared the Passover.

While they were eating,
    he took bread, said the blessing,
    broke it, gave it to them, and said,
    "Take it; this is my Body."
Then he took a cup, gave thanks, and gave it to them,
    and they all drank from it.
He said to them,
    "This is my Blood of the covenant,
    which will be shed for many.
Amen, I say to you,
    I shall not drink again the fruit of the vine
    until the day when I drink it new in the Kingdom of God."
Then, after singing a hymn,
    they went out to the Mount of Olives.

The Gospel of the Lord.

2.

Mark 15:16-20   They clothed him in purple and weaving a crown of thorns, placed it on him.

✢ **A reading from the holy Gospel according to Mark**

The soldiers led Jesus away inside the palace,
   that is, the praetorium, and assembled the whole cohort.
They clothed him in purple and,
   weaving a crown of thorns, placed it on him.
They began to salute him with, "Hail, King of the Jews!"
   and kept striking his head with a reed and spitting upon him.
They knelt before him in homage.
And when they had mocked him,
   they stripped him of the purple cloak,
   dressed him in his own clothes,
   and led him out to crucify him.

The Gospel of the Lord.

3.

Luke 22:39-44   He was in such agony and he prayed so fervently, that his sweat became like drops of blood.

✢ **A reading from the holy Gospel according to Luke**

Jesus went, as was his custom, to the Mount of Olives,
   and the disciples followed him.
When he arrived at the place he said to them,
   "Pray that you may not undergo the test."
After withdrawing about a stone's throw from them and kneeling,
   Jesus prayed, saying, "Father, if you are willing,
   take this cup away from me;
   still, not my will but yours be done."
And to strengthen him an angel from heaven appeared to him.
He was in such agony and he prayed so fervently
   that his sweat became like drops of blood
   falling on the ground.

The Gospel of the Lord.

4.

John 19:31-37   One soldier thrust his lance into his side, and immediately Blood and water poured out.

☩ **A reading from the holy Gospel according to John**

Since it was preparation day,
> **in order that the bodies might not remain on the cross on the sabbath,**
> **for the sabbath day of that week was a solemn one,**
> **the Jews asked Pilate that their legs be broken**
> **and they be taken down.**

So the soldiers came and broke the legs of the first
> **and then of the other one who was crucified with Jesus.**

But when they came to Jesus and saw that he was already dead,
> **they did not break his legs,**
> **but one soldier thrust his lance into his side,**
> **and immediately Blood and water flowed out.**

An eyewitness has testified, and his testimony is true;
> **he knows that he is speaking the truth,**
> **so that you also may come to believe.**

For this happened so that the Scripture passage might be fulfilled:
> ***Not a bone of it will be broken.***

And again another passage says:
> ***They will look upon him whom they have pierced.***

The Gospel of the Lord.

THE MOST SACRED HEART OF JESUS

995 READING I FROM THE OLD TESTAMENT

1.

Exodus 34:4-6, 8-9   The Lord, the Lord, a merciful and gracious God.

A reading from the Book of Exodus

Early in the morning Moses went up Mount Sinai
   as the LORD had commanded him,
   taking along the two stone tablets.

Having come down in a cloud, the LORD stood with Moses there
   and proclaimed his name, "LORD."
Thus the LORD passed before him and cried out,
   "The LORD, the LORD, a merciful and gracious God,
   slow to anger and rich in kindness and fidelity."
Moses at once bowed down to the ground in worship.
Then he said, "If I find favor with you, O LORD,
   do come along in our company.
This is indeed a stiff-necked people; yet pardon our wickedness and sins,
   and receive us as your own."

The word of the Lord.

2.

Deuteronomy 7:6-11   The Lord set his heart on you and chose you.

A reading from the Book of Deuteronomy

Moses said to the people:
"You are a people sacred to the LORD, your God;
he has chosen you from all the nations on the face of the earth
to be a people peculiarly his own.
It was not because you are the largest of all nations
that the LORD set his heart on you and chose you,
for you are really the smallest of all nations.
It was because the LORD loved you
and because of his fidelity to the oath he had sworn to your fathers,
that he brought you out with his strong hand
from the place of slavery,
and ransomed you from the hand of Pharaoh, king of Egypt.
Understand, then, that the LORD, your God, is God indeed,
the faithful God who keeps his merciful covenant
down to the thousandth generation
toward those who love him and keep his commandments,
but who repays with destruction the person who hates him;
he does not dally with such a one,
but makes him personally pay for it.
You shall therefore carefully observe the commandments,
the statutes, and the decrees which I enjoin on you today."

The word of the Lord.

3.

Deuteronomy 10:12-22   Yet in his love for your fathers, the Lord chose you, their descendants.

A reading from the Book of Deuteronomy

Moses said to the people:
"And now, Israel, what does the LORD, your God, ask of you
but to fear the LORD, your God, and follow his ways exactly,
to love and serve the LORD, your God,
with all your heart and all your soul,
to keep the commandments and statutes of the LORD
which I enjoin on you today for your own good?
Think! The heavens, even the highest heavens,
belong to the LORD, your God,
as well as the earth and everything on it.
Yet in his love for your fathers the LORD was so attached to them
as to choose you, their descendants,
in preference to all other peoples, as indeed he has now done.
Circumcise your hearts, therefore, and be no longer stiff-necked.
For the LORD, your God, is the God of gods,
the LORD of lords, the great God, mighty and awesome,
who has no favorites, accepts no bribes;
who executes justice for the orphan and the widow,
and befriends the alien, feeding and clothing them.
So you too must befriend the alien,
for you were once aliens yourselves in the land of Egypt.
The LORD, your God, shall you fear, and him shall you serve;
hold fast to him and swear by his name.
He is your glory, he, your God,
who has done for you those great and terrible things
which your own eyes have seen.
Your ancestors went down to Egypt seventy strong,
and now the LORD, your God,
has made you as numerous as the stars of the sky."

The word of the Lord.

4.

Isaiah 49:13-15   Even if she should forget, I will never forget you.

A reading from the Book of the Prophet Isaiah

Sing out, O heavens, and rejoice, O earth,
  break forth into song, you mountains.
For the Lord comforts his people
  and shows mercy to his afflicted.

But Zion said, "The Lord has forsaken me;
  my Lord has forgotten me."
Can a mother forget her infant,
  be without tenderness for the child of her womb?
Even should she forget,
  I will never forget you.

The word of the Lord.

5.

Jeremiah 31:1-4   With an age-old love I have loved you.

A reading from the Book of the Prophet Jeremiah

At that time, says the Lord,
  I will be the God of all the tribes of Israel,
  and they shall be my people.
    Thus says the Lord:
The people that escaped the sword
  have found favor in the desert.
As Israel comes forward to be given his rest,
  the Lord appears to him from afar:
With age-old love I have loved you;
  so I have kept my mercy toward you.
Again I will restore you, and you shall be rebuilt,
  O virgin Israel;
Carrying your festive tambourines,
  you shall go forth dancing with the merrymakers.

The word of the Lord.

6.

A reading from the Book of the Prophet Ezekiel

Thus says the Lord GOD:
I myself will look after and tend my sheep.
As a shepherd tends his flock
   when he finds himself among his scattered sheep,
   so will I tend my sheep.
I will rescue them from every place where they were scattered
   when it was cloudy and dark.
I will lead them out from among the peoples
   and gather them from the foreign lands;
   I will bring them back to their own country
   and pasture them upon the mountains of Israel
   in the land's ravines and all its inhabited places.
In good pastures will I pasture them,
   and on the mountain heights of Israel
   shall be their grazing ground.
There they shall lie down on good grazing ground,
   and in rich pastures shall they be pastured
   on the mountains of Israel.
I myself will pasture my sheep;
   I myself will give them rest, says the Lord GOD.
The lost I will seek out,
   the strayed I will bring back,
   the injured I will bind up,
   the sick I will heal,
   but the sleek and the strong I will destroy,
   shepherding them rightly.

The word of the Lord.

7.

Hosea 11:1, 3-4, 8c-9   My heart is overwhelmed.

A reading from the Book of the Prophet Hosea

Thus says the LORD:
When Israel was a child I loved him,
    out of Egypt I called my son.
Yet it was I who taught Ephraim to walk,
    who took them in my arms;
I drew them with human cords,
    with bands of love;
I fostered them like one
    who raises an infant to his cheeks;
Yet, though I stooped to feed my child,
    they did not know that I was their healer.

My heart is overwhelmed,
    my pity is stirred.
I will not give vent to my blazing anger,
    I will not destroy Ephraim again;
For I am God and not a man,
    the Holy One present among you;
    I will not let the flames consume you.

The word of the Lord.

996 READING I FROM THE NEW TESTAMENT DURING THE SEASON OF EASTER

1.

Revelation 3:14b, 20-22   I will dine with him and he with me.

A reading from the Book of Revelation

**""The Amen, the faithful and true witness,
the source of God's creation, says this:**

**"""Behold, I stand at the door and knock.
If anyone hears my voice and opens the door,
then I will enter his house and dine with him
and he with me.
I will give the victor the right to sit with me on my throne,
as I myself first won the victory
and sit with my Father on his throne.**

**"""Whoever has ears ought to hear
what the Spirit says to the churches."""**

The word of the Lord.

2.

Revelation 5:6-12   With your Blood you purchased us for God.

A reading from the Book of Revelation

I, John, saw standing in the midst of the throne
    and the four living creatures and the elders
    a Lamb that seemed to have been slain.
He had seven horns and seven eyes;
    these are the seven spirits of God sent out into the whole world.
He came and received the scroll
    from the right hand of the One who sat on the throne.
When he took it, the four living creatures and the twenty-four elders
    fell down before the Lamb.
Each of the elders held a harp and gold bowls filled with incense,
    which are the prayers of the holy ones.
They sang a new hymn:
    "Worthy are you to receive the scroll
        and to break open its seals,
        for you were slain and with your Blood you purchased for God
        those from every tribe and tongue, people and nation.
    You made them a kingdom and priests for our God,
        and they will reign on earth."
I looked again and heard the voices of many angels
    who surrounded the throne
    and the living creatures and the elders.
They were countless in number, and they cried out in a loud voice:
        "Worthy is the Lamb that was slain
            to receive power and riches, wisdom and strength,
            honor and glory and blessing."

The word of the Lord.

997 RESPONSORIAL PSALM

1.

Isaiah 12:2-3, 4bcd, 5-6

R⃒. (3) **You will draw water joyfully from the springs of salvation.**

God indeed is my savior;
  I am confident and unafraid.
My strength and my courage is the LORD,
  and he has been my savior.
With joy you will draw water
  at the fountain of salvation.

R⃒. **You will draw water joyfully from the springs of salvation.**

Give thanks to the LORD, acclaim his name;
  among the nations make known his deeds,
  proclaim how exalted is his name.

R⃒. **You will draw water joyfully from the springs of salvation.**

Sing praise to the LORD for his glorious achievement;
  let this be known throughout all the earth.
Shout with exultation, O city of Zion,
  for great in your midst
  is the Holy One of Israel!

R⃒. **You will draw water joyfully from the springs of salvation.**

2.

Psalm 23:1-3, 4, 5, 6

R℟. (1) The Lord is my shepherd; there is nothing I shall want.

The Lord is my shepherd; I shall not want.
   In verdant pastures he gives me repose;
Beside restful waters he leads me;
   he refreshes my soul.
He guides me in right paths
   for his name's sake.

R℟. The Lord is my shepherd; there is nothing I shall want.

Even though I walk in the dark valley
   I fear no evil; for you are at my side
With your rod and your staff
   that give me courage.

R℟. The Lord is my shepherd; there is nothing I shall want.

You spread the table before me
   in the sight of my foes;
You anoint my head with oil;
   my cup overflows.

R℟. The Lord is my shepherd; there is nothing I shall want.

Only goodness and kindness follow me
   all the days of my life;
And I shall dwell in the house of the Lord
   for years to come.

R℟. The Lord is my shepherd; there is nothing I shall want.

3.

Psalm 25:4-5ab, 6 and 7bc, 8-9, 10 and 14

℞. (6a) **Remember your mercies, O Lord.**

Your ways, O Lord, make known to me;
   teach me your paths,
Guide me in your truth and teach me,
   for you are God my savior.

℞. **Remember your mercies, O Lord.**

Remember that your compassion, O Lord,
   and your kindness are from of old.
In your kindness remember me,
   because of your goodness, O Lord.

℞. **Remember your mercies, O Lord.**

Good and upright is the Lord;
   thus he shows sinners the way.
He guides the humble to justice,
   he teaches the humble his way.

℞. **Remember your mercies, O Lord.**

All the paths of the Lord are kindness and constancy
   toward those who keep his covenant and his decrees.
The friendship of the Lord is with those who fear him,
   and his covenant, for their instruction.

℞. **Remember your mercies, O Lord.**

4.

Psalm 33:1-2, 4-5, 11-12, 18-19, 20-21

℟. (5b) **The earth is full of the goodness of the Lord.**
  or:
℟. (Matthew 11:29b) **Learn from me, for I am gentle and humble of heart.**

Exult, you just, in the Lord;
  praise from the upright is fitting.
Give thanks to the Lord **on the harp;**
  with the ten-stringed lyre chant his praises.

℟. **The earth is full of the goodness of the Lord.**
  or:
℟. **Learn from me, for I am gentle and humble of heart.**

For upright is the word of the Lord,
  and all his works are trustworthy.
He loves justice and right;
  of the kindness of the Lord **the earth is full.**

℟. **The earth is full of the goodness of the Lord.**
  or:
℟. **Learn from me, for I am gentle and humble of heart.**

But the plan of the Lord **stands forever;**
  the design of his heart, through all generations.
Blessed the nation whose God is the Lord,
  the people he has chosen for his inheritance.

℟. **The earth is full of the goodness of the Lord.**
  or:
℟. **Learn from me, for I am gentle and humble of heart.**

But see, the eyes of the Lord **are upon those who fear him,**
  upon those who hope for his kindness,
To deliver them from death
  and preserve them in spite of famine.

℟. **The earth is full of the goodness of the Lord.**
  or:
℟. **Learn from me, for I am gentle and humble of heart.**

Our soul waits for the LORD,
>   who is our help and our shield.
For in him our hearts rejoice;
>   in his holy name we trust.

R℣. The earth is full of the goodness of the Lord.
>   or:
R℣. Learn from me, for I am gentle and humble of heart.

5.

Psalm 34:2-3, 4-5, 6-7, 8-9, 17-18, 19 and 23

R℣. (9a) Taste and see the goodness of the Lord.

I will bless the LORD at all times;
>   his praise shall be ever in my mouth.
Let my soul glory in the LORD;
>   the lowly will hear me and be glad.

R℣. Taste and see the goodness of the Lord.

Glorify the LORD with me,
>   let us together extol his name.
I sought the LORD, and he answered me
>   and delivered me from all my fears.

R℣. Taste and see the goodness of the Lord.

Look to him that you may be radiant with joy,
>   and your faces may not blush with shame.
When the poor one called out, the LORD heard,
>   and from all his distress he saved him.

R℣. Taste and see the goodness of the Lord.

The angel of the LORD encamps
>   around those who fear him, and delivers them.
Taste and see how good the LORD is;
>   blessed the man who takes refuge in him.

R℣. Taste and see the goodness of the Lord.

(cont.)

The LORD confronts the evildoers,
    to destroy remembrance of them from the earth.
When the just cry out, the LORD hears them,
    and from all their distress he rescues them.

℞. Taste and see the goodness of the Lord.

The LORD is close to the brokenhearted;
    and those who are crushed in spirit he saves.
But the LORD redeems the lives of his servants;
    no one incurs guilt who takes refuge in him.

℞. Taste and see the goodness of the Lord.

6.

Psalm 103:1-2, 3-4, 6-7, 8 and 10

℞. (see 17) **The Lord's kindness is everlasting to those who fear him.**

Bless the LORD, O my soul;
    and all my being, bless his holy name.
Bless the LORD, O my soul,
    and forget not all his benefits.

℞. The Lord's kindness is everlasting to those who fear him.

He pardons all your iniquities,
    he heals all your ills.
He redeems your life from destruction,
    he crowns you with kindness and compassion.

℞. The Lord's kindness is everlasting to those who fear him.

The LORD secures justice
    and the rights of all the oppressed.
He has made known his ways to Moses,
    and his deeds to the children of Israel.

℞. The Lord's kindness is everlasting to those who fear him.

Merciful and gracious is the LORD,
    slow to anger and abounding in kindness.
Not according to our sins does he deal with us,
    nor does he requite us according to our crimes.

℞. The Lord's kindness is everlasting to those who fear him.

998 READING II FROM THE NEW TESTAMENT

1.

Romans 5:5-11   The love of God has been poured out into our hearts.

A reading from the Letter of Saint Paul to the Romans

Brothers and sisters:
Hope does not disappoint,
 because the love of God has been poured out into our hearts
 through the Holy Spirit who has been given to us.
For Christ, while we were still helpless,
 died at the appointed time for the ungodly.
Indeed, only with difficulty does one die for a just person,
 though perhaps for a good person
 one might even find courage to die.
But God proves his love for us
 in that while we were still sinners Christ died for us.
How much more then, since we are now justified by his Blood,
 will we be saved through him from the wrath.
Indeed, if, while we were enemies,
 we were reconciled to God through the death of his Son,
 how much more, once reconciled,
 will we be saved by his life.
Not only that,
 but we also boast of God through our Lord Jesus Christ,
 through whom we have now received reconciliation.

The word of the Lord.

2.

Ephesians 1:3-10   In accord with the riches of his grace that he lavished upon us.

A reading from the Letter of Saint Paul to the Ephesians

Blessed be the God and Father of our Lord Jesus Christ,
   who has blessed us in Christ
   with every spiritual blessing in the heavens,
   as he chose us in him, before the foundation of the world,
   to be holy and without blemish before him.
In love he destined us for adoption to himself through Jesus Christ,
   in accord with the favor of his will,
   for the praise of the glory of his grace
   that he granted us in the beloved.

In him we have redemption by his Blood,
   the forgiveness of transgressions,
   in accord with the riches of his grace that he lavished upon us.
In all wisdom and insight, he has made known to us
   the mystery of his will in accord with his favor
   that he set forth in him as a plan for the fullness of times,
   to sum up all things in Christ, in heaven and on earth.

The word of the Lord.

3.

Ephesians 3:8-12   To preach to the Gentiles the inscrutable riches of Christ.

A reading from the Letter of Saint Paul to the Ephesians

Brothers and sisters:
To me, the very least of all the holy ones, this grace was given,
   to preach to the Gentiles the inscrutable riches of Christ,
   and to bring to light for all what is the plan of the mystery
   hidden from ages past in God who created all things,
   so that the manifold wisdom of God
   might now be made known through the Church
   to the principalities and authorities in the heavens.

This was according to the eternal purpose
  that he accomplished in Christ Jesus our Lord,
  in whom we have boldness of speech
  and confidence of access through faith in him.

The word of the Lord.

  4.

Ephesians 3:14-19   To know the love of Christ that surpasses all knowledge.

A reading from the Letter of Saint Paul to the Ephesians

Brothers and sisters:
I kneel before the Father,
  from whom every family in heaven and on earth is named,
  that he may grant you in accord with the riches of his glory
  to be strengthened with power through his Spirit in the inner self,
  and that Christ may dwell in your hearts through faith;
  that you, rooted and grounded in love,
  may have strength to comprehend with all the holy ones
  what is the breadth and length and height and depth,
  and to know the love of Christ that surpasses knowledge,
  so that you may be filled with all the fullness of God.

The word of the Lord.

  5.

Philippians 1:8-11   With the affection of Christ Jesus.

A reading from the Letter of Saint Paul to the Philippians

Brothers and sisters:
God is my witness,
  how I long for all of you with the affection of Christ Jesus.
And this is my prayer:
  that your love may increase ever more and more
  in knowledge and every kind of perception,
  to discern what is of value,
  so that you may be pure and blameless for the day of Christ,
  filled with the fruit of righteousness
  that comes through Jesus Christ
  for the glory and praise of God.

The word of the Lord.

6.

1 John 4:7-16   Let us love one another.

A reading from the first Letter of Saint John

Beloved, let us love one another,
  because love is of God;
  everyone who loves is begotten by God and knows God.
Whoever is without love does not know God, for God is love.
In this way the love of God was revealed to us:
  God sent his only-begotten Son into the world
  so that we might have life through him.
In this is love:
  not that we have loved God, but that he loved us
  and sent his Son as expiation for our sins.
Beloved, if God so loved us,
  we also must love one another.
No one has ever seen God.
Yet, if we love one another, God remains in us,
  and his love is brought to perfection in us.

This is how we know that we remain in him and he in us,
  that he has given us of his Spirit.
Moreover, we have seen and testify
  that the Father sent his Son as savior of the world.
Whoever acknowledges that Jesus is the Son of God,
  God remains in him and he in God.
We have come to know and to believe in the love God has for us.

God is love, and whoever remains in love
  remains in God and God in him.

The word of the Lord.

999 ALLELUIA VERSE AND VERSE
BEFORE THE GOSPEL

1.

See Matthew 11:25

**Blessed are you, Father, Lord of heaven and earth;
you have revealed to little ones the mysteries of the Kingdom.**

2.

Matthew 11:28

**Come to me, all you who labor and are burdened,
and I will give you rest, says the Lord.**

3.

Matthew 11:29ab

**Take my yoke upon you and learn from me,
for I am meek and humble of heart.**

4.

John 10:14

**I am the good shepherd, says the Lord;
I know my sheep, and mine know me.**

5.

John 15:9

**As the Father loves me, so I also love you.
Remain in my love.**

6.

1 John 4:10b

**God loved us and sent his Son
as expiation for our sins.**

1000 GOSPEL

1.

Matthew 11:25-30   I am meek and humble of heart.

✠ **A reading from the holy Gospel according to Matthew**

At that time Jesus answered:
"I give praise to you, Father, Lord of heaven and earth,
  for although you have hidden these things
  from the wise and the learned
  you have revealed them to the childlike.
Yes, Father, such has been your gracious will.
All things have been handed over to me by my Father.
No one knows the Son except the Father,
  and no one knows the Father except the Son
  and anyone to whom the Son wishes to reveal him.

"Come to me, all you who labor and are burdened,
  and I will give you rest.
Take my yoke upon you and learn from me,
  for I am meek and humble of heart;
  and you will find rest for yourselves.
For my yoke is easy, and my burden light."

The Gospel of the Lord.

2.

✝ **A reading from the holy Gospel according to Luke**

Tax collectors and sinners were all drawing near to listen to Jesus,
  but the Pharisees and scribes began to complain, saying,
  "This man welcomes sinners and eats with them."
So Jesus addressed this parable to them.
"What man among you having a hundred sheep and losing one of them
  would not leave the ninety-nine in the desert
  and go after the lost one until he finds it?
And when he does find it,
  he sets it on his shoulders with great joy
  and, upon his arrival home,
  he calls together his friends and neighbors and says to them,
  'Rejoice with me because I have found my lost sheep.'
I tell you, in just the same way
  there will be more joy in heaven over one sinner who repents
  than over ninety-nine righteous people
  who have no need of repentance.

"Or what woman having ten coins and losing one
  would not light a lamp and sweep the house,
  searching carefully until she finds it?
And when she does find it,
  she calls together her friends and neighbors
  and says to them,
  'Rejoice with me because I have found the coin that I lost.'
In just the same way, I tell you,
  there will be rejoicing among the angels of God
  over one sinner who repents."

The Gospel of the Lord.

3.

Luke 15:1-3, 11-32   Now we must celebrate and rejoice because your
brother was dead and has come back to life.

✛ **A reading from the holy Gospel according to Luke**

Tax collectors and sinners were all drawing near to listen to Jesus,
but the Pharisees and scribes began to complain, saying,
"This man welcomes sinners and eats with them."
So Jesus addressed this parable to them.
"A man had two sons, and the younger son said to his father,
'Father give me the share of your estate that should come to me.'
So the father divided the property between them.
After a few days, the younger son collected all his belongings
and set off to a distant country
where he squandered his inheritance on a life of dissipation.
When he had freely spent everything,
a severe famine struck that country,
and he found himself in dire need.
So he hired himself out to one of the local citizens
who sent him to his farm to tend the swine.
And he longed to eat his fill of the pods on which the swine fed,
but nobody gave him any.
Coming to his senses he thought,
'How many of my father's hired workers
have more than enough food to eat,
but here am I, dying from hunger.
I shall get up and go to my father and I shall say to him,
"Father, I have sinned against heaven and against you.
I no longer deserve to be called your son;
treat me as you would treat one of your hired workers."'
So he got up and went back to his father.
While he was still a long way off,
his father caught sight of him, and was filled with compassion.
He ran to his son, embraced him and kissed him.
His son said to him,
'Father, I have sinned against heaven and against you;
I no longer deserve to be called your son.'
But his father ordered his servants,
'Quickly bring the finest robe and put it on him;
put a ring on his finger and sandals on his feet.

Take the fattened calf and slaughter it.
Then let us celebrate with a feast,
    because this son of mine was dead, and has come to life again;
    he was lost, and has been found.'
Then the celebration began.
Now the older son had been out in the field
    and, on his way back, as he neared the house,
    he heard the sound of music and dancing.
He called one of the servants and asked what this might mean.
The servant said to him,
    'Your brother has returned
    and your father has slaughtered the fattened calf
    because he has him back safe and sound.'
He became angry,
    and when he refused to enter the house,
    his father came out and pleaded with him.
He said to his father in reply,
    'Look, all these years I served you
    and not once did I disobey your orders;
    yet you never gave me even a young goat to feast on with my friends.
But when your son returns
    who swallowed up your property with prostitutes,
    for him you slaughter the fattened calf.'
He said to him,
    'My son, you are here with me always;
    everything I have is yours.
But now we must celebrate and rejoice,
    because your brother was dead and has come to life again;
    he was lost and has been found.'"

The Gospel of the Lord.

4.

John 10:11-18   A good shepherd lays down his life for the sheep.

✠ **A reading from the holy Gospel according to John**

**Jesus said:
"I am the good shepherd.
A good shepherd lays down his life for the sheep.
A hired man, who is not a shepherd
   and whose sheep are not his own,
   sees a wolf coming and leaves the sheep and runs away,
   and the wolf catches and scatters them.
This is because he works for pay and has no concern for the sheep.
I am the good shepherd,
   and I know mine and mine know me,
   just as the Father knows me and I know the Father;
   and I will lay down my life for the sheep.
I have other sheep that do not belong to this fold.
These also I must lead, and they will hear my voice,
   and there will be one flock, one shepherd.
This is why the Father loves me,
   because I lay down my life in order to take it up again.
No one takes it from me, but I lay it down on my own.
I have power to lay it down, and power to take it up again.
This command I have received from my Father."**

The Gospel of the Lord.

5.

John 15:1-8   Remain in me as I remain in you.

✠ **A reading from the holy Gospel according to John**

Jesus said to his disciples:
"I am the true vine, and my Father is the vine grower.
He takes away every branch in me that does not bear fruit,
    and every one that does he prunes so that it bears more fruit.
You are already pruned because of the word that I spoke to you.
Remain in me, as I remain in you.
Just as a branch cannot bear fruit on its own
    unless it remains on the vine,
        so neither can you unless you remain in me.
I am the vine, you are the branches.
Whoever remains in me and I in him will bear much fruit,
    because without me you can do nothing.
Anyone who does not remain in me
    will be thrown out like a branch and wither;
    people will gather them and throw them into a fire
    and they will be burned.
If you remain in me and my words remain in you,
    ask for whatever you want and it will be done for you.
By this is my Father glorified,
    that you bear much fruit and become my disciples."

The Gospel of the Lord.

6.

John 15:9-17   Love one another as I love you.

✠   **A reading from the holy Gospel according to John**

Jesus said to his disciples:
"As the Father loves me, so I also love you.
Remain in my love.
If you keep my commandments, you will remain in my love,
    just as I have kept my Father's commandments
    and remain in his love.

"I have told you this so that my joy may be in you
    and your joy may be complete.
This is my commandment: love one another as I love you.
No one has greater love than this,
    to lay down one's life for one's friends.
You are my friends if you do what I command you.
I no longer call you slaves,
    because a slave does not know what his master is doing.
I have called you friends,
    because I have told you everything I have heard from my Father.
It was not you who chose me, but I who chose you
    and appointed you to go and bear fruit that will remain,
    so that whatever you ask the Father in my name he may give you.
This I command you: love one another."

The Gospel of the Lord.

7.

John 17:20-26   You loved them as you loved me.

☩ **A reading from the holy Gospel according to John**

Jesus raised his eyes to heaven and said:
"Holy Father, I pray not only for these,
   but also for those who will believe in me through their word,
   so that they may all be one,
   as you, Father, are in me and I in you,
   that they also may be in us,
   that the world may believe that you sent me.
And I have given them the glory you gave me,
   so that they may be one, as we are one,
   I in them and you in me,
   that they may be brought to perfection as one,
   that the world may know that you sent me,
   and that you loved them even as you loved me.
Father, they are your gift to me.
I wish that where I am they also may be with me,
   that they may see my glory that you gave me,
   because you loved me before the foundation of the world.
Righteous Father, the world also does not know you,
   but I know you, and they know that you sent me.
I made known to them your name and I will make it known,
   that the love with which you loved me
   may be in them and I in them."

The Gospel of the Lord.

8.

John 19:31-37   One of the soldiers thrust his lance into his side and
immediately Blood and water flowed out.

✠ **A reading from the holy Gospel according to John**

Since it was preparation day,
   in order that the bodies might not remain on the cross on the sabbath,
   for the sabbath day of that week was a solemn one,
   the Jews asked Pilate that their legs be broken
   and they be taken down.
So the soldiers came and broke the legs of the first
   and then of the other one who was crucified with Jesus.
But when they came to Jesus and saw that he was already dead,
   they did not break his legs,
   but one soldier thrust his lance into his side,
   and immediately Blood and water flowed out.
An eyewitness has testified, and his testimony is true;
   he knows that he is speaking the truth,
   so that you also may come to believe.
For this happened so that the Scripture passage might be fulfilled:
   Not a bone of it will be broken.
And again another passage says:
   They will look upon him whom they have pierced.

The Gospel of the Lord.

1001 THE HOLY SPIRIT

The readings for Pentecost, nos. 62–63, or those for Confirmation, nos. 764–768, are used.

1002 THE BLESSED VIRGIN MARY

The readings from the Common of the Blessed Virgin Mary, nos. 707–712, are used.

I. THE BLESSED VIRGIN MARY, MOTHER OF THE CHURCH

The following readings for the votive Mass of Mary, Mother of the Church, may also be used in the votive Mass for the Blessed Virgin Mary.

FIRST READING

First Option

Genesis 3:9-15, 20   I will put enmity between your offspring and hers.

A reading from the Book of Genesis

After Adam had eaten of the tree,
  the Lord God called to him and asked him, "Where are you?"
He answered, "I heard you in the garden;
  but I was afraid, because I was naked,
  so I hid myself."
Then he asked, "Who told you that you were naked?
You have eaten, then,
  from the tree of which I had forbidden you to eat!"
The man replied, "The woman whom you put here with me—
  she gave me fruit from the tree, and so I ate it."
The Lord God then asked the woman,
  "Why did you do such a thing?"
The woman answered, "The serpent tricked me into it, so I ate it."

Then the Lord God said to the serpent:
  "Because you have done this, you shall be banned
    from all the animals
    and from all the wild creatures;
  On your belly shall you crawl,
    and dirt shall you eat
    all the days of your life.
  I will put enmity between you and the woman,
    and between your offspring and hers;
  He will strike at your head,
    while you strike at his heel."

The man called his wife Eve,
  because she became the mother of all the living.

The word of the Lord.

OR Second Option

Acts 1:12-14   All these devoted themselves with one accord to prayer together with Mary, the mother of Jesus.

A reading from the Acts of the Apostles

**After Jesus had been taken up into heaven,
  the Apostles returned to Jerusalem
  from the mount called Olivet, which is near Jerusalem,
  a sabbath day's journey away.**

**When they entered the city
  they went to the upper room where they were staying,
  Peter and John and James and Andrew,
  Philip and Thomas, Bartholomew and Matthew,
  James son of Alphaeus, Simon the Zealot,
  and Judas son of James.
All these devoted themselves with one accord to prayer,
  together with some women,
  and Mary the mother of Jesus, and his brothers.**

The word of the Lord.

RESPONSORIAL PSALM

Judith 13:18bcde, 19

℟. (15:9d) **You are the highest honor of our race.**

**Blessed are you, daughter, by the Most High God,
  above all the women on earth;
and blessed be the Lord God,
  the creator of heaven and earth.**

℟. **You are the highest honor of our race.**

**Your deed of hope will never be forgotten
  by those who tell of the might of God.**

℟. **You are the highest honor of our race.**

ALLELUIA

℟. Alleluia, alleluia.

Blessed are you, holy Virgin Mary, deserving of all praise;
from you rose the sun of justice, Christ the Lord.

℟. Alleluia, alleluia.

GOSPEL

John 19:25-27   Woman, behold your son. Behold your mother.

✠   A reading from the holy Gospel according to John

Standing by the cross of Jesus were his mother
    and his mother's sister, Mary the wife of Clopas,
    and Mary Magdalene.
When Jesus saw his mother and the disciple whom he loved
    he said to his mother, "Woman, behold, your son."
Then he said to the disciple,
    "Behold, your mother."
And from that hour the disciple took her into his home.

The Gospel of the Lord.

II. THE MOST HOLY NAME OF MARY

The following readings for the votive Mass of the Holy Name of Mary may also be used in the votive Mass for the Blessed Virgin Mary.

FIRST READING

First Option

Galatians 4:4-7   God sent his Son, born of a woman.

A reading from the Letter of Saint Paul to the Galatians

Brothers and sisters:
When the fullness of time had come, God sent his Son,
   born of a woman, born under the law,
   to ransom those under the law,
   so that we might receive adoption as sons.
As proof that you are sons,
   God sent the Spirit of his Son into our hearts,
   crying out, "Abba, Father!"
So you are no longer a slave but a son,
   and if a son then also an heir, through God.

The word of the Lord.

OR Second Option

Ephesians 1:3-6, 11-12   He chose us in him before the foundation of the world.

A reading from the Letter of Saint Paul to the Ephesians

Blessed be the God and Father of our Lord Jesus Christ,
  who has blessed us in Christ
  with every spiritual blessing in the heavens,
  as he chose us in him, before the foundation of the world,
  to be holy and without blemish before him.
In love he destined us for adoption to himself through Jesus Christ,
  in accord with the favor of his will,
  for the praise of the glory of his grace
  that he granted us in the beloved.

In him we were also chosen,
  destined in accord with the purpose of the One
  who accomplishes all things according to the intention of his will,
  so that we might exist for the praise of his glory,
  we who first hoped in Christ.

The word of the Lord.

RESPONSORIAL PSALM

Luke 1:46-47, 48-49, 50-51, 52-53, 54-55

℟. (49) **The Almighty has done great things for me, and holy is his Name.**
  or:
℟. **O Blessed Virgin Mary, you carried the Son of the eternal Father.**

"My soul proclaims the greatness of the Lord,
  my spirit finds joy in God my savior."

℟. **The Almighty has done great things for me, and holy is his Name.**
  or:
℟. **O Blessed Virgin Mary, you carried the Son of the eternal Father.**

"For he has looked with favor on his lowly servant;
From this day all generations will call me blessed.
   The Almighty has done great things for me,
   holy is his Name."

℟. The Almighty has done great things for me, and holy is his Name.
   or:
℟. O Blessed Virgin Mary, you carried the Son of the eternal Father.

"He has mercy on those who fear him
   in every generation.
He has shown the strength of his arm,
   he has scattered the proud in his conceit."

℟. The Almighty has done great things for me, and holy is his Name.
   or:
℟. O Blessed Virgin Mary, you carried the Son of the eternal Father.

"He has cast down the mighty from their thrones,
   and has lifted up the lowly.
He has filled the hungry with good things,
   and the rich he has sent away empty."

℟. The Almighty has done great things for me, and holy is his Name.
   or:
℟. O Blessed Virgin Mary, you carried the Son of the eternal Father.

"He has come to the help of his servant Israel
   for he has remembered his promise of mercy,
   the promise he made to our fathers,
   to Abraham and his children for ever."

℟. The Almighty has done great things for me, and holy is his Name.
   or:
℟. O Blessed Virgin Mary, you carried the Son of the eternal Father.

ALLELUIA

See Luke 1:45

℟. Alleluia, alleluia.

**Blessed are you, O Virgin Mary, who believed
that what was spoken to you by the Lord would be fulfilled.**

℟. Alleluia, alleluia.

GOSPEL

Luke 1:39-47   Blessed is she who believed.

☩   **A reading from the holy Gospel according to Luke**

**Mary set out
    and traveled to the hill country in haste
    to a town of Judah,
    where she entered the house of Zechariah
    and greeted Elizabeth.
When Elizabeth heard Mary's greeting,
    the infant leaped in her womb,
    and Elizabeth, filled with the Holy Spirit,
    cried out in a loud voice and said,
    "Most blessed are you among women,
    and blessed is the fruit of your womb.
And how does this happen to me,
    that the mother of my Lord should come to me?
For at the moment the sound of your greeting reached my ears,
    the infant in my womb leaped for joy.
Blessed are you who believed
    that what was spoken to you by the Lord
    would be fulfilled."**

And Mary said:

> **"My soul proclaims the greatness of the Lord;
>   my spirit rejoices in God my savior."**

The Gospel of the Lord.

1003 THE HOLY ANGELS

The readings for the feast of the Archangels on September 29, no. 647, or those for the memorial of the Guardian Angels, October 2, no. 650, are used.

1004 SAINT JOSEPH

The readings for the solemnity of Joseph on March 19, no. 543, or those for the memorial of Joseph the Worker, on May 1, no. 559, are used.

1005 ALL THE HOLY APOSTLES

The readings for the feast of Simon and Jude on October 28, no. 666, are used.

1006 SAINTS PETER AND PAUL, APOSTLES

The readings for the memorial of the Dedication of the Churches of Peter and Paul on November 18, no. 679, are used.

1007 SAINT PETER, APOSTLE

The readings for the feast of the Chair of Peter on February 22, no. 535 are used.

1008 SAINT PAUL, APOSTLE

The readings for the feast of the Conversion of Paul on January 25, no. 519, are used.

1009 ONE HOLY APOSTLE

The readings for the feast of the Apostle are used. But if two Apostles are honored together, and the texts of the readings are not appropriate for a votive Mass for one of them alone, the readings for Simon and Jude, on October 28, no. 666, are used.

1010 ALL THE SAINTS

The readings for the solemnity of All Saints on November 1, no. 667, are used.

MASSES FOR THE DEAD

MASSES FOR THE DEAD

1011 READING I FROM THE OLD TESTAMENT

1.

2 Maccabees 12:43-46   He acted in an excellent and noble way as he had the resurrection of the dead in view.

A reading from the second Book of Maccabees

Judas, the ruler of Israel,
   took up a collection among all his soldiers,
   amounting to two thousand silver drachmas,
   which he sent to Jerusalem to provide for an expiatory sacrifice.
In doing this he acted in a very excellent and noble way,
   inasmuch as he had the resurrection of the dead in view;
   for if he were not expecting the fallen to rise again,
   it would have been useless and foolish to pray for them in death.
But if he did this with a view to the splendid reward
   that awaits those who had gone to rest in godliness,
   it was a holy and pious thought.
Thus he made atonement for the dead
   that they might be freed from this sin.

The word of the Lord.

2.

Job 19:1, 23-27a   I know that my Vindicator lives.

A reading from the Book of Job

Job answered Bildad the Shuhite and said:
Oh, would that my words were written down!
   Would that they were inscribed in a record:
That with an iron chisel and with lead
   they were cut in the rock forever!
But as for me, I know that my Vindicator lives,
   and that he will at last stand forth upon the dust;
Whom I myself shall see:
   my own eyes, not another's, shall behold him;
And from my flesh I shall see God;
   my inmost being is consumed with longing.

The word of the Lord.

3.

Long Form

Wisdom 3:1-9   As sacrificial offerings he took them to himself.

A reading from the Book of Wisdom

The souls of the just are in the hand of God,
  and no torment shall touch them.
They seemed, in the view of the foolish, to be dead;
  and their passing away was thought an affliction
  and their going forth from us, utter destruction.
But they are in peace.
For if before men, indeed they be punished,
  yet is their hope full of immortality;
Chastised a little, they shall be greatly blessed,
  because God tried them
  and found them worthy of himself.
As gold in the furnace, he proved them,
  and as sacrificial offerings he took them to himself.
In the time of their visitation they shall shine,
  and shall dart about as sparks through stubble;
They shall judge nations and rule over peoples,
  and the LORD shall be their King forever.
Those who trust in him shall understand truth,
  and the faithful shall abide with him in love:
Because grace and mercy are with his holy ones,
  and his care is with his elect.

The word of the Lord.

OR Short Form

Wisdom 3:1-6, 9   As sacrificial offerings he took them to himself.

A reading from the Book of Wisdom

The souls of the just are in the hand of God
  and no torment shall touch them.
They seemed, in the view of the foolish, to be dead;
  and their passing away was thought an affliction
  and their going forth from us, utter destruction.
But they are in peace.

For if in the eyes of men, indeed they be punished,
    yet is their hope full of immortality;
Chastised a little, they shall be greatly blessed,
    because God tried them,
    and found them worthy of himself.
As gold in the furnace, he proved them,
    and as sacrificial offerings he took them to himself.
Those who trust in him shall understand truth,
    and the faithful shall abide with him in love:
Because grace and mercy are with his holy ones,
    and his care is with his elect.

The word of the Lord.

    4.

Wisdom 4:7-15   An unsullied life, the attainment of old age.

A reading from the Book of Wisdom

The just man, though he die early,
    shall be at rest.
For the age that is honorable comes not
    with the passing of time,
    nor can it be measured in terms of years.
Rather, understanding is the hoary crown for men,
    and an unsullied life, the attainment of old age.
He who pleased God was loved;
    he who lived among sinners was transported—
Snatched away, lest wickedness pervert his mind
    or deceit beguile his soul;
For the witchery of paltry things obscures what is right
    and the whirl of desire transforms the innocent mind.
Having become perfect in a short while,
    he reached the fullness of a long career;
    for his soul was pleasing to the LORD,
    therefore he sped him out of the midst of wickedness.
But the people saw and did not understand,
    nor did they take this into account.

The word of the Lord.

5.

Isaiah 25:6a, 7-9   He will destroy death forever.

A reading from the Book of the Prophet Isaiah

On this mountain the LORD of hosts
  will provide for all peoples.
On this mountain he will destroy
  the veil that veils all peoples,
The web that is woven over all nations;
  he will destroy death forever.
The Lord GOD will wipe away
  the tears from all faces;
The reproach of his people he will remove
  from the whole earth; for the LORD has spoken.

  On that day it will be said:
"Behold our God, to whom we looked to save us!
  This is the LORD for whom we looked;
  let us rejoice and be glad that he has saved us!"

The word of the Lord.

6.

Lamentations 3:17-26   It is good to hope in silence for the saving help of
the Lord.

A reading from the Book of Lamentations

My soul is deprived of peace,
  I have forgotten what happiness is;
I tell myself my future is lost,
  all that I hoped for from the LORD.
The thought of my homeless poverty
  is wormwood and gall;
Remembering it over and over
  leaves my soul downcast within me.
But I will call this to mind,
  as my reason to have hope:

The favors of the LORD are not exhausted,
  his mercies are not spent;
They are renewed each morning,
  so great is his faithfulness.

My portion is the Lord, says my soul;
    therefore will I hope in him.

Good is the Lord to one who waits for him,
    to the soul that seeks him;
It is good to hope in silence
    for the saving help of the Lord.

The word of the Lord.

7.

Daniel 12:1-3   Many of those who sleep in the dust of the earth shall awake.

A reading from the Book of the Prophet Daniel

In those days, I, Daniel, mourned
    and heard this word of the Lord:
At that time there shall arise
    Michael, the great prince,
    guardian of your people;
It shall be a time unsurpassed in distress
    since nations began until that time.
At that time your people shall escape,
    everyone who is found written in the book.

Many of those who sleep in the dust of the earth shall awake;
Some shall live forever,
    others shall be an everlasting horror and disgrace.
But the wise shall shine brightly
    like the splendor of the firmament,
And those who lead the many to justice
    shall be like the stars forever.

The word of the Lord.

1012 READING II FROM THE NEW TESTAMENT DURING THE SEASON OF EASTER

1.

Long Form

Acts 10:34-43   He is the one appointed by God as judge of the living and the dead.

A reading from the Acts of the Apostles

Peter proceeded to speak, saying:
"In truth, I see that God shows no partiality.
Rather, in every nation whoever fears him and acts uprightly
  is acceptable to him.
You know the word that he sent to the children of Israel
  as he proclaimed peace through Jesus Christ, who is Lord of all,
  what has happened all over Judea,
  beginning in Galilee after the baptism
  that John preached,
  how God anointed Jesus of Nazareth
  with the Holy Spirit and power.
He went about doing good
  and healing all those oppressed by the Devil,
  for God was with him.
We are witnesses of all that he did
  both in the country of the Jews and in Jerusalem.
They put him to death by hanging him on a tree.
This man God raised on the third day and granted that he be visible,
  not to all the people, but to us,
  the witnesses chosen by God in advance,
  who ate and drank with him after he rose from the dead.
He commissioned us to preach to the people
  and testify that he is the one appointed by God
  as judge of the living and the dead.
To him all the prophets bear witness,
  that everyone who believes in him
  will receive forgiveness of sins through his name."

The word of the Lord.

OR Short Form

Acts 10:34-36, 42-43   He is the one appointed by God as judge of the living and the dead.

A reading from the Acts of the Apostles

Peter proceeded to speak, saying:
"In truth, I see that God shows no partiality.
Rather, in every nation whoever fears him and acts uprightly
      is acceptable to him.
You know the word that he sent to the children of Israel
      as he proclaimed peace through Jesus Christ, who is Lord of all.
He commissioned us to preach to the people
      and testify that he is the one appointed by God
      as judge of the living and the dead.
To him all the prophets bear witness,
      that everyone who believes in him
      will receive forgiveness of sins through his name."

The word of the Lord.

   2.

Revelation 14:13   Blessed are the dead who die in the Lord.

A reading from the Book of Revelation

I, John, heard a voice from heaven say, "Write this:
      Blessed are the dead who die in the Lord from now on."
"Yes," said the Spirit,
      "let them find rest from their labors,
      for their works accompany them."

The word of the Lord.

3.

Revelation 20:11–21:1   The dead were judged according to their deeds.

A reading from the Book of Revelation

I, John, saw a large white throne and the one who was sitting on it.
The earth and the sky fled from his presence
      and there was no place for them.
I saw the dead, the great and the lowly, standing before the throne,
      and scrolls were opened.
Then another scroll was opened, the book of life.
The dead were judged according to their deeds,
      by what was written in the scrolls.
The sea gave up its dead;
      then Death and Hades gave up their dead.
All the dead were judged according to their deeds.
Then Death and Hades were thrown into the pool of fire.
(This pool of fire is the second death.)
Anyone whose name was not found written in the book of life
      was thrown into the pool of fire.

Then I saw a new heaven and a new earth.
The former heaven and the former earth had passed away,
      and the sea was no more.

The word of the Lord.

4.

Revelation 21:1-5a, 6b-7   There shall be no more death.

A reading from the Book of Revelation

I, John, saw a new heaven and a new earth.
The former heaven and the former earth had passed away,
   and the sea was no more.
I also saw the holy city, a new Jerusalem,
   coming down out of heaven from God,
   prepared as a bride adorned for her husband.
I heard a loud voice from the throne saying,
   "Behold, God's dwelling is with the human race.
He will dwell with them and they will be his people
   and God himself will always be with them as their God.
He will wipe every tear from their eyes,
   and there shall be no more death or mourning, wailing or pain,
   for the old order has passed away."

The One who sat on the throne said,
   "Behold, I make all things new.
I am the Alpha and the Omega,
   the beginning and the end.
To the thirsty I will give a gift
   from the spring of life-giving water.
The victor will inherit these gifts,
   and I shall be his God,
   and he will be my son."

The word of the Lord.

1013 RESPONSORIAL PSALM

1.

Psalm 23:1-3, 4, 5, 6

R̸. (1) **The Lord is my shepherd; there is nothing I shall want.**
or:
R̸. (4ab) **Though I walk in the valley of darkness, I fear no evil, for you are with me.**

The LORD** is my shepherd; I shall not want.**
   In verdant pastures he gives me repose;
Beside restful waters he leads me;
   he refreshes my soul.
He guides me in right paths
   for his name's sake.

R̸. **The Lord is my shepherd; there is nothing I shall want.**
   or:
R̸. **Though I walk in the valley of darkness, I fear no evil, for you are with me.**

Even though I walk in the dark valley
   I fear no evil; for you are at my side
With your rod and your staff
   that give me courage.

R̸. **The Lord is my shepherd; there is nothing I shall want.**
   or:
R̸. **Though I walk in the valley of darkness, I fear no evil, for you are with me.**

You spread the table before me
   in the sight of my foes;
You anoint my head with oil;
   my cup overflows.

R̸. **The Lord is my shepherd; there is nothing I shall want.**
   or:
R̸. **Though I walk in the valley of darkness, I fear no evil, for you are with me.**

Only goodness and kindness follow me
   all the days of my life;
And I shall dwell in the house of the Lord
   for years to come.

℞. The Lord is my shepherd; there is nothing I shall want.
   or:
℞. Though I walk in the valley of darkness, I fear no evil, for you are with me.

   2.

Psalm 25:6 and 7b, 17-18, 20-21

℞. (1) To you, O Lord, I lift my soul.
   or:
℞. (3a) No one who waits for you, O Lord, will ever be put to shame.

Remember that your compassion, O Lord,
   and your kindness are from of old.
In your kindness remember me,
   because of your goodness, O Lord

℞. To you, O Lord, I lift my soul.
   or:
℞. No one who waits for you, O Lord, will ever be put to shame.

Relieve the troubles of my heart;
   and bring me out of my distress.
Put an end to my affliction and my suffering;
   and take away all my sins.

℞. To you, O Lord, I lift my soul.
   or:
℞. No one who waits for you, O Lord, will ever be put to shame.

Preserve my life and rescue me;
   let me not be put to shame, for I take refuge in you.
Let integrity and uprightness preserve me,
   because I wait for you, O Lord.

℞. To you, O Lord, I lift my soul.
   or:
℞. No one who waits for you, O Lord, will ever be put to shame.

3.

Psalm 27:1, 4, 7 and 8b and 9a, 13-14

℟. (1a) **The Lord is my light and my salvation.**
   or:
℟. (13) **I believe that I shall see the good things of the Lord in the land of the living.**

The LORD is my light and my salvation;
   whom should I fear?
The LORD is my life's refuge;
   of whom should I be afraid?

℟. **The Lord is my light and my salvation.**
   or:
℟. **I believe that I shall see the good things of the Lord in the land of the living.**

One thing I ask of the LORD;
   this I seek:
To dwell in the house of the LORD
   all the days of my life,
That I may gaze on the loveliness of the LORD
   and contemplate his temple.

℟. **The Lord is my light and my salvation.**
   or:
℟. **I believe that I shall see the good things of the Lord in the land of the living.**

Hear, O LORD, the sound of my call;
   have pity on me, and answer me.
Your presence, O LORD, I seek.
   Hide not your face from me.

℟. **The Lord is my light and my salvation.**
   or:
℟. **I believe that I shall see the good things of the Lord in the land of the living.**

I believe that I shall see the bounty of the Lord
   in the land of the living.
Wait for the Lord with courage;
   be stouthearted, and wait for the Lord.

℞. The Lord is my light and my salvation.
   or:
℞. I believe that I shall see the good things of the Lord in the land of the living.

4.

Psalm 42:2, 3, 5cdef; 43:3, 4, 5

℞. (42:3) My soul is thirsting for the living God: when shall I see him face to face?

As the hind longs for the running waters,
   so my soul longs for you, O God.

℞. My soul is thirsting for the living God: when shall I see him face to face?

Athirst is my soul for God, the living God.
   When shall I go and behold the face of God?

℞. My soul is thirsting for the living God: when shall I see him face to face?

I went with the throng and led them in procession
   to the house of God.
Amid loud cries of joy and thanksgiving,
   with the multitude keeping festival.

℞. My soul is thirsting for the living God: when shall I see him face to face?

Send forth your light and your fidelity;
   they shall lead me on
And bring me to your holy mountain,
   to your dwelling-place.

℞. My soul is thirsting for the living God: when shall I see him face to face?

Then will I go in to the altar of God,
   the God of my gladness and joy;
Then will I give you thanks upon the harp,
   O God, my God!

(cont.)

R℣. My soul is thirsting for the living God: when shall I see him face to face?

Why are you so downcast, O my soul?
    Why do you sigh within me?
Hope in God! For I shall again be thanking him,
    in the presence of my savior and my God.

R℣. My soul is thirsting for the living God: when shall I see him face to face?

5.

Psalm 63:2, 3-4, 5-6, 8-9

R℣. (2b) **My soul is thirsting for you, O Lord my God.**

O God, you are my God whom I seek;
    for you my flesh pines and my soul thirsts
    like the earth, parched, lifeless and without water.

R℣. My soul is thirsting for you, O Lord my God.

Thus have I gazed toward you in the sanctuary
    to see your power and your glory,
For your kindness is a greater good than life;
    my lips shall glorify you.

R℣. My soul is thirsting for you, O Lord my God.

Thus will I bless you while I live;
    lifting up my hands, I will call upon your name.
As with the riches of a banquet shall my soul be satisfied,
    and with exultant lips my mouth shall praise you.

R℣. My soul is thirsting for you, O Lord my God.

You are my help,
    and in the shadow of your wings I shout for joy.
My soul clings fast to you;
    your right hand upholds me.

R℣. My soul is thirsting for you, O Lord my God.

6.

Psalm 103:8 and 10, 13-14, 15-16, 17-18

℟. (8a) **The Lord is kind and merciful.**
  or:
℟. (37:39a) **The salvation of the just comes from the Lord.**

Merciful and gracious is the Lord,
  slow to anger, and abounding in kindness.
Not according to our sins does he deal with us,
  nor does he requite us according to our crimes.

℟. **The Lord is kind and merciful.**
  or:
℟. **The salvation of the just comes from the Lord.**

As a father has compassion on his children,
  so the Lord has compassion on those who fear him.
For he knows how we are formed,
  he remembers that we are dust.

℟. **The Lord is kind and merciful.**
  or:
℟. **The salvation of the just comes from the Lord.**

Man's days are like those of grass;
  like a flower of the field he blooms;
The wind sweeps over him and he is gone,
  and his place knows him no more.

℟. **The Lord is kind and merciful.**
  or:
℟. **The salvation of the just comes from the Lord.**

But the kindness of the Lord is from eternity,
  to eternity toward those who fear him,
And his justice toward children's children
  among those who keep his covenant
  and remember to fulfill his precepts.

℟. **The Lord is kind and merciful.**
  or:
℟. **The salvation of the just comes from the Lord.**

7.

Psalm 116:5, 6, 10-11, 15-16ac

R̸. (9) **I will walk in the presence of the Lord in the land of the living.**
  or:
R̸. **Alleluia.**

Gracious is the Lord and just;
  yes, our God is merciful.

R̸. **I will walk in the presence of the Lord in the land of the living.**
  or:
R̸. **Alleluia.**

The Lord keeps the little ones;
  I was brought low, and he saved me.

R̸. **I will walk in the presence of the Lord in the land of the living.**
  or:
R̸. **Alleluia.**

I believed, even when I said,
  "I am greatly afflicted";
I said in my alarm,
  "No man is dependable."

R̸. **I will walk in the presence of the Lord in the land of the living.**
  or:
R̸. **Alleluia.**

Precious in the eyes of the Lord
  is the death of his faithful ones.
O Lord, I am your servant,
  you have loosed my bonds.

R̸. **I will walk in the presence of the Lord in the land of the living.**
  or:
R̸. **Alleluia.**

8.

Psalm 122:1-2, 4-5, 6-7, 8-9

℟. (1) **I rejoiced when I heard them say: let us go to the house of the Lord.**
   or:
℟. (see 1) **Let us go rejoicing to the house of the Lord.**

I rejoiced because they said to me,
   "We will go up to the house of the Lord."
And now we have set foot
   within your gates, O Jerusalem.

℟. **I rejoiced when I heard them say: let us go to the house of the Lord.**
   or:
℟. **Let us go rejoicing to the house of the Lord.**

To it the tribes go up,
   the tribes of the Lord.
According to the decree for Israel,
   to give thanks to the name of the Lord.
In it are set up judgment seats,
   seats for the house of David.

℟. **I rejoiced when I heard them say: let us go to the house of the Lord.**
   or:
℟. **Let us go rejoicing to the house of the Lord.**

Pray for the peace of Jerusalem!
   May those who love you prosper!
May peace be within your walls,
   prosperity in your buildings.

℟. **I rejoiced when I heard them say: let us go to the house of the Lord.**
   or:
℟. **Let us go rejoicing to the house of the Lord.**

Because of my relatives and friends
   I will say "Peace be within you!"
Because of the house of the Lord, our God,
   I will pray for your good.

℟. **I rejoiced when I heard them say: let us go to the house of the Lord.**
   or:
℟. **Let us go rejoicing to the house of the Lord.**

9.

Psalm 130:1-2, 3-4, 5-6ab, 6c-7, 8

℟. (1) **Out of the depths, I cry to you, Lord.**
   or:
℟. (see 50) **I hope in the Lord, I trust in his word.**

Out of the depths I cry to you, O LORD;
   LORD, hear my voice!
Let your ears be attentive
   to my voice in supplication.

℟. **Out of the depths, I cry to you, Lord.**
   or:
℟. **I hope in the Lord, I trust in his word.**

If you, O LORD, mark iniquities,
   LORD, who can stand?
But with you is forgiveness,
   that you may be revered.

℟. **Out of the depths, I cry to you, Lord.**
   or:
℟. **I hope in the Lord, I trust in his word.**

I trust in the LORD;
   my soul trusts in his word.
My soul waits for the LORD
   more than the sentinels wait for the dawn.

℟. **Out of the depths, I cry to you, Lord.**
   or:
℟. **I hope in the Lord, I trust in his word.**

More than the sentinels wait for the dawn,
   let Israel wait for the LORD,
For with the LORD is kindness
   and with him is plenteous redemption.

℟. **Out of the depths, I cry to you, Lord.**
   or:
℟. **I hope in the Lord, I trust in his word.**

And he will redeem Israel
   from all their iniquities.

℟. **Out of the depths, I cry to you, Lord.**
   or:
℟. **I hope in the Lord, I trust in his word.**

10.

Psalm 143:1-2, 5-6, 7ab and 8ab, 10

℟. (1a) **O Lord, hear my prayer.**

O LORD, hear my prayer;
   hearken to my pleading in your faithfulness;
   in your justice answer me.
And enter not into judgment with your servant,
   for before you no living man is just.

℟. **O Lord, hear my prayer.**

I remember the days of old;
   I meditate on all your doings;
   the works of your hands I ponder.
I stretch out my hands to you;
   my soul thirsts for you like parched land.

℟. **O Lord, hear my prayer.**

Hasten to answer me, O LORD;
   for my spirit fails me.
At dawn let me hear of your mercy,
   for in you I trust.

℟. **O Lord, hear my prayer.**

Teach me to do your will,
   for you are my God.
May your good spirit guide me
   on level ground.

℟. **O Lord, hear my prayer.**

1014 READING II FROM THE NEW TESTAMENT

1.

Romans 5:5-11   Since we are now justified by his Blood, we will be saved through him from the wrath.

A reading from the Letter of Saint Paul to the Romans

Brothers and sisters:
Hope does not disappoint,
   because the love of God has been poured out into our hearts
   through the Holy Spirit who has been given to us.
For Christ, while we were still helpless,
   died at the appointed time for the ungodly.
Indeed, only with difficulty does one die for a just person,
   though perhaps for a good person
   one might even find courage to die.
But God proves his love for us
   in that while we were still sinners Christ died for us.
How much more then, since we are now justified by his Blood,
   will we be saved through him from the wrath.
Indeed, if, while we were enemies,
   we were reconciled to God through the death of his Son,
   how much more, once reconciled,
   will we be saved by his life.
Not only that,
   but we also boast of God through our Lord Jesus Christ,
   through whom we have now received reconciliation.

The word of the Lord.

2.

Romans 5:17-21   Where sin increased, grace overflowed all the more.

A reading from the Letter of Saint Paul to the Romans

Brothers and sisters:
If, by the transgression of the one,
   death came to reign through that one,
   how much more will those who receive the abundance of grace
   and of the gift of justification
   come to reign in life through the one Jesus Christ.

In conclusion, just as through one transgression
   condemnation came upon all,
   so, through one righteous act,
   acquittal and life came to all.
For just as through the disobedience of the one man
   the many were made sinners,
   so through the obedience of the one
   the many will be made righteous.
The law entered in so that transgression might increase
   but, where sin increased, grace overflowed all the more, so that,
   as sin reigned in death,
   grace also might reign through justification for eternal life
   through Jesus Christ our Lord.

The word of the Lord.

3.

Long Form

Romans 6:3-9   We too might live in newness of life.

A reading from the Letter of Saint Paul to the Romans

Brothers and sisters:
Are you unaware that we who were baptized into Christ Jesus
   were baptized into his death?
We were indeed buried with him through baptism into death,
   so that, just as Christ was raised from the dead
   by the glory of the Father,
   we too might live in newness of life.

For if we have grown into union with him through a death like his,
   we shall also be united with him in the resurrection.
We know that our old self was crucified with him,
   so that our sinful body might be done away with,
   that we might no longer be in slavery to sin.
For a dead person has been absolved from sin.
If, then, we have died with Christ,
   we believe that we shall also live with him.
We know that Christ, raised from the dead, dies no more;
   death no longer has power over him.

The word of the Lord.

OR Short Form

Romans 6:3-4, 8-9   We too might live in newness of life.

A reading from the Letter of Saint Paul to the Romans

Brothers and sisters:
Are you unaware that we who were baptized into Christ Jesus
  were baptized into his death?
We were indeed buried with him through baptism into death,
  so that, just as Christ was raised from the dead
  by the glory of the Father,
  we too might live in newness of life.

If, then, we have died with Christ,
  we believe that we shall also live with him.
We know that Christ, raised from the dead, dies no more;
  death no longer has power over him.

The word of the Lord.

4.

Romans 8:14-23   We also groan within ourselves as we wait for adoption, the redemption of our bodies.

A reading from the Letter of Saint Paul to the Romans

Brothers and sisters:
Those who are led by the Spirit of God are sons of God.
For you did not receive a spirit of slavery to fall back into fear,
  but you received a spirit of adoption,
  through which we cry, *Abba*, "Father!"
The Spirit itself bears witness with our spirit
  that we are children of God,
  and if children, then heirs,
  heirs of God and joint heirs with Christ,
  if only we suffer with him
  so that we may also be glorified with him.

I consider that the sufferings of this present time are as nothing
  compared with the glory to be revealed for us.
For creation awaits with eager expectation
  the revelation of the children of God;
  for creation was made subject to futility,

not of its own accord but because of the one who subjected it,
in hope that creation itself
would be set free from slavery to corruption
and share in the glorious freedom of the children of God.
We know that all creation is groaning in labor pains even until now;
and not only that, but we ourselves,
who have the firstfruits of the Spirit,
we also groan within ourselves
as we wait for adoption, the redemption of our bodies.

The word of the Lord.

5.

Romans 8:31b-35, 37-39   What will separate us from the love of Christ?

A reading from the Letter of Saint Paul to the Romans

Brothers and sisters:
If God is for us, who can be against us?
He did not spare his own Son
but handed him over for us all,
will he not also give us everything else along with him?
Who will bring a charge against God's chosen ones?
It is God who acquits us.
Who will condemn?
It is Christ Jesus who died, rather, was raised,
who also is at the right hand of God,
who indeed intercedes for us.
What will separate us from the love of Christ?
Will anguish, or distress or persecution, or famine,
or nakedness, or peril, or the sword?

No, in all these things, we conquer overwhelmingly
through him who loved us.
For I am convinced that neither death, nor life,
nor angels, nor principalities,
nor present things, nor future things,
nor powers, nor height, nor depth,
nor any other creature will be able to separate us
from the love of God in Christ Jesus our Lord.

The word of the Lord.

6.

Romans 14:7-9, 10c-12   Whether we live or die, we are the Lord's.

A reading from the Letter of Saint Paul to the Romans

Brothers and sisters:
No one lives for oneself,
   and no one dies for oneself.
For if we live, we live for the Lord,
   and if we die, we die for the Lord;
   so then, whether we live or die, we are the Lord's.
For this is why Christ died and came to life,
   that he might be Lord of both the dead and the living.
Why then do you judge your brother?
Or you, why do you look down on your brother?
For we shall all stand before the judgment seat of God;
   for it is written:

   As I live, says the Lord, every knee
     shall bend before me,
     and every tongue shall give praise to God.

So then each of us shall give an accounting of himself to God.

The word of the Lord.

7.

Long Form

1 Corinthians 15:20-28   So too in Christ shall all be brought to life.

A reading from the first Letter of Saint Paul to the Corinthians

Brothers and sisters:
Christ has been raised from the dead,
   the firstfruits of those who have fallen asleep.
For since death came through a man,
   the resurrection of the dead came also through man.
For just as in Adam all die,
   so too in Christ shall all be brought to life,
   but each one in proper order:
   Christ the firstfruits;
   then, at his coming, those who belong to Christ;

then comes the end,

when he hands over the Kingdom to his God and Father.

For he must reign until he has put all his enemies under his feet.

The last enemy to be destroyed is death,

for "he subjected everything under his feet."

But when it says that everything has been subjected,

it is clear that it excludes the one who subjected everything to him.

When everything is subjected to him,

then the Son himself will also be subjected

to the one who subjected everything to him,

so that God may be all in all.

The word of the Lord.

OR Short Form

1 Corinthians 15:20-23   So too in Christ shall all be brought to life.

A reading from the first Letter of Saint Paul to the Corinthians

Brothers and sisters:

Christ has been raised from the dead,

the firstfruits of those who have fallen asleep.

For since death came through a man,

the resurrection of the dead came also through man.

For just as in Adam all die,

so too in Christ shall all be brought to life,

but each one in proper order:

Christ the firstfruits;

then, at his coming, those who belong to Christ.

The word of the Lord.

8.

1 Corinthians 15:51-57   Death is swallowed up in victory.

A reading from the first Letter of Saint Paul to the Corinthians

Brothers and sisters:
Behold, I tell you a mystery.
We shall not all fall asleep, but we will all be changed,
  in an instant, in the blink of an eye, at the last trumpet.
For the trumpet will sound,
  the dead will be raised incorruptible,
  and we shall be changed.
For that which is corruptible must clothe itself with incorruptibility,
  and that which is mortal must clothe itself with immortality.
And when this which is corruptible clothes itself with incorruptibility
  and this which is mortal clothes itself with immortality,
  then the word that is written shall come about:

  Death is swallowed up in victory.
  Where, O death, is your victory?
  Where, O death, is your sting?

The sting of death is sin,
  and the power of sin is the law.
But thanks be to God who gives us the victory
  through our Lord Jesus Christ.

The word of the Lord.

9.

2 Corinthians 4:14–5:1   What is seen is transitory, but what is unseen
is eternal.

A reading from the second Letter of Saint Paul to the Corinthians

Brothers and sisters:
Knowing that the One who raised the Lord Jesus
  will raise us also with Jesus
  and place us with you in his presence.
Everything indeed is for you,
  so that the grace bestowed in abundance on more and more people
  may cause the thanksgiving to overflow for the glory of God.

Therefore, we are not discouraged;
rather, although our outer self is wasting away,
our inner self is being renewed day by day.
For this momentary light affliction
is producing for us an eternal weight of glory beyond all comparison,
as we look not to what is seen but to what is unseen;
for what is seen is transitory, but what is unseen is eternal.

For we know that if our earthly dwelling, a tent,
should be destroyed,
we have a building from God,
a dwelling not made with hands, eternal in heaven.

The word of the Lord.

10.

2 Corinthians 5:1, 6-10   We have a building from God, eternal in heaven.

A reading from the second Letter of Saint Paul to the Corinthians

Brothers and sisters:
We know that if our earthly dwelling, a tent,
should be destroyed,
we have a building from God,
a dwelling not made with hands,
eternal in heaven.

We are always courageous,
although we know that while we are at home in the body
we are away from the Lord,
for we walk by faith, not by sight.
Yet we are courageous,
and we would rather leave the body and go home to the Lord.
Therefore, we aspire to please him,
whether we are at home or away.
For we must all appear before the judgment seat of Christ,
so that each may receive recompense,
according to what he did in the body, whether good or evil.

The word of the Lord.

11.

Philippians 3:20-21   He will change our lowly bodies to conform to his glory.

A reading from the Letter of Saint Paul to the Philippians

Brothers and sisters:
Our citizenship is in heaven,
**   and from it we also await a savior, the Lord Jesus Christ.**
He will change our lowly body
**   to conform with his glorified Body**
**   by the power that enables him also**
**   to bring all things into subjection to himself.**

The word of the Lord.

12.

1 Thessalonians 4:13-18   Thus we shall always be with the Lord.

A reading from the first Letter of Saint Paul to the Thessalonians

We do not want you to be unaware, brothers and sisters,
**   about those who have fallen asleep,**
**   so that you may not grieve like the rest, who have no hope.**
For if we believe that Jesus died and rose,
**   so too will God, through Jesus,**
**   bring with him those who have fallen asleep.**
Indeed, we tell you this, on the word of the Lord,
**   that we who are alive,**
**   who are left until the coming of the Lord,**
**   will surely not precede those who have fallen asleep.**
For the Lord himself, with a word of command,
**   with the voice of an archangel and with the trumpet of God,**
**   will come down from heaven,**
**   and the dead in Christ will rise first.**
Then we who are alive, who are left,
**   will be caught up together with them in the clouds**
**   to meet the Lord in the air.**
Thus we shall always be with the Lord.
Therefore, console one another with these words.

The word of the Lord.

13.

2 Timothy 2:8-13   If we have died with him we shall also live with him.

A reading from the second Letter of Saint Paul to Timothy

Beloved:
Remember Jesus Christ, raised from the dead, a descendant of David:
  such is my Gospel, for which I am suffering,
  even to the point of chains, like a criminal.
But the word of God is not chained.
Therefore, I bear with everything for the sake of those who are chosen,
  so that they too may obtain the salvation that is in Christ Jesus,
  together with eternal glory.
This saying is trustworthy:
  If we have died with him
    we shall also live with him;
  if we persevere
    we shall also reign with him.
  But if we deny him
    he will deny us.
  If we are unfaithful
    he remains faithful,
    for he cannot deny himself.

The word of the Lord.

14.

1 John 3:1-2   We shall see him as he is.

A reading from the first Letter of Saint John

Beloved:
See what love the Father has bestowed on us
  that we may be called the children of God.
Yet so we are.
The reason the world does not know us
  is that it did not know him.
Beloved, we are God's children now;
  what we shall be has not yet been revealed.
We do know that when it is revealed we shall be like him,
  for we shall see him as he is.

The word of the Lord.

15.

1 John 3:14-16   We know that we have passed from death to life because we love our brothers.

A reading from the first Letter of Saint John

Beloved:
We know that we have passed from death to life
   because we love our brothers.
Whoever does not love remains in death.
Everyone who hates his brother is a murderer,
   and you know that no murderer has eternal life remaining in him.
The way we came to know love
   was that he laid down his life for us;
   so we ought to lay down our lives for our brothers.

The word of the Lord.

1015 ALLELUIA VERSE AND VERSE BEFORE THE GOSPEL

1.

See Matthew 11:25

**Blessed are you, Father, Lord of heaven and earth;
you have revealed to the childlike the mysteries of the Kingdom.**

2.

Matthew 25:34

**Come, you who are blessed by my Father, says the Lord;
inherit the kingdom prepared for you from the foundation of the world.**

3.

John 3:16

**God so loved the world that he gave his only-begotten Son,
so that everyone who believes in him might have eternal life.**

4.

John 6:39

**This is the will of my Father, says the Lord,
that I should lose nothing of all that he has given to me,
and that I should raise it up on the last day.**

5.

John 6:40

**This is the will of my Father, says the Lord,
that everyone who sees the Son and believes in him may have eternal life,
and I shall raise him on the last day.**

6.

John 6:51

**I am the living bread that came down from heaven,
says the Lord;
whoever eats this bread will live forever.**

7.

John 11:25a, 26

**I am the resurrection and the life, says the Lord;
whoever believes in me will never die.**

8.

See Philippians 3:20

**Our true home is in heaven,
and Jesus Christ, whose return we long for,
will come from heaven to save us.**

9.

2 Timothy 2:11-12a

**If we die with Christ, we shall live with him,
and if we persevere we shall also reign with him.**

10.

Revelation 1:5a, 6b

**Jesus Christ is the firstborn from the dead;
glory and power be his forever and ever. Amen.**

11.

Revelation 14:13

**Blessed are those who have died in the Lord;
let them rest from their labors for their good deeds go with them.**

1016 GOSPEL

1.

Matthew 5:1-12a   Rejoice and be glad, for your reward will be great in heaven.

✝ **A reading from the holy Gospel according to Matthew**

When Jesus saw the crowds, he went up the mountain,
  and after he had sat down, his disciples came to him.
He began to teach them, saying:
  "Blessed are the poor in spirit,
    for theirs is the Kingdom of heaven.
  Blessed are they who mourn,
    for they will be comforted.
  Blessed are the meek,
    for they will inherit the land.
  Blessed are they who hunger and thirst for righteousness,
    for they will be satisfied.
  Blessed are the merciful,
    for they will be shown mercy.
  Blessed are the clean of heart,
    for they will see God.
  Blessed are the peacemakers,
    for they will be called children of God.
  Blessed are they who are persecuted for the sake of righteousness,
    for theirs is the Kingdom of heaven.
  Blessed are you when they insult you and persecute you
    and utter every kind of evil against you falsely because of me.
  Rejoice and be glad,
    for your reward will be great in heaven."

The Gospel of the Lord.

2.

Matthew 11:25-30   Come to me and I will give you rest.

✠ **A reading from the holy Gospel according to Matthew**

At that time Jesus answered:
"I give praise to you, Father, Lord of heaven and earth,
    for although you have hidden these things
    from the wise and the learned
    you have revealed them to the childlike.
Yes, Father, such has been your gracious will.
All things have been handed over to me by my Father.
No one knows the Son except the Father,
    and no one knows the Father except the Son
    and anyone to whom the Son wishes to reveal him.

"Come to me, all you who labor and are burdened,
    and I will give you rest.
Take my yoke upon you and learn from me,
    for I am meek and humble of heart;
    and you will find rest for yourselves.
For my yoke is easy, and my burden light."

The Gospel of the Lord.

3.

Matthew 25:1-13   Behold the bridegroom! Come out to him!

✠ **A reading from the holy Gospel according to Matthew**

Jesus told his disciples this parable:
"The Kingdom of heaven will be like ten virgins
  who took their lamps and went out to meet the bridegroom.
Five of them were foolish and five were wise.
The foolish ones, when taking their lamps,
  brought no oil with them,
  but the wise brought flasks of oil with their lamps.
Since the bridegroom was long delayed,
  they all became drowsy and fell asleep.
At midnight, there was a cry,
  'Behold, the bridegroom! Come out to meet him!'
Then all those virgins got up and trimmed their lamps.
The foolish ones said to the wise,
  'Give us some of your oil,
  for our lamps are going out.'
But the wise ones replied,
  'No, for there may not be enough for us and you.
Go instead to the merchants and buy some for yourselves.'
While they went off to buy it,
  the bridegroom came
  and those who were ready went into the wedding feast with him.
Then the door was locked.
Afterwards the other virgins came and said,
  'Lord, Lord, open the door for us!'
But he said in reply,
  'Amen, I say to you, I do not know you.'
Therefore, stay awake,
  for you know neither the day nor the hour."

The Gospel of the Lord.

4.

Matthew 25:31-46   Come, you who are blessed by my Father.

✠ **A reading from the holy Gospel according to Matthew**

Jesus said to his disciples:
"When the Son of Man comes in his glory,
  and all the angels with him,
  he will sit upon his glorious throne,
  and all the nations will be assembled before him.
And he will separate them one from another,
  as a shepherd separates the sheep from the goats.
He will place the sheep on his right and the goats on his left.
Then the king will say to those on his right,
  'Come, you who are blessed by my Father.
Inherit the kingdom prepared for you from the foundation of the world.
For I was hungry and you gave me food,
  I was thirsty and you gave me drink,
  a stranger and you welcomed me,
  naked and you clothed me,
  ill and you cared for me,
  in prison and you visited me.'
Then the righteous will answer him and say,
  'Lord, when did we see you hungry and feed you,
  or thirsty and give you drink?
When did we see you a stranger and welcome you,
  or naked and clothe you?
When did we see you ill or in prison, and visit you?'
And the king will say to them in reply,
  'Amen, I say to you, whatever you did
  for one of these least brothers of mine, you did for me.'
Then he will say to those on his left,
  'Depart from me, you accursed,
  into the eternal fire prepared for the Devil and his angels.
For I was hungry and you gave me no food,
  I was thirsty and you gave me no drink,
  a stranger and you gave me no welcome,
  naked and you gave me no clothing,
  ill and in prison, and you did not care for me.'

Then they will answer and say,
   'Lord, when did we see you hungry or thirsty
   or a stranger or naked or ill or in prison,
   and not minister to your needs?'
He will answer them, 'Amen, I say to you,
   what you did not do for one of these least ones,
   you did not do for me.'
And these will go off to eternal punishment,
   but the righteous to eternal life."

The Gospel of the Lord.

5.

Long Form

Mark 15:33-39; 16:1-6   Jesus gave a loud cry and breathed his last.

✠ **A reading from the holy Gospel according to Mark**

At noon darkness came over the whole land
   until three in the afternoon.
And at three o'clock Jesus cried out in a loud voice,
   "Eloi, Eloi, lema sabachthani?"
   which is translated,
   "My God, my God, why have you forsaken me?"
Some of the bystanders who heard it said,
   "Look, he is calling Elijah."
One of them ran, soaked a sponge with wine, put it on a reed,
   and gave it to him to drink, saying,
   "Wait, let us see if Elijah comes to take him down."
Jesus gave a loud cry and breathed his last.
The veil of the sanctuary was torn in two from top to bottom.
When the centurion who stood facing him
   saw how he breathed his last he said,
   "Truly this man was the Son of God!"

When the sabbath was over,
   Mary Magdalene, Mary, the mother of James, and Salome
   bought spices so that they might go and anoint him.
Very early when the sun had risen,
   on the first day of the week, they came to the tomb.
They were saying to one another,
   "Who will roll back the stone for us
   from the entrance to the tomb?"
When they looked up,
   they saw that the stone had been rolled back;
   it was very large.
On entering the tomb they saw a young man
   sitting on the right side, clothed in a white robe,
   and they were utterly amazed.
He said to them, "Do not be amazed!
You seek Jesus of Nazareth, the crucified.

He has been raised; he is not here.
Behold the place where they laid him."

The Gospel of the Lord.

OR Short Form

Mark 15:33-39   Jesus gave a loud cry and breathed his last.

☩ **A reading from the holy Gospel according to Mark**

At noon darkness came over the whole land
   until three in the afternoon.
And at three o'clock Jesus cried out in a loud voice,
   "Eloi, Eloi, lema sabachthani?"
   which is translated,
   "My God, my God, why have you forsaken me?"
Some of the bystanders who heard it said,
   "Look, he is calling Elijah."
One of them ran, soaked a sponge with wine, put it on a reed,
   and gave it to him to drink, saying,
   "Wait, let us see if Elijah comes to take him down."
Jesus gave a loud cry and breathed his last.
The veil of the sanctuary was torn in two from top to bottom.
When the centurion who stood facing him
   saw how he breathed his last he said,
   "Truly this man was the Son of God!"

The Gospel of the Lord.

6.

Luke 7:11-17   Young man, I tell you, arise!

✠ **A reading from the holy Gospel according to Luke**

Jesus journeyed to a city called Nain,
   and his disciples and a large crowd accompanied him.
As he drew near to the gate of the city,
   a man who had died was being carried out,
   the only son of his mother, and she was a widow.
A large crowd from the city was with her.
When the Lord saw her,
   he was moved with pity for her and said to her,
   "Do not weep."
He stepped forward and touched the coffin;
   at this the bearers halted,
   and he said, "Young man, I tell you, arise!"
The dead man sat up and began to speak,
   and Jesus gave him to his mother.
Fear seized them all, and they glorified God, exclaiming,
   "A great prophet has arisen in our midst,"
   and "God has visited his people."
This report about him spread through the whole of Judea
   and in all the surrounding region.

The Gospel of the Lord.

7.

Luke 12:35-40   You also must be prepared.

✠ **A reading from the holy Gospel according to Luke**

Jesus said to his disciples:
"Gird your loins and light your lamps
   and be like servants who await their master's return from a wedding,
   ready to open immediately when he comes and knocks.
Blessed are those servants
   whom the master finds vigilant on his arrival.
Amen, I say to you, he will gird himself,
   have them recline at table, and proceed to wait on them.
And should he come in the second or third watch
   and find them prepared in this way,
   blessed are those servants.

Be sure of this:
    if the master of the house had known the hour
    when the thief was coming,
    he would not have let his house be broken into.
You also must be prepared, for at an hour you do not expect,
    the Son of Man will come."

The Gospel of the Lord.

    8.

Luke 23:33, 39-43   Today you will be with me in Paradise.

✝ **A reading from the holy Gospel according to Luke**

When the soldiers came to the place called the Skull,
    they crucified Jesus and the criminals there,
    one on his right, the other on his left.

Now one of the criminals hanging there
    reviled Jesus, saying,
    "Are you not the Christ?
    Save yourself and us."
The other man, however, rebuking him, said in reply,
    "Have you no fear of God,
    for you are subject to the same condemnation?
And indeed, we have been condemned justly,
    for the sentence we received corresponds to our crimes,
    but this man has done nothing criminal."
Then he said,
"Jesus, remember me when you come into your Kingdom."
He replied to him,
    "Amen, I say to you,
    today you will be with me in Paradise."

The Gospel of the Lord.

9.

Long Form

Luke 23:44-46, 50, 52-53; 24:1-6a   Father, into your hands I commend
my spirit.

✠ **A reading from the holy Gospel according to Luke**

It was about noon and darkness came over the whole land
   until three in the afternoon
   because of an eclipse of the sun.
Then the veil of the temple was torn down the middle.
Jesus cried out in a loud voice,
   "Father, into your hands I commend my spirit";
   and when he had said this he breathed his last.
Now there was a virtuous and righteous man named Joseph who,
   though he was a member of the council,
   went to Pilate and asked for the Body of Jesus.
After he had taken the Body down,
   he wrapped it in a linen cloth
   and laid him in a rock-hewn tomb
   in which no one had yet been buried.

At daybreak on the first day of the week
   the women took the spices they had prepared
   and went to the tomb.
They found the stone rolled away from the tomb;
   but when they entered,
   they did not find the Body of the Lord Jesus.
While they were puzzling over this, behold,
   two men in dazzling garments appeared to them.
They were terrified and bowed their faces to the ground.
They said to them,
   "Why do you seek the living one among the dead?
He is not here, but he has been raised."

The Gospel of the Lord.

OR Short Form

Luke 23:44-46, 50, 52-53   Father, into your hands I commend my spirit.

✠ **A reading from the holy Gospel according to Luke**

It was about noon and darkness came over the whole land
 until three in the afternoon
 because of an eclipse of the sun.
Then the veil of the temple was torn down the middle.
Jesus cried out in a loud voice,
 "Father, into your hands I commend my spirit";
 and when he had said this he breathed his last.

Now there was a virtuous and righteous man named Joseph who,
 though he was a member of the council,
 went to Pilate and asked for the Body of Jesus.
After he had taken the Body down,
 he wrapped it in a linen cloth
 and laid him in a rock-hewn tomb
 in which no one had yet been buried.

The Gospel of the Lord.

10.

Long Form

Luke 24:13-35   Was it not necessary that the Christ should suffer these things and enter into his glory?

☩ **A reading from the holy Gospel according to Luke**

That very day, the first day of the week,
   two of the disciples of Jesus were going
   to a village called Emmaus, seven miles from Jerusalem,
   and they were conversing about all the things that had occurred.
And it happened that while they were conversing and debating,
   Jesus himself drew near and walked with them,
   but their eyes were prevented from recognizing him.
He asked them,
   "What are you discussing as you walk along?"
They stopped, looking downcast.
One of them, named Cleopas, said to him in reply,
   "Are you the only visitor to Jerusalem
   who does not know of the things
   that have taken place there in these days?"
And he replied to them, "What sort of things?"
They said to him,
   "The things that happened to Jesus the Nazarene,
   who was a prophet mighty in deed and word
   before God and all the people,
   how our chief priests and rulers both handed him over
   to a sentence of death and crucified him.
But we were hoping that he would be the one to redeem Israel;
   and besides all this,
   it is now the third day since this took place.
Some women from our group, however, have astounded us:
   they were at the tomb early in the morning
   and did not find his Body;
   they came back and reported
   that they had indeed seen a vision of angels
   who announced that he was alive.
Then some of those with us went to the tomb
   and found things just as the women had described,
   but him they did not see."
And he said to them, "Oh, how foolish you are!

How slow of heart to believe all that the prophets spoke!
Was it not necessary that the Christ should suffer these things
   and enter into his glory?"
Then beginning with Moses and all the prophets,
   Jesus interpreted to them what referred to him
   in all the Scriptures.
As they approached the village to which they were going,
   Jesus gave the impression that he was going on farther.
But they urged him, "Stay with us,
   for it is nearly evening and the day is almost over."
So he went in to stay with them.
And it happened that, while he was with them at table,
   he took bread, said the blessing,
   broke it, and gave it to them.
With that their eyes were opened and they recognized him,
   but he vanished from their sight.
Then they said to each other,
   "Were not our hearts burning within us
   while he spoke to us on the way and opened the Scriptures to us?"
So they set out at once and returned to Jerusalem
   where they found gathered together
   the Eleven and those with them, who were saying,
   "The Lord has truly been raised and has appeared to Simon!"
Then the two recounted
   what had taken place on the way
   and how he was made known to them in the breaking of the bread.

The Gospel of the Lord.

OR Short Form

Luke 24:13-16, 28-35   Was it not necessary that the Christ should suffer these things and enter into his glory?

✠ **A reading from the holy Gospel according to Luke**

That very day, the first day of the week,
  two of the disciples of Jesus were going
  to a village called Emmaus, seven miles from Jerusalem,
  and they were conversing about all the things that had occurred.
And it happened that while they were conversing and debating,
  Jesus himself drew near and walked with them,
  but their eyes were prevented from recognizing him.
As they approached the village to which they were going,
  he gave the impression that he was going on farther.
But they urged him, "Stay with us,
  for it is nearly evening and the day is almost over."
So he went in to stay with them.
And it happened that, while he was with them at table,
  he took bread, said the blessing,
  broke it, and gave it to them.
With that their eyes were opened and they recognized him,
  but he vanished from their sight.
Then they said to each other,
  "Were not our hearts burning within us
  while he spoke to us on the way and opened the Scriptures to us?"
So they set out at once and returned to Jerusalem
  where they found gathered together
  the Eleven and those with them, who were saying,
  "The Lord has truly been raised and has appeared to Simon!"
Then the two recounted
  what had taken place on the way
  and how he was made known to them in the breaking of the bread.

The Gospel of the Lord.

11.

John 5:24-29   Whoever hears my word and believes has passed from death to life.

☩ **A reading from the holy Gospel according to John**

Jesus answered the Jews and said to them:
"Amen, amen, I say to you, whoever hears my word
  and believes in the one who sent me
  has eternal life and will not come to condemnation,
  but has passed from death to life.
Amen, amen, I say to you, the hour is coming and is now here
  when the dead will hear the voice of the Son of God,
  and those who hear will live.
For just as the Father has life in himself,
  so also he gave to the Son the possession of life in himself.
And he gave him power to exercise judgment,
  because he is the Son of Man.
Do not be amazed at this,
  because the hour is coming in which all who are in the tombs
  will hear his voice and will come out,
  those who have done good deeds
  to the resurrection of life,
  but those who have done wicked deeds
  to the resurrection of condemnation.

The Gospel of the Lord.

12.

John 6:37-40   Everyone who sees the Son and believes in him may have eternal life and I shall raise him on the last day.

✠ **A reading from the holy Gospel according to John**

Jesus said to the crowds:
"Everything that the Father gives me will come to me,
  and I will not reject anyone who comes to me,
    because I came down from heaven not to do my own will
    but the will of the one who sent me.
And this is the will of the one who sent me,
    that I should not lose anything of what he gave me,
    but that I should raise it on the last day.
For this is the will of my Father,
    that everyone who sees the Son and believes in him
    may have eternal life,
    and I shall raise him on the last day."

The Gospel of the Lord.

13.

John 6:51-59   Whoever eats this bread will live forever, and I will raise them up on the last day.

✠   **A reading from the holy Gospel according to John**

Jesus said to the crowds:
"I am the living bread that came down from heaven;
   whoever eats this bread will live forever;
   and the bread that I will give is my Flesh
   for the life of the world."

The Jews quarreled among themselves, saying,
   "How can this man give us his Flesh to eat?"
Jesus said to them,
   "Amen, amen, I say to you,
   unless you eat the Flesh of the Son of Man and drink his Blood,
   you do not have life within you.
Whoever eats my Flesh and drinks my Blood
   has eternal life,
   and I will raise him on the last day.
For my Flesh is true food,
   and my Blood is true drink.
Whoever eats my Flesh and drinks my Blood
   remains in me and I in him.
Just as the living Father sent me
   and I have life because of the Father,
   so also the one who feeds on me
   will have life because of me.
This is the bread that came down from heaven.
Unlike your ancestors who ate and still died,
   whoever eats this bread will live forever."

The Gospel of the Lord.

14.

Long Form

John 11:17-27   I am the resurrection and the life.

✠ A reading from the holy Gospel according to John

When Jesus arrived in Bethany, he found that Lazarus
    had already been in the tomb for four days.
Now Bethany was near Jerusalem, only about two miles away.
Many of the Jews had come to Martha and Mary
    to comfort them about their brother.
When Martha heard that Jesus was coming,
    she went to meet him;
    but Mary sat at home.
Martha said to Jesus,
    "Lord, if you had been here,
    my brother would not have died.
But even now I know that whatever you ask of God,
    God will give you."
Jesus said to her,
    "Your brother will rise."
Martha said to him,
    "I know he will rise,
    in the resurrection on the last day."
Jesus told her,
    "I am the resurrection and the life;
    whoever believes in me, even if he dies, will live,
    and everyone who lives and believes in me will never die.
Do you believe this?"
She said to him, "Yes, Lord.
I have come to believe that you are the Christ, the Son of God,
    the one who is coming into the world."

The Gospel of the Lord.

OR Short Form

John 11:21-27   I am the resurrection and the life.

✠ **A reading from the holy Gospel according to John**

Martha said to Jesus,
  "Lord, if you had been here,
    my brother would not have died.
But even now I know that whatever you ask of God,
    God will give you."
Jesus said to her,
    "Your brother will rise."
Martha said to him,
    "I know he will rise,
    in the resurrection on the last day."
Jesus told her,
    "I am the resurrection and the life;
    whoever believes in me, even if he dies, will live,
    and everyone who lives and believes in me will never die.
Do you believe this?"
She said to him, "Yes, Lord.
I have come to believe that you are the Christ, the Son of God,
    the one who is coming into the world."

The Gospel of the Lord.

15.

John 11:32-45   Lazarus, come out!

☩ **A reading from the holy Gospel according to John**

When Mary came to where Jesus was and saw him,
  she fell at his feet and said to him,
  "Lord, if you had been here,
  my brother would not have died."
When Jesus saw her weeping and the Jews who had come with her
    weeping,
  he became perturbed and deeply troubled, and said,
  "Where have you laid him?"
They said to him, "Sir, come and see."
And Jesus wept.
So the Jews said, "See how he loved him."
But some of them said,
  "Could not the one who opened the eyes of the blind man
  have done something so that this man would not have died?"

So Jesus, perturbed again, came to the tomb.
It was a cave, and a stone lay across it.
Jesus said, "Take away the stone."
Martha, the dead man's sister, said to him,
  "Lord, by now there will be a stench;
  he has been dead for four days."
Jesus said to her,
  "Did I not tell you that if you believe
  you will see the glory of God?"
So they took away the stone.
And Jesus raised his eyes and said,
  "Father, I thank you for hearing me.
I know that you always hear me;
  but because of the crowd here I have said this,
  that they may believe that you sent me."
And when he had said this,
  he cried out in a loud voice,
  "Lazarus, come out!"
The dead man came out,
  tied hand and foot with burial bands,
  and his face was wrapped in a cloth.

So Jesus said to the crowd,
    "Untie him and let him go."

Now many of the Jews who had come to Mary
    and seen what he had done began to believe in him.

The Gospel of the Lord.

16.

Long Form

John 12:23-28   If it dies, it produces much fruit.

✠ A reading from the holy Gospel according to John

Jesus said to his disciples:
"The hour has come for the Son of Man to be glorified.
Amen, amen, I say to you,
    unless a grain of wheat falls to the ground and dies,
    it remains just a grain of wheat;
    but if it dies, it produces much fruit.
Whoever loves his life will lose it,
    and whoever hates his life in this world
    will preserve it for eternal life.
Whoever serves me must follow me,
    and where I am, there also will my servant be.
The Father will honor whoever serves me.

"I am troubled now. Yet what should I say?
'Father, save me from this hour'?
But it was for this purpose that I came to this hour.
Father, glorify your name."
Then a voice came from heaven,
    "I have glorified it and will glorify it again."

The Gospel of the Lord.

OR Short Form

John 12:23-26   If it dies, it produces much fruit.

✠ **A reading from the holy Gospel according to John**

Jesus said to his disciples:
"The hour has come for the Son of Man to be glorified.
Amen, amen, I say to you,
> **unless a grain of wheat falls to the ground and dies,**
> **it remains just a grain of wheat;**
> **but if it dies, it produces much fruit.**

Whoever loves his life will lose it,
> **and whoever hates his life in this world**
> **will preserve it for eternal life.**

Whoever serves me must follow me,
> **and where I am, there also will my servant be.**

The Father will honor whoever serves me."

The Gospel of the Lord.

17.

John 14:1-6   In my Father's house there are many dwellings.

✠ **A reading from the holy Gospel according to John**

Jesus said to his disciples:
"Do not let your hearts be troubled.
You have faith in God; have faith also in me.
In my Father's house there are many dwelling places.
If there were not,
> **would I have told you that I am going to prepare a place for you?**

And if I go and prepare a place for you,
> **I will come back again and take you to myself,**
> **so that where I am you also may be.**

Where I am going you know the way."
Thomas said to him,
> **"Master, we do not know where you are going;**
> **how can we know the way?"**

Jesus said to him, "I am the way and the truth and the life.
No one comes to the Father except through me."

The Gospel of the Lord.

18.

John 17:24-26   I wish that where I am they also may be with me.

✠ **A reading from the holy Gospel according to John**

Jesus raised his eyes to heaven and said:
"Father, those whom you gave me are your gift to me.
I wish that where I am they also may be with me,
   that they may see my glory that you gave me,
   because you loved me before the foundation of the world.
Righteous Father, the world also does not know you,
   but I know you, and they know that you sent me.
I made known to them your name and I will make it known,
   that the love with which you loved me
   may be in them and I in them."

The Gospel of the Lord.

19.

John 19:17-18, 25-39   And bowing his head he handed over his Spirit.

✝ **A reading from the holy Gospel according to John**

So they took Jesus, and, carrying the cross himself,
   he went out to what is called the Place of the Skull,
   in Hebrew, Golgotha.
There they crucified him, and with him two others,
   one on either side, with Jesus in the middle.

Standing by the cross of Jesus were his mother
   and his mother's sister, Mary the wife of Clopas,
   and Mary Magdalene.
When Jesus saw his mother and the disciple whom he loved,
   he said to his mother, "Woman, behold, your son."
Then he said to the disciple,
   "Behold, your mother."
And from that hour the disciple took her into his home.

After this, aware that everything was now finished,
   in order that the Scripture might be fulfilled,
   Jesus said, "I thirst."
There was a vessel filled with common wine.
So they put a sponge soaked in wine on a sprig of hyssop
   and put it up to his mouth.
When Jesus had taken the wine, he said,
   "It is finished."
And bowing his head, he handed over the Spirit.

Now since it was preparation day,
   in order that the bodies might not remain on the cross on the sabbath,
   for the sabbath day of that week was a solemn one,
   the Jews asked Pilate that their legs be broken
   and they be taken down.
So the soldiers came and broke the legs of the first
   and then of the other one who was crucified with Jesus.
But when they came to Jesus and saw that he was already dead,
   they did not break his legs,
   but one soldier thrust his lance into his side,
   and immediately Blood and water flowed out.

An eyewitness has testified, and his testimony is true;
>   he knows that he is speaking the truth,
>   so that you also may come to believe.

For this happened so that the Scripture passage might be fulfilled:
>   *Not a bone of it will be broken.*

And again another passage says:
>   *They will look upon him whom they have pierced.*

After this, Joseph of Arimathea,
>   secretly a disciple of Jesus for fear of the Jews,
>   asked Pilate if he could remove the Body of Jesus.

And Pilate permitted it.

So he came and took his Body.

Nicodemus, the one who had first come to him at night,
>   also came bringing a mixture of myrrh and aloes
>   weighing about one hundred pounds.

The Gospel of the Lord.

FUNERALS FOR BAPTIZED CHILDREN

1017 READING I FROM THE OLD TESTAMENT

1.

Isaiah 25:6a, 7-9   He will destroy death forever.

A reading from the Book of the Prophet Isaiah

On this mountain the LORD of hosts
   will provide for all peoples.
On this mountain he will destroy
   the veil that veils all peoples,
The web that is woven over all nations;
   he will destroy death forever.
The Lord GOD will wipe away
   the tears from all faces;
The reproach of his people he will remove
   from the whole earth; for the LORD has spoken.

      On that day it will be said:
"Behold our God, to whom we looked to save us!
   This is the LORD for whom we looked;
   let us rejoice and be glad that he has saved us!"

The word of the Lord.

2.

Lamentations 3:22-26   It is good to hope in silence for the saving help of the Lord.

A reading from the Book of Lamentations

The favors of the LORD are not exhausted,
   his mercies are not spent;
They are renewed each morning,
   so great is his faithfulness.
My portion is the LORD, says my soul;
   therefore will I hope in him.

Good is the LORD to one who waits for him,
   to the soul that seeks him;
It is good to hope in silence
   for the saving help of the LORD.

The word of the Lord.

1018 READING I FROM THE NEW TESTAMENT DURING THE SEASON OF EASTER

1.

Revelation 7:9-10, 15-17   God will wipe away every tear from their eyes.

A reading from the Book of Revelation

I, John, had a vision of a great multitude,
   which no one could count,
      from every nation, race, people, and tongue.
They stood before the throne and before the Lamb,
   wearing white robes and holding palm branches in their hands.
They cried out in a loud voice:
   "Salvation comes from our God, who is seated on the throne,
      and from the Lamb.

   "For this reason they stand before God's throne
      and worship him day and night in his temple.
      The One who sits on the throne will shelter them.
   They will not hunger or thirst anymore,
      nor will the sun or any heat strike them.
   For the Lamb who is in the center of the throne
      will shepherd them
      and lead them to springs of life-giving water,
      and God will wipe away every tear from their eyes."

The word of the Lord.

2.

Revelation 21:1a, 3-5a   There shall be no more death.

A reading from the Book of Revelation

I, John, saw a new heaven and a new earth.
I heard a loud voice from the throne saying,
  "Behold, God's dwelling is with the human race.
He will dwell with them and they will be his people
  and God himself will always be with them as their God.
He will wipe away every tear from their eyes,
  and there shall be no more death or mourning, wailing or pain,
  for the old order has passed away."

The One who sat on the throne said,
  "Behold, I make all things new."

The word of the Lord.

1019 RESPONSORIAL PSALM

1.

Psalm 23:1-3, 4, 5, 6

R͠. (1) **The Lord is my shepherd; there is nothing I shall want.**

The Lᴏʀᴅ is my shepherd; I shall not want.
  In verdant pastures he gives me repose;
Beside restful waters he leads me;
  he refreshes my soul.
He guides me in right paths
  for his name's sake.

R͠. **The Lord is my shepherd; there is nothing I shall want.**

Even though I walk in the dark valley
  I fear no evil; for you are at my side
With your rod and your staff
  that give me courage.

R͠. **The Lord is my shepherd; there is nothing I shall want.**

You spread the table before me
  in the sight of my foes;
You anoint my head with oil;
  my cup overflows.

R͠. **The Lord is my shepherd; there is nothing I shall want.**

Only goodness and kindness follow me
  all the days of my life;
And I shall dwell in the house of the Lᴏʀᴅ
  for years to come.

R͠. **The Lord is my shepherd; there is nothing I shall want.**

2.

Psalm 25:4-5ab, 6 and 7bc, 20-21

R͠. (1) **To you, O Lord, I lift up my soul.**

Your ways, O Lᴏʀᴅ, make known to me;
  teach me your paths,
Guide me in your truth and teach me,
  for you are God my savior.

R͠. **To you, O Lord, I lift up my soul.**

(cont.)

Remember that your compassion, O LORD,
   and your kindness are from of old.
In your kindness remember me,
   because of your goodness, O LORD.

℟. To you, O Lord, I lift up my soul.

Preserve my life, and rescue me;
   let me not be put to shame, for I take refuge in you.
Let integrity and uprightness preserve me,
   because I wait for you, O LORD.

℟. To you, O Lord, I lift up my soul.

   3.

Psalm 42:2, 3, 5cdef; 43:3, 4, 5

℟. (42:3) **My soul is thirsting for the living God: when shall I see him face to face?**

As the hind longs for the running waters,
   so my soul longs for you, O God.

℟. My soul is thirsting for the living God: when shall I see him face to face?

Athirst is my soul for God, the living God.
   When shall I go and behold the face of God?

℟. My soul is thirsting for the living God: when shall I see him face to face?

I went with the throng
   and led them in procession to the house of God.
Amid loud cries of joy and thanksgiving,
   with the multitude keeping festival.

℟. My soul is thirsting for the living God: when shall I see him face to face?

Send forth your light and your fidelity;
   they shall lead me on
And bring me to your holy mountain,
   to your dwelling-place.

℟. My soul is thirsting for the living God: when shall I see him face to face?

Then will I go in to the altar of God,
   the God of my gladness and joy;

Then will I give you thanks upon the harp,
   O God, my God!

℟. My soul is thirsting for the living God: when shall I see him face to face?

Why are you so downcast, O my soul?
   Why do you sigh within me?
Hope in God! For I shall again be thanking him,
   in the presence of my savior and my God.

℟. My soul is thirsting for the living God: when shall I see him face to face?

   4.

Psalm 148:1-2, 11-13a, 13c-14

℟. (13a) Let all praise the name of the Lord.
   or:
℟. Alleluia.

Praise the LORD from the heavens,
   praise him in the heights;
Praise him, all you his angels,
   praise him, all you his hosts.

℟. (13a) Let all praise the name of the Lord.
   or:
℟. Alleluia.

Let the kings of the earth and all peoples,
   the princes and all the judges of the earth,
Young men too, and maidens,
   old men and boys,
Praise the name of the LORD,
   for his name alone is exalted.

℟. (13a) Let all praise the name of the Lord.
   or:
℟. Alleluia.

His majesty is above earth and heaven,
   and he has lifted up the horn of his people.
Be this his praise from all his faithful ones,
   from the children of Israel, the people close to him. Alleluia.

℟. (13a) Let all praise the name of the Lord.
   or:
℟. Alleluia.

1020 READING II FROM THE NEW TESTAMENT

1.

Romans 6:3-4, 8-9   We believe that we shall also live with him.

A reading from the Letter of Saint Paul to the Romans

Brothers and sisters:
Are you unaware that we who were baptized into Christ Jesus
   were baptized into his death?
We were indeed buried with him through baptism into death,
   so that, just as Christ was raised from the dead
   by the glory of the Father,
   we too might live in newness of life.

If, then, we have died with Christ,
   we believe that we shall also live with him.
We know that Christ, raised from the dead, dies no more;
   death no longer has power over him.

The word of the Lord.

2.

Romans 14:7-9   Whether we live or die, we are the Lord's.

A reading from the Letter of Saint Paul to the Romans

Brothers and sisters:
No one lives for oneself,
   and no one dies for oneself.
For if we live, we live for the Lord,
   and if we die, we die for the Lord;
   so then, whether we live or die, we are the Lord's.
For this is why Christ died and came to life,
   that he might be Lord of both the dead and the living.

The word of the Lord.

3.

1 Corinthians 15:20-23   So too in Christ shall all be brought to life.

A reading from the first Letter of Saint Paul to the Corinthians

Brothers and sisters:
Christ has been raised from the dead,
  the firstfruits of those who have fallen asleep.
For since death came through a man,
  the resurrection of the dead came also through man.
For just as in Adam all die,
  so too in Christ shall all be brought to life,
  but each one in proper order:
  Christ the firstfruits;
  then, at his coming, those who belong to Christ.

The word of the Lord.

4.

Ephesians 1:3-5   He chose us in him, before the foundation of the world,
to be holy.

A reading from the Letter of Saint Paul to the Ephesians

Blessed be the God and Father of our Lord Jesus Christ,
  who has blessed us in Christ
  with every spiritual blessing in the heavens,
  as he chose us in him, before the foundation of the world,
  to be holy and without blemish before him.
In love he destined us for adoption to himself through Jesus Christ,
  in accord with the favor of his will.

The word of the Lord.

5.

1 Thessalonians 4:13-14, 18   We shall be with the Lord forever.

A reading from the first Letter of Saint Paul to the Thessalonians

We do not want you to be unaware, brothers and sisters,
    about those who have fallen asleep,
    so that you may not grieve like the rest, who have no hope.
For if we believe that Jesus died and rose,
    so too will God, through Jesus,
    bring with him those who have fallen asleep.
Therefore, console one another with these words.

The word of the Lord.

1021 ALLELUIA VERSE AND VERSE BEFORE THE GOSPEL

1.

See Matthew 11:25

**Blessed are you, Father, Lord of heaven and earth;
you have revealed to the childlike the mysteries of the Kingdom.**

2.

John 6:39

**This is the will of my Father, says the Lord,
that I should lose nothing of all that he has given to me,
and that I should raise it up on the last day.**

3.

2 Corinthians 1:3b-4a

**Blessed be the Father of compassion and God of all encouragement,
who encourages us in our every affliction.**

1022 GOSPEL

1.

Matthew 11:25-30   You have hidden these things from the wise and the learned and have revealed them to the childlike.

☩ **A reading from the holy Gospel according to Matthew**

At that time Jesus answered:
"I give praise to you, Father, Lord of heaven and earth,
 for although you have hidden these things
 from the wise and the learned
 you have revealed them to the childlike.
Yes, Father, such has been your gracious will.
All things have been handed over to me by my Father.
No one knows the Son except the Father,
 and no one knows the Father except the Son
 and anyone to whom the Son wishes to reveal him.

"Come to me, all you who labor and are burdened,
 and I will give you rest.
Take my yoke upon you and learn from me,
 for I am meek and humble of heart;
 and you will find rest for yourselves.
For my yoke is easy, and my burden light."

The Gospel of the Lord.

2.

Mark 10:13-16   The Kingdom of heaven belongs to little children.

☩ **A reading from the holy Gospel according to Mark**

People were bringing children to Jesus that he might touch them,
 but the disciples rebuked them.
When Jesus saw this he became indignant, and said to them,
 "Let the children come to me; do not prevent them,
 for the Kingdom of God belongs to such as these.
Amen, I say to you,
 whoever does not accept the Kingdom of God like a child
 will not enter it."
Then he embraced the children and blessed them,
 placing his hands on them.

The Gospel of the Lord.

3.

Long Form

John 6:37-40   This is the will of my Father, that I should not lose anything of what he gave me.

☩ **A reading from the holy Gospel according to John**

Jesus said to the crowds:
"Everything that the Father gives me will come to me,
   and I will not reject anyone who comes to me,
    because I came down from heaven not to do my own will
    but the will of the one who sent me.
And this is the will of the one who sent me,
   that I should not lose anything of what he gave me,
   but that I should raise it on the last day.
For this is the will of my Father,
   that everyone who sees the Son and believes in him
   may have eternal life,
   and I shall raise him on the last day."

The Gospel of the Lord.

OR Short Form

John 6:37-39   This is the will of my Father, that I should not lose anything of what he gave me.

☩ **A reading from the holy Gospel according to John**

Jesus said to the crowds:
"Everything that the Father gives me will come to me,
   and I will not reject anyone who comes to me,
    because I came down from heaven not to do my own will
    but the will of the one who sent me.
And this is the will of the one who sent me,
   that I should not lose anything of what he gave me,
   but that I should raise it on the last day."

The Gospel of the Lord.

4. (For a child who had already received the Eucharist)

John 6:51-58   Whoever eats this bread will live forever, and I will raise him up on the last day.

✝ **A reading from the holy Gospel according to John**

Jesus said to the Jews:
"I am the living bread that came down from heaven;
   whoever eats this bread will live forever;
   and the bread that I will give is my Flesh
   for the life of the world."

The Jews quarreled among themselves, saying,
   "How can this man give us his Flesh to eat?"
Jesus said to them,
   "Amen, amen, I say to you,
   unless you eat the Flesh of the Son of Man and drink his Blood,
   you do not have life within you.
Whoever eats my Flesh and drinks my Blood
   has eternal life,
   and I will raise him on the last day.
For my Flesh is true food,
   and my Blood is true drink.
Whoever eats my Flesh and drinks my Blood
   remains in me and I in him.
Just as the living Father sent me
   and I have life because of the Father,
   so also the one who feeds on me
   will have life because of me.
This is the bread that came down from heaven.
Unlike your ancestors who ate and still died,
   whoever eats this bread will live forever."

The Gospel of the Lord.

5.

John 11:32-38, 40   If you believe, you will see the glory of God.

☩ **A reading from the holy Gospel according to John**

When Mary [the sister of Lazarus]
    came to where Jesus was and saw him,
    she fell at his feet and said to him,
    "Lord, if you had been here,
    my brother would not have died."
When Jesus saw her weeping and the Jews who had come with her weeping,
    he became perturbed and deeply troubled, and said,
    "Where have you laid him?"
They said to him, "Sir, come and see."
And Jesus wept.
So the Jews said, "See how he loved him."
But some of them said,
    "Could not the one who opened the eyes of the blind man
    have done something so that this man would not have died?"

So Jesus, perturbed again, came to the tomb.
It was a cave, and a stone lay across it.
Jesus said to her,
    "Did I not tell you that if you believe
    you will see the glory of God?"

The Gospel of the Lord.

6.

John 19:25-30   Behold, your mother.

✠ **A reading from the holy Gospel according to John**

**Standing by the cross of Jesus were his mother
and his mother's sister, Mary the wife of Clopas,
and Mary Magdalene.
When Jesus saw his mother and the disciple whom he loved
he said to his mother, "Woman, behold, your son."
Then he said to the disciple,
"Behold, your mother."
And from that hour the disciple took her into his home.**

**After this, aware that everything was now finished,
in order that the Scripture might be fulfilled,
Jesus said, "I thirst."
There was a vessel filled with common wine.
So they put a sponge soaked in wine on a sprig of hyssop
and put it up to his mouth.
When Jesus had taken the wine, he said,
"It is finished."
And bowing his head, he handed over the spirit.**

The Gospel of the Lord.

FUNERALS FOR CHILDREN WHO DIED BEFORE BAPTISM

1023 READING I FROM THE OLD TESTAMENT

1.

Isaiah 25:6a, 7-8   He will destroy death forever.

A reading from the Book of the Prophet Isaiah

On this mountain the LORD of hosts
 will provide for all peoples.
On this mountain he will destroy
 the veil that veils all peoples,
The web that is woven over all nations;
 he will destroy death forever.
The Lord GOD will wipe away
 the tears from all faces.

The word of the Lord.

2.

Lamentations 3:22-26   It is good to hope in silence for the saving help of the Lord.

A reading from the Book of Lamentations

The favors of the LORD are not exhausted,
 his mercies are not spent;
They are renewed each morning,
 so great is his faithfulness.
My portion is the LORD, says my soul;
 therefore will I hope in him.

Good is the LORD to one who waits for him,
 to the soul that seeks him;
It is good to hope in silence
 for the saving help of the LORD.

The word of the Lord.

1024 RESPONSORIAL PSALM

Psalm 25:4-5ab, 6 and 7b, 17 and 20

℟. (1) **To you, O Lord, I lift up my soul.**

Your way, O Lord, make known to me;
  teach me your paths.
Guide me in your truth and teach me,
  for you are God my savior.

℟. **To you, O Lord, I lift up my soul.**

Remember that your compassion, O LORD,
  and your kindness are from of old.
In your kindness remember me,
  because of your goodness, O LORD.

℟. **To you, O Lord, I lift up my soul.**

Relieve the troubles of my heart;
  bring me out of my distress.
Preserve my life and rescue me;
  let me not be put to shame, for I take refuge in you.

℟. **To you, O Lord, I lift up my soul.**

1025 ALLELUIA VERSE AND VERSE BEFORE THE GOSPEL

1.

2 Corinthians 1:3b-4a

Blessed be the Father of compassion and God of all encouragement, who encourages us in our every affliction.

2.

Revelation 1:5a, 6b

Jesus Christ is the firstborn from the dead; glory and kingship be his forever and ever. Amen.

1026 GOSPEL

1.

Matthew 11:25-30   You have hidden these things from the wise and the learned and have revealed them to the childlike.

✝ **A reading from the holy Gospel according to Matthew**

At that time Jesus answered:
  "I give praise to you, Father, Lord of heaven and earth,
  for although you have hidden these things
  from the wise and the learned
  you have revealed them to the childlike.
Yes, Father, such has been your gracious will.
All things have been handed over to me by my Father.
No one knows the Son except the Father,
  and no one knows the Father except the Son
  and anyone to whom the Son wishes to reveal him.

"Come to me, all you who labor and are burdened,
  and I will give you rest.
Take my yoke upon you and learn from me,
  for I am meek and humble of heart;
  and you will find rest for yourselves.
For my yoke is easy, and my burden light."

The Gospel of the Lord.

2.

Mark 15:33-46   Jesus gave a loud cry and breathed his last.

✝ **A reading from the holy Gospel according to Mark**

At noon darkness came over the whole land
  until three in the afternoon.
And at three o'clock Jesus cried out in a loud voice,
  "Eloi, Eloi, lema sabachthani?"
  which is translated,
  "My God, my God, why have you forsaken me?"
Some of the bystanders who heard it said,
  "Look, he is calling Elijah."
One of them ran, soaked a sponge with wine, put it on a reed,
  and gave it to him to drink, saying,
  "Wait, let us see if Elijah comes to take him down."

Jesus gave a loud cry and breathed his last.

The veil of the sanctuary was torn in two from top to bottom.

When the centurion who stood facing him
  saw how he breathed his last he said,
  "Truly this man was the Son of God!"

There were also women looking on from a distance.

Among them were Mary Magdalene,
  Mary the mother of the younger James, and of Joses, and Salome.

These women had followed him when he was in Galilee
  and ministered to him.

There were also many other women
  who had come up with him to Jerusalem.

When it was already evening,
  since it was the day of preparation,
  the day before the sabbath, Joseph of Arimathea,
  a distinguished member of the council,
  who was himself awaiting the Kingdom of God,
  came and courageously went to Pilate
  and asked for the Body of Jesus.

Pilate was amazed that he was already dead.

He summoned the centurion
  and asked him if Jesus had already died.

And when he learned of it from the centurion,
  he gave the Body to Joseph.

Having bought a linen cloth, he took him down,
  wrapped him in the linen cloth,
  and laid him in a tomb that had been hewn out of the rock.

Then he rolled a stone against the entrance of the tomb.

The Gospel of the Lord.

3.

John 19:25-30   Behold, your mother.

✠ **A reading from the holy Gospel according to John**

Standing by the cross of Jesus were his mother
and his mother's sister, Mary the wife of Clopas,
and Mary Magdalene.
When Jesus saw his mother and the disciple whom he loved
he said to his mother, "Woman, behold, your son."
Then he said to the disciple,
"Behold, your mother."
And from that hour the disciple took her into his home.

After this, aware that everything was now finished,
in order that the Scripture might be fulfilled,
Jesus said, "I thirst."
There was a vessel filled with common wine.
So they put a sponge soaked in wine on a sprig of hyssop
and put it up to his mouth.
When Jesus had taken the wine, he said,
"It is finished."
And bowing his head, he handed over the spirit.

The Gospel of the Lord.

TABLE OF READINGS

Weekdays, Year I, are indicated by WI following the Lectionary number; Year II by WII; Proper of the Saints by PS; Commons by COM; Ritual Masses by RM; Masses for Various Needs by MVN; Votive Masses by VM; and Masses for the Dead by MD.

Genesis 1:1-19 329WI

Genesis 1:11-12 912MVN

Genesis 1:14-18 902MVN

Genesis 1:20–2:4a 330WI

Genesis 1:26–2:3 559PS 882MVN 907MVN

Genesis 1:26-28, 31a 801RM

Genesis 2:4b-9, 15-17 331WI

Genesis 2:4b-9, 15 882MVN 907MVN

Genesis 2:18-25 332WI

Genesis 2:18-24 801RM

Genesis 3:1-8 333WI

Genesis 3:9-24 334WI

Genesis 3:9-15, 20 689PS 707COM 1002VM

Genesis 4:1-15, 25 335WI

Genesis 4:3-10 882MVN 897MVN

Genesis 6:5-8; 7:1-5, 10 336WI

Genesis 8:6-13, 20-22 337WI

Genesis 9:1-13 338WI

Genesis 11:1-9 339WI

Genesis 12:1-9 371WI

Genesis 12:1-7 707COM

Genesis 12:1-4a 737COM 743RM 811RM 857MVN

Genesis 13:2, 5-18 372WI

Genesis 14:18-20 785RM 976VM

Genesis 15:1-12, 17-18 373WI

Genesis 15:1-6, 18a 751RM

Genesis 16:1-12, 15-16 374WI

Genesis 17:1, 9-10, 15-22 375WI

Genesis 17:1-8 751RM

Genesis 17:3-9 254WI 254WII

Genesis 18:1-15 376WI

Genesis 18:16-33 377WI

Genesis 19:15-29 378WI

Genesis 21:5, 8-20 379WI

Genesis 22:1-19 380WI

Genesis 23:1-4, 19; 24:1-8, 62-67 381WI

Genesis 24:48-51, 58-67 801RM

Genesis 27:1-5, 15-29 382WI

Genesis 28:10-22a 383WI

Genesis 28:11-18 817RM

Genesis 32:22-32 384WI

Genesis 35:1-4, 6-7a 751RM

Genesis 37:3-4, 12-13a, 17b-28 234WI 234WII

Genesis 41:55-57; 42:5-7a, 17-24a 385WI

Genesis 44:18-21, 23b-29; 45:1-5 386WI

Genesis 46:1-7, 28-30 387WI

Genesis 49:2, 8-10 193WI 193WII

Genesis 49:29-32; 50:15-26a 388WI

Exodus 1:8-14, 22 389WI

Exodus 2:1-15a 390WI

Exodus 3:1-6, 9-12 391WI 857MVN

Exodus 3:11-15 983VM

Exodus 3:13-20 392WI

Exodus 11:10–12:14 393WI

Exodus 12:1-8, 11-14 969VM

Exodus 12:21-27 976VM 989VM

Exodus 12:37-42 394WI

Exodus 14:5-18 395WI

Exodus 14:21–15:1 396WI

Exodus 16:1-5, 9-15 397WI

Exodus 16:2-4, 12-15 785RM 976VM

Exodus 17:1-7 236WI 236WII

Exodus 17:3-7 756RM

Exodus 19:1-2, 9-11, 16-20b 398WI

Exodus 20:1-17* 399WI

Exodus 23:20-23 650PS

Exodus 24:3-8 400WI 785RM 976VM 989VM

Exodus 32:7-14 247WI 247WII 719COM

Exodus 32:15-24, 30-34 401WI

Exodus 33:7-11; 34:5b-9, 28 402WI

Exodus 34:4b-6, 8-9 995VM

Exodus 34:29-35 403WI

Exodus 40:16-21, 34-38 404WI

* Readings with a longer and shorter option are indicated with an asterisk.
The numbers in the columns are the Lectionary reference numbers, not the page numbers.

Leviticus 19:1-2, 11-18 224WI 224WII
Leviticus 19:1-2, 17-18 737COM
Leviticus 23:1, 4-11, 15-16, 27, 34b-37 405WI
Leviticus 25:1, 8-17 406WI

Numbers 3:5-9 770RM
Numbers 6:22-27 882MVN 902MVN
Numbers 11:4b-15 407WI
Numbers 11:11b-12, 14-17, 24-25a 770RM
Numbers 12:1-13 408WI
Numbers 13:1-2, 25–14:1, 26-29, 34-35 409WI
Numbers 20:1-13 410WI
Numbers 21:4-9 252WI 252WII 638PS
Numbers 24:2-7, 15-17a 187WI 187WII

Deuteronomy 1:9-14 775RM
Deuteronomy 4:1, 5-9 239WI 239WII
Deuteronomy 4:32-40 411WI
Deuteronomy 6:1-7 748RM
Deuteronomy 6:3-9 623PS 737COM 780RM
Deuteronomy 6:4-13 412WI
Deuteronomy 7:6-11 995VM
Deuteronomy 8:2-3, 14b-16a 785RM 976VM
Deuteronomy 8:7-18 917MVN
Deuteronomy 10:8-9 719COM 737COM
Deuteronomy 10:12-22 413WI 995VM
Deuteronomy 10:17-19 927MVN
Deuteronomy 24:17-22 922MVN 927MVN
Deuteronomy 26:16-19 229WI 229WII
Deuteronomy 30:1-4 867MVN
Deuteronomy 30:10-14 780RM 838MVN
Deuteronomy 30:15-20 220WI 220WII
    751RM
Deuteronomy 31:1-8 414WI
Deuteronomy 34:1-12 415WI

Joshua 3:7-10a, 11, 13-17 416WI
Joshua 8:30-35 817RM
Joshua 24:1-13 417WI
Joshua 24:1-2a, 15-17, 18b-25a 751RM
Joshua 24:14-29 418WI

Judges 2:11-19 419WI
Judges 6:11-24a 420WI
Judges 9:6-15 421WI
Judges 11:29-39a 422WI
Judges 13:2-7, 24-25a 195WI 195WII

Ruth 1:1, 3-6, 14b-16, 22 423WI
Ruth 2:1-3, 8-11; 4:13-17 424WI

1 Samuel 1:1-8 305WII
1 Samuel 1:9-20 306WII
1 Samuel 1:24-28 198WI 198WII
1 Samuel 3:1-10, 19-20 307WII
1 Samuel 3:1-10 811RM 857MVN
1 Samuel 4:1-11 308WII
1 Samuel 8:4-7, 10-22a 309WII
1 Samuel 9:1-4, 17-19; 10:1a 310WII
1 Samuel 15:16-23 311WII
1 Samuel 16:1-13 312WII
1 Samuel 16:1b, 6-13a 719COM
1 Samuel 17:32-33, 37, 40-51 313WII
1 Samuel 18:6-9; 19:1-7 314WII
1 Samuel 24:3-21 315WII
1 Samuel 26:2, 7-9, 12-13, 22-23 958MVN

2 Samuel 1:1-4, 11-12, 19, 23-27 316WII
2 Samuel 5:1-7, 10 317WII
2 Samuel 6:12b-15, 17-19 318WII
2 Samuel 7:1-5, 8b-12, 14a, 16 200WI
    200WII
2 Samuel 7:1-5, 8b-11, 16 707COM
2 Samuel 7:4-17 319WII
2 Samuel 7:4-5a, 12-14a, 16 543PS
2 Samuel 7:18-19, 24, 29 320WII
2 Samuel 11:1-4a, 5-10a, 13-17 321WII
2 Samuel 12:1-7a, 10-17 322WII
2 Samuel 15:13-14, 30; 16:5-13a 323WII
2 Samuel 18:9-10, 14b, 24-25a, 30–19:3
    324WII
2 Samuel 24:2, 9-17 325WII

1 Kings 2:1-4, 10-12 326WII
1 Kings 3:4-13 328WII
1 Kings 3:11-14 725COM 882MVN
1 Kings 8:1-7, 9-13 329WII
1 Kings 8:22-23, 27-30 330WII 701COM
1 Kings 8:55-61 943MVN
1 Kings 10:1-10 331WII
1 Kings 11:4-13 332WII
1 Kings 11:29-32; 12:19 333WII
1 Kings 12:26-32; 13:33-34 334WII
1 Kings 17:1-6 359WII
1 Kings 17:7-16 360WII
1 Kings 18:20-39 361WII
1 Kings 18:41-46 362WII
1 Kings 19:1-8 790RM
1 Kings 19:4-9a, 11-15a 737COM 811RM
    852MVN
1 Kings 19:4-8 785RM 796RM 976VM

1 Kings 19:9a, 11-16 363WII
1 Kings 19:16b, 19-21 737COM 811RM
  857MVN
1 Kings 19:19-21 364WII
1 Kings 21:1-16 365WII
1 Kings 21:17-29 366WII

2 Kings 2:1, 6-14 367WII
2 Kings 4:18b-21, 32-37 250WI 250WII
2 Kings 5:1-15a 237WI 237WII
2 Kings 5:9-15a 751RM
2 Kings 11:1-4, 9-18, 20 369WII
2 Kings 17:5-8, 13-15a, 18 371WII
2 Kings 19:9b-11, 14-21, 31-35a, 36 372WII
2 Kings 20:1-6 933MVN
2 Kings 22:8-13; 23:1-3 373WII
2 Kings 24:8-17 374WII
2 Kings 25:1-12 375WII

1 Chronicles 15:3-4, 15-16; 16:1-2 621PS
  707COM

2 Chronicles 5:6-10, 13–6:2 701COM
2 Chronicles 24:17-25 370WII
2 Chronicles 24:18-22 713COM

Ezra 1:1-6 449WI
Ezra 6:7-8, 12b, 14-20 450WI
Ezra 9:5-9 451WI

Nehemiah 2:1-8 457WI
Nehemiah 8:1-4a, 5-6, 7b-12 458WI
Nehemiah 8:2-4a, 5-6, 8-10 780RM 816RM

Tobit 1:3; 2:1a-8 353WI
Tobit 2:9-14 354WI
Tobit 3:1-11a, 16-17a 355WI
Tobit 6:10-11; 7:1, 9-17; 8:4-9a 356WI
Tobit 7:6-14 801RM
Tobit 8:4b-8 737COM 801RM
Tobit 11:5-17 357WI
Tobit 12:1, 5-15, 20 358WI
Tobit 12:6-13 529PS 737COM

Judith 8:2-8 737COM

Esther 4:17, n; p-r; aa-bb, gg-hh 227WI 227WII
Esther 4:17b-17e, 17i-17l 877MVN 882MVN
  938MVN
Esther 4:17b-17g, 17l 737COM

1 Maccabees 1:10-15, 41-43, 54-57, 62-64
  497WI
1 Maccabees 2:15-29 500WI
1 Maccabees 2:49-52, 57-64 877MVN
1 Maccabees 4:36-37, 52-59 501WI
1 Maccabees 4:52-59 817RM
1 Maccabees 6:1-13 502WI

2 Maccabees 6:18-31 498WI
2 Maccabees 6:18, 21, 24-31 713COM
2 Maccabees 7:1, 20-31 499WI
2 Maccabees 7:1, 20-23, 27b-29 713COM
2 Maccabees 7:1-2, 9-14 576PS 713COM
2 Maccabees 12:43-46 1011MD

Job 1:6-22 455WII
Job 3:1-3, 11-17, 20-23 456WII 790RM
Job 7:1-4, 6-11 790RM
Job 7:12-21 790RM
Job 9:1-12, 14-16 457WII
Job 19:1, 23-27a 1011MD
Job 19:21-27 458WII
Job 19:23-27a 790RM 796RM
Job 31:16-20, 24-25, 31-32 882MVN 922MVN
Job 38:1, 12-21; 40:3-5 459WII
Job 42:1-3, 5-6, 12-16 460WII

Proverbs 2:1-9 597PS 806RM
Proverbs 3:27-34 449WII
Proverbs 4:7-13 806RM
Proverbs 8:22-31 707COM
Proverbs 9:1-6 785RM 976VM
Proverbs 21:1-6, 10-13 450WII
Proverbs 30:5-9 451WII
Proverbs 31:10-13, 19-20, 30-31 540PS
  691PS 737COM

Ecclesiastes 1:2-11 452WII
Ecclesiastes 3:1-11 453WII
Ecclesiastes 11:9–12:8 454WII

Song of Songs 2:8-14 197WI 197WII 811RM
Song of Songs 2:8-10, 14, 16a; 8:6-7a 801RM
Song of Songs 3:1-4a 603PS
Song of Songs 8:6-7 530PS 731COM
  811RM 852MVN

Wisdom 1:1-7 491WI
Wisdom 2:1a, 12-22 248WI 248WII 969VM
Wisdom 2:23–3:9 492WI

Wisdom 3:1-9* 615PS 644PS 713COM
   1011MD
Wisdom 4:7-15 1011MD
Wisdom 6:1-11 493WI
Wisdom 7:7-10, 15-16 522PS 641PS
   725COM
Wisdom 7:22–8:1 494WI
Wisdom 9:9-11, 13-18 790RM
Wisdom 13:1-9 495WI
Wisdom 18:14-16; 19:6-9 496WI

Sirach 1:1-10 341WI
Sirach 2:1-13 342WI
Sirach 2:7-13 616PS 737COM
Sirach 3:19-26 737COM
Sirach 4:12-22 343WI
Sirach 5:1-10 344WI
Sirach 6:5-17 345WI
Sirach 15:1-6 625PS 675PS 725COM
Sirach 17:1-13 346WI
Sirach 17:20-28 347WI
Sirach 24:1-2, 5-7, 12-16, 26-30 707COM
Sirach 26:1-4, 16-21 632PS 658PS 737COM
   801RM
Sirach 35:1-15 348WI
Sirach 36:1-2a, 5-6, 13-19 349WI
Sirach 39:1, 5-8 775RM
Sirach 39:8-14 672PS 725COM
Sirach 42:15-26 350WI
Sirach 44:1, 9-13 351WI
Sirach 44:1, 10-15 606PS
Sirach 47:2-13 327WII
Sirach 48:1-15 368WII
Sirach 48:1-4, 9-11 186WI 186WII
Sirach 50:24-26 943MVN
Sirach 51:1-12 713COM
Sirach 51:11-17 983VM
Sirach 51:17-27 352WI

Isaiah 1:10, 16-20 231WI 231WII
Isaiah 1:10-17 389WII
Isaiah 2:1-5 175WI 175WII 872MVN
Isaiah 4:2-6 175WI 175WII
Isaiah 6:1-8 388WII 687PS 719COM
Isaiah 6:1-2a, 3-8 775RM
Isaiah 6:1, 6-8 857MVN
Isaiah 7:1-9 390WII
Isaiah 7:10-14; 8:10 545PS 707COM
Isaiah 7:10-14 196WI 196WII
Isaiah 9:1-6 627PS 707COM 887MVN

Isaiah 10:5-7, 13-16 391WII
Isaiah 11:1-10 176WI 176WII
Isaiah 11:1-4a 764RM
Isaiah 25:6-10a 177WI 177WII 963MVN
Isaiah 25:6a, 7-9 1011MD 1017MD
Isaiah 25:6a, 7-8b 1023MD
Isaiah 26:1-6 178WI 178WII
Isaiah 26:7-9, 12, 16-19 392WII
Isaiah 29:17-24 179WI 179WII
Isaiah 30:19-21, 23-26 180WI 180WII
Isaiah 32:15-18 882MVN 887MVN
Isaiah 35:1-10 181WI 181WII 790RM
Isaiah 38:1-6, 21-22, 7-8 393WII
Isaiah 40:1-11 182WI 182WII
Isaiah 40:25-31 183WI 183WII
Isaiah 41:8-10, 13-14 877MVN
Isaiah 41:13-20 184WI 184WII
Isaiah 42:1-7 257WI 257WII
Isaiah 42:1-3 764RM
Isaiah 44:1-5 811RM
Isaiah 44:1-3 751RM
Isaiah 45:6b-8, 18, 21b-25 189WI 189WII
Isaiah 48:17-19 185WI 185WII
Isaiah 49:1-6 258WI 258WII 587PS
Isaiah 49:8-15 246WI 246WII
Isaiah 49:13-15 995VM
Isaiah 50:4-9a 259WI 259WII 958MVN
   969VM
Isaiah 52:7-10 526PS 665PS 683PS
   719COM
Isaiah 52:13–53:12 790RM 969VM 982VM
Isaiah 53:1-5, 10-11 933MVN
Isaiah 54:1-10 190WI 190WII
Isaiah 55:1-3, 6-9 892MVN
Isaiah 55:6-13 912MVN
Isaiah 55:6-9 948MVN
Isaiah 55:10-11 225WI 225WII 780RM
Isaiah 56:1-3a, 6-8 191WI 191WII
Isaiah 56:1, 6-7 701COM 827MVN
   872MVN
Isaiah 57:15-19 887MVN
Isaiah 58:1-9a 221WI 221WII
Isaiah 58:6-11 630PS 676PS 737COM
   882MVN 922MVN
Isaiah 58:9b-14 222WI 222WII
Isaiah 60:1-6 827MVN 872MVN
Isaiah 61:1-3a, 6a, 8b-9 260WI 260WII
   764RM
Isaiah 61:1-3a 581PS 673PS 719COM
   770RM 790RM 833MVN 843MVN

Isaiah 61:9-11 573PS 707COM 811RM
  852MVN
Isaiah 63:7-9 943MVN
Isaiah 65:17-21 244WI 244WII
Isaiah 66:10-14c 531PS 649PS

Jeremiah 1:1, 4-10 397WII
Jeremiah 1:1, 7-19 634PS
Jeremiah 1:4-10 586PS
Jeremiah 1:4-9 719COM 770RM 775RM
  843MVN 857MVN
Jeremiah 2:1-3, 7-8, 12-13 398WII
Jeremiah 3:14-17 399WII
Jeremiah 7:1-11 400WII
Jeremiah 7:23-28 240WI
Jeremiah 11:18-20 249WI 249WII
Jeremiah 13:1-11 401WII
Jeremiah 14:17-22 402WII
Jeremiah 15:10, 16-21 403WII
Jeremiah 17:5-10 233WI 233WII
Jeremiah 18:1-6 404WII
Jeremiah 18:18-20 232WI 232WII
Jeremiah 20:7-9 737COM 857MVN
Jeremiah 20:10-13 255WI 255WII
Jeremiah 23:5-8 194WI 194WII
Jeremiah 26:1-9 405WII
Jeremiah 26:11-16, 24 406WII
Jeremiah 28:1-17 407WII
Jeremiah 30:1-2, 12-15, 18-22 408WII
Jeremiah 31:1-7 409WII
Jeremiah 31:1-4 995VM
Jeremiah 31:31-37 811RM
Jeremiah 31:31-34 410WII 751RM 892MVN
Jeremiah 31:31-32a, 33-34a 801RM

Lamentations 2:2, 10-14, 18-19 376WII
Lamentations 3:17-26 938MVN 1011MD
Lamentations 3:22-26 1017MD 1023MD

Baruch 1:15-22 459WI
Baruch 4:5-12, 27-29 460WI

Ezekiel 1:2-5, 24-28c 413WII
Ezekiel 2:8–3:4 414WII
Ezekiel 3:16-21 612PS 719COM 882MVN
Ezekiel 9:1-7; 10:18-22 415WII
Ezekiel 12:1-12 416WII
Ezekiel 16:1-15, 60, 63 417WII
Ezekiel 16:59-63 417WII
Ezekiel 18:1-10, 13b, 30-32 418WII

Ezekiel 18:21-28 228WI 228WII
Ezekiel 18:21-23, 30-32 948MVN
Ezekiel 24:15-24 419WII
Ezekiel 28:1-10 420WII
Ezekiel 34:1-11 421WII
Ezekiel 34:11-16 578PS 700PS 719COM
  827MVN 995VM
Ezekiel 36:23-28 422WII
Ezekiel 36:24-28 751RM 756RM 764RM
  862MVN 867MVN
Ezekiel 37:1-14 423WII
Ezekiel 37:15-19, 21b-22, 26-28 867MVN
Ezekiel 37:21-28 256WI 256WII
Ezekiel 43:1-7a 424WII
Ezekiel 43:1-2, 4-7a 701COM
Ezekiel 47:1-9, 12 245WI 245WII 756RM
Ezekiel 47:1-2, 8-9, 12 671PS 701COM

Daniel 1:1-6, 8-20 503WI
Daniel 2:31-45 504WI
Daniel 3:14-20, 91-92, 95 253WI 253WII
Daniel 3:25, 34-43 238WI 238WII 877MVN
  938MVN
Daniel 5:1-6, 13-14, 16-17, 23-28 505WI
Daniel 6:12-28 506WI
Daniel 7:2-14 507WI
Daniel 7:9-10, 13-14 614PS 647PS
Daniel 7:15-27 508WI
Daniel 9:4b-10 230WI 230WII
Daniel 12:1-3 1011MD
Daniel 13:1-9, 15-17, 19-30, 33-62 251WI
  251WII

Hosea 2:16, 17b-18, 21-22 383WII
Hosea 2:16b, 17b, 21-22 681PS 731COM
  827MVN
Hosea 2:16, 21-22 811RM 852MVN
Hosea 6:1-6 242WI 242WII
Hosea 8:4-7, 11-13 384WII
Hosea 10:1-3, 7-8, 12 385WII
Hosea 11:1-4, 8c-9 386WII
Hosea 11:1, 3-4, 8c-9 749RM 995VM
Hosea 14:2-10 241WI 241WII

Joel 1:13-15; 2:1-2 465WI
Joel 2:12-18 219WI 219WII 948MVN
Joel 2:21-24, 26-27 917MVN
Joel 2:23a–3:1-3a 764RM
Joel 3:1a-5 862MVN
Joel 4:12-21 466WI

Amos 2:6-10, 13-16 377WII
Amos 3:1-8; 4:11-12 378WII
Amos 5:4, 14-15, 21-24 892MVN
Amos 5:14-15, 21-24 379WII
Amos 7:10-17 380WII
Amos 8:4-6, 9-12 381WII
Amos 9:11-15 382WII

Jonah 1:1–2:1, 11 461WI
Jonah 3:1-10 226WI 226WII 462WI
  948MVN
Jonah 3:10–4:11 872MVN
Jonah 4:1-11 463WI

Micah 2:1-5 394WII
Micah 4:1-4 897MVN
Micah 5:1-4a 636PS 707COM
Micah 6:1-4, 6-8 395WII
Micah 6:6-8 598PS 737COM
Micah 7:7-9 243WI 243WII
Micah 7:14-15, 18-20 235WI 235WII 396WII

Nahum 2:1-3; 3:1-3, 6-7 411WII

Habakkuk 1:12–2:4 412WII

Zephaniah 2:3–3:12-13 737COM
Zephaniah 3:1-2, 9-13 188WI 188WII
Zephaniah 3:14-18 572PS
Zephaniah 3:14-18a 197WI 197WII 827MVN
Zephaniah 3:14-15 943MVN
Zephaniah 3:16-20 867MVN

Haggai 1:1-8 452WI
Haggai 1:15b–2:9 453WI

Zechariah 2:5-9, 14-15a 454WI
Zechariah 2:14-17 601PS 680PS 707COM
Zechariah 8:1-8 455WI
Zechariah 8:20-23 456WI 872MVN
Zechariah 9:9-10 897MVN
Zechariah 12:10-11; 13:6-7 969VM

Malachi 3:1-4, 23-24 199WI 199WII
Malachi 3:1-4 524PS
Malachi 3:13-20a 464WI

Matthew 1:1-16, 18-23* 636PS 712COM
Matthew 1:1-17 193WI 193WII
Matthew 1:16, 18-21, 24a 543PS

Matthew 1:18-25 988VM
Matthew 1:18-24 194WI 194WII
Matthew 2:13-15, 19-23 712COM 931MVN
Matthew 2:13-18 698PS
Matthew 4:12-17, 23-25 212WI 212WII
Matthew 4:18-22 684PS
Matthew 5:1-12 359WI 359WII
Matthew 5:1-12a 576PS 611PS 667PS
  742COM 768RM 795RM 805RM
  815RM 866MVN 881MVN 886MVN
  891MVN 896MVN 1016MD
Matthew 5:2-12a 763RM
Matthew 5:13-19 512PS 574PS 588PS
  610PS 694PS 730COM
Matthew 5:13-16 360WI 360WII 654PS
  742COM 763RM 774RM 805RM
Matthew 5:14-19 784RM
Matthew 5:17-19 239WI 239WII 361WI
  361WII
Matthew 5:20-26 228WI 228WII 362WI
  362WII
Matthew 5:20-24 886MVN 901MVN
Matthew 5:23-24 822RM
Matthew 5:27-32 363WI 363WII
Matthew 5:33-37 364WI 364WII
Matthew 5:38-48 886MVN 891MVN
  962MVN
Matthew 5:38-42 365WI 365WII
Matthew 5:43-48 229WI 229WII 366WI
  366WII
Matthew 6:1-6, 16-18 219WI 219WII 367WI
  367WII
Matthew 6:7-15 225WI 225WII 368WI
  368WII
Matthew 6:9-13 749RM
Matthew 6:19-23 369WI 369WII
Matthew 6:24-34 370WI 370WII
Matthew 6:31-34 906MVN 911MVN
Matthew 7:1-5 371WI 371WII
Matthew 7:6, 12-14 372WI 372WII
Matthew 7:7-12 227WI 227WII
Matthew 7:7-11 942MVN 947MVN
Matthew 7:15-20 373WI 373WII
Matthew 7:21-29 374WI 374WII 552PS
  567PS 641PS 730COM
Matthew 7:21, 24-29* 805RM
Matthew 7:21, 24-27 178WI 178WII
Matthew 7:21-27 598PS 742COM
Matthew 8:1-4 375WI 375WII 795RM
Matthew 8:5-17* 376WI 376WII 795RM

Matthew 8:5-11 175WI 175WII

Matthew 8:14-17 937MVN

Matthew 8:18-22 377WI 377WII

Matthew 8:23-27 378WI 378WII

Matthew 8:28-34 379WI 379WII

Matthew 9:1-8 380WI 380WII 952MVN

Matthew 9:9-13 381WI 381WII 643PS

Matthew 9:14-17 382WI 382WII

Matthew 9:14-15 221WI 221WII

Matthew 9:18-26 383WI 383WII

Matthew 9:27-31 179WI 179WII

Matthew 9:32-38 384WI 384WII

Matthew 9:35–10:1, 6-8 180WI 180WII

Matthew 9:35–10:1 612PS

Matthew 9:35-38 544PS 571PS 645PS
724COM 774RM 779RM 861MVN

Matthew 10:1-5a 774RM

Matthew 10:1-7 385WI 385WII

Matthew 10:7-15 386WI 386WII

Matthew 10:7-13 580PS

Matthew 10:16-23 387WI 387WII

Matthew 10:17-22 517PS 562PS 696PS
718COM 881MVN

Matthew 10:22-25a 560PS

Matthew 10:24-33 388WI 388WII

Matthew 10:26-33 881MVN

Matthew 10:28-33 515PS 615PS 644PS
718COM

Matthew 10:34–11:1 389WI 389WII

Matthew 10:34-39 538PS 585PS 646PS
718COM

Matthew 11:11-15 184WI 184WII

Matthew 11:16-19 185WI 185WII

Matthew 11:20-24 390WI 390WII

Matthew 11:25-30 557PS 563PS 624PS
651PS 659PS 742COM 763RM 795RM
815RM 856MVN 947MVN 1000VM
1016MD 1022MD 1026MD

Matthew 11:25-27 391WI 391WII

Matthew 11:28-30 183WI 183WII 392WI
392WII

Matthew 12:1-8 393WI 393WII

Matthew 12:14-21 394WI 394WII

Matthew 12:38-42 395WI 395WII

Matthew 12:46-50 396WI 396WII 601PS
680PS 712COM

Matthew 13:1-9 397WI 397WII 916MVN

Matthew 13:10-17 398WI 398WII

Matthew 13:16-17 606PS

Matthew 13:18-23 399WI 399WII

Matthew 13:24-30 400WI 400WII

Matthew 13:31-35 401WI 401WII

Matthew 13:36-43 402WI 402WII

Matthew 13:44-46 403WI 403WII 516PS
628PS 648PS 675PS 742COM

Matthew 13:47-53 404WI 404WII

Matthew 13:47-52 730COM

Matthew 13:54-58 405WI 405WII 559PS

Matthew 14:1-12 406WI 406WII

Matthew 14:12-16, 22-26 789RM

Matthew 14:13-21 407WI 407WII

Matthew 14:22-36 407WI, 408WI 407WII,
408WII

Matthew 14:22-33 679PS

Matthew 15:1-2, 10-14 408WI 408WII

Matthew 15:21-28 409WI 409WII

Matthew 15:29-37 177WI 177WII

Matthew 15:29-31 795RM

Matthew 16:13-23 410WI 410WII

Matthew 16:13-19 535PS 568PS 591PS
672PS 682PS 700PS 706COM 724COM
831MVN

Matthew 16:13-18 748RM

Matthew 16:24-28 411WI 411WII

Matthew 16:24-27 663PS 699PS 742COM
755RM 768RM 815RM 856MVN
866MVN

Matthew 17:1-9 614PS

Matthew 17:10-13 186WI 186WII

Matthew 17:14-20 412WI 412WII

Matthew 17:22-27 413WI 413WII

Matthew 18:1-5, 10, 12-14 414WI 414WII

Matthew 18:1-5, 10 650PS

Matthew 18:1-5 523PS 549PS 631PS
649PS 742COM

Matthew 18:12-14 182WI 182WII

Matthew 18:15-20 415WI 415WII 831MVN
842MVN 956MVN

Matthew 18:19-22 871MVN

Matthew 18:21–19:1 416WI 416WII

Matthew 18:21-35 238WI 238WII

Matthew 19:3-12 417WI 417WII 736COM
742COM 815RM 856MVN

Matthew 19:3-6 805RM

Matthew 19:13-15 418WI 418WII

Matthew 19:16-26 513PS

Matthew 19:16-22 419WI 419WII

Matthew 19:23-30 420WI 420WII

Matthew 19:27-29 533PS 597PS 619PS
742COM

Matthew 20:1-16a 421WI 421WII
Matthew 20:17-28 232WI 232WII
Matthew 20:20-28 605PS 826RM 847MVN
  851MVN
Matthew 20:25-28 774RM
Matthew 21:23-27 187WI 187WII
Matthew 21:28-32 188WI 188WII
Matthew 21:33-43, 45-46 234WI 234WII
Matthew 22:1-14* 422WI 422WII
Matthew 22:15-21 886MVN
Matthew 22:34-40 423WI 423WII 540PS
  583PS 630PS 669PS 742COM
Matthew 22:35-40 760RM 805RM
Matthew 23:1-12 231WI, 424WI 231WII,
  424WII
Matthew 23:8-12 510PS 522PS 600PS
  633PS 724COM 730COM 810RM
Matthew 23:13-22 425WI 425WII
Matthew 23:23-26 426WI 426WII
Matthew 23:27-32 427WI 427WII
Matthew 24:4-13 592PS
Matthew 24:42-51 428WI 428WII
Matthew 25:1-13 429WI 429WII 681PS
  692PS 736COM 742COM 815RM
  967MVN 1016MD
Matthew 25:14-30* 430WI 430WII 623PS
  686PS 742COM 768RM 866MVN
  886MVN 911MVN
Matthew 25:31-46* 224WI 224WII 539PS
  594PS 742COM 886MVN 926MVN
  931MVN 932MVN 1016MD
Matthew 25:31-40 673PS 795RM
Matthew 26:14-25 259WI 259WII
Matthew 26:47-56 975VM
Matthew 27:33-50 975VM
Matthew 28:8-15 261WI 261WII
Matthew 28:16-20 528PS 662PS 724COM
  831MVN 847MVN 876MVN
Matthew 28:18-20 755RM 760RM

Mark 1:1-8, 14-15 952MVN
Mark 1:7-11 209WI 209WII
Mark 1:9-11 755RM 760RM 768RM
Mark 1:14-20 305WI 305WII 526PS 556PS
  665PS 724COM 779RM
Mark 1:21-28 306WI 306WII
Mark 1:29-39 307WI 307WII
Mark 1:35-39 569 784RM
Mark 1:40-45 308WI 308WII
Mark 2:1-12 309WI 309WII 795RM

Mark 2:13-17 310WI 310WII
Mark 2:18-22 311WI 311WII
Mark 2:23-28 312WI 312WII
Mark 3:1-6 313WI 313WII
Mark 3:7-12 314WI 314WII
Mark 3:13-19 315WI 315WII
Mark 3:20-21 316WI 316WII
Mark 3:22-30 317WI 317WII
Mark 3:31-35 318WI 318WII 569PS 658PS
  691PS 742COM 815RM 856MVN
  866MVN
Mark 4:1-20 319WI 319WII
Mark 4:1-10, 13-20* 602PS 637PS 730COM
Mark 4:1-9 866MVN
Mark 4:21-25 320WI 320WII
Mark 4:26-34 321WI 321WII
Mark 4:26-29 916MVN
Mark 4:35-41 322WI 322WII 795RM
  942MVN
Mark 5:1-20 323WI 323WII
Mark 5:18-20 947MVN
Mark 5:21-43* 324WI 324WII
Mark 6:1-6 325WI 325WII
Mark 6:7-13 326WI 326WII
Mark 6:14-29 327WI 327WII
Mark 6:17-29 634PS
Mark 6:30-34 328WI 328WII 842MVN
Mark 6:34-44 213WI 213WII 926MVN
Mark 6:45-52 214WI 214WII
Mark 6:53-56 329WI 329WII
Mark 7:1-13 330WI 330WII
Mark 7:14-23 331WI 331WII
Mark 7:24-30 332WI 332WII
Mark 7:31-37 333WI 333WII
Mark 8:1-10 334WI 334WII
Mark 8:11-13 335WI 335WII
Mark 8:14-21 336WI 336WII
Mark 8:22-26 337WI 337WII
Mark 8:27-33 338WI 338WII
Mark 8:31-34 974VM
Mark 8:34–9:1 339WI 339WII
Mark 9:2-13 340WI 340WII
Mark 9:2-10 614PS
Mark 9:14-29 341WI 341WII
Mark 9:30-37 342WI 342WII
Mark 9:34-37 521PS 742COM
Mark 9:38-40 343WI 343WII
Mark 9:41-50 344WI 344WII
Mark 10:1-12 345WI 345WII
Mark 10:6-9 805RM

Mark 10:13-16 346WI 346WII 595PS
742COM 755RM 760RM
Mark 10:17-30* 529PS 742COM
Mark 10:17-27 347WI 347WII 861MVN
Mark 10:24b-30 815RM
Mark 10:28-31 348WI 348WII
Mark 10:28-30 861MVN
Mark 10:32-45 349WI 349WII
Mark 10:46-52 350WI 350WII 795RM
Mark 11:11-26 351WI 351WII
Mark 11:27-33 352WI 352WII
Mark 12:1-12 353WI 353WII 974VM
Mark 12:13-17 354WI 354WII
Mark 12:18-27 355WI 355WII
Mark 12:28b-34* 241WI, 356WI 241WII,
356WII 760RM
Mark 12:35-37 357WI 357WII
Mark 12:38-44* 358WI 358WII
Mark 14:12-16, 22-26 826RM 981VM 994VM
Mark 14:32-41 975VM
Mark 14:55-65 975VM
Mark 15:1-15 975VM
Mark 15:16-20 975VM 981VM 994VM
Mark 15:33-46 1026MD
Mark 15:33-39; 16:1-6* 975VM 1016MD
Mark 16:9-15 266WI 266WII
Mark 16:15-20 525PS 555PS 685PS
724COM 795RM 851MVN 876MVN
937MVN
Mark 16:15-16, 19-20 755RM
Mark 16:15-18 519PS

Luke 1:5-25 195WI 195WII
Luke 1:5-17 586PS
Luke 1:26-38 196WI 196WII 545PS 627PS
653PS 689PS 712COM 815RM
Luke 1:39-56 572PS 622PS
Luke 1:39-55 947MVN
Luke 1:39-47 712COM 1002VM
Luke 1:39-45 197WI 197WII
Luke 1:46-56 198WI 198WII
Luke 1:57-66, 80 587PS
Luke 1:57-66 199WI 199WII
Luke 1:67-79 200WI 200WII
Luke 2:1-14 712COM
Luke 2:15b-19 712COM
Luke 2:16-21 988VM
Luke 2:22-40* 524PS
Luke 2:22-35 202WI 202WII
Luke 2:27-35 712COM

Luke 2:33-35 639PS
Luke 2:36-40 203WI 203WII
Luke 2:41-52 712COM
Luke 2:41-51 573PS
Luke 2:41-51a 543PS
Luke 3:7-18 896MVN
Luke 3:23-28 210WI 210WII
Luke 4:14-22a 215WI 215WII
Luke 4:16-30 431WI 431WII
Luke 4:16-22a 768RM
Luke 4:16-21 260WI 260WII 784RM
Luke 4:24-30 237WI 237WII
Luke 4:31-37 432WI 432WII
Luke 4:38-44 433WI 433WII
Luke 5:1-11 434WI 434WII 541PS 655PS
724COM 779RM 861MVN
Luke 5:12-16 216WI 216WII
Luke 5:17-26 181WI 181WII
Luke 5:27-32 222WI 222WII
Luke 5:33-39 435WI 435WII
Luke 6:1-5 436WI 436WII
Luke 6:6-11 437WI 437WII
Luke 6:12-19 438WI 438WII 666PS
Luke 6:20-26 439WI 439WII
Luke 6:27-38 440WI 440WII 678PS 695PS
742COM 962MVN
Luke 6:36-38 230WI 230WII
Luke 6:39-42 441WI 441WII
Luke 6:43-49 442WI 442WII
Luke 6:43-45 547PS 579PS 608PS 730COM
Luke 7:1-10 443WI 443WII
Luke 7:11-17 444WI 444WII 632PS
1016MD
Luke 7:19-23 189WI 189WII 795RM
Luke 7:24-30 190WI 190WII
Luke 7:31-35 445WI 445WII
Luke 7:36-50 446WI 446WII 952MVN
Luke 8:1-3 447WI 447WII
Luke 8:4-15 448WI 448WII
Luke 8:4-10a, 11b-15 768RM
Luke 8:16-18 449WI 449WII
Luke 8:19-21 450WI 450WII
Luke 9:1-6 451WI 451WII
Luke 9:7-9 452WI 452WII
Luke 9:11b-17 789RM 981VM
Luke 9:18-22 453WI 453WII
Luke 9:22-25 220WI 220WII
Luke 9:23-26 527PS 553PS 718COM
Luke 9:28b-36 614PS
Luke 9:43b-45 454WI 454WII

Luke 9:46-50 455WI 455WII

Luke 9:49-56 871MVN

Luke 9:51-56 456WI 456WII

Luke 9:57-62 457WI 457WII 566PS 617PS
    652PS 664PS 683PS 742COM 815RM
    861MVN

Luke 10:1-9 520PS 532PS 581PS 661PS
    687PS 724COM 774RM 847MVN
    851MVN

Luke 10:1-12 458WI 458WII

Luke 10:5-6, 8-9 795RM

Luke 10:13-16 459WI 459WII

Luke 10:17-24 460WI 460WII 947MVN

Luke 10:21-24 176WI 176WII 768RM

Luke 10:25-37 461WI 461WII 795RM
    931MVN

Luke 10:38-42 462WI 462WII 530PS 607PS
    736COM 742COM 815RM 856MVN

Luke 11:1-4 463WI 463WII

Luke 11:5-13 464WI 464WII 795RM

Luke 11:14-23 240WI 240WII

Luke 11:15-26 465WI 465WII

Luke 11:27-28 466WI 466WII 613PS
    621PS 712COM 815RM

Luke 11:29-32 226WI, 467WI 226WII,
    467WII

Luke 11:37-41 468WI 468WII

Luke 11:42-46 469WI 469WII

Luke 11:47-54 470WI 470WII

Luke 12:1-7 471WI 471WII

Luke 12:8-12 472WI 472WII

Luke 12:13-21 473WI 473WII

Luke 12:15-21 886MVN 921MVN

Luke 12:32-34 584PS 616PS 742COM

Luke 12:35-44 774RM 795RM 810RM

Luke 12:35-40 511PS 548PS 742COM
    886MVN 906MVN 967MVN 1016MD

Luke 12:35-38 474WI 474WII

Luke 12:39-48 475WI 475WII

Luke 12:49-53 476WI 476WII

Luke 12:54-59 477WI 477WII

Luke 13:1-9 478WI 478WII

Luke 13:10-17 479WI 479WII

Luke 13:18-21 480WI 480WII

Luke 13:22-30 481WI 481WII

Luke 13:31-35 482WI 482WII

Luke 14:1-6 483WI 483WII

Luke 14:1, 7-11 484WI 484WII

Luke 14:12-14 485WI 485WII 886MVN
    926MVN

Luke 14:15-24 486WI 486WII

Luke 14:25-33 487WI 487WII 578PS
    582PS 609PS 693PS 742COM 861MVN

Luke 15:1-10 488WI 488WII 1000VM

Luke 15:1-3, 11-32 235WI 235WII 896MVN
    952MVN 1000VM

Luke 16:1-8 489WI 489WII

Luke 16:9-15 490WI 490WII

Luke 16:19-31 233WI 233WII 886MVN
    926MVN

Luke 17:1-6 491WI 491WII

Luke 17:7-10 492WI 492WII

Luke 17:11-19 493WI 493WII 921MVN
    947MVN

Luke 17:20-25 494WI 494WII

Luke 17:26-37 495WI 495WII

Luke 18:1-8 496WI 496WII 942MVN

Luke 18:9-14 242WI 242WII 795RM

Luke 18:35-43 497WI 497WII

Luke 19:1-10 498WI 498WII 706COM

Luke 19:11-28 499WI 499WII

Luke 19:41-44 500WI 500WII

Luke 19:45-48 501WI 501WII

Luke 20:27-40 502WI 502WII

Luke 21:1-4 503WI 503WII

Luke 21:5-11 504WI 504WII

Luke 21:12-19 505WI 505WII

Luke 21:20-28 506WI 506WII

Luke 21:29-33 507WI 507WII

Luke 21:34-36 508WI 508WII 967MVN

Luke 22:14-20, 24-30 774RM

Luke 22:14-20 982VM

Luke 22:24-30 565PS 635PS 656PS
    724COM 847MVN 886MVN

Luke 22:24-27 810RM

Luke 22:39-44 981VM 994VM

Luke 22:39-43 937MVN

Luke 23:33-34, 39-46 975VM

Luke 23:33, 39-43 1016MD

Luke 23:39-46 967MVN

Luke 23:44-46, 50, 52-53; 24:1-6a* 1016MD

Luke 24:13-35* 263WI 263WII 789RM
    981VM 1016MD

Luke 24:35-48 264WI 264WII 974VM

Luke 24:44-53 755RM 876MVN

Luke 24:44-48 784RM

Luke 24:46-48 952MVN

John 1:1-18* 204WI 204WII

John 1:1-5, 9-14, 16-18 755RM

John 1:19-28 205WI 205WII
John 1:29-34 206WI 206WII 755RM
John 1:35-51* 861MVN
John 1:35-42 207WI 207WII 743RM
  779RM
John 1:43-51 208WI 208WII
John 1:45-51 629PS 779RM
John 1:47-51 647PS
John 2:1-11 210WI 210WII 531PS
  712COM 805RM
John 2:13-22 671PS 706COM
John 3:1-8 267WI 267WII
John 3:1-6 755RM 760RM
John 3:7b-15 268WI 268WII
John 3:13-17 638PS
John 3:16-21 269WI 269WII 755RM 763RM
John 3:22-30 217WI 217WII
John 3:31-36 270WI 270WII
John 4:5-42* 236WI 236WII
John 4:5-14 760RM
John 4:19-24 706COM 822RM
John 4:43-54 244WI 244WII
John 5:1-16 245WI 245WII
John 5:17-30 246WI 246WII
John 5:24-29 1016MD
John 5:31-47 247WI 247WII
John 5:33-36 191WI 191WII
John 6:1-15 271WI 271WII 789RM 981VM
John 6:16-21 272WI 272WII
John 6:22-29 273WI 273WII
John 6:24-35 789RM 981VM
John 6:30-35 274WI 274WII
John 6:35-40 275WI 275WII 795RM
John 6:37-40* 1016MD 1022MD
John 6:41-50 789RM 800RM 981VM
John 6:44-51 276WI 276WII
John 6:44-47 760RM
John 6:51-58 789RM 800RM 981VM
  1016MD 1022MD
John 6:52-59 277WI 277WII
John 6:53-58 795RM
John 6:60-69 278WI 278WII
John 7:1-2, 10, 25-30 248WI 248WII
John 7:14-18 784RM
John 7:34b-39a 760RM 768RM
John 7:40-53 249WI 249WII
John 8:1-11 251WI 251WII
John 8:12-20 251WI 251WII
John 8:21-30 252WI 252WII
John 8:31-42 253WI 253WII

John 8:51-59 254WI 254WII
John 9:1-41* 243WI 243WII
John 9:1-7 760RM 795RM
John 10:1-10 279WI 279WII
John 10:11-18 279WI 279WII 795RM
  1000VM
John 10:11-16 577PS 670PS 688PS
  724COM 774RM 847MVN 871MVN
John 10:22-30 280WI 280WII
John 10:31-42 255WI 255WII
John 11:1-45* 250WI 250WII
John 11:17-27* 1016MD
John 11:19-27 607PS
John 11:32-45 1016MD
John 11:32-38, 40 1022MD
John 11:45-56 256WI 256WII
John 11:45-52 871MVN 876MVN
John 12:1-11 257WI 257WII
John 12:23-28* 1016MD
John 12:24-26 596PS 618PS 642PS 660PS
  718COM 774RM 815RM
John 12:31-36a 822RM 974VM
John 12:44-50 281WI 281WII 748RM
  755RM
John 13:1-15 871MVN
John 13:16-20 282WI 282WII
John 13:21-33, 36-38 258WI 258WII
John 14:1-6 283WI 283WII 1016MD
John 14:6-14 561PS 988VM
John 14:7-14 284WI 284WII
John 14:15-23, 26-27 763RM
John 14:15-17 768RM
John 14:21-26 285WI 285WII
John 14:23-29 842MVN 891MVN
John 14:23-26 768RM
John 14:27-31a 286WI 286WII
John 15:1-11 755RM 760RM
John 15:1-8 287WI 287WII 534PS 542PS
  604PS 657PS 677PS 742COM 815RM
  831MVN 856MVN 866MVN 937MVN
  1000VM
John 15:1-6 763RM
John 15:9-17 518PS 537PS 564PS 599PS
  690PS 724COM 742COM 774RM
  815RM 837MVN 847MVN 861MVN
  947MVN 1000VM
John 15:9-12 805RM 886MVN 901MVN
John 15:9-11 288WI 288WII
John 15:12-17 289WI 289WII 956MVN
John 15:12-16 805RM

John 15:18-21, 26–16:4 881MVN
John 15:18-21, 26-27 768RM
John 15:18-21 290WI 290WII 536PS
  551PS 620PS 718COM 866MVN
John 15:26–16:4a 291WI 291WII
John 16:5-11 292WI 292WII
John 16:5b-7, 12-13a 768RM
John 16:12-15 293WI 293WII
John 16:16-20 294WI 294WI
John 16:20-23a 295WI 295WII
John 16:20-22 947MVN
John 16:23b-28 296WI 296WII
John 16:29-33 297WI 297WII
John 17:1-11a 298WI 298WII 871MVN
John 17:6, 14-19 774RM
John 17:11b, 17-23 831MVN 837MVN
  876MVN
John 17:11b-19 299WI 299WII 550PS
  575PS 640PS 718COM 871MVN
  881MVN
John 17:20-26* 300WI 300WII 554PS
  570PS 589PS 625PS 674PS 742COM
  805RM 815RM 871MVN 1000VM
John 17:24-26 1016MD
John 19:17-18, 25-39 1016MD
John 19:25-30 1022MD
John 19:25-27 639PS 712COM 1002VM
John 19:28-37 975VM
John 19:31-37 981VM 994VM 1000VM
John 19:31-35 760RM
John 20:1-2, 11-18 603PS
John 20:2-8 697PS
John 20:11-18 262WI 262WII
John 20:19-23 774RM 891MVN
John 20:24-29 593PS
John 21:1-14 265WI 265WII 789RM 981VM
John 21:15-19 301WI 301WII 590PS
John 21:15-17 514PS 558PS 626PS
  724COM 774RM 831MVN 847MVN
John 21:20-25 302WI 302WII

Acts of the Apostles 1:3-8 765RM 873MVN
Acts of the Apostles 1:12-14 653PS
  708COM 1002VM
Acts of the Apostles 1:15-17, 20-26 564PS
Acts of the Apostles 2:1-6, 14, 22b-23, 32-33
  765RM
Acts of the Apostles 2:1-11 863MVN
Acts of the Apostles 2:14, 22-33 261WI
  261WII

Acts of the Apostles 2:14a, 22-24, 32-36
  726COM
Acts of the Apostles 2:14a, 36-40a, 41-42
  752RM
Acts of the Apostles 2:36-41 262WI 262WII
Acts of the Apostles 2:42-47 786RM 807RM
  812RM 818RM 828MVN 853MVN
  977VM
Acts of the Apostles 3:1-10 263WI 263WII
  590PS 791RM 984VM
Acts of the Apostles 3:11-26 264WI 264WII
Acts of the Apostles 3:11-16 791RM
Acts of the Apostles 3:13-15, 17-19 893MVN
Acts of the Apostles 4:1-5, 18-21 878MVN
Acts of the Apostles 4:1-12 265WI 265WII
Acts of the Apostles 4:8-12 566PS 791RM
  984VM
Acts of the Apostles 4:13-21 266WI 266WII
Acts of the Apostles 4:23-31 267WI 267WII
  878MVN
Acts of the Apostles 4:32-37 268WI 268WII
Acts of the Apostles 4:32-35 738COM
  812RM
Acts of the Apostles 5:17-26 269WI 269WII
Acts of the Apostles 5:27b-32, 40b-42
  878MVN 984VM
Acts of the Apostles 5:27-33 270WI 270WII
Acts of the Apostles 5:34-42 271WI 271WII
Acts of the Apostles 6:1-7 272WI 272WII
Acts of the Apostles 6:1-7b 771RM
Acts of the Apostles 6:8-10; 7:54-59 696PS
Acts of the Apostles 6:8-15 273WI 273WII
Acts of the Apostles 7:44-50 702COM
Acts of the Apostles 7:51–8:1a 274WI 274WII
Acts of the Apostles 7:55-60 714COM
  959MVN
Acts of the Apostles 8:1b-8 275WI 275WII
Acts of the Apostles 8:1, 4, 14-17 765RM
Acts of the Apostles 8:26-40 276WI 276WII
  771RM
Acts of the Apostles 8:26-38 752RM
Acts of the Apostles 9:1-22 519PS
Acts of the Apostles 9:1-20 277WI 277WII
Acts of the Apostles 9:31-42 278WI 278WII
Acts of the Apostles 10:1, 33-34a, 37-44
  765RM
Acts of the Apostles 10:34-43* 970VM
  1012MD
Acts of the Apostles 10:34a, 37-43 786RM
  977VM

Acts of the Apostles 10:37-43 771RM
Acts of the Apostles 11:1-18 279WI 279WII
Acts of the Apostles 11:19-26 280WI
   280WII 873MVN
Acts of the Apostles 11:21b-26, 13:1-3 580PS
Acts of the Apostles 11:27-30 883MVN
   923MVN
Acts of the Apostles 12:1-11 591PS
Acts of the Apostles 12:24–13:5a 281WI
   281WII
Acts of the Apostles 13:13-25 282WI
   282WII
Acts of the Apostles 13:22-26 587PS
Acts of the Apostles 13:26-33 726COM
   970VM
Acts of the Apostles 13:26b-33 283WI
   283WII
Acts of the Apostles 13:32-39 791RM
Acts of the Apostles 13:44-52 284WI 284WII
Acts of the Apostles 13:46-49 532PS
   720COM 873MVN
Acts of the Apostles 14:5-18 285WI 285WII
Acts of the Apostles 14:19-28 286WI 286WII
Acts of the Apostles 14:21-23 776RM
Acts of the Apostles 15:1-6 287WI 287WII
Acts of the Apostles 15:7-21 288WI 288WII
Acts of the Apostles 15:22-31 289WI 289WII
Acts of the Apostles 16:1-10 290WI 290WII
Acts of the Apostles 16:11-15 291WI 291WII
Acts of the Apostles 16:22-34 292WI 292WII
Acts of the Apostles 17:15, 22–18:1 293WI
   293WII
Acts of the Apostles 18:1-8 294WI 294WII
Acts of the Apostles 18:9-18 295WI 295WII
Acts of the Apostles 18:23-28 296WI 296WII
Acts of the Apostles 19:1-8 297WI 297WII
Acts of the Apostles 19:1b-6a 765RM
Acts of the Apostles 20:17-18a, 28-32, 36
   568PS 690PS 720COM 771RM
Acts of the Apostles 20:17-27 298WI 298WII
Acts of the Apostles 20:28-38 299WI 299WII
Acts of the Apostles 22:3-16 519PS
Acts of the Apostles 22:30; 23:6-11 300WI
   300WII
Acts of the Apostles 25:13b-21 301WI
   301WII
Acts of the Apostles 26:19-23 577PS
   720COM
Acts of the Apostles 28:7-10, 11-16, 30-31
   679PS

Acts of the Apostles 28:7-10 934MVN
Acts of the Apostles 28:16-20, 30-31 302WI
   302WII

Romans 1:1-7 467WI
Romans 1:16-25 468WI
Romans 2:1-11 469WI
Romans 3:21-30 470WI
Romans 4:1-8 471WI
Romans 4:13, 16-18, 22 543PS
Romans 4:13, 16-18 472WI
Romans 4:20-25 473WI
Romans 5:1-2, 5-8 765RM
Romans 5:1-5 525PS 716COM
Romans 5:5-11 998VM 1014MD
Romans 5:12, 15b, 17-19, 20b-21 474WI
Romans 5:12, 17-19 710COM
Romans 5:17-21 1014MD
Romans 6:2-14 949MVN
Romans 6:2-4, 12-14 863MVN
Romans 6:3-11* 752RM 812RM
Romans 6:3-9* 1014MD
Romans 6:3-4, 8-9 1020MD
Romans 6:3-5 757RM
Romans 6:12-18 475WI
Romans 6:19-23 476WI
Romans 7:18-25a 477WI
Romans 8:1-11 478WI
Romans 8:1-4 610PS
Romans 8:12-17 479WI
Romans 8:14-17, 26-27 749RM
Romans 8:14-23 1014MD
Romans 8:14-17 765RM 792RM
Romans 8:18-30 883MVN 939MVN
Romans 8:18-27 792RM
Romans 8:18-25 480WI
Romans 8:22-27 657PS
Romans 8:26-30 481WI 533PS 740COM
Romans 8:26-27 765RM
Romans 8:28-39 761RM
Romans 8:28-32, 35, 37-39 752RM
Romans 8:28-32 757RM
Romans 8:28-30 636PS 710COM
Romans 8:31b-39 482WI 538PS 592PS
   716COM 863MVN 939MVN
Romans 8:31b-35, 37-39 792RM 802RM
   1014MD
Romans 9:1-5 483WI
Romans 10:8-13 748RM
Romans 10:9-18 684PS 873MVN

Romans 11:1-2a, 11-12, 25-29 484WI
Romans 11:29-36 485WI
Romans 12:1-2, 9-18* 802RM
Romans 12:1-13 812RM 863MVN
Romans 12:3-13 670PS 722COM 953MVN
Romans 12:4-8 771RM
Romans 12:5-16a 486WI
Romans 12:9-16b 572PS 928MVN
Romans 13:8-10 487WI
Romans 14:7-12 488WI
Romans 14:7-9, 10c-12 964MVN 1014MD
Romans 14:7-9 1020MD
Romans 15:14-21 489WI
Romans 16:3-9, 16, 22-27 490WI

1 Corinthians 1:1-3 986VM
1 Corinthians 1:1-9 428WII
1 Corinthians 1:3-9 944MVN
1 Corinthians 1:10-13 868MVN
1 Corinthians 1:17-25 429WII
1 Corinthians 1:18-25 556PS 574PS 663PS
    722COM 728COM 792RM 972VM
1 Corinthians 1:22-31 812RM 853MVN
1 Corinthians 1:26-31 430WII 516PS
    527PS 645PS 740COM
1 Corinthians 2:1-10a 617PS 693PS
    728COM
1 Corinthians 2:1-5 431WII 781RM
1 Corinthians 2:10b-16 432WII 567PS
    728COM
1 Corinthians 3:1-9 433WII
1 Corinthians 3:18-23 434WII
1 Corinthians 3:6-10 918MVN
1 Corinthians 3:9c-11, 16-17 704COM
    828MVN
1 Corinthians 4:1-5 435WII 558PS
    722COM
1 Corinthians 4:6b-15 436WII
1 Corinthians 5:1-8 437WII
1 Corinthians 6:1-11 438WII
1 Corinthians 6:13c-15a, 17-20 596PS 802RM
1 Corinthians 7:25-35 569PS 734COM
    812RM 853MVN
1 Corinthians 7:25-31 439WII
1 Corinthians 7:29-31 903MVN
1 Corinthians 8:1b-7, 11-13 440WII
1 Corinthians 9:16-19, 22b-27 441WII
1 Corinthians 9:16-19, 22-23 685PS
    722COM 776RM 848MVN
1 Corinthians 10:14-22 442WII

1 Corinthians 10:14-22a 823RM
1 Corinthians 10:16-21 820RM
1 Corinthians 10:16-17 786RM 797RM
    979VM
1 Corinthians 10:31–11:1 609PS
1 Corinthians 11:17-26, 33 443WII
1 Corinthians 11:23-26 786RM 797RM
    823RM 844MVN 979VM
1 Corinthians 12:3b-7, 12-13 828MVN
    848MVN 863MVN
1 Corinthians 12:4-13 765RM
1 Corinthians 12:4-11 776RM
1 Corinthians 12:12-14, 27-31a 444WII
1 Corinthians 12:12-22, 24b-27 792RM
1 Corinthians 12:12-13 752RM, 757RM
1 Corinthians 12:31–13:13* 445WII 631PS
    740COM 761RM 953MVN
1 Corinthians 12:31–13:8a 802RM
1 Corinthians 15:1-11* 446WII
1 Corinthians 15:1-8* 561PS 748RM
1 Corinthians 15:12-20 447WII 792RM
1 Corinthians 15:20-24a, 25-28* 1014MD
1 Corinthians 15:20-27 622PS
1 Corinthians 15:20-23 1020MD
1 Corinthians 15:35-37, 42-49 448WII
1 Corinthians 15:51-57 1014MD
1 Corinthians 15:54b-57 621PS

2 Corinthians 1:1-7 359WI
2 Corinthians 1:18-22 360WI
2 Corinthians 3:1-6a 722COM
2 Corinthians 3:4-11 361WI
2 Corinthians 3:15–4:1, 3-6 362WI
2 Corinthians 4:1-2, 5-7 547PS 602PS 635PS
    655PS 722COM 771RM 844MVN
2 Corinthians 4:7-15 363WI 517PS 605PS
    640PS 662PS 716COM
2 Corinthians 4:10-18 934MVN
2 Corinthians 4:14–5:1 1014MD
2 Corinthians 4:16-18 792RM
2 Corinthians 5:1, 6-10 792RM 1014MD
2 Corinthians 5:14-21 364WI
2 Corinthians 5:14-20 511PS 664PS
    722COM 771RM 844MVN 858MVN
2 Corinthians 5:14-17 603PS
2 Corinthians 5:17–6:2 893MVN
2 Corinthians 5:20–6:2 219WI 219WII
2 Corinthians 6:1-10 365WI
2 Corinthians 6:4-10 575PS 654PS
    716COM

Colossians 1:24–2:3 437WI

Colossians 1:24-29 554PS 722COM
  844MVN 848MVN

Colossians 2:6-15 438WI

Colossians 3:1-11 439WI

Colossians 3:1-4 812RM

Colossians 3:9b-17 752RM 868MVN
  883MVN

Colossians 3:12-17 440WI 579PS 740COM
  802RM 807RM 812RM 944MVN
  986VM

Colossians 3:12-15 888MVN 959MVN

Colossians 3:14-15, 17, 23-24 559PS

1 Thessalonians 1:1-5, 8b-10 425WI

1 Thessalonians 2:1-8 426WI

1 Thessalonians 2:2b-8 571PS 626PS
  722COM 844MVN

1 Thessalonians 2:9-13 427WI

1 Thessalonians 3:7-13 428WI

1 Thessalonians 4:1-3a, 7-12 812RM

1 Thessalonians 4:1b-2, 9-12 908MVN

1 Thessalonians 4:1-8 429WI

1 Thessalonians 4:9-11 430WI

1 Thessalonians 4:13-18* 431WI 1014MD

1 Thessalonians 4:13-14, 18 1020MD

1 Thessalonians 5:1-6, 9-11 432WI

1 Thessalonians 5:16-24 761RM

2 Thessalonians 1:1-5, 11b-12 425WII

2 Thessalonians 2:1-3a, 14-17 426WII

2 Thessalonians 3:6-10, 16-18 427WII

2 Thessalonians 3:6-12, 16 908MVN

1 Timothy 1:1-2, 12-14 441WI

1 Timothy 1:15-17 442WI

1 Timothy 2:1-8 443WI 873MVN

1 Timothy 2:5-8 868MVN

1 Timothy 3:1-13 444WI

1 Timothy 3:8-10, 12-13 771RM

1 Timothy 3:14-16 445WI

1 Timothy 4:12-16 446WI 771RM

1 Timothy 5:3-10 740COM

1 Timothy 6:2c-12 447WI

1 Timothy 6:6-11, 17-19 883MVN 918MVN

1 Timothy 6:13-16 448WI

2 Timothy 1:1-3, 6-12 355WII

2 Timothy 1:1-8 520PS

2 Timothy 1:6-14 771RM

2 Timothy 1:13-14; 2:1-3 544PS 549PS
  595PS 686PS 722COM 728COM

2 Timothy 2:8-13; 3:10-12 699PS 551PS
  716COM

2 Timothy 2:8-15 356WII

2 Timothy 3:8-13 1014MD

2 Timothy 3:10-17 357WII

2 Timothy 3:10-12, 14-15 776RM

2 Timothy 3:14-17 781RM

2 Timothy 3:22b-26 589PS

2 Timothy 4:1-8 358WII

2 Timothy 4:1-5 534PS 548PS 588PS 694PS
  722COM 728COM 781RM 848MVN

2 Timothy 4:6-8, 17-18 591PS

2 Timothy 4:10-17b 661PS

Titus 1:1-9 491WII

Titus 1:1-5 520PS

Titus 2:1-8, 11-14 492WII

Titus 3:1-7 493WII

Titus 3:4-7 752RM

Philemon 7-20 494WII

Hebrews 1:1-6 305WI

Hebrews 2:5-12 306WI

Hebrews 2:14-18 307WI 524PS

Hebrews 3:7-14 308WI

Hebrews 4:1-5, 11 309WI

Hebrews 4:12-16 310WI

Hebrews 4:12-13 781RM

Hebrews 4:14-16; 5:7-9 792RM

Hebrews 5:1-10 311WI 771RM 834MVN
  858MVN

Hebrews 5:7-9 639PS 972VM

Hebrews 6:10-20 312WI

Hebrews 7:1-3, 15-17 313WI

Hebrews 7:25–8:6 314WI

Hebrews 8:6-13 315WI

Hebrews 9:2-3, 11-14 316WI

Hebrews 9:11-15 786RM 979VM 992VM

Hebrews 9:15, 24-28 317WI

Hebrews 10:1-10 318WI

Hebrews 10:4-10 545PS

Hebrews 10:11-18 319WI

Hebrews 10:12-23 982VM

Hebrews 10:19-25 320WI

Hebrews 10:22-25 752RM

Hebrews 10:32-39 321WI

Hebrews 10:32-36 642PS 716COM

Hebrews 11:1-7 340WI
Hebrews 11:1-2, 8-19* 322WI
Hebrews 11:13-16 928MVN
Hebrews 11:32-40 323WI
Hebrews 12:1-4 324WI
Hebrews 12:2-13 878MVN
Hebrews 12:4-7, 11-15 325WI
Hebrews 12:18-19, 21-24 326WI
Hebrews 12:18-19, 22-24 704COM 979VM
  992VM
Hebrews 13:1-2, 7-8, 17-18 807RM
Hebrews 13:1-3, 14-16 928MVN
Hebrews 13:1-8 327WI
Hebrews 13:8-15 820RM
Hebrews 13:15-17, 20-21 328WI

James 1:1-11 335WII
James 1:2-4, 12 716COM 939MVN
James 1:12-18 336WII
James 1:19-27 337WII
James 2:1-9 338WII
James 2:14-24, 26 339WII
James 2:14-17 695PS 740COM
James 3:1-10 340WII
James 3:13-18 341WII 883MVN 888MVN
James 4:1-10 342WII 883MVN 898MVN
James 4:13-17 343WII
James 4:13-15 903MVN
James 5:1-6 344WII
James 5:7-8, 16c-18 913MVN
James 5:9-12 345WII
James 5:13-20 346WII
James 5:13-16 792RM 934MVN

1 Peter 1:3-9 347WII 792RM 812RM
  853MVN 878MVN
1 Peter 1:8-12 586PS
1 Peter 1:10-16 348WII
1 Peter 1:17-21 979VM 992VM
1 Peter 1:18-25 349WII
1 Peter 2:2-5, 9-12 350WII
1 Peter 2:4-10 863MVN
1 Peter 2:4-5, 9-10 752RM 757RM
1 Peter 2:4-9 704COM 828MVN
1 Peter 3:1-9 740COM 802RM
1 Peter 3:14-17 515PS 646PS 716COM
1 Peter 4:7-13 351WII
1 Peter 4:7b-11 521PS 541PS 740COM
  771RM
1 Peter 4:12-19 558PS 620PS 716COM

1 Peter 5:1-4 514PS 535PS 656PS 682PS
  722COM 771RM 807RM
1 Peter 5:5b-14 555PS

2 Peter 1:2-7 353WII
2 Peter 1:16-19 614PS
2 Peter 3:12-15a, 17-18 354WII

1 John 1:1-4 697PS 781RM
1 John 1:5–2:2 557PS 698PS 949MVN
1 John 2:1-5 893MVN
1 John 2:3-11 202WI 202WII
1 John 2:12-17 203WI 203WII
1 John 2:18-25 512PS
1 John 2:18-21 204WI 204WII
1 John 2:22-28 205WI 205WII
1 John 2:29–3:6 206WI 206WII
1 John 3:1-3 667PS
1 John 3:1-2 792RM 1014MD
1 John 3:7-10 207WI 207WII
1 John 3:11-21 208WI 208WII
1 John 3:14-18 539PS 594PS 599PS 678PS
  740COM 953MVN
1 John 3:14-16 1014MD
1 John 3:18-24 802RM
1 John 3:22–4:6 212WI 212WII
1 John 4:7-16 607PS 633PS 740COM
  812RM 998VM
1 John 4:7-12 802RM
1 John 4:7-10 213WI 213WII
1 John 4:9-15 868MVN
1 John 4:11-18 214WI 214WII
1 John 4:19–5:4 215WI 215WII
1 John 5:1-5 542PS 560PS 583PS 611PS
  716COM 740COM
1 John 5:4-8 979VM 992VM
1 John 5:5-13 209WI 209WII 216WI 216WII
1 John 5:14-21 210WI 210WII

2 John 4-9 495WII

3 John 5-8 496WII

Jude 17, 20b-25 352WII

Revelation 1:1-4; 2:1-5a 497WII
Revelation 1:5-8 260WI 260WII 970VM
  977VM 990VM
Revelation 2:8-11 536PS
Revelation 3:1-6, 14-22 498WII

TABLE OF
RESPONSORIAL PSALMS
AND
CANTICLES

I. RESPONSORIAL PSALMS

Psalm 1   185, 220, 233, 344, 464, 469, 476, 479, 497, 549, 595, 598, 652, 674, 739, 808

Psalm 2   212, 267, 283, 879

Psalm 3   323, 498

Psalm 4   360

Psalm 5   365, 378, 437

Psalm 6   793

Psalm 7   249

Psalm 8   264, 306, 330, 472, 753, 884, 904

Psalm 9   412, 465, 502

Psalm 10   394

Psalm 11   302

Psalm 12   340

Psalm 13   481, 636

Psalm 15   337, 372, 449, 498, 537, 739

Psalm 16   261, 300, 361, 364, 418, 441, 513, 534, 546, 583, 619, 651, 664, 721, 739, 777, 824, 845, 859

Psalm 17   250, 384, 447, 455, 499

Psalm 18   255, 327, 412

Psalm 19   224, 310, 341, 352, 380, 399, 458, 468, 495, 542, 561, 590, 641, 643, 657, 666, 684, 686, 727, 748, 782, 829, 840, 845, 849, 854, 874

Psalm 21   310, 421

Psalm 22   324, 486, 766, 924, 971

Psalm 23   177, 251, 328, 421, 493, 510, 516, 535, 565, 578, 659, 668, 677, 700, 721, 739, 749, 753, 758, 766, 772, 787, 798, 824, 869, 978, 997, 1013, 1019

Psalm 24   196, 318, 320, 434, 477, 478, 491, 503, 524, 667, 777, 813

Psalm 25   187, 199, 238, 355, 356, 668, 793, 829, 997, 1013, 1019, 1024

Psalm 26   378

Psalm 27   179, 243, 257, 271, 327, 363, 432, 458, 487, 488, 668, 753, 758, 762, 793, 813, 829, 845, 854, 859, 879, 1013

Psalm 28   443

Psalm 29   336

Psalm 30   190, 244

Psalm 31   232, 274, 323, 367, 527, 536, 553A, 596, 639, 692, 696, 715

Psalm 32   325, 333, 347, 471, 753

Psalm 33   197, 262, 272, 339, 350, 371, 385, 429, 430, 433, 445, 471, 476, 743, 803, 813, 997

Psalm 34   188, 225, 248, 269, 270, 338, 359, 369, 370, 379, 492, 515, 517, 529, 533, 540, 550, 552, 554, 570, 574, 591, 597, 604, 607, 609, 611A, 631, 660, 678, 699, 715, 739, 753, 758, 787, 793, 798, 803, 808, 813, 849, 978, 997

Psalm 36   398

Psalm 37   321, 331, 342, 387, 435, 492, 518, 547, 560, 579, 589, 672, 693, 727

Psalm 40   307, 314, 318, 422, 443, 474, 514, 545, 548, 566, 556A, 584, 602, 637, 656, 687, 694, 721, 813, 859, 978, 982, 991

Psalm 41   965, 971

Psalm 42   237, 279, 484, 753, 762, 793, 798, 1013, 1019

Psalm 43   453

Psalm 44   308

Psalm 45   439, 622, 681, 709, 733, 813, 854

Psalm 46   245, 671, 703

Psalm 47   295, 296, 316

Psalm 48   326, 372, 390

Psalm 49   343, 344, 447, 904

Psalm 50   231, 311, 335, 348, 377, 379, 389, 395, 400, 500

Psalm 51   219, 221, 226, 242, 321, 322, 366, 387, 408, 410, 418, 422, 753, 894, 950

Psalm 52   433

Psalm 54   436

Psalm 55   342, 971

Psalm 56   314, 448

Psalm 57   289, 315

Psalm 59   403

Psalm 60   371

Psalm 61   762

Psalm 62   437, 469

Psalm 63   352, 603, 753, 762, 793, 813, 1013
Psalm 65   362, 762, 914
Psalm 66   275, 276, 415, 753
Psalm 67   191, 281, 406, 829, 874, 919
Psalm 68   297, 298, 299, 479
Psalm 69   259, 390, 405, 406, 460, 485, 971
Psalm 71   195, 258, 358, 397, 586, 634, 793
Psalm 72   176, 193, 194, 213, 214, 215, 889, 899
Psalm 74   376
Psalm 77   411
Psalm 78   309, 397, 416, 638, 787, 978
Psalm 79   230, 349, 374, 402, 459
Psalm 80   186, 316, 386, 884, 940
Psalm 81   241, 333, 405, 407
Psalm 82   493
Psalm 84   330, 400, 404, 441, 507, 703, 772, 813, 819, 845, 859
Psalm 85   181, 189, 315, 362, 382, 396, 420, 424, 474, 864, 884, 889, 899, 940, 954
Psalm 86   222, 324, 463, 793, 960
Psalm 87   280, 456
Psalm 88   456, 457
Psalm 89   200, 260, 282, 309, 312, 317, 319, 370, 543, 555, 581, 588, 611, 626, 670, 673, 682, 688, 721, 753, 772, 835
Psalm 90   334, 354, 428, 452, 454, 559, 793, 904, 909
Psalm 91   353, 383, 650
Psalm 92   808
Psalm 93   268, 341, 388
Psalm 94   336, 391, 484
Psalm 95   236, 240, 308, 410, 508, 703, 819
Psalm 96   182, 202, 203, 204, 288, 351, 425, 426, 431, 504, 520, 526, 541, 544, 571, 617, 635, 655, 665, 683, 721, 766, 772, 829, 849, 874
Psalm 97   305, 368, 429, 466, 614, 697
Psalm 98   205, 206, 207, 284, 294, 317, 348, 365, 430, 434, 467, 470, 489, 505, 580, 679, 689, 777, 829, 874
Psalm 99   361, 403
Psalm 100   208, 290, 350, 435, 444, 448, 473, 506, 772, 813, 864, 869, 884, 954
Psalm 101   444
Psalm 102   252, 338, 392, 408, 455, 793, 935
Psalm 103   183, 235, 301, 325, 345, 346, 364, 377, 391, 402, 511, 523, 557, 563, 739, 749, 793, 803, 864, 950, 960, 997, 1013
Psalm 104   329, 331, 766, 914

Psalm 105   234, 254, 263, 307, 373, 385, 386, 388, 392, 466, 472, 488, 496
Psalm 106   247, 332, 334, 374, 381, 401, 409, 419, 721
Psalm 107   423, 884, 914, 924, 929
Psalm 109   482
Psalm 110   311, 313, 319, 512, 558, 568, 690, 721, 772, 787, 829, 845, 978
Psalm 111   312, 347, 368, 445, 446, 461, 465, 483
Psalm 112   339, 353, 354, 367, 487, 490, 496, 539, 594, 601A, 616, 618, 623, 630, 645, 676, 695, 739, 803, 854, 884, 924
Psalm 113   415, 442, 467, 564, 627, 709, 864, 945, 985
Psalm 114   416
Psalm 115   285, 380, 384, 1013
Psalm 116   278, 305, 337, 363, 393, 442, 620A, 772, 787, 798, 978, 991, 1013
Psalm 117   277, 463, 519. 525, 532, 556, 577, 593, 612, 663, 685, 721, 766, 772, 829, 874
Psalm 118   178, 265, 266, 446, 819, 869, 971
Psalm 119   229, 273, 328, 335, 343, 345, 357, 360, 373, 381, 407, 414, 431, 450, 451, 460, 468, 477, 494, 495, 497, 501, 522, 567, 600, 608, 610, 625, 633, 648, 675, 727, 782, 819
Psalm 121   359, 762, 929
Psalm 122   175, 287, 450, 478, 489, 703, 819, 869, 884, 889, 1013
Psalm 123   355, 793, 829, 854, 879, 884, 940
Psalm 124   389, 475, 538, 562, 575, 576, 592, 620, 698, 715, 879
Psalm 126   449, 480, 528, 551, 553, 585, 605, 615, 640, 642, 642A, 644, 646, 654, 662, 715, 753, 919
Psalm 127   884, 909
Psalm 128   332, 356, 375, 424, 427, 480, 658, 739, 803
Psalm 130   228, 462, 470, 894, 950, 1013
Psalm 131   485, 486, 582, 623A, 624, 632, 649, 669, 739
Psalm 132   320, 329, 369, 606, 621
Psalm 135   382
Psalm 136   394, 417
Psalm 137   375, 457
Psalm 138   227, 292, 647, 945
Psalm 139   426, 427, 440, 459, 462, 491, 587
Psalm 141   346
Psalm 143   793, 1013
Psalm 144   313, 453, 482, 502

Psalm 145   184, 246, 286, 340, 383, 428, 432, 436, 438, 439, 481, 490, 629, 661, 766, 787, 798, 803, 945, 978

Psalm 146   357, 366, 404, 423, 494

Psalm 147   180, 209, 216, 239, 349, 413, 483, 782, 787, 978

Psalm 148   293, 413, 521, 530, 569, 628, 733, 803, 854, 1019

Psalm 149   210, 217, 291, 351, 425, 438, 452, 500

Psalm 150   440, 499

II. OLD TESTAMENT CANTICLES

Exod 15:1-17   395, 396

Deut 32:3-41   401, 411, 414, 419, 420

1 Sam 2:1-8   198, 306, 573, 709

1 Chr 29:10-12   326, 501, 703, 945

Tob 13:2-9   358, 451, 929

Jdt 13:18-20   531, 613, 690A, 709, 1002

Isa 12:2-6   417, 475, 572, 985, 997

Isa 38:10-16   393, 793, 935

Jer 31:10-13   256, 399, 409, 454, 869

Dan 3:52-56   253, 398, 503

Dan 3:57-87   504, 505, 506, 507, 508

Jonah 2:3-8   461

III. NEW TESTAMENT CANTICLES

Luke 1:46-55   376, 601, 653, 680, 709, 1002

Luke 1:69-75   322, 464, 473

Lectionary for Mass, Classic edition,
was designed by Frank Kacmarcik, Obl.S.B.
The text was set at The Liturgical Press
in Cheltenham typeface
designed by Bertam Goodhue.

National Publishing Company, Philadelphia,
Pennsylvania, printed the book on
Domtar Volume Opaque paper,
and the endsheets are Beckett Blazer Blue.
It is bound in red Sturdite,
Morocco embossed, over binderboard.

The book was completed on the feast of
Saint Elizabeth of Hungary, 2001.